English-Korean • Korean-English

Dictionary of Accounting Terms

영한 · 한영
회계용어사전

English-Korean • Korean-English

Dictionary of Accounting Terms

영한 · 한영

회계용어사전

신 · 장 · 판

엮은이 박재완朴載完

서울대학교에서 경영학을 공부했으며, 미국 텍사스 오스틴대학에서 회계학 박사 학위를
받았다. 현재 동국대학교 회계학과 교수로 있다. 주요 논문으로 「Reporting Strategies in a
Multi-location Audit Environment」(1992), 「Allocating a Fixed Audit Budget over Time」(1995),
「Strategic Audit Timing Plans」(1995), 「경쟁시장에서의 감사수수료와 감사의 품질」(1996),
「회계감사의 경제적 가치결정모형」(1996), 「감사위험과 통계적 표본크기의 결정」(1996),
「Minimizing Organizational Losses Due to Theft」(1996), 「Allocation Internal Audit Resources
to Minimize Organizational Losses due to Theft」(1998) 등이 있다.

영한·한영 회계용어사전

신장판1쇄 인쇄일 2017년 3월 8일
신장판1쇄 발행일 2017년 3월 15일

펴낸곳 도서출판 일빛
펴낸이 이성우
엮은이 박재완

등록일 1990년 4월 6일(제10-1424호)
주소 03993 서울시 마포구 동교로27길 12 동교씨티빌 201호(동교동 198-9)
전화 02) 3142-1703~1704 팩스 02) 3142-1706

값 20,000원
ISBN 978-89-5645-179-4 91320

글머리에

학교에서 회계 원리 과정을 가르칠 때 회계는 기업의 언어라고 가르칩니다. 따라서 여러분은 회계가 조직 특히 기업의 여러 가지 활동을 화폐적으로 측정하는 기본적인 정보 시스템이므로 회계적 용어를 모르면 기업의 경영 과정을 논하기가 매우 어렵다는 사실을 깨달았을 것입니다.

특히 국제화 시대에 우리 나라 기업들이 해외에 시장을 개척하고 외국인 경영자를 모셔오고 하는 과정에서 영문으로 표시된 회계 문서를 접할 기회가 급속도로 확장되고 있습니다. 이러한 국제화 환경 아래에서 기업인이 필요로 하는 회계 지식과 영어 능력의 결합이 매우 중요한 경쟁 우위를 확보할 수 있을 것으로 믿습니다.

이 사전은 국제화 시대에 기업인이 갖추어야 할 영문 회계 용어에 대한 기본 지식의 확충과 영문 회계 서류를 작성하고 이해하는 데 도움을 제공하기 위해 출간되었습니다. 재무회계, 원가회계, 관리회계 용어를 비롯하여 회계감사 용어를 포함한 회계 전분야에 대한 용어를 포함하고 있어 전문 회계사나 회계학을 공부하는 학생들에게도 유용할 것으로 기대합니다. 또한 금융 용어 및 금융 관련 법률 용어를 포함시켜 관련 분야에 대한 용어를 포괄적으로 다루고 있어 금융 관련 업무나 외국인 회사에 근무하는 직장인에게도 유용할 것으로 생각합니다.

모쪼록 이 사전이 회계와 관련된 모든 분들께 좋은 벗이 되어 항상 함께하길 바랍니다.

끝으로 이 사전의 출간을 결심하고 오랜 시간 조력을 아끼지 않은 일빛 편집부에게 감사의 마음을 전합니다.

박재완

일러두기

• 영한(英韓) 부분

1. 표제어의 선정 및 배열

(1) 표제어는 주로 미국 문헌과 자료에서 선정하였지만, 미국 용어와는 다른 영국 용어 가운데 특히 철자 등이 다른 것과 영국 특유의 용어에 대해서는 (영)이라고 표시해두었다.

　　예: chargeable transfer (영)과세대상이 되는 자산양도(증여)

　　　　financial accounts   (영)재무제표, 재무보고서

(2) 공공 기관명 및 문헌명 가운데 특히 중요한 것은 표제어로 삼았다. 또한 문헌명은 이탤릭체로 표시하였다.

(3) 표제어는 원칙적으로 소문자로 표시하였으며 고유 명사의 머리글자, 약어, 기타 특별한 경우에 한해서 대문자를 사용하였다.

(4) 표제어는 원칙적으로 단수 형태로 표시하였으며, 회계 용어는 일관되게 복수형을 사용하는 용어에 한해서는 복수형으로 표시하였다.

　　예: earnings 이익, 가득이익

(5) 표제어가 단수형인 경우에도 그 복수형의 의미가 다른 용어에 대

해서는 (pl)의 다음에 그 번역어를 표시하였다.

　　예 : holding 1) 소유, 보유, 보유고, 보유품 2) (pl) 소유주식, 소유지(地)

(6) 표제어에 약어가 있는 경우에는 그 약어를 표제어의 뒤에 괄호를 써서 표시하고, 약어 그 자체도 표제어로 표시하였다.

　　예 : first-in, first-out method(FIFO)

　　　　FIFO(first-in, first-out method)

(7) 표제어는 알파벳순으로 배열하였다. 또한 표제어가 두 단어 이상으로 구성되어 있는 경우에도 그것을 한 단어로 보고 알파벳순으로 배열하였다.

2. 동의어 및 참조어

(1) 표제어에 동의어가 있는 경우에는 번역어 = 뒤에 동의어를 표시했다.

　　예 : inventory 재고자산, 재고품 = stock

(2) 반의어, 유사어 그 외 참조어는 ▶ 뒤에 표시했다.

　　예 : acquiring company 매수기업 ▶ acquired company

　　　　fundamental accounting concept 회계의 기초개념 ▶ accounting
　　　　principle

(3) 동의어, 참조어가 복수로 있는 경우에는 쉼표로 구별하고 알파벳순으로 나열하였다.

3. 번역어

(1) 번역어가 복수로 있는 경우에, 그 번역어가 간단히 환언할 수 있는 경우에는 쉼표로 나누어 표시하였다.

　　예: accounting period 회계기간, 회계연도

(2) 번역어가 복수로 있는 경우에, 그 번역어가 환언할 수 없는 경우에는 1), 2), 3)……처럼 번호를 매겨서 구별하였다.

　예: stock 1) 주식, 지분 2) 주권 3) 저량 4) 재고자산(영)

● **한영(韓英) 부분**

(1) 표제어는 영한 부분의 번역어를 중심으로 회계 경리에 관계된 중요한 용어를 선정하였다.

(2) 표제어는 ㄱ, ㄴ, ㄷ순으로 배열하였다.

(3) 표제어에 대응하는 영어 번역어가 복수로 있는 경우에는 쉼표로 구별하였다.

　예: 매도호가 ask price, asked price, asking price, offered price

영한편

English-Korean

A

AAA(accumulated adjustment account) 적립금 정산회계

AAA(American Accounting Association) 미국회계학회

AAER(Accounting and Auditing Enforcement Release) 회계 · 감사 시행통첩

AAT(Association of Accounting Technicians) 회계기능자협회

abacus 주판

Abacus 시드니대학 출판부(Sidney University Press)에서 발행하는 회계전문 잡지. 1965년 창간. 연2회 발행.

abandoned property 유기물(遺棄物)

abandonment 1) 폐기, 제거 2) 유기(遺棄), 보험위탁 3) 인도

abandonment method 폐기법
= retirement method, retirement system ▶ appraisal system

abandonment value 폐기가치

abatement 1) 감액 2) 취소, 공제, 경감, 3) 무효, 실효

abatement claim 감액청구

ABB(activity based budgeting) 활동기준예산

abbreviated accounts (영)약식재무제표, 요약재무제표
▶ abridged accounts, modified accounts

abbreviation 생략형, 단축, 약어, 약자

ABC(activity based costing) 활동기준원가

ABC(General Assignment Benefit of Creditors) 재산청산신탁

ABC analysis (재고관리)ABC분석
= ABCD analysis, XYZ analysis

ABCD analysis (재고관리)ABCD분석
= ABC analysis

ABC inventory classification ABC재고분류 ▶ ABC analysis

ABEND(abnormal end of task) 과업의 비정상적 종료

ability theory of taxation 담세능력설, 능력과세설 ▶ benefit principle

ability to pay 지불능력

ABM(activity based management) 활동기준관리

abnormal cost 비정상적 원가
▶ normal cost

abnormal end of task(ABEND) 과업의 비정상적 종료

abnormal item 특별항목
= extraordinary item

abnormal loss 비정상 손실 ▶ normal loss, shrinkage, spoilage, waste

abnormal shrinkage 비정상 감손, 비정상 감모 ▶ shrinkage

abnormal spoilage 비정상 공손
▶ defective work, normal spoilage, shrinkage, spoilage, spoiled work, waste

abnormal waste   비정상 감손, 비정상
　　작업 폐기물 ▶ normal
　　waste, waste

abort   중지

above-normal earning   초과수익력

above-normal profit   초과이익

above par   액면초과, 할증

above the line   1) 경상손익계산 = top
　　line ▶ below the line, bottom
　　line 2) 경상지출의

above the line' deductions   경상손익
　　계산시 차감항목

abridged accounts   (영)약식재무제표
　　▶ abbreviated accounts,
　　medium sized company, small
　　company

absenteeism   1) 상습적인 결근, 계획적
　　인 결근, 장기결석 2) 부재지주
　　제도

absolute bill of sale   무조건 매매증서
　　▶ conditional bill of sale

absolute difference   절대차이

absolute error   절대오차 ▶ relative
　　error

absolute expression   절대식, 절대표현
　　형식

absolute insolvency   절대적 채무초과
　　▶ insolvency

absolute liability   절대적 책임

absolute performance measure   절대
　　적 성과 측정

absolute probability   절대확률 = state
　　probability

absolute-truth approach   완전진실성
　　접근법 ▶ conditional truth
　　approach, costly truth approach

absolute value   절대치 ▶ check digit,
　　modulus

absorb   부담하다, 배부하다

absorbed burden   제조간접비배부액
　　= absorbed overhead, applied
　　overhead

absorbed cost   1) 전부원가 ▶ partial
　　cost 2) 배부원가

absorbed overhead   제조간접비배부액
　　= applied burden ▶ absorption
　　rate

absorption account   배부계정, 평가계정
　　= offset account, valuation
　　account ▶ contra account

absorption approach to target pricing
　　전부원가법에 의한 목표가격
　　설정 ▶ contribution pricing

absorption cost   전부원가 = full cost
　　▶ partial cost

absorption costing   전부원가계산
　　= absorption cost system, full
　　costing, full absorption costing,
　　full cost accounting, total
　　costing
　　▶ conventional costing
　　▶ 직접원가계산 (direct costing)

absorption cost system   전부원가계산
　　= absorption costing

absorption income   전부원가계산에 의
　　거한 손익 ▶ contribution
　　income

absorption rate   배부율

abstract   발췌, 적요서, 개요, 줄거리

a/c(account)   계정

ACA   (1. Associate of the Institute of
　　Chartered Accountants in
　　Englandand Wales 2. Associate
　　of theInstitute of Chartered

Accountants in Ireland), 칙허(왕
이 허가한)회계사협회 준회원
ACAE(associated corporate accounting
executive)   국제회계사협회
(Association of International
Accountants)의 전문시험 수험자
acc.(acceptance)   인수, 수령
ACCA(Associate of the Chartered
Association of Certified
Accountants)   칙허 공인회계
사협회 준회원
accelerated amortization   가속상각
▶ accelerated depreciation
accelerated cost recovery system
(ACRS)   가속상각제도, 가속
원가회수제도 ▶ accelerated
depreciation, modified
accelerated cost recovery
system
accelerated depreciation   가속상각(법)
accelerated method   가속상각법
acceleration clause   기한의 이익상실
조항, 단축조항, 변제기일
acceleration time   가속시간
accept the whole   전부수령
acceptance(acc.)   1) 인수, 어음 인수
2) 수령, 승낙, 승인 3) 화물인수
acceptance and guarantee   지불 승낙
acceptance commission   (환)어음인수
수수료
acceptance credit   인수조건부 신용장
= usance L/C
acceptance of bill of exchange   어음
인수 ▶ bill of exchange
acceptance of offer   청약의 승낙
acceptance rate   인수환시세, 외화표시
수입어음결제시세

acceptance region   채택역
acceptance sampling inspection   수용
표본조사에 의한 검사
acceptance test   인수검사
accepting house   (영)어음인수회사
acceptor   어음인수인
access control   접근통제, 접근제어, 접
근관리 ▶ accounting control,
application control, general
control
accession   동산이 다른 동산에 첨부된 것
accessory equipment   부속설비
accident and health insurance benefit
사고 및 건강보험 수익
accident error   우발적 오류
accident insurance   사고보험
accommodation   1) 융통어음의 발행, 융
통 2) 대체품
accommodation acceptance   융통어음
인수 ▶ accommodation note
accommodation bill   융통어음, 금융어
음 = accommodation note,
finance bill, non value bill
▶ accommodation acceptance,
accommodation paper
accommodation note   융통어음, 금융
어음 = accommodation bill
accommodation paper   융통어음
= accommodation note
accommodation party   명의신탁 당사
자, 융통 서명인, 융통어음 발행
인(인수인, 배서인), 융통 당사자
accommodation shipment   대체품 출하
accommodator   융통인, 조정인
accomodation   편의용
accord and satisfaction   1) 대물변제
2) 원계약에 대체하는 새로운

계약과 만족스런이행

account(a/c) 1) 계정 2) 외상매출채권

accountability 1) 회계책임 2) 회사책임

accountability center 책임중심점
▶ accountability, responsibility center

account analysis 계정분석

account analysis approach 계정분석법 = account classification, cost analysis by account classification

accountancy 회계, 회계업, 회계직, 회계 전문직

Accountancy (영)영국·웨일즈의 칙허회계사협회(The Institute of Chartered Accountants in England and Wales)에서 발행하는 월간지. 1938년 창간

accountant 회계 전문가, 회계사, 경리·회계 담당자 ▶ certified public accountant

Accountant (영)런던의 Gee&co.,Ltd.가 발행하는 회계전문 잡지. 1874년 창간된 주간지

accountant's fee 감사 보수

accountant's legal liability 회계사의 법적 책임 ▶ accountant's responsibility

accountant's lexicon 회계용어

accountant's lien 회계사의 유치권

Accountant's Magazine 스코틀랜드 칙허회계사협회 (The Institute of Chartered Accountants in Scotland)의 기관지. 1897년 창간된 월간지.

accountant's opinion 회계사의 의견

accountant's rate of return 회계적 자본이익율 = accounting rate of return, average rate of return

accountant's report 회계사의 보고서 ▶ auditor's report

accountant's responsibility 회계사의 책임 ▶ accountant's legal liability

Accountants International Study Group(AISG) 회계사 국제연구그룹

account balance 계정 잔고

account books 회계장부, 외상매출 채권장, 외상판매장 ▶ accounting books, books of accounting, financial books

account classification 계정 분류법 = cost analysis by account classification, account analysis approach

account code 계정과목 코드 ▶ account number

account day (증권거래소) 그 주일 결제 거래의 정산일 = settlement day

account due 미수금 ▶ account receivable, accrued revenue

account form 계정 형식 ▶ report form

account groups 계정그룹

accounting 1) 회계 ▶ accounting information 2) 회계학

accounting action (법원에) 계산 청구

accounting adjustment of prior period 전기손익수정, 전기오류수정

accounting adjustments of earlier period 전기손익수정

accounting alternative 회계 대체안

▷ alternative accounting principle

Accounting and Auditing Enforcement Release(AAER)   회계 · 감사 시행통보

Accounting and Business Research   영국 · 웨일즈 칙허회계사협회 (The Institute of Chartered Accountants in England and Wales)가 발행하는 회계연구잡지. 1970년에 창간된 계간지.

Accounting and Finance   호주와 뉴질랜드 회계사협회(Accounting Association of Australia and New Zealand)가 발행하는 회계잡지. 연 2회 발행.

Accounting and Reporting Standards for Corporate Financial Statements   회사 재무제표에 관한 회계 및 보고기준

accounting audit   회계감사

accounting axiom   회계공리 = accounting postulate

accounting base   회계기준, 회계상의 기초, 회계방법 ▷ accounting standard, accounting policy

accounting beta   회계 베타 ▷ beta

accounting books   회계장부 = account books, books of account, financial books

accounting change   회계상의 변경

accounting characteristic   회계특성 = accounting quality

accounting choice   회계방법 선택

accounting concept   회계개념, 회계용어 ▷ accounting postulate, accounting principle, basic

assumption, fundamental accounting assumption, fundamental accounting concept

accounting control   회계통제, 회계관리

accounting convention   1) 회계관행 2) 회계공준 ▷ accounting axiom, accounting postulate, basic concept

accounting criteria   회계규준

accounting cycle   1) 회계순환과정 2) 회계처리 수속의 과정 = bookkeeping cycle

accounting data   회계자료

accounting date   (영)결산일 = closing date ▷ balance sheet date

accounting department   회계부문, 경리부 = accounting division, accounting section

accounting disclosure   회계공시

accounting division   회계과, 경리과 = accounting department, accounting section

accounting earnings   회계적 이익 = earnings

accounting entity   회계실체 ▷ accounting unit

accounting equation   회계등식 = accounting formula

accounting error   회계상의 오류 ▷ fraud

accounting estimate   1) 회계상의 추정, 견적 2) 회계추정치

accounting estimate change   회계상의 추정의 변경 ▷ change in accounting estimate

accounting evidence　회계증거
　　▶ audit evidence
accounting firm　회계법인
accounting for business enterprise
　　기업회계
accounting for capital project fund
　　자본예산기금 회계
accounting for changes in specific
　　prices　개별가격 변동회계
　　▶ accounting for changes in
　　the general price level, current
　　cost accounting, current value
　　accounting
accounting for changes in the general
　　price level　일반 물가변동
　　회계, 일반 물가수준 변동회계,
　　일반 구매력 변동회계
　　= constant dollar accounting,
　　constant purchasing power
　　accounting, general purchasing
　　power accounting
　　▶ accounting for changes in
　　specific prices
accounting for changes in the
　　purchasing power of money
　　화폐구매력 변동회계
　　= constant purchasing power
　　accounting, stabilized
　　accounting
accounting for changing money value
　　화폐가치 변동회계 = constant
　　purchasing power accounting
accounting for changing prices
　　물가변동회계 = accounting for
　　inflation, inflation accounting
accounting for contingency
　　우발사건의 회계

　　▶ contingency, contingent
　　asset, contingent liability
accounting for control　통제회계
　　▶ accounting for planning
accounting for decision making
　　의사결정회계 = decision
　　accounting ▶ accounting for
　　performance evaluation
accounting for equity　자본 회계, 지분
　　회계
accounting for external reporting　외
　　부보고 회계, 재무회계
　　▶ accounting for decision
　　making, financial accounting
accounting for fiduciary funds　수탁
　　형기금의 회계
accounting for inflation　인플레이션
　　회계, 물가변동회계
　　= accounting for changing
　　prices, inflation accounting
accounting for internal reporting　내
　　부보고 회계, 관리회계
　　= managementaccounting,
　　managerial accounting
　　▶ accounting for external
　　reporting, financial accounting
accounting for inventory　재고자산
　　회계
accounting for investment　투자자
　　산회계
accounting for lease　리스 회계
accounting for longterm investment
　　투자유가증권의 회계처리
accounting for manufacturing cost
　　제조원가계산
accounting formula　회계등식
　　= accounting equation

accounting for nonexchange transaction 비교환거래의 회계

accounting for not-for-profit organization 비영리 사업체 회계, 비영리법인 회계

accounting for overhead 제조간접비 회계

accounting for ownership equity 자본회계

accounting for performance evaluation 성과평가회계 = performance accounting ▶ decision accounting

accounting for planning 계획회계 ▶ accounting for control

accounting for proprietary funds 사업형 기금의 회계

accounting for public enterprise 공기업회계 ▶ accounting for business enterprise

accounting for reorganization 구조조정의 회계

accounting for special assessments 특별부과에 대한 회계

accounting for special revenue funds 특별수익기금의 회계

accounting for the general fund 일반기금의 회계

Accounting Historians Journal 미국 회계사학회(The Academy of Accounting Historians)의 기관지. 1977년에 창간되어 연 2회 발행.

Accounting Horizons 미국 회계학회 (American Accounting Association) 에서 발행하고 있는 계간 회계 연구지.

accounting identity 회계 항등식

accounting information 회계정보 ▶ accounting, accounting information system, financial reporting

accounting information of human resources 인적자원 회계정보

accounting information standard 회계정보기준 = standard for accounting information

accounting information system(AIS) 회계정보 시스템 ▶ accounting information, management information system

Accounting Interpretations 회계해석

accounting in units of current purchasing power 현행 구매력회계 = accounting for changes in the general price level, constant purchasing power accounting

accounting in units of general purchasing power 일반 구매력회계, 일반 구매력 변동회계 = accounting for changes in the general price level, constant purchasing power accounting

accounting literature 회계학의 문헌

accounting loss 회계상의 손실

accounting machine 회계기

accounting measure 회계측정치

accounting method 회계처리방법

accounting model of human resources 인적자원 회계모델 ▶ human resources accounting

accounting number 회계수치
accounting objectives 회계목적
accounting officer (각 도청의) 세 출감
시관
accounting period 회계기간, 회계연도
= financial year, fiscal year
accounting period in case of merger
합병의 경우 회계연도
accounting policy 회계방침, 회계정책
accounting postulate 회계공준
= accounting axiom,
accounting convention
accounting practice 회계실무
accounting principle 1) 회계원칙
= generally accepted
accounting principles,
accounting standard 2) 회계원
리
Accounting Principles Board(APB)
회계원칙심의회 ▶ APB
Opinion, Financial Accounting
Standards Board, Accounting
Standards Executive
Committee
accounting Principles Board opinion
회계원칙위원회 의견서
accounting procedure 회계절차
▶ accounting postulate,
accounting standard
accounting process 회계과정
accounting profession 회계 전문가, 직
업회계사(공인회계사), 회계인
accounting profit 회계상의 이익
▶ generally accepted
accounting principles
accounting quality 회계정보의 특성
= accounting characteristic

accounting quasi-measurement
유사 회계측정, 비공식 회계측
정
accounting rate of return(ARR) 1) 회
계적 이익률 = accountant's rate
of return 2) 회계이익률법. (회계
상의 이익)÷(투자금액) = ROI
(return on investment) ▶ pay
back method, netpresent value
method, IRR method
accounting rate of return method 회
계적 이익률법
▶ discounted cash flow
method
accounting record 회계기록
accounting reference date (영)회계기
준일
accounting reference period (영)회
계기준기간
accounting reports 회계 보고서
Accounting Research Bulletin(ARB)
회계연구공보 ▶ *Accounting*
Terminology Bulletin
Accounting Research Division(ARD)
회계조사 연구부
▶ *Accounting Research Study*
Accounting Research Monograph
(ARM) 회계연구 모노그래프
Accounting Research Study(ARS) 회
계연구총서 ▶ *Accounting*
Research Division
accounting return on equity 회계적
자기자본익률
accounting return on investment
method 회계적 이익률법
▶ accounting rate of return
Accounting Review 미국 회계학회

(American Accounting Association)
의 기관지. 1926년 창간된 계간
지.

accounting section 경리부, 회계부
= accounting department,
accounting division

Accounting Series Release(ASR) 회
계연속통첩(通牒) ▶ Financial
Reporting Release(FRR)

accounting services 재무제표 작성업
무(회계업무대행)

accounting standards 회계기준
= accounting principle

Accounting Standards Board(ASB)
회계기준심의회 ▶ Financial
Reporting Council

Accounting Standards Committee
(ASC) 회계기준위원회
▶ Accounting Standards
Board, Financial Reporting
Council, Accounting Standards
Steering Committee

Accounting Standards Division(ASD)
회계기준부 ▶ Accounting
Standards Executive
Committee

Accounting Standards Executive
Committee(AcSEC) 회계
기준 집행위원회 ▶ Accounting
Principles Board, Accounting
Standards Division

Accounting Standards Steering
Committee(ASSC) 회계기
준 운영위원회 ▶ Accounting
Standards Committee

accounting system 회계제도, 회계시스
템, 계정체계, 회계조직

accounting technician 회계기능자
accounting terminology 회계용어
Accounting Terminology Bulletin
(ATB) 회계용어공보
▶ Accounting Research
Bulletin

accounting theory 회계이론
Accounting Trends and Techniques
미국 대기업의 재무보고 실무
를 조사한 AICPA 연차 정기간
행물. 여기에는 연감, 보고서에
서 얻은 구체적인 실무, 용어,
실태 등의 조사 결과가 일람표
로 예시되고 있다.

accounting unit 회계실체 = accounting
entity ▶ business entity

accounting year 회계연도 = accounting
period, fiscal year, operating
period ▶ closing date

account number 1) 계정과목 번호
2) 계좌번호

account payable 매입채무, 외상매입금

account payable ledger 외상매입금 원
장 ▶ account receivable
ledger, customer's ledger,
creditor's ledger

account payable register 매입처계정
기입장, 매입처원장

account receivable 매출채권, 외상매
출금, 수취계정, 장부 채권
= account due ▶ accrued
revenue

account receivable collection period
외상매출금 회수기간 = debtor
days ratio

account receivable ledger 외상매출금
원장, 매출처원장 ▶ account

payable ledger, creditor's
ledger

account receivable management   외
상매출금 관리

account receivable turnover   외상매
출금 회전율
▶ receivable turnover ratio

accounts   1) 재무제표, 계산서류
= financial statement
▶ statutory accounts   2) 외상
매출금   3) 서면에 청구되지
않은 지급을 청구할 수 있는 권
리

accounts book   회계장부, 재무장부
= book of accounts, financial
book

accounts for a financial year   회계연
도 재무제표, 회계년도 계산서
류

accounts payable   1) 외상매입금 2) 매
입채무, 지불채무

accounts payable clerk   외상매입금 담
당자

accounts payable subsidiary ledger
외상매입금 보조원장

accounts receivable   1) 외상매출금 2)
매출채권

accounts receivable subsidiary ledger
외상매출금 보조원장

accounts receivable turnover   외상매
출금 회전율

accounts receivable turnover ratio
외상매출금 회전율, 매출액÷
외상매출채권▶ inventory
turnover ratio, turnover ratio

accounts receivable write off   외상매
출금 상각

account stated   확정계정(서), 채무확인
(서), 정해진 계산

accredited investor   유산 (有産) 투자가

accrediting agency   설정기관

accretion   증가(增價), 자연적 증가

accrual   1) 발생, 발생항목 2) 예정

accrual accounting   발생주의 회계
= accrual system   ▶ accrual
basis, cash basis

accrual basis   발생주의, 실현주의, 발생
기준 = accrual concept   ▶ cash
basis, realization basis

accrual basis accounting   발생주의 회계

accrual basis of accounting   발생주의
회계

accrual concept   발생주의 = accrual
basis

accrual method   발생주의 방법

accrual of expenses   비용의 발생

accruals   1) 발생항목 2) 세법상 미지급
계상항목

accruals and deferrals   수익비용의 발
생과 이연

accrual swap   금리발생형 스왑

accrual system   발생주의 회계
= accrual accounting

accrued asset   발생자산 ▶ accrued
income, accrued charge

accrued benefit cost method   미지급
효익 · 비용방식, 발생급부 원
가방식   ▶ projected benefit
cost method, unit credit
method, step-rate method

accrued benefit valuation method   발
생급부 평가방식   ▶ retirement
benefit plan

accrued charge   미지급비용

accrued depreciation   1) 감가상각누계액 = accumulated depreciation ▶ reserve for depreciation, allowance for depreciation 2) 발생원가 ▶ reproduction cost, physical depreciation, functional obsolescence, external obsolescence

accrued dividend   미지급배당, 발생배당

accrued expense   1) 미지급비용 2) 발생비용

accrued income   미수수익 ▶ accrued asset, accrued charge

accrued income tax   미지급법인세, 미지급소득세 ▶ deferred income tax

accrued interest   미지급이자, 미지급이자 할인율, 미수이자, 경과이자

accrued item   발생항목

accrued liability   1) 미지급비용 2) 미지급부채 3) 발생된(실현된) 채무

accrued pension expense   미지급 연금비용

accrued pension liability   미지급 연금채무

accrued postretirement benefit cost   미지급 퇴직후 연금지급채무비용

accrued/prepaid pension cost   미지급/선지급 연금비용

accrued receivable   미수채권

accrued rent   미지급임차료

accrued revenue   미수수익

accrued tax on income   미지급법인세

accrued wage   미지급임금

accumulated   누적

accumlated adjustments account(AAA)   적립금 정산회계

accumulated benefit obligation(ABO)   1) 누적급부채무 2) 미래 급여 수준이 당기와 같다고 가정한 경우의 연금채무

accumulated benefits approach   누적적 이익 접근법

accumulated depreciation   감가상각누계액 = accrued depreciation ▶ reserve for depreciation, allowance for depreciation

accumulated dividend   누적이익 배당

accumulated earnings   이익잉여금, 유보이익, 준비금

accumulated earnings and profits(AEP)   누적소득과 누적이익

accumulated earnings tax(AET)   유보이익 과세

accumulated fund   기본금, 자본기금 = capital fund

accumulated income tax prepayment   장기 선납세금

accumulated other comprehensive income   기타 포괄이익의 누계액

accumulated physical inventory listing   재고표

accumulated plan benefits   연금급부 누적액

accumulated postretirement benefit obligation   퇴직후 누적급부채무

accumulated postretirement benefit obligation(APBO)   종업원

이 이미 근무를 완료한 기간에
대응하는 미래의 퇴직 후 연금
지급의무의 누적액

accumulated stock 1) 누적주 2) 잉여
재고, 잉여품

accumulation and maintenance trust
누적이자신탁

accumulative stock 누적이익 배당주
▷ preferred stock

accuracy 1) 정확 2) 정확성 3) 정확도

ACE(adjusted current earnings) 조정
후 당기이익

achievement motive 달성동기

acid test ratio 1) 당좌비율, 산성시험비
율 2) (당좌자산)÷(유동부채),
current ratio = quick ratio

acknowledgement 증명서, 승인, 공식
승인서, 영수서, 사례의 말

ACM(Association for Computing
Machinery) 미국 계산기학회

ACMA(Associate of Chartered Institute of
Management Accountants)
(영)칙허 관리회계사협회 준회원

acquiescence 묵인 (默認)

acquired company 피(被) 매수기업
▷ acquiring company

acquiring company 매수기업
= acquiring enterprise
▷ acquired company

acquiring enterprise 매수기업
= acquiring company
▷ acquired company

acquisition (타회사의) 취득, 매수
= purchase, take over
▷ amalgamation, business
combination, merger, pooling
of interests, uniting of interests

acquisition accounting 취득회계, 매
수회계 = purchase accounting
▷ merger accounting, pooling
of interests, uniting of interests

acquisition cost 취득원가 = historical
cost, acquisition value

acquisition cost theory 취득원가주의
= historical cost basis

acquisition date 취득일

acquisition indebtedness 주택취득채
무

acquisition of a company 회사의 인수

acquisition of business 기업매수

acquisition of common stock 주식취
득

acquisition of equipment 설비의 취득

acquisition of property 유형 자산의
취득

acquisition planning 취득계획

acquisition price 취득원가
= acquisition cost, historical
cost

acquisition process 취득과정

acquisition value 취득가액
= acquisition cost

acquittance 해약장, (채무의) 면제, 해제,
채무소멸증서

acreage 면적

ACRS(accelerated cost recovery system)
가속상각제도, 가속원가회수제
도 ▷ accelerated depreciation,
modified accelerated cost
recoverysystem

AcSEC(Accounting Standards Executive
Committee) 회계기준 실행
위원회

ACT(advance corporation tax) 예납법

인세, 선급법인세
▶ imputation system

Act for Prevention of Frauds and
Perjurices   사기와 위증 방
지법

action   행동대체안, 활동, 행위

action for damages   손해배상청구

action for lost profit   멸실이익 배상청
구

action for price   가격 배상청구

activation   활동화, 활성화, 활용화, 기동

active account   활동계정 ▶ sleeping
account

active income   활동소득

active market   활발한 시장

active program   활동, 실행 프로그램

active station   활동 단말기

active trust   활동적 신탁

activity   활동, 작업, 사용, 활용

activity analysis   활동분석

activity cost   활동비 ▶ capacity cost,
product cost, variable cost

activity level   조업도 = level, volume,
operation level

activity method   생산량비례법
= production method, units of
production method

activity ratio   1) 활동비율 2) 사용률
= turnover ratio

acts discreditable   신용실추행위

acts of God   불가항력, 자연현상

actual absorption costing   실제전부원
가계산 ▶ actual cost basis,
direct costing, direct cost
system

actual achievement   실적(實績)

actual address   실제주소, 절대주소

= real address ▶ absolute
address

actual authority   실질적 대리권

actual burden rate   제조간접비 실제
배부율 = actual overhead rate

actual cost   실제원가 ▶ historical cost,
standard cost

actual cost accounting   실제원가계산
= actual cost basis ▶ future
cost accounting

actual cost accounting system   실제
원가계산제도 = actual
absorption costing ▶ direct
costing, direct cost system

actual cost basis   실제원가계산
= actual cost accounting

actual costing   실제원가계산

actual damages   실질적인 손해배상

actual eviction   사실상의 점유 박탈

actual expected standard cost   현실
적 표준원가 = expected actual
standard cost

actual expense   실비, 실제 비용

actual factory overhead   실제 제조간
접비, 제조간접비 실제 발생액

actual fixed cost   실제 고정비, 고정비
실제 발생액

actual fraud   사실상의 부정, 실질적인
사기(詐欺)

actual hour   실제발생시간

actual implied authority   묵시의 대리
권

actual interest rate   실질이자율

actual key   실제 키

actual labor hour(ALH)   실제 작업시
간

actual labor rate(AR)   실제임률

= actual wage rate

actually expectable standard cost 현실적 표준원가 = expected actual standard cost

actual manufacturing cost 실제제조원가

actual normal cost accounting 실제정상원가계산

actual notice 실질적 통지

actual overhead costs 실제 발생한 제조간접비

actual overhead rate 제조간접비 실제배부율 = actual burden rate

actual price(AP) 실제 가격

actual quantity(AQ) 실제소비수량

actual residual value 실제잔존가액

actual return on plan assets 연금자산의 실제수익, 연금기금의 실제수익

actual return rate 실제수익률

actual transaction 실제거래

actual variable cost 실제 변동비, 변동비 실제 발생액

actual volume 실제 조업도, 실제 활동수준

actual wage rate 실제임률 = actual labor rate

actuarial asset value 보험수리에 의한 자산가치

actuarial cost method 보험수리에 의한 원가계산법

actuarial method 보험수리법

actuarial present value 보험수리상 현가

actuarial present value of accumulated plan benefits 연간급부 누적액의 보험수리 현재가치

actuarial valuation 보험수리가치, 보험수리평가 ▶ actuary

actuary 보험계리인, 보험수리사

adapter 접속기

adaptive control 최적제어, 적응제어

adaptive system 적응시스템

added disclosure 추가공시

added value 부가가치 = value added

added value analysis 부가가치 분석

added value per employee 종업원 1인당 부가가치액

added value statement 부가가치 계산서 = value added statement

additional allowance 추가수당

additional amount 가산금

additional cost of material 재료의 추가비용

additional investment and drawing 파트너의 추가 출자 및 인출

additional liability 추가계상채무

additional mark up 추가가격인상 ▶ retail inventory method

additional minimum liability 최저연금 채무추가액

additional paid in capital 자본잉여금, 주식불입잉여금, 부가적 불입자본 ▶ paid in capital

additional pension liability 추가연금채무

additional standard deductions 표준할증상각

additional terms 추가조항

addition and betterment 증설 및 개량 ▶ capital expenditure

addition and betterment reserve 증설 및 개량적립금, 증개축적립금 ▶ addition and betterment, capital expenditure

addition theorem of probability   확률의 덧셈 정리 = addition theory of probability

addition theory of probability   확률의 덧셈 정리 = addition theorem of probability

additive congruential method   가산 합동법

additive linear model   가산선형모델

address   번지, 주소 ▶ absolute address, relative address

address check   주소 검사 = address checking

address constant   주소 정수 ▶ base address

address format   주소 형식

addressing   주소 지정

address modification   주소 변경, 주소 수정

address part   주소록, 번지부

address reference   주소 참조

address register   주소 레지스터 ▶ address, register

address space   주소 공간

address stop   주소 정지

address track   주소 트랙

address translation   주소 변환

address translator   주소 변환기 ▶ address, real address, virtual address

ademption   유증의 철회

adequacy   타당성

adequacy of disclosure   적정한 공시

adequate assurance of performance   적절한 이행보증서

adequate disclosure   적정한 공시

adequate document   적정한 서류

adhesion contract   부합(附合) 계약, 약관계약, 부종계약

adjudicated incompetent   무능력자

adjudication   파산선고

adjudication order   파산자에 대한 지불명령 = bankruptcy order ▶ bankruptcy notice

adjunct account   부가계정 ▶ contra account, offset account

adjusted basis   수정주의

adjusted cost basis   수정원가주의

adjusted current earnings(ACE)   조정 후 당기이익 ▶ alternative minimum tax, regular tax

adjusted trial balance   수정 후 시산표

adjusting entry   수정분개, 수정기입 = adjustment

adjusting journal entry(AJE)   수정분개

adjustment   수정, 정리, 기말정리, 결산정리 = adjusting entry

adjustment account   수정계정, 정산계정

adjustment item   수정항목, 조정항목

adjustment of financial statements of prior periods   과년도 재무제표 수정 ▶ restatement

adjustment of revenue recognition   수입인식의 조정

administered price   관리가격

administration   경영, 경영관리, 집행, 행정

administration cost   1) 일반관리비 = administration expense, administration overhead 2) 신탁관리비용

administration cost variance   일반관리비 차이

administration of estate   상속재산의
    관리
administration of trust   신탁의 관리
administration overhead   일반관리비
    = administration cost
administration period   유산관리기간
administrations   행정기관
administrative act   행정행위, 관리행위
administrative activity   행정활동
administrative agency   행정대리인
administrative and maintenance
    expense   유지관리비
administrative control   운영관리 통제,
    관리통제 ▶ accounting control
administrative data processing   사무
    데이터 처리, 사무관리 데이터
    처리 = business data
    processing
administrative environment   관리 환
    경요인
administrative expense   일반관리비,
    관리비, 경비 = administration
    cost, administration overhead
administrative expense budget   일반
    관리비 예산 ▶ advertising
    expense budget
administrative function   경영관리 기능,
    경영기능
administrative order   행정규정, 행정
    명령
administrative power   경영능력, 관리
    능력
administrative proceeding   관리소송
    절차
administrator   1) 관리인, 유산관리인,
    집행인 2) 관리자, 이사
administrator of bequest   유산관리인

administratrix   여자 집행인
admission   입장료, 입회금
admission of a new partner   새 파트
    너의 입회(가입)
Admission of Securities to Listing
    유가증권 상장 인가규정
admission tax   입장세
adoption   채택
ADRS(asset depreciation range system)
    자산 감가상각 탄력제도,
    ADR 제도
ad valorem   종가
ad valorem duty   종가세 ▶ specific
    duty, specific tax
ad valorem freight   종가운임
ad valorem goods   종가과세품, 종가품
    목
ad valorem tariff   종가세율, 종가관세
    ▶ specific tax
ad valorem tax   종가세 ▶ specific
    duty
advance   전도금, 선급금, 선수금
advance buying   계절 전 매입
advance corporation tax(ACT)   선불
    법인세, 예납법인세
    ▶ corporation tax, franked
    investment income, franked
    payment, mainstream
    corporation tax, qualifying
    distribution
advance freight   선불운임
advance from customer   선수금
advance on construction   건설공사 전
    도금
advance payment   전도금, 선급금
advance receipt   선수금
advance received   선수금

advance received on incident   위탁매
입에 대한 선수금

advance refunding   재적립채무의 사전
부담 ▶ early extinguishment

advance royalty   선불 로열티

advantage   우위성

adventure   모험, 투기적 사업

adverse claim   소유자의 의사에 반하는
이용

adverse effect   불리한 영향

adverse opinion   부적정 의견
▶ auditor'sopinion, auditor's
report, except opinion

adverse opinion report   부적정 의견
보고서 ▶ unqualified report

adverse possession   1) 불법점유 2) 적
대적 점유 3) 적대적 고유한
취득시효

adverse selection   역선택

adverse variance   불리한 차이
= unfavorable variance
▶ favorable variance

advertising   광고

advertising cost   광고선전비
= advertising expense

advertising expense   광고선전비
= advertising cost

advertising expense budget   광고선전
비 예산
▶ administrative expense
budget

advertising rate   광고료

advice and pay(A/P)   통지 지불
= dispatch note ▶ delivery
note

advising bank   통지은행

advisor   증권고문(顧問)업자

advisory service   자문업무, 고문 서비
스

AEP(accumulated earnings and profits)
누적소득과 누적이익

AET(accumulated earnings tax)   유보
이익 과세

affairs   기업업무, 영업활동, 사항

affiliate   관계회사 = affiliated
enterprise, affiliated company

affiliated and controlled corporation
관계회사와 지배회사

affiliated company   1) 관계회사, 계열
회사, 동계회사 = affiliate
2)지배·종속관계의 회사 3) 관
련회사 ▶ associated company
(영), equity method, affiliation
4) 자회사 = subsidiary

affiliated enterprise   관계회사, 관련기
업 = affiliate, affiliated
company ▶ subsidiary

affiliated entity   관계사업체

affiliated group   관계회사그룹

affiliation   제휴, 연맹, 관계 ▶ affiliated
company, affiliate, subsidiary

affirmation of fact   사실 확언

affirmative action   1) 차별철폐조처
2) 긍정적 활동, 확정적 행위

affirmative answer   긍정적 회답

affirmative confirmation   적극적 조회
확인 = positive confirmation
▶ negative confirmation

affirmative easement   적극적 지역권

affirmative waste   적극적 훼손

AFIPS(American Federation of
Information Processing
Societies)   미국 정보처리학회
연합회

after-acquired property 사후취득재산

after-acquired property clause 사후취득재산 포괄담보조항

after-closing trial balance 마감후 시산표, 이월 시산표 = post-closing trial balance

after cost 사후비용

after-image 갱신 후 이미지

after market 신규 발행 후의 시장 = secondary market ▶ primary market

aftertax cash inflow 세금공제 후 현금유입액

after the fact control 사후관리 ▶ before the fact control

AFUDC(allowance for funds used during construction) 건설기간 중의 자금비용

age allowance (영)노령자 공제

age discrimination 연령차별

Age Discrimination in Employment Act 고용시 연령차별에 관한 법

aged trial balance 구 시산표

ageing 연수조사, 연령조사 = aging

ageing for debtors (영)수취계정의 연수조사 = aging of accounts receivable

ageing of accounts receivable (영)수취계정의 연수조사 = ageing for debtors ▶ ageing

agency 1) 대리,대리권, 대리행위 2) 대리점, 특약점 3) 정부기관

agency bookkeeping 대리인 부기, 대리점 부기 ▶ proprietorship bookkeeping

agency by estoppel 금반언(禁反言)에 의한 대리

agency by necessity 사무관리

agency contract 대리계약

agency cost 대리원가

agency fund 1) 대리기금 2) 정부기금 (청, 국 등 미국 정부기관의 기금)

agency head 국장

agency law 대리법

agency obligation 대리예치금

agency of federal government 연방 정부기관

agency problem 대리인 문제 = principal-agent relationship

agency relationship 대리관계

agency theory 대리인 이론 ▶ management stewardship

agenda 1)협의사항, 의사일정, 처리사항 2) 과제

agent 대리인, 대리점, 특약점

agent and third party 대리인과 제3자

agent coupled with an interest 이해관계가 있는 대리인

agent's lien 대리인의 담보권

agent's warranty 대리인의 담보책임

aggregate 총합치

aggregate amount 합계금액, 총계, 누계, 합계수치

aggregate basis 총괄기준 ▶ individual basis, individual item basis, lower of cost or market basis

aggregate expression 집합체식

aggregation 총합, 총계, 집계, 통합, 합산

aggregative costing 제품원가계산 = product costing

aggressive security 공격적 증권

A

▶ defensive security, beta

aging 1) 기간, 시기 2) 연수조사, 연령조사 = ageing (영) ▶ aging schedule

aging of accounts receivable 외상매출금의 연령조사

aging of debtors 매출채권의 연령조사

aging schedule 연령조사표

agio 환전수수료, 주식 프리미엄, 환전업

AGM(annual general meeting) 연차주주총회

agreed bid 합의에 의한 주식 공개매입 = agreed takeover ▶ take-over bid

agreed takeover 합의에 의한 주식 공개매입

agreed-upon procedure 사전에 합의된 감사절차

agreement 일치, 계약, 협정, 동의

agreement of financial statements with accounting records 재무제표와 회계 기록의 일치

agreement to sell 매도계약

agricultural accounting 농업회계

agricultural bookkeeping 농업부기

AIA(American Institute of Accountants) 미국 회계사협회

AI(artificial intelligence) 인공지능

AICM(Grad)(Associate of the Institute of Credit Management) 여신관리협회 준회원의 약칭

AICPA(American Institute of Certified Public Accountants) 미국 공인회계사협회

AICPA responsibilities in tax practice 세무실무에서 AICPA의 책임

AICPA Special Committee on

Financial Reporting 미국 공인회계사협회(AICPA) 재무보고특별위원회 = Jenkins Committee ▶ business reporting

AICPA statement of position(SOP) AICPA의 의견표명서

AIMR (Association for Investment Management and Research) 투자관리연구협회

air bill 항공화물 운송장 = air waybill

air consignment note 항공 운송장 = air waybill

air damage 공수손해

air waybill(AWB) 항공화물 운송장, 항공화물 수취증 = air bill

AIS(accounting information system) 회계정보 시스템

AISG(Accountants International Study Group) 회계사 국제연구 단체

AJE(adjusting journal entry) 수정분개

alcohol fuels credit 알코올 연료 세액공제

algebraic method of cost allocation 연립방정식법에 의한 원가배분 ▶ direct distribution method, reciprocal distribution method, step ladder distribution method

ALI(American Law Institute) 미국 법률협회

alias 별명

alien corporation 외국적 회사, 외국적 법인, 외국회사 = foreign corporation

alignment 일직선(을 이루기), 정렬

alimony 이혼 위자료, 이혼한 배우자에게 지급하는 보조금

**alimony or separate maintenance
payment**   위자료와 별거유
지수당

all-capital earnings rate   총자본이익
률

all financial resource   총재무자원

all inclusive basis   포괄주의 = all
inclusive concept ▶ current
operating basis, current
operating performance concept

all inclusive concept   포괄주의 = all
inclusive basis, clean surplus
concept ▶ current operating
performance concept

all inclusive income statement   포괄
주의 손익계산서 = all inclusive
type of income statement ▶ all
inclusive concept, current
operating performance concept,
current operating performance
income statement

all inclusive theory   포괄주의 이론
▶ selective theory

all inclusive type of income statement
포괄주의 손익계산서 = all
inclusive income statement
▶ all inclusive concept,
current operating performance
concept, current operating
performance income statement

allocable cost   배분가능원가

allocate   배부하다

allocated contract   분할계약

allocated cost   배부원가 = distributed
cost ▶ direct charging

allocated stock   1) 특정 용도 원재료
2) 예비재고 = appropriate
stock, assigned stock,
earmarked stock, reserved
stock

**allocate the differential to the assets
and liabilities of S**   S의 자
산 및 부채에 대한 차이의 배부

allocation   1) 배분, 배부 2) 할당, 배당

allocation basis   배부기준

allocation cost   배부원가, 배부비

allocation model   배부 모델

allocation of cost   비용 배부

**allocation of income and deductions
among taxpayers**   납세자
간의 소득 및 비용의 배부

allocation of income tax   소득세 기간
배부 ▶ deferred income tax

allocation of partnership income (loss)
파트너십의 이익(손실)의 분배

allocation of principal and income
원금과 소득의 배부

allocation of resources   자원의 배부

allocation of service department cost
보조부문비의 배부

allocation of tax expense   세금비용의
배부 ▶ interperiod tax
allocation, tax allocation

allocation period   배부기간

allocation process   자원배분 과정

allocation variance   배부차이

allotment   할당, 배부, 배당, 예산배부

allotment certificate   할당증권, 주식할
당증 = allotment letter
▶ allotment

allotment letter   (영)주식 할당통지서
= allotment certificate, letter of
allotment

allotment of share   주식의 할당

allotted capital   할당완료자본
= issued capital

allotted share   할당완료주식 = issued
share ▶ authorised capital,
paid-up capital, unallotted
share

allotted share capital   할당완료 주식
자본 = issued share capital

allottee   (신주의) 할당권 소유자

allowable cost   허용원가

allowable level of audit risk   감사인이
허용할 수 있는 수준의 감사 위
험

allowable level of detection risk   감사
인이 허용할 수 있는 수준의 적
발위험

allowance   1) 충당금 = provision
▶ reserve 2) 수당, 보수, 급여
액 3) 할인, 에누리 4) 소득공
제 5) 지출예산 6) 허용치, 허
용량

allowance for bad debt   대손충당금
= allowance for doubtful
accounts, allowance for
uncollectable accoun,

allowance for depreciation   감가상각
누계액, 감가상각충당금
= accumulated depreciation,
reserve for depreciation

allowance for doubtful account   대손
충당금 (의심스러운 계정에 대한
충당금) = allowance for bad debt,
allowance for uncollectables,
bad-debt provision

allowance for doubtful receivables   대
손충당금

allowance for earnings on

shareholder's investment
주식투자이익준비금
▶ regulated operation

**allowance for funds used during
construction(AFUDC)**   건
설기간 중의 자금비용

**allowance for inventory decline to
market**   재고자산 시가 하락
충당금

allowance for inventory valuation
재고자산 평가충당금

allowance for losses on repossessions
상품환입손실충당금

allowance for purchases discount
매입할인충당금

allowance for repairs   수선충당금

**allowance for retirement and
severance**   퇴직급여충당금
= reserve for retirement
allowance

allowance for sales discount   매출할
인충당금 = provision for
discount allowance

allowance for sales rebate   매출할인
충당금

allowance for sampling risk   표본위
험 허용치

allowance for uncollectables   대손충
당금 = allowance for bad debt,
allowance for doubtful
accounts

allowance method   충당금 방식
▶ direct write-off method

allowance to reduce deferred tax assets
이연법인세자산 감소를 위한
충당금

allowance to reduce deferred tax asset

A

to expected realizable value
이연법인세 자산을 기대 · 실
현가능가액으로 감소시키기 위
한 충당금

allowance to reduce inventory to LIFO
후입선출법 원가수정충당금
= last-in, first-out reserve

all-round price   포괄가격, 제비용 포함
가격

alpha factor used in expotential
smoothing   지수평활법에
있어서 알파 요소

alpha risk   알파 위험, 제1종 위험
▶ beta risk

alpha value market related risk   알파
치 시장관련 리스크 ▶ beta
value, nonmarket related risk

alteration   변경, 개조

alteration switch   변경 스위치, 변경용
스위치

alternate routing   대체경로 지정

alternate track   대체트랙, 교대트랙
= alternative track

alternate valuation date   평가일 교체

alternative   대체안

alternative accounting principle   대체
적 회계기준

alternative accounting rule   대체적
회계기준 = alternative
accounting principle

alternative auditing procedure   대체
적 감사절차

alternative demand   선택수요

alternative hypothesis   대립가설
▶ null hypothesis

alternative measures   대체적 측정치

alternative method   대체적 방법

alternative minimum tax(AMT)   대체
적 최소과세 ▶ adjusted
current earnings, regular tax

alternative procedure   대체적 절차

alternatives to bankruptcy   파산대체

alternative track   대체트랙, 교대트랙
= alternate track

alternative way   대체적 방법

ALU(arithmetic and logic unit)   산술논
리 연산장치

AMA(American Management Association)
미국 경영자협회

AMA(American Marketing Association)
미국 마케팅협회

amalgamation   합병, 합동, 회사합병
= consolidation, merger
▶ business combination,
purchase of business

AM(amplitude modulation)   진폭변조

ambiguities in negotiable instruments
교부성 증서의 모호성

ameliorative waste   개량적 훼손

a memorandum on
balance-sheet audits   대차
대조표 감사에 대한 비망기록
▶ venfication of financial
statements

amended auditor's report   정정감사
보고서, 수정감사보고서

amended budget   수정예산 = revised
budget

amended return   수정 세무 신고서

amended tax return   수정 세무 신고
= revised return

American Accounting Association
(AAA)   미국 회계학회

American Association of Public

Accountants   미국 공공회
계사협회
**American Association of University
    Instructors in Accounting**
    미국 대학 회계학담당 교원학회
American Depositary Receipts(ADR)
    미국 예탁증권
American Economic Review   미국 경
    제학회 (American Economics
    Association)의 학회지
**American Federation of Information
    Processing Societies(AFIPS)**
    미국 정보처리학회 연합회
**American Institute of Accountants
    (AIA)**   미국 회계사학회
**American Institute of Certified Public
    Accountants(AICPA)**   미국
    공인회계사협회
American law   미국법
**American Management Association
    (AMA)**   미국 경영자협회
**American Marketing Association
    (AMA)**   미국 마케팅협회
**American National Standards Institute
    (ANSI)**   미국 규격협회
American option   미국형 옵션
        ▶ option, European option
**American Society Mechanical
    Engineers**   미국 기계기술
    자협회
**American Standard Code for
    Information Interchange
    (ASCII)**   정보교환용 미국 표
    준코드 = American National
    Standard Code for Information
    Interchange
American Stock Exchange(AMEX)   미

국 증권거래소 ▶ New York
Stock Exchange
American with Disabilities Act(ADA)
    심신장애 미국민법
AMEX(American Stock Exchange)   미
    국 증권거래소
amortizable loan   할부상환 대부
amortization   할부상환, 상각, 할부상각,
    상각비 ▶ depletion,
    depreciation
amortization fund   상각기금 ▶ fund
    for retirement of bond
amortization money table   할부상환
    금표 = amortization table
amortization of bond discount   사채
    할인 · 발행차금상각
    = amortization of discount of
    debentures
amortization of discount on debentures
    사채할인발행차금상각
    = amortization of bond
    discount
amortization of goodwill   영업권의 상
    각 ▶ goodwill
amortization of intangible assets   무
    형고정자산 상각비
amortization of prior service cost   과
    거근무비용의 상각
**amortization of unrecognized gain or
    loss**   미인식 손익의 상각
**amortization of unrecognized prior
    service cost**   미인식 과거근
    무비용의 상각
**amortization of unrecognized
    transition obligation(UTO)**
    미인식 이전(移轉)채무의 상각
amortization payment   할부금

= amortization rent

amortization table　할부상각표, 상각표

amortized cost　(유효이자율법을 적용한)
상각비, 상각원가

amortized the differential for the year
연간차이의 상각

amount　1) 금액, 가액, 수치　2) 현금

amount and variety of information
다종다량의 정보

amount brought forward　전기이월
(액)= balance brought forward
▶ amount carried forward

amount carried forward　차기이월(액)
= balance carried forward
▶ amount brought forward

amount due　만기결제액, 만기지불액,
기일상환액

amount earned for equity　주주지분
이익 = earnings available for
ordinary, earnings for equity

amount of annuity　복리연금종가, 연
금종가

amount of cash　현금액

amount of investment　투자액

amount paid to subconstructor　하청
업자 지급액

amounts initially recorded　원시장부
기입가액 = historical cost

amounts of net assets　순자산액

AMT(alternative minimum tax)　대체적
최소과세

analyser　증권분석가, 재무분석가
= analyst (애널리스트)

analysis department　분석부문, 분석과,
조사과

analysis for credit　신용분석 = credit
analysis

analysis for credit purpose　신용분석

analysis of balance sheet　대차대조표
분석 = balance sheet analysis

analysis of budget variance　예산차이
분석 = budget variance
analysis

analysis of cost variance　원가차이분
석 = cost variance analysis

analysis of financial statements　재무
제표분석, 재무분석
= financial statements analysis

analysis of income statement　손익계
산서 분석 = income statement
analysis

analysis of market　시장분석

analysis of material efficiency variance
직접재료비 소비량차이 분석,
직접재료비 능률차이 분석
▶ analysis of material price
variance

analysis of material price variance
재료 가격차이 분석
▶ analysis of material
efficiency variance

analysis of material quantity variance
재료 수량차이 분석
▶ analysis of material price
variance

analysis of past experience　실적분석
법 = historical analysis

analysis of post-due receivables　만기
경과 채권분석

analysis of profitability　수익성분석

analysis of surplus　잉여금분석, 잉여
금분석표 = surplus analysis

analysis of the rate of firm growth
성장성분석

A

analysis of variance 차이분석

analysis of time series 시계열분석

analysis of variance from budget 예산차이분석 = budget variance analysis, budget variation analysis

analysis of wage variance 노무비차이분석

analysis paper 분석표

analysis report 분석보고서

analysis sheet 명세표, 내역표, 분석표

analyst 증권분석가, 재무분석가, 애널리스트 = security analyst

analysts' report 애널리스트 보고서

analytical accounting 분석적 회계

analytical evidence 분석적 증거

analytical procedures 분석적 검토 절차

analytical process type of production 분해형 생산, 분해공정형 생산

analytical review(AR) 분석적 검토

analytical review procedure 분석적 검토절차

analytical work sheet 분석용 정산표

analytic approach 분석적 어프로우치, 분석적 접근법

analyzing cost behavior 원가행태의 분석

ancillary credit business 부수적 신용사업

AND 논리곱

AND gate 논리곱 게이트, 논리곱 회로, 논리곱 소자

AND operation 논리곱 연산, AND연산 ▶ conjunction

Anglo-American Law 영미법

annotation (컴퓨터 프로그램의) 주석, 주

annual accounts 연차계산서류, 연차재무제표 = final accounts
▶ financial accounts, financial statements

annual allowance 세비, 연차수당

annual audit 연도감사, 연차감사

annual budget 연도예산, 연간예산

annual cash inflow 연간 현금흐름 유입액

annual demand 연간 수요량

$$Q = 2aD/k$$

D = 연간수요량 (annualdemand for inventory in units)

a = 1회당 주문비용 (cost of placing order)

k = 재고 1단위당 재고유지비용 (average costs of carring on a unit for one year)

annual earnings 연간이익, 연도이익

annual exclusion 연간공제액

annual general meeting(AGM) 연차사원총회, 정례주주총회
▶ annual meeting of shareholders, annual shareholders' meeting, extraordinary general meeting, ordinary resolution

annual inventory 연차 재고자산

annualized overhead rate 제조간접비 연간배부율

annualized profit method 연간이익 비교법

annual meeting 정기총회

annual meeting of shareholders 정기주주총회 = annual shareholders' meeting

annual percentage rate(APR) 연간여
신부담 요율

annual physical count 기말 실지재고

annual profit and loss 연차손익

annual programmed budget 연차 프
로그램 예산

annual report 연차보고서 ▶ financial
highlight, financial statements

annual report and accounts 연차보고
서

annual report to stockholders 주주용
연차보고서 ▶ Form 10-K

annual result 연간성과

annual return 연차신고서 ▶ Gazette

annual shareholder's meeting 정기
주주총회 = annual meeting of
shareholders

annual value 연차 순사용료

annuitant 연금수령자

annuities and pensions 연금

annuity 연금 ▶ pension

annuity bond 무기한채권, 연금채권
= perpetual bond

annuity certain 기간보장연금, 확정연
금 ▶ life annuity

annuity contracts 연금계약

annuity depreciation 연금법 감가상각

annuity due 1) 선불연금 (연금의 미래가
치 계산상에서) 2) 기수불 연금
▶ ordinary annuity

annuity in advance 선불연금 (연금의 미
래가치 계산상에서)

annuity method 연금법

annuity method of depreciation 연금
식 감가상각법, 연금법

annuity payable in advance 선불 정
액연금 ▶ ordinary annuity

anonymous association 익명조합

**ANSI(American National Standards
Institute)** 미국 규격협회

answerback 응답

antecedent debt 기존의 채무

antecedent party 이서인

antedate 후일부, 전일부 = backdate
▶ postdate

antedated 후일부

**anticipated and planned
manufacturing variances**
원가차이중 정상적인 것

anticipated loss 기대손실

anticipated transaction 예상거래, 예
정거래

anticipation 예측

anticipation control 예정 콘트롤

anticipation of repudiation 지불거절
의 예상

anticipatory breach 직전의 계약 불이
행, 기한전 계약불이행

anticipatory breach of contract 이행
기일전의 계약위반

anticipatory repudiation 1) 이행기일
전 이행거절 2) 선행하는 지불
거절

anti dilution 반희석화 ▶ dilution

antidilutive 반희석화

anti fraud 사기의 방지, 부정방지
= antifraud

anti fraud provisions 사기방지조항

antitrust 반트러스트, 독점금지

A/P(advice and pay) 통지불

APB(Accounting Principles Board) 회계
원칙심의회

APB Opinion 회계원칙심의회의 의견
서, APB 의견서 ▶ APB,

APB Statement
APB Statement   APB에서 발행하는 보
고서 ▶ APB, APB Opinion
APC(Auditing Practices Committee)   감
사실무위원회
aperture   항목설정범위
apparent authority   외견상 대리권, 표
현대리, 표현상의 권한
apparent ownership   외견상 소유권
appeal   공소, 상고
applicability   적용가능성
applicable tax rate   적용세율
application   1) 중요한 회계업무 2) 신
청서
application basis   배부기준
application control   응용통제, 적용통
제 ▶ accounting control,
general control
application for registration   등록신청
application for shares   주식청약, 주식
신청
application money   신청금, 주식청약
증거금
application of fund   자금의 운영
application of manufacturing expense
제조간접비의 배부
= application of overhead
application of overhead   제조간접비의
배부 = application of
manufacturing expense
applied cost   원가배부액
applied factory burden   제조간접비 배
부액 = applied manufacturing
burden
applied factory overhead   제조간접비
배부액 = apportioned factory
overhead

applied manufacturing burden   제조
간접비 배부액 = applied
factory burden, applied factory
overhead
applied manufacturing expense   제조
간접비 배부액
applied overhead   제조간접비 배부액
= factory overhead applied
▶ factory overhead
applied research   응용연구
appoint   지정, 기일지정
appointment   1) 지정 2) 임명, 임용
3) 약속
apportioned factory overhead   제조
간접비 배부액 = applied
factory overhead
apportionment of cost variance   원가
차액의 배부
appraisal   1) 평가, 사정 2) 감정 3) 견
적 4) 사정가액, 사정액, 평가
액 = valuation
appraisal capital   감정 자본
appraisal fee   감정비용
appraisal method of depreciation   감
가상각의 평가법, 감가상각의
간접법 ▶ appraisal system
appraisal of asset   자산의 감정, 자산의
평가
appraisal right   주식매수청구권
appraisal surplus   재평가 적립금
= appreciation surplus
▶ revaluation, revaluation
reserve
appraisal system   평가법
▶ replacement system,
retirement system
appraisal value   감정가치, 사정가치

appraisement　(재산 등의) 평가, 감정
　　= appraisal
appraiser　감정인
appreciation　1) 평가증 ▶ depreciation
　　2) 평가익 ▶ appraisal surplus,
　　appreciation surplus　3) 통화의
　　가치상승　4) 소유한 자산의 시
　　장가격 상승　5) 증가(增價)
appreciation surplus　재평가적립금
　　▶ appraisal surplus
appropriated earned surplus　처분된
　　이익잉여금 ▶ retained
　　earnings, unappropriated
　　earned surplus
appropriated RE　처분 이익잉여금
appropriated retained earnings　처분
　　된 이익잉여금
appropriated stock　1) 예비주　2) 예비
　　재고 = reserved stock
appropriate interest rate　적정이율
appropriateness　타당성
appropriation　1) 이익유보　2) 충당금
　　3) 지출권한　4) 할당예산액　5)
　　처분
appropriation of retained earnings
　　이익잉여금의 처분
appropriation statement　이익처분계
　　산서
approval　승인
approval sale　시용판매 = sale on
　　approval
approved method for the
　　preparation of balance
　　sheet statement　공인 대
　　차대조표 작성방법 ▶ Uniform
　　Accounting, Verification of
　　Financial Statements

approved pension scheme　적격연금
　　제도
approved vendor list　승인완료업자 리
　　스트
approximate amount　개략적 금액, 근
　　사치
approximate cost　개략적 원가, 견적원
　　가
approximate measure　개략적 측정치
approximate rate-of-return method
　　개략적 이익률법
approximate value　개산가액, 근사치
approximation　근사치
APR(annual percentage rate)　연간여신
　　부담료율
aqactual quantity of input used in
　　production　생산에 사용된
　　실제투입량
AR(analytical review)　분석적 검토
ARB(Accounting Research Bulletin)　회
　　계연구공보
arbitrage　차액취득매매
arbitrage broker　차액취득 매매업자
　　= arbitragist
arbitrage operation　차액취득 매매행
　　위
arbitragist　차액취득 매매업자
　　= arbitrage broker
arbitrary cost allocation　자의적 원가
　　배분
arbitration　조정, 중재
architecture　구조
archive　보존, 보관(하다)
ARD(Accounting Research Division)　회
　　계연구조사부
area　영역, 기억영역, 구역
area franchise　구역 프랜차이즈

area variable 구역변수
argument 독립변수
argument list 독립변수 리스트
arithmetical instruction 산술명령
    = arithmetic instruction
    ▶ arithmetic operation
arithmetic average 산술평균
    ▶ geometric mean
arithmetic check 연산검사, 산술검사
    ▶ application control,
    crossfooting
arithmetic data 산술적 자료
arithmetic instruction 산술명령
    = arithmetical instruction
    ▶ arithmetic operation
arithmetic mean 산술평균
arithmetic operation 산술연산, 사칙
    연산 ▶ arithmetic instruction
arithmetic weighted average 가중평
    균
ARM(Accounting Research Monograph)
    회계연구 모노그래프
arm's length principle 공정거래의 원
    칙
arm's length transaction 1) 공정한 거
    래 2) 독립기업간의 거래
ARQ(automatic request for repetition)
    자동반복요구
arrangement 동의
array 배열 ▶ subscript
arrear certificate 연체이자증서
arrear of interest 연체이자
arrears 연체료, 체납금
arrival draft 도착 후 일람불어음
arrival notice 도착통지, 착선통지
ARS(Accounting Research Study) 회계
    연구총서

article 1) 정관, 계약, 규약, 조항, 항목
    2) 상품, 물품
article consigned 위탁적송품, 적송품
    = consignments-out
articles of association 1) 통상정관
    2) (미국 회사의) 정관 = articles
    of incorporation
articles of copartnership 파트너십 합
    의서
articles of incorporation 정관
articles of partnership 조합규약, 합명
    회사의 정관 = partnership
    agreement, partnership articles
articulation 1) 유기(有機)성 2) 증감연
    관, 상호관련
articulation statement 계정연관표
artifical person 가공인물
artificial intelligence (AI) 인공지능
    ▶ expert system
artificial language 인공언어
artificial monetary 인위적인 화폐단위
artificial monetary unit 인위적인 화
    폐단위
artisan's lien 기능공(직공)의 선취특권,
    대리인의 유치권
ASA(American Standards Association)
    미국 규격협회
ASB(Accounting Standards Board) 회
    계기준심의회
ASB(Auditing Standards Board) 감사
    기준심의회
ASC(Accounting Standards Committee)
    회계기준위원회
ASCII(American Standard Code for
    Information Interchange) 정
    보교환용 미국 표준코드
ASD(Accounting Standards Division) (미

국 공인회계사협회의) 회계기준부

a single statment　단일재무제표

as is sale　현재의 상태로 매매, 현재의 상
태로 매각

ask price　매도호가 = asked price,
asking price, offered price
▶ bid price

**ASME(American Society of Mechanical
Engineers)**　미국 기계기술자
협회

**ASOBAC(A Statement of Basic Auditing
Concepts)**　기초적 감사개념
에 관한 보고서

**ASOBAT(A Statement of Basic
Accounting Theory)**　기초적
회계이론에 관한 보고서

aspiration level　희망수준, 요구수준

ASR(Accounting Series Release)　회계연
속통첩

ASR(automatic send/receive)　자동송수
신장치

**ASSC(Accounting Standards Steering
Committee)**　회계기준운영위
원회

assembly order　조립지시서
= assembly production order

assembly production order　조립지시
서 = assembly order

assertion　단언, 단정, 주장, 의사표시

assessed level of control risk　통제위
험 평가수준 ▶ assertion,
control risk, detection risk,
substantive tests

assessing　(사람, 사물의) 가치를 평가하다

assessing control risk　통제위험 평가
▶ assertion, internal control
structure

assessment　평가(액), 사정(액), 세액, 할당
금, 추징금

assessment of control risk　통제 위험
평가

assessment rate of collateral　담보평
가율

assessments　1) 부과 (賦課), 부과금
2) 사전평가

assessor　재산평가인, 감정인, 사정인,
세액사정인

asset　자산

asset accounting　자산회계

asset basis　자산기준

asset capitalization　자산계상

asset cover　자산배율 ▶ dividend
cover, equity dividend cover

asset depreciation range system(ADRS)
자산의 감가상각 탄력제도, 법
정허용 내용연한, 연수

asset devaluation　자산의 가치하락

**asset found or received
as contribution**　발견자산
(우발자산) 또는 수증자산

asset inflow　자산유입액

asset-liability approach　자산부채법

asset life　자산 내용연수

asset outflow　자산유출액

asset register　고정자산 대장 = fixed
asset register

asset revaluation　자산재평가
▶ revaluation

asset turnover　자산회전율 = capital
turnover

asset turnover ratio　자산회전율
= turnover of asset

asset valuation　자산평가

asset value　자산가치

assignation 양도, 할당, 지정

assigned cost 유도원가 = derived cost

assigned stock 1) 예비주 2) 예비재고
= reserved stock

assignee 양수인

assignment 1) 양도, 지정양도, 양도증
서, 양도담보 2) 할당, 배분
3) 임무, 일

assignment for benefit of creditor
채권자를 위한 양도

assignment of contract 계약의 양도

assignment of interest 지분의 양도

assignment of negotiable instrument
교부성 증서의 양도

assignment of partnership 지분의
양도

assignment of partnership interest
파트너십 지분의 양도

assignment of receivable 채권 양도

assignment of right 채권의 양도, 계약
상 권리의 양도

assignment problem 할당 문제

assignment statement 할당명세서

assignment technique 원가배분법
▶ cost allocation

**assignment to identifiable net assets
and goodwill** 식별 가능
한 순자산 및 영업권에 할당

assignor 양도인

assigns 지정

assistant 1) 보좌의, 보조의, 보조인
2) 보좌관

assistant manager 부관리자, 부지배인

assisted area (영)개발조성지역
▶ special assisted area, special
development area

associate (회계사협회 등의) 준회원

▶ fellow

associated company 1) 관계회사, 계열
회사, 동계회사 ▶ affiliated
company 2) 반수(半數)소유회
사 ▶ fifty-percent-owned
company 3) 관련회사 (영)
▶ related company

association 조합, 사단(社團), 협회, 연
합, 기업연합

**Association for Computing Machinery
(ACM)** 미국 계산기학회

**Association of Accounting Technicians
(AAT)** (영) 회계기능자협회

Association of Corporate Treasurers
(영)재무담당자협회

Association of International Accountants
(영)국제회계 전문가협회

association with financial statements
재무제표와 연계

associative memory 연상기억장치
= associative storage

associative storage 연상기억장치
= associative memory

assumed rate of interest 예정이율

assumption 1) 인수, 인계, 취임 2) 공
준 3) 전제

assumption of accounting 회계상의
가정 ▶ convention of
accounting, postulate of
accounting

assumption of a stable monetary unit
화폐가치 안정의 가정

assumption of duties 의무의 인수

assumption of risk 위험의 인수

assurance 1) 보증, 확신 2) 보험

assurance of performance 이행의 보
증

A Statement of Basic Accounting Theory(ASOBAT) 기초적 회계이론에 관한 보고서

A Statement of Basic Auditing Concepts(ASOBAC) 기초적 감사개념에 관한 보고서

asymmetric information 비대칭 정보

ATB(Accounting Terminology Bulletin) 회계용어 공보

ATM(automatic teller machine) 현금자동지급기

attachment 담보권 설정, 압류

attachment of security interest 담보물권의 설정

attainability 달성가능성

attainable standard 달성가능 표준

attendance bonus 정시 보너스

attendance time 근무 총시간수, 총노동시간

attention interruption 처리방해

attenuation distortion 1) 왜곡된 회석화 2) (전류, 전압의) 감쇠되어 일그러짐

attestation 입증 업무 ▶ attest function, audit

attestation clause (문서가 진짜라는) 증명 문구

attestation engagement 입증업무

attestation standard 입증 업무 기준

attest function 입증 기능 ▶ attestation, fair presentation

attest service 입증 업무

attitude and attitude change 태도와 태도변동

attorney 변호사, 의뢰인

attorney at law 대리인의 변호사

attributable fixed cost 귀속가능

고정비 ▶ direct fixed cost

attributable profit 귀속시켜야 할 이익, 가산되어야 할 이익, 배분가능 이익 ▶ long-term contract

attribute 속성 = attribution, property

attribute measured 측정속성 = measurement attribute

attribute sampling 속성표본조사

attribution 1) 속성 = attribute 2) 배분

AU 감사기준

auction 경매

auction market 경매시장

audio frequency 음성 주파수

audio response unit 음성 응답장치

audit 1) 감사 2) 감사하다

audit adjustments 감사상의 수정사항

audit and accounting guide 감사 및 회계 가이드

audit and appeal procedure 감사 및 항소절차

audit around the computer 컴퓨터 주변 감사 ▶ auditing through the computer, audit with the computer

audit certificate 감사 보고서

audit check list 감사점검표 ▶ audit planning, audit program

Audit Commission for Local Authorities in England and Wales 영국 · 웨일즈 지방자치단체 감사위원회 ▶ Commission for Local Authority Accounts in Scotland

audit committee 감사위원회

audit completion 감사종결

audit difference 감사상의 차이

audited financial statements 감사받

은 재무제표

audit effectiveness　감사의 유효성

audit effectiveness and efficiency　감사 유효성과 능률

audit efficiency　감사의 효율

audit engagement　감사계약

audit evidence　감사증거
= examination evidence

audit fee　감사보수

audit file　감사조서 ▶ audit working paper

audit finding　감사상의 발견사항

audit function　감사기능 ▶ audit of financial statements

audit guide　감사 가이드

audit hooks　컴퓨터에 내장된 감사프로그램을 가동시키는 기능의 장치

audit indicator　감사표지(법)

auditing　감사 ▶ management's responsibility for financial statements

Auditing : A Journal of Practice & Theory　미국 회계학회의 감사연구부문 (The Auditing Section, American Accounting Association)이 발행하는 감사전문잡지. 연 2회 발행.

auditing around the computer　컴퓨터 주변 감사 ▶ auditing through the computer, auditing with the computer

auditing for note receivable　받을 어음 감사

auditing interpretation　감사지침

auditing postulate　감사공준

Auditing Practices Committee(APC)　감사실무위원회 ▶ Accounting Standards Committee

auditing procedure　감사절차 ▶ audit technique

auditing research　감사 연구

Auditing Research Monograph　감사연구논문

auditing responsibilities　감사책임

auditing standard　감사기준

Auditing Standards and Guidelines (ASG)　감사기준 및 감사준칙

Auditing Standards and Procedures (ASP)　감사기준과 감사절차

Auditing Standards Board(ASB)　감사기준심의회 ▶ Statement on Auditing Standards

Auditing Standards Executive Committee(Aud SEC)　감사기준 집행위원회 ▶ Auditing Standard Board

auditing standards literature　감사기준서

auditing technique　감사기술 ▶ audit procedure

auditing through the computer　컴퓨터를 통한 감사, 컴퓨터 처리 감사 ▶ auditing around the computer, auditing with the computer

auditing with technology　전산화된 환경하에서 감사

auditing with the computer　컴퓨터 이용 감사 ▶ auditing around the computer, auditing through the computer

audit inquiry letter to legal counsel　고문변호사에 대한 질문서

audit log　감사 로그

audit manual 감사 매뉴얼 ▶ audit outline

audit module 감사 모듈

audit monitoring routine 감사 모니터링 루틴 ▶ audit module

audit note 감사 노트 = audit notebook ▶ working paper

audit notebook 감사 노트, 감사 수첩 = audit note ▶ working paper

audit objective 감사목적

audit of batch system 배치시스템의 감사

audit of financial statements 재무제표 감사 ▶ review of financial statements

audit of on-line system 온라인 시스템의 감사

audit of purchasing department 구매부 감사

audit of revenue 수익 감사

audit of service-center 외부 용역업체의 감사

audit opinion 감사의견

auditor 감사인 ▶ external auditor

auditor's certificate 감사보고서, 감사증명서

auditor's independence 감사인의 독립성

auditor's liability 감사인의 책임 = auditor's responsibility

auditor's report 감사보고서 = audit report ▶ accountants' report

auditor's responsibility 감사인의 책임 = auditor's liability

auditors' remuneration 감사 보수

auditor-submitted documents 감사인이 제출하는 문서

audit outline 감사요약표 ▶ audit manual

audit planning 감사계획, 감사계획의 입안 = audit program

audit procedure 감사절차, 감사수속 ▶ audit technique

audit process 감사과정

audit program 1) 감사 프로그램 2) 감사계획, 감사절차서 ▶ audit planning

audit report 감사보고서 = auditor's report

audit reporting 감사보고

audit responsibility 감사책임

audit risk 감사위험

audit routine 감사루틴

audit sampling 표본감사, 감사 표본추출 ▶ sampling

audit schedule 감사일정

audit scope 감사범위 ▶ audit scope limitation, scope limitation

audit scope limitation 감사범위의 제한 = scope limitation ▶ audit scope

audit sensitive position 감사에 민감한 상태

Audits of Corporate Accounts 회사 재무제표의 감사

audit software 감사 프로그램, 감사 소프트웨어 ▶ auditing with the computer, generalized audit software

audit standard 감사기준

audit strategy 감사전략

audit supervision 감사감독, 감사지도

audit technique 감사기술 ▶ auditing procedure

audit testing   시사(試査) ▶ detailed
          audit, internal control system

audit test program   감사용 프로그램

audit through the computer   컴퓨터
          를 통한 감사, 컴퓨터 처리 감
          사 ▶ audit software, computer-
          assisted audit techniques,
          integrated test facility

audit timing   감사시기

audit trail   감사증적

audit value   감사가액

audit working paper   감사조서
          ▶ audit file, current working
          paper, current file, permanent
          file, permanent working paper

**Aud SEC(Auditing Standards Executive
          Committee)**   감사기준 집행
          위원회

Australian Accountant   호주 회계사
          협회(Australian Society of
          Accountants)의 기관지. 1916년
          에 *Federal Accountant*라는 이
          름으로 발간되었지만, 1936년
          에 *Australian Accountant*라고
          명칭을 변경하여 연 11회 발간.

authentication   인증, 확인 ▶ disital
          signature

authorised auditor   (영)관허감사인
          = statutory auditor

authorised capital   (영)수권자본
          = authorized capital, authorised
          share capital, nominal capital
          ▶ paid-up capital, uncalled
          capital, uncalled share capital

authorised minimum   (영)수권 최저자
          본액 ▶ authorised capital,
          certificate to commence
          business

authorised share capital   (영)수권주
          식자본 = nominal share capital

authorised unit trust   (영)정부의 허가
          를 받은 단위형 투자신탁

authoritative support   권위 있는 지지
          ▶ Generally Accepted
          Accounting Principles

authority   1) 권한, 직권 2) 권위

authority by estoppel   금반언(앞서 한
          말에 대한 반대의견 주장 금지)
          에 의한 대리권

authority model   외국(外局) 모델

authority of agent   대리권한

authority support   권위에의 지지

authority to inquire and inspect   질
          문검사권 ▶ audit and
          intelligence

authorization   1) 승인, 인증 2) 허가
          3) 수권, 인가증서

authorization code   승인 코드

authorized audit   강제감사
          ▶ voluntary audit

authorized capital   수권자본
          = authorised capital

authorized share   수권자본

authorized stock   수권주식

authorized sub-agent   승인된 부대리인

auto-abstract   자동초록, 자동작성초록
          = automatic abstract

autocorrelation   자기상관 관계

auto-index   색인 자동작성

automated workpaper software   자
          동화된 감사조서 소프트웨어

automatic abstract   자동초록 = auto-
          abstract

automatic calling   자동발신, 자동호출

automatic calling unit(ACU)   자동호
출 장치 ▶ automatic dialling
unit

automatic carriage   자동운송기구

automatic perfection   담보설정상의 자
동적 완전화, 자동적 완성

automatic programming   자동프로그
래밍

automatic repetition system   자동연송
방식

automatic request for repetition(ARQ)
자동반복요구

automatic retry and diagnosis   자동
재시행과 진단 장치

automatic send/receive(ASR)   자동
송수신장치

automatic stay   자동정지

automatic teller machine(ATM)   현금
자동지급기

automatic transfer service   자동대체
서비스

automatic warranty   자동적 담보책임

automation   1) 자동화, 2) 오토메이션

autonomous branch   독립채산점, 자립
적 지점, 독립적 지점

autonomy   자주성, 자유재량권, 자치권

auxiliary book   보조부 ▶ main book

auxiliary department   보조부문
= service department,
subsidiary department
▶ manufacturing department,
production department,
producing department

auxiliary operation   보조조작

auxiliary storage   보조기억장치, 보조
기억기구 ▶ magnetic disk,
magnetic drum

availability   사용가능도, 이용가능도, 가
용성, 가용도

available asset   이용가능자산

available evidence   입수가능한 증거

available-for-sale(AFS)   매각가능한 유
가증권

available-for-sale securities   매각가능
유가증권

available hour   작업가능시간

available time   1) 납품기간, 납기 2) 사
용가능시간, 가용시간

aval   유통증권보증, 어음보증

AVCO(average cost)   1) 평균원가
2) 평균원가법

average   1)평균법 2) 평균, 평균치, 표
준치

average absolute deviation   평균절대
편차 ▶ deviation

average accumulated expenditure
during construction   건설
또는 제조기간 중의 평균 누적
지출액

average capacity   평균조업도 = normal
capacity ▶ practical capacity,
theoretical capacity

average corporate tax rate   평균법인
세율

average cost(AVCO)   1) 평균원가
2) 평균원가법 = average cost
method

average cost flow assumption   평균
원가흐름의 가정

average cost method   평균원가법

average cost of capital   평균자본비용

average cost of carring on a unit for
one year   재고 1단위당 연
간 재고유지비용

average cost of production   생산평균
원가

average difference technique   평균차
이법

average for the year constant dollar
기중 평균통일 달러 ▶ end of
the year constant dollar

average historical performance   평균
적인 역사적 업적, 평균조업도
(average volume)

average inventory   평균재고자산, 평균
재고

average inventory method   평균원가
법 ▶ first-in, first-out method;
last-in, first-out method

average investment   평균 투자액

average labor rate   평균임률 = average
wage rate ▶ labor rate

average method   평균법

average net account receivable   평균
매출채권 순액

average number of days in inventory
평균 재고일수

average number of shares outstanding
평균 사외 유통 주식수

average personal tax rate   평균개인세율

average rate of return   평균자본이익
율 = accountant's rate of
return, accounting rate of return

average remaining service periods
평균 잔존 용역 제공 기간

average return on investment   평균
투자수익(률) ▶ return on
investment

average return on investment method
평균투자수익률법

average unit cost   평균단위원가

average unit cost method   평균단가법,
평균단위원가법 ▶ moving
average cost method, periodic
average method

average wage   평균임금 ▶ average
wage rate

average wage rate   평균임율
= average labor rate ▶ wage
rate

avoidable cost   회피가능원가
= escapable cost
▶ discretionary cost, sunk
cost, unavoidable cost

avoidable fixed cost   회피가능고정비
▶ escapable fixed cost,
inescapable fixed cost,
unavoidable fixed cost

avoidable interest   회피가능이자 (그 자
산을 구입 또는 제조하지 않았으면
발생하지 않았을 이자)

award   재정(裁定), 낙찰, 상

axiom   공리(公理) ▶ going concern

B

BA(bank acceptance, banker's acceptance)
은행인수어음

BAA(British Accounting Association)   영
국 회계학회

baby bond   소액사채, 소액채권

backdate   1) 전일부 2) 소급적용
= antedate, predate ▶ postdate

backdoor listing   부정 상장

backed bond   저당부 채권

background information   배경 설명

background job   배경 일(처리)
▶ background processing

background processing   배경 처리
▶ background job

backing   이서, 배서

backing storage   보조 기억장치

backlog   1) 비축물, 주문 잔고, 현품 주문
2) 체화(滯貨), 잔무, 미처리분
= backlogging ▶ order backlog

backlog adjustment   소급 수정
= catch-up adjustment

backlog depreciation   소급 상각액, 회
수 상각액 = catch up
depreciation

backlogging   현품 주문, 주문 잔고, 체
화(滯貨), 잔무, 미처리분
= backlog

back margin   역마진 ▶ rebate

back-office   증권회사의 수수(사무) 부분

back order   주문 잔고, 미처리 주문

back-to-back credit   다른 통화끼리의

융자

back-to-back loan   다른 통화끼리
의 상호대부

backwardation   1) 인도유예금 2) 현물
고

backwardation rate   인도유예금리

backward reading   역방향판독

bad debt   대손, 불량채권 = doubtful debt

bad debt expense   대손상각비 ▶ bad
debt provision

bad debt provision   대손충당금
= allowance for doubtful
accounts, allowance for
uncollectibles

bad debt recovered   상각채권 추심이
익 = bad debt recovery

bad debt recovery   상각채권 추심액
(이익)

bad debt reserve   대손충당금

bad faith   부정(不正)

badwill   부(負)의 영업권(대변 계상의 영업
권) = negative goodwill

bailed goods   위탁물품

bailed property   기탁재산

bailee   수탁인, 수탁자 ▶ bailment

bailment   기탁, 위탁 = deposit ▶ bailor

bailor   기탁자, 위탁인 ▶ bailment

bailout factor   1) 투자위험의 회피요인
▶ bailout period 2) 과세유보
요인 3) 베일아웃 요인

bailout period   1) 긴급회수기간, 투자

대상 설비의 판매가치를 가미
한 회수기간 ▶ bailout factor,
payback method, payback period
2) 과세유보기간

balance 1) 잔액, 계정잔액 ▶ balance
off, close off, off-balance-sheet
financing 2) 대차계정, 기재된
장부의 끝, 결산의 결과, 차액,
부족액, 이월금 3) 잔존가액
4) 평형, 균형, 조화, 일치 5) 계
량, 견적, 평가, 비교량

balance account 잔액계정

balance at the bank 은행예금잔액

balance brought forward 전기이월
(고), 앞 페이지 이월(액)
= amount carried forward
▶ balance carried forward

balance carried forward 차기이월(고),
다음 페이지 이월(액) = amount
carried forward ▶ balance
brought forward

balanced fund 밸런스형 펀드, 밸런스
형 투자신탁 ▶ income fund,
mutual fund

balanced station 평형국 = combined
station

balance form 잔고식, 계정형식

balance off 마감 = close off ▶ balance

balance of international payment
국제수지표, 국제수지

balance of national economy 국민경
제의 균형

balance sheet (B/S) 대차대조표
▶ position statement, profit
and loss statement

balance sheet account 대차대조표 계
정 = balance account

▶ income statement account

balance sheet analysis 대차대조표 분
석 ▶ balance sheet, income
statement analysis

balance sheet approach 대차대조표적
방법

balance sheet asset value 대차대조표
순자산액

balance sheet audit 대차대조표 감사

balance sheet classification 대차대조
표의 분류

balance sheet date 대차대조표일
= closing date

balance sheet equation 대차대조표 등
식

balance sheet form 대차대조표의 양식

balance sheet item 대차대조표 항목

balancing adjustment 평형공제, 평형
부과

balancing charge 평형부과

balancing figure 장부의 끝을 맞추기
위한 수치, 잔고, 차액

band 대역

band of investment technique 이자율
합성법 ▶ capitalization rate

bank 은행

bank acceptance 은행인수 어음
= banker's acceptance

bank account 은행계정, 은행계좌

bank accounting 은행회계

bank agreement 은행계정조정표
= bank reconciliation
▶ bank reconciliation
schedule, bank reconciliation
statement

bank balance 은행예금잔고

bank bill 은행권, 지폐

bank book 당좌예금 출납장

bank bookkeeping 은행부기

bank card 은행카드

bank casher's check payable to a bearer 은행원이 지참인에게 지불하는 수표(어음)

bank charge 은행수수료

bank confirmation 은행확인장, 은행조회서 = bank report

bank credit 은행 당좌대, 은행신용

bank credit arrangement 은행 대출한도

bank cutoff statements 은행 기간귀속 보고서

bank deposit 은행예금

bank discount 은행할인료

bank draft(B/D) 은행(발행) 환어음

banker 은행가, 금융업자, 은행원

banker's acceptance(BA) 은행 인수, 은행 인수어음 = bank acceptance

banker's acceptance bill 은행 인수어음

banker's commercial credit 은행 신용장

banker's discount 은행할인료, 단리할인료

banker's discount method 은행할인법

banker's draft(B/D) 은행(발행) 어음, 은행 환어음 = bank draft

banker's order 자동 대체계좌, 은행환 = standing order

banker's payment 지불수단 어음

banker's ratio 은행가 비율

bank examination 은행 검사

bank giro (영)은행예금 대체계좌 제도

▶ giro

bank holiday 은행 휴업일 ▶ business day

Banking Act of 1933 1933년 은행법

banking and thrift industry 은행 및 저축산업

bank interest 은행 이자

bank line 은행 여신한도액

bank loan 은행 차입, 은행 론

bank mandate 은행 위임서

bank note(BN) 은행권 = bank bill

Bank of England 영국은행

bank overdraft 당좌차월

bank rate 은행 수수료

bank reconciliation 은행잔고조정(표), 은행계정조정표

bank reconciliation schedule 은행잔고조정표 = bank agreement, bank reconciliation statement

bank reconciliation statement 은행잔고조정표 = bank agreement, bank reconciliation schedule

bank register 당좌예금 출납장 = bank book

bank remittance 송금환 = remittance bill

bank remittance bill 송금 환어음

bank report 은행 거래보고서 = bank confirmation

bankrupt 파산, 도산, 파산자 ▶ bankruptcy

bankruptcy 도산, 부도, 파산 ▶ bankrupt, insolvency

bankruptcy court 연방 파산재판소

bankruptcy estate 파산재단

bankruptcy law 파산법

bankruptcy notice 파산 고지

bankruptcy order 파산 명령

bankruptcy petition 파산 주장, 파산 신청

bankruptcy prediction 파산 예측

bankruptcy proceeding 파산 절차

Bankruptcy Reform Act 개정연방파 산법

Bankruptcy Reform Act of 1978 1978년 파산구제법

bankruptcy sense insolvency 부채 총 액이 자산 총액을 넘는 것

bank service charge 은행수수료

bank statement 은행잔고명세서, 은행 잔고증명서

bank statement rule 은행잔고증명서 규칙

bank transaction 은행 거래

bank transfer 은행간 대체계좌 = credit transfer

bank transfer schedule 은행간의 이 체 스케줄, 은행이체명세서

bar 1) 100만 포인트 2) 장벽 3) 법정, 변호사 업계

bar code 바코드 ▶ bar code reader

bar code reader 바코드 읽기 장치 ▶ bar code

bargain and sale 토지 매매계약 및 대 금 지불

bargain and sale deed 거래양도증서

bargained amount 거래가액

bargained for 거래

bargained-for exchange 교환매매

bargainee 매수자

bargainer 매도자

bargain money 계약금, 착수금, 보증금

bargain price 할인가격, 특별가격, 계약 가격, 협정가격

bargain purchase 할인 구입

bargain purchase option(BPO) 염가 구입선택권, 할인구입권리

bargain renewal option 염가갱신 선 택권

bargain sale 바겐세일, 염가판매

barrister 1) (영)법정 변호사 2) (일반 적으로) 변호사

barter 물물교환, 교환무역제, 구상무역제

barter change 물물교환

barter exchange 물물교환

barter transaction 현물교환거래, 바터 거래

base 저(底), 기수, 기저(基底)

base case system evaluation (BCSE) 기본 케이스 시스템 평가법

base item 기본 항목

baseline budget 기본 예산 ▶ budget period, current budget

base of relative sales value 판매가비 례기준 = relative sales value method

base of taxation 과세표준

base period 기준 기간

base price 기준 단가 ▶ basing point price

base rate 1) 기본급, 기초 임금률 = basic rate 2) (은행의) 최저대 출이율

base stock 기초 잔액, 기준 재고, 정상 재고 = normal stock

base stock inventory valuation 기준 재고법, 정상 재고법 = base stock method

base stock method 기준 재고법, 정상 재고법 ▶ normal stock method

B

base value of share 주식의 기초가액
base year 기준연도, 기준연차
basic accounting theory 기본회계이론
basic allowance 기본허용금액
basic assumption 기본적 가정
　　　▶ accounting postulate,
　　　fundamental accounting
　　　concept
basic concept 기본적 제개념
basic cost 기본 원가 ▶ current
　　　standard
basic design 기본 설계 ▶ detail design
basic earnings per share(EPS) 기본
　　　1주당 이익 = primary earnings
　　　per share
basic financial statement 기본 재무
　　　제표 = primary financial
　　　statements
basic precision 기본 정밀도
basic principle of accounting 회계의
　　　기본 원칙
basic rate 1) 기초 임금률, 기본급
　　　= base rate, basic wage rate
　　　2) (소득세의) 기초 세율(영)
basic research 기초 연구
　　　▶ fundamental research
basic standard cost 기준 표준원가
　　　= bogy standard cost, fixed
　　　standard cost, static standard
　　　cost ▶ current standard cost
basic standard cost accounting 기준
　　　표준원가계산 = basic standard
　　　costing
basic standard costing 기준 표준원가
　　　계산 = basic standard cost
　　　accounting, basic standard cost
　　　system ▶ basic standard cost

basic standard cost system 기준 표준
　　　원가계산 = basic standard
　　　costing
basic wage rate 기준 임금률, 기준급률
　　　= base rate, basic rate
basing point price 기점 가격 ▶ base
　　　price
basis 기초(基礎), 근거
basis of apportionment (제조간접비의)
　　　배부기준
basis of assessment 부과의 기초
basis of bargain 교섭의 기초
**basis of performance of the services
　　　required** 요구된 서비스 수행
　　　기준
basis of property acquired by gift 증
　　　여로 취득한 자산의 기초가격
basis period (영)(소득세를 산정하기 위
　　　한) 기준 기간 ▶ current-year
　　　basis, preceding-year basis
basis point (이율을 표시할 때의) 100분
　　　의 1포인트
basket purchase 일괄구입
　　　= lump-sum purchase
batch 재화의 한 묶음, 재화 1회분 = lot
　　　▶ batch quantity, on-line
　　　process
batch control 일괄통제, 배치통제
　　　▶ batch total
batch control total 일괄통제 합계
　　　= batch total
batch cost 일괄원가, 배치원가 = lot
　　　cost
batch costing 일괄원가계산 = lot
　　　costing ▶ batch cost, lot cost
batching technique 배치기법
batch job 일괄작업

batch processing 일괄처리 ▶ on-line real time system, real time processing

batch processing system 일괄처리방식

batch production 일괄생산 = lot production

batch quantity 묶음 량 ▶ batch

batch ticket 일괄전표

batch total 일괄통제 합계 = batch control total ▶ batch control

battle of forms 서식전쟁, 서식의 대결

battle of forms problem 서식전쟁 문제

Bayes' theorem 베이즈의 정리

B/C(bill for collection) 대금징수 어음, 징수 어음

BCSE(base case system evaluation) 기본 케이스 시스템 평가법

B/D(bank draft, banker's draft) 은행(발행) 환어음

B/D(brought down) 전기이월

BDV(budget day value) 예산 제시일에 있어서 자산 평가액

B/E (bill of exchange) 환어음

beam deflection 빔 편향

bear 약세, 파는 쪽 ▶ bull

bearer (어음. 수표의) 소지인, 보유자

bearer bond 무기명식 채권, 지참인 지급 사채 ▶ registered bond

bearer check 지참인 지급 어음(수표)

bearer debenture 무기명 사채

bearer paper 무기명식 증서, 지참인 지불식 증권

bearer security 무기명 증권, 지참인 지급 증권

bearer share 무기명 주식

bearer stock 무기명 주식

bear market 약세 시장, 하향 시세의 시장 ▶ bull market

bear raid 의도적인 투매

Bedbug letter 불평 편지

before-image 전 이미지, 갱신전 이미지

before tax 세금공제전 ▶ pretax accounting income

before the fact control 사전 관리 = motivation control ▶ after the fact control

beginning balance 기초잔액, 개시잔액 = initial balance

beginning inventory 기초재고 = initial inventory, opening inventory ▶ cost of goods sold

beginning of the period 기초

beginning of year(BOY) 기초, 연초

beginning raw material 원재료 기초잔액

beginning retained earnings balance 이익잉여금 기초잔액

beginning WIP(work in process) 기초재공품

beginning work in process(WIP) 기초재공품 ▶ beginning inventory

behavioral accounting 행동회계 ▶ behavioral science

behavioral science 행동과학 ▶ interdisciplinary approach

behavioral system 행동 시스템 ▶ behavioral science

behavioral theory of the firm 기업의 행동이론

bell-shaped curve 벨형 곡선 = normal curve

B

below cost   원가 이하

below par   액면 이하

below the line   1) 비경상항목 또는 이익처분 ▶ above the line, bottom line, top line 2) 승부의 행방에 직접 관계가 없는 것

below the line deduction   비경상항목의 공제 ▶ above-the line deduction

benchmark   벤치마크, 기준점, 기준치 = benchmark test

benchmark problem   벤치마크 문제, 기본수준 문제

benchmark test   벤치마크 시험, 벤치마크 테스트 = benchmark

beneficial owner   실질적 소유권자 또는 수익자

beneficial title   실질적 소유권

beneficiary   1) 수익권자, 수혜자 2) 수익자(受益者) 3) 보험금 수취인 4) L/C의 피지불인

beneficiary certificate   수익증권

benefit   1) 이익, 효익 2) (영)국민보험의 급부(금전, 현물, 서비스) 3) (세금의) 면제

benefit-cost analysis   비용·효익분석 = cost/benefit analysis ▶ benefit/cost ratio, cost/effectiveness analysis

benefit-cost ratio   비용·효익 비율 = profitability index

benefit due to loss carryback   결손금 소급공제에 의한 효익

benefit due to loss carryforward   결손금 이월공제에 의한 효익

benefit for bargain   매매에 대한 이익

benefit information   효익(편익) 정보

benefit information date   급부(효익, 편익) 정보일

benefit obligation   연금채무

benefit principle   수혜원칙 ▶ ability theory of taxation

benefits   1) 퇴직연금 2) 편익

benefit security   급부(효익, 이익) 보장

benefits of servicing   서비스에 따른 이익

BEP (break-even point)   손익분기점

bequest   동산의 유증(遺贈), 유산 = legacy

bereavement pay   (근친상을 당하여 근무처를 쉴 때 주는) 수당

best estimator   최적 추정량

best unbiased estimator   최적 불편 추정량

beta distribution   베타(β) 분포

beta risk   베타 위험, 제2종 위험, 제2종의 오류를 범하는 리스크 = type II risk

beta service   베타 서비스 ▶ beta

beta value   베타치, 베타 = beta ▶ alpha value, market related risk, non-diversifiable risk, non-market related risk, portfolio, systematic risk, unsystematic risk

betterment   개선, 개량 = improvement ▶ capital expenditure, maintenance, repair

betterment expense   개선비, 개량비 ▶ capital expenditure

betting   도박

betting and wagering contract   도박계약

between merchants   상인간의 거래

between nonmechants   상인과 비상인

간의 거래

B/F(brought forward)   전 페이지 이월

BFOQ   진정한 직업자격

BFP(bona fide purchaser)   선량한 구매자, 선의(善意)의 유상(有償) 취득자

bias   편향(偏向), 편의, 치우침 ▶ bias in measurement

bias distortion   편향 왜곡 ▶ bias

bias in measurement   측정상의 편향

bid   입찰, (사는 사람이) 가격을 제시하다

bid and asked price   호가(呼價)

bid bond   입찰 보증금, 입찰 보증서 = tender bond, tender guarantee

bidding expense   입찰비, 입찰 경비

bidirectional flow   양방향 흐름

bid price   입찰 가격 ▶ asked price

bifurcation   분기

Big Bang   (영)빅뱅, 금융혁명 ▶ May Day

big-bath approach   빅 배스 접근(영업실적이 나쁜 연도에 다음 연도의 성과를 높게 하기위해 당해 성과를 더욱 낮추고자 하는 방법)

Big Board   뉴욕 증권거래소(속칭)

big brother   강력한 권력을 갖고 있는 기관

big business   대기업, 대규모 회사, 대형 사업

Big Eight   8대 회계사무소 ▶ Big Six

big GAAP   대규모 공개회사의 일반적으로 인정된 회계원칙 ▶ little GAAP

Big Six   6대 회계사무소 ▶ Big Eight

big-ticket lease   (영)고액 물건 리스

bilateral contract   쌍방계약, 쌍무계약

bilateral mistake   상호 착오

bilateral offer   쌍방적 신청

bilateral offercontract   쌍방청약계약, 쌍무청약계약

bilateral transaction   쌍방 거래

bill   1) 청구서, 어음 ▶ bill of exchange, note 2) 계정서, 계산서 3) 증권, 증서 4) 지폐 5) 법안, 의안 6) 표, 목록, 명세서 7) 소장(訴狀), 조서

bill broker   어음 중개인

bill collector   어음 매집인

bill for collection(B/C)   대금징수 어음 ▶ bill receivable

bill in foreign currency   외화표시(환)어음 = foreign currency bill

billing   대금 청구

billing machine   청구서 작성기

billing rate   청구료율 = charge rate

billings on construction   공사청구액

billings on LT contract   미성공사선수금

bill of credit   신용장

bill of dishonor   부도어음 = dishonored bill

bill of exchange(B/E)   환어음 = draft ▶ promissory note

bill of lading (B/L)   1) 선하증권 2) 화물 적하증 ▶ waybill

bill of materials(B/M)   재료시방서, 재료명세서 = material specification, production specification ▶ production order

bill of parcels   화물선적명세서

bill of sale   매도증

bill payable(B/P, BP)   1) 지불어음 ▶ note payable 2) 보통지불환

bill payable book　　지불(지급)어음 기입장

bill receivable(B/R, BR)　　1) 받을 어음 ▶ note receivable 2) 보통징수환 ▶ bills for collection (B/C)

bill receivable book　　(받을)수취어음 기입장

bills bought　　매입외국환 ▶ selling exchange

bills of exchange　　환어음

bills of lading　　선하증권, 운송증권

bin card　　저장품 카드 = bin tag

binder　　가보험증권, 구두계약 보험증서

bindex system　　바인더식 장부제

binding contract　　구속력이 있는 계약

binding slip　　가보험증서

binomial distribution　　이항분포

bin record　　저장품 기록

bin tag　　저장품 카드 = bin card

BIOC　　통상의 영업과정에서의 동산 취득자

bipolar transmission　　복류식 운송

bit　　비트

bits per second(bps)　　초당 비트 전송량 = bit per second

B/L(bill of lading)　　1) 선하증권 2) 화물적하증

black-box testing　　블랙박스 테스팅 ▶ white-box testing

black economy　　지하경제

black market　　암시장(법률에 위반하면서 상품 또는 외국통화를 매매하는 시장)

Black Monday　　암흑의 월요일 ▶ Black Thursday

black paper　　흑서(현행 제도 · 정책을 비판한 문서) ▶ Blue Paper, Green Paper

Black Thursday　　암흑의 목요일

blank　　공백, 공백문자

blank character　　공백문자 = space character

blank check　　백지수표

blank endorsement　　백지 배서, 부기명식 배서 ▶ special endorsement 기명식배서

blanket brand　　통일상표, 공동상표

blanket order　　1) 일괄제조지시서 2) 일괄주문

blanket policy　　특정가능한 재산 대상 가입 보험

blanket price　　포괄가격(공통가격)

blanket rate　　1) 총괄배부율 ▶ individual rate 2) 종목별배부율

blanket rate method　　총괄배부율법

blanking　　공백화

blending of CCA and GPLA　　현행원가 및 일반물가 변동회계의 결합 = (현재원가회계와 일반물가변동회계) ▶ current cost/constant purchasing power accounting, integration of CCA and GPLA

blending problem　　(제품상) 혼합문제

block　　블록 ▶ blocking, blocking factor

block check　　블록 검사

blocked currency　　사용제한 통화

blocking　　블로킹 ▶ blocking factor(블록화 요소), deblocking(블록화)

blocking factor　　블로킹 요소 ▶ block, blocking

block sales　　대량판매

block sampling　　구획 샘플링, 구획표본조사

Blue Book　　1) (영)청서 ▶ Black Paper,

Green Paper 2) 공무원 명부

blue chip   우량주

Blue Sky Law   청공(靑空)법(부정유가
증권 발행의 규제를 목적으로 하는
법)

B/M(bill of material)   재료명세서

BN(bank note)   은행권

board   회, 회의, 이사회, 위원회

board meeting   회의(임원회, 이사회, 전
무회의)

Board of Customs and Excise   (영)간
접세 세무국 ▶ Commissioner
of Customs and Excise

board of directors   이사회, 임원(任員)
회(會), 전무(상무)회

**Board of Governors of the Federal
Reserve System(FRB)**   연
방준비제도이사회

Board of Inland Revenue   내국세입위
원회

board of trade   1) 상품거래소
▶ commodity futures, financial
futures 2) (영)상무성

board of trustees   재산 관리인

Board's Rules of Procedures   FASB
의 절차규칙

body corporate   법인 = corporation

body of persons   단체, 조직체, 집단

bogus dividend   위조배당(배당가능 이익
이 없는 상태에서의 배당)

bogy standard   측정척도표준, 기본표준
= basic standard ▶ current
standard

bogy standard cost   기본표준원가
= basic standard cost, fixed
standard cost, static standard
cost

BOM(bill of materials)   재료명세서

bona fide   선량한

bona fide cost   진정원가(진실원가)

bona fide occupational qualification
성실한 직업상의 자격

bona fide purchase(BFP)   선량한 구
매, 선의(善意)의 유상(有償)
취득

bona fide purchaser(BFP)   선량한 구
매자(채권자 포함), 선의(善意)
의 유상(有償) 취득자

bona fide seniority and merit system
진정한 선임권 제도

bona vacantia   귀속불명물, 무주물

bond   1) 공사채, 사채 ▶ debenture 2) 지
급보증서

bond agreement   사채 계약

bond authorized   수권사채

bond certificate   사채권 ▶ stock
certificate 주권

bond conversion   사채의 전환
▶ conversion, convertible
bond(전환사채)

bond discount   사채할인발행차금, 사채
할인료

bond discount accumulation   (액면가
이하로 취득한 사채의) 장부가액
의 증액 ▶ bond premium
amortization

bond discount amortization   사채할인
발행차금 상각

bond dividend   사채배당 ▶ stock
dividend(주식배당)

bonded area   보세지역 ▶ bonded
system(보세제도)

bonded goods   보세화물

bonded system   보세제도 ▶ bonded

area
bonded warehouse 보세창고
bond fund 채권투자신탁 ▶ stock fund
(주식투자신탁)
bond holder 사채권자 ▶ creditor
bond indenture 사채신탁계약, 사채계
약
bonding company 사채보증회사
bond interest 사채이자
bond investment 회사채투자
bond issue cost 사채발행비 = bond
issue expense
bond issued at a discount 할인발행사
채 ▶ bond issued at a premium
bond issued at a premium 할증발행
사채 ▶ bond issued at a
discount
bond issue expense 사채발행비
bond outstanding 유통사채, 미상환사
채 ▶ bond unissued 미발행사
채
bond payable (미상환) 사채 ▶ bond
outstanding
bond payable subscribed 인수완료사
채
bond premium 사채할증금, 사채할증
발행차금 ▶ bond discount,
bond issue
bond premium amortization 사채할
증발행차금 상각 ▶ bond
discount amortization
bond rating 사채등급 ▶ bond rating
of Moody's Investors Service,
Inc.
**bond rating of Moody's Investors
Service, Inc.** 무디스사의 채
권등급

bond redemption 사채상환 ▶ bond
refunding
bond refunding 사채의 차환 ▶ bond
redemption
bonds outstanding method 미상환 사
채 잔액비례법
bonds payable 사채
bond subscription receivable 사채
미불입금
bonds with detachable stock warrant
분리형 신주인수권부 사채
bonds with stock purchase warrant
신주인수권부 사채, 워런트채
bond transfer tax 사채이전세
bond trustee 채권 수탁자 ▶ indenture
신탁계약서
bond unissued 미발행사채
bond valuation 사채평가
bond washing 채권 세탁, 사채 유통
= dividend washing
bond with datachable stock warrant
분리형 신주인수권부사채
▶ detachable stock warrant
bonus 보너스, 상여금, 특별수당
bonus agreement 상여지불협약
bonus issue 특별발행, 무상신주발행
▶ bonus share(무상배당주, 무
상주식)
bonus method(new partners) 보너스법
bonus plan 보너스제도
bonus pool 보너스 지급한도총액
bonus share 무상배당주, 무상주식
= free share
book audit 장부감사
book calculation of inventory 장부상
재고량
book cost 장부원가 ▶ gross book

value 장부상총액

book entry　　장부기입

book inventory　　장부재고법, 계속기록
법 = perpetual inventory method
▶ inventory method, physical
inventory

book keeper　　부기계, 기록계

bookkeeping　　부기

bookkeeping cycle　　부기의 일련의 순
환과정　= accounting cycle
(회계순환)

bookkeeping system　　장부조직

book of account　　회계장부 = financial
book

book of final entry　　원장 ▶ book of
original entry

book of original entry　　원시기입 장부,
제1차 기입 장부 = book of
prime entry ▶ book of final
entry, book of secondary entry

book of prime entry　　원시기입 장부,
제1차 기입 장부 = book
of original entry

book of secondary entry　　제2차 기입
장부 ▶ book of original entry,
book of prime entry

book value(BV)　　장부가액 = carrying
amount

book value approach　　장부가액접근법
= market value approach

book value method　　장부가액법

book value of common stock　　보통주
1주당 장부가치

book value per share of common stock
보통주 1주당 장부가치 ▶ book
value

boot　　단수결제금, 교환차액

boot given　　교환차금을 매각할 경우

boot received　　교환차금을 취득한 경우

bore-holes　　(석유, 수맥 탐사) 시추공사,
시굴공사

borrow digit　　차(빌린) 수

borrowed capital　　차입자본, 타인자본,
융자자본 = debt capital loan
capital

borrowed stock　　차(빌린)주

borrowing　　차입(借入), 임차(賃借), 차
입금 ▶ borrowed capital, debt
capital(차입자본)

borrowing cost　　차입비용

borrowing rate　　차입금리

BOS(basic operation system)　　기본적 운
용시스템

Boston ledger　　보스턴식 장부

both days included　　양일(兩日) 포함

both-way communication　　양방향
동시통신 ▶ either-way
communication, two-way
communication

bottle neck problem　　애로문제, 병목문
제

bottom line　　1) 순이익(순손실) P/L의 마
지막 숫자　2) 최종결과, 총결과
3) 요점, 가장 중요한 사항
4) 전환시점 ▶ above the line,
below the line, top line

bottom-up type budget　　아래에서 위로
전달되는 유형의 예산 ▶ top-
down type budget

bought day book　　매입장 = purchase
book

bought ledger　　매입처원장 = creditor
ledger, purchase ledger

bought out parts　　구입부품

boundary 경계

boundary alignment 한계선

boundary protection 경계보호

bound book 장정(裝幀)장부

bounty 조성금, 보조금, 상여금

BOY(beginning of year) 기초, 연초

BP(bill payable) 1) 지급어음 2) 보통지급환어음

BR(bill receivable) 1) 받을어음 2) 보통받을환어음

branch 1) 지점, 지사 2) 분기

branch accounting 지점회계

branch balance sheet 지점 대차대조표

branch control 지점 통제, 지점 예산

branch current account 지점 계정

branch instruction 분기명령
    = decision instruction

branch office 지점 ▶ home office

branch point 분기점

brand 1)명예, 브랜드 2)품질, 종류
    3)낙인

breach 불이행(不履行)

breach of contract 계약위반, 계약의 불이행

breach of trust 신탁의무위반

breach of warranty 보증위반

break 중단

break-even 손익분기점

break-even analysis 손익분기점분석
    ▶ break-even model (손익분기점모델), cost-volume-profit analysis (원가–조업도–이익 분석)

break-even chart 손익분기도표, 이익도표 = profit chart, profit graph ▶ break-even analysis, break-even point analysis, cost-volume-profit analysis,

cost-volume-profit graph

break-even method 손익분기점법
    = break-even point method

break-even model 손익분기모형
    ▶ break-even point analysis, cost-volume-profit analysis, cost-volume-profit relationship

break-even point 손익분기점

break-even point analysis 손익분기점 분석 ▶ cost-volume-profit relation analysis

break-even point method 손익분기점법 = break-even method

break-even sales 손익분기 매출액

break-even volume 손익분기 조업도 = break-even sale

breaking-down time 분류시간

breakpoint 중지점, 구분점

bribe 뇌물

bribery 증회, 수회(뇌물의)

brief exposition 요약설명

British Accounting Association (BAA)
    영국회계학회

broad-band 광(廣)지역대, 광주파수지역대

broker 1) 브로커 중매인 ▶ brokerage firm 2) 주식매매 중개인, 증권회사

brokerage 1) 중개, 중매 2) 중개업
    3) 중개수수료

brokerage commission 중개수수료

brokerage firm 증권회사 = broker

brokers 증권중개인

brokers and dealers in securities 증권발행 · 유통업

broker's fee 수수료

brought down(B/D) 전기이월

▶ brought forward
brought forward(B/F) 차기이월
▶ brought down
B/S (balance sheet) 대차대조표
Bubble Act 버블(거품)법
bubble company 거품회사
budget 예산 ▶ forecast, plan
budget allowance 예산허용액
**budget allowance based on actual
hours** 실제시간에 기초한
변동예산
**budgetary accounting for the general
funds** 일반기금의 예산회계
**budgetary accounting for the special
revenue funds** 특별수익 기
금의 예산회계
budgetary appropriation 예산의 계상
budgetary authority 예산한도액
budgetary comparison schedule 예산
비교명세서
budgetary control 예산통제
▶ budgetary planning and
control
budgetary control organization 예산
통제조직
budgetary control system 예산통제제
도
budgetary fund balance 기금잔액예산
budgetary planning and control 예산
계획과 통제 ▶ budgetary
control
budgetary price 예산가격
budgetary procedure 예산과정
budgetary system 예산제도
▶ budgetary control system
budget audit 예산감사
budget calendar 예산 캘린더

▶ budget cycle
budget ceiling 예산한도(상한)
budget center 예산중심점, 예산통제상
중심점
budget committee 예산위원회
budget consciousness 예산의식
budget cost allowance 예산원가 허용
액
budget cycle 예산편성과정 ▶ budget
calendar
budget day value(BDV) (영)예산제시
일에서의 자산평가액
budget department 예산과, 예산처
= budget division
budget director 예산사무담당자
budget division 1) 예산과 2) 예산부문
= budget department
budgeted activity 예산 조업도
▶ budgeted volume
budgeted activity level 예산 조업도
수준, 예산활동수준
budgeted balance sheet 예산(추정)
대차대조표 = forecasted
balance sheet
budgeted capacity 예산 조업도
= budgeted volume
budgeted cost 예산 원가
budgeted financial statement 견적
(예산) 재무제표 = forecasted
financial statements
budgeted hours 예산 조업도
budgeted income statement 예산(추정)
손익계산서 = forecasted income
statement
budgeted statement 예산(추정) 재무
제표, 견적재무제표
▶ master budget(종합예산)

budgeted volume   예산 조업도
= budgeted activity, budgeted
capacity, expected annual
activity, expected annual
volume, master budget activity,
master budget volume
▶ normal volume

budgetee   예산집행자

budget executive   예산통제 적임자, 예
산담당자

budget for capital expenditure   자본
지출예산

budget for order-cost   주문획득비 예산
▶ budget for order-filling cost

budget for order-filling cost   주문처
리비 예산 ▶ budget for order-
getting cost

budget guideline   예산편성방침
▶ budget preparation

budgeting   1) 예산 2) 예산작성, 예산편
성, 예산관리
= budget preparation

budgeting manual   예산관리규정, 예산
편람

budgeting policy   예산편성방침
= budget guideline

budget of head office   본부예산

budget period   예산기간

budget preparation   예산편성
= budgeting ▶ budget guideline

budget report   예산보고서
= performance report

budget revision variance   예산수정차
이

budget sheet   예산표

budget simulation   예산 시뮬레이션

▶ budget simulation model,
business simulation

budget simulation model   예산 시뮬레
이션모델 ▶ budget simulation

budget system   1) 예산체계 2) 예산제도

budget variance   예산차이(controllable
variance) ▶ capacity variance,
efficiency variance

budget variance analysis   예산실적 차
이분석, 예산차이분석 = analysis
of budget variance, analysis of
variance from budget

buffer   1) (파산 등의 방지를 위한) 잉여금
(준비금) 2) 완충역, 완충기억장
치, 완충기억기구 ▶ buffer
storage

buffer pool   완충지역 풀

buffer stock   완충재고

buffer unit   완충역구성단위

bug   버그

Building and Loan Association
(영)건축금융조합, 주택구입조
합 ▶ building society

building residual technique   건물잔여
법 ▶ income approach, land
residual technique

Building Society   (영)주택금융조합
= Building and Loan
Association ▶ housing
association

built-in check   내장(內裝)검사, 고유검사

built-in function   내장기능, 고유기능

built-in stabilizer   자동안정장치

bulk purchase   대량구매 ▶ lump sum
purchase

bulk service system   집단서비스시스템

bulk transfer   대량 이전

bull 강세쪽(증권시장 및 상품시장에서 가격이 상승한다고 믿고 자신의 자금을 유가증권 또는 다른 재산에 투자) ▶ bear

Bulldog bond 불독 본드 ▶ Samurai bond, Yankee bond

Bulletins of Committee on Acounting Procedure 회계절차위원회의 회계연구공보

bull market 강세시장 ▶ bear market

burden 제조간접비, 경비 = factoryexpense, factory overhead, manufacturing expense, manufacturing overhead

burden center 간접비중심점, 간접부문

burden of proof 증거의 책임

burden rate 제조간접비배부율 = manufacturing overhead rate, overhead rate ▶ combined burden rate

burden rate of conversion cost 가공비배부율 ▶ burden rate of manufacturing department expenses

burden rate of manufacturing department expenses 제조부문비배부율 ▶ burden rate of conversion cost

Bureau of Internal Revenue 내국세입국

burst (증권시장에서의) 과열, 돌발사태

burst mode (증권시장에서의) 과열, 돌발장세

business 1) 경영, 사업 2) 기업, 기업체

business accounting 기업회계

business activity 사업활동, 기업활동, 경영활동

business administration 기업경영, 경영관리 = business management

business affair 기업사상, 기업거래

business analysis 경영분석

business combination 기업합동, 기업결합 ▶ amalgamation, consolidation, merger, pooling of interest concept, purchase concept

business company 사업회사

business consultant 경영조언, 경영자문

business data processing 사무데이터처리 = administrative data processing

business day (영)경영일, 은행영업일 ▶ non-business day

business decision 경영적 의사결정

business energy credit 영업상 소요되는 에너지에 대한 세액공제

business enterprise 기업, 기업체, 영리기업

business entity 기업실체 ▶ separate entity concept

business entity principle 기업실체의 원칙

Business Expansion Scheme (영)기업진흥정책

business failure 기업도산 (倒産)

business finance 기업재무, 경영재무

business forecasting 1) 기업예측, 경영예측 2) 경기예측

business game 비즈니스게임, 경영게임 = management game

business gifts 업무상 증여

business income 기업이익, 기업소득

business income and deductions　사업 소득과 공제

business indicator　경기지표, 경기지수 = index of business condition

business information　기업정보

business interruption　경영방해

business judgment rule　경영판단 불개입의 원칙, 영리판단 불개입의 원칙

business license　경영면허

business machine　사무기계

business management　경영관리 = business administration ▶ business planning

business meal　사업상의 식사

business name　기업명

business operations audit　업무감사

business plan　경영계획 ▶ business policy

business planning　경영계획 ▶ business management

business policy　경영방침 ▶ business planning, business plan

business purposes　사업목적

business reorganization　사업 재조정

business report　경영보고서, 사업보고서

business researcher　비즈니스 조사기관

business result　기업실적, 영업실적

business review　기업의 검토

business risk　영업위험 ▶ financial risk

business segment　사업 영역 구분

business simulation　경영 시뮬레이션 ▶ budget simulation, business game

business structure　경영구조

business trust　기업합동, 사업신탁

business use of home　주거지의 사업상 이용

business worth　기업가치

business year　회계연도, 사업연도, 회계기간

buyer　구입자, 매입자

buyer credit　바이어 신용, 구매자의 신용 ▶ suppliers credit

buyer's remedies for breach of contract　계약위반에 대한 매수인의 구제

buyers in the ordinary course of business　일상적인 영업 활동의 구매자, 동산 취득자

buying exchange　매입환출

buying off　매수, 뇌물 = buying over

buying out　영업권 취득 ▶ management buyout

buying over　매수, 뇌물 = buying off

buying price　매수가격

buying up　매수, 매점(買占)

buy or make analysis　구입 또는 자가 제조 의사결정

buy-sell agreement　매매계약

by acquiescence　묵인에 의한

by-law　부속정관, 부칙, 업무규칙 ▶ articles of association, articles of incorporation

by operation of law　법의 운용

by-passing　오해

by performance　이행

by-product　부산물 ▶ main product, joint-product

by-product cost　부산물원가

▶ by-product
by-product method 부산물법

by-product proceed 부산물 처리의
수익(수취금)

C

CA(chartered accountant) 공인회계사,
(영) 칙허회계사
CAAT(computer-assisted audit technique)
컴퓨터를 이용한 감사기법
CACA(Chartered Association of Certified
Accountants, ACCA) 공인
회계사협회
CAD(computer aided design) 컴퓨터 지
원 설계
CAI(computer aided instruction) 컴퓨
터 지원 학습 = computer-
assisted instruction
calculated value 수정시장가격
calculus 산법, 미분적분학
calculus of variation 변분법, 변분학
calendar variance 역일차이
call 1) (프로그래밍에서) 호출 2) 매수약정
▶ call option
callable 수시 상환 가능한
callable bond 상환사채, 수시상환가능
사채 ▶ callable security
callable obligation 임의상환가능사채
callable preferred stock 상환우선주
callable security 상환조건부 유가증권
callable stock 상환주, 상환가능주식, 임
의상환주식
call-back pay 최저보장급여 = call-in
pay
call directing code(CDC) 완선지정코

드
called party 피호출측, 피호출 가입자
▶ calling party
called-up capital (영)불입청구 주식자
본 ▶ issued share capital,
paid-up share capital
called-up share capital (영)불입청구
된 주식자본
calling party 호출측 ▶ called party
calling sequence 호출(呼出) 열(列)
calling up (영)(미불입된 주식자본의) 불입
요구
call-in pay 특별최저보장급 = call-back
pay
call loan 콜 대부금 ▶ call money
call money 콜 차입금 ▶ call loan
call option 콜 옵션, 매수선택권 ▶ put
option
call premium 상환프리미엄
call price 상환가격
call provision 임의상환조건
call rate 콜 금리 = rate of call
CA Magazine 캐나다 공인회계사협회
의 기관지(The Canadian Institute
of Chartered Accountants)
Canadian Institute of Chartered
Accountants(CICA) 캐나
다 공인회계사협회
canceled check 은행 결재완료 수표, 지

불된 수표

cancellable lease 해약가능 리스
▶ capital lease, finance lease, noncancellable lease, operating lease

cancellation 변제(辨濟), 계약 해제, 말소

cancellation table entry (영)취소분개
= elimination journal entry, work sheet elimination

cancelled check 결제완료된 수표

cancelled stock 소각 주식

cap 상한금리

CAP(Committee on Accounting Procedure) 회계절차심의위원회 ▶ APB

CAPA(Confederation of Asian and Pacific Accountants) 아시아·태평양 회계사연맹

capacity 1) 능력, 생산능력, 조업도
2) 기억용량 = storage capacity

capacity cost 생산설비원가 ▶ activity cost, fixed cost, period cost, product cost, variable cost

capacity costing 생산설비에 대한 원가계산

capacity planning 용량계획

capacity ratio 조업도비율

capacity resources 생산능력, 설비능력
▶ capacity, size of capacity

capacity size 생산능력규모, 설비능력규모

capacity to act as surety 보증인으로서의 능력

capacity to be agent 대리인의 자격

capacity to be principal 본인의 자격

capacity to pay 지불능력

capacity usage ratio 생산설비 조업률, 가동률

capacity variance 조업도차이
= overhead volume variance, volume variance, utilization variance ▶ budget variance, controllable variance, efficiency variance

capital 자본, 자본금 ▶ equity, equity of security holders, legal capital, net assets, net worth, paid-in capital

capital a/c 자본계정

capital accumulation plan 자본축적계획

capital addition 추가설비투자

capital allowance 자본적 지출공제, 세무감가상각 ▶ first year allowance, investment tax credit

capital asset 자본적 자산, 고정자산
= fixed asset, long-lived asset, permanent asset ▶ capital gain, current asset

capital asset pricing model(CAPM) 자본자산가격결정모델, 자본자산평가모델 ▶ beta, market portfolio

capital balance 자본계정의 잔액

capital budget 자본예산 = capital budgeting

capital budget decision 자본예산에 관한 의사결정

capital budgeting 자본예산 = capital budget, construction budget, capital expenditure budget, investment budget, plant and equipment budget ▶ capital investment decision

capital change　자본변동

capital charge　자본비용

capital committed　수탁자본

capital contribution　자본납입

capital cost　자본비

capital demand curve　자본수요곡선

capital duty　(영)증자세금

capital employed　사용자본 ▶ net
capital employed

capital employed turnover ratio　총
자본회전율(총자산÷매출액)

capital expenditure　자본적 지출
▶ betterment, revenue
expenditure

capital expenditure budget　자본지출
예산 ▶ capital budgeting,
capital investment decision

capital formation　자본축적, 자본구성

capital fund　(영)기본금, 자본기금
= accumulated fund

capital gain　자본이득 ▶ capital loss,
holding gain and loss

capital gain and loss　자본이득과 손실
▶ capital gain tax

capital gain tax(CGT)　자본이득세

capital goods　자본재 ▶ consumption
goods, producer's goods,
production goods

capital graph　자본도표 ▶ contribution
graph, cost-volume-profit
graph

capital improvement　자본적 지출
▶ maintenance charge,
maintenance cost, maintenance
expense

capital in excess of stated value　액면

초과액(주식발행 초과금)

capital input　자본투입

capital in real term　실질자본

capital introduced　자본금, 출자금

capital investment　설비투자, 자본투하

capital investment decision　투자결정
▶ capital budgeting, capital
expenditure budget

capital issue　1) 주식발행 2) 주권, 주식

capitalization　1) 자본화, 수익의 자본환
원 ▶ capitalization of earning
2) 산업화, 취득원가산입
▶ capital expenditure

capitalization issue　자본화 주식발행
= bonus issue, stock dividend
▶ right issue

capitalization method　자본화 방법
▶ capitalization rate, direct
capitalization, income approach,
mortgage-equity capitalization,
straight-line capitalization

capitalization of earning　수익의 자
본화

capitalization of interest　이자비용의
자본화, 이자비용의 자산계상액

capitalization of interest cost　지급이
자의 자본화 ▶ interest on
constructions

capitalization of lease　리스의 자본화

capitalization of reserve　준비금의 자
본화 ▶ capitalization

capitalization rate　자본화율
▶ income approach, risk rate,
safe rate

capitalized lease　자본화리스
▶ operating lease, sales-type
lease

capitalized value   자본화가치
　　▶ capitalization
capitalizing versus expensing   자본화
　　대 비용화
capital lease   자본리스, 자본화리스
　　▶ direct financing lease,
　　finance lease, operating lease,
　　sales-type lease
capital lease obligation   자본리스 채무
capital leverage   자본레버리지, 재무레
　　버리지
capital loss   1) 자본손실 2) 고정자산처
　　분손 ▶ capital gain, capital
　　profit, holding gain and loss
capital maintenance   자본유지
　　▶ financial capital
capital maintenance adjustment   자
　　본유지수정
capital maintenance concept   자본유
　　지개념
capital market   자본시장
capital market analysis   자본시장분석
capital market line(CML)   자본시장선
　　▶ security market line, market
　　portfolio
capital paid-in excess of per value
　　　　1) 액면초과금 2) 주식발행초과
　　금 = share premium, paid-in
　　surplus ▶ capital surplus,
　　stated value
capital projects funds   자본투자 프로
　　젝트 기금
capital rationing   자본배분
capital recovery factor   자본회수계수,
　　원금회수계수
capital recovery method   자본회수법
capital redemption reserve   (영)자본

상환적립금 ▶ treasury stock,
　　redeemable share
capital reserve   자본잉여금,자본준비금
　　▶ capital surplus, revenue
　　reserve
capital resources   자금의 원천
capital stock   1) 자본금 2) 자사주식
capital stock outstanding   사외 유통
　　주식
capital stock subscribed   청약된 자본
　　금 ▶ capital stock subscription
　　receivable
capital stock subscription receivable
　　미수주식청약금
capital stock transactions   주식거래
capital structure   자본구성, 자본구조
　　▶ financial structure
capital surplus   자본잉여금
　　▶ appraisal capital, paid-in
　　capital, paid-in surplus
capital transactions   자본거래
capital transfer tax(CTT)   (영)자산양
　　도세 ▶ death duty, death tax,
　　estate duty, inheritance tax
capital turnover   자본회전율, 총자본회
　　전율
capital turnover ratio   총자본회전율
capital value   자본가치
CAPM(capital asset pricing model)   자
　　본자산가격결정모델, 자본자
　　산평가모델
capsule information   요약정보
card   카드
card book   카드식 장부, 카드식 원장
cardinal number   기수
card system of bookkeeping   전표식
　　부기

career employee 상시종업원 = career laborer ▶ casual laborer

career laborer 상시노동자 = career employee ▶ casual laborer

caretaker 관리인

carriage 1) 운반대, (타이프라이터의) 캐리지, 운반 2) 운임

carriage control tape 운반제어테이프 = carriage tape, control tape

carriage forward 운임 도착지 지불 ▶ carriage free

carriage free 운임 발송지 지불(운임무료) ▶ carriage forward

carriage in (영)운임, 운임 도착지 지불 = freight in, transportation in ▶ carriage out, carriage forward, freight out

carriage-inward (영)인취운임, 매입운임 = freight-in

carriage note 화물인환증

carriage out (영)지불운임, 운임 발송지 지불 = freight out ▶ carriage in, distribution cost, freight in, transportation in

carriage outward 지불운임, 운임 발송지 지불 = carriage out

carriage paid 운임 발송지 지불

carried down(c/d) 전기이월 = brought down ▶ carried forward

carried forward(c/f) 차기이월, 이월액 ▶ carried forward

carrier 1) 운송업자, 운수회사 2) 반송파

carrier case 운송인에 의한 배달이 예정된 계약

carrier's note 운송목록

carrier system 반송방식, 반송시스템

= consignment note, waybill

carryback of operating loss 결손금의 소급 ▶ carryforward of operating loss

carryforward of operating loss 결손금의 이월 ▶ carryback of operating loss

carryforwards 이월액

carrying amount 장부가액 = book value ▶ gross book value, gross carrying amount, net book value, net carrying amount

carrying amount of the payable 채무의 장부가액

carrying charge 1) 보관비, 유지비 = carrying cost 2) 상승가액

carrying cost 보관비 = stockholding cost

carrying value(CV) 장부가액 ▶ book value, carrying amount

carrying value(CV) of loan 대여금의 장부가액

carrying value of loan receivable 대여금의 장부가액

carryover 이월, 이월품 = carryover of deficit

carryover of deficit 결손금의 이월

carryover of tax attribute 세법상 속성의 이월

car tax 자동차세

cartel 카르텔, 기업연합

cartography 지도의 제작방법

CASB(Cost Accounting Standards Board) 원가계산기준심의회

cascade-type turnover tax 다단계 매출세, 누적형 매출세

case law 판례법

case method　사례연구법 = case study method

case-of-need　부도 연락인

case study　사례연구

case study method　사례연구법 = case method

cash　1) 법정통화　2) 현금, 예금 ▶ cash equivalent, legal tender, monetary asset, quick asset, petty cash

cash and cash equivalent　현금 및 현금등가물

cash at bank　요구불예금

cash at bank and in hand　보유현금과 요구불예금

cash basis　현금주의, 현금기준 ▶ accrual basis = receipts and payments basis

cash basis accounting　현금주의회계 ▶ accrual basis accounting

cash basis financial statement reports 현금기준 재무제표

cash basis statement of changes in financial position　현금기준에 의한 재무상태변동표 ▶ fund statement

cash before delivery(CBD)　대금선불 조건판매 ▶ cash on delivery

cash book(CB)　현금출납장

cash budget　현금예산 ▶ financial budget, operating budget

cash collection basis　현금회수기준 = collection basis

cash concept　현금주의 ▶ accrual concept

cash consequence　현금적 결말 ▶ cash-to-cash cycle

cash control　현금관리 ▶ physical control

cash conversion cycle　현금화 과정

cash crop　환금작물, 시장용 작물 = money crop

cash cycle　영업순환, 현금순환

cash disbursement　현금지출 ▶ cash outlay

cash disbursement journal　현금지출 분개장

cash discount(CD)　현금할인, 매출할인

cash dispenser(CD)　현금자동지불기 = cash-dispending machine

cash dividend　현금배당 ▶ stock dividend

cash donation　기부금 ▶ donation, gift, grant

cash equivalent　현금등가물 = equivalent to cash

cash equivalent value　현금등가액

cash float　잔돈, 적은 액수의 돈 ▶ change fund

cash flow　현금흐름

cash flow accounting　현금흐름회계

cash flow analysis　현금흐름분석 ▶ cash flow

cash flow budget　현금흐름예산 = cash budget

cash flow coverage　현금흐름보상률

cash flow from financing activities 재무활동에 의한 현금흐름

cash flow from investing activities 투자활동에 의한 현금흐름

cash flow from operating activities 영업활동에 의한 현금흐름

cash flow hedge　현금흐름에 대한 헤지

cash flow per share　1주당 현금흐름

= fund flow per share ▶ cash flow

cash flow statement 현금흐름, 현금흐름 계산서 ▶ cash report

cash fund 현금예금자금 ▶ cash float

cashier 현금출납계

cashier's check 은행의 자기앞 수표 = bank draft

cash in bank 요구불예금

cash inflow 1) 내부현금유입액 2) 현금유입액, 화폐유입액 ▶ cash outflow

cash in hand 보유현금 = cash on hand

cash in transit 은행미기입예금

cash journal 현금출납장, 금전출납장

cash keeper 출납계

cash limit 현금사용상한, 현금지출제한

cash limit system 사용현금제한제도

cash management 현금예금관리

cash management account(CMA) 투자형 예금구좌

cash on delivery(COD) 현금인도

cash on delivery sale 현금인도판매 = collect on delivery sale

cash on hand 보유현금 = cash in hand

cash on hand and demand deposit 보유현금과 요구불예금

cash or stock award 현금 또는 주식 지급

cash outflow 외부현금흐름, 현금유출액

cash outlay 현금지출 = cash disbursement, cash payment

cash outlay cost 현금지출원가

cash over and short a/c 현금과부족계정 = cash shortage and overage

cash paid for dividend 비상으로 지급된 공액

cash paid for income taxe 법인세로 지급된 금액

cash paid for interest 이자로 지급된 금액

cash paid for operating expense 영업비용으로 지급된 금액

cash paid to suppliers 매입대금 지출액

cash payback method 현금회수법 = payback method

cash payment 현금지불 ▶ cash outlay

cash payment journal 현금지급장 ▶ cash receipt journal

cash planning 현금계획

cash purchase 현금매입, 현금구입

cash ratio 현금비율

cash receipt 현금수입(액)

cash receipt and disbursement 현금수지

cash receipt and outlay 현금수지

cash receipt and payment 현금수지

cash receipt journal 현금수입장, 입금대장 ▶ cash payment journal

cash received from customer 매출채권의 회수, 매출 현금회수액

cash reconciliation(fourcolumn) 현금검증표

cash record 현금기록

cash recovery rate 현금회수율 ▶ corporate recovery rate

cash register 현금등록기

cash remittance 현금송금

cash report 자금보고서, 현금수지보고서 ▶ cash statement

cash resource 현금자원

cash sale 현금판매 ▶ credit sale

cash shop 현금점 = cash store

C

cash shortage 현금부족

cash statement 현금보고서 ▶ cash report

cash surrender value 해약반려금, 해약현금가치

cash surrender value of life insurance 생명보험 계약의 해약반환금

cash terms 현금지불조건

cash-to-cash cycle 영업순환과정
▶ cash consequence

cash transaction 현금거래

cash value 1) 현금가치, 시가 2) (생명보험 관련) 해약반려금

cash with order(CWO) 현금주문

casual hand 임시고용노동자, 자유노동자, 임시공 = casual laborer, casual worker

casuality insurance 1) 재해보험 2) 상해보험

casual laborer 임시고용노동자, 자유노동자, 임시공 = casual hand
▶ career laborer

casual sales 우발적 판매

casualty loss 재해손실

CAT(Committee on Accounting Terminology) 회계용어위원회

catalog 1) 목록 2) 목록에 등록

cataloged procedure 등록완료절차
▶ cataloged data set

cataloging 등록

catastrophe reserve 재해손실준비금

catch-up adjustment 소급수정
= backlog adjustment

catch-up depreciation 소급상각
= backlog depreciation

category 종류, 카테고리

causal cost control 원인별 원가관리

causation 인과

cause-and-effect logic 인과관계, 인과법칙

cause of action 1) 소송원인 2) 권리발생원인

CB(cash book) 현금예금출납장

CB(convertible bonds) 전환사채

CBD(cash before delivery) 대금수취후 판매

CCA(current cost accounting) 현행원가회계

CCAB(Consultative Committee of Accountancy Bodies) (영)회계단체합동자문위원회

CCA Monitoring Working Party CCA감시작업부회
▶ Inflation Accounting Sub-Committee

CCA Sub-Committee CCA소위원회
▶ CCA

CCB(command control block) 지령제어블록

c.c.c.(cwmni cyfyngedig cyhoeddus) 공모유한책임회사

CCE(current cash equivalent) 현행현금등가물

c/d(carried down) 전기이월

CD(cash discount) 현금할인

CD(cash dispenser) 현금자동지급기

CD(certificate of deposit) 양도성예금증서

CED(consumers' expenditures deflator) 소비지출디플레이터

ceiling 최고한계(가격, 임금 등)

Central Bank 중앙은행

central corporate expense 1) 일반본

사관리비 2) 본부비
▶ general corporation costs, corporation costs

central exchange 중앙(증권)거래소

central filing 중앙집권 관리방식

centralization 집중화
▶ decentralization

centralization of management 경영권의 집중

centralized management 중앙집권관리
▶ decentralized management

centralized organization 중앙집권적 조직 ▶ decentralized organization

centralized processing 중앙집권적 처리 ▶ distributed processing

central market 중앙시장

central role 중심적 역할

central service 본부관리업무

central tendency 평균치

CEO(chief executive officer) 최고경영책임자

CEP(current earnings and profits) 당기소득과 당기이익

CERCLA(Comprehensive Environmental, Compensation and Liability Act) 포괄적 환경대처보상책임법

certainty 확실성 ▶ uncertainty

certainty equivalent 확실성등가(액)

certainty equivalent return 확실성등가수익율

certificate 1) 증서, 증명서 2) 채권, 주권 = stock certificate

Certificate in Management Accounting (CMA) 공인관리회계사자격증

certificate of authority 영업 허가증

certificate of bank balance 은행잔고 증명서, 예금잔고증명서

certificate of deposit(CD) 양도성예금증서 ▶ commercial paper, treasury bond

certificate of dissolution 해산증명서

certificate of exemption (영)회사법 요건면제증명서

certificate of incorporation 1) 정관
= articles of association, memorandum of association
▶ registrar of companies
2) 회사설립증명서

certificate of insurance 보험증명서, 보험승인장

certificate of limited partnership 한정 파트너십의 증명서

certificate of necessity 필요시설증명서

certificate of origin 원산국증명서, 원산지증명서

certificate of partnership 파트너십 허가증

certificate of title 소유권 증명서

certificate to commence business (영)개업면허증 ▶ allotted sharecapital, authorised minimum, private company, public company

certification 인증(認證)

certification of audit 감사증명

Certified Accountant(Chartered Association of Certified Accountants) 공인회계사협회의 기관지 또는 월간지

certified check 은행의 지불보증수표,

은행이 인수한 수표

certified financial statements　감사된 재무제표

certified information system auditor (CISA)　공인정보시스템 감사인

certified mail　등기 우편

certified management accountant (CMA)　공인관리회계사

certified public accountant(CPA)　공인회계사 ▶ chartered accountant

certified security　인증증권

cestui que trust　신탁수익자

c/f(carried forward)　차기이월

C&F(cost and freight)　운임포함

CFA(Chartered Financial Analyst)　공인증권분석사

CFO(chief financial officer)　최고재무관리자, 재무담당자

CFR(cost and freight)　운임포함

CGS(cost of goods sold)　매출원가

CGT(capital gain tax)　자본이득세

Chaflin doctrine　채플린 독트린

chain of title　소유권의 사슬

chairman's report　회장보고서 ▶ chairman's review, chairman's statement, directors' report

chamber of commerce　상업회의소

chance constrained programming　확률적 계획법, 확률제약계획법

chancellor　왕의 재판을 담당하는 산하 기구

change　1) 변경, 개정 2) 교환, 취체, 양체 ▶ exchange 3) 취인소 ▶ exchange

changed neighborhood condition　주위상황의 변화

change dump　1) 양체용 자금 2) 잔돈

change fund　1) 양체자금 2) 잔돈

change in accounting estimate　회계추정치의 변경

change in accounting principle　회계원칙의 변경

change in accounting principle and practice　회계방침의 변경

change in capital strucrure　자본구성의 변동

change in classification　(재무제표상의) 분류의 변경

change in class of net asset of not-for-profit organization　비영리조직의 순자산액의 변동

change in employment　이적

change in estimate　회계상 추정의 변경

change in financial position　재무상태변동

change in market value　시가변동

change in permanently restricted net assets　영구구속순자산의 변동

change in reporting entity　보고실체의 변경

change in statement format　재무제표양식의 변경

change in temporarily restricted net assets　일시구속순자산의 변동

change in unrestricted net assets　비구속순자산의 변동

change in value of money　화폐가치의 변동

change of auditors　감사인 교체

change of standard cost　표준원가의
변경 ▶ basic standard cost,
current standard cost

changing price　가격변동, 물가변동
▶ accounting for changing
prices, inflation accounting

**changing price and financial
reporting**　가격변동과 재무
보고

changing price level　물가수준의 변동

**changing the base period of index
number**　물가지수의 기준
년도 변경

channel　통신로 ▶ multiplexer channel,
selector channel

channel of distribution　유통경로

character display　문자표시장치
= character display device

character display device　문자표시장
치 = character display

characteristic　1) 지수부(부동소수점표시의)
2) 지수(대수의) 3) 특징

characteristic line　특성선 ▶ market
portfolio

characteristic of partnership　파트너
쉽의 특징

character recognition　문자인식

charge　1) 차변기입(차기), 차변기입하다
▶ debit, credit 2) 외상 3) 수
익부과분 4) 비용, 손실 발생액
▶ cost, expense 5) 요금, 대금,
청구금액 6) 담보 7) 물상담보
부채무 보증계약

chargeable gain　과세대상이 되는 자산
처분익

chargeable labor cost　과세대상이 되는
인건비

chargeable transfer　(영)과세대상이 되
는 자산양도(증여)

charge account　외상거래계정 = credit
account

charge-a-plate　크레디트카드
= charge card, charge plate,
credit card

charge by way of legal mortgage　담
보물의 저당권 ▶ equitable
mortgage, estate mortgage by
way of lease

charge card　크레디트카드
= charge-a-plate, charge plate,
credit card

charge off　자산의 비용처리

charge plate　크레디트카드 = charge-a-
plate, charge card, credit card

charge rate　청구 요율 = billing rate

charges forward　제비용 선불

charges here　제비용 지불

charging lien　형평법상의 유치권

charitable company　(영)자선회사, 공
익회사

charitable contribution　자선기부

charitable gift　(gift tax) 자선적 증여

charitable purpose　공익목적, 비영리
목적 ▶ not for profit
organization

charitable trust　자선신탁, 공익신탁

charity　1) 자선단체, 자선사업, 공익단체
2) 자선행위

charity to charity exception　특정물품
에 대한 금전적인 의무와 담보
권 혹은 임대차를 표창하는 문
서

chart　계층구조도, 계층도

C

charter 1) 칙허장 (royal charter) 2) 날인증서 (deed) 3) 양도증서 4) 대차계약서 5) 특별면제 6) 특권

chartered accountant(CA) (영)칙허(공인)회계사 ▶ certified public accountant

Chartered Accountant in Australia 오스트레일리아 공인회계사협회의 기관지. 1930년 창간한 월간지 (Institute of Chartered Accountants in Australia)

Chartered Association of Certified Accountants(CACA, ACCA) 공인회계사협회

chartered company (영)칙허회사, 특허회사 ▶ charter

chartered corporation (영)칙허법인, 특허법인

chartered financial analyst(CFA) 공인증권분석사 ▶ Institute of Chartered Financial Analysts

Chartered Institute of Management Accountants(CIMA) (영)공인관리회계사협회

charter party 용선(傭船)증서, 용선계약서

chartist 주가도표전문가

chart of account 계정조직

chart of accounting books system 장부조직도

chattels 동산(動産), 가재(家財)

chattels mortgage 동산양도저당

chattels paper 동산(재산)저당증권, 특정물품에 대한 금전적인 의무와담보권 혹은 임대차를 표창하는 문서

chattels personal 본래의 동산, 인적 동산

chattels real 부동산상의 동산, 물적 동산

cheap money 저금리 자금

Chebyschev inequality 체비세프부등식

Chebyshev's theorem 체비세프이론

check 1) 수표 2) 감정서 3) 검사

check book 수표장

check card 크레디트카드 = check guarantee card

check guarantee card 크레디트카드 = check card

checking 조합, 대조 ▶ checking account, checking slip, checking posting, footing, vouching

checking account 당좌예금구좌 = current account (영)

checking posting 전기(轉記) 대조 = retracing of book

checking program 검사 프로그램

checking slip 전표(傳票) 대조

check list 검사목록, 점검표

check off 공제

check received 수령한 수표, 지불한 수표

check register 수표기입장

checksum 검사합계

check trading 수표거래

check up 조합, 검사

check writer 증권인쇄기, 수표금액인쇄기

cheque 수표 = check

cheque card 크레디트카드 = check card

chest 1) (공공시설) 금고 2) 자금

chief accountant　기업회계심의관, 주임회계심사관

chief cashier　출납책임자

chief executive officer(CEO)　최고경영책임자

chief financial officer(CFO)　최고재무관리자, 재무담당자, 재무총괄경영자 ▶ chief executive officer

chief operating decision maker　최고경영상의 의사결정자, 영업정책의 최고의사결정자

child care credit　자녀보호 세액공제

child support　자녀 양육비

child tax credit　자녀세액공제

Chinese Wall　정보의 장벽

Chi-square(x^2) -distribution　카이제곱분포

Chi-square(x^2) test　카이제곱검정

chit　비망(備忘)용 전표, 신분증명서

chit book　서류송달부, 편지접수부

choice　선택

choice of an attribute　속성의 선택

choice of a scale of measurement　측정척도의 선택

chose in action　1) 무체재산(無體財産) ▶ chose in possession 2) 채권 3) 일정액의 화폐와 동산을 법적으로 취득할 수 있는 권리

chose in possession　유체재산 ▶ chose in action

chronological record　연대순기록, 발생순서의 기록

chronometer　정밀 시계

church law　교회법

CIA(Committee on Internal Auditing)　내부감사위원회

CIA(Controller's Institute of America)　공인내부감사사

CICA(Canadian Institute of Chartered Accountants)　캐나다 공인회계사

CIF(cost, insurance and freight)　운임 · 보험료 포함 가격조건

CIMA(Chartered Institute of Management Accountants)　공인관리회계사협회

CIPFA(Chartered Institute of Public Finance and Accountancy)　재정 · 공공회계 공인협회

CIR(Commissioner of Inland Revenue)　내국세입국의 감독관

circuit　항소 법원이 담당하는 지역

circulating asset　순환자산, 유동자산, 운전자산 = current asset, floating asset

circulating capital　유동자산 ▶ current asset

circulating fund　유동자금, 운전자금

circumstance　환경요인

circumstantial evidence　상황증거

CISA(certified information system auditor)　공인정보시스템 감사인

citadel of privity　당사자의 최후의 거점

city　(영)상업, 금융의 중심지역

city code on take-overs and mergers　(영)매수, 합병관계에 있는 시티코드

civil action　민사 소송

civil law　민사법

Civil Rights Act　시민권법

claim　청구, 청구권, 미수(未收)채권, 클레임

claim adjustment expense 보험금 지
불액
claim, filing of bankruptcy 파산의 신
청, 우선순위
claim for refund 세금 환급 청구
claim in foreign currency 외화채권
claim to cash 현금청구권, 현금청구액
claim to debtor's estate 채무자 재산
에 대한 청구
claim to money 화폐청구권
claimant company (영)세액공제신청회
사 ▶ group relief, 75 percent
subsidiary
class 구분
class cost system 등급별 종합원가계
산, 조별 종합원가계산 ▶ lot
cost system
class gift 단체 증여
classical variable sampling 전통적인
변수 표본감사
classification 분류
classification of accounts 계정분류
classification of cost by department
원가의 부문별 분류
▶ classification of cost by
nature or product
classification of cost by nature 원가
의 성격별 분류 ▶ classification
of cost by department or product
classification of cost by product 원가
의 제품별 분류 ▶ classification
of cost by nature or department,
direct cost, indirect cost,
semidirect cost
classification of trust 신탁의 분류
classified balance sheet 구분식(보고식)
대차대조표

classified statement of profit and loss
구분식(보고식) 손익계산서
class interval 급간격(級間隔)
class mark 급대표치(級代表値)
class of share 주식의 종류(분류)
class of stock 주식의 분류
class of transaction 거래의 분류(종류)
class voting 특정 종류의 주식을 가진
자들만의 의결
claused bill of lading 조건부 선하(船荷)
증권
clean acceptance (수표의) 단순인수
Clean Air Act 대기정화법
clean bill 환어음 ▶ documentary bill
clean bill of draft 환어음
▶ documentary bill
clean hands 구제를 구하는 측이 잘못이
없어야 함
clean opinion 적정의견 = unqualified
opinion ▶ standard opinion
clean surplus approach 포괄주의
= all inclusive income statement
Clean Water Act 수질정화법
clearance 1) 수표교환, 결제 = clearing
2) 통관수속, 출입항인가서
clearing 결제 = clearance
clearing bank 시중은행
clearing house 1) 수표교환소 2) (무역
수지결산에 대한) 청산소
clearing house balance 수표교환 후
잔고
clerical check 사무적인 체크
clerical error 기장상 오류
clerical work 사무적 작업
client 1) 의뢰인, 피감사회사 2) 고객
client interest 고객의 이익
client representation 피감사회사의 진

술서, 고객 진술서

client representation letter 경영자 확
인서

Clifford trust 클리포드 신탁

cliff vesting 일시적 권리확정

cllable preferred stock 상환우선주식

clock card 출근표 = gate card, in-and-
out card ▶ time

close company (영)회사

close corporation 주식비공개회사
▶ open corporation

closed corporation 폐쇄회사 ▶ private
company, public corporation

closed-end fund 폐쇄형 투자신탁
▶ investment trust, mutual
fund, open-end fund

closed-end investment company 폐쇄
형 투자신탁회사 ▶ open-end
investment trust

closed job cost sheet 마감된 개별 원
가계산표 ▶ job cost sheet

closed loop verification 폐쇄 루프 입증

closed mortgage 폐쇄식 저당

closed mortgage bond 폐쇄식 저당부
사채

closed shop 폐쇄방식 ▶ open shop,
union shop

closely held company 비공개회사

closely held corporation 비공개회사

closely held enterprise 비공개 회사

close off 계정(장부)마감 = balance off

closing 마감

closing a department 부문의 폐지

closing adjustment 결산수정

closing agreement and compromise
종결합의와 타협

closing a segment 세그먼트(부문)의 폐

지

closing balance 기말잔고 ▶ opening
balance

closing balance account 대차대조표계
정의 마감

closing corporation 폐쇄회사 ▶ open
corporation

closing date 결산일 = terminal date

closing entry 마감분개

closing price 종가(終價) ▶ opening
price

closing process 결산절차

closing rate(CR) 결산일환율
= current rate → historical rate

closing rate method 결산일환율법
= current rate method ▶ foreign
currency financial statements,
temporal method

closing rate/net investment method
결산일환율/순투자법 ▶ closing
rate method, cover concept,
temporal method

closing stock 재고자산 기말잔고
= ending inventory

closing trial balance 이월시산표

cluster analysis 집단분석

CM (contribution margin) 공헌이익

CMA(cash management account) 투자
형 예금구좌

**CMA(certificate in management
accounting)** 관리회계사 인
정증

CMA(certified management accountant)
공인관리회계사

**CMAP(Committee on Management
Accounting Practice)** 관리
회계 실무위원회

CMA sampling 금액누적 표본감사

CMA-The Management Accounting Magazine 캐나다 관리회계사협회(Society of Management Accountants of Canada)의 기관지. 1926년 창간

CMDM(Committee on Managerial Decision Model) 경영의사결정모형 위원회

CML(capital market line) 자본시장선
▶ security market line, market portfolio

CMS(conversational monitor system) 회화형 모니터시스템

coacceptor 공동인수인

Cobb-Douglas function 콥-더글라스 함수

COBRA(Consolidated Budget Reconciliation Act) 연방포괄예산조정법

Cochran's theorem 코크런정리

CoCoA(continuously contemporary accounting) 계속적 현대회계

COD(cash on delivery) 현금인도

COD(collect on delivery) 인도에 대한 대금추심

COD sale (cash on delivery sale) 대금인수(수취) 후 판매

CODASYL(Conference for Data Systems Languages) 데이터시스템 언어협의회

code 1) 부호, 코드 = coding scheme 2) (전기통신)코드 3) 정보 4) 법전

code of professional conduct 공인회계사직업윤리규정
= professional responsibility (전문가로서의 책임)

Code of Professional Conduct AICPA의 직업윤리규정

code of professional ethics 직업윤리규정

code set 코드집합

codicil 유언보충서

codification of auditing standards and procedures 감사기준과 감사절차의 편찬

codification of statements on auditing procedures 감사절차개요서 = Statement of Auditing Procedures

coefficient of constraint 제약계수
▶ technical coefficient

coefficient of rank correlation 순위상관계수

coefficient of variation 변동계수
▶ standard deviation

co-factor 공통인자

cognitive dissonance 인지적 부조화

cognitive style 인지적 스타일

cognitive style approach 인지스타일접근법

coinsurance 1) 비례전보보험, 공동보험 2) 공통보험자

coinsurance clause 공동보험 조항

collapsible corporations 붕괴법인, 청산법인

collar 컬러, 상한금리와 하한금리의 조합

collate 대조하다

collateral 담보, 담보물건, 부담보(副擔保)

collateral bond 담보부사채

collateral good 담보물

collateral loan 1) 담보부대여금 2) 부담보대여금

collateral security 1) (제3자 제공) 담보
(물) 2) 부담보

collateral trust bond 증권담보사채

collating sequence 순번, 대조순번, 대
조순서 = sequence

collator 대조기(機)

collected in advance 선수금, 전수금

collectibility 회수가능성

collectibility of receivable 채권의 회
수가능성

collecting agent 징수대리기관, 징수대
리업

collecting bank (채권)징수은행

collecting taxes 징세(徵稅)

collection basis 회수기준 = cash
collection basis

collection expense 대금회수비용

collection guarantor 추심 보증인

collection method 회수기준 방법

collection of debt 채권회수

collective time 합계시간

collect on delivery 대금인수 후 인도,
현금인도

collect on delivery sale 대금인수 후
판매 = cash on delivery(COD)

collector of taxes 조세징수자 = tax
collector

collinearity 공선성(共線性)

collusion 공모(共謀), 결탁

column 열(列), 행

columnar journal 다행식 분개장

columnar ledger 다행식 원장

columnar type of variable budget 다
행식 변동예산 = table type of
variable budget ▶ formula
type of variable budget

column split (카드의) 행 분할

comaker 공동 발행인

combination 1) 합동, 결합 2) 조합
3) 합병 = business combination

combination circuit 조합된 회로

combination of business 기업결합, 기
업합동 = business combination
▶ amalgamation, consolidation,
merger

**combination of the production and the
straight-line method** 생산
량 · 정액복합상각법. 복합생산
량비례법 ▶ modified units of
production method

**combined balance sheet of home office
and branch** 본지점결합 대
차대조표

combined burden rate 결합제조간접
비 배부율 ▶ burden rate

combined financial statement 1) 결
합재무제표 ▶ consolidated
financial statements 2) 본지점
의 결합(총합) 재무제표
▶ home-branch accounting

**combined income and retained
earnings statement** 결합
손익 및 이월이익잉여금처분계
산서

combined income statement 결합 손
익계산서

**combined income statement of home
office and branch** 본지점
결합 손익계산서

combined overhead rate 결합 간접비
배부율 ▶ overhead rate

combined revenue 연결수익

combined segment revenue 총수익

combined statement 결합재무제표, 합

C

병재무제표 = combined
financial statement
▶ consolidated financial
statement, group financial
statement

**combined statement of income and
retained earnings**   결합 손익
및 이월이익잉여금처분계산서

combined station   복합(複合)국(局)
= balanced station

combined transport document(CTD)
복합운송증권

combined variance   결합차이

combined work sheet   결합정산표

comfort letter   조사보고서

comfort letter for underwriter   증권
인수회사(간사(幹事)증권회사)의
조사보고서 = letter
forunderwriter

comment   주석(注釋) = annotation, note,
remark

comment letter   SEC의 코멘트 레터

commercial bank   상업은행

commercial bookkeeping   상업부기

commercial code   상법

commercial court   상사재판소

commercial document   상업상의 서류

commercial efficiency   상업상의 능률

commercial expense   영업비
= distribution cost, marketing
cost ▶ manufacturing cost,
selling and general
administrative cost

commercial injury   상업적 손해

commercial law   상법

commercial letter of credit written   영
업신용장(발행측)

commercial loss   상업적 손해

commercial paper(CP)   기업어음, 상
업증권, 유가증권 ▶ Negotiable
instruments (교부성 증서),
promissory note

commercial transaction   상업적 거래

commission   1) 수수료 2) 명령, 지시
3)위원회 4) 의뢰,주문 5) 위임

commissioner   1) 장관, 국장, 감독관
2) 위원,이사

**Commissioner for the General
Purposes of the Income Tax**
(영)국세불복심판관 = General
Commissioner

**Commissioner for the Special Purposes
of the Income Tax Acts**
(영)특별국세불복심판관
= Special Commissioner

Commissioner of Customs and Excise
(영) 간접세징수관

**Commissioner of Inland Revenue
(CIR)**   (영)내국세 입국커미
셔너

**Commission for Local Authority
Accounts in Scotland**   (영)
스코틀랜드 지방자치단체의 감
사위원회 ▶ Audit
Commission for Local
Authorities in England and
Wales

**commission on issue of shares and
debentures**   주식과 사채 발
행 수수료

commission receivable   미수수수료

commission to consignees   판매위탁수
수료

commitment   1) 판매계약, 거래계약 2)

위탁, 위임 3) 의무, 미수행채무

commitment and contingent liability
계약채무 및 우발채무

commitment fee   계약수수료

commitment letter   계약의무조항이 표
시된 서류

committed capacity cost   생상설비기
초원가, 확정원가 = committed
cost ▶ discretionary cost,
engineered cost

committed cost   확정고정비, 생산설비
기초원가 = committed capacity
cost ▶ capacity cost,
discretionary cost, engineered
cost, managed cost

committed fixed cost   생산설비기초
원가, 확정고정비 = committed
cost ▶ discretionary cost,
engineered cost

committee of inspection   조사위원회

Committee of Sponsoring Organizations
(COSO)   자문 조직위원회

**Committee on Accounting Concepts
and Standards**   회계개념
및 기준위원회

Committee on Accounting Procedure
(CAP)   회계절차심의위원회

**Committee on Accounting
Terminology(CAT)**   회계
용어위원회

Committee on Auditing Procedure
(CAP)   감사절차위원회

Committee on Internal Auditing(CIA)
내부감사위원회

**Committee on Management
Accounting Practice(CMAP)**
관리회계실무위원회

**Committee on Managerial Decision
Model(CMDM)**   경영의사
결정모델위원회

**Committee on Statement of Cost
Accounting Principles
(CSCAP)**   원가계산기준위원
회

commodity   상품

commodity draft   상품대금징수어음

commodity futures   선물상품, 상품 선
물거래

commodity market   상품시장

common   보통

common capacity cost   공통시설원가,
공통고정원가 = common fixed
cost ▶ specific capacity cost

common carrier   공공운송인, 통신사
업자, 전신전화회사

common cost   공통비 = joint cost
▶ direct cost, indirect cost,
individual cost, overhead

common difference   공식적으로 허용
되는 오차

common fixed cost   공통고정비
= common capacity cost

common language   공통언어

common law   관습법, 불문율, 민법, 일
반법 ▶ equity

common law liability to client   의뢰
인에 대한 민법상의 책임

common law liability to nonclient
비의뢰인에 대한 민법상의 책임

common law lien   민법상의 유치권

common law property   부부별산제

common logarithm   상용대수(常用對數)

common ownership case   부착된 동산
의 소유자와 부동산의 소유자

가 동일한 경우

common property　공유재산

common ratio　공비(公比)

common scheme　공통된 계획

common segment　공통부분

common share　보통주 = common stock

common shares outstanding　사외유
통발행 보통주식수

common size balance sheet　백분율 대
차대조표, 비율표시 대차대조
표, 공통형 대차대조표 = one
hundred percentage balance
sheet ▶ common size income
statement

common size income statement　백분
율 손익계산서, 비율표시 손익
계산서, 공통형 손익계산서
= one hundred percentage
income statement ▶ common
size balance sheet

common stock　자본금, 보통주식
= common share ▶ deferred
stock, preferred stock

common stock equivalent　보통주식 상
당증권, 보통주식 등가물

common stockholder's equity　보통
주주 자기자본

commoriente　동일사고사망자

communicability　전달성 ▶ software
requirements specification

communication　전달, 통신

communication channel　통신채널

communication common carrier　전
신전화회사

communication control　통신제어

communication control character　전
송제어문자, 통신제어문자

= transmission control character

communication control program(CCP)
통신제어프로그램

communication control unit(CCU)　통
신제어장치, 통신제어기구, 회선
제어장치 ▶ communication
control character

communication device　통신장치

communication line　통신회선

communication link　통신링크

communication network　통신네트워크

communication processor(CP)　통신
용 프로세서

communication region　연결영역, 연결
구역

communication system　통신시스템

communication task　통신과업

community at large　지역사회 전체

community property　공유재산제

Companies Acts　(영)회사법

companies bill　회사법 법안, 회사법 개
정안

companies registration office　(영)회
사 등기사무소 ▶ London
Gazette, registered company

company　1) 회사, 상사 2) 친교 3)
친구, 동료 4) 집단

company law　회사법 = corporation law

company limited by guarantee　(영)보
증유한회사 = guarantee
company ▶ registered company

comparability　비교가능성, 비교성
▶ consistency

comparative analysis　비교분석

comparative balance sheet　비교대차
대조표

comparative figure　전기(前期)의 비교

대응수치, 전기의 비교액
= corresponding amount
▶ comparative balance sheet,
comparative profit and loss
statement

comparative financial statement   비교
재무제표

comparative fund statement   비교자
금계산서

comparative income statement   비교
손익계산서

comparative international accounting
비교국제회계

comparative negligence   비교 과실, 과
실상쇄

comparative profit and loss statement
비교손익계산서 ▶ comparative
balance sheet, comparative
figure, corresponding amount

comparative unit method   건설비 비
교법 ▶ quantity survey method,
unit-in-place method

comparator   비교기(器)

comparing   비교

comparison   비교

comparison analysis   비교분석

comparison operator   비교연산자

compatibility   호환성, 양립성

compensated absence   유급휴가
▶ paid educational leave, paid
vacation

compensated surety   유상(有償)보증인,
배상보증인

compensating balance   1) 양건예금, 보
상예금 2) 사용제한예금 잔고

compensating balance arrangement
사용제한예금 잔고정리

compensation   1) 수당, 보수(報酬)
▶ salary 2) 보장 3) 보상금

compensation cost   보상비용

compensation expense   보상비용

compensatory damage   보상적 손해
배상

compensatory plan   보수(報酬)제도

competence   능력, 적격성, 자격

competence of evidence   증거력

competent and sufficient evidential
matter   적격하고 충분한 증
거

competing method   경합하는 모든 방법

competition with corporation   회사와
의 경쟁

compilation   1) 대리작성 업무
▶ audit, compilation of
financial statements, review
2) 편집, 작성

compilation and review service   대리
작성 및 검토 업무

compilation engagement   재무제표 대
리작성계약

compilation of financial statement
재무제표 대리작성

compilation procedure   대리작성업무
절차

compilation report   대리작성업무보고
서 ▶ review

compilation test   작성 테스트

compiler   편집자, 편찬자 = compiling
program ▶ generator,
interpreter, language processor,
translator

complement   보수(補數)

complete audit   정밀감사, 전부감사
= detailed audit

C

complete auditing　전부감사, 완전감사
complete checking　완전대조
completed contract method　완료기준,
　공사완성 기준 ▶ percentage
　of completion method,
　realization basis
completed job method　공사완성기준
　▶ long-term construction
　work contract, percentage of
　completion method
**completed job method for long-term
　contract**　장기공사계약에
　의한 공사완성기준
　▶ construction-type contract,
　percentage of completion
　method for long-term contract
completed long-term contract　장기
　공사계약
completed sales basis　판매기준
　= sales basis of revenue
　recognition ▶ installment
　method, percentage of
　completion method
complete integration　완전한 통합
complete liquidation　완전 청산
completeness　완전성, 충분성, 망라(網
　羅)성 ▶ representative
　faithfulness ▶ software
　requirements specification
complete set of financial statement
　전체 재무제표
completing the audit　감사의 종결
completion of field work　현장작업의
　종료
completion of production basis　생
　산완성수익기준
completion of production method　생

산기준, 완료기준
complex capital structure　복잡한 자
　본구성
complex constant　복소(複素)정수, 복소
　수
complex data　복합데이터
complex trust (exemption)　복합합병
compliance　법령준수, 준거(準據)
compliance attestation　준거 감사
compliance audit　준거감사, 준수감사
　▶ compliance test
compliance auditing　법령 준거감사
compliance test　법령 준거 테스트, 준
　거성 테스트
compliance testing　준거성 감사
　= compliance test
compliance test report　준거성 감사
　보고서
**compliance with aspect contractual
　agreement or regulatory
　requirement**　계약조항 혹
　은 감독관청 규정으로의 준거성
complication　합의(含意), 암시
　▶ conditional implication
component　1) 구성요소, 요인, 구성분
　자 2) 구성부품 3) 기계장치,
　소자
component unit　부속기관
composite contribution margin　가중
　평균 공헌이익
composite depreciation　복합상각
　▶ group depreciation
**composite depreciation by straight-line
　method**　복합상각법
composite life　복합내용연수
composite rate　(영)합성세율
composite rate method　복합상각법

▶ group rate method

composite stock price table   복합주가
표 ▶ NYSE Common Stock
Index

composite transaction   복합거래

composite useful life   복합내용연수

composition   1) 타협, 화해, 화의 2) 채
무일부변제계약 3) 일부변제금,
시담금(示談金) 4) 성질 5) 구성,
조직, 구조

composition agreement   조정합의, 채
무의 일부변제 합의

composition agreement with creditor
채권자와의 화의

composition plan   채무구성계획

compound discount   복수할인
= mathematical discount

compounding   복리계산

compounding interest   복리

compound interest   복리이자
▶ compounding interest

compound interest method   복리상각
법 = equal annual-payment
method ▶ annuity method,
sinking fund method

compound sum   복리원리합계

**comprehensive annual financial
report(CAFR)**   총괄 연간
재무제표

comprehensive basis   포괄적 기준

comprehensive basis of accounting
포괄적 회계기준

**comprehensive basis of accounting
other than GAAP**
GAAP 이외의 포괄적 회계원칙

comprehensive budget   포괄예산, 총괄
예산, 종합예산 = master budget

**Comprehensive Environmental,
Compensation and Liability
Act(CERCLA)**   포괄적 환
경대처보상책임법

comprehensive income   포괄적 이익,
포괄이익 ▶ earnings

comprehensive income tax allocation
소득세의 완전기간배분
= comprehensive tax allocation

comprehensive loss   포괄적 손실

comprehensive tax allocation   소득세
의 완전기간배분
= comprehensive income
tax allocation, full provision
basis ▶ deferred income tax,
income tax allocation

comptroller   1) 감사관 2) 회계검사관
3) 파산감사관 = controller
▶ controllership

Comptroller and Auditor General
(영)회계검사원장

comptroller's department   회계감사
부 = controller's department

comptrollership   회계감사관
= controllership

compulsory contribution   강제적인
납입금

compulsory disposition   강제처분

compulsory execution   강제집행

compulsory liquidation   강제청산
= compulsory winding up

compulsory sales by auction   강제경
매

compulsory winding up   (영)강제해산
= compulsory liquidation
▶ voluntary liquidation,
voluntary winding up

computational complexity   계산의 복
잡성
**computation of cstate or trust taxable
income**   유산 및 신탁의 과
세소득 계산
computer account   컴퓨터 계좌
computer aided design(CAD)   컴퓨터
이용(지원) 설계 ▶ computer-
aided instruction, computer-
aided manufacturing
computer aided instruction(CAI)   컴
퓨터 지원 교육 = computer
assisted instruction
computer aided manufacturing(CAM)
컴퓨터 원용(援用) 제조
computer application control activity
컴퓨터 적용 통제활동
computer architecture   컴퓨터 건축
**computer assisted audit techniques
(CAAT)**   컴퓨터를 이용한 감
사기법 ▶ audit software, audit
through the computer
computer assisted instruction   컴퓨
터 지원 학습 = computer-aided
instruction(CAI)
computer assisted management   컴퓨
터 지원 사무관리
computer auditing   컴퓨터 감사
▶ auditing through the
computer, auditing with the
computer
computer audit program   컴퓨터 감사
프로그램 = computer audit
software ▶ auditing with the
computer, generalized audit
software
computer audit software   컴퓨터 감사

소프트웨어 = computer audit
program ▶ auditing with the
computer, generalized audit
software
**computer based accounting
information system**   컴퓨
터 이용 회계정보 시스템
= computerized accounting
system
computer center   중앙처리장치 = EDP
center, electronic data-
processing center
computer control activity   컴퓨터 통
제활동
computer crime   컴퓨터 범죄
computer facility   컴퓨터 시설
computer file   컴퓨터 파일
computer general control activities
컴퓨터에 관한 일반 통제 활동
computer generated report   컴퓨터
로 생성한 보고서
computerized accounting system   전
산화된 회계시스템
= computer- based accounting
information system
computerized audit tool   전산화된 감
사수단
computerized control   전산화된 통제
computer programmed control   컴퓨
터로 프로그램화된 통제
computer readable form   컴퓨터 판독
가능 형태
computer utility   컴퓨터 효용
concatenation   연결
concatenation character   연결문자
concealment   1) 은폐, 은닉 2) 보험금
의 지불 보류 3) 사실의 불고

지(不告知)

concentration of credit risk   모든 금
        융상품에 연계된 신용 리스크
        의 집중

concentrator   집중시키는 장치

concept   개념

concept framework   개념구조

concept framework project   개념구조
        프로젝트

concept of earnings   이익 개념

concept of maintenance of operating
        capability   조업능력유지 개
        념 ▶ net operating assets

concept of matching costs with
        revenues   비용 · 수익대응
        개념 = matching principle

conceptual base   개념적 기초, 이론적
        토대

conceptual design   개념설계

conceptual framework   개념적 체계,
        개념구조 ▶ statement of
        financial accounting concept

conceptual framework for financial
        reporting   재무보고에 대한
        개념 구조

conceptual framework project   개념
        적 체계 프로젝트 ▶ Trueblood
        Committee, Wheat Committee

conceptual schema   개념도표

concession   1) 특권부여 2) 양보, 승인
        3) 면허, 특허 4) 영업허가,
        토지사용권 5) 조계(租界), 거
        류지 6) 값을 깎음

concurrent   병행, 동시병행

concurrent access   동시접근

concurrent estate   공유 재산권, 공동적
        부동산권

concurrent interest   동시발생 이익

concurrent interest in real property
        동시발생 이익

concurrent job   동시작업, 공동작업

concurrent operation   병행연산, 병행
        조작, 동시조작

concurrent peripheral operation(CPO)
        동시주변조작

concurrent processing   병행처리, 동시
        처리 ▶ multiprocessing,
        multiprogramming

concurrent testing   동시적 시사, 병행
        테스트

concurring review of report   감사보
        고서의 제2차 사열

condensation   1) 응축화, 간결화 2) 요
        약수치

condensed financial information   요
        약재무정보

condensed financial statement   요약
        재무제표

condition   1) 계약조항 2) 상태, 상황
        3) 지위, 신분 4) 조건, 요약
        조건, 제약 5) (pl) 지불조건

conditional bill of sale   (영)조건부 매
        매증서 ▶ absolute bill of sale

conditional delivery   조건부 전달

conditional endorsement   조건부 이서
        (裏書) = conditional indorsement

conditional financing   조건부 융자
        ▶ conditional payment

conditional gift   조건부 증여

conditional implication   함의(含意)
        = complication

conditional indorsement   조건부 이서
        = conditional endorsement

conditional loan   조건부 차입

▶ conditional payment

conditional loss 조건부 손실, 기회손실
= cost of prediction error,
opportunity loss

conditional order 조건부 지시

conditional payment 조건부 지불액
▶ conditional financing,
conditional loan

conditional probability 조건부 확률

conditional promise 조건부 약속

conditional sale 조건부 매매

conditional sale agreement 조건부 판
매계약 ▶ conditional sale

conditional truth approach 조건적 진
실성 ▶ absolute-truth
approach, costly-truth approach

condition concurrent 동시조건, 동시
조항

condition precedent 정지조건, 정지조
항, 선행조건

condition subsequent 해제조건, 해제
조항, 후행조건

conduct 행위

confederated state 국가 연합

**Confederation of Asian and Pacific
Accountants(CAPA)** 아시
아태평양 회계사연맹

**Conference on Accounting and
Education** 회계교육회의

**Conference On Data Systems
Languages(CODASYL)**
데이터시스템용어협의회

confidence level 신뢰성 수준

confidential relationship 친밀한 관계

configuration 기기(器機)구성, 구성

confirmation 확인, 조회

confirmation of account receivable

외상매출금 잔액의 조회확인

confirmation request 조회 요청서

confirmatory note 확인증서

confirmatory value 확증적 가치

confirmed credit 확인된 신용장
= confirmed letter of credit

confirmed letter of credit 확인된 신용
장 = confirmed credit

confirming house 수입대행업자
= London shipper

conflict of interest 이해상충, 이익상
반행위

conflict of interest statement 이해상
충에 관한 진술서

conformity 1) 통일성, 일치, 연합
2) 준거, 복종

conformity with GAAP 일반적으로
인정된 회계원칙의 준거(準據)

confounding method 혼돈법

conglomerate 복합기업
▶ diversified company

conglomerate company 복합기업, 다
각화기업

conglomerate financial statement
복합기업재무제표

conglomerate merger 복합적 합병

conglomerate reporting 복합기업보
고서

congruence 목표 일치, 정합성(整合性)

conjunction 연결

connected graph 연결그래프(도표)

consecutive 연속

consensual contract 낙성(諾成)계약

consensual lien 합의에 의한 담보권

consensus 합의

consensus ad idem (계약당사자간의)합의

consent dividend 동의배당금

consent letter 동의 서한 = consent
    statement in published
    prospectuses
consent statement in published
    prospectuse 공표된 사업
    전망서에 포함된 동의 서한
    = consent letter
consequence 1) 귀결 2) 성과 3) 경향
consequential damage 1) 파생적 손
    해, 결과적 손해, 간접손해 2) 손
    해배상
conservation of central management
    time 중앙 경영자 시간의 보
    호
conservatism 보수주의 ▶ prudence
conservative procedure 보수적 절차
consideration 고려사항 대가
consideration for contract 계약의 대
    가
consigned goods 위탁품
consigned inventory 위탁재고
consignee (위탁판매의) 수탁자, 하수인
    (荷受人) ▶ consignor
consignment 1) 적송품 2) 위탁, 위탁
    판매, 수탁판매
consignment inward 수탁품
    ▶ consignment outward
consignment inward ledger 수탁판매
    원장
consignment note 항공화물수취증
    = air waybill
consignment outward 적송품
    ▶ consignment inward
consignment purchase 매수위탁
consignment sale 위탁판매
    = consignment selling
consignment selling 위탁판매

    = consignment sale
consignment sheet 화물인수증
    = waybill
consignor 위탁자, 송하인 ▶ consignee
consistency 1) 일관성
    ▶ comparability 2) 계속성
    ▶ software requirements
    specification
consistency standard 계속성의 원칙
consistent estimator 일치추정량
consol (영)콘솔 공채, 정리 공채
    ▶ consol market, consols
console 1) 컨소울 2) 조작 테이블
console function 조작탁월기능
consolidate and blanket mortgage 포
    괄저당사채
consolidated accounts (영)연결재무제
    표 = consolidated financial
    statements ▶ group accounts
consolidated annuity (영)정리공채
    = consols
consolidated balance 연결란, 연결잔고
consolidated balance sheet 연결대차
    대조표 ▶ consolidated
    financial statement, consolidated
    income statement, parent
    company, subsidiary
consolidated balance sheet working
    paper 연결대차대조표 정산
    표
consolidated bond 정리사채
Consolidated Budget Reconciliation
    Act of 1985 포괄재정조정
    1985년법
consolidated company 연결회사
    ▶ consolidated balance sheet,
    consolidated financial statement,

consolidated income statement

consolidated equity　연결지분, 친회사
　　(주주)지분 = majority interest

consolidated excess　연결초과액
　　= consolidated goodwill

consolidated financial information
　　연결재무정보

**consolidated financial statement
　　subsequent to acquisition**
　　회기말에 연결재무제표의 작성
　　(매입법의 경우)

consolidated financial statement　연
　　결재무제표 ▶ full
　　consolidation, group accounts

Consolidated Fund　(영)정리공채자금

consolidated fund statement　연결자
　　금계산서

consolidated goodwill　합병시 영업권
　　= consolidated excess,
　　consolidation goodwill

**consolidated income and expenditure
　　account**　(영)연결손익계산
　　서(비영리사업)

consolidated income statement　연결
　　손익계산서 ▶ consolidated
　　balance sheet

consolidated profit　연결이익

consolidated profit and loss account
　　연결손익계산서 = consolidated
　　income statement

consolidated ratio　합병비율

consolidated return　연결납세신고서
　　= consolidated tax return
　　▶ consolidated return system

consolidated return system　연결납세
　　제도 ▶ consolidated return

consolidated statement of cash flow

연결현금흐름표

**consolidated statement of changes in
　　financial position**　연결재
　　무상태변동표

consolidated statement of income　연
　　결손익계산서

**consolidated statement of retained
　　earnings**　연결이익잉여금
　　처분계산서

**consolidated statement of source and
　　application of fund**　연결
　　자금계산서 = consolidated
　　funds statement

consolidated statement workpaper
　　연결정산표

consolidated stockholders' equity
　　연결지분

consolidated subsidiary　연결자회사

consolidated surplus　연결잉여금

consolidated tax provision　연결납세
　　담보금

consolidated tax return　연결납세 신
　　고서 = consolidated return

consolidated working paper　연결정
　　산표 = consolidating working
　　paper

consolidating financial statement
　　연결재무제표 = consolidated
　　financial statements

consolidating working paper　연결정
　　산표 = consolidated working
　　paper

consolidation　1) 신설합병
　　▶ amalgamation, business
　　combination, merger　2) 연결
　　(재무제표작성)

Consolidation Act　(영)통합법

consolidation by purchase   매수에 의
한 연결 ▶ consolidation by
pooling of interest
consolidation criteria   연결기준, 연결
범위 = scope of consolidation
consolidation excess   연결초과액
= consolidated goodwill
consolidation journal entry   연결분개
consolidation policy   연결방침
▶ consolidated financial
statement, preconsolidation
adjustment
consol market   콘솔(정리)시장, 콘솔공
채시장 ▶ consol
consols   콘솔공채 = consol, consolidated
annuity
consortium   1) 조합, 협회 2) 국제 석유
자본연합 3) (저개발국을 원조하
는 선진국의) 채권국 회의
conspicuous   현저한
conspiracy   1) 공모, 음모 2) 동시발생
constant   1) 정관 2) 고정정보
constant dollar   불변가격, 일정가격, 항
상가격 = constant purchasing
power ▶ constant dollar
accounting, current purchasing
power accounting, general
price-level accounting,
purchasing power unit, unit of
measurement
constant dollar accounting   불변가격
회계, 불변달러화 가격회계, 불
변화폐회계, 안전가치회계 또
는 일반구매력회계 = constant
purchasing power accounting
▶ current cost, historical cost
constant dollar bases   불변화폐가치기

준
constant dollar measurement   불변
가격에 의한 측정 ▶ constant
dollar accounting
constant dollar reporting   불변가격
에 의한 보고
constant functional currency   통일기
능통화, 항상기능통화
▶ functional currency,
nominal functional currency
constant order   정량발주주문
= constant order-quantity
system, quantity system, two
bin system ▶ reorder point
constant order cycle system   정시발주
제도 ▶ constant order quantity
system
constant order quantity system   고정
주문량 발주제도 ▶ constant
order cycle system
constant purchasing power   불변가격
구매력, 불변적 구매력, 항상구
매력, 일반구매력 = constant
dollar ▶ constant dollar
accounting, constant dollar
measurement
**constant purchasing power accounting
(CPP accounting)**   불변구매
력회계, 일반구매력회계, 현재
구매력회계 = accounting for
changes in the general price
level, accounting in units of
current purchasing power
▶ general price level adjusted
statement, purchasing power
gain or loss
constant purchasing power unit   불변

C

구매력 단위, 항상구매력 단위

constant variance 등(等)분산

constituent 1) 지지모체 2) 구성단체 3) 용역이용자

constraining factor 제약요인
▶ constraint

constraint 일반적 제약, 제약조건
▶ constraining factor

construct contract 공사계약

construction account receivable 공사외상매출금, 건설공사미수금

construction bond 건설증서

construction budget 건설예산 = capital budget, capital expenditure budget, investment budget, plant and equipment budget

construction in process 건설가계정 = construction in progress, construction suspense account

construction in progress 미완성공사

construction inventory 미완성공사, 건설중 재고자산

construction mortgage 건설업자가 지어 주고 있는 건물에 대한 모기지(담보부대여)

construction order 공사지시서, 건설지시서

construction other than building 구축물

construction period cost 건설기간중 원가

construction revenue 공사수익

construction suspense account 미완성공사 = construction in process

construction type contract 청부공사계약, 건설공사계약

▶ completed job method for long-term contract, percentage of completion method for long-term contract

construction work in progress 건설중인 자산

constructive accounting 분석적 회계 = analytical accounting

constructive bailment 추정 위탁

constructive eviction 퇴거의제, 고유박탈

constructive fraud 의제(擬制) 사기(詐欺), 추정적인 사기, 준기망, 의제기망

constructive intent 추정 의도

constructive notice 의제통지, 추정적 통지

constructive service comment and letter 전문가의 건설적 의견을 담은 서신

constructive trust 의제(擬制)신탁, 추정신탁, 법정신탁

consular invoice 영사(領使)증명송장

consultation 상담, 협의

Consultative Committee of Accountancy Bodies (CCAB) 회계단체합동자문위원회
▶ Accounting Standards Board, Financial Reporting Council

Consultative Committee on International Telegraphy and Telephony(CCITT) 국제전신전화자문위원회

Consultative Group of ASC 회계기준위원회자문그룹
▶ Consultative Committee of

Accountancy Bodies

consultative model   협의형 모델

consulting partner   컨설팅 파트너
▶ partner

consulting service   컨설팅 서비스

consumer   소비자 ▶ producer

Consumer Credict Protectoin Act   소
비자신용보호법

consumer credit   소비자신용
▶ consumer's loan

consumer goods   소비재, 소비자 상품,
소비자 물품

consumerism   소비자중심주의, 소비자
보호운동

consumer price index(CPI)   소비자 물
가지수 ▶ general index of
retail price, wholesale price
index

consumer price index for all urban
consumer(CPI-U)   전국의
도시 소비자물가지수

consumer price index for urban
consumers(CPI-U)   전국도
시 소비자의 소비자물가지수

consumers' expenditures deflator
(CED)   소비자 지출 디플레
이터

consumers' goods   소비재
= consumption goods
▶ capital goods, producers'
goods, production goods

consumers' loan   소비자금융
▶ consumer credit

consumers' risk   소비자위험
▶ producers' risk

consumption function   소비함수

consumption goods   소비재

= consumers' goods ▶ capital
goods, producer's goods,
production goods

contango   주식결제유예예금, 주식결제 연
기이자, (영)증권결제유예

contemner   재판소 경멸자 = contemnor

contemnor   재판소 경멸자 = contemner

contention   회선쟁탈, 경쟁

contention system   경쟁시스템

contents of the comprehensive annual
financial report(CAFR)
총괄 연간재무보고서의 내용

contingency   우발사항, 우발현상, 우발
사건, 우발채무 ▶ contingent
liability, contingent loss

contingency fund   우발위험부담금

contingency planning   재해대책입안,
긴급대책회의 ▶ contingency
plan

contingency processing   우발처리

contingency reserve   우발손실준비금
▶ contingent liability

contingency table   분할표

contingency theory   우연성이론

contingent asset   우발자산

contingent claim security   조건부 증권
▶ option

contingent consideration   우발적 대가

contingent fees   성공 보수

contingent gain   우발이득, 우발이익
▶ contingent loss, extraordinary
gain, unusual item

contingent interest   우발이자

contingent liability   우발채무
▶ allowance, contingent asset

contingent liability audit   우발채무감
사

contingent liability on bill endorsed
　　배서된 수표(어음)에 대한 우발
　　채무
contingent loss　우발손실 ▶ contingent
　　gain, extraordinary loss, unusual
　　item
contingent project　상호의존적 프로젝
　　트 ▶ mutually exclusive
　　project
contingent remainder　불확정 잔여권
contingent remainder in fee simple
　　무조건 상속 재산에서 불확정
　　잔여권
contingent reminder　불확정 독촉장
contingent rental　조건부 임차료, 미확
　　정 임대차료, 우발적 임차료
contingent stock agreement　조건부
　　주식계약
continuation agreement　계속 계약
continuation control　계속적 통제
continuation of debt　채무의 계속
　　▶ debt restructuring,
　　refinancing debt
continuation statement　계속 보고서
continue　계속
continued distribution method　연속
　　배분법 ▶ reciprocal
　　distribution method
continuing auditor　계속감사인
continuing franchise fee　계속적인 프
　　랜차이즈료
continuing obligation　(영)계속적 개
　　서(改書)의무
continuing operation　1) 계속적 조업
　　(영업, 사업)활동　2) 연속생산방
　　식 ▶ income from
　　continuing operations

**continuing professional education
　　(CPE)**　계속적인 전문직업인
　　교육
continuity　계속성 = consistency
continuity of activity　사업활동의 계속
　　성
continuity principle　계속기업의 원칙
continumm　연속체
continuous audit　계속적 감사 ▶ return
　　audit
continuous auditing　계속감사
continuous budget　계속형 예산
　　= evolving budget, progressive
　　budget, rolling budget
continuous compounding　연속복리 계
　　산
continuous discounting　연속할인
continuous inventory　계속 재고정리,
　　연속 재고조사 ▶ cycle count
continuous inventory method　계속기
　　록법, 장부재고조사법
　　= perpetual inventory method
　　▶ physical inventory taking
**continuously contemporary accounting
　　(CoCoA)**　계속적 현행회계
　　▶ current cash equivalent
continuous manufacturing　연속생산
　　형태 ▶ discrete manufacturing
continuous operation　연속적 기업활
　　동
continuous operation costing　(영)종
　　합원가계산 = process costing
　　▶ job order costing
continuous physical inventory　계속
　　실지재고조사, 항시 실지재고
　　조사
continuous probability distribution

연속형 확률 분포

continuous process costing   공정별 종
합원가계산 = departmental
process cost system ▶ job-
order costing, process costing

continuous process cost system
공정별 종합원가계산 시스템

continuous processing   연속생산
▶ continuing operation

continuous process production   연속
공정별생산

continuous random variable   연속형
확률변수 ▶ discrete random
variable

continuous stock checking   연속적 재
고조사 = cyclic stock check
▶ continuous inventory, cycle
count

continuous testing   계속적 시사

continuous use   계속적 이용

continuous variable   연속변수
= continuous random variable

continuous working paper   영구 조서
= permanent file, permanent
working paper ▶ audit file,
current file

continuum   연속성

contra account   평가계정, 차감계정
= offset account ▶ adjunct
account, negative asset account

contract   계약, 계약서

contract cost   계약별 비용, 계약별 원가

contract costing   계약별 원가계산
▶ contract cost

contract for sale of goods   물품판매
계약

contract for sale of land   토지매매

계약

contract for service   (영)용역계약

contract for the supply of a service
(영)용역제공계약

contract guarantee   계약수행보증

contract negotiation   계약교섭

contract of employment   고용계약
= contract of service, service
contract

contract of sale of goods   물품판매 계
약

contract of service   고용계약 = contract
of employment, service contract

contractor   계약자

contract price   계약가격, 계약가(價)
▶ firm price

contract pricing   계약가격결정

contract rate   계약이자율

contractual defense   계약상의 항변

contractual liability   계약상의 책임, 계
약 책임

contract under seal   날인(捺印) 증서

contract value   계약가치

contract work account receivable   청
부공사 미수금, 도급공사 미수금

contradictory evidence   반증 증거

contra equity account   자본차감 계

contra stockholders' equity item
자본조정 항목

contra to cost of sales   매출원가의 차
감

contributed capital   1) 납입자본
= invested capital, paid-in
capital 2) 주식 발행으로 인하여
회사가 받는 대가의 합계액

contributed surplus   납입잉여금, 자본
잉여금 = paid-in surplus

contributing factor   공헌요인

contribution   1) 기부, 분담 2) 기부금,
분담액, 갹출금

contribution approach   공헌이익 접근
법 ▶ marginal income
approach, net profit approach,
residual income approach

**contribution approach to target
pricing**   공헌이익을 이용한
목표가격결정 = contribution
pricing ▶ absorption approach
to target pricing

contribution graph   공헌이익도표, 한
계이익도표 ▶ capital graph,
contribution profit graph, cost-
volume-profit graph

contribution income statement   공헌
이익 손익계산서

contribution margin   공헌이익, 한계
이익 ▶ marginal income, net
profit, residual income

contribution margin approach   공헌
이익접근법, 공헌이익법

contribution margin ratio   공헌이익
률, 한계이익율

contribution margin variance   한계이
익차이, 공헌이익차이 ▶ sales
quantity variance

contribution pricing   공헌이익가격 결
정법 = contribution approach
to target pricing ▶ absorption
approach to target pricing

contribution profit approach   공헌
이익법 = contribution approach
▶ net profit approach

contribution profit graph   공헌이익
도표, 한계이익도표 ▶ capital

graph, cost-volume-profit graph

contribution surplus   납입잉여금, 자
본잉여금 = paid-in surplus
▶ capital surplus

**contribution to certain retirement
plan**   특정한 퇴직연금계획
에 대한 납입금

contributor   기부자

contributory   1) 기여 2) 청산출자자

contributory negligence   기여과실

contributory plan   갹출(據出)제 연금제
도

control   1) 지배, 통제 2) 제어 3) 관리

control account   통제계정, 포괄계정
= controlling account
▶ controlled account

control accounting   통제회계

control activity   통제활동

control area   통제구역, 제어구역

control budget   통제예산, 제어예산
▶ planning budget

control environment   통제환경, 제어환
경

control factor unit   작업량측정단위

control format item   통제형식 항목

control function   통제기능 = control
operation ▶ application
control, general control

controllability   통제가능성
▶ controllability of cost,
controllable cost, responsibility
accounting

controllability of cost   원가의 통제가
능성

controllable burden   통제가능 간접비
= controllable overhead

controllable capacity cost   통제가능한

생산설비 기초원가
▶ uncontrollable capacity cost

controllable contribution 통제가능
공헌이익

controllable cost 통제가능원가, 관리
가능비용 ▶ uncontrollable
cost, non-controllable cost

controllable expense 관리가능경비,
통제가능경비 ▶ controllable
cost

controllable investment 통제가능투
자액

controllable overhead 통제가능간접
비 = controllable burden
▶ controllable cost

controllable profit 통제가능이익
▶ controllable cost,
uncontrollable profit

controllable variable 통제가능변수

controllable variance 통제 차이
▶ capacity variance

controlled account 통제계정
▶ control account

controlled company 종속회사, 피지배
회사, 자회사 = subsidiary
▶ controlling company, holding
company, parent company

controlled foreign company 재외 자
회사, 재외 종속회사 ▶ controlled
company, controlling company,
subsidiary

controlled group 지배회사그룹

controlled parameter 통제된 모수

controlled reprocessing 재처리법

controlled storage allocation 통제된
저장장소 배분

controlled variable 통제가능변수, 제

어가능변수, 피제어변수

controller of audit 감사책임자

controller's department 감사부(部)
= comptroller's department

controllership 감사 = comptrollership

Controller's Institute of America
미국 컨트롤러 협회

controlling 감사하는, 통제하는

controlling account 통제계정, 총괄계
정 = control account
▶ controlled account

controlling company 모회사, 지배회사
▶ controlled company,
subsidiary

controlling function 관리적 기능, 관리
직능

controlling person 지배자

control objective 통제목표

control operation 제어기능, 제어조작
= control function

control panel 1) 조작반, 제어 2) 배선반

control period 통제기간 ▶ control
report

control procedure 통제절차, 내부통제
절차 ▶ accounting system,
control environment

control program 통제프로그램

control report 통제보고서 ▶ control
period

control risk 통제위험 ▶ assertion,
detection risk, inherent risk,
internal control structure

control section(CSECT) 제어구역

control set 내부통제의 정비상황에 관
한 질문서, 평가표를 한 조로
한 서류

control total 통제합계, 조사합계

▶ control total check

control total check 통제합계검사

control type budget 통제형 예산

convenant 계약조항

convention 1) 관행 ▶ accounting convention 2) 대회, 집회 3)협정

conventional costing 전통적 전부원가계산 ▶ absorption costing, absorption cost system, direct costing, full absorption costing, full cost accounting, full costing, total costing, variable costing

conventional retail method 전통적 소매재고법

convention of accounting 회계관행, 회계공준 = accounting convention ▶ assumption of accounting, postulate of accounting

convention of periodicity 회계기간기준 = periodicity concept, time-period concept, time-period principle ▶ accounting convention, accounting period, accounting postulate

conversion 1) 환산, 차환, 변환, 전환, 이행 ▶ translation 2) 횡령

conversion cost 가공비, 직접노무비와 제조간접비 ▶ direct material cost, indirect cost

conversion from fund financial statement to financial statement 기금 재무제표에서 정부단위 재무제표로의 전환

conversion of debt 사채의 전환 ▶ convertible bond, loan stock

conversion of liability 부채의 전환

conversion parity 전환비율, 전환가격

conversion period 전환기간

conversion price 전환가격 ▶ convertible bond, conversion ratio

conversion ratio 전환비율

conversion right 전환권

convert 1) 변환하다 2) 이행하다

convertibility 환금(換金)가능성, 전환가능성

convertible asset 환금가능한 자산, 전환가능한 자산

convertible bond(CB) 전환사채 = convertible debt ▶ conversion price, conversion ratio

convertible debenture 전환사채 = convertible bond

convertible debt 전환사채 = convertible bond, convertible debenture

convertible preferred stock 전환우선주, 전환가능우선주, 전환사채 ▶ preferred stock

convertible ratio 전환비율 = conversion ratio ▶ conversion price

convertible security 전환증권

convertible share 전환주식 = convertible stock

convertible stock 전환주식 = convertible share

convertible unsecured loan stock (CULS) (영)전환무담보사채

convex programming 볼록형 계획

법, 철(凸)형 계획

conveyance 양도

cooperative audit 협동감사
= coordinate audit

coordinate audit 협동감사
= cooperative audit

coordination 조정 ▶ planning

coowner 공동 소유자

coproduct 연산품 = joint product

copy 카피, 복사

copyright 저작권

copyright law 저작권법

corporate bond 사채

corporate cost 1) 일반본사관리비
▶general corporate cost 2) 본부
비 ▶ central corporate expense

corporate expense 본부비

corporate income tax 법인소득세
= corporation income tax

corporate joint venture 합병(주식) 회
사, 공동사업회사

corporate model 기업모델 ▶ planning

corporate readjustment 준갱생(準更
生) = quasi reorganization

corporate recovery rate 기업회수율
= cash recovery rate

corporate reorganization 법인의 조
직변경

corporate report (영)회사보고서

corporate slush fund 회사의 뇌물자금

corporate social accounting 회사의
사회회계

corporate social reporting 기업의 사
회적 보고

corporate social responsibility 기업
의 사회적 책임

corporate strategy 기업전략

corporation 기업, 주식회사, 법인

corporation aggregate 집합법인
▶ corporation sole

corporation by estoppel 금반언에 의
한 회사, 법인

corporation cost 회사비용

corporation income tax 법인세, 법인
소득세 = corporate income tax

corporation law 회사법 ▶ commercial
law, company law

corporation opportunity 회사의 거래
기회

corporation opportunity rule 이사나
임원 그리고 대주주는 회사가
현실적인 거래를 가지고 있는
재산이나 거래기회를 자기이익
으로 전용해서는 안 된다는 규
칙

corporation sole 단독법인
▶ corporation aggregate

corporation tax(CT) (영)법인세, 법인
소득세 ▶ corporate income
tax, imputation system, income
tax

Corporation Tax Acts (영)법인세법,
법인소득세법

corporator 주주, 법인의 일원, 조합원
= member

corporte bankruptcy 회사의 파산

corpus 신탁재산

correction 수정, 정정, 시정

correction of error 오류수정

correction term 수정사항

corrective control 수정적 통제

corrective maintenance 사후보수, 사
후보전, 수리, 보수

corrective maintenance time 수리보

수시간

correctness 1) 정확성, 확실성 2) 정당성
correlated return 수익률의 상관관계
correlation 상관관계 ▶ negative correlation, positive correlation
correlation analysis 상관분석, 상관관계분석
correlation between product sales 제품판매량간의 상관관계
correlation coefficient 상관계수
correlation diagram 상관도
correlation matrix 상관행렬
correlation table 상관표
correspondence 1) 대응, 유사 2) 통신
correspondent 1) 거래처 은행 2) 통신원, 기자
corresponding amount 전기의 비교 대응 수치 = comparative figure
corridor 허용범위
Corridor approach 코리도어 방식
corroborating evidence 확인적 증거, 입증적 증거
corroborating evidential matter 확인적 증거, 입증적 증거
corroboration 입증
COSA(cost of sales adjustment) (영)매출원가 수정
cost 1) 원가 2) 비용 ▶ acquisition cost, cost basis, historical cost, cost accounting
cost account 원가계정 ▶ cost control account
cost accounted for 산출원가 ▶ cost to account for
cost accounting 원가계산, 원가회계, 원가계산제도 ▶ costing, manufacturing cost accounting, marketing cost accounting
cost accounting cycle 원가계산과정
cost accounting department 원가계산과(課)
cost accounting organization 원가계산조직
cost accounting standard 원가계산기준
Cost Accounting Standards Board (CASB) 원가계산기준심의위원회
cost accounting system 원가계산제도 ▶ special cost study
cost accumulation 원가집계 ▶ cost assignment, cost distribution
cost adjusted fair value method 시가를 반영한 원가법
cost allocation 원가(비용) 배분 = cost assignment
cost analysis 원가분석 ▶ cost measurement, cost variance analysis
cost analysis by account classification 계정과목별 원가분석 = account analysis approach, account classification
cost and benefit analysis 비용·효익분석, 비용·효과분석 = cost-benefit analysis
cost and freight(C&F/CFR) 운임포함원가, 운임포함 가격조건 ▶ cost, insurance and freight
cost apportionment 원가배부 = cost allocation, cost attribution
cost approach 원가법 ▶ depreciation, economic age, economic life, income approach, market-data-

approach, reproduction cost,
sales comparison approach

cost ascertainment   원가산정 = cost
finding

cost assignment   원가배분 = cost
allocation, cost apportionment,
cost attribution

cost attach   원가의 귀속성

cost attribution   원가배분 = cost
allocation, cost apportionment
▶ cost distribution

cost audit   원가감사

cost based pricing   원가기초 가격결정

cost based pricing model   1) 원가가산
가격결정 ▶ cost reimbursement
2) 원가기초 가격결정모델
▶ cost-plus contract, cost-plus
markup, cost-plus-pricing

cost base transfer price   원가에 기초
한 대체가격

cost basis   원가기준, 원가주의 = cost
concept, cost convention, cost
method ▶ cost

cost before adjustment   수정전 원가

cost behavior   원가행태

cost behavior analysis   원가행태분석,
원가예측

cost behavior pattern   원가변동행태
▶ fixed cost, variable cost

cost-benefit   비용 · 효익, 비용 · 편익

cost-benefit analysis   비용 · 효익분석

cost-benefit approach   비용 · 편익법

cost-benefit relationship   비용 · 효익
관계

cost card   원가카드, 원가계산표

cost center   원가중심점 ▶ investment
center, profit center

cost classification   원가분류

cost concept   원가개념, 원가주의
= cost basis, cost convention,
cost method

cost consciousness   원가의식

cost control   원가통제, 원가관리

cost convention   원가법, 원가주의
= cost basis, cost method
▶ historical cost accounting

cost curve   원가곡선 = long-run cost
curve, short-run cost curve

cost data   원가자료

cost department   원가부문

cost departmentalization   부문별 원가
계산

cost depletion   취득원가에 의한 감모
상각

cost distribution   원가배분 ▶ cost
allocation

cost driver   원가동인

cost-effective   경제적인

cost-effectiveness   원가효율, 비용유효
도, 비용효과 ▶ cost efficiency

cost-effectiveness analysis   경제적인
분석

cost efficiency   원가능률 ▶ cost
effectiveness

cost engineer   원가기사, 원가공학 전문
가

cost equation   원가행태방정식

cost estimation   원가예측, 원가추정
▶ cost standard

cost estimation method   원가추정방법

cost finding   원가산정, 부문별 · 제품별
원가집계 = cost ascertainment

cost flow   원가 흐름

cost flow and production flow   원가

흐름과 생산흐름

cost flow assumption 원가흐름의 가정
(재고자산 평가 방법) ▶ average
cost method, first-in first-out
method, last-in first-out method

cost flow method 원가흐름법

cost for trial manufacture 시작품(試
作品) 원가

cost from previous department 전공
정비

cost function approximation 원가함
수추정

cost incurred 발생원가

cost indifference point 원가 무차별점

costing 원가계산, 원가측정 ▶ cost
accounting system

costing convention 원가계산실무

costing nonmanufacturing activity
비(非)제조활동의 원가계산

costing period 원가계산기간

costing system 원가계산제도

costing unit 원가단위, 원가계산단위,
원(原)단위

cost, insurance and freight(CIF)
운임과 보험료를 포함한 원가,
운임 및 보험료 포함 가격조건
▶ cost and freight, free on
board

cost justification 가격의 정당성을 증
명하는 원가계산

cost ledger 원가원장

cost less accrued depreciation
감가상각누계액 공제 후 원가
= cost less accumulated
depreciation

costly-truth approach 비용·편익적
진실성접근법 ▶ absolute-truth

approach, conditional-truth
approach

cost management 원가관리 ▶ cost
control, cost reduction

cost management organization 원가
관리조직

cost measurement 원가측정, 원가계산
▶ cost analysis

cost measurement error 원가측정의
오류

cost method 원가법, 원가주의
= cost basis, cost concept, cost
convention ▶ historical cost
accounting

cost object 원가대상(對象) = cost
objective ▶ cost unit

cost of acquisition 취득원가

cost of by-product 부산물 원가
▶ by-product

cost of capital 자본비용 = capital cost

cost of capital of preferred stock 우
선주의 자본비용

cost of capital on division's assets 부
서별 투하자본의 비용

cost of common stock 보통주의 자본
비용

cost of completion and disposal 완성
과 처분에 관련된 비용 ▶ net
realizable value

cost of conversion 가공비

cost of debt 타인자본비용

cost of defective work 공손품원가
▶ defective work

cost of equity 자기자본비용

cost of external equity 자기자본의 자
본비용

cost of getting order 주문획득비용

= order-getting cost

cost of goods available for sale   판매
　　　가능상(제)품의 원가

cost of goods manufactured   제조원가,
　　　제품제조원가

cost of goods manufactured statement
　　　제품제조원가명세서

cost of goods purchased   구입원가, 취
　　　득원가 = cost of purchase

cost of goods sold(CGS)   매출원가, 판
　　　매원가 = cost of sales,
　　　production cost of sales

cost of goods sold budget analysis   매
　　　출원가예산분석

cost of inventory   재고자산의 취득원가

cost of living   생계비

cost of material issued   재료사용액

cost of money   현금차입비용

cost of new equity   신주발행비용
　　　▶ cost of capital

cost of normal spoilage   정상공손비

cost of placing an order   1회당 발주
　　　비용

cost of prediction error   예측오차의 원
　　　가 = conditional loss, opportunity
　　　loss ▶ predicton error

cost of preferred stock   우선주의 자본
　　　비용 ▶ cost of capital

cost of production   제조원가

cost of production budget   제조원가
　　　예산, 제조비용 예산
　　　▶ manufacturing budget,
　　　production volume budget

cost of production report   제조원가
　　　보고서

cost of purchase   취득(매입)원가 ▶ cost
　　　of goods purchased

cost of raising capital   자본조달비용
　　　▶ cost of capital

cost of reproduction   재생산원가

cost of retained earnings   유보이익의
　　　자본비용 ▶ cost of capital

cost of sales   매출원가 = cost of goods
　　　sold

cost of sales adjustment(COSA)   (영)
　　　매출원가의 수정 ▶ current
　　　cost operating profit,
　　　depreciation adjustment, value
　　　to the business

cost of services   서비스 원가

**cost of spoiled goods and defective
　　　work**   공손품(불량품) 원가
　　　▶ cost of defective work

cost of spoiled units   공손품원가

cost or market principle   저가주의

cost or market rule   저가법

cost percentage   원가율 = cost/retail
　　　ratio ▶ retail inventory
　　　method, retail method

cost-performance   원가 · 성과
　　　▶ performance

cost-performance ratio   비용 · 성과비율

cost period   원가계산기간

cost-plus contract   원가보상계약, 원가
　　　가산계약, 원가가산방식 = cost-
　　　plus markup, cost-plus pricing

cost-plus-fixed fee contract   원가가산
　　　고정수수료 계약

cost-plus markup   원가가산방식 = cost-
　　　plus contract, cost-plus pricing

cost-plus pricing   원가가산 가격결정
　　　방법

cost pool   원가집계액

cost prediction   원가예측 ▶ cost

C

estimation

cost principle   원가주의 = cost basis
  ▶ historical cost accounting

cost rate   원가율

cost reapportionment   원가재배분
  = cost reassignment, cost
  redistribution, cost retracing

cost reassignment   원가재배분 = cost
  reapportionment, cost
  redistribution, cost retracing

cost recover method   원가회수법

cost recovery   원가회수

cost recovery method   원가회수법,
  원가보상법 = deferral method
  ▶ flow through, investment
  tax credit

cost redistibution   원가재배분

cost reduction   원가소멸, 원가감소(오로
  지 고정비의 소멸에 이용)

cost reimbursement   원가보상 ▶ cost
  based pricing model

cost reimbursement contract   원가보
  상계약 ▶ cost recovery method

cost report   원가보고서

cost residuary   원가잔류 ▶ cost
  stickness

cost responsibility   원가책임
  ▶ responsibility accounting

cost-retail ratio   원가율 = cost
  percentage

cost retracing   원가재배분 = cost
  reapportionment, cost
  reassignment, cost redistribution

cost saving   원가절감, 원가절약

cost separation   원가분해

cost sheet   원가계산표 ▶ job cost sheet

cost standard   원가표준 ▶ physical

standard, price standard, standard
cost

cost stickness   원가잔류 ▶ cost
  residuary

cost subsequent to acquisition of PPE
  고정자산 취득후 원가

cost summary account   원가십계계정

cost to date   누적원가

cost unit   원가단위 ▶ cost objective

cost utility analysis   비용효용분석

cost variability   원가변동성
  ▶ determination of cost
  behavior pattern

cost variance analysis   원가차이분석
  ▶ budget variance analysis

cost variance statement   원가차이보고
  서

cost-volume-profit analysis   CVP분석,
  원가 · 조업도 · 이익분석
  ▶ break-even analysis

cost-volume-profit graph   CVP도표
  ▶ cost-volume-profit analysis

cost-volume-profit relationship
  CVP의 관계, 원가 · 조업도 ·
  이익의 관계 ▶ cost-volume
  relationship

cost-volume relationship   원가 · 조업
  도관계 = cost-volume-profit
  relationship ▶ cost-volume-
  profit analysis

cosurety   (채무의) 공동 보증인, 연대보증
  인

cotenants   공동 세입자

council   평의회(評議會), 협의(協議)

**Council for the Securities Industries
  (CSI)**   (영)증권업협의회

Council of Institute   공인회계사협의회

이사회

Council of State Goverments 주(州)
정부평의회

counter 계수기, 계산기

counterfoil 예비부분, 부본(副本)

counteroffer 역청약, 반대청약, 수정
청약, 반대 신청인

counter stock 점두주(占頭株) ▶ OTC
stock

country risk 국가 위험도

count sheet 개수를 적은 표

coupled with an interest 이익과 결부
된 대리

coupon 사채이자율

coupon bond 이자부 사채 ▶ registered
bond

coupon fund 이자부 자금 ▶ interest
bearing security, interest coupon

coupon rate 액면, 표시 이율

court 재판소

Court of Appeals 합중국 공소재판소
항소법원

court trust 법정신탁

covariability in earnings 이익의 동시
변동성

covariance 공분산(共分散)

covariance of sales 판매량의 공분산

covenant 1) 계약조항, (증서에 규정
된) 약속 2) 날인증서

covenant against encumbrance 부동
산상에 저당권이 설정되어 있
지 않다는 약속

covenant for future assurance 증서
등기에 문제 발생시 양도인이
등기하는데 필요한 행위를 해
주겠다는 약속

covenant for quiet enjoyment 양수인

의 부동산 이용이 제3자의 합
법적 소유권 주장에 의해 방해
받지 않는다는 약속

covenant of right to convey 양도인이
부동산상의 권리를 양도할 수
있는 권한을 가지고 있다는 보
장

covenant of seisin 양도인이 양도하려
는 부동산의 재산권, 이익을 가
지고 있다는 보장

covenant of warranty 담보책임의 약
속

cover 대체품의 취득, 방지

coverage ratio 장기지불능력비율

cover concept 상쇄보전개념 ▶ closing
rate method, net investment

covering 매입할인

covering contract 매입할인계약

cover note 보험인수증, 가(假)증서

CP(command processor) 지령처리프로
세서

CP(commercial paper) 상업어음, 기업어음

CP(communication processor) 통신용
프로세서

CPA(certified public accountant) 공인
회계사 ▶ chartered accountant

CPA firm 공인회계사법인

CPA Journal 뉴욕주 공인회계사협회
(New York State Society of
Certified Public Accountants)의 기
관지. 1930년에 *The New York
Certified Public Accountant*로
창간된 월간지.

CPE(continuing professional education)
계속적 전문직업인교육

CPI(consumer price index) 소비자물가
지수

CPI-U(consumer price index for all urban consumers) 전국 도시의 소비물가지수

CPO(concurrent peripheral operation) 동시조달 조작

CPP(current purchasing power) accounting 현행구매력회계

CPU(central processing unit) 중앙처리장치, 중앙연산처리장치

CR(closing rate) 결산일 환율 = current rate ▶ historical rate

CR(closing rate, current rate) 결산일 시세

Cr.(creditor) 대변

CRC(cyclic redundancy check) 순환적 중복 검사

creation 성립

creation of 대리의 성립, 신탁의 형성

creation of partnership 파트너쉽 회사의 설립

creation of secret or hidden reserve 비밀적립금의 설정

creative accounting 창조적 회계, 창조적 회계조작 ▶ false accounting

credibility 신빙성

credit 1) 대변 = creditor 2) 신용 ▶ on credit, credit grantor

credit account 대변계정 = charge account

credit agency 신용조사기관 = credit reporting agency, mercantile agency

credit analysis 신용분석 = analysis for credit, analysis for credit purpose

credit audit 신용감사

credit balance 1) 차변잔액 2) 여신잔고

credit balance sheet 신용대차대조표

credit beneficiary 권리자가 부담하고 있는 채무의 이행을 목적으로 제3자에게 이행하도록 하는 경우의 제3수익자

credit budget 신용예산 ▶ cash budget

credit bureau 신용조사기관 = credit agency, credit-reporting agency

credit card 신용카드

credit decision 신용제공 의사결정, 여신의사결정

credit department 신용심사 부문

credit department audit 신용조사부의 감사

credit exchange 지급어음 ▶ debit exchange

credit for adoption expenses 입양비용에 대한 세액공제

credit for rehabilitation expenditures 재건축 지출에 대한 세액공제

credit for the elderly and the disabled 노령자와 장애인에 대한 세액공제

credit goodwill 부의 영업권

credit grantor 여신자 ▶ credit

credit insurance 신용보험

credit life insurance 소비자신용생명보험

credit limit 신용한도, 여신(與信)한도

credit line 대출한도액

credit loss 대손추정액

credit management 신용관리

credit memo 대변 메모

credit memorandum 신용거래비망표, 대변비망표, 대변표 ▶ credit note

credit note(C/N) 신용거래비망표, 신용

거래표

creditor(cr.)　1) 대변 = credit 2) 채권자
　▶ ordinary creditor, preferred
　creditor, secured creditor 3) (pl.)
　채권액

creditor beneficiary　채권자가 수익자
　인 경우, 채권수혜자

creditor beneficiary contract　채권자
　수익자계약

creditor ledger　외상매입처 원장
　= bought ledger, purchase
　ledger

creditor's committee　채권자 위원회,
　채권단 ▶ creditors' committee

creditors days ratio　매입채무 만류(挽
　留)일수 = days purchases in
　accounts payable ratio

creditors' committee　채권단

creditor's meeting　채권자 집회

creditors' voluntary liquidation　채
　권자의 임의청산 = creditors'
　voluntary winding up

creditors' voluntary winding up　(영)
　채권자의 임의해산 = creditors'
　voluntary liquidation
　▶ compulsory winding up,
　members' voluntary winding up,
　voluntary winding up

creditors' voluntary wind up　채권
　자의 임의해산

credit policy　신용정책

credit rating　신용등급책정

credit rating agency　신용조사기관, 신
　용등급책정기관 ▶ credit
　reporting agency, credit agency,
　credit bureau

credit reporting agency　신용조사기관

　▶ credit agency, credit bureau,
　credit rating agency

credit risk　신용위험

credits　세액공제

credit sale　신용판매, 외상판매, 외상매
　출 ▶ 현금매출(cash sales)

credit sale agreement　외상판매계약

credit slip　입금표 = paying-in slip

credit term　신용조건, 여신조건

crime　범죄

criminal law　형사법

criminal liability　형사법상의 책임

criteria　규준(規準)

critical path method(CPM)　크리티컬
　패스 방법(어떤 프로젝트의 최단
　경로를 컴퓨터로 분석하여 가장 유
　효한 순서를 결정하는 방법)

critical region　기각(棄却) 지역

critical success factor　중요 성공요인

CRJE(conversational remote job entry)
　회화형 원격작업입력

crop basis　회수기준 ▶ realization
　basis

cross allocation　상호배부 = reciprocal
　allocation

cross allocation method　상호배부법
　= reciprocal distribution method
　▶ direct distribution method,
　step ladder distribution method

cross cast　(영)횡단적 검사= cross
　footing

cross entry　대체기입

crossfooting　금액의 교차검증 = cross
　cast

crossfooting test　금액의 교차검증
　= crossfoot test

crossfoot test　금액의 교차검증

= crossfooting test

cross-holding 상호협조

crossing 1) 횡선수표 2) 횡단 3) 교차

crossing offer 교차청약

crossover analysis 교차분석

cross sectional data 횡단면의 데이터

cross section analysis 횡단면 분석

cross section of an array 배열의 단면

cross slip 대체전표

CS 경영 자문업무에 관한 기준 보고서

CSCAP(Committee on Statement of Cost Accounting Principles) 원가 계산기준위원회

CSI(Council for the Securities Industry) 증권업협의회

CT(corporation tax) 법인세

CTD(combined transport document) 복합운송증권

CTT(capital transfer tax) (영)자산양도세, 자산증여세 ▶ death duty, death tax, estate duty, inheritance tax

CULS(convertible unsecured loan stock) 무담보전환사채

cum-call 지불포함

cum-dividend 배당부 ▶ ex dividend

cum-drawing 추첨부

cum-right (신주인수권의) 권리부

cum testamento annexo 유언집행자가 없을 때의 유산관리(인)

cumulative 누적식

cumulative accounting adjustment 누적적 회계수정

cumulative distribution function 누적분포함수

cumulative dividend 누적배당

cumulative effect 누적효과, 누적적 영

향액

cumulative effect of accounting change 회계변경의 누적적 영향액

cumulative effect of a change in accounting principle 회계 원칙변경에 의한 누적적 영향

cumulative effect of the change 회계 변경의 누적적 영향

cumulative effects 누적적 영향액

cumulative effect type 누적적 영향액 을 표시하는 타입

cumulative frequency distribution 누적빈도분포

cumulative frequency table 누적빈도 분포표

cumulative method 누가법, 누적법 ▶ non-cumulative method

cumulative monetary amount(CMA) sampling 누적 화폐금액 표본조사

cumulative monetary sampling 누적 화폐단위표본조사

cumulative preference share 누적적 우선주

cumulative preferred stock 누적적 우선주 ▶ dividend in arrears

cumulative translation adjustment 누적 환산조정액

cumulative voting 누적투표, 집중투표

cumulative voting system 집중투표제 도

cure conformity 적합한 치유

cure nonconformity 부적합한 치유

currency 1) 통화, 대용통화 2) 통화 유통액 3) 유통시장

currency note 1) (영)1달러 지폐 2) 은행권 ▶ treasury note

currency restriction 통화제한

currency swap 통화교환

currency translation 통화환 ▶ closing
　　　　rate method, temporal method

current 유동

current account 1) 당좌예금(구좌)
　　　　2) 당좌지분계정

current arrangement 유동성배열법

current asset 유동자산 = circulating
　　　　asset, floating asset, liquid asset
　　　　▶ fixed asset, long-lived asset,
　　　　long-term asset, normal operating
　　　　cycle basis, one year rule

current asset investment 단기투자
　　　　자산 = short-term investment
　　　　▶ fixed asset investment,
　　　　long-term investment

current asset management 유동자산
　　　　관리

current assets turnover 유동자산 회
　　　　전율 = turnover of current assets

current attainable standard 현재달
　　　　성가능한표준

current budget 당좌예산 ▶ baseline
　　　　budget

current cash equivalent(CCE) 현행
　　　　화폐등가액 ▶ continuously
　　　　contemporary accounting

current control report 단기적 통제
　　　　보고서 ▶ control report

**current cos-constant purchasing
　　　　power accounting** 현행원
　　　　가통일구매력 회계
　　　　= current cost-constant dollar
　　　　accounting, integration of CCA
　　　　and GPLA

current cost 1) 현행원가, 현재원가, 시

가 2) 재조달원가, 대체원가
　　　　▶ current replacement cost,
　　　　direct pricing, replacement
　　　　cost, value to the business

current cost account (영)현행원가 재
　　　　무제표 ▶ historic cost account

current cost accounting(CCA) 현행
　　　　원가회계, 시가주의 회계
　　　　= current cost/nominal dollar
　　　　accounting ▶ holding gain or
　　　　loss, operating income

current cost basis 현행원가기준
　　　　▶ current cost accounting

**current cost-constant dollar
　　　　accounting** 현행원가-불
　　　　변화폐 회계 = current cost-
　　　　constant purchasing power
　　　　accounting, integration of CCA
　　　　and GPLA

**current cost-constant purchasing
　　　　power** 현행원가-불변(항
　　　　상) 구매력

current cost control 일상적 원가관리

current cost depreciation 현행원가
　　　　감가상각

current cost earnings 현행원가이익
　　　　= current cost profit

current cost income 현행원가이익, 시
　　　　가주의 이익

current cost information 현행원가 정
　　　　보, 시가정보 ▶ current cost
　　　　accounting

current cost loss 현행원가손실
　　　　▶ current cost profit

current cost-nominal dollar accounting
　　　　현행원가-명목화폐 회계
　　　　= current cost accounting

current cost-nominal functional currency accounting 현행원가-명목기능통화 회계 ▶ foreign currency, functional currency

current cost operating income 현행원가영업이익 = current cost operating profit ▶ income from continuing operation

current cost operating profit 현행원가영업이익 = current cost operating income ▶ income from continuing operations

current cost or lower recoverable amount 현행원가 또는 회수가능액 ▶ value to the business

current cost profit 현행원가이익 = current cost earnings ▶ current operating income

current cost profit attributable to shareholder (영)주주귀속 현행원가이익

current cost reserve (영)현행원가 준비금 ▶ cost of sales adjustment, current cost accounting, depreciation adjustment, gearing adjustment, monetary working capital adjustment

current deposit 당좌예금 ▶ demand deposit

current earnings 당기의 손익

current earnings and profits(CEP) 당기소득과 당기이익

current entry cost 현행구입 원가 ▶ current cost, replacement cost

current entry value 현행구입가격 ▶ current exit value

current exchange rate 현행환율

current exit value 현행판매가치, 매각 시가 ▶ current entry value

current fair value 현행공정가치, 현행 판매시장가치 ▶ current market value

current file 1) 당좌계정철 2) 당기 감사 조서 ▶ audit file, audit working paper, current working paper, permanent file

current financial resource measurement 현행재무자원측정치

current finding cost 현재탐사가치

current-first order 유동성배열 ▶ fixed-first order

current-first order arrangement 유동성배열법 ▶ fixed-first order arrangement

current fund 유동기금, 당좌자금 ▶ fund

current generation 현세대

current gross margin 현행원가에 의한 매출총이익

current ideal standard cost 현행이상 적 표준원가

current income 당기이익 = current net income

current income before tax 세공제전 당기순이익

current investment 단기투자 ▶ long-term investment

current liability 유동부채 = short-term liability, short-term obligation ▶ fixed liability, long-term liability

current line pointer   현재 포인터 라인

currently attainable standard   현행
달성가능표준원가
▶ perfection standard

currently attainable standard cost
현행달성가능한 표준원가
▶ ideal standard cost, standard
cost

current market price   현행시장가격,
시가(時價)

current market value   현행시장가격
▶ current cost, current entry
value, current exit value, current
fair-value, historical cost

current net income   당기순이익
= current income

currentnoncurrent classification
유동 · 비유동분류 ▶ monetary-
non-monetary classification

current-noncurrent method   유동 ·
비유동법 ▶ closing rate
method, monetary nonmonetary
method, temporal method

current operating basis   당기업적주의
▶ all inclusive basis

current operating income   당기영업
이익 ▶ current cost profit

**current operating performance
concept**   당기업적주의
▶ all-inclusive concept, income
attributable to ordinary activity

**current operating performance income
statement**   당기업적주의에
의한 손익계산서 ▶ all-inclusive
income statement

current operating profit   당기영업이

익 ▶ operating profit

current period   당기

current portion of long-term debt   유
동성장기부채 장기차입금 가운
데 1년 이내에 지불기일이 도
래하는 것

current practice   현행(회계)실무

current price   현행가격, 시가 = market
price, quotation ▶ current
value

current proceed   현재현금수령액

**current purchasing power accounting
(CPP accounting)**   (영)현행
구매력변동회계

current purchasing power unit   현행
구매력단위 ▶ purchasing
power unit

current rate   1) BS에서의 환율, 결산일
현행환율 2) 외화환산비율
= closing rate ▶ historical rate

current rate method   결산일 현행환율
법 = closing rate ▶ currency
translation, temporal method

current ratio   유동비율, (유동자산)÷(유
동부채) ▶ acid-test ratio,
liquidity ratio

current record   현재기록

current replacement cost   현행대체
원가 = current cost ▶ direct
pricing, indexing

current replacement cost accounting
현행대체원가회계 = current
cost accounting
▶ replacement cost accounting

current replacement price   현행대체
가격

current replacement value   현행대체

가격, 재조달가격 = current
replacement cost

current report   당기 보고서, 임시 보고
서

current reproduction cost   현행재생
산원가, 재제조원가 ▶ current
replacement cost

current revenue   당기수익

current selling price   현행판매가액

current service cost   현근무비 = normal
pension cost ▶ past service
cost, retirement benefit plan

current standard   당기표준 ▶ basic
standard cost, bogy standard
cost, current standard cost

current standard cost   당기표준원가
▶ bogy standard, current
standard

current standard cost accounting   당
기표준원가회계 ▶ basic
standard cost, current standard
cost

current tax expense or benefit   법인
세등(당년도분)

current transaction   경상거래

current value   1) 현행원가, 시가 2)현
재가치 ▶ current cost, net
realizable value, present value,
replacement cost

current value accounting(CVA)   현행
가치회계, 시가주의회계
▶ continuously contemporary
accounting, current cost
accounting, present value
accounting, replacement cost
accounting, value accounting

current working paper   당기감사조서

▶ permanent working paper

current-year basis   (영)당년소득 과세
주의 ▶ basis period

curtailment   단축, 소멸, 축소

curtesy   홀아비 유산권

curve fitting   곡선적합(표준 또는 가설에
의하여 수량적, 경험적인 정보를 곡
선으로 표시하는 절차)

curve generator   곡선발생기

custodial in nature   보관의 성질

custodian   1) 보호자, 보관기관, 보관자
2) 재산관리인

custodian bank   보관은행, 수탁은행
▶ American Depositary
Receipts

custodian trustee   보관수탁자
▶ managing trustee

custody   보관, 보존, 감시, 관리 ▶ safe
custody

custom   실습

customer   거래처, 매출처, 고객

customers' account   매출처계정

customer's deposit   소비자의 계약금

customers' ledger   매출처원장

customer's NSF check   부도수표

customer specified product   특주품,
특별주문품

customized audit program   전용감사
프로그램 ▶ customized audit
software

customized audit software   전용감사
소프트웨어 ▶ customized
audit program

customs duty   관세

customs house   세관

cut   절단

cutoff   1) 절단, 차단 2) 컷 오프 3) 결

산일, 마감일

cutoff date 결산일, 마감일

cutoff rate 기각율, 각하율, 절사율

cutoff statements 기간귀속 보고서

cutting a melon 특별배당
= melon-cutting ▶ melon

CVA(current value accounting) 현행
가치회계, 시가주의회계

CVP(cost-volume-profit) **relationship**
C · V · P관계 ▶ cost-volume-
profit analysis

cwmni cyfyngedig cyhoeddus(c.c.c.)
(영)공모유한책임회사
= public limited company

CWO(cash with order) 현금주문

cybernetics 인공두뇌

cycle 주기, 순환

cycle billing 주기적 청구서작성

cycle count 연속재고수량조사

▶ continuous stock-checking,
cyclic stock check

cycle inventory system 순환재고조사
법, 연속재고조사법

cycles per second 주기/초

cycle stock 순환재고

cycle time 사이클 타임, 순환주기

cyclic code 순회부호 ▶ parity bid,
parity check, redundancy check

cyclic redundancy check(CRC) 순환
적중복성검사

cyclic shift 주기적 이동

cyclic stock check 계속적 재고조사
= continuous stock-checking

cyclic storage 순환기억장치

cylinder 원주, 기둥

cy pres doctrine 씨 프레스 원칙(가급적
근사원칙)

D

DA(depreciation adjustment) (영)감가
상각비 수정

DA(development area) (영)개발지역

D/A(documentary against acceptance)
인수 후 인도

DAF(delivered at frontier) 국경인도 조
건

daily allowance 일당

daily cash balance book 현금 일일 잔
액 기입장, 현금잔고 일차(日次)
기입장

daily jobtime report 일일작업시간보

고서

daily production 일일생산량

daily production report 일일제조보
고서

daily time ticket 작업시간표, 작업시
간보고서 = time ticket ▶ clock
card

daily trial balance 일계표

daily wage 일급(日給), 일당

damaged goods 파손품, 손상품

damages 손상, 손해, 손해배상
▶ exclusions

damages for physical injury or physical sickness 신체적 상해나 질병에 대한 배상금

damping 제동, 감폭

DARPA(Defense Advanced Research Projects Agency) 방위 선진 연구 기획청

data 자료 ▶ information

data acquisition 데이터 수집

data administration function 데이터 관리기능

database 데이터베이스

database administrator(DBA) 데이터베이스 관리자

database management 데이터베이스 관리

database management system(DBMS) 데이터베이스 관리 시스템 ▶ data base

database system 데이터베이스 시스템

date 날짜

dated retained earnings 날짜가 표시된 이익잉여금

date of acquisition 매수일자, 취득일

date of auditor's report 감사보고 날짜

date of business combination 기업결합일

date of combination 기업결합일

date of combination consolidated financial statement 기업결합일의 연결재무제표

date of combination consolidated financial statement purchase accounting 매수 직후의 연결재무제표작성(퍼체이스법의 경우)

date of combination financial statement pooling

accounting 매수 직후의 연결재무제표 작성(지분풀링법의 경우)

date of completion of field work 감사 절차 종료일 · 현장작업 종료일

date of declaration 배당선언일, 명의개서 변환정지일 ▶ date of record, record date

date of record 명의서 교환 정지일 = record date ▶ date of declaration

dating of the independent auditor's report 감사보고의 날짜

dating the audit report 감사보고서 일자 결정

daybook 1) 일기장 2) 출입장

daybook cash journal 현금출납장

day duty allowance 일직료

day of maturity 만기일

day order 당일유효주문 ▶ good till cancelled

days purchases in accounts payable ratio 외상매입채무 보유일수 = creditors days ratio

days sales in inventory 평균재고일수 = number of days stock held

days to run 할인일수

day-to-day control 일상관리 = interim control

day-to-day operation 일상의 영업 활동

day to sell inventory 평균재고일수 = days' sales in inventory, number of days' stock

daywork 1) 일근(日勤) 2) 일중근무, 일용근무, 일급노동

D/B(documentary bill) 화환어음

DBA(data base administrator) 데이터

베이스 관리자

DBMS(data base management system)
데이터베이스 관리시스템

DCF(discounted cash flow) 할인된 현금
흐름

**DDB method(double declining-balance
method)** 이중체감잔액법

DDP(delivered duty paid) 지정인도, (관
세를 포함하는) 조건

DDP(distributed data processing) 분산
처리, 분산형 데이터 처리

deadlock 교착상태

dead stock 1) 사장품(死藏品), 불량품
= frozen stock 2) (농장, 목장 등
의) 자산, 공구 ▶ livestock

dealer 판매회사, 판매업자

dealing cost 거래비용

deallocation 배당 해제, 배당 취소

death 사망

death duty (영)상속세 = estate duty
▶ capital transfer tax, death
tax, inheritance tax

death tax (영)상속세 = estate tax,
inheritance tax

debenture 1) 무담보사채 ▶ bond,
debenture stock 2) 증권화한
채무 3) 기명 채무증서 4) 담
보차입계약서

debenture bond 무담보사채
▶ unsecured bond

debenture holder 증권 소지인, 사채권자

debenture interest 사채이자 = bond
interest

debenture redemption reserve 사채
상환적립금, 감채적립금
= sinking fund reserve
▶ sinking fund

debenture stock (영)담보부 사채
= debenture bond, mortgage
bond ▶ unsecured loan stock

debenture stock certificate 담보부 사
채권증서

debit 차변 = debtor

debit and credit 차변과 대변

debit balance 차변 잔액

debit exchange (수표)수입교환물, 교환
지속수표 ▶ credit exchange

debit note 채무거래장부 ▶ credit note

debit slip 지급전표, 차변전표

deblocking 비블록화 ▶ blocking

debt 부채, 차입, 채무 ▶ liability,
obligation

debt adjustment plan 채무 조정계획

debt agreement 채무계약서

debt and equity 차입과 지분

debt assumption 채무인수계약

debt capital 타인자본 = borrowed
capital, borrowing, loan capital
▶ contributed capital, paid-in
capital

debt factoring 채권의 매입 ▶ invoice
discounting

debt financed portfolio stock 채권으
로 자금조달된 유가증권 주식
명세서

debt financing 부채에 의한 자금조달
▶ equity financing, self
financing

debt instrument 채권

debt issue cost 사채발행비

**debt issued with stockpurchase
warrant** 주식매수인수권부
사채, 주식구입보증부사채, 신
주인수권부사채

D

debt obligation　사채와 유사한 채무

debt ratio　부채비율 = ratio of total liability to net worth
▶ worth to debt ratio

debt restructure　불량채권채무의 재조정

debt restructuring　1) 채무의 재조정 2) 채무의 특별조건 변경 = refinancing debt
▶ continuation of debt, extinguishment of debt, retirement of debt

debt security　부채증권, 채무증권, 사채권

debt security holder　사채권 보유자

debt service fund　부채상환기금

debt service payment　부채상환

debt to equity ratio　부채자본비율

debt adjusting　채무이행조정

debt · asset ratio　부채 · 자산비율

debt collecting　대여금징수

debtor (Dr.)　1) 차변 = debit 2) (pl.) 채무액

debtor account　차변계정

debtor-creditor agreement　채무자 · 채권자 간의 용도를 제한한 신용공여계약 ▶ debtor-creditor-supplier agreement, tied loan

debtor-creditor relationship　채무자와 채권자의 관계

debtor-creditor-supplier agreement　채무자-채권자-판매업자 간의 용도를 제한한 신용공여계약
▶ tied loan, debtor-creditor agreement

debtor days ratio　매출채권 회수기간, (영)매출채권 회수일수

= accounts receivable collection period

debtor in possession　점유를 계속하는 채무자

debtor's estate　파산재단

debtors ledger　매출채권원장 = sales ledger, sold ledger

debt paying ability　채무변제능력

decay constant　감쇠정수(減衰定數)

decedent　사망자

decentralization　분권화 = decentralized management
▶ centralization, divisionalization

decentralized data processing　분산 데이터처리

decentralized management　분권관리 = decentralization
▶ centralized management

decentralized organization　분권적 조직 ▶ centralized organization, division

decentralized processing　분리적 처리

decimal　1) 10 2) 10진, 10진수, 10진법

decision　의사결정

decision accounting　의사결정회계
▶ performance accounting

decision analysis　의사결정분석

decision instruction　판단명령 = discrimination instruction

decision maker　의사결정자

decision making　의사결정

decision making process　의사결정 과정

decision making under uncertainty　불확실한 상태에서의 의사결정

decision relevant information　의사결정 관련정보

decision significance   의사결정의 중요
성

decision support system(DSS)   의사
결정 지원시스템 ▶ anagement
information system

decision symbol   결정기호, 판단기호

decision table   의사결정표

decision theory   의사결정이론
▶ statistical decision theory,
theory of game

decision theory approach   의사결정
이론 접근법

decision tree   의사결정 수(樹)

decision usefulness   의사결정에 대한
유용성

decision variable   의사결정 변수

deck   카드의 한 벌 = card deck

declaration   선언 = directive

declaration date   배당선언일

declaration of dividend   배당선언, 배
당결의 = dividend
announcement

declaration of solvency   (영)지불가능
선언

declaration of trust   신탁의 선언

declaratives   선언부분, 선언

declared dividend   공시된 배당

decline in inventory market value   재
고자산의 시가 하락

declining balance(DB)   체감잔액법

declining balance method   체감잔액
법 = diminishing balance
method, fixed percentage of
book value method, reducing
balance method, reducing
installment method

decomposition approach to variance

analysis   분해적 차이 분석
법

decrease   하락

decree of court   법전 명령

decrement   감소분, 감소량

decremental cost   감소분 원가

decrepitude   노쇠한 상태, 노후화
= deterioration and decay

dedicated channel   전용채널

dedicated line   전용회선

dedicated service   전용서비스

dedication   전용(초用)

deductible   손금산입

deductible clause   공제조항

deductible expense   과세 공제비 목록

deductible temporary difference
공제가능 일시적 차이

deduction   1) 연역, 연역법 ▶ induction,
inductive method 2) 공제, 공
제액 3) (pl.) 손실금

deduction at source   (영)원천징수 과
세, 원천징수

**deduction for interest on education
loans**   교육적 대출에 대한
이자의 공제

deduction of foreign tax   외국세액 공
제 = foreign tax credit

deductive method   1) 연역법 2) 공제법
= deductive system ▶ inductive
method

deductive system   연역법 = deductive
method

deed   1) 날인증서, (부동산 양도등의) 증서
2) 행위, 사실, 공적 ▶ escrow

deed of arrangement   (영)채무정리에
대한 자산 양도증서

deed of partnership   조합규약서

= partnership deed

deed of trust 신탁증서, 신탁양도 = trust deed

deep discount bond 초(超)할인사채

de facto corporation 사실상의 법인, 회사

defalcation 1) 배임, 횡령 2) 위탁금 유용, 부당유용액

default 1) 채무불이행 2) 불이행, 위약 3) 생략, 줄여서 해석

defaulting on contract 계약불이행

default option 연체시 옵션

default premium 연체이자

defeasance 1) 무효, 파기 2) 권리소멸 조건

defeasance and quasi-defeasance 채무소멸과 준채무소멸 = insubstance defeasance

defeasance of outstanding debt 미결제 채무의 결제

defective goods 불량품, 공손품, 결함제품 = defective unit

defective unit 공손품 = defective goods, defective work ▶ spoilage work, spoiled goods, spoiled unit, spoiled work

defective work 공손품 ▶ defective unit

defective work cost 공손품원가, 공손비 ▶ spoilage cost

defective work report 공손품보고서

defense 항변(抗辯), 항변 사유

defenses of surety 보증인의 항변사유

defensive security 방어적 증권 ▶ aggressive security

deferment 1) 유예, 거치 2) 이연하다

deferral 이연, 이연항목

deferral method (세무조정상의) 이연법 = cost reduction method

deferred account 이연계정 ▶ deferred asset, deferred items, deferred liability

deferred advertising expense 이연광고비

deferred annuity 거치연금 = deferred perpetuity ▶ immediate perpetuity

deferred approach 이연법

deferred asset 이연자산 ▶ deferred charges

deferred bonus and compensation 이연된 급여와 상여금

deferred charge 이연비용, 이연자산

deferred compensation 이연된 급료, 이연된 보수, 이연보상 ▶ compensated absences

deferred compensation contract 보수이연계약

deferred cost 이연원가 ▶ deferred revenue

deferred credit 이연 대변항목, 이연수익

deferred debt 이연 차변항목, 이연비용 ▶ preferential debt

deferred entry 거치하는 입구

deferred exit 거치하는 출구

deferred gain 이연이득

deferred GP-1 이연 GP-1

deferred gross margin 이연매출총이익

deferred gross profit 이연매출총이익 환급

deferred gross profit on installment sales 할부판매 이연매출총이익

deferred income tax credit 이연법인
세대(貨) = deferred income tax
charge

deferred item 이연항목 ▶ deferred
account

deferred liability 이연부채 ▶ deferred
account

deferred maintenance 이연된 보수유
지비

deferred method 이연법 = deferral
method ▶ flow through

deferred ordinary share 후배적(後配
的) 보통주 ▶ deferred share

deferred payment 지불의 연기, 후불,
연불

deferred payment contract 연불판매,
할부판매계약 ▶ installment
sale

deferred payment sale 할부판매, 연불
판매

deferred perpetuity 거치한 영구연금
= deferred annuity ▶ immediate
perpetuity

deferred profit-sharing plan 거치형
이익분배 계획 ▶ money-
purchase plan

deferred rental revenue 선수임대료
= rent received in advance,
unearned rent revenue
▶ prepaid rental expense

deferred revenue 이연수익 = deferred
credit, deferred income, payment
in advance, prepayment received
▶ deferred charge, deferred
cost

deferred share 후배주(後配株)
= deferred stock ▶ common

stock, ordinary share, preferred
stock

deferred stock 후배주 = deferred share
▶ common stock, deferred
ordinary share, preferred share,
preferred stock

deferred tax 이연법인세

deferred tax asset 이연법인세차

deferred tax asset valuation allowance
이연법인세차의 평가준비금
(충당금)

deferred tax charge 이연법인세차
= deferred tax debit ▶ deferred
tax credit

deferred tax credit 이연법인세대

deferred tax debit 이연법인세차

deferred tax expense or benefit 이연
법인세 등 법인세 조정액

deferred tax liability 이연법인세대

**deferred tax related to business
investment** 기업투자와 관
련된 법인세이연

deficiency 결함, 차손, 부족액, 채무초과

deficiency action 채무변제에 부족한
경우 부족액 청구소송

deficiency judgment 담보부족금 판결,
부족분 지급 판결

deficiency letter 정정지시서 ▶ letter
of comment

deficit 결손금, 손실금

deficit finance 적자재정

defined benefit pension plan 확정급
부형 연금제도, 연금액 보증제
도(일부이익을 연금으로 적립하는
방식) = defined benefit plan,
defined benefit scheme

defined benefit plan 연금액보증제도,

정액 연금제도 = defined benefit pension plan, defined benefit scheme ▶ retirement benefit plan

defined benefit postretirement benefit plan 확정급부형 퇴직후급 부제도

defined benefit scheme 확정급부형 연금 = defined benefit plan ▶ retirement benefit plan

defined compensation plan 확정급부형 보상제도 ▶ retirement benefit plan

defined contribution pension plan 확정납입형 연금제도, 정액납입금 연금제도

defined contribution plan 정액납입제도 ▶ retirement benefit plan

definite and certain 확실 및 명백

definite integration 정적분

definiteness 확정성, 명확성

deflation 디플레이션

degree of completion [종합원가계산] 완성도

degressive cost 체감비 ▶ progressive cost

degree of inequality 소득분포의 불평등도 ▶ Lorenz curve

de jure corporation 법률상의 회사, 적법의 법인

delay distortion 지연여파, 지연의 왜곡

delayed time system 대기방식

delay equalizer 지연등화기

delay line 지연선

delay of payment 지급연기

del credere 보증대리

del credere agent 지불보증 대리인

delegation 이양(移讓)

delegation of contract 계약의 위임

delegation of duty 계약상 권리의 위양(委讓), 의무의 위임

deletion 폐기

deliberation 평의(評議)

delict 불법행위, 위법행위

delinquent account receivable 불량채권계정, 회수지연채권계정 = overdue account ▶ bad debt

delinquent tax 체납세액

delisting 상장폐지, 상장정지, 상장제외 ▶ listing

delivered at frontier(DAF) 국경인도조건

delivered duty paid(DDP) 지시인도조건

delivered on rail 차량인도조건 = free on rail

delivered to order 지시자인도

delivering goods 재화의 인도

delivery 1) (상품, 제품의)인도, 교부(交付) 2) (물품의) 배송, 발송

delivery alone 단독 교부

delivery at station 역에서 인도

delivery basis 인도기준 ▶ sales basis

delivery date 납기, 납입예정일

delivery equipment 운반구

delivery note 물품서, 납품서

Delphi technique 델피법

demand bill 요구불어음 = draft at sight, sight bill, sight draft

demand deposit 요구불예금 ▶ current deposit

demand draft 요구불환어음, 일람출급환어음 = demand bill, sight bill, sight draft

demand instrument　요구불증권

demand loan　단기융자, 당좌대월(대부)
　　= call loan

demand note　요구불수표 = sight note

demand paging　요구시의 호출

demerger　(영)1) 회사분할 2) (사업부, 자
　　회사의) 본사에서의 독립

demise　1) (유언에 관련된 임대차 계약 등의)
　　권리양도, 부동산 권리 등의 설
　　정 2) 토지임대차 3) 재산양도
　　의 원인 소멸 4) 왕위, 통치권
　　의 이전

demographic data　인구통계데이터
　　▶ census

demolition　해체, 해체공사

demolition cost　해체비, 철거비
　　= dismantling expense

demonstrative legacy　유언자의 현금
　　증여

demurrage　1) 선박의 정박료 2) 초과
　　시간 사용료

denial of discharge　면책의 부인, 채무
　　면제의 부인

denial of opinion　(감사인의) 의견 거절
　　= disclaimer of opinion

denomination　액면금액

denominator　1) 분모, 공(公)분모(分母)
　　▶ 분자 (numerator) 2) 표준,
　　수준

denominator level　기준조업도

denominator variance　조업도차이
　　= production volume variance

denominator volume　(간접비 배부에서
　　선택하는) 기준조업도

density　밀도

department　부(部), 부문(部門)

departmental accounting　부문별 회계

departmental allocation cost　부문배
　　부비

departmental audit　부문감사
　　= department audit

departmental budget　부문예산
　　= department budget

departmental burden　부문간접비
　　= departmental overhead,
　　indirect departmental expense

departmental burden rate　부문제조
　　간접비배부율 = departmental
　　overhead rate

departmental charge　부문비
　　= departmental cost, department
　　cost

departmental cost　부문비
　　= departmental charge,
　　department cost

departmental cost accounting　부문별
　　원가계산 =departmental
　　costing, departmental cost
　　system

departmental cost allocation　부문별
　　원가배부

departmental costing　부문별 원가계산
　　▶ departmental process cost
　　system

departmental cost summary　부문비
　　집계표

departmental cost system　부문별 원가
　　계산 = departmental cost
　　accounting

departmental expense　부문비
　　=departmental cost, department
　　cost

departmental expense budget　부문비
　　예산 ▶ manufacturing expense

budget

departmental expense ledger 부문비
원장

departmental expense variance 부문
비 차이

departmental factory expense rate
부문별 제조간접비율

departmental function 부문기능

departmental hour method 부문시간
율법

departmental hour rate 부문별 시간
율 ▶ machine hour rate

departmentalization 부문화, 부문별,
부문배부

**departmental job order cost
accounting** 부문별 개별 원
가계산 ▶ job order costing

departmental operation report 부문
별 영업보고서

departmental overhead 부문간접비
▶ manufacturing expense,
manufacturing overhead

departmental overhead ledger 부문
별 제조간접비 원장

departmental overhead rate 부문별
제조간접비 배부율 ▶ plant-
wide overhead rate

departmental process cost system
공정별 종합원가계산
= continuous process cost
system ▶ job order costing,
process cost system

departmental rate 부문별 배부율
▶ blanket rate, differential
rate, plant-wide overhead rate

departmental system 분과(分課)제도

departmental work-in-process 부문
별 재공품

department audit 부문감사
= departmental audit

department budget 부문예산
= departmental budget

department charge 부문비
= departmental charge

department cost 부문비, 통상적으로
부문에서 발생하는 총코스트
= departmental cost

department cost collecting sheet 부
문비집계표

department cost distribution sheet
부문비배부표 = department
expense distribution sheet

department cost sheet 부문별 원가 계
산표 ▶ cost sheet

department expense distribution sheet
부문비배부표 = department cost
distribution sheet

department manager 부문책임자, 부
문관리자, 부문장(長)

**Department of Trade and Industry
(DTI)** (영)상무성, 통상산업
성(省)

department process cost system 공정
별 종합원가계산 = continuous
process cost system ▶ job-
order costing, process costing

department store accounting 백화점
회계

department variance on overhead 부
문별 제조간접비차이

departure from GAAP GAAP로부터
이탈

dependent company 종속회사, 자회사
▶ parent company, subsidiary

company

dependent project   상호의존적 프로젝트 ▶ independent project

dependent variable   종속변수 ▶ independent variable

depletion   감모상각, 감모상각비 ▶ depreciation

depletion base   감모상각기초액

deposit   1) 예금, 공탁금, 증거금, 예납금, 보증금, 착수금 2) 창고, 보관소 3) 매장물

depositary bank   수탁은행 ▶ American Depositary Receipt

deposit book   예금기입장

deposit certificate   예금증서

deposit for preparation of tax   납세준비예금

deposit in transit   은행 미기입예금, 미달(未達)수표, 미달현금 ▶ cash in transit

deposit liability   예금채무

deposit method   예금기준

depositor   예금자, 공탁자

deposit rate   예금이율

deposit received   요구불예금

deposit received for guarantee   요구불예금 보증서

deposit slip   은행의 예입전표

deposit taker   (영)예금업자, 예금업무 ▶ deposit taking business

deposit taking business   (영)예금사업 ▶ deposit taker, deposit taking company

deposit taking company   예금사업회사 ▶ deposit-taking business

depreciable amount   감가상각가능가액, 상각대상가액

depreciable asset   감가상각자산

depreciable cost   상각원가, 감가상각가능가액 ▶ depreciation base

depreciable life   내용연수 = service life, useful life

depreciated value   미상각잔액, 감가상각누계액 공제 후 가액 ▶ net book value, net carrying amount, written down value

depreciation   1) 감가상각 ▶ accumulated depreciation, amortization, depletion, depreciation method 2) 감가상각비 = depreciation charge, depreciation expense 3) 통화의 가치하락 ▶ appreciation 4) 감가, 감가수정 → reproduction cost

depreciation adjustment(DA)   (영)감가상각비 수정 ▶ cost of sales adjustment, current cost accounting, current operating profit

depreciation base   감가상각기초액, 감가상각가능가액 ▶ depreciable cost

depreciation charge   감가상각비 = depreciation expense

depreciation cost   감가상각비 ▶ depreciation expense

depreciation expense   감가상각비 ▶ depreciation cost

depreciation fund   감가상각기금

depreciation method   감가상각방법 ▶ declining balance method, straight line method, sum-of-the-years' digits method, units of production method

D

depreciation of dollar　달러의 가치 하락, 화폐의 가치 하락
　　▶ depreciation
depreciation rate　1) 감가상각율
　　▶ cost approach, effective age, recapture rate　2) 감가율
depreciation rule　(영)감가상각기준
depreciation unit　감가상각단위
　　▶ composite depreciation, group depreciation, unit depreciation
deprival value　박탈가치　▶ value to the business
deputy Special Commissioner　(영)특별국세불복심판관보좌
　　▶ Special Commissioner
deregulation　(법적 규제의) 완화
derivative　파생금융상품
derivative action　주주대표소송
derivative instrument　파생금융상품
derivative method　유도법(誘導法)
　　▶ inventory method
derived cost　유도원가 = assigned cost
derived measurement　유도된 측정, 파생적 측정　▶ fundamental measurement
descent law　주(州)의 상속법
descriptive information　기술(記述)정보
designated fund　지정기금
design law　의장법
design patent　의장특허
design review　디자인 논평
desk research　탁상(卓上)조사　▶ test marketing
despatch note　발송통지서, 소포송장 = advice note, dispatch note

destination carrier case　목적지 운송의 경우
destination case　목적지 조건의 경우
destination contract　목적지 계약
destruction　파괴
destructive read　파괴적 판독
detachable　분리가능한
detachable stock purchase warrants　분리형 신주인수권
detachable stock warrant　분리형 신주인수권 증서　▶ bond with detachable stock warrant, nondetachable stock warrant, stock purchase warrant
detachable warrant　분리형 신주인수권 증서　▶ warrant
detail audit　정밀감사, 세부감사, 세밀감사 = detailed audit　▶ audit of financial statements, balance sheet audit, complete checking, test check
detail checking　정밀조사　▶ detailed audit
detail design　상세 설계　▶ basic design
detailed audit　정밀감사 = complete audit, detail audit　▶ audit of financial statements, balance sheet audit, complete checking, detail checking, test check
detailed budget　세목(細目)예산
detail file　명세 파일 = trans-action file
detection of fraud　사기(詐欺) 또는 부정의 발견
detection risk　적발위험　▶ assertion, control risk, inherent risk
detective control　적발통제
deterioration　(재고자산의) 품질저하, (감

가상각자산의) 시간경과에 따른
가치하락, 노후화

deterioration and decay 노후화
= decrepitude

determinable fee 확정가능한 재산권

determination of cost behavior pattern
원가행태의 결정 ▶ cost
behavior, cost variability

detour 우회(迂廻)

detrimental reliance 불이익적 신뢰

devaluation 평가절하 = devaluation of
currency ▶ revaluation

devaluation of currency 통화의 평가
절하 ▶ revaluation

devastavit 유산관리의무 위반

development 1) 개발, 조성, 개발(조성)
지, 단지 2) 발전, 전개

development area(DA) (영)개발지역

development control 개발통제

development cost 개발비

development expenditure 개발비

development land tax (DLT) (영)개발
용지(用地)세

development life cycle 개발생애주기

development stage enterprise 개발단
계기업

**development stage enterprise
accounting** 개발단계 기업
에 대한 회계처리

development support library 개발지
원 자료실, 개발원조 자료실

**development type stratigraphic test
well** 개발형 지질층위식 추
정(錐井)

development well 개발 우물

deviation 1) 이탈 (정해진 일에서 벗어남)
2) 편차

deviation condition 이탈상황

deviation rate 이탈률

device 기기, 장치, 기구

devise 부동산의 유증(遺贈) ▶ bequest,
legacy

de-watering 도수(導水)공사

diagnosis 진단

diagnostic function test 기능진단 테
스트

diagnostic program 진단 프로그램

diagnostic routine 진단적 루틴

diagonal model 대각선 모델 = single
index model

diagram 도표, 도(圖)

dial exchange 자동교환국, 자동교환

dictating machine 자동청취녹음기

dies non (영)휴업일 = non-business day

difference 차(差), 차이, 다른점

difference estimation method 차액추
정법, 차이추정법 = mean-per-
unit difference method, mean-
per-unit method, ratio
estimation method

differential 1) 차이 2) 투자제거차액

differential a/c 차이계정

differential analysis 차액분석
= differential cost and revenue
analysis, incremental analysis
▶ incremental cost, incremental
profit, incremental revenue

differential analyzer 미분해석기

**differential and comparative cost
analysis** 차액 및 비교원가
분석 = differential cost and
revenue analysis ▶ incremental
cost, incremental profit,
incremental revenue

D

differential cost　차액원가
　　▶ decremental cost,
　　incremental cost, special cost
　　study

differential cost analysis　차액원가분
　　석 ▶ special cost study

differential cost and revenue analysis
　　차액원가수익분석 = differential
　　analysis, differential and
　　comparative cost analysis
　　▶ special cost study

differential cost decision　차액원가
　　의사결정

differential fixed cost　차액고정비

differential profit　차액이익
　　▶ incremental profit

differential profit analysis　차액이익
　　분석 ▶ differential cost and
　　revenue analysis

differential rate　운임차(差)

differential revenue　차액수익
　　▶ incremental revenue

differential variable cost　차액변동비

differentiation　1) 미분법 2) 분화, 파생,
　　특수화, 구별

diffusion index　1) 경기동향지수, 경기
　　지수 2) 보급율

diluted earnings per share(EPS)　희
　　석화된 1주당 이익

**diluted earnings per share of common
　　stock**　희석 후 보통주식 1주
　　당 순이익

dilution　희석화 ▶ earnings per share

dilutive security　희석화 증권

dimension　차원(次元)

diminished radix complement　체감기
　　수(基數)의 보수(補數) = radix-
minus-one complement

diminishing balance method　체감잔
　　액법 = declining balance
　　method, reducing balance
　　method

direct allocation　직접배분법
　　▶ reciprocal allocation,
　　sequential allocation, step-down
　　allocation

direct allocation method　직접배분법
　　= direct distribution method
　　▶ reciprocal distribution
　　method, sequential allocation

direct and material effect　직접적이며
　　중요한 영향

direct capitalization　직접자본화법
　　▶ over-all rate, straightline
　　capitalization

direct charge　직접비

direct charging　직접비 부과

direct control feature　직접제어기구

direct cost　직접원가, 직접비 ▶ indirect
　　cost, period cost, product cost

direct cost center　직접비 원가중심점

direct costing　직접원가계산
　　= variable costing
　　▶ absorption costing,
　　cost-volume-profit analysis,
　　full costing

direct costing income　직접원가계산
　　손익 ▶ absorption income

direct cost of sales　변동매출원가
　　= direct production cost of sales

direct cost system　직접원가계산제도
　　▶ actual absorption costing,
　　actual cost basis, direct costing

direct debit　(은행의) 계좌 개설

direct departmental fixed cost   부문
　　직접고정비
direct department cost   부문직접비
direct distribution method   직접배분
　　법 ▶ reciprocal distribution
　　method, step ladder distribution
　　method
directed beam scan   유향(有向)검사
　　= directed scan
directed scan   유향검사 = directed beam
　　scan
direct evidence   직접적인 증거
　　▶ indirect evidence
direct expense   직접비용 ▶ indirect
　　expense
direct file   직접편성 파일 = direct data
　　set ▶ direct access
direct financial interest   직접적인 경
　　제상의 이익
direct financing lease   직접금융리스
　　▶ leveraged lease, operating
　　lease, sales-type lease
direct fixed cost   직접 고정비
　　= attributable fixed cost,
　　separable fixed cost, specific
　　capacity cost, traceable
　　fixed cost ▶ common fixed
　　cost
direct hour   직접노동시간 = direct labor
　　hour
direct hours yield   직접작업시간수율
direct instruction   직접명령
directional testing   시사의 방향
directive   1) 선언 = declaration 2) 지령
　　= order
direct labor   1) 직접노무비 2) 직접작
　　업 3) 직접공 ▶ direct labor

　　cost
direct labor budget   직접노무비예산
　　= direct labor cost budget
direct labor cost   직접노무비 ▶ direct
　　wage, indirect labor cost
direct labor cost budget   직접노무비
　　예산 = direct labor budget
direct labor cost method   직접노무비
　　법 ▶ direct wage method
direct labor cost variance   직접노무비
　　차이 = direct labor variance
　　▶ direct labor rate variance,
　　direct labor usage variance
direct labor efficiency variance   직접
　　노무비 작업시간차이, 직접노
　　무비 능률차이 ▶ direct labor
　　rate variance
direct labor hour   직접노동시간, 직접
　　작업시간
direct labor hour method   직접노동
　　시간법
direct labor mix variance   노동배합
　　차이 = labor mix variance
　　▶ direct labor yield variance
direct labor rate variance   직접노무
　　비 임률차이
direct labor standard   직접노무비표준
　　▶ direct material standard,
　　labor rate standard, labor time
　　standard
direct labor total variance   직접노무
　　비차이 ▶ direct labor
　　efficiency variance, direct labor
　　price variance
direct labor usage variance   작업시간
　　차이, 노동시간차이 = labor
　　hour variance, labor time

D

variance ▶ direct labor mix
variance

direct labor variance   직접노무비차이
= direct labor cost variance

direct labor work ticket   직접작업시
간 보고서

direct labor yield variance   직접노동
수율차이 = labor yield variance
▶ direct labor mix variance

direct loan   직접차입

direct loan origination cost   대부직접
비(채권자측 부담분)와
nonrefundable loan fee (채무자측
부담분)가 발생한 경우의 처리

direct manufacturing labor   직접노
무비

direct material   1) 직접재료비 = direct
material cost, raw material cost
2) 직접재료

direct material analysis sheet   직접
재료비 분석표

direct material budget   직접재료비 예
산

direct material cost   직접재료비
= direct material ▶ direct labor
cost

direct material cost budget   직접재료
비예산

direct material cost method   직접재료
비법

direct material cost variance   직접재
료비차이 = direct material
variance

direct material inventory   직접재료
재고량

direct material price variance   직접
재료비 가격차이 ▶ direct

material usage variance

direct material purchase budget   직
접재료 구매예산

direct material standard   직접재료 표
준 ▶ direct labor standard,
material price standard, material
quantity standard

direct material total variance   직접재
료비차이 총계 ▶ direct
material price variance, direct
material usage variance

direct material usage variance   직접
재료비 소비량차이 ▶ direct
material price variance

direct material variance   직접재료비
차이 = direct material cost
variance

direct method   직접법, 직접배분법

direct method of cost allocation   직접
배분법 = direct distribution
method ▶ reciprocal allocation,
reciprocal distribution method,
step-down allocation, step ladder
distribution method

director   1) 이사, 역원, 중역, 장관, 국장
2) 관리자, 지휘자, 교장

direct organization   직접편성

directors' emolument   (영)관리자의
보수

directors' report   (영)관리자의 보고
서 ▶ annual return, chairman'
s statement

directory   등록부

directory file   등록부 파일

directory provisions   임의 규정

direct posting   직접 전기(轉記)

direct pricing method   직접적 가격 결

정방식 ▶ indexation, method based on the use of indexes

direct production cost of sales 매출원가에 대한 직접비 = direct cost of sales

direct relationship   [직접원가계산] 정비례

direct selling activity   직접주문활동

direct selling cost   직접판매비
▶ indirect selling cost

direct stock   직접재료 · 부품재고 = productive stock

direct tax   직접세 ▶ indirect tax

direct variable cost   직접변동비
▶ direct fixed cost

direct wage method   직접임금법
▶ direct labor cost method

direct worker   직접공

direct write-off method   (대손처리상의) 직접상각법, 직접감액법
▶ allowance method, indirect method

disable   사용금지

disabled access credit   장애인 접근 세액공제

disabling   박탈하는

disabling restraint   박탈적인 제한

disadvantages of corporation   법인조직의 단점

disaffirm   부인하다, (전의 판결을) 파기하다

disaffirmance   계약의 취소, 부인

disaggregation   분할

disaster dump   재해 쓰레기를 버리다

disaster loss   재해손실

disaster recovery plan   재해 복구계획

disbursement   (현금, 수표 등의) 지불

disbursement book   현금지급장

discharge   1) (의무, 책임의) 해제, 회계책임의 해제(면제) 2) 해고, 면직 3) 의무의 이행(상환) 4) 채무면제 ▶ charge

discharge in bankruptcy   파산 면책

discharge of bankrupt   파산인의 채무면제

discharge of contract   계약의 소멸, 계약의 해소

discharge of contractual obligation 계약 의무의 해소

discharge of indebtedness   채무의 면제

discharge of party   당사자의 면제

discharge or release   삭감 또는 면제

disciplinary system   징계 장치

disclaimed report   의견거절보고서

disclaimer   1) 배제(排除), 기권, 부인 2) 부인자, 포기자 3) 의견거절 4) 보증책임의 부인

disclaimer of opinion   의견거절

disclaimer of title warranty   소유권 담보책임의 포기

disclaimer of warranty   보증책임의 부인, 담보책임의 포기

disclosed principal   공시(공개)된 본인, 밝혀진 본인

disclosure   1) 공시 2) 기업내용공시 3) 공시제도 = disclosure system

disclosure in financial statement   재무제표 공시

disclosure of accounting policy   회계방침의 공시

disclosure of enterprise wide information   세그먼트레벨이 아닌 기업레벨 정보의 공시

D

disclosure of information about multiple reportable segment 복수 세그먼트를 보유하는 기업의 공시정보

disclosure philosophy 공시주의 = disclosure requirement
▶ merit regulation, regulatory philosophy

disclosure practice 공시실무

disclosure principle 공시의 원칙

disclosure requirement 공시요구사항
▶ regulatory philosophy

disclosure system 공시제도

discontinuance actuarial valuation 비연속의 연금금액평가

discontinuance of operation 사업의 중단

discontinued operation 1) 정지된 사업부문의 이익 2) 사업부의 폐지 3) 중단된 영업활동
▶ extraordinary item, inter-period allocation, prior-period adjustment, tax effect accounting

discount 1) 할인, 할인액, 감가 2) 할인율 3) 어음할인 4) 짐작 5) (차입금의) 이자, 선급이자

discount allowed 허용된 할인액
▶ discount received

discount amortization 할인액 상각

discount broker 어음할인 중개인

discounted cash flow 할인된 현금흐름
▶ present value

discounted cash flow method 현금흐름의 할인율법 ▶ internal rate of return method, present value method

discounted free cash flow method 여유 현금흐름의 할인법
▶ discounting excess earnings approach, excess earnings power approach, master valuation approach, number of years method

discounted future revenue 미래수익의 할인 ▶ discounted value

discounted payback method 할인회수기간법 = discounted payback period method ▶ cash flow, discount rate, payback method, payback period method, present value

discounted payback period method 할인회수기간법 = discounted payback method

discounted present value 할인현재가치

discounted value 할인가치 ▶ face value

discount expense 할인료

discount factor 할인계수

discount house 1) 할인상사, 어음할인업자 2) 대형할인매장
▶ discount store

discounting 할인 ▶ discount rate

discounting criteria 할인기준
▶ discount factor

discounting excess earnings approach 초과수익할인법 ▶ discounted free cash flow method

discounting note receivable 어음할인

discount on acquisition 구매할인, 취득할인 = purchased goodwill

discount on bond payable 사채발행

할인료, 사채발행차금
▶ premium on bond payable

discount on forwarding contract　예
약상의 할인

discount on note receivable　어음의 할
인

discount on sale of stock　주식할인발
행 ▶ capital in excess of par
value

**discount or premium on a forward
contract**　선물계약의 할인
액 또는 할증액

discount or premium on debt　채권의
할인액 또는 할증액

discount rate　할인율 ▶ discount factor,
discounting, future value,
present value, time value of
money

discount received　매입할인 ▶ discount
allowed

discount store　대형할인점 ▶ discount
house

discovery　발견

discovery basis　발견기준

discovery sampling　색출표본조사
▶ acceptance sampling,
estimation sampling, sampling,
statistical sampling

discovery value　발견가치

discovery value accounting　발견가치
계정 ▶ discovery value

discrete manufacturing　개별생산형태
▶ continuous manufacturing

discrete programming　분산형 계획법

discrete representation　분산적 표현

discrete view　4분기를 독립된 회계 단
위로 보는 관점, 분리적 관점

discretionary cost　자유재량원가
= managed cost, programmed
cost ▶ capacity cost, committed
cost, policy cost

discretionary expense　자유재량비, 회
피가능비 ▶ avoidable cost,
escapable cost

discretionary expense center　자유재
량원가중심 ▶ expense center

discretionary fixed cost　자유재량고정
비 ▶ discretionary cost,
discretionary fixed cost approach

discretionary fixed cost approach　자
유재량고정비법▶ discretionary
cost, discretionary fixed cost,
engineered variable cost
approach, short-range profit
planning

discretionary trust　재량, 일임신탁

discretionary variable cost　자유재량
변동비 ▶ discretionary fixed
cost

discriminant analysis　판별(함수)분석
▶ discriminant function,
multivariate analysis

discriminant function　판별함수
▶ discriminant analysis

discrimination　차별, 구별

discrimination instruction　판단명령
= decision instruction

discussion memorandum(DM)　토의
자료

**discussion with the representatives of
the audited organization**
감사받은 조직의 대표자와 회
의 ▶ audit function

disfunctional consequence　역기능효

과

dishonor 거절

dishonored bill 부도어음 = bill of
dishonor

dishonored check 부도수표

dishonored note 부도어음

dishonored note receivable 부도어음
▶ distressed loan

dismantling expense 파괴비용, 철거
비용 = demolition cost

disparate impact 차별적 효과

dispatcher 급파(急派)하는 사람

dispatching 급파한

dispatching priority 지명순위

dispatch note 발송통지서, 소포송장
= advice note, despatch note

dispatch rule 발신(發信)주의

disperson 분산

displacement 변위

display 1) 표시 2) 표시하다 3) 표시장
치

disposable income 가처분소득

disposable personal income 가처분
개인소득

disposable profit 처분가능이익
▶ distributable income, profit
available for dividend

disposal 고정자산의 매각 또는 처분

disposal account 제거자산계정

disposal date 매각일, 처분일

disposal of a segment of a business
사업부문의 처분

disposal value 처분가액 ▶ scrap value

disposition 1) 매각, 처분, 처리 2) 배치
3) 자유 재량권, 양도

disposition of under and overapplied
overhead 과대 및 과소제

조간 접비배부액처리

dispute 분쟁(紛爭)

dissector 해부기구

dissimilar asset 이종(異種)자산, 다른
자산

dissolution 해산

dissolution of corporation 법인의 해
산

distinction 구별

distortion 왜곡

distress 1) 자구적 동산 차압 2) 차압한
동산, 압류동산

distressed loan 대손(貸損) ▶ bad debt,
dishonored note receivable,
doubtful account, uncollectible
receivable

distress pricing 에누리가격 ▶ distress
selling

distress selling 투매, 덤핑 ▶ distress
pricing

distributable income 분배가능이익, 처
분가능이익

distributable net income(DNI) 처분
가능순이익

distributable profit 분배가능이익, 처
분가능이익 = profit available
for distribution

distributed computer system 분산적
컴퓨터시스템 ▶ distributed
processing

distributed cost 배부원가 = allocated
cost

distributed data processing 분산적
자료처리

distributing activity 유통활동

distribution 배부, 분포, 분배

distribution basis 배부기준

distribution basis of calculating EPS
배당과세 전 1주당 이익 계산표
▶ earnings per share, net basis
of calculating EPS

distribution channel 유통경로 = trade
channel

distribution cost 판매비, 배급비, 영업
비, 유통비, 물류비, 배송비

distribution cost accounting 유통원
가계산

distribution cost analysis 유통비분석
▶ marketing cost analysis

distribution cost budget 유통비예산

distribution entry 판매처 기입

distribution expense 판매비

distribution in kind 현물분배

distribution list 판매처 목록

distribution of departmental expense
부문비의 배부 ▶ distribution
of service departmental cost

distribution of estate 상속재산의 배부

distribution of expense 간접비의 배부
▶ distribution ofmanufacturing
expense

distribution of manufacturing expense
생산원가의 배부 ▶ distribution
of expense

distribution of profit 이익의 배분
▶ profit available for
distribution

distribution of property 재산의 분배

distribution of service departmental
cost 보조부문비의 배부
▶ distribution of departmental
expense

distribution overhead 간접판매비, 간
접영업비 ▶ factory overhead

distribution rate 배부율

distribution sheet 배부표, 제조간접비
배부표

distribution to owner 출자자에 대한
분배, 소유주에 대한 배부

distribution to related persons 관계
자에게 배부

distributor 1) 분배자 2) 유통상의 주체,
도매업자

district court 지방법원(1심 법원)

District Court 연방지방재판소

disturbance term 교란항목 = error
term, residual term

disutility for effort 노력에 대한 비효
용

divergent interest 다양한 이해관계

diverse interest 다양한 이해관계

diversifiable risk 분산가능한 위험
= unsystematic risk
▶ diversified investment,
market related risk, non-market
related risk, portfolio, systematic
risk

diversification 1) 분산투자
▶ international diversification
2) 경영다각화

diversified company 복합기업, 다각화
기업 ▶ conglomerate

diverted hour 직접공의 간접작업시간

diverted hour ratio 직접공의 간접작업
시간 비율

diverted time 여유시간

divestiture 기업분할, 자산의 분할
▶ divestment liquidation,
spin-off, split-off, split-up

divestiture of subsidiary 자회사 재
편성

D

divided column journal 다행식 분개
장, 다간식 분개장

divided journal system 분할 분개장
제도

divided ownership case 분할된 소유권
의 경우

dividend 1) 배당, 이익배당금 ▶ scrip
dividend, stock dividend,
property dividend 2) 채권자 분
배금 3) 공채 이자액

dividend announcement 배당선언
= declaration of dividend

dividend cover (영)배당배율 ▶ asset
cover, dividend payout, pay-out
ratio

dividend declared 배당선언

dividend equalization reserve 배당
평균적립금 ▶ reserve

dividend in arrear (누적적 배당우선주
의) 누적 미지급 배당금
▶ cumulative preference share,
cumulative preferred stock

dividend income 배당소득, 배당금 수
익

dividend in kind 현물배당 ▶ cash
dividend, dividend on stock,
property dividend, scrip
dividend

dividend mandate 배당금의 은행 불입
통지서

dividend-off 배당락(落) = ex dividend

dividend on stock 주식배당
▶ dividend in kind

dividend payable 미지급배당금

dividend payment 배당금 지급
▶ dividend, dividend rate

dividend payout 배당성향, 배당지급률

= dividend payout ratio, payout
ratio ▶ dividend cover, equity
dividend cover

dividend payout ratio 배당성향, 배당
지급률 = payout ratio
▶ dividend payment, dividend
policy, dividend rate

dividend per share(DPS) 1주당 배당
금 ▶ dividend rate, earnings
per share, payout ratio

dividend policy 배당정책 ▶ dividend
payment, dividend payout ratio,
dividend rate

dividend rate 배당율 ▶ dividend
payment

dividend receivable 미수배당금

dividend received 수취배당금

dividend received deduction(DRD)
수취배당금의 익금불산입, 배당
공제

dividend right 배당청구권

dividend stripping 과세회피적 배당정책

dividend warrant 배당금 지급증서

dividend washing 배당과세 워싱
= bond washing

dividend yield 배당이율

divisible contract 가분(可分)계약

divisible profit 배당가능이익

division 1) 사업부 2) 부(部)

divisional accounting 사업부별 회계

divisional capital 사업부별 사용자본
= divisional capital employed
▶ divisional control, divisional
profit

divisional capital employed 사업부별
사용자본 = divisional capital

divisional contribution 사업부 공헌

이익 = divisional contribution margin

divisional contribution margin   사업부 공헌이익 = divisional contribution

divisional control   사업부관리, 사업부 통제, 부문관리 ▶ divisional capital, divisional profit

divisionalization   사업부화 ▶ decentralization

divisional organization   사업부제(制) 조직 ▶ functional organization

divisional performance evaluation   사업부 업적평가

divisional profit   사업부이익

divisional reporting   사업부문별 보고

divisional return on investment   사업부 투자이익률

division capital   사업부 자본

division header   사업부의 장(長)

division name   사업부 명칭

division of corporate regulation   기업 규제부(部)

division of corporation finance   기업 재무부

division of enforcement   업무집행부

division of investment management   투자관리부

division of market regulation   증권 시장 규제부

division of professional ethics   직업 윤리 부서

division of profit or loss   손익의 배분

division of responsibility   책임 분담

division profit   사업부이익

division system   사업부제도

DLT(Development Land Tax)   (영)개발 용지세

DM(discussion memorandum)   토의 자료

DMLH(direct manufacturing labor hours)   직접노동시간

doctrine   원리, 학설, 정책

doctrine of cy pres   가급적 근사주의

doctrine of respondeat superior   사용자 책임의 원칙, 상급자 책임주의

doctrine of stare decisis   선례(先例) 구속의 원칙

doctrine of substantial performance   실질적 이행의 원칙

document   1) 문서, 서류, 전표 2) 증권, (물품에 대한) 증서

document against acceptance(D/A)   인수인도조건 ▶ document against payment, documentary bill

document against payment(D/P)   지불인도조건 ▶ document against acceptance

documentary bill(D/B)   환어음 = documentary bill of exchange, documentary demand for payment, documentary draft ▶ document against acceptance, document against payment

documentary collateral   증서상의 담보물, 서면담보

documentary credit   신용장, 상업 신용장 = letter of credit

documentary demand for payment   환어음 = documentary bill, documentary bill of exchange, documentary draft ▶ document

D

against acceptance, document
against payment

documentary draft　환어음
= documentary bill

documentary evidence　문서적 증거

documentation　1) 문서, 문서화 2) 기
술, 감사조서의 기술

**document containing audited financial
statement**　감사 받은 재무
제표를 포함하는 서류

document of title　소유권 증권, 소유권
증서, 권리증서, 권언증서

document processing fee　리스계약서
작성비용

document reference edge　장부기준 기
록

dogmatism　독단적 태도, 신조주의, 교
조주의

dollar magnitude　금액적 중요성

dollars to break-even　[CVP분석] 손
익분기점의 매출액

dollar unit method　금액단위 후입선
출법

dollar unit sampling　금액단위 샘플링

dollar value　달러가치, 화폐가치

dollar value LIFO　화폐가치입선출법
▶ dollar value LIFO
inventory

dollar value LIFO inventory　화폐가
치후입선출법에 의한 재고자산
가액 ▶ dollar value LIFO

dollar year method　적수법(積數法)

domain　정의구역, 영역

domestic book keeping　가계 부기

domestic corporation　주(州)내 법인,
내국법인

domestic exchange　내국의 환어음

▶ foreign exchange

domicile　주소

domicile by birth　본래주소 = domicile
of origin ▶ domicile of choice

domicile by operation of law　법정 주
소 = domicile of dependency

domiciled bill　지급장소 지정 어음

domicile of a bill　(환어음의) 지급지

domicile of choice　선택 주소

domicile of dependency　법정주소
= domicile by operation of law
▶ domicile by birth

domicile of origin　본래주소 = domicile
by birth

dominant tenement　분할된 일부 토지

dominium　(대륙법에서의) 소유권

donated capital　증여자본, 수증자본

donated surplus　증여잉여금
▶ contributed surplus, paid-in
surplus

donated treasury stock　수증자사주,
수증자기주

donatio mortis causa　사인증여(死因贈
與) = gift causa mortis

donation　1) 수증 ▶ nonreciprocal
transaction 2) 증여, 기부금

donative transaction　증여적 거래

done beneficiary　수증수익자, 수증자
가 수익자인 경우

donee　수증자 ▶ donor

donee beneficiary contract　수증수익
자계약

donor　기증자 ▶ donee

donor imposed restriction　기증자에게
부과하는 구속 ▶ donor
restriction

donor restriction　기증자 구속

▶ donor-imposed restriction

dormant account　휴면계정

dormant company　(영)휴면(休眠)회사

dormant partner　익명조합원 ▶ secret partner, silent partner, sleeping partner

double account system　복식회계제도

double declining balance method(DDB vmethod)　2배 정률법, 이중 체감잔액법 = double-rate declining balance method

double distribution method　상호배 부법 = reciprocal distribution method

double entry　복식기입

double entry bookkeeping　복식부기

double extension method　이중계산법 = double extention technique

double extension technique　이중계산 법 = double extention method

double posting　이중전기

double precision　2배 정밀도

double-rate declining balance method　이중체감잔액법, 이중체감법 = double declining-balance method

double representation　이중대리

double taxation　이중과세

double taxation relief　이중과세회피 ▶ double taxation, international double tax

doubtful account　불량채권 ▶ allowance for doubtful account, bad debt

doubtful bill receivable　불량수취어음

doubtful debt　불량채권, 대손 = bad debt

doubtful receivable　불량채권, 대손 = doubtful debt, uncollectible account

dower　과부유산권

Dow Jones industrial average　다우 존스 공업주 30종 평균

down payment　1) 자기투자자본 ▶ equity, mortgage equity capitalization 2) 할부의 첫 지 불금

downstream　자회사에 대한 판매 ▶ consolidated financial statements, upstream

down stream merger　자회사 합병

D/P(document against payment)　지불인 도조건

DP(dynamic programming)　동적 계획 법

Dr.(debtor)　차변

draft　환어음 = bill of exchange

draft at a tenor　기한부어음 = time bill ▶ draft at sight, sight bill

draft at sight　일람출급어음 = demand bill

Dragnet clause　드래그너트 조항

drawback　환불금, 관세환급금

drawee　1) 인수인, 지급인 2) 환어음 수 취인 ▶ presenting bank

drawer　(환어음, 수표의 경우) 어음발행인, 증권의 발행인

drawing　인출, 인출금 = private drawing

drawing number　제도 번호

dry trust　수탁인이 할 일이 남아 있지 않은 신탁

DSS(decision support system)　의사결정 지원시스템

dual basis of distribution 복수기준 배
부법 = dual method of
allocation

dual currency bond 이중통화 채권 발
행

dual custody technique 이중보관법

dual dating 이중날짜, 이중보고서 일자

dual method of allocation 복수기준
배부법 = dual basis of
distribution

dual operation 쌍방연산
▶ conjunction, disjunction

dual plan 병기(倂記)법 ▶ single plan,
partial plan

**dual presentation of earnings per
share** 1주당 이익의 이중 표
시 ▶ fully diluted earnings per
share, primary earnings per
share

dual pricing 이중가격설정, 복수대체가
격

dual purpose sampling 이중목적 표
본감사

dual purpose test 이중목적시사

dual transaction assumption 거래의
이중가정

dual transfer pricing system 이중 이
전가격제도

due audit care 감사상의 정당주의
▶ due professional care

due care 1) 정당한 주의(注意), 상당한
주의 2) 주의(主意) 의무
▶ due professional care

due diligence 적절한 주의

due from agency 대리점 대여 ▶ due to
agency

due from consignee 위탁판매 미수금,

적송품 미수금 ▶ consignment

due from FC dealer 외화표시 채권 채
무 판매자에 대한 채권

due from proprietor 점주(店主)대여
▶ due to proprietor

due negotiation 정당 교부

due on sales clause 부동산을 양도하면
채무의 상환기일이 만기가 되는
조건

due process 정당한 절차

due professional care 전문가의 정당
한 보호 = professional due care

due to agency 대리점차입 ▶ due from
agency

due to consignor 수탁판매미수금

due to FC dealer 외화표시 채권채무
판매자에 대한 채무

due to proprietor 점주(店主)차입

dummy data 모의 자료

dummy stock 명의주

duplicate receipt 영수증의 부본

duplication check 이중검사

duplication factor 복사요소

durable year 내용연수 = service life,
useful life

duration (회사의) 존속기간

Durbin Watson test 회귀분석에서 자
기상관관계를 검사하는 검증기
법

duress 협박, 강요, 강박(强迫)

duty 1) 관세 = duty of custom, import
duty 2) 국세 3) 공과금 4) 직무
5) 의무

duty of care 주의(主意)의무

duty of compensation 보상의무

duty of custom 관세 = duty, import
duty

duty of due care   주의의무
duty of excise   소비세 = excise duty
duty of fiduciary   신의의무
duty of loyalty   충성의무, 충실의무
duty of reimbursement   변상의무
duty to mitigate damage   손해경감 의
　무
duty to pay rent   임차료 지급의무
dyadic Boolean operation   2향(向) 불
　린연산
dyadic Boolean operator   2향 불린연
　산자 ▶ dyadic operation
dynamic analysis   동태분석
dynamic budget   동태예산 = flexible
　budget, variable budget

dynamic dispatching   동적인 신속 처
　리
dynamic economy   동적 경제
dynamic inventory model   동적인 재
　고모델
dynamic model (DYNAMO)   동적 모델
dynamic programming(DP)   동적 계
　획법
dynamic ratio   동태비율
dynamic relocation   동적 재배치
dynamic resource allocation   동적 자
　원배분 = dynamic allocation
dynamic statements   동태적 계산표
DYNAMO(dynamic model)   동적 모델

E

E

EAA(European Accounting Association)
　유럽회계학회
E and OE(errors and omissions excepted)
　오류 및 누락은 제외
earier period   전기(前期)
earliest point   [종합원가계산] 가장 빠
　른점
early extinguishment of debt   부채의
　조기상환 = early redemption of
　bond
early redemption of bond   사채의 조
　기상환
earmarked stock   예비재고 = allocated
　stock, reserved stock
earned   가득
earned income   1) 가득(稼得)이익 2) 노

　동소득
earned income credit(refund)   소득 세
　액공제
earned surplus   이익잉여금 = retained
　earnings
earned surplus statement   이익잉여금
　계산서
earnest money   보증금
earnest money on contract   계약 보증
　금
earning capacity   수익력, 수익가득능력
　= earning power
earning power   수익력 = earning
　capacity
earnings   이익, 가득이익
earnings and losses   손익

earnings and profits　소득과 이익

earnings available for dividends　배당가능이익 = profits available for dividends

earnings available for ordinary　(영)보통주식의 이익 = amount earned for equity, earnings for equity

earnings basis　(영)발생기준

earnings before interest and after tax (EBIAT)　(영)세금납부후 지급이자 공제전 이익

earnings before interest and tax(EBIT)　(영)지급이자와 세금공제전 이익

earnings cycle　이익창출과정

earnings distribution and appropriation　이익배분과 처분 ▶ dividend, retained earnings

earnings for equity　(영)보통주식의 이익 = amount earned for equity, earnings available for ordinary

earnings per share(EPS)　1주당 이익, 1주당 순이익 ▶ dividend per share, dividend rate, pay-out ratio

earnings recognition　수익의 인식 ▶ revenue recognition

earnings related contribution　이익관련 기부금

earnings retained for use in the business　임의 적립금 = reserve

earnings statement　손익계산서, 이익계산서 = income statement

earnings summary　손익총괄표

earnings tax　이득세 ▶ accumulated earnings tax, income tax

earnout　합병회계에서의 추가지출

easement　지역권

easement appurtenant　부종적 지역권

easement by prescription　시효에 의한 지역권

easement in gross　독립적 지역권

easy dollar　저리자금

easy payment　할부납입, 분할지급, 월부지급 = installment

easy payment system　할부판매제도

EBIAT(earnings before interest and after tax)　세금납부 후 지급이자 공제전 이익

EBIT(earnings before interest and tax)　지급이자와 세금 공제전 이익

EBQ(economic batch quantity)　경제적 일괄(묶음)생산량

EC(European Community)　유럽공동체

EC Directive(European Community Directive)　EC지령서

ECGD(Export Credits Guarantee Department)　(영)수출신용보증국

echo check　반향(反響)검증 ▶ echo checking system

echo suppressor　반향검증

ECMA(European Computer Manufacturers' Association)　유럽 전자계산기 공업회

econometric model　계량경제학 모델

econometrics　계량경제학

economic activity　경제활동

economic affair　경제사건, 경제사상(事象) = economic event

economic age　경제적 내용연수 = economic life

▶ costapproach, depreciation, effective age, physical age, physical life

economic batch quantity (EBQ)   경제적 일괄생산량

economic benefit   경제적 효익, 경제적 편익

economic circulation relationship (ecocirc. relationship)   경제순환관계

economic consequence   경제적 영향

economic decision   경제적 의사결정

economic entity   경제실체, 기업실체

economic entity assumption   기업 실체의 가정

economic environment   경제환경

economic event   경제사상(事象), 경제사건 = economic affair

economic feasibility   경제적 실행가능성(타당성)

economic fluctuation   경제변동

economic happening   경제적 사정

economic impact   경제적 경향, 경제적 충격

economic income   경제적 이익
▶ subjectivity in accounting

economic indicator   경제지표

economic interest   경제적 이익, 경제적 이해관계

economic life   경제적 내용연수 = economic age

economic life of investment   투자의 경제적 내용연수

economic limit   경제적 한계

economic lot size(ELS)   경제적 생산단위규모 ▶ economic order quantity

economic manufacturing quantity (EMQ)   경제적 생산수량
▶ economic purchase quantity

economic measurement   경제적 측정

economic obligation   경제적 채무

economic order quantity(EOQ)   경제적 주문량, 경제적 발주량, 최적 발주량 = optimal purchasing lot size

economic phenomena   경제현상
▶ economic manufacturing quantity

economic resource   경제적 자원

economic service life   경제적 내용연수 = useful economic life

economic statistics   경제통계

economic things   경제적 사항

economic value   경제가치 ▶ present value, value in use

economic value added(EVA)   경제적 부가가치, 잔여 이익법(residual income method)의 한 종류, 세공제후이익― (투하자본×가중평균자본코스트율)

economic welfare   경제적 복지, 경제적 후생

economies of scales   규모의 경제, 규모의 경제성

economist   이코노미스트, 경제학자

economy   경제계(界), 경제사회, 경제, 경제성

ECU(European Currency Unit)   유럽통화단위

ED(exposure draft)   공개초안

Edinburgh Gazette   (영)관보
▶ Exchequer Chambers, London Gazette,

E

registeredcompany, Registrar of
Companies

edit   편집 ▶ edit check

edit check   편집검사

edit directed transmission   편집지시
전송

edit mode   편집모드

EDP(electronic data processing)   전자
데이터 처리

EDPAA(EDP Auditors Association)
EDP감사인협회

EDP audit   EDP감사 = EDP auditing

EDP auditing   EDP감사 = EDP audit

EDP Auditors Association(EDPAA)
EDP감사인협회

EDP audit specialist   EDP감사전문가

EDP center   EDP센터, 컴퓨터 센터

EDP environment   EDP환경

EDP function   EDP기능

EDPS(electronic data processing system)
EDP시스템

EDR(European Depositary Receipt)   유
럽주예탁증권

educational and medical exclusion
교육 및 의료공제 제외

educational testing   교육 테스트

education cost   교육훈련비

EE(engineering economy)   엔지니어링
경제, 공학경제

EEC(European Economic Community)
유럽경제공동체

**EFFAS(European Federation of Financial
Analysis Societies)**   유럽재무
분석가 연합회

effective   유효(有效)

effective address   유효한 주소

effective age   유효경과연수 = effective

life ▶ depreciation rate,
remaining economic life

effective data transfer   효율적인 데이
터 전송

effective date   효력발생일, 발효일

effective date of the readjustment   재
수정유효일

effective gross income   유효총수익
▶ capitalization rate, income
approach

effective income tax rate   유효소득세율

effective interest   실질금리, 유효이자,
유효금리

**effective interest amortization rate
method**   유효이자율법

effective interest method   유효이자율
법

effective interest rate   유효이자율
▶ coupon rate, nominal

effectiveness   유효성, 효과성
▶ efficiency

effectiveness of offer   청약의 유효
interest rate

effective rate of discount   유효할인율

effective rate of interest   유효이율

effective speed   유효속도

effective statutory tax rate   법정유효
세율 = effective income tax rate

effective tax rate   유효(실효)세율
= effective income tax rate

effective yield   유효이자율

effective yield method   유효이자율법

effect of computer on internal control
컴퓨터가 내부 통제에 미치는 영
향

effect of strike   (스트라이크)에 의한 손실

effectual demand   유효수요 = effective

demand ▶ latent demand

efficiency   1) 능률, 능력, 효율성
▶ effectiveness 2) 효율
▶ usability

efficiency audit   효율감사

efficiency cost   능률원가

efficiency ratio   능률비율

efficiency variance   능률차이
= overhead efficiency variance
▶ price variance

efficiency wage   능률임금

efficient capital market   효율적 자본
시장 ▶ efficient market
hypothesis

efficient estimator   유효추정량

efficient frontier   효율적인 영역
▶ efficient portfolio, portfolio

efficient market   효율적 시장
▶ efficient market hypothesis,
semistrong form efficient
market, strong form efficient
market

efficient market approach   효율적 시
장접근법

efficient market hypothesis   효율적 시
장가설 ▶ efficient capital
market

efficient portfolio   효율적 포트폴리오
▶ efficient frontier, portfolio

effort and accomplishment   노력과 성
과 ▶ basic concept, concept of
matching costs with revenue

EFTS(electronic funds transfer system)
전자자금결제시스템

EGM(extraordinary general meeting)
(영) 임시주주총회, 임시사원총회

EIA(Electronic Industries Association)

전자공업협회

eighty-twenty(80/20)   8할 대 2할의 법칙

EITF(Emerging Issues Task Force)   긴
급문제 전문위원회, 발생문제
전문위원회

either-way communication   양방향 교
대통신 = two-way alternate
communication ▶ both-way
communication

elective share   유류분(遺留分)

electric light power charge   광열비

electric power department   전력부문

electric rate   전력료

electronic calculator   전자식 탁상 계산
기

electronic commerce   전자상거래

electronic computer   전자계산기

electronic data interchange (EDI)   전
자자료교환제도

electronic data processing(EDP)   전자
데이터 처리

electronic data-processing center   전
자데이터 처리센터 = computer
center, EDP center

**electronic data processing system
(EDPS)**   전자데이터 처리
시스템

electronic form   전자양식

electronic funds transfer(EFT)
전자자금이체

electronic funds transfer system(EFTS)
전자자금결제시스템

electronic mail   전자우편

electronic spreadsheet   전자 스프레드
시트

electrostatic storage   정전기억장치

element   1) (집합의) 구성요소 = member

(of a set) 2) 형태별 분류

elementary item 기본항목

element error rate 구성요소의 오류율

element expression 요소식(式)

element of cost 원가요소

element of financial statement 재무제
표의 구성요소

element variable 요소변수

eligibility requirement 자격요건

eliminate 상계

eliminating entry 1) 제거분개
2) 연결소거란

elimination 제거분개

elimination journal entry 제거분개
= cancellation table entry, work
sheet elimination

**elimination of intercompany profit and
loss** 내부손익제거

**elimination of intercompany
transaction** 연결회사간 거
래의 상쇄제거

Ellwood-method 엘우드 방법, 저당 –
자기자본 자본화방식
= mortgage-equity capitalization
▶ income approach

ELS(economic lot size) 경제적 생산단
위 규모

embedded audit module 내장된 감사
모듈

embedded derivative instruement
부수적 파생상품

embezzled 횡령

embezzlement 착복, 횡령

emblements 1) 근로과실 2) (차지인의)
작물수득권, 자기작물

embossment 부조(浮彫)

emergency 비상사태, 긴급시

emergency maintenance 긴급보수

emergency maintenance time 긴급보
수시간

**Emergency Planning and Community
Right to Know Act** 비상
계획 및 지역주민 알권리보호
법: 위험물질과 독극물을 소유
한 사람과 기업은 주정부에 사
실을 통고해야 한다는 법

Emerging Issues Task Force(EITF)
긴급문제 전문위원회, 발생문제
전문위원회

Emerson efficiency bonus plan 에머
슨식 임금할증제도

emolument 보수, 임금, 봉급

emphasis of a matter 특정사항의 강조

empirical probability 경험적 확률

empirical research 실증연구

employee 종업원, 노동자

employee benefit 종업원 복리후생비

employee benefit laws 고용급부법

employee benefit plan 종업원 복리후
생계획

employee pension fund 종업원 연금
기금

employee report 종업원 보고서

**Employee Retirement Income Security
Act(ERISA)** 종업원 퇴직소
득보장법

employee safety 피고용자의 안전

Employee Safety Laws 노동안전법

employee savings plan 종업원 저축계
획

employee's benefit fund 종업원 복리
후생기금 = employee welfare
fund

employee's bonus expense 종업원 상

여

employee's deposit   종업원 예금

employee's deposit received   종업원
예수금

employee's flotation expense   종업원
모집비

employee's relief fund   종업원 상부상
조기금

employee stock option plan   종업원 주
식매입선택권제도

employee stock ownership plan(ESOP)
종업원 지주제도, 우리사주제도

employee stock purchase plan   종업
원 지주제도

employee's training expense   종업원
훈련비

employee welfare fund   종업원 복리
후생기금 = employee's benefit
fund

employer   사용주, 고용주

employer employee relationship   고
용주, 피고용인 관계

employer payroll tax   고용관계세

employer's liability insurance   고용
주 책임보험

employer social security credit   고용
주 사회보장 세액공제

employment   고용

employment agency   직업소개소, 직업
안정소

employment discrimination   고용차별

Employment Discrimination Law
고용차별 금지 관련법

employment report   (영)고용보고서

empowerment zone employment credit
강화지역의 고용세액공제

EMQ(economic manufacturing quantity)

경제적 생산량

emulation   1) 경쟁, 대항 2) (전자) 에뮬
레이터 이용기술

emulator   1) 경쟁자, 모방자 2) (전자) 에
뮬레이터, 모방기

emulator generation   에뮬레이터 생성

EMV(expected monetary value)   기대화
폐가치, 기대치

enacted tax rate   손금이 되는 사업연
도의 유효세율

**en bloc system of domestic exchange
settlement**   내국환어음 집
중결제제도

encryption   암호화

encumbrance   1) 채무, 저당, 담보 2) 유
치권, 담보권 3) 부양가족, 자식
4) 권리원인의 하자(瑕疵)

end   1) 기말, 연도말 2) 부문, 부분 3) 궁
극적 목적

Endangered Species Act   멸종위기 동
물보호법

ending balance   기말잔액, 기말잔고

ending inventory   재고자산 기말잔액
= closing stock

ending inventory budget   기말재고 예산

ending raw material   원재료 기말재고
액 ▶ 원재료 기초 재고액
(beginning raw material)

ending retained earnings balance
이익잉여금 기말잔액
▶ retained earnings

ending WIP   기말재공품

end of a period   기말 현재

end of message (EOM)   메시지의 종료

end of month   월말

end of the year constant dollar   기말
불변화폐 ▶ average for the

year constant dollar

endogenous variable　　내생변수
　　▶ exogenous variable

endorsed bill　　배서어음 = endorsed
　　note

endorsed note　　배서어음 = endorsed
　　bill

endorsee　　피배서인 ▶ endorser

endorsement　　배서(背書), 이서
　　=indorsement

endorsement and delivery　　배서 및 교
　　부

endorsement in blank　　백지배서
　　▶ special endorsement

endorsement of negotiable instrument
　　교부성 증권의 배서

endorsement to order　　지시식 배서

endorsement without recourse
　　소구권이 없는 배서

endorser　　배서인 ▶ endorsee

endorser for accommodation　　융통어
　　음배서인

endowment　　1) 기부, 기부금　2) 기금,
　　기본재산　3) 양로자금, 양로보
　　험

endowment contract　　기부행위, 기부
　　계약(서)

endowment fund　　기금, 기본금, 기부 기
　　금

endowment policy　　양로보험증권

endowment principal　　기금의 원본

end point　　종점

end product　　최종산출물

end user　　최종 이용자

energy cost　　동력비

enforceable promise　　법적 강제력이 있
　　는 약속

engagement　　1) 계약, 약속　2) 고용계약,
　　고용시간　3) (pl) 채무액　4) 감사
　　계약

engagement letter　　감사계약서 = letter
　　of engagement

engagement planning and other
　　responsibilities　　감사계획
　　과 기타 책임, 업무계획

engineered cost　　공학적 원가

engineered standard　　공학적 표준

engineered variable cost approach
　　공학적 변동비 접근법
　　▶ discretionary fixed cost
　　approach

engineering and drafting department
　　설계 · 제도부문

engineering approach　　공학적 접근법

engineering changes to product　　제품
　　에 대한 공업기술의 변화

engineering cost　　공학적 원가
　　= engineered cost ▶ committed
　　cost, discretionary cost

engineering department　　기술부

engineering economy(EE)　　공학경제

engineering estimates based on ideal
　　performance　　[표준원가계
　　산] 이상적인 상태에 기초한 공
　　학적 추정치

engineering technological analysis
　　공학적 분석

engineering variable　　공학기술적 변수

English book keeping　　영국식 부기

English form of balance sheet　　영국
　　식 대차대조표

English Institute　　영국협회

English law　　영국법

ENQ(enquiry character)　　질문문자, 연

구문자

enrollment 등록, 등기, 기재

entering wedge 주위 상황의 변화의 항변 사유를 이용할 수 없도록 하는 사유

enterprise 1) 사업, 기업 2) 조직체

enterprise continuity 기업의 계속성

enterprise operation 경영활동, 영업활동

Enterprise Resource Planning(ERP) 전사적 자원계획

enterprise's performance 기업성과, 기업실적

enterprise theory 기업실체이론
▶ entity theory

enterprise value 기업가치

enterprise zone (영)(환경대신 지정의) 기업지구(지역)

entertainment expense 접대비, 유흥비

entire board 전원이사회

entire surplus 총잉여금

entitlement 양도(讓渡)

entity 1) 기업실체, 사업단위, 법적 주체 2) 지분

entity classification 기업실체 분류

entity concept 기업실체개념

entity convention 기업실체의 공준

entity equity theory 주주지분이론
▶ equity theory, issue equity theory

entity theory 기업실체이론
▶ proprietorship theory, residual equity, residual equity theory

entrance 1) 입구 2) 기입, 기장 = entry, entry point

entrepreneur 기업가

entropy 1) (점진적)일률화, 무변화, 혼돈 2) (질의) 저하

entrusting 위탁

entry 기장, 기입 = entrance

entry clerk 기장계(係)

entry condition 기입조건

entry name 입구명

entry point 입구 = entrance, entry

entry price 유입가격 = input price
▶ current cost, exit price

environment 제(諸) 환경

environmental accounting 환경회계

environmental accounting model 환경회계모델

environmental compliance audit 환경준거감사

environmental data 환경자료

environmental disruption 공해, 환경파괴

environmental disruption cost 공해대책비 ▶ environment protection cost

environmental information 환경정보

environmental liability 환경상의 책임

environmental loss time 외부요인에 의한 손실시간 = external loss time ▶ down time

Environmental Protection Agency (EPA) 환경보호청

environmental regulation 환경법, 환경규정

environmental remediation 환경보존

environment protection cost 환경보호비 ▶ environmental disruption cost

EOM(end of message) 메시지의 종료

EOQ(economic order quantity) 경제적

주문량
EPA(Environmental Proottection Agency) 환경보호청
epilogue 발문(跋文), 후기(後記)
EPQ(economic purchase quantity) 경제적 구입량
EPS(earnings per share) 1주당 이익
EPS(external page storage) 외부기록 기억장치
equal annual payment method 복리상각법 = compound interest method
equal credit opportunity 동등한 신용기회
Equal Credit Opportunity Act 동등한 신용기회 보장법, 신용기회평등법
Equal Employment Opportunity Commission 고용기회 균등위원회
equal installment depreciation 균등상각법 = straight-line depreciation
equalizer 동등하게 하는 것
Equal Pay Act 동일임금법, 임금균등법
equal right 평등의 권리
equated time of payment 평균지급기일 ▶ equation of payment
equation manipulation 분식(粉飾), 겉모양을 장식
equation method 등식법에 의한 손익분기분석
equation of payment 기일평균법 ▶ equated time of payment
equipment 장치, 기기, 설비, 시설
equipment check 설비검사, 입출력 장치 검사

equipment failure 설비장애
equipment note 설비구입 지급어음, 설비 신탁어음
equipment purchased 설비구입
equipment replacement decision 설비대체의 의사결정
equipment sold 설비매각
equipment subsidiary ledger 설비 관리보조원장 ▶ plant ledger
equipment trust certificate 설비신탁증서
equitable conversion 형평법상의 재산의 전환
equitable lien 형평법상의 유치권
equitable mortgage 형평법상의 양도담보, 형평법상의 저당권 ▶ legal mortgage
equitable obligation 형평법상의 의무(채무)
equitable remedy 형평법상의 구제절차
equitable right of redemption 수여(授與)권
equitable servitude 형평법상의 용역권(지역권과 채취권)
equitable title 1) 형평법상의 소유권 2) 경제적 편익
equity 1) 지분 ▶ down payment, mortgage equity capitalization 2) 자기자본, 자기지분, 주주지분 ▶ owners equity 3) 형평법 ▶ common law
equity accounting 지분회계
equity capital (영)지분자본 = ordinary share
equity capital to total asset 자기자본비율
equity dividend 자기자본배당

equity dividend cover 배당율
▶ asset cover, dividend payout, payout ratio

equity financing 자기자본조달, 주식 발행에 의한 자본조달
▶ debt financing, self financing

Equity Funding case Equity Funding 회사 사건

equity holder 지분권자, 지분증권 보유자

equity in earning of unconsolidated subsidiary and affiliated company 연결되지 않은 관련회사의 지분이익

equity instrument 지분상품

equity in subsidiary 종속회사지분

equity law 형평법

equity method 지분법

equity method investment 지분법 적용대상투자자산

equity method investor 지분법 적용 대상투자자

equity method of accounting 지분법에 의한 회계처리

equity of redemption 형평법상의 수여권, 상환권, 회수의 권리

equity of security holder 증권보유자의 지분 ▶ capital

equity ratio 자기자본비율

equity revaluation 지분의 재평가
▶ current value accounting, inflation accounting

equity security 지분유가증권, 지분증권

equity security holder 지분증권의 소유자 (주주)

equity sense insolvency 만기 채무의 상환 불능

equity share (영)지분주식
▶ equity capital

equity share capital (영)지분주식자본

equity shareholder 보통주식

equity structure 자본구성

equity theory 지분이론

equity transfer 지분이전

equity trust 지분신탁 ▶ mortgage trust

equity turnover 자본회전율 = sale to net worth

equivalence 등가, 등량, 등치

equivalent 등가액, 등가물, 동등물

equivalent binary digit 등가 2진행수

equivalent production 완성품환산량, 등가생산량 ▶ equivalent whole unit

equivalent to cash 현금등가물, 현금등가액 = cash equivalent

equivalent unit 완성품환산량

equivalent unit of production(EUP) 제품의 완성품환산량

equivalent unit of work 완성품환산량 = equivalent production, equivalent whole unit

equivalent whole unit 완성품 총환산량 ▶ equivalent production

ERISA(Employee Retirement Income Security Act) 종업원 퇴직소득보장법

ERISA plan ERISA 연금제도

erosion of capital 자본 잠식

ERP(enterprise resource planning) 전사적 자원계획

error 1) 오류 ▶ fraud 2) 오차 3) 실수, 과실, 착오

error and omission excepted(E&OE)
오류와 누락의 제외

error burst   갑작스러운 실수

error condition   오류상태, 착오상태

error control   1) 오류제어 2) 에러 통
제

error control character   오류통제문자

error control procedure   오류통제과
정

error control system   오류통제방식

error correcting system   오류정정방식

error correction   오류정정, 오류수정
= error control

error detection   오류발견

error excepted(EE)   오류제외

error flag   오류표시

error handling   오류처리

error message   오류메세지

error of calculation   계산상 오류
▶ error of omission

error of mistake in writing   오기(誤記)
에 의한 오류
▶ offsetting error

error of omission   누락오류 ▶ error
of(accounting) principle, error of
calculation

error of the first kind   제1종 오류
▶ error of the second kind

error of the second kind   제2종 오류
▶ error of the first kind

error range   오차범위

error rate   오차율, 오류율

error ratio   오차율, 오류율

error recovery procedure   오류수정
과정

error span   오차, 오차범위

error term   오류항목 = residual term

ESA (European System of Integrated
Economic Accounts)   EC 가
맹국민 경제계정 총합시스템

escalator clause   신축조항 ▶ escalator
system, price adjustment clause

escalator system   신축조항제도
▶ escalator clause

escapable cost   회피가능원가
= avoidable cost
▶ inescapable cost, unavoidble
cost

escapable fixed cost   회피가능고정비
= avoidable fixed cost
▶ inescapable fixed cost,
unavoidable fixed cost

escape clause   면제조항, 면책조항
= exclusion clause, exemption
clause

escrow   조건부 날인증서, 조건부 증서
▶ deed

ESOP(employee stock ownership plan)
종업원 지주제도, 우리사주제
도

ESPRIT(European Strategic Programm
for R&D in Information
Technologies)   유럽정보기술
연구개발전략계획

essential characteristic   본질적 특징

essential element of contract   계약의
중요 요소

establishment of corporation   법인설
립

estate   1) 부동산 권리 ▶ excluded
property 2) 개인재산, 유산
3) 소유지 4) 지위, 신분

estate agent   부동산중개업자, 부동산
관리인

estate at will　무기한부 재산권

estate duty　유산세, 상속세
= death duty

estate for life　생애 부동산권

estate for years　기한부 재산권

estate of bankruptcy　파산재단

estate owner　형평법상의 토지소유자

estate tax　상속세 = death tax, inheritance tax

estate tax deduction　상속세 공제액

estate tax formula　상속세 공식

estimate　1) 견적, 측정, 추정, 평가　2) 견적서, 계산서, 개산치(槪算値)
= estimating

estimate cost　추정원가, 측정원가
= estimated charge, estimated cost, estimated expense
▶ predetermined cost, standard cost

estimate cost accounting　추정원가 계산 = estimated cost system

estimate cost card　추정원가표

estimate cost system　추정원가계산
= estimated cost system
▶ standard cost accounting

estimated activity level　추정 활동수준

estimated amount of uncollectable account　회수불능채권 추정액, 대손추정액

estimated annual effective tax rate　추정 연간유효세율

estimated annual effect tax rate　추정 연간유효세율

estimated annual tax rate　추정 연간 세율

estimated balance sheet　추정 대차대조표 ▶ estimated financial

statements, estimated income statement, projected financial statements

estimated burden rate　예정배부율
▶ burden rate

estimated cash purchase price　견적 현금구입가격, 추정매입원가

estimated charge　추정된 비용, 견적 원가 = estimated cost, estimated expense ▶ standard cost

estimated cost　추정원가
= estimated charge, estimate cost, estimated expense
▶ standard cost

estimated cost accounting　추정원가 계산 = estimated cost system

estimated cost of construction work　추정공사원가

estimated cost system　추정원가계산
= estimated cost accounting
▶ actual cost basis, standard cost accounting

estimated current value　추정현행가치

estimated current value of asset　추정현행가치, 추정시가

estimated economic life of leased property　리스물건의 경제적 내용연수

estimated exit value　추정판매가치
▶ current market value, expected exit value, net realized value, net settlement value

estimated expense　추정비용
= estimated charge, estimated cost ▶ standard cost

estimated expired value 추정소멸가
치
estimated figure 추정수치, 예정수치
estimated financial statement 추정
재무제표 ▶ estimated balance
sheet, estimated income
statement
estimated income statement 추정손
익계산서 = estimated profit
and loss statement ▶ estimated
balance sheet, estimated
financial statement
**estimated incremental cash outflow
and inflow** 추정증분 현금
유출입액
estimated liability 추정부채
estimated litigation liability 추정 소
송부채
estimated loss from bad debt 대손 예
상액, 예상대손손실, 견적 대손
상각
estimated net realizable value method
추정 순실현가치방법
estimated overhead cost 예정제조간
접비
estimated overhead distribution rate
예정간접비배부율 ▶ burden
rate, overhead rate
estimated price 예정가격, 추정가격
estimated procedure in valuation 추
정평가법
estimated profit 추정이익
estimated profit and loss statement
추정손익계산서 = estimated
income statement ▶ estimated
financial statement
estimated purchase 구입견적액

estimated rate 예정율, 견적표
estimated rate distribution 예정배부
estimated realizable value 추정실현
가능가액
▶ recoverable value
estimated residual service life 추정
잔여내용연수
estimated residual value 추정잔존가액
**estimated residual value of leased
property** 리스물건의 추정
잔존가치
estimated revenue 추정이익
estimated salvage value 추정잔존가액
= estimated scrap value
estimated scrap value 추정잔존가액
= estimated salvage value
estimated selling price 추정판매가격,
예상판매가격
estimated standard 예정표준원가, 견
적원가기준
estimated tax 예정납세액
estimated tax payable 추정미지급세액
estimated tax payment 예정납세비용,
조세추정액 납부
estimated usable period 추정사용가능
기간, 추정내용연수
estimated value 평가액, 견적액
estimated volume 예정 조업도수준
= estimated activity level
estimated wage rate 예정임률
estimated warranty expense 판매보
증비
estimated warranty liability 판매
보증충당금
estimate of sales 예상판매액
estimate premium claim outstanding
추정 미인도경품 채무

▶ premium expense

estimation   1) 견적, 추정 2) 판단, 의견

estimation sampling   추정표본조사

▶ discovery sampling

estoppel   금반언(禁反言), 먼저 주장에 반
대되는 진술을 뒤에 하는 것을
금지(자기의 행위에 대한 상대방
의 신뢰를 보호하기 위한 개념)

estoppel by certification   인증에 의한
금반언

estoppel by deed   증서에 의한 금반언

ethic ruling   윤리규칙, 윤리규정

EUP(equivalent unit of production)   제
품의 완성품환산량

EUP for material   원재료완성품환산량

Eurobond   유로채권

Euro dollar market   유로달러시장

European Accounting Association
(EAA)   유럽회계학회

European Community(EC)
유럽공동체

European Community Directive
(EC Directive)   EC지령서

European Computer Manufacturers'
Association(ECMA)   유럽
전자계산기협회

European Currency Unit(ECU)   유럽
통화단위

European Depositary Receipt(EDR)
유로예탁증서 ▶ American
Depositary Receipt

European Economic Community(EEC)
유로경제공동체

European Federation of Financial
Analysis Societies(EFFAS)
유럽재무분석협회연합회

European Foundation for

Management Development
(EFMD)   유럽경영개발재단

European Strategic Programme for
R&D in Information
Technologies(ESPRIT)
유럽정보기술연구개발 전략계
획

European System of Integrated
Economic Accounts(ESA)
EC가맹국 국민경제계정 총합
시스템

evading tax   탈세 = tax evasion

evaluation   평가

evaluation period   (예산, 실적비교의) 평
가기간

event   사건, 사상(事象)

event approach   사상접근법
▶ event theory, value approach

event occurring after the balance sheet
date   후속사건 ▶ post
balance sheet event

event subsequent to balance sheet date
후속사건 = event occurring
after the balance sheet date,
event subsequent to the date of
financial statements, post
balance sheet event

event subsequent to the date of
financial statements   후속
사건 = event occurring after
the balance sheet date, event
subsequent to balance sheet
date, post balance sheet event

event theory   사상이론 ▶ value approach

eventuality   우발성, 가능성

eviction   추방

evidence   증거

E

evidential document 증거서류
evidential matter 증거(물건), 증거자료
evolving budget 연속형 예산
= continuous budget,
progressive budget, rolling
budget
exact sampling theory 정밀표본이론
examination 1) 검사, 조사, 감사
2) 감사업무 ▶ audit
examination by reference 조사
examination evidence 감사증거
= audit evidence
examination of financial statements
재무제표감사
examination of transaction 거래검증
examination report 조사업무 보고서
ex ante optimum program 사전최적
계획 ▶ ex post optimum
analysis, ex post optimum
program
ex bounded warehouse 보세창고인도
except for opinion 예외사항에 의한 한
정의견 = with-the-exception-of
opinion
exception 1) 예외사항, 제외사항 2) 거
액손익항목
exceptional item 예외적 항목
▶ extraordinary item, prior
year adjustment
exception condition 예외조건
exception message 예외메세지
exception principle 예외원칙
exception report 예외보고서
exception reporting 한정보고, 예외보
고
except opinion (영)예외사항에 의한 한
정의견 ▶ adverse opinion,

disclaimer of opinion, subject
to opinion
excess 1) 과다, 초과액, 여분 2) 자산이
부채를 초과한 가액 3) (수리
계산서상의) 지출초과액
excess earning power 초과수익력
▶ goodwill
excess earning power approach
초과수익력접근법
▶ discounted free cash flow
approach, master valuation
approach, number of years
method
excessive profit 초과이윤, 부당이득, 폭
리
excess material requisition 재료초과
사용청구서, 초과재료 출고표
▶ materials requisition
excess of cost over book value acquired
취득장부가액을 초과하는 원가
excess of cost over net asset acquired
연결차변차익
excess of debt 채무초과
excess or deficiency 과부족
▶ deficiency, excess
excess over estimate 견적초과액
excess present value 초과현재가치
▶ net present value
excess present value index 초과현재
가치지수, 현재가치 수익성지
수
excess present value index method
현재가치 지수법
excess present value (profitability) index
수익성지수법
excess profit 초과이익 ▶ normal profit
margin

excess profit tax   초과이윤세

excess stock   과잉재고

exchange   1) 교환 2) 환어음 3) 거래소,
　　　교환소

exchangeability   교환가능성, 교환가치

Exchange Act   거래소법, 증권거래소법
　　　▶ Integrated Disclosure System

exchange bank   외국환은행

exchange broker   환어음중매인

exchange buffering   교환완충방식

exchange check   교환어음

exchange control   어음관리, 외국환 관
　　　리

exchange economy   교환경제

exchange gain   환차익 = exchange
　　　profit ▶ exchange loss

exchange loss   환차손 ▶ exchange
　　　gain

exchange of insurance policy   보험
　　　증권의 교환

exchange of nonmonetary asset   비화
　　　폐성자산의 교환

exchange profit   환차익
　　　= exchange gain, foreign
　　　exchange gain

exchange rate   환산율, 환율

exchange risk   환위험

exchange service   교환서비스

exchange transaction   교환거래

exchange value   교환가치

Exchequer   (영)대장성

exchequer bill   (영)국고증권
　　　= exchequer bond

exchequer bond   (영)국채

Exchequer Chambers   대장성 의회
　　　▶ Edinburgh Gazette,
　　　Registered Company, Registrar

　　　of Company

Excise   (영)간접세세무국

excise duty   간접세 = duty of excise

excise licence   간접세면허

excise tax   간접세

excluded property   과세대상외 재산
　　　▶ estate

exclusion   1) 비과세 2) 공제, 제외

exclusion clause   제외사항, 면책조항,
　　　면제조항 = escape clause,
　　　exemption clause

exclusive agent   독점대리인

exclusive reference   배타적 참조

exclusive segment   제외부문

ex-coupon(XC)   권리락

ex-coupon price of bond   채권의 권리
　　　락가격

exculpatory clause   면책조항

ex-dividend(XD)   배당락 ▶ cum-
　　　dividend, dividend-off, ex-
　　　dividend date

ex-dividend date   배당락 기일
　　　▶ cum-dividend, ex-dividend

executed   이행완료

executed contract   이행완료 계약

executed trust   수탁인의 할 일이 남아
　　　있지 않은 신탁 1) 강제집행
　　　2) 형의 집행, 집행영장 3) 날인
　　　증서(deed)의 작성 4) (유언서의)
　　　작성 5) 계약의 이행 6) 실행

execution creditor   집행채권자
　　　▶ execution debtor

execution cycle   명령실행단계

execution debtor   집행채무자
　　　▶ execution creditor

execution time   실행시간, 실행시

executive   임직원, 중역, 경영관리자

E

executive committee 집행위원회

executive director 상무이사

executive officer 업무집행위원
▶ chief executive officer

executive program 감시프로그램
= supervisor, supervisory
program

executive routine 감시일과

executive vice prresident 부(副)사장

executor 유언집행자, 상속재산 관리인
(남성)

executor according to the tenor 유언
집행자

executor dative (영)재판소 지명의 유
언집행자

executor de son tort 무권(無權)유언
= executor in his own wrong

executor in his own wrong 무권유언
집행자 = executor de son tort

executor nominate 유언서 상의 유언
집행자

executorship 유언집행자의 책임, 자격

executory 미이행

executory commitment 미이행계약
▶ executory contract

executory contract 미이행계약
▶ executory commitment

executory cost 미확정원가, 미확정 비
용(리스거래)

executory interest 미래의 점유권을 가
진 재산권

executory promise 미이행 약속

executrix 유언집행자, 상속재산 관리인
(여성) ▶ executor

exemplary damage 징벌적 손해배상

exemplification 1) 표본 2) 실증, 예시

exempt 면책(免責)

exemption 면책, 공제

exemption clause 면책조항, 면제조항,
제외사항 = escape clause,
exclusion clause

exemption of debt 채무면제

exempt organization 비과세 조직

exempt property (파산재단에서) 제외 재
산

exempt security 면책증권

exercise of warrant 신주인수권의 행사

exercise price 권리행사가격

ex factory 공장인도가격 = ex works

exhaustion 고갈, 감모, 소모

exhibit 첨부서류, 부표(付漂)

existence 실재성

existence or occurrence 실재성 또는
발생

existing practice 현행의 회계실무

existing structure 기존 건축물

exit 출구

exit price 유출가격 = output price
▶ entry price, net realizable
value

exogenous variable 외생변수
▶ endogenous variable

exoneration 1) 면제(免除) 2) 배상 또는
상환 요구

exor 유언집행자

expectation 예측(기대치) = expected
value

expectation interest 기대이자

expectation of life 기대내용연수, 견적
내용연수 = expected life

expected actual activity 기대실제활동
량, 기대실제조업도 = budgeted
volume, master-budget activity,
master-budget volume

▶ normal volume

expected actual capacity   기대실제
조업도

expected actual performance level
기대실제업적수준 ▶ expected
actual standard cost

expected actual standard cost   현실적
표준원가 = currently attainable
standard cost ▶ expected actual
performance level, normal cost,
normal standard cost

expected amount of misstatement
기대왜곡표시금액

expected annual activity   연간기대조
업도 = expected annual capacity
▶ budgeted activity, master
budget activity, master budget
volume

expected annual capacity   연간기대
조업도 = expected annual
volume, master budget activity,
master budget volume
▶ budgeted activity, budgeted
capacity, budgeted volume,
expected annual activity,
expected annual capacity

expected annual volume   연간기대조
업도 = expected annual capacity

expected deviation rate   기대이탈율

expected exit value   기대매각가치
= estimated exit value, net
realizable value ▶ current
market value, net realized
value, net settlement value

expected fixed cost   고정비 예정(예측)
액, 특별한 고정제조간접비의
예측액 ▶ 변동비 예측액

(expected variable cost)

expected frequency   기대횟수

**expected future years of service
periods**   연수합계법에 의한
미래내용년수

expected income   기대이익

expected increase in annual net income
매년의 순이익 증가 예측액

**expected incremental cash outflow and
inflow**   예상 증분현금 유출
입액

expected life   기대내용연수, 견적내용
연수 = expectation of life

expected misstatement   기대왜곡표
시금액

expected monetary value(EMV)   기대
화폐치, 기대치 = expected
payoff, expected value

expected payoff   기대금액 = expected
monetary value

expected population deviation rate
모집단의 기대이탈율

**expected postretirement benefit
obligation**   예측 퇴직후 급
부채무

expected profit   기대이익

expected rate of occurrence   기대발생
율

expected return   기대수익

expected return rate   기대수익률

expected standard   기대수준, 목표수준

expected standard cost   현실적 표준
원가 ▶ 이상표준원가(ideal
standard cost) 〉 정상표준원가
(normal standard cost) 〉 현실적
표준원가

expected utility   기대효용

expected value   기대가치, 기대치
▶ average, random variable

expected value of perfect information
완전정보의 기대치

expected variable cost   변동비 예정액,
특별한 변동 제조간접비의 예
정액 ▶ 고정비 예정(예측)액
(expected fixed cost)

expected volatility   예상변동률

expected volume   예정조업수준

expediency accounting   회계의 응급처
치 처리

expediting plan   작업진보계획

expenditure   지출, 지출액, 소비량, 경비

expenditure classification   지출의 분류

expenditure classification for
         governmental funds   정
부 기금의 지출 분류

expense   비용, 원가 (cost), 경비
▶ expired cost

expense arising from outside
         manufacture   외주(外注) 가
공비

expense book   비용명세장

expense budget   비용예산

expense center   비용센터
▶ discretionary expense center

expense distribution   비용배부

expense paid   비용지급액

expense rate   경비율 = expense ratio
▶ overhead rate

expense ratio   경비비율 = expense rate
▶ overhead rate

experience adjustment   실적조정
▶ retirement benefit plan

experimental manufacturing cost   시
험작품비

experiment and research expense
시험연구비 = experimental
research expense

experimentation   실험, 시험

expert   전문가

expert section of the prospectus   (사
업, 계획 등의) 미래전망보고서
중의 전문가 부분

expert system   전문가시스템
▶ artificial intelligence

expiration   1) 소멸 2) 만기, 경과 3) 소비

expiration date   만기일

expired cost   소멸원가
▶ asset, expense, loss

expiry date   (식품의) 최종기한, 사용기
한, 실효기일

explained variation   설명되는 변동

explanation   보충사항, 설명사항

explanation of transaction   거래의 설
명

explanatory foreword   (영)취지서

explanatory language   설명문

explanatory matter   보충적 설명사항

explanatory note   주기(注記)

explanatory paragraph   설명 문단

explanatory variable   설명 변수

explicit cost   명시적 비용 ▶ implicit
cost

explicit cost of capital   명시적 자본 비
용 ▶ implicit cost of capital

explicit declaration   명시적 선언

exploration cost   탐사비, 조사비, 시굴
비, 채광비

exploratory well   시굴정(井)

explusion from AICPA   AICPA로 부
터의 제명

exponent   1) (부동소수점 표시의) 누승지

수 2) 전형(典型) 3) 설명자, 인
도자

exponential annuity   정률상승연금
▶ level annuity

export bill   수출어음

export credit   수출신용

**Export Credits Guarantee Department
(ECGD)**   (영)수출신용 보증
국

export quota system   수출할당제도
▶ import quota system

export sales   수출 판매

exposed net asset position   순자산 노
출상태 ▶ exposed net
liability position

exposed net liability position   순부채
노출상태 ▶ exposed net asset
position

ex post optimum analysis   사후최적분
석 ▶ ex ante optimum program,
ex post optimum program, ex
post variance, forecasting
variance, opportunity cost
variance

ex post optimum program   사후최적
계획 ▶ ex ante program, ex
post analysis

ex post research   회고적 연구, 사후적
연구

ex post variance   사후차이
= opportunity cost variance

exposure draft(ED)   공개초안

exposure period   검증기간, (초안의) 공
개기간, 검토기간

express   명시적 보증, 명백한 보증

express authority   명시적 대리권

express easement   지역권의 표시

express grant   명시적 부여

expression   표현

express reservation   명시적 유보

express trust   명시(明示)신탁
▶ implied trust, presumptive
trust

express warranty   명시적 보증, 명백한
보증, 명시한 보증책임

express will   명시한 의사(意思)

expropriation   공용징수, 수용, 강제매입

expulsion   제명(除名)

expulsion clause   변제기일연장조항

EXQ(ex quay)   (수입항) 부두인도

ex quay(EXQ)   (수입항) 부두인도

ex right   권리락 ▶ cum-right, right-on

EXS(ex ship)   (수입항) 본선인도

ex ship(EXS)   (수입항) 본선인도, 착선
(着船)인도

ex store   점두(店頭)인도

extended trial balance   정산표, 확장한
시산표

Extensible markup language(EML)
EML 언어

extension   1) 연장, 연기, 확대 2) 채무변
제 3) 연기승인서

extension clause   연장 조항

extension plan   (채무) 연장 계획

extent of test   시사범위

exterior   외장재

external accounting   외부보고회계
▶ external reporting, financial
accounting, managerial
accounting

external analysis   외부분석 ▶ internal
analysis

external aspect   외부적 측면

external audit   외부감사 ▶ internal

E

audit

external auditor 외부감사인
▶ internal auditor

external bond 외채 ▶ foreign bond

external confirmation 외부확인

external economy and external diseconomy 외부경제와 외부불경제

external event 외부사건

external evidence 외부증거 = extrinsic evidence ▶ internal evidence

external financial reporting 외부 재무보고

external function 외부함수

external fund 외부자금 ▶ internal fund

external interruption 외부방해

external label 외부라벨

external loss time 외부요인에 의한 손실시간 = environmental loss time

external merge 외부조합

external name 외부명(名)

external obsolescence 외부요인에 의한 진부화 ▶ cost approach, depreciation, functional obsolescence, physical deterioration

external procedure 외부절차, 외부처리과정

external reconstruction (영)새 회사 설립을 위한 회사재건

external reference 외부참조

external report 외부보고서 ▶ internal report

external report accounting 외부보고 회계 ▶ internal report accounting, management

accounting, managerial accounting

external reporting 외부보고
▶ external accounting

external reporting system 외부보고 제도 ▶ internal reporting system

external transaction 외부거래
▶ internal transaction

external user 외부정보이용자

external valuation 외부평가

extinction (채권 등의) 소멸

extinctive prescription 소멸시효

extinguishment (권리, 의무, 계약에 관한) 소멸, 변제(辨濟)

extinguishment of bonds payable 사채의 상환

extinguishment of debt 부채상환, 채무계약의 해제, 채무의 상각
▶ renancing debt, restructuring, debt restructuring

extinguishment of hypothec 저당권의 소멸

extract 추출하다, 골라내다

extract instruction 추출 지시

extractive industries 원료채굴산업

extractive industry 채취산업, 추출산업

extranet 익스트라넷

extraordinary 특별한, 이상한

extraordinary charge 특별손실, 임시적 비용, 임시손실
▶ extraordinary loss, non-recurring charge

extraordinary depreciation 1) 특별감가, 비경상적 감가, 이상감가 2) 임시상각, 특별상각

extraordinary gain   특별이익
  ▶ contingent gain, contingent
  loss, unusual item
extraordinary gain or loss   특별손익
extraordinary general meeting(EGM)
  (영)임시주주총회, 임시사원총
  회
extraordinary income and charge
  (영)특별손익 = extraordinary
  gain and loss, extraordinary
  item ▶ exceptional item
extraordinary item   1) 특별손익항목
  2) 임시항목, 비경상적 항목, 이
  상(異常)항목 3) 기타항목
extraordinary loss   특별손실, 경상외
  손실, 이상손실
  ▶ extraordinary gain or loss,
  extraordinary item, non-
  recurring item, non-recurring
  loss
extraordinary profit and loss   특별손
  익, 임시손익, 비경상적 손익

  ▶ non-periodical profit and
  loss, non-recurring profit and
  loss
extraordinary repair   특별수선, 임시
  수선 = major repair ▶ ordinary
  repair
extraordinary repairs expense   특별
  수선비, 임시수선비
  ▶ ordinary repairs expense
extraordinary resolution   (영)비상결의
  ▶ ordinary resolution, special
  resolution
extrapolation   추론(推論)
extra worker   임시고용노동자
extreme duress   극도의 강박(强迫)
extrinsic evidence   외부증거 = external
  evidence ▶ internal evidence
extrinsic motivation   외적동기
  ▶ intrinsic motivation
EXW(ex works)   공장인도(가격)
ex works(EXW)   공장인도(가격)
  = ex factory

F

F(favorable variance)   유리한 차이
  ▶ variance
FA(Finance Act)   재정법
fabrication   1) 제조, 구성 2) 위조
face amount   액면가액, 액면액
  = face value ▶ discount value,
  discounted value, market value
face value   1) 액면(額面), 표시가액, 권
  면가액, 권면액 = face amount

  ▶ discount 2) 변제액
facilities   설비
facility   1) 시설, 설비 2) 편익 3) 기능
facility management   시설관리, 설비
  관리
facsimile(FAX)   팩스, 복사(複寫)전송
facsimile signal level   복사전송신호 레
  벨
fact discovered after report issued

감사보고서 제출후 발견사항

factor 1) 도매상, 채권매수업자, 중매인, 채권금융회사 2) 요소, 인자, 요인 3) 인수(因數)

factorage 1) 대리업 2) 중개수수료

factor cost 요소비용

factor cost principle 요소비용원칙

factorial 계승 (어느 특정의 수와 그것에 선행하는 모든 정의 정수와의 곱)

factoring 팩토링, 매출채권의 매각, 외상 매출채권의 매수

factoring of receivable 외상매출금의 팩토링

factor of production 생산요소

factor's lien 채권매수업자 유치권

factory accounting 공장회계
▶ factory bookkeeping

factory administration department 공장관리부문

factory bookkeeping 공장부기
▶ factory accounting, manufacturing bookkeeping

factory burden 제조간접비 = factory overhead

factory cost 공장원가, 제조원가, 판매 품의 제조원가
= manufacturing cost ▶ factory expense, production cost

factory cost report 제조원가보고서
= cost report

factory expense 제조간접비 = factory burden, factory overhead, manufacturing expense
▶ factory cost

factory expense budget 제조간접비 예산 = factory overhead budget

factory fitting 공장비품

factory general expense 공장일반관 리비

factory ledger 공장원장

factory ledger system 공장원장시스템

factory management 공장관리

factory office supply 공장사무용 소모 품 ▶ factory supplies

factory order 제조명령 = production order

factory overhead 제조간접비 = factory burden, factory expense, factory overhead cost, indirect factory cost, indirect manufacturing cost, manufacturing burden, manufacturing expense, manufacturing indirect cost, manufacturing overhead, manufacturing overhead cost, oncost, overhead, overhead cost(expense), production overhead, production overhead cost

factory overhead applied 배부된 제조 간접비, 제조간접비의 배부액
= applied overhead ▶ factory overhead

factory overhead budget 제조간접비 예산 = factory expense budget, manufacturing expense budget, manufacturing overhead budget

factory overhead cost 제조간접비
▶ factory overhead

factory overhead expense distribution sheet 제조간접비배부표
= manufacturing overhead distribution sheet

factory overhead incurred 제조간접

비 발생액

factory payroll 제조관계 지급임금 내
역 명세표

factory supply 공장소모품, 공장소모품
비

**facts existed at the date of auditor's
report** 감사보고 날짜의 시
점에서 존재했던 사실

FAF(Financial Accounting Foundation)
재무회계재단

FAF(Financial Analyst Federation) 재
무분석가 연합회

**FAIA(Fellow of the Association of
International Accountants)**
국제회계사협회 정회원의 칭호

fail safe 시스템이 고장났을 때 안전성
을 확보하기 위해 설계된 시스
템 ▶ fail soft

fail soft 컴퓨터의 하드웨어나 소프트웨
어 손상이 있는 경우에 주변처
리기능을 종료시키도록 설계된
시스템 ▶ fail safe

failure 1) 태만, 불이행 2) 고장

failure log 고장 기록

failure rate 고장률

failure to warn 경고실패

fair 공정

FAIR CREDIT BILLING ACT 공정
신용지불 청구법

FAIR CREDIT REPORTING ACT
공정신용 보고법

FAIR DEBT COLLECTION ACT
소비자인 채무자로부터 부채상
환을 독촉하는방법을 규제하는
법

Fair Debt Collection Practices act 공
정채권회수법

Fair Labor Standards Act 연방공정
노동기준서

fair market price 공정시장가격
▶ fair value

fair market value(FMV) 공정시장가
치 ▶ fair value

fairness 공정성 ▶ justice

fairness test 공정성 테스트

fair presentation 적정표시

fair price 공정거래가격, 적정시장가격
▶ fair value

fair rate of return 공정수익율

fair trade 공정거래

fair value 공정가격, 공정가치 ▶ arm's
length transaction, fair market
price, fair market value

fair value adjusted cost method 공정
가액 조정 원가법

fair value adjustment a/c 공정가액 조
정 계정

**fair value and credit risk disclosures of
financial instrument (other
than derivatives)** 금융상품
의 공정가액 및 신용위험 공시
— SFAS 107

fair value hedge 공정가치 헤지, 시가
변동에 대한 헤지

fair value measurement 공정가액평
가의원칙

fair value of plan asset 연금자산의 공
정가액

fair value of the leased property 리
스자산의 공정가격

fair values 공정가액, 공정가치

faithfulness 충실성 ▶ verifiability

faithful representation 충실한 표현

false accounting (영)부정경리, 불법 회

계조작 ▶ creative accounting,
window dressing

falsification　위조, 반증, 문서위조

Family and Medical Leave Act(FMLA)
　가족 · 의료휴가법

family bookkeeping　가계부기

family corporation　동족회사

family partnership　가족조합

fancy price　터무니 없는 가격

**FAPA(Fellow of the Association of
　Authorised Public
　Accountants)**　AAPA
　(Association of Authorised Public
　Accountants) 정회원의 칭호

fare　운임, 요금

far-end crosstalk　원안수화

farm accounting　농업회계

farm bookkeeping　농업부기

farm price method　농장가격법, 정상법

farm product　농업에서 생산 · 사용되
　는 물품

FAS(free alongside ship)　선측(船側) 인
　도조건

**FAS(statement of financial accounting
　standards)**　재무회계기준

**FASAC(Financial Accounting Standards
　Advisory Committee)**　재무
　회계기준자문위원회

**FASB(Financial Accounting Standards
　Board)**　재무회계기준심의회

FASB concepts series　재무회계기준
　심의회의 제개념 목록 = SFAC

FASB concepts statement　FASB 개념
　보고서

FASB interpretation　FASB 해석지침

FASB standards　FASB 기준 보고서

FASB technical bulletin　FASB 적용

지침

fault　장애, 고장

fault-tolerant design　오차허용설계

favorable to surety　보증인에 유리

favorable variance　유리한 차이
　　▶ unfavorable variance,
　　variance analysis

FAX(facsimile)　복사전송

**FCA(Fellow of the Institute of Chartered
　Accountants in England and
　Wales, Fellow of the Institute of
　Chartered Accountants in
　Ireland)**　잉글랜드와 웨일즈
　의 칙허회계사협회와 아일랜드
　칙허회계사협회 정회원의 칭호

FCC(federal communications commission)
　연방통신위원회

**FCCA(Fellow of the Chartered
　Association of Certified
　Accountants)**　(영)공인회계
　사협회 정회원의 칭호

**FCMA(Fellow of the Chartered Institute
　of Management Accountants)**
　(영)관리회계사 칙허협회 정회
　원의 칭호

**FCPA(Fellow of the Institute of Certified
　Public Accountants in Ireland)**
　아일랜드 공인회계사 정회원의
　칭호

**FCT(Fellow of the Association of
　Corporate Treasurers)**
　(영)재무담당자협회 정회원의
　칭호

**FCWA(Fellow of the Institute of Cost and
　Works Accountants)**
　(영)원가회계사협회 정회원의
　칭호

FDIC(Federal Deposit Insurance Corporation)   연방예금보험회사

FDM(frequency division multiplex)   주파수 분할 다중통신방식

FDP(field development program)   분야 개발 프로그램

FDX(full duplex)   전 2종

FE(field engineer)   부문 기술자

FE(format effector)   서식제어분자

feasance   (계약, 의무의) 이행

feasibility   실행가능성

feasibility study   실행가능성 조사, 실행가능성 연구

Federal Age Discrimination in Employment Act   고용상의 연령차별 금지법

Federal Bankruptcy Code   연방파산법

Federal Bankruptcy Court   연방파산법원

Federal Bankruptcy Reform Sct of 1944   1944년 개정 연방파산법

Federal Communications Commission (FCC)   연방통신위원회

Federal Consolidated Budget Reconciliation Act(COBRA)   연방포괄예산조정법

federal court   연방재판소

Federal Deposit Insurance Corporation (FDIC)   연방예금보험회사

Federal Employment Discrimination Law   연방고용차별금지법

Federal Environmental Protection Law   환경보호법

Federal Environment Pesticide Control Act   연방환경살충제 관리법

Federal Fair Labor Standards Act   공정노동기준서

federal fund   연방준비은행 준비금

federal income tax expense   연방법인세 비용

Federal Insecticide, Fungicide and Rodenticide Act   연방 살충제, 방균제, 살균제법

Federal Insurance Contributions Act (FICA)   연방보험납입금법

Federal National Mortgage Association(FNMA)   연방 · 전국저당협회

Federal Power Commission(FPC)   연방 전력위원회

Federal Reserve Bank(FRB)   연방 준비은행

Federal Reserve Board(FRB)   연방준비위원회

Federal Reserve System(FRS)   연방준비제도

Federal Saving and Loan Insurance Corporation(FSLIC)   연방저축 · 대부보험회사

Federal Savings and Loan Association   연방 저축 · 대부조합

Federal Securities Acts   연방증권법

Federal Securities Statutes   연방증권법

Federal Social Securty Act   연방사회보험법, 연방사회보장법

federal state   연방 국가

federal tax lien   연방세금 담보권

Federal Trade Commission(FTC)   연방통상위원회

Federal Trade Commission Improvement Act   연방 거

래위원회 개선법

Federal Unemployment Tax Act(FUTA)
연방 실업보험세법, 연방실업
세법

fee 1) 요금, 수수료, 보수(報酬), 사례(謝
禮) 2) 봉토, 영지

fee and commission received 수입수
수료

fee conditional 조건부 소유권

feedback 피드백, 귀환

feedback control 피드백 통제

feedback control system 피드백 통제
시스템

feedback effect 피드백 효과

feedback loop 피드백 부호

feedback mechanism 피드백 기구

feedback system 피드백 방식

feedback value 피드백 가치
        ▶ predictive value

feeder organization 지류 조직

fee determinable 특약조건소유권

feedforward 피드 포워드

feed hole 조출(계속 내보내는)구멍

fee for service 수입수수료

fee in tail 직계비속에 한정된 부동산권

fees 수취수수료

fees for service 수취수수료

fee simple 완전소유권, 무조건 상속재
산권

fee simple absolute 절대적 단순 부동
산권

fee simple defeasible 소멸 조건부 단
순 부동산권

fee simple determinable 소멸 조건부
단순 부동산권

fee simple servant rule 공동고용의 준
칙

**fee simple subject to a condition
        subsequent** 해제 조건부 단
순 부동산권

fee tail 상속제한 영지권, 직계비속에
한정된 부동산권

FEI(Financial Executives Institute) 재
무저당중역협회

fellow 1) (대학의)특별연구원 2) (회계사
협회 직업단체의) 정회원, 특별회
원

**Fellow of the Institute of Chartered
        Accountants in England &
        Wales(FCA)** 잉글랜드와
웨일즈의 정회원

fellow subsidiary 형제회사

FFA (free from alongside) 선측인도조건

fiar 단순영지권 소유자
        ▶ fee simple

fiat 1) 법령, 명령, 인가 2) 규약

fiat money 법정불환지폐

Fibonacci number 피보나치 수

Fibonacci search 피보나치 탐색

Fibonacci series 피보나치 수열

FICA 연방 보험납입금법

FICA tax 연방보험납입금세

**FICM(Fellow of the Institute of Credit
        Management)** 여신관리협회
정회원의 칭호

fictitious asset 의제자산

fictitious name statute 가상 이름법

fictitious payee rule 가공의 수취인 규
정

fictitious profit 가공이익 ▶ paper
        profit

Fictitious Rule 의제(擬制)법

fidelity bond 1) 신용(책임)보험 2) 신원
보증 3) 충실증서

fiduciary   수탁자

fiduciary accounting   1) 수탁회사책임 2) 신탁회계 3) 부동산회계

fiduciary duty   1) 신탁의무, 신탁인정 의무 2) 신의성실의무

fiduciary fund financial statement 수탁형기금 재무제표

fiduciary fundstrust and agency 수탁형 기금신탁 및 대리기금

fiduciary loan   신용대부, 무담보대부

fiduciary relationship   신인(信認)관계

fiduciary responsibility   수탁책임

field   1) 광산구역 2) 필드, 분야 = item

field audit   현장감사

field check   1) 분야검사 ▶ format check, input control 2) 필드 검증

field development program(FDP) 분야개발 프로그램

field engineer(FE)   분야기술자

field office   지방사무소

field size check   필드 크기 검증

field study   현장조사

field test   현장검사

field warehousing   현장창고제, 현지 보관, 필드 창고

field work   분야 작업, 현장 업무, 현장 작업

field work standard   (감사)실시기준

FIFO(first-in, first-out method)   선입 선출법

FIFO WIP assumption   선입선출법의 재공품 가정

fifty-percent-owned company   50%소 유회사 ▶ associated company

figurative constant   표의 정수, 형상 정수

figure   수자, 수치, 합계(금액, 수량) 가격

FII(franked investment income)   (영)납 세완료후 투자이익

file   1) 파일 2) 신청, 등기, 등록

file quality maintenance   파일 품질관리

file retention period   파일 보존기간 ▶ file label

file updating   파일갱신

file usage control   파일 사용통제

filing   제출, 신고서 제출

filing and payment of tax   세금의 신 고와 납부

filing date   신고서 제출일

filing of audit working paper   감사조 서의 제출

filing requirement   세금신고 조건

filing status   신고 자격

filing system   신고 체계

filler   1) 충당문자 2) 여과기

FIN   기준서의 상세한 해석

final accounts   (영)결산재무제표, 연차 재무제표 = annual accounts

final adjustment   기말수정분개

final audit   기말감사 ▶ interim audit

final dividend   기말배당

final injunction   최후법정금지명령 = permanent injunction, perpetual injunction ▶ interlocutory injunction

final pay plan   최종급여기준연금 ▶ retirement benefit plan

final settlement   (채무의)변제완료, 채무 잔액의 지불

final value of annuity   연금종가

finance   금융, 재무, 재정

Finance Act(FA)   (영)재정법

finance bill   융통어음, 금융어음 = accommodation bill

F

Finance Bill　(영)재정법 초안
finance charge　재무비용
finance company　금융회사, 할부금융
　회사 = finance house
finance forecast and projection　재무
　예측과 계획
finance house　금융회사, 할부금융 회사
　= finance company
finance lease　금융리스 = financial lease
　▶ operating lease
finance subsidiary　금융자회사
Finance System Council(FSC)　재무
　제도 심의회
financial accounting　재무회계
　= accounting for external
　reporting ▶ accounting for
　internal reporting, managerial
　accounting, related party
Financial Accounting Foundation(FAF)
　재무회계재단 ▶ Financial
　Accounting Standards Board
financial accounting reporting cycle
　재무회계보고 순환과정
financial accounting standards
　재무회계기준
Financial Accounting Standards
　Advisory Committee
　재무회계기준 자문위원회
　▶ Financial Accounting
　Standards Board
Financial Accounting Standards Board
　(FASB)　재무회계기준 심의
　회 ▶ American Institute of
　Certified Public Accountants,
　Financial Accounting
　Foundation
financial accounts　(영)재무제표, 재무

보고서 ▶ annual accounts,
　financial statements
financial activity　자금조달활동, 재무
　활동
financial advisor　재무 고문(顧問)
financial aggregate　재무적 총합계액,
　통합치
financial amount　화폐액
financial analysis　재무분석
financial analyst　재무분석가, 증권분
　석가
Financial Analyst Federation(FAF)
　재무분석가 연합회
Financial Analyst Journal Financial
　Analyst Federation : FAF
　발행의 기관지. 1945년에
　Analysts Journal 창간, 격월제
　발행
financial aspect　재무적 측면
financial audit　재무감사, 재무제표감사
financial book　재무장부, 회계장부
　= account book, book of
　account
financial budget　재무예산 ▶ cash
　budget, operating budget
financial capital　재무자본, 화폐(현금)
　자본 = monetary capital
　▶ capital maintenance,
　physical capital
financial capital concept　화폐자본 개
　념, 재무적 자본개념
financial capital maintenance　화폐
　자본유지, 재무자본유지
　▶ maintenance of operating
　capability, physical capital
　maintenance
financial capital maintenance concept

화폐자본 유지개념

financial community   금융증권업계,
　　재계(財界)

financial comparision   재무비교

financial condition   재무상태

financial department   재무부서

financial document   (어음, 환어음상의)
　　지급수단용 증권

financial effect   재무적 영향

financial enterprise   금융업

Financial Executive   재무담당협회의
　　기관지, 1933년에 Cotroller의
　　잡지명으로 창간, 1963년에
　　현 잡지명으로 개칭한 월간지

financial executive insitute   재무담당
　　중역회의

**Financial Executive Research
　　Foundation(FERF)**   재무
　　담당자 연구재단(재무담당직원
　　연구단체)

financial expense   재무비용

financial flexibility   재무적 탄력성
　　▶ nearness to cash

financial flow   재무흐름

financial forecast   재무예측

Financial forecast and projection
　　예측 재무제표

financial future   금융선물거래

financial gearing   재무레버리지
　　= financial leverage

financial group   융자단

financial gurantee written   (보증자측의)
　　채무보증

financial highlight   재무상의 중심 부분

financial history   재무경과

financial impact   재무적 영향

financial information   재무정보

financial information system   재무정
　　보시스템

financial in nature   재무적 성질

financial institution   금융기관

financial instrument   금융상품

financial interest   경제적 이해관계자,
　　투자관계자

financial interest in client   고객에 대
　　한 경제적 이해

financial intermediary   금융중개업

financial lease   금융리스 ▶ capital
　　lease, operation lease, sale and
　　leaseback

financial leverage   재무 레버리지
　　= financial gearing
　　▶ leverage, operating leverage

financial management   재무관리

financial market   금융시장

financial organization   금융기관

financial performance   재무적 성과

financial planning   재무계획

financial policy   재무정책

financial position   재정상태, 재무상태

financial position statement   대차대조
　　표, 재무상태표 ▶ statement of
　　change in financial position,
　　statement of financial position,

financial prediction   재무예측

financial press   경제신문

financial projection   재무전망

financial questionnaire   재무질문서

financial ratio   재무비율

financial report   재무회계보고서

financial reporting   재무회계보고
　　▶ accounting information

Financial Reporting Council(FRC)
　　재무회계보고평의회

F

▶ financial Reporting Pannel

financial reporting practice   재무회계
보고실무

financial reporting release   재무회계
보고통첩(通牒)

**Financial Reporting Review Pannel
(FRRP)**   재무보고검토 심사
회 ▶ Standard Board, Financial
Reporting Council

financial reporting standard   재무회
계 보고기준

financial report survey   재무회계보고
조사서

financial resource   재무적 자원

**Financial resource measurement
focus**   재무자원의 측정초점

financial revenue   재무수익, 금융수익

financial risk   재무위험 ▶ business
risk

financial section   재무 분야

financial situation   재무상태 = financial
conditon

financial solvency   재무유동성

financial state   재정상태, 재무상태

financial statement   재무제표

financial statement analysis   재무제표
분석, 재무분석, 경영분석

financial statement assertion   재무제
표 주장

financial statement audit   재무제표
감사

**financial statement for state and
local governments**   주정
부와 지방정부의 재무제표

financial statement method   재무제
표법 = internal rate of return
method, net present value

method, payback period

**financial statement prepared for use in
other country**   다른 나라에
서 사용되는 재무제표

financial statement presentation   재
무제표의 표시

financial structure   재무구성, 자본 구
성, 자금조달구조 ▶ capital
structure

financial transaction   재무거래

financial year   회계연도, 사업연도

financier   개인금융업자

financing   자금조달

financing activity   재무활동

financing cycle   재무순환과정

financing lease   금융리스

financing method   자금조달법

financing statement   1) 재무보고서
2) 담보권을 기재한 문서, 융자
보고서

financing statement filing   융자보고서
의 제출

financing structure   자금조달구조

financing transaction   자금조달거래

finder   발견자, 습득자

finder's fee   1) lessee의 중개수수료
2) 소개수수료, 발견자 보수
▶ commission

fine bill   (영)우량어음

fine paper   우량어음

fine rate   최우량이자율, 최우량할인율

finished goods   제품, 완성품

finished goods budget   제품예산

finished goods control account   제품
계정

finished goods held for sale   판매를
위한 제품, 완성품

finished goods inventory   제품재고(량)

finished goods ledger   제품원장

finished goods on hand   재고제품

finished goods stock   제품재고량
= finished parts stock, finished
product stock

finished part   완성부품, 자가제조품
= finished part stock

finished part goods   완성부품 = finished
part, manufactured part
▶ purchased part

finished part stock   완성부품의 재고
= finished goods stock

finished product   제품, 완성품 semi-
finished stock, work in process

finished product goods ledger   제품
원장 ▶ finished goods controll
account

finished product stock   (영)완성품 재
고 = finished goods stock

finished stock   완성품 = finished product

finishing   가공, 마무리, 성과

finite population   유한모집단(有限母
集團)

fire damage   화재손실

fire insurance   화재보험

fire policy   화재보험증권

firm   1) 상사조합, 상사, 상회 2) (일반적
인)회사, 사무소 3) 조합원
(partner)의 총칭 4) 회계사무소
▶ company, corporation,
partnership

firm commitment   1) 외화표시 확인(행
위)계약 2) 전액인수
▶ stand-by agreement,
underwriting agreement

firm name   조합 · 합명회사의 명칭

firm offer   확정신청, 확정주문, 강력한
청약, 회답기한부 주문

firm price   확정가격, 고정가격

firm price contract   확정가격계약
= fixed price contract

first audit   초도감사 ▶ repeat audit

first cost   기초원가, 요소별 원가, 제조
직접비 = flat cost, prime cost
▶ direct cost, shutdown cost

first creditors' metting   최초의 채권
자집회, 제1회 채권자집회

first-in, first-out(FIFO)   선입선출법
= firstin, firstout(FIFO)

first-in, first-out method(FIFO)   선입
선출법 ▶ average inventory
method, last-in firat-out method

first in on hand   선입보존법 = last-in
first-out method

first meeting of directors   제1회 이사
회

first mortgage bond   이심저당부 사채

first quarter   제1사분기 ▶ second
quarter, third quarter

first standard of field work   제1실시
기준

first year allowance(FYA)   (영)초년도
상각 ▶ capital, allowance,
initial allowance, writing down
allowance

fiscal period   회계기간, 회계연도
= fiscal year

fiscal policy   재무정책, 재정정책

fiscal year   회계연도, 회계기간
= fiscal period
▶ year of assessment

Fisher'ideal index   피셔의 이상적 지수

fishery   1) 어업권 2) 어업, 수산업, 수산

F

회사

fitting   조작, 부속기구 ▶ fixture

fixed amount   확정금액

fixed amount in money   금액상 확정
금액

fixed asset   고정자산 = capital asset,
long-lived asset ▶ intangibile
asset, investment, tangible asset

fixed asset intended for disposal   제
거 또는 매각이 예정된 고정자산

fixed asset investment   장기투자
▶ current asset investment,
long-term investment, short-
term investment

fixed asset ledger   고정자산원장
= plant ledger

fixed asset ratio   고정비율 = fixed asset
to net worth ratio, ratio of net
worth to fixed asset

fixed asset register   고정자산대장
= asset register

fixed asset statement   고정자산 증감
변동표

fixed asset to net worth ratio   고정
비율 = fixed asset ratio, ratio
of net worth to fixed asset

fixed asset turnover   고정자산회전

fixed asset turnover ratio   고정자산
회전율

fixed asset unit   고정자산 처리단위

fixed award   정액보장

fixed benefit plan   정액급부금제도

fixed budget   고정예산 = static budget
▶ flexible budget, variable
budget

fixed capital   고정자본 ▶ variable
capital

fixed charge   1) 고정비 = fixed cost
▶ floating charge 2) 확정 부
채, 고정담보

fixed charge coverage   고정비배율
▶ times floating charge

fixed cost   고정비, 고정적 비용
= standing cost ▶ capacity
cost, committed capacity cost,
committed cost, fixed expense
cost, managed cost,
programmed capacity cost,
programmed cost

fixed exchange rate   고정환율, 고정
시세 ▶ flexible change rate,
floating exchange rate

fixed exchange rate system   고정환율
제도

fixed expense   고정비 ▶ fixed
overhead cost

fixed factory burden   고정제조간접비
= fixed factory overhead, fixed
overhead, fixed overhead
▶ variable factory overhead

fixed factory overhead   고정제조간접
비 = fixed factory burden, fixed
manufacturing overhead, fixed
overhead variable factory
overhead

fixed factory overhead variance   고정
제조간접비차이

fixed first order arrangement
고정성 배열법 ▶ current-first
order arrangement

fixed income   확정 보수, 확정 수입

fixed income security   확정 이자부 증
권

fixed installment method   정액법

= straight-line method
▶ declining balance method,
fixed percentage method

fixed length record   고정길이 기록기

fixed liability   고정부채 ▶ current
liability

fixed link pack area   고정연계팩지역

fixed manufacturing overhead   고정
제조간접비 = fixed factory
overhead

fixed manufacturing overhead applied
배부된 고정제조간접비

fixed overhead   고정제조간접비
= fixed factory overhead

fixed overhead allocation   고정제조
간접비의 배부

fixed overhead cost   고정제조간접비
= fixed product overhead cost,
fixed cost

fixed page   고정 페이지

fixed percentage method   정률법
= declining balance method,
fixed percentage on reducing
balance method
▶ depreciation, production
method, straight-line method

fixed percentage of book value method
정률법 = fixed percentage on
declining base method

**fixed percentage on declining base
method**   정률법 = fixed
percentage of book value
method

**fixed percentage on reducing balance
method**   체감잔액법, 정률
법 = declining balance method
depreciation,production

method, straight- line method

fixed percentage rule   고정백분율기준
= percentage rule

fixed point arithmetic   고정소수점 연
산

fixed point part   고정소수점부분

fixed point representation   고정소수
점표시

fixed point representation system   고
정소수점표시법

fixed price   1) 고정가격 ▶ maximum
price, minimum price 2) 정가,
정찰가격

fixed price contract   확정가격계약
= firm price contract

fixed production overhead cost   고정
제조간접비 = fixed overhead
cost ▶ fixed cost

fixed radix notation   고정기수표시법
= fixed radix notation system

**fixed selling, general and
administrative expense**
[CVP분석]고정 판매비 및 일
반관리비

fixed standard cost   고정 표준원가
= basic standard cost

fixed stock option   정액 스톡옵션

fixed storage   고정기억장치
= read-only storage

fixed tangible   유형고정자산
▶ land, plant and equipment

fixing   가격결정회의

fixture   1) 부동산에 첨부된 동산, (토지,
건물의) 부대물, 정착물 2) 조작
(造作)

fixture and fitting   부대설비, 부대
기구, 부대물

flag   깃발, 표식 = switch indicator
flagging on account   미결계정
= earmarked account, rubricated account
flat cost   기준원가, 기초원가
= prime cost, first cost
▶ direct cost, shutdown cost
flat lease   정액요금리스, 운용리스
▶ percentage lease, straight lease
flat price   균일가격 ▶ flat quotation
flat quotation   균일가격 ▶ flat price
flexed budget   변동예산
flexibility   신축성
flexible budget   변동예산, 탄력성예산
= flexiblebudgeting, variable budget ▶ flexed budget
flexible budget allowance   변동예산 허용액 ▶ flexible budget
flexible budgeting   변동예산 = flexible budget, variable budget,
▶ fixed budget
flexible budget variance   변동예산 차이 ▶ flexible budget
flexible exchange rate   변동환율, 변동 시세 ▶ fixed exchange rate, floating exchange rate
flip-flop   (방향, 의견의) 급변, 전환
= bistable trigger circuit
float   1) 변동시세제도, 변동환율제도 2) 통화, 流通貨 3) 부동상태
floating asset   유동자산
floating capital   유동자본, 운전자본
floating charge   유동담보, 포괄담보
floating debt   유동부채
floating exchange rate   변동환율
▶ fixed exchange rate, flexible

exchange rate
floating exchange rate system   변동 환율제도
floating head   부동(浮動)부분
floating lien   유동 담보
floating money   일시적 여유자금
floating point   부동소수점
floating point arithmetic   부동소수점 연산
floating point base   부동소수점기수
(基數) = floating point radix
▶ floating point representation
floating point constant   부동소수점 상 수
floating point radix   부동소수점기수
floating point representation   부동소 수점표시, 부동소수점표시법
floating rate   1) 변동이율 2) 변동시세
floating rate certificate of deposit
(FRCD)   변동이자부 예금증서
floating rate note(FRN)   변동이자 부 채권
floor   하한금리
floor-to-floor time   가공시간
flotation   1) (증권의)모집, 발행, 기채(起 債) 2) (회사의)설립
flotation cost   발행비
flow   흐름
flowchart   흐름도 = flow diagram
flow diagram   흐름도 = flowchart
flow direction   흐름방향
flowline   흐름 선(線)
flow-of-fund   자금순환
flow-of-fund analysis   자금순환분석
flow of unit   생산량의 흐름
flow through method   당기인식법, 일 괄공제법 ▶ deffered method

FLSA 연방공정노동기준서

fluctuation (가격의) 변동

flying head 부동(浮動)부분 = floating head

flying spot scanner 비(飛)점 주사기구, 부(浮)점 주사기구

FMLA(Family and Medical Leave Act) 가족의료휴가법

FMV(fair market value) 공정시장가치

FNMA(Federl National Mortgage Association) 연방전국저당협회

FOB(free on board) 1) 본선인도(가격) 2) 제비용 무료

FOB airport 항공인도(가격)

FOB destination 선적지 인도조건, 본선인도 가격조건의 목적지

FOB destination(shipping point) 도착지 (선적지) 기준

FOB of particular term 특별규정의 본선인도가격조건

FOB seller's place of shipment 본선인도가격조건의 선적지의 판매처

FOB shipping point 목적지(도착지) 인도조건

FOB the place of destination FOB 목적지

FOB the place of shipment FOB 선적지

folding 접는

folio 장수 (페이지)

font 글자체

footing 합계, 합산

footnote 주석, 각주(脚注) = note
▶ headnote

footnote disclosure 주석공시

footnote to financial statement 재무제표의 주석

FOR(free on rail) 철도화차인도

forbearance 부작위(不作為)

forcasted transaction 미계약 예정거래

forced sale 강제매매, 경매처분

force majeure 불가항력(不可抗力)

for collection 징수

for deposit only 예입이 된

forecast 예측, 추정 ▶ estimate, projection

forecast and projection 추정과 프로젝션

forecasted balance sheet 추정대차대조표 = budgeted balance sheet

forecasted financial statement 추정재무제표 = budgeted financial statements

forecasted income statement 추정 손익계산서 = estimated income statement

forecasted transaction 예상거래

forecasting 예측, 예보, 견적, 추정

forecasting sales 판매액 예측

forecasting variance 예측차이
▶ ex post optimum analysis, opportunity cost variance

forecast of cash 현금예측

forecast of sales 판매액 예측

forecast profit and loss statement 추정손익계산서 = forecasted income statement

foreclosure 1) 차압 2) 유질(流質)처분 (處分), 담보권 실행매각 3) 담보물을 찾을 권리의 상실, 수여권의 상실

F

foreclosure sale 담보물의 매각
foregift (임대차계약의)권리금, 보증금
foreground 전경(前景)
foreground initiation 전경개시
foreground initiated background 전경기변경
foreground initiating 전경제기
foreground job 전경작업
foreground message processing program 전경 메시지 처리 프로그램
foreground processing 전경부 처리
foreground program 전경 프로그램
foreground region 전경영역
foreign asset 재외자산
foreign bill of exchange 외국환어음 ▶ inland bill of exchange
foreign bond 외채(外債) ▶ external bond
foreign branch 외국지점, 해외지점
foreign capital 외자(外資), 외국자본
foreign corporate bond 외국사채
foreign corporation 1) 외국기업, 외국회사, 외국법인 = alien corporation 2) 주(州)의 법인
Foreign Corrupt Practices Act 외국부패방지법
foreign currency 외화(外貨), 외국통화
foreign currency bill 외국환어음 = bill in foreign currency
foreign currency denominated forcasted transaction 외화에 의한 미계약 예정거래에 대한 해지
foreign currency financial statement 외화표시 재무제표 = foreign statements ▶ closing rate

method, foreign currency translation, temporal method
foreign currency fluctuation 외환 시세변동, 외국환율변동
foreign currency hedge 외환 헤지
foreign currency loan 외국환 차입금
foreign currency receivable 외화 표시채권
foreign currency receivables and payables 외화표시채권·채무 ▶ closing rate, current rate, foreign currency translation, one-transaction perspective, two-transaction perspective
foreign currency swap 외환 스왑
foreign currency transaction 외국환 거래, 외환거래 ▶ foreign currency receivables and payables, foreign currency translation
foreign currency transaction adjustment 외환거래조정금액
foreign currency transaction gain 외환거래이익
foreign currency transaction gain and loss 환손익, 외환거래손익
foreign currency transaction loss 외환거래손실
foreign currency translation 외화 환산, 외화환산회계 ▶ closing rate method, foreign currency financial statements, foreign currency receivables and payables, temporal method
foreign currency translation adjustment

외화환산 조정계정

foreign earned income exclusion 외
국소득공제

foreign entity 재외사업체, 재외사업 단
위 ▶ foreign operation

foreign exchange 외국환표기 단기어
음 ▶ domestic exchange

foreign exchange gain 외화환산차익
= exchange gain , exchange
profit

foreign exchange rate 외국환율, 외국
환시세

foreign government bond 외국국채

foreign investment 해외투자

foreign money order 외국우편환증권,
해외송금환 = overseas money
order

foreign operation 해외종속회사, 재외
영업활동체, 재외사업
▶ foreign entity

foreign statement 외화표시재무제표
= foreign currency financial
statement

foreign tax 외국세

foreign tax credit 외국세액공제
= deduction foreign tax

foreseeable party 예견가능 당사자, 예
상가능 제3자

foreseen party 예견당사자

foreseen third party 예상된 제3자

forfeiture 1) 몰수 2) 실권, 벌과금

forgery 위조(僞造), 변조

forgivable loan 변제조건부 융자
▶ goverment grant

form 서식, 양식, 형식, 용지

Form 10-K 연례보고서(annual report),
연차보고서양식

Form 10-Q 분기별보고서(quarterly
report)양식, 반기보고서양식

Form 8-K 임시보고서양식, 수시보고서
양식(current report)

formal arrangement 공식결제, 공식
계약

formal budget 정규예산

formal contract 정식계약

formal logic 형식이론

formal organization 형식조직, 공식
조직 ▶ informal organization

forman 직장, 직장주임

form and content of advice to client
고객에 대한 조언의 형태 및 내
용

form and substance 실질우선성

format 서식, 형식, 양식

format check 서식검사 ▶ field check

format effortor(FE) 서식제어문자
= layout character

format expense 창립비 = organization
expense, preliminary expense

format for account 재무제표양식

formation of corporation 법인의 설립

formation of partnership 합자회사
의 설립

Former Companies Act (영) 舊회사법

form feed character(FF) 서식전송, 용
지전송

form of business organization 기업
형태

form of qualification 한정의견의 방식

Form UCC-1 융자보고서

formula and secret process 화학식 소
유권에 대한 비밀제조법 권리

formula investing 공식을 이용한 투자

formula method 공식법

formula plan　공식계획

formulation of problem　문제의 정형화

formula type of variable budget　변동예산의 공식유형

for sale of goods　상품판매계약

for sale of land　토지판매계약

fortuious event　우발적 사건

fortune　1) 부, 재산　2) 운, 행운

for value　유상(有償), 대가를 주고

forward bargain　선물거래

forward contract　선물계약, 선인도계약

forward delivery　선인도

forward distribution　선물환계약

forward exchange　선물외국환, 선물외국환율 ▶ forward rate, spot dealing, spot exchange dealing, spot exchange rate, spot rate

forward exchange contract　선물환 계약, 선물환계약에 수반한 손익

forward exchange rate　선물환시세
　▶ spot exchange rate, spot rate

forward financial statement　미래재무제표 ▶ estimated financial statements

forwarding agent　통운업자, 화물 취급자

forwarding report　출하보고서

forward looking information　장래정보, 미래정보

forward price　선물가격

forward quotation　선물시세

forward rate　선물계약 레이트, 선물환시세, 예약시세

forward reading　순독(順讀)

forward transaction　선물거래

FOT(free on truck)　화차인도

foundation　1) 기초, 기초공사, 기초 구조　2) 재단　3) 기금

foundation collateral　재단저당, 재단담보

FPC(Federal Power Commission)　연방동력위원회

fractile　(통계) 분위(分位) = quantile

fractional currency　보조통화, 보조화폐

fractional equity retention　대부신탁채권의 미판매분

fractional programming　분수계획법

fractional share　단주(端株)

fractional share warrant　단주인수권증서

fractional year depreciation　감가상각의 분할계산

fraction of share　배당시의 단주

fragmentation　분할, 단편화

frame　열(列) = row

frame number　열의 번호

frame of reference　준거조항

framing　구성, 틀

framing bit　구성단위

franchise　프랜차이즈, 특권영업면허, 가맹권(加盟權)

franchise agreement　프랜차이즈 계약

franchisee　프랜차이즈 가맹자

franchise fee revenue　프랜차이즈료수익

franchise tax　1) 특별사업세 2) 면허세　3) 특권세　4) 각주의 법인세법상의 연차등록세

franchisor　프랜차이즈 주재자

franked investment income (FII)　(영)　납세후 투자이익 ▶ imputation system

franked payment ▶ imputation system

franked SORP (ASC승인)업종별 회계 실무 권고서 ▶ Statement of Recommended Practice

fraud 1) 허위표시 2) 부정, 허위, 사기 (詐欺) ▶ error

fraud in execution 작성상의 사기

fraud in factum 유언을 작성하는 것이 라고 속여 계약서에 서명하게 하는 것

fraud in inducement 증서상의 기망, 유인(誘引)상의 사기

fraud in the execution or factum 문 서작성상의 사기

fraud in the inducement 유인(誘因)상 의 사기

fraud risk factor 부정 위험 요인

fraudulent act 부정행위

fraudulent conveyance 사해적(詐害的) 재산양도, 사해행위

fraudulent financial reporting 부정 (不正)한 재무보고

fraudulent misrepresentation 악의 (惡意)의 왜곡표시

fraudulent preference (영)부정우선 지불, 사기적 편파행위

fraudulent trading 불공정거래

fraudulent transfer 사해적 양도

FRB(Board of Governors of the Federal Reserve System) 연방준비 제도이사회

FRB(Federal Reserve Bank) 연방준비 은행

FRB(Federal Reserve Board) 연방준비 위원회

FRC(Financial Reporting Coyncil) 재무

보고평의회

FRCD(floating rate certificate of deposit) 변동이율예금증서

free alongside 선측인도

free alongside ship(FAS) 선측인도 조건

free balance 실제잔고 = order cover

free capital 자유자본

free depreciation 자유상각

free distribution 무상교부

freedom from bias 불편성(不偏性) ▶ neutrality, quantification, relevance, verifiability

free economy 자유경제 ▶ planned economy

free enterprise (자본주의 경제체제하에서 의)자유기업(제도)

free float 자유변동, 환율의 자유변동제

free form from alongside (FFA) 선측 인도

freehand method 수묘법(手描法) ▶ method of selected point

freehold ▶ leasehold, property

freeholder (영)(부동산에대한)자유보유 권, 자유보유부동산 ▶ leaseholder

freehold estate 자유토지 부동산권

freehold land (영)자유토지보유자 ▶ leasehold land

freehold property (영)자유보유부동 산, 자유보유재산 ▶ property

free issue 무상교부 = bonus issue

free issue system 자유발행제도

freely negotiable credit 자유매수 신 용장

free market 자유시장

free of charge(FOC) 전비용이 포함된,

무료의, 제비용무료의

free on board(FOB) 본선인도가격
▶ cost, insurance and freight

free on rail(FOR) 화차인도가격
= free on truck ▶ free on board

free on truck(FOT) 화차인도가격
= free on rail

free rent 리스료의 지불액이 제로인 경우

free rent / uneven payment 리스료의 지불액이 제로인 경우/다른 기간 보다 소액인 경우

free routing 임의 경로지정

free share 무상주 = bonus stock

free share distribution 주식의 무상교부

free transferability of interest 주식양도의 자유

freight 운임 ▶ freight-in, freight-out

freightage 화물운송(료), 운임

freight collect 운임도착지불, 운임선지불방식

freightin 매입운임 = freight-in

freight-in 인수운임, 매입운임
= carriage-inward, freightin
▶ freight-out

freightout 운반비 = freight-out

freight-out 발송운임, 지불전송료
= carriage-out, freightout
▶ freight-in

freight rate 운임율

frequency 주파수

frequency distribution 도수분포(度數), 횟수분포

frequency division multiplex (FBM) 주파수분할 다중통신방식

frequency shift keying(FSK) 주파수변위방식

fresh start 새로운 출발

fresh start method 신출발법 ▶ quasi-reorganizatiion aproach

fresh start procedure 신출발법, 신규출발법

fringe benefit 경제적 이익, 후생급부

fringe benefit plan 복리후생제도

FRN(floating rate note) 변동이자부 채권

frolic 환락, 피고용인의 작업궤도에서 이탈한 경우

front office 본부, 본사, 본점

frozen asset 동결자산

frozen fund 회수불능자금 = frozen loan

frozen loan 회수불능대부금 = frozen fund

frozen stock 냉동품, 동결품 = dead stock

FRR(financial reporting release) 재무보고 통첩(通牒)

FRS(Federal Reserve System) 연방준비제도

fruit 1) (pl) 성과, 결과, 수익 2) 과실, 열매

frustration 1) 이행불능 계약목적 달성불능 2) 욕구불만

FSC(Financial System Council) 재무제도심의회

FSCA(Fellow of the Society of Company and Commercial Accountants) 회사·상업회계사협회의 정회원

FSIA(Fellow of the Society of Investment Analysts) 투자분석가협회 정회원의 칭호

**FSLIC(Federal Saving and Loan
     Insurance Corporation)**   연
     방저축대부보험회사
FTC(Federal Trade Commission)   연방
     통상위원회
F-test   F검정
FTIT(Fellow of the Institute of Taxation)
     조세협회 정회원칭호
FTL(federal tax lien)   연방세금 담보권
fuel cost   연료비 = fuel expense
fuel expense   연료비
full absorption costing   전부원가계산
     = full costing
full accrual method   완전발생기준, 완
     전발생주의(부동산회계)
full adder   전부가산법 = three-input
     adder
full and fair disclosure   완전하고 공정
     한 공시
**full, articulated set of financial
     statements**   충분하고 상호
     유기성을 가진 한 조의 재무제
     표
full capacity   완전조업도 = maximum
     capacity
full consolidation   전부연결
     ▶ consolidated financial
     statements, proportional
     consolidation
full cost   전부원가 = fully allocated cost,
     fully distributed cost
full cost accounting   전부원가계산
     = full costing
full cost approach   전부원가법 = full
     cost basis
full cost basis   전부원가법 = full cost
     approach

full costing   전부원가계산 = absorption
     cost system, full absorption
     costing, full cost accounting,
     full cost system, total costing
full costing method   총발생원가 자산
     계상방식 ▶ reserve recognition
     accounting, successful effort
     costing
full cost method   전부원가법
full cost principle   전부원가 원칙
full cost system   전부원가계산 = full
     costing
full disclosure   완전공시, 충분한 명료
     표시(공개명시)
full disclosure principle   완전공시의
     원칙
full eligibility   완전자격
full eligibility date   모든 자격 취득일
full endorsement   기명식배서
full equity method   완전지분법
full performance   완전이행, 전부이행
full product cost transfer price   총원
     가 가산에 기준한 이전 가격
full provision basis   완전 세(稅)효과
     회계, 소득세의 완전기간배분
     = comprehensive tax allocation
full subtracter   전부감산법
fullword   모든 언어
fully allocated cost   완전배부원가
     = full cost
fully depreciated asset   상각완료자산
fully diluted earnings per share   (영)
     완전희석화 1주당이익 ▶ basic
     earnings per share, dual
     presentation of earnings per share
fully distributed cost   완전배부원가
     = full cost

F

fully owned subsidiary　전액소유자회계, 완전소유자회계

fully paid share　(영)불입완료주식, 전액납입완료주식 ▶ called-up share capital, paid-up share capital, partly paid share

fully participating　완전참가

fully participating preferred stock　완전참가적 우선주

fully secert trust　완전비밀신탁 = secert trust ▶ halfsecret trust

function　1) 함수　2) 기능, 직능, 작용, 목적, 직무

functional　모든 함수의

functional accounting　직능별 회계

functional analysis　기능분석, 함수분석

functional auditing　직능별 감사

functional authority　기능별 권한, 직능별권한 ▶ line authority, staff authority

functional classification　직능별 분류

functional cost　기능별 원가분류

functional cost classification　기능별 원가회계 = cost element

functional costing　기능별 원가계산법, 직능별 원가계산법

functional currency　기능통화 = local currency ▶ closing rate method, foreign currency translation, reporting currency

functional decentralization　직능적 분권제 = decentralization

functional decomposition　직능분할 ▶ structured design

functional depreciation　기능적 감가 ▶ inadequacy, obsolescence, physical depreciation

functional design　기능설계

functional diagram　기능도(圖)

functional division　직능별 부문

functional fixation　기능적 고정화

functional obsolesence　기능적 진부화, 기능적 감가 ▶ cost approach, depreciation, external obsolesence, physical deterioration

functional organization　기능적 조직 ▶ divisional organization

functional pricing　기능적 가격측정법 = unit pricing

functional requirement　기능적 요구 ▶ non-functional requirement, requirement

functional unit　기능단위

functioning　기능

function key　기능 키

function part　기능부, 조작부 = operation part, operator part

function reference　함수인용, 함수참조

function table　함수표

fund　1) 자금 ▶ fund concept, working capital　2) 기금

fund accounting　기금회계, 수지(收支) 회계

fundamental accounting assumption　회계의 기본적 전제, 회계공준

fundamental accounting concept　(영) 회계의 기초개념 ▶ accounting principle, convention

fundamental analysis　(투자의) 기본 분석 ▶ technical analysis

fundamental concept　기본 컨셉, 기본 개념

fundamental recognition criteria and

guidance   기본적 인식기준 및 지침

fundamental research   기초적 조사
▶ basic research

fundamentals   근본원리

fundamental sector   (국민소득회계상의) 기본부문

fund asset   연금자산

fund balance   (회계단위에서의) 기금 순재산, 기금잔고 = fund equity

fund balance sheet   기금대차대조표

fund budget   자금예산

fund concept   자금개념

fund debt   1) 기한부 국채 (영)
▶ teminable annuity, unfuned debt 2) 고정부채, 장기부채
3) 사채발행차입금 = boned debt

funded status   조금조달상태

fund equity   (회계단위에서의) 기금 순재산, 기금잔고 = fund balance

fund financial statement   기금재무제표

fund flow   자금흐름

fund flow accounting   자금흐름회계, 자금수지회계

fund flow per share   1주당 자금흐름
= cash flow per share ▶ cash flow

fund flow statement   자금흐름계산서

fund for retirement of bond   사채 상환기금 ▶ amortization fund, sinking fund

fund from operation   영업활동에 의한 자금

funding   적립, 기금 설립 ▶ retirement benefit plan

funding agency   자금제공기관, 기금 적립기관

funding policy   적립보험계약

fund in hand   보유자금, 현금보유고
▶ fund on hand

fund obligation   기금채무

fund on hand   보유자금 ▶ fund in hand

fund provided by operation   영업활동에 의해 공급된자금

fund raising   자금조달

fund statement   자금계산서
= statement of change in financial position

fund theory   자금이론

fungible asset   대체가능자산
▶ weighted averae, weighted average price

furnishing   비품

fusion   기업결합, 기업활동

FUTA (Federal Unemplotment Tax Act)   연방실업자구제세법, 연방실업보험세법

FUTA tax   연방실업세

future advance   장래권

future amount   미래현금금액
▶ teminal value

future cashflow   미래현금흐름

future cost   미래원가 ▶ actual cost, future value, historical cost, past cost, present cost

future cost accounting   미래원가계산
▶ actual cost accounting

future deductible amount   미래 손금이 되는 금액

future economic benefits   미래의 경제적 효익

future goods   미확정상품

future interest   장래(將來)권, 미래권

F

future interest in real property　부동
산의 미래이익
future price　선물가격
future revenue　미래수익
future sacrifice of economic benefit
　　미래의 경제적 효익의 희생
futures contract　선물(先物)계약
future service　미래의 용역
futures interest　선물 구입권
futures purchase and sale　선물매매
future taxable income　미래 과세되는
　　수입
future tax rate　실제로 과세될 때의 세율

future value(FV)　미래가치, 종가
　　▶ future cost
future value of annuity　연금의 미래
　　가치
future value of an ordinary annuity
　　연금의 미래가치
future value of money　화폐의 미래 가
　　치　▶ time value of money (화
　　폐의 시간가치)
FV of asset received　자산취득의 미래
　　가치
FYA(first year allowance)　(영) 초년도
　　상각

G

**GAAP (Generally Accepted Accounting
　　Princing principles)**　일반
　　적으로 인정된 회계원칙
GAAP departure　일반적으로 인정된
　　회계원칙의 위배
**GAAS (Generally Accepted Auditing
　　Standards)**　일반적으로 인
　　정된 감사기준
**G & A expense (general and
　　administrative expense)**　일
　　반관리비
gage　저당물, 담보
gain　1) 이익 ▶ expense, revenue 2) 이
　　득 ▶ capital gain, loss 3) 주가
　　시세의 상승 4) 주가상승 기업
**gain and loss from early extinguishment
　　of debt**　채무의 조기상환에
　　의해 생긴 손익

gain and loss on business property
　　사업자산의 이익과 손실
gain contingency　우발이익, 우발이득
　　▶ loss contingency
gain from appreciation of security
　　유가증권평가익
**gain from decline in purchasing power
　　of net amount owed**　순부
　　채액에 관련된 구매력의 하락
　　에 기인하는 이득 ▶ monetary
　　gain or loss, purchasing power
　　gain or loss
**gain from decline in the value of
　　money**　화폐가치 하락에 따
　　른 이익 = purchasing power
　　gain on monetary items
　　▶ loss from decline in the
　　value of money, purchasing

power gain or loss on net monetary items

gain from forgiveness of debt   채무면제익

gain from reduction of capital stock   감자차익

gain from troubled debt restructuring   변제곤란한 차입금의 재조정에 의한 이익

gain on conversion of stock   주식전환이익

gain on disposal of equipment   설비처분이익

gain on redemption of stock   주식상환익

gain on sale   처분이익

gain on sale of equipment   설비매각이익

gain on sale of securities   유가증권 처분이익

gain on sale of treasury stock   자기주식처분익 ▶ profit on treasury stock

gain or loss   손익

gain or loss in purchasing power   구매력 손익

gain or loss on disposal of fixed asset   고정자산처분손익 ▶ gain or loss on sales of fixed asset

gain or loss on foreign currency exchange or translation   환차손익

gain or loss on redemption of bond   사채상환손익

gain or loss on retirement of fixed asset   고정자산처분손익

gambling   1) 내기 2) 투기 ▶ speculation

gambling loss   투기손실

gambling winning   도박소득

game theory   게임이론

Gantt chart   간트 도표

GAO (Governmental Accounting Office)   회계감사원

gap period   갭 기간

garnishee   제3채무자

garnishee order   권리차압명령

garnishee proceeding   권리차압절차

garnishment   채권차압 통고, 채권압류

GAS(Government Auditing Standard)   정부감사기준

GASB(Governmental Accounting Standard Board)   정부회계기준 심의회, 지방정부회계기준 심의회

GASB Statement   정부회계기준 심의회 보고서

gate   입구, 문

gate card   출근표 = clock card

GATT(General Agreement on Tariffs and Trade)   관세와 무역에 관한 일반협정

Gaussian distribution   가우시안 분포 ▶ normal distribution

Gazette   (영) 관보(官報) ▶ annual return

GDP (gross domestic products)   1) 국내총생산 2) 국내총생산물

gearing   (영) 레버리지, 보통주자본 이외의 장기자본이 보통주 이익에 공헌 ▶ financial leverage, leverage, trading on the equity

gearing adjustment   (영) 기어링 조정액, 부채조정액 ▶ gearing proportion, monetary working capital, net borrowing, net

G

operating assets

gearing proportion　(영) 기어링 조정율,
부채조정율 ▶ gearing,
adjustment, net borrowing, net
operating assets

gearing ratio　우선자본비율 ▶ gearing,
prior charge capital

general acceptance　1) 일반인수 2) (일
반적으로 인정되는 회계원칙 요건
의) 일반적 승인성
▶ generally accepted
accounting principles

general account　일반계정

General Accounting Office (GAO)　회
계검사원

general administrative cost　일반관리
비 ▶ general cost

general administrative expense　일반
관리비 = general and
asdministrative expense
▶ selling expense

general administrative expense budget
일반관리비 예산

general administrative expense ledger
일반관리비 원장

general agent　포괄대리인

**General Agreement on Tariffs and
Trade (GATT)**　관세와 무역
에 관한 일반협정 = general
administrative expense
▶ selling expense

**general and administrative expense
(G & A expense)**　일반관리비

**general assignment for benefit of
creditor**　재산 청산 신탁

general audit　일반감사

general business credit　일반적인 영업

상 세액공제

general carrier　운송인

general commissioner　(영) 국세불복
심판관

**general concept of negotiable
instrument**　교부성 증서의
일반 개념

general contingency reserve　일반우
발손실준비금

general control　일반통제

general control for computer　컴퓨터
에 대한 일반통제

general corporation cost　본사비
▶ central corporate expense,
corporation cost

general cost　일반비 = general expense
▶ general administrative cost

general credit　매수은행 부지정 신용
장, 무조건신용장 = negotiation
credit, open credit

general crossing　일반횡선

general disclaimer　일반적 포기(抛棄),
일반적 책임해제

general expense　일반비 = general cost
▶ indirect departmental
overhead cost

general file　일반사항조사철

general fixed asset　일반고정자산

**general fixed asset account group
(GFAAG)**　일반고정자산 계
정그룹

general fund　일반기금

general gift　일반증여 ▶ specific gift

general index of retail price　소매물가
지수 ▶ wholesale price index

general inflation　일반물가상승, 일반물
가수준의 상승 ▶ general price-

level change

general information   일반정보

general intangible   (특허권, 상표권) 무체재산. 일반무형재산

generalization   일반이론, 일반화, 보편화

generalized audit program   범용 감사 프로그램 ▶ computer audit program

generalized audit software   범용 감사 소프트웨어, 일반화된 감사 소프트웨어

general journal   일반분개장

general ledger   총계정원장, 원장

general ledger controlling account   총계정원장의 통제계정

general ledger treatment   총계정원장의 처리

general ledger trial balance   총계정원장의 잔액시산표

general long term debt   일반고정부채

general long term debt account group   일반고정부채 계정그룹

generally accepted accounting principle (GAAP)   일반적으로 인정된 회계기준

generally accepted auditing standard (GAAS)   일반적으로 인정된 감사기준

general meeting of stockholder   주주총회

general obligation fund   일반공채

general operating expense   일반영업활동비, 일반영업비

general partner   1) 무한책임 파트너, 무한책임사원 2) 일반파트너

general partnership   1) 일반 파트너십

2) 합명회사, 통상조합
 ▶ limited partnership

general price index   일반물가변동지수, 일반물가지수

general price level accounting (GPLA)   일반물가(수준)변동회계
 = accounting for changes in the general price level, constant purchasing power accounting

general price level adjusted statement   일반물가수준 수정재무제표
 ▶ constant purchasing power accounting

general price level change   일반물가변동 = general inflation

general price level index   일반물가지수 ▶ consumer's price index, wholesale price index

general purchasing power   일반구매력

general purchasing power accounting (GPPA)   일반구매력회계
 = constant purchasing power accounting

general purchasing power of the dollar   달러의 일반구매력, 화폐구매력

general purpose external financial reporting   일반목적 외부재무보고

general purpose financial statement   일반목적 재무제표, 일반목적 보고서

general purpose governmental unit   일반목적 정부단위

general purpose statement   일반목적 재무제표

general questionnaire   전반적인 질문

G

서

general rate   (영) 일반 부동산세 ▶ rate

general reserve   별도적립금
▶ allowance, reserve

general solicitation   일반 권유(勸誘)

general standard   일반기준

general standard of auditing   감사일
반기준

general supervision department   총무
부

general tax revenue   일반세수입(一般
税收入)

general undertaking   (영) USM상장 일
반협정 ▶ Green Book, listing
agreement

general warranty deed   일반적 담보
책임 증서

generation skipping tax   세대를 뛰어
넘은 세금

generator   생성프로그램

generic name   총칭 (總稱), 총칭명

geographical segment   지역별 부문, 지
역별 구획 ▶ segmental
reporting, segment reporting

geographical segment information
지역별 부문정보 ▶ industry
segment information, segment
reporting

geographic area   소재지

geographic information   지리정보

geographic segment report   지역별 부
문보고 ▶ segmental reporting,
segment reporting

geological and geographical cost   지
질학과 지리학적 원가
= G&G cost

geometric mean   기하평균

▶ arithmetric mean

GFA and GLTD account group   일반
고정자산 및 일반고정부채 계
정그룹

**G&G cost (geological and geographical
cost)**   지질학과 지리학적 원
가

Giffen's goods   기펜 재화

gift   증여(贈與) ▶ cash donation,
donation, grant

gift and estate taxation   증여세와 상속
세

gift certificate   증여권

gift expense   증여 비용

gift inter vivos   생전(生前)증여

gift mortis causa   사인(死因)증여
= donatio mortis causa

gift on account of death   유증(遺贈)

gift splitting   증여 분할, 증여 분배

gift tax   증여세

gift tax formula   증여세 공식

gift tax return   증여세 신고서

gilt   (영) 영국정부발행의 국채
= gilt-edged security

gilt-edged security   금제 증권, 금테 증
권 = gilt, government security

giro   은행(우편) 대체제도 ▶ bank giro

glamour stock   성장주, 인기주(株), 소
형성장주

Glass-Steagall Act   글래스 · 스티걸 법

global value of business   기업가치, 기
업평가액(에 대한 회계)

global variable symbol   대구역 변수
기호, 대구역 가변기호

glossary   용어 해설

glut   공급과잉, 재고과다

GNMA (Government National Mortgage

Association) 정부전국 저당
협회

GNP (gross national products) 국민총
생산

GNP deflator GNP 디플레이터
= GNP implict deflator

GNP implict deflator GNP 디플레이
터 = GNP deflator ▶ implict
deflator

goal 목표, 최종목표

going concern 계속기업, 영속기업
▶ axiom, going concern value,
postulate, quitting concern

going concern assumption 계속기업
의 공준, 계속기업의 가정
▶ convention, postulate

going concern concept 계속기업의 개
념

going concern consideration 계속기
업 고려사항

going concern principle 계속기업의
원칙

going concern value 계속기업의 가치

going private 주식의 비공개 ▶ going
public

going public 주식의 공개, 주식의 상장

gold basis 금본위제

gold bloc 금본위제 지역

golden handcuff 소유자의 업무집행
조건의 기업매수

golden handshake (고액의) 퇴직금

golden parachute (감사인에 대한) 임기
보장제도

golden share 특권주

Gompertz curve 굼페르츠 곡선

good debt 우량대부

good faith 성실

good faith purchaser 선의(善意)의 유
상(有償)취득자

good faith purchaser for value 대가
를 치른 선의(善意)의 구입자

good for the week 금주 동안 유효

goodness-of-fit test 적합도 검정 = test
goodness of fit

good paper 일류상업어음

goods 재화, 물품, 상품, 상제품

goods available for sale 판매가능상품
= cost of goods available for
sale

goods held for sale 판매를 위해 소유
하고 있는 상품

goods in process 재공품 = work-in-
process, work in process

goods in transit 미달상품, 미착상품, 운
송중인 물품

goods on approval 시송품(試送品)

goods on consignment 적송품
= consignment

goods on consignment-in 수탁품

goods on consignment-out 위탁품, 적
송품

goods on hand 재고품, 수탁품재고

goods received note(GRN) 상품수령
증, 품목수령증

goods sold on credit 외상판매상품
▶ credit sale

goods sold on installment 할부판매상
품

good till cancelled(GTC) 취소유효
▶ day order

good title 정당한 권원(權原)

goodwill 영업권 ▶ excess earnings
power

goodwill amortization 영업권상각

goodwill method   영업권법
goodwill on consolidation   연결영업
권, 합병영업권
goodwill recorded   계상된 영업권
governing and oversight body   통제
와 감독기관
governing body   감독기관
government   정부기관
Government Accountants Journal
미국정부회계담당자협회가 발
행하는 공공회계에 관련된 기
관지
governmental accounting   정부회계
Governmental Accounting Standard
Board (GASB)   정부회계기
준심의회
governmental agency   정부기관
governmental auditing   정부감사
governmental auditing responsibility
정부감사의 책임
governmental auditing standard   정
부감사기준
governmental fund   정부형 기금
▶ general fund, special
revenuefund, capital projects
fund, debt service fund
Governmental National Mortgage
Association(GNMA)   정부
전국저당협회
governmental organization   정부기
관
governmental regulatory agency's
standard   정부규제기관의
기준
governmental regulatory organization
정부규제기관
government assistance   정부원조, 정

부조성(助成) ▶ governmental
grant
Government Auditing Standards(GAS)
정부 감사기준
government grant   국고보조금, 정부
조성금
▶ forgivable loan,
governmental assistance
government guarantee   정부보증(채권)
government owned   공적(公的) 소유
government sector   정부부문
government security   정부증권, 국채
government sponsored entity   정부
가 지원하는 기관
government stock   (영) 국채, 장기국채
= gilt-edged security,
government security
▶ treasury bill
governmentwide financial statement
정부단위 재무제표
GPLA (general price level accounting)
일반물가수준변동회계
GPPA (general purchasing power
accounting)   일반구매력회계
GPSS (general purpose systems simulator)
일반목적제도 시뮬레이터
grace period   특혜기간
gradation   우선순위, 등급표기
grade   1) 등급, 정도 2) 성적
graded vesting   단계적 권리확정
graduated tax rate   단계세율
grandfather-father-son method   조
부·부·자 방법
grant   보조금, 교부금 ▶ subsidy,
subvention
grant deed   거래양도증서
grantee index   양수인 색인

grant in aid 조성금(助成金)

grantor 교부자

grantor-grantee index 양도 · 양수인 색인

grantor trust 자익(自益)신탁

graphic 도형(圖形)

graphic analysis 도표분석

graphic analysis program 도표분석 프로그램

graphic character 도표문자

graphic display program 도표표시 프로그램

graphic form 도표형식

graphic job processing 도표작업처리

graphic presentation 도표를 통한 보고, 도표표시

graphic statement 도표식 보고서

gratuitous agent 무상대리인

gratuitous agreement 무상의 양도

gratuitous bailee 무상의 기부 수여자

gratuitous promise 무상의 약속

Gray code 그레이 코드 = reflect binary code

greater quorum 정족수(투표권이 있는 주식의 과반수 이상 출석)

greenback 그린 지폐, (미)달러 지폐

Green Book (영국, 이탈리아 등의) 정부 간행물, (미국에서 외국인 노동자 에게 발행하는) 공문서, 입국허가 증 ▶ general undertaking, Yellow Book

green card 입국허가증 ▶ white card, yellow card

green mail (영) 주식의 고액매수 요구

Green Paper (영) 정부의 견해를 발표 하는 문서

grid 격자(格子)

GRM (gross rent multiplier) 총임대 료 승수

GRN (goods received note) 상품수령증, 품목수령증

gross amount of purchase 총매입량

gross book value 감가상각누계액 공제 전 장부가액 = gross carrying amount

gross carrying amount 장부가총액, 감가상각누계액 공제 전 장부가 액 = gross book value

gross cash flow 총현금흐름 ▶ cash flow

gross cost 총원가 ▶ gross manufacturing cost

gross current replacement cost 총현 행대체원가, 감가상각비 공제 전 현행대체원가

gross dividend 총배당 ▶ imputation system

gross dividend per share 1주당 총배 당

gross dividend yield 총주가배당율

gross domestic product (GDP) 국내 총생산, 국내총생산물 ▶ gross national product

gross estate 총유산액

gross income 총익금, 총수입, 총소득

gross income multiplier 총수익승수 = gross rent multiplier

gross income on individual return 개인소득세 신고시의 총수익

gross investment 총투자 ▶ net investment

gross investment in a lease 리스 총투 자액, 리스투자 미회수 총액

gross invoice price 총송장가격 ▶ net

invoice price

gross loss 매출총손실 ▶ gross margin,
gross profit

gross loss on sales 매출총손실 ▶ gross
profit on sales

gross manufacturing cost 총제조원가
▶ factory cost , manufacturing
cost

gross margin 매출총이익 = gross profit
▶ gross loss

gross margin method 매출총이익률법
= gross profit method

gross margin on sale 매출총이익

gross margin percentage 매출총이익
률 = gross margin ratio, gross
profit percentage

gross margin ratio 매출총이익률
= gross profit percentage

gross method 총액법

gross national product(GNP) 국민총
생산 ▶ gross domestic
product, net national product

**gross national product implict price
deflator (GNP deflator)** 총
합물가지수 ▶ implict deflator

gross negligence 과실의 추정

gross operating spread 총영업이익폭

gross premium 총보험료

gross profit 매출총이익 = gross margin
▶ gross loss

gross profit method 매출총이익법

gross profit on sales 매출총이익

gross profit percentage 매출총이익률
= gross margin percentage,
gross margin ratio

gross profit percentage method 매출
총이익률법

gross profit ratio 매출총이익률 = gross
margin ratio, gross profit
percentage

gross profit ratio test 매출총이익률
검사 ▶ gross profit ratio

gross profit realized 이연할인매출 이
익 환입

gross profit test 매출총이익 검사

gross receipt 총수입

gross rent multiplier (GRM) 총임대료
승수 = gross income multiplier
▶ over-all rate

gross residual value 총잔존가액

gross sales 총매출액

gross turnover (영) 총매출액

gross up 공제하기 전의 총액

gross up method 그로스업 방식, 총액
식 = imputation system
▶ mainstream corporation tax

gross value 연간임대차가액 ▶ group
account

gross working capital 총운전자본

group (영) 기업집단

group account (영) 그룹재무제표, 기
업집단재무제표
= group financial statements
▶ consolidated financial
statements

**group and composite method of
depreciation** 종합상각법

group code 집단부호

group company (영) 기업집단구성회
사, 그룹구성회사 ▶ group
relief

group depreciation 조별상각
▶ composite depreciation, unit
depreciation

group depreciation method 조별상각법

group dynamics 그룹역동학

grouped record 그룹화 기록

group financial statement 기업집단 재무제표 = group accounts ▶ consolidated financial statements, consolidated accounts

group income (영) 그룹 내 배당소득

group indicate 그룹표시, 집단표시

grouping sheet 분류집계표

group item 집단항목

group mark 그룹 마크

group number 그룹번호

group of user 회계정보의 이용자 집단

group-rate method 조별상각법 ▶ composite rate method

group relief (영) 그룹세액공제 ▶ group company

group term insurance 그룹 기간 보험

growing crop 육성중인 작물 ▶ crop basis

growth stock 성장주(株)

GTC (good till cancelled) 취소유효

guarantee 담보

guarantee company (영) 보증유한회사 = company limited by guarantee

guaranteed bond 보증부 사채

guarantee deposit received 예수보증금

guaranteed residual value 보증잔존가액

guarantee for replacement 상품대체보증

guarantee for service 서비스에 대한 보증

guarantor 보증인

guarantor of collection 회수보증인

guarantor payment 지불보증인

guaranty 1) 보증, 보증계약, 담보 2) 보증인 ▶ debtor-creditor relationships(채권자와 채무자의 관계)

guaranty contract 보증계약

guaranty for collection 징수 보증

guaranty for payment 지불 보증

guardian 후견인

guidance 지침

Guidance Note (영) 안내서 ▶ Technical Release

H

H

half a bar 50만

half-secret trust 반(半)익명신탁

half-yearly report 반기보고서 ▶ interim report, quarterly report

Halon gas fire extinguisher 할론 가스 소화기

Halsey premium plan 할시 할증임금제도

halt instruction 휴지명령, 정지명령, 중

단명령 = pasue instruction

Hamming code 해밍 코드

Hamming distance 해밍 거리

haphazard sampling 우연표본조사, 임의표본조사

haphazard selection 임의표본추출법

harmonic mean 조화평균

harmonization 조화화, 일치

Harvard Businesss Review 하버드 대학 대학원 경영학연구과 (Harvard University Graduate School of Businesss Admlnistration)의 기관지. 1922년 창간 격월간지

hash total 해시 합계 ▶ batch control, batch total

HCA(historical cost accounting, historic cost accounting) 취득원가주의회계, 역사적 원가회계

HDC(holder in the course) 정당한 절차에 의한 소지인

HDR(header label) 표제, 색인표

header 표제, 제자(題子)

heading 표제, 색인, 차례

head lease 주(主)리스

headnote 두주(頭注), 두서(頭書) ▶ footnote

head office 본점, 본사 = home office ▶ branch

head office ledger 본사원장

Health Insurance Portability and Accountability Act 회사 간 누적건강보험 및 보고책임 법률

heating expense 난방비, 광열비

heat light and power 광열동력비

heavy industry 중공업 ▶ light industry

hedge (손실, 위험에 대한) 방지책

= hedging

hedge accounting 위험분산회계

hedge fund 헷지펀드

hedging 1) (손실, 위험에 대한) 방지책 = hedge 2) (商)연계매매

heirs (유언이 없었을 때) 상속인

heirs per stripes 대습(代襲) 상속인

held-to-maturity security 만기보유증권

hereditament 상속재산

heuristic approach 휴리스틱 접근법

heuristic method 휴리스틱 접근법

heuristic program 휴리스틱 프로그램

heuristic programing 휴리스틱 계획법

HIDC(holder in due course) 정당한 소지인

hidden line 음선(陰線),

hidden reserve 비밀적립금 = secret reserve

hierarchical database 계층적 데이터베이스

hierarchical structure 계층구조

hierarchy 계층구조

hierarchy of needs theory 욕구단계설, 욕구계층설 = needs hierarchy theory

HIFO(highest-in, first-out method) 최고가격선출(先出)법

highest and best use 최고유효사용

highest-in, first-out method(HIFO) 최고가격선출법

highlights 재무정보요약 ▶ annual report, financial highlight, selected financial data

high-low chart 고 · 저점 도표

high-low method 고 · 저점법 = high-low point method

high-low point method   고 · 저점법
　　= high-low method ▶ regression
　　analysis, scattergarph method
high-order digit   최고위숫자
high-order position   고순위
high speed carry   고속이동
high street bank   시중은행
hindsight   사후판단편견
hire charge   임차료
hire-purchase   (영)매수선택권부 임차
hire-purchase contract   (영)매수선택
　　권부 임대차계약서
hirer   임차인
historical analysis   역사적 분석법, 실적
　　분석법 = analysis of past
　　experience
historical buying price   역사적 구입
　　가격 = historical cost
　　▶ historical selling price
historical cost   취득원가, 역사적 원가
　　= historical buying price
historical cost account   (영)역사적 원
　　가 재무제표 ▶ current cost
　　accounts
historical cost accounting(HCA)   역사
　　적 원가회계, 취득원가주의회
　　계 ▶ currett cost accunting,
　　inflation accounting
historical cost accounting rules   (영)
　　취득원가주의 회계의 제규칙
historical cost basis   취득원가주의, 취
　　득원가기준 = acquisition cost
　　theory
historical cost-constant dollar
　　accounting   취득 원가-불변
　　화폐가치회계, 취득원가통일구
　　매력회계, 수정원가회계

　　= historical cost-constant
　　purchasing power accounting
historical cost-constant purchasing
　　power accounting   취득원
　　가-불변구매력회계, 수정원가
　　회계 = historical cost-constant
　　dollar accounting ▶ accounting
　　for changes in the general price
　　level
historical cost convention   역사적 원
　　가관행, 역사적 원가주의
　　= cost basis, cost concept, cost
　　convention, cost nethod
　　▶ historical cost accounting
historical costing   실제원가계산(엄격한
　　실제원가회계) = historical cost
　　system ▶ actual cost
　　accounting
historical cost/nominal dollar
　　accounting   취득원가/명목
　　달러(화폐)회계 = historical cost
　　accounting
historical cost system   역사적 원가회계
　　= historical costing ▶ actual
　　cost accounting, actual cost
　　basis, actual cost system
historical financial information   역사
　　적 재무정보, 취득원가주의에
　　의한 재무정보
historical financial statement   취득 원
　　가주의에 의한 재무제표
historical overhead rate   제조간접비
　　실제배부율
historical price   역사적 가격
　　▶ historical cost
historical proceed   실제 현금수령액
historical rate   거래발생일 비율, 취득

H

시 비율 ▶ closing rate, current rate

historical selling price 역사적 매각원가, 역사적 판매가격
▶ historical buying price

historical value 역사적 가치 ▶ current market value

hit ratio 성공율

holder 소지인(所持人)

holder by due negotiation 정당한 교부에 의한 소지인

holder in due course 정당한 절차에 의한 소지인

holder in the course 정당한 소지인

holder through a holder in due course 정당한 소지인을 통한 소지인

holding 1) 소유, 보유, 보유고, 보유품 2) (pl) 소유주식, 소유지(地)

holding company 1) 지주(持株)회사 2) 친회사

holding cost 보관비, 재고비용
= inventory carrying cost

holding gain 보유이익 ▶ current cost accounting holding loss, realized holding gain, unrealized holding gain

holding gain and loss 보유손익
▶ capital gain

holding loss 보유손실 ▶ holding gain

holiday pay 휴일임금, 휴일근무수당

holograph will 자율유언서

home-branch accounting 본지점회계
▶ combined financial statement

home currency 본국통화, 자국통화
▶ local currency

home office 본점(本店) = head office
▶ front office

home office control 본점계정

home pages 홈페이지

home product 국산품

homestead (부속 건물이 있는) 주택

homogeneity of cost in relation to revenue 수익에 관련 있는 원가의 동질성

horizontal check 수평검사

horizontal flowchart 수평흐름도

horizontal merger 수평적 합병
▶ conglomerate merger, vertical merger

horizontal privity 수평적 상호관계

horizontal tabulation character(HT) 수평도표작성문자

hospital accounting 병원회계

hotchpot 재산병합

hot meney 금리선호형 국제이동자본

hourly burden plan 시간률법

hourly rate 시간임률

household bookkeeping 가계부기

housekeeping 가정의

housekeeping operation 가계부기연산
= overhead operation

housing association 주택구입조합, 주택건설협회 ▶ building and loan association, building society

Howey test 하우이 테스트(SEC가 규정하는 특자자산의 적격성에 대한 네 가지 조건)

HRA(human resource accounting) 인적자산회계 = human asset accounting ▶ accounting model of human resource

human asset accounting 인적자산회계, 인간자산회계 = human

resource accounting

human control   대인통제

human engineering   조작성 ▶ usability

human information processing   인적
정보처리

human resource   인적자원

human resource accounting(HRA)
인적자원회계 = human asset
accounting

human service organization   인적 용
역제공기관

humidity control   습도조절

hundred   백(百)

Hyde Guideline   ▶ Morpeth Committee

hypergeometric distribution   초기하
분포

hyperinflation   초(超)인플레이션

hypertext markup language(HTML)
HTML언어

hypothec   저당권

hypothecated asset   담보제공자산
= pledged asset

hypothecation   담보계약

hypothecation agreement   담보계약

hypothec bank   산업은행

hysteresis loop   이력(履歷)곡선

I

IA(initial allowance)   (영)기초고율상각

IA(intermediate area)   (영)중(中)규모 개
발지역

IAA(Institute of Adminisrative Accountants)
관리회계인 협회

**IAAA(Inter-American Accounting
Association)**   남북아메리카
회계사연합, 미국대륙회계연합

IAG(International Auditing Guideline)
감사의 국제적 지침

**IAG/RSs(International Guidelines on
Auditing and Related Services)**
감사 및 감사관련업무에 대한
국제 지침

**IAPC(International Auditing Practices
Committee)**   국제감사실무
위원회

IAS(International Accounting Standards)
국제회계기준

**IASC(International Accounting Standards
Committee)**   국제회계기준
위원회

IASG(Inflation Accounting Steering Group)
(영)물가변동회계 운영위원회

**IBRD(International Bank for
Reconstruction and
Development)**   국제부흥개발
은행

IC(import certificate)   수입증명서

IC(integrated circuit)   집적회로

ICA(integrated communication adapter)
통신통합어댑터

**ICA(International Communication
Association)**   국제통신협회

ICA(International Congress of Accountants)
국제회계사회의

ICAEW(Institute of Chartered Accountants in England and Wales) 잉글랜드와 웨일즈의 공인회계사협회

ICAI(Institute of Chartered Accountants in Ireland) 아일랜드의 공인회계사협회

ICAS(Institute of Chartered Accountants of Scotland) 스코틀랜드의 공인회계사협회

ICC(International Computation Center) 국제계산센터

ICC(Interstate Commerce Commission) 주제(州際)상무위원회

ICCAP(International Committee for the Coordinations of the Accountancy Profession) 회계업무국제협조위원회

ICFA(Institute of Chartered Financial Analysts) 공인재무분석가협회

ICM(Institute of Credit Management) 여신관리협회

ICMA(Institue of Cost and Management Accountants) 원가 · 관리회계사협회

iconic model 화상 모형

ICQ(internal control questionaire) 내부통제질문서

ICWA(Institute of Cost and Works Accountants) 원가계산회계사협회

ID(industrial dynamics) 산업동력학, 산업원동력

ID card(identification card) ID카드, 신분증

ideal capacity 이상적 조업도 = full capacity, maximum capacity, theoretical capacity ▶ expected actual capacity, normal capacity, practical capacity

ideal standard cost 이상(理想) 표준 원가 ▶ normal standrd cost

identifiable asset 식별가능자산, 고유자산 = segment asset ▶ segmental reporting

identifiable intangible asset 식별가능한 무형자산 ▶ unidentifiable intangible asset

identifiable net assets 식별가능한 순자산

identification 1) 식별(識別) 2) 신분증명, 동일하다는 증명 3) 특정, 특정화

identification card (ID card) ID카드, 신분증

identification of goods 상품의 식별

identified cost method 개별법 = specific cost method

identifier 식별자(子)

identifying segment 세그먼트의 결정

identity 정체성, 동일성, 본질

IDF (intermediate distributing frame) 중간단자반, 중간배선반

idle asset 유휴(遊休)자산

idle capacity cost 유휴설비비용, 유휴생산능력비용 ▶ capacity cost

idle capacity ratio 유휴생산능력비율

idle character 유휴문자

idle cost 유휴비, 무효원가 ▶ idle hour

idle equipment 유휴설비 ▶ idle machine

idle facility 유휴시설

idle hour 유휴시간 ▶ idle cost

idle machine   유휴기계 ▶ idle
    equipment
idle plant   유휴공장설비
idle property   유휴자산
idle time   1) 대기시간 2) 유휴시간
idle time cost   불로(不勞)임금, 부동(不
    動)노무비 ▶ labor cost
IDP(integrated data processing)   집중자
    료처리, 통합데이터처리
**IEC(International Electrotechnical
    Commission)**   국제전기표준
    회의
IEE(Institute of Electrical Engineers)
    전기기술자협회
**IEEE(Institute of Electrical and Electronic
    Engineers)**   전기 · 전자기술
    자협회
IFA(International Fiscal Association)
    국제재정협회
**IFAC(International Federation of
    Accountants)**   국제회계사연맹
ifconverted method   전환가정법
    ▶ if-converted method
if converted method   전환가정법, 전환
    가정방식 = ifconverted method
**IFIP(International Federation for
    Information Processing)**   정
    보처리학회 국제연합
**IFRB(International Frequency
    Registration Board)**   국제 주
    파수등록회의
IIA(Institute of Internal Auditors)   내부
    감사인협회
illegal   위법(違法)
illegal act   위법행위
illegal act by client   의뢰인에 의한 불
    법행위

**illegal act having direct and material
    effect**   재무제표에 직접적이
    며 중요한 영향을 미치는 위법
    행위
illegal act having indirect effect   재무
    제표에 간접적인 영향을 미치는
    위법행위
illegal character   위법(違法)문자
illegality   위법성, 불법행위
illegality of contract   계약의 불법성
illegal payment   부정지출
illicit gain   부정이익
illusory promise   가공의 약속
illustration   예시(例示)
illustrative financial statement   도표
    로 본 재무제표
illustrative transaction   도표로 본 거래
**IMA(Institute of Management
    Accountants)**   관리회계사협회
image   상(象), 영상(映像)
image dissector   해상기구
image processing   이미지 처리
IMF(International Monetary Fund)
    국제통화기금
immaterial asset   중요하지 않은 자산
immediate acceptance   즉시인수
immediate family   근친자
immediate perpetuity   즉시지불연금
immovable   부동산
**IMPACT(Inventory Management
    Program and Control
    Technique)**   재고관리 프로
    그램과 제어기법
impact day   1) 회사가 두번째로 주식을
    일반에게 제공하는 날짜 2) 증
    권의 공모 조건이 공표되는 날
impact loan   용도제약이 없는 외화차관

impact printer 충격식 인쇄장치

impaired capital 손상자본
▶ impairment

impairment 1) 손상, 감가 2) (자본금의)
결손 ▶ impaired capital 3) 채
무초과액 4) 대손평가액의 계상

impairment long-lived asset 장기
자산의 감손

impairment of value 자산가치의 감소,
고정자산의 진부화

imperfect competition 불완전경쟁

impersonal account 물적 계정

impersonal entity 비인적(非人的) 실체

impersonal ledger 비인명계정원장
= general ledger, nominal
ledger, private ledger

impersonal security 물적 담보
▶ personal security

implementability 실현가능성
▶ implementation, software
requriements specification

implementation 실현, 구체화
▶ implementability

implementation guide 적용지침

implementation service 이행 서비스

implication 함의, 내포, 묵시
= conditional implication,
IFTHEN operation

implicit cost 비명시적(묵시적) 비용
▶ explicit cost

implicit cost of capital 비명시적 자본
비용 ▶ explicit cost of capital

implicit declaration 암묵적 선언

implicit deflator 종합물가지수 = GNP
implicit deflator

implicit rate 포괄이자율

implicit rate computed by lessor 리

스임대인의 요율산정상의 계산
이자율 = interest rate implicit
in the lease ▶ lessee's
incremental borrowing rate

implied actual authority 묵시(默示)의
대리권

implied authority 묵시적 대리권

implied contract 묵시계약

implied trust 묵시신탁 = presumptive
trust ▶ express trust

implied warranty 묵시적 보증, 묵시
적 보증책임

implied warranty for a merchantability
상품성에 관한 묵시적 보증책임

**implied warranty for fitness of
particular purpose** 묵시의
특정목적 적합성 책임

**implied warranty of fitness for a
particular purpose** 특정
목적의 적합성에 관한 묵시적
보증책임

implied warranty of habitability 거
주가능성에 대한 묵시적 담보책
임

implied warranty of merchantability
묵시의 상품적합성 보증

implied warranty of title 소유권 보증
책임

**important feature of the FASB
guidance** FASB 지침서의
중요사항

import bill 수입어음 ▶ export bill

import certificate(IC) 수입증명서

import charge 수입제비용

import credit 수입신용, 수입금융

import duty 수입관세 = duty, duty of
custom

import letter of credit 수입신용장
▶ export letter of credit

import quota system 수입할당제
▶ export quota system

imposed budget 강제 예산
▶ participation, participative budgeting

imposition 1) 과세(課稅) 2) 세금 3) 부과(賦課)

impossibility 불가능, 이행불능

imposter rule 사칭시 규정

imposters rule 사기법

impostor (타인을 사칭하는) 사기꾼

impracticability 실행 불가능

impressed stamp 납세증지

imprest cash 정액전도 소액현금

imprest fund 정액전도자금

imprest imprest 정액자금 전도제도

imprest petty cash system 정액 소액현금 전도제도

improper action 면제되지 않는 채무자

improper delivery 부적절한 인도

improper packing 부적절한 포장

improvement 개량, 증축 = betterment
▶ repair

improvement cost 개량비

improvement expense 개량비

impulse 충격 = pulse

imputation system (영)귀속계산제도 = gross up method

imputation transaction 귀속거래

imputed cost 부가원가, 내재원가
▶ opportunity cost

imputed interest 내재이자, 귀속이자

imputed interest rate 잠재적 이자율

IMS (information management system) 정보관리시스템

inactive employee 휴직 종업원

inactive program 비활동 프로그램

inactive station 비활동 단말기

inactive stock 비인기주(株) ▶ glamour stock

inadequacy 부적응화 ▶ functional depreciation, obsolescence, physical depreciation

inadequate disclosure 불충분한 공시

in-and-out time card 출근표 = clock card ▶ time ticket

incapacity 무능력

incentive 장려(奬勵), 유인(誘因)
▶ motivation

incentive contract 인센티브계약

incentive payment system 인센티브제 = incentive system
▶ incentive wage

incentive stock option plan 자사주 구입 선택 장려제도

incentive system 인센티브제
= incentive payment system
▶ incentive wage

incentive wage 인센티브급여
▶ incentive payment system, incentive system

inception of lease 리스의 개시점

inception of the lease 리스의 개시일

incidence of audit testing 감사의 발생

incidental beneficiary 부수적인 수익자

incidental beneficiary 우연적 수익자, 우연적인 제3자

incidental beneficiary contract 부수적 수익자계약

incidental cost 부수비용

incidental or peripheral transaction

부수적 또는 주변적 거래

incidentals time　잡(雜)시간
= miscellaneous time

incidental transaction　부수적 거래
= peripheral transaction

income　1) 이익　2) 소득

income account　손익계산서 = income
statement, profit and loss
statement

income and expenditure account
수지(收支)계산서 = revenue
account

income approach　1) 손익법　2) 수익환
원법　3) 수익방식 ▶ cost
approach, market data approach

**income attributable to ordinary
activity**　경상손익

income available to common share
보통주 배당가능이익

**income available to common
shareholder**　보통주에 대
한 배당가능이익

income basis　이율근거

income before extraordinary item　특
별손익전 이익

income before tax　세전 이익 ▶ pretax
accounting income

**income before unusual or infrequent
item and income tax**　비경
상적이거나 비반복적인 항목전
의 세차감전 이익

income beneficiary　수익(收益)의 수익
자(受益者)

income bond　수익사채 ▶ bond

income budget　손익예산
= operating budget, profit and
loss budget

income deduction　이익공제항목

income determination　이익결정, 이익
산정 ▶ income measurement

income distribution deduction　소득
배분공제

income elasticity　소득탄력성

income from consolidated operation
연결이익

income from continuing operation　계
속적 영업활동에 의한 이익
▶ current cost operating profit

income from discontinued operation
중단된 영업활동에 대한 이익
▶ income from continuing
operations

income from investment　투자수익

income from operation　영업이익

income fund　자금수입 ▶ balance
fund, mutual fund

income measurement　이익측정
▶ income determination

income on construction　공사이익

income on long-tern construction　장
기도급공사이익

income or earnings statement　손익
계산서

income producing real estate　이익을
가득하는 부동산

income realization　이익의 실현

income recognition　이익의 인식
▶ income realization, revenue
recognition

income sheet　손익계산서, 손익표
= income statement

income statement　손익계산서
= earnings statement, profit and
loss statement

income statement account   손익계산서 계정 ▶ balance sheet account

income statement analysis   손익계산서 분석 = analysis of income statement ▶ balance sheet analysis

income statement audit   손익계산서 감사

income statement item in constant dollars   일반구매력으로 표시된 손익계산서 항목

income statement ratio   손익계산서 비율

income summary account   집합손익계정

income tax   1) 소득세 2) 법인세, 법인소득세

income tax allocation   법인세 기간배분

income taxation of estate and trust   유산과 신탁에 대한 소득세

income tax bases   소득세 기준

income tax deferred   이연법인세

income tax expense   법인세비용

income tax expense-current   법인세 비용-당기분

income tax expense-deferred   법인세 비용-이연분

income tax liability   미지급 소득세

income tax month   소득세 계산상의 1개월

income tax payable   미지급법인세, 미지급소득세

income tax prepayment   예납법인세

income tax return   법인세신고서, 소득세신고서

income tax return preparer   소득세신고 작성자

income tax withholding   원천소득세 예수금

income transaction   손익거래

incoming partner   신임 파트너

incompetence   무능력

incompetent   1) 무능력의, 무자격의 2) 무능력자

incomplete record   불완전기록

inconsistency   일관성 결여

incorporated accounting technician   (영)(등록)회계기능사

incorporated administrative accountant   (영)(등록)관리회계사

incorporated company and commercial accountant   (영)(등록)회사·상사회계사

incorporation   회사, 회사설립

incorporation by reference   참조조입(組入)방식

incorporator   발기인(發起人), 정관을 작성하여 등록하는 자

Incoterms(International Commercial Terms)   국제상업용어

increase and decrease method   증감법

increase in inflation   인플레이션하의 상승

increasing annuity   증액연금

increasing charge method of depreciation   체증감가상각법

incremental allowance   증분허용액

incremental allowance for projected misstatement   예측 왜곡표시금액에 대한 증분허용치

incremental analysis   증분분석

▶ incremental cost, incremental profit, incremental revenue

incremental benefit 증분이익
　▶ differential cost, incremental cost

incremental borrowing rate 임차인의 한계차입이자율, 가중차입율
　= lessee's incremental borrowing rate

incremental budget 증분주의 예산, 증분예산 ▶ ordinary incremental budget, priority incremental budget, zero-base budget

incremental comparison method 증분비교법 ▶ incremental analysis

incremental computer 증분계산기

incremental cost 증분원가
　▶ differential cost, relevant cost

incremental direct cost 증분직접비

incremental integrator 증분적분기

incremental profit 증분이익
　▶ incremental cost, incremental revenue

incremental representation 증분표현법, 증분표시법 = incremental representation system

incremental revenue 증분수익
　▶ incremental analysis, incremental cost, incremental profit

incremental share 부가적 발행 주식

incumbrance 1) 토지부담
　= encumbrance 2) 방해물, 장해물

incurred 발생

indefinite reversal criteria 무기한 철거 규준

indemnification 배상, 보상

indemnifier 손해보상자

indemnity 손해보상(금), 손해보상계약

indemnity agreement 손실보상계약, 손해배상계약

indemnity contract 손해 보전(補塡) 보증계약, 변상계약, 배상계약

indent 위탁매입, 매입위탁

indent invoice 위탁매입송장

indent ledger 수탁매입원장

indenture 신탁계약서 ▶ bond trustee

independence 독립성, (감사인의) 독립성

independence in appearance 외관상 독립성 ▶ independence in reality

independence in reality 실제적 독립성, 사실상 독립성
　▶ independence in appearance

independent 독립

independent accountant 독립 회계인

independent auditor 독립 감사인

independent check 독립적 체크

independent contractor 1) 독립적 도급인, 청부(請負)인 2) 독립계약자, 독립된 계약직

independent cost 독립원가, 개별원가
　▶ joint cost

independent in fact and appearance 사실상, 외관상의 독립

independent project 독립프로젝트
　▶ dependent project

independent trustee 발행기업으로 부터 독립한 신탁인

independent utility program 독립 효용프로그램

independent variable　독립변수
　　= controllable variable
　　▶ dependent variable
indeterminate term liability　미확정
　　부채
index　1) 지수 2) 색인 3) 지표
indexation　지수법 = indexing, method
　　based on the use of index
　　▶ current cost accounting,
　　direct pricing
indexation allowance　(영)물가지수 공
　　제법,
indexed sequential access method
　　(ISAM)　색인순차 접근방식
indexing　1) 지수법, 지수화 = indexation
　　2) 지표첨부, 색인첨부
index method　지수법
index number　지수(指數)
index number of price　물가지수
　　▶ index number
index of business condition　경기지수,
　　경기지표 = business indicator
index of business indicator　경기지수
index of retail price　소매물가지수
　　= general index of retail prices
index of wage　임금지수 = wage index
index register　지수레지스터
indicator　1) 지표(指標) 2) 표식(標識), 표
　　시자
indicia of ownership　물건의 점유와 함
　　께 물건의 소유권을 상징하는
　　문서
indicia of title　물건의 소유권을 상징하
　　는 문서
indifference curve　무차별곡선
indirect audit evidence　간접증거
　　▶ indirect evidence

indirect cost　간접비 ▶ direct cost
indirect cost center　간접비 중심점
　　= service cost center
indirect cost pool　간접비 집계액 = cost
　　pool
indirect departmental cost　부문간접
　　비 ▶ direct department cost
indirect departmental expense　부문
　　간접비 = departmental burden
indirect evidence　간접증거 ▶ direct
　　evidence
indirect expense　간접비용 ▶ direct
　　expense
indirect factory cost　제조간접비
　　= factory overhead
indirect factory material　공장소모품,
　　공장소모품비 = factory supply
indirect instruction　간접명령
indirect labor　1) 간접노동 2) 간접노
　　무비 = indirect labor cost
indirect labor cost　간접노무비
　　▶ direct labor cost
indirect manufacturing cost　제조간
　　접비 = factory overhead
indirect material　1) 간접재료 2) 간접
　　재료비 = indirect material cost
indirect material cost　간접재료비
　　▶ direct write-off method
indirect method　간접법
indirect selling cost　간접판매비
　　▶ direct selling cost
indirect stock　소모품, 간접재료재고
　　= non-productive stock
indirect tax　간접세
indirect wage　간접임금
individual accounts　(영)개별재무제표
individual activity report　개별업무 보

고서 ▶ cost report

individual basis　개별기준 ▶ aggregate basis, lower of cost of market basis

individual change method　개별변동법(법인세회계)

individual cost　개별원가 ▶ common cost

individual depreciation　개별상각 = unit depreciation ▶ group depreciation, composite depreciation

individual financial statement　개별재무제표 = consolidated financial statements

individual goal　개인목표

individual item basis　개별항목기준 = individual basis ▶ aggregate basis, lower of cost or market value

individually significant item　개별적으로 중요한 항목

individual rate　개별배부율 ▶ blanket rate

individual retirement account(IRA)　개인퇴직연금계정, 개인퇴직금구좌제도 = qualified pension plan

individuals　개인

individual wage rate　개별임률

indorsee　피배서인(被裏書人), 양수인(讓受人)

indorsement　이서(裏書) = endorsement ▶ blank endorsement, conditional endorsement

indorsement in blank　백지식 이서 = endorsement in blank

indorser　이서인, 양도인 ▶ indorsee

induced conversions of debt　전환사채의 유도된 전환

induction　1) 귀납법, 귀납적 결론 = inductive method ▶ deduction 2) 제출(提出)

induction coil　유도 코일

inductive inference　귀납적 추리(추론) = inductive reasoning

inductive method　귀납법 = induction ▶ deduction

inductive reasoning　귀납적 추리(추론) = inductive inference

industrial accounting　공업회계 = manuhacturing accounting

industrial combination　기업결합 ▶ business combination

industrial concentration　기업집중

industrial data processing　산업용 데이터 처리, 공업용 데이터 처리

industrial design　공업디자인

industrial dynamics (ID)　산업동력학, 산업원동력

industrial engineering method　산업공학적 방법, 기술적 예측법 ▶ cost analysis, regression analysis

industrial member　(영)산업계에 근무하는 칙허회계사 ▶ public accountant, public practice

industrial revenue bond　미국 면세(免稅) 지방국채 ▶ tax exempt security

industry(pl.)　업종(業種)

industry audit guide　업종별 감사안내서

industry bookkeeping　공업부기

industry outlook　업계예측

industry practice   업계관행
industry ratio   업계평균비율
industry segment   1) 사업별 부문 2) 산
    업 분류표, 산업별 부문 보고서
    ▶ segment reporting
industry segment reporting   사업별
    부문보고서 ▶ geographical
    segment reporting, segment
    reporting
inefficient user   비효율적인 자원이용자
inescapable cost   회피불능원가
    = unavoidable cost
inescapable fixed cost   회피불능고정비
    = unavoidable fixed cost
    ▶ avoidable fixed cost,
    escapable fixed cost
infancy   미성년
infant   미성년자
infinite pad method   무한 패드법
infinite population   무한 모(母)집단
infix notation   삽입표기법, 중간표기법
inflation   1) 인플레이션 2) 일반물가변
    동
inflation accounting   물가변동회계
    = accounting for changing
    prices ▶ constant purchasing
    power accounting, current cost
    accounting group
**Inflation Accounting Steering Group
    (IASG)**   (영)물가변동회계
    운영위원회 ▶ Hyde Guideline
Inflation Accounting Sub-Committee
    (영)물가변동회계소위원회
    ▶ Neville Report, CCA
    Monitoring Working Party
influential variables   영향변수
informal contract   비공식계약

informal organization   비공식조직
    ▶ formal organization
information about geographic area
    지역별 매출액 등에 관한 정보
information about major customer
    중요 거래처에 관한 정보
**information about product and
    service**   제품서비스 정보
**information about segment profit or
    loss**   부문별 손익정보
information accounting standards   정
    보회계기준
informational needs   정보수요
information and communication   정
    보와 전달, 정보 및 의사교환
information bit   정보단위
information economics   정보경제학
information feedback system   정보피
    드백시스템
information hiding   정보은폐
    ▶ data abstraction design
information interchange   정보교환
information management system(IMS)
    정보관리시스템
information needs   정보 수요
information network   정보망
information on forecast   예측정보
information on forecasted profit   이
    익예측정보
information overload   정보과다
information processing   정보처리
    = data processing
information report   정보보고서
    ▶ control report
information requirement   정보요건
information retrieval (IR)   정보검색
information science   정보과학

information separator(IS) 정보분리
문자 = separating character

information system 정보조직, 정보시
스템

information system master
development plan 정보시
스템 종합개발계획

information technology 정보기술

information theorist 정보이론의 연구
자

information theory 정보이론

infrequency (or nonrecurring) of
occurrence 비반복적(발생
이 비경제적 또는 반복적으로 발생
하지 않는 것)

infrequent event 비반복적 사건

infrequent item 비반복적 사항

in good faith 선의(善意)로

in good faith modification 선의에 의
한 계약 변경

ingredient 요소(要素)

inherent authority 선천적 대리권

inherent risk 고유위험, 고유 리스크
▶ assertions, control risk,
detection risk, internal control
structure

inheritance 상속

inheritance duty 상속세 = inheritance
tax

inheritance tax 상속세 = death tax,
estate tax, inheritance duty

inherited error 이월오차, 유전(遺傳)
오차

inhibiting signal 금지신호, 억지(抑止)
신호

in-house 구내(構內)

in-house computer system 구내 컴퓨

터 시스템

initial allowance(IA) (영)기초 고율상
각 ▶ capital allowance, first-
year allowance, writing down
allowance

initial audit 초도(初度)감사 ▶ running
audit

initial balance 기초잔고 = beginning
balance

initial capital 기금(생명보험업), 기초자본

initial direct cost (리스 계약상) 초기직
접비용

initial franchise fee 초기 프랜차이즈료

initial goods in process 기초재공품
▶ work in process

initial inventory 기초재고자산
= beginning inventory

initial investigation 예비적 조사
▶ pilot test

initial investment 초기투자

initial investment in a partnership 파
트너십의 형성

initial investment outlay 원시(原始) 투
자액

initialization 초기설정

initial margin 기본증거금

initial markup 최초이윤
▶ maintained markup

initial net investment 초기 순투자

initial public offering(IPO) 신규상장,
최초의 공모(公募)

initial reaction to the report of the
inflation accounting
committee (영)물가변동회
계 위원회보고서에 대한 최초
반응 ▶ Morpeth Committee

initial recognition 제1차적 인식

injunction 금지, 금지명령, 금지청구
　　▶ preliminary injunction,
　　temporary injunction
injured party 피해자
injury (원고의) 손해
inland bill of exchange 내국환어음
inland check 내국수표
inland market 국내시장
inland money order 내국송금대체
Inland Revenue(IR) (영)내국세입청
Inland Revunue Commissioner(IRC)
　　(영)내국세입위원회
inline processing 즉시처리
innkeeper 숙박업자
innkeeper's lien 여관업자의 유치권,
　　담보권
innocent misrepresentation 선의(善
　　意)의 부실표시, 오도 의도가 없
　　는 거짓표시
innocent purchaser for value 선량한
　　구매자
in order rule 순서대로 규칙
inplementation service 시행 업무
input 1) 입력 2) 입력자료 (data) = input
　　data 3) 입력처리(process) 4) 투
　　입, 투하 5) 유입
input method 투하법 ▶ output method
input-output(IO) 입출력
input-output accounting 투입산출회
　　계 ▶ input-output analysis
input-output analysis 투입산출분석
　　▶ input-output accounting
input-output table 투입산출표
input price 투입가액
input tax (영)투입세(投入稅) ▶ output
　　tax
input value 투입 가치

inquiring 질문
inquiry 질문, 조회, 조사
inquiry notice 조회 통지
inquiry of a client's lawyer 의뢰인
　　변호사에 대한 질문, 의뢰처 변
　　호사로의 질문
inquiry software 조회용 소프트웨어
inquiry station 조회용단말기
insane person 정신장애자
insanity 정신장애
inscribed security 기명증권
inscribed share 기명주권 (記名株券)
inscribed stock 기명주권
inside information 내부정보 = insider
　　information ▶ insider trading
insider 기업내부자 ▶ insider trading
insider dealing 내부자거래, 내부정보를
　　이용하는 불공정거래
insider information 내부자정보, 내부
　　정보 = inside information
　　▶ insider trading
insider trading 내부자거래 ▶ insider
　　information
insincerity 부정(不正)
insolvency 지불불능
insolvency in the bankruptcy sense
　　채무초과(채무의 합계액이 자산의
　　시가를 초과한 상태)
insolvency in the equity sense
　　(만기일에 채무자가 채무를 변제하
　　지 못하는) 지불불능
insolvency practitioner (영)파산관재인
Insolvency Practitioners Association
　　(IPA) 파산관재인협회
insolvency test 지불불능 테스트
inspection 1) 실사(實査) 2) 검수, 검사
　　3) 사열

inspection department 검사부, 검수부
▶ purchase department

inspection expense 검사비

inspection report 검수전표, 검수보고서, 조사보고서

inspector 검사계(係)

inspector of tax (영)세금사정의 감찰관

install AR-1 할부외상매출금

installation 1) 취임(就任) 2) 설치, 가설, 도입

installation account payable 할부 미지급금 ▶ installation account receivable

installation account receivable 할부매출채권, 할부외상판매금

installation basis 할부기준

installation bond 분할상환채, 할부 지급채권

installation charge 설치비
▶ installation fee

installation contract 할부매매계약

installation cost 설치비 ▶ installation fee

installation expense 설치비
▶ installation fee

installation fee 설치비 ▶ installation charge, installation cost, installation expense

installation method 할부기준
▶ completed sales basis

installation revenue recognition method 할부수익의 인식방법

installation sale 할부판매, 할부매출
▶ credit sale, hire purchase

installation time 설비기간, 설치조정시간, 설치시간

installment contract 할부계약

installment land contract 할부토지매매

installment liquidation 분할분배방식

installment method 할부기준, 할부기준법

installment sales method 할부판매법

install sale 할부판매

Institute of Accountants and Bookkeepers 회계인협회

Institute of Administrative Accountants(IAA) 관리회계인협회

Institute of Certified Public Accountants in Ireland 아일랜드의 공인회계사협회

Institute of Chartered Accountants in England and Wales(ICAEW) 잉글랜드와 웨일즈의 공인회계사협회

Institute of Chartered Accountants in Ireland(ICAI) 아일랜드 공인회계사협회

Institute of Chartered Accountants of Scotland(ICAS) 스코틀랜드의 공인회계사협회

Institute of Chartered Financial Analysts(ICFA) 공인재무분석가협회

Institute of Cost and Management Accountants(ICMA) 원가관리회계사협회

Institute of Cost and Works Accountants(ICWA) 원가회계사협회

Institute of Credit Management(ICM) 여신관리협회

**Institute of Electrical and Electronic
  Engineers(IEEE)**   전기 · 전
  자기술자협회
Institute of Electrical Engineers(IEE)
  (영)전기기술자협회
Institute of Financial Executive   재무
  관리자협회
Institute of Internal Auditors(IIA)
  내부감사인협회
**Institute of Management Accounting
  (IMA)**   관리회계협회
**Institute of Taxation in England and
  Wales**   아일랜드와 웨일즈
  의 조세협회
institution   조직체
institutional investor   기관투자가
instruction   명령
instrument   1) 기구, 기계 2) 증서, 증거
  문 3) (금융)상품, 증권 4) (일정
  금액에 대한) 권리증서
instrument of credit   신용증권
in-substance defeasance   실질계약 해
  제조건
insurable interest   피보험이익
insurance   1) 보험 2) 운송보험료
insurance amount   보험금액
insurance binder   보험가계약서
insurance certificate   보험인수증
insurance clause   보험약관
insurance company   보험회사
insurance contract   보험계약
insurance cost   보험료
insurance dividend   보험계약자 배당금
insurance expense   지급보험료
  ▶ insurance premium, prepaid
  insurance premium, insurance
  prepaid

insurance policy   보험증서, 보험증권
insurance premium   보험료
insurance prepaid   선급보험료
  ▶ insurance expense,
  insurance premium, prepaid
  insurance premium
insurance proceed   보험금
insurance rate   보험 요율
insurance value   보험가액
insured   보험계약자, 피보험인, 피보험자
insurer   보험회사, 보험자
insurer liability   보험자의 책임
intangible   무형자산, 무형재산
  = intangible asset
intangible asset   1) 무형자산, 무형고정
  자산 = intangible ▶ fixed
  asset, tangible asset 2) 계상의
  상한액
intangible assets-deferred pension cost
  무형고정자산-이연연금비용
intangible collateral   무체 담보물
intangible development cost   개발비
  ▶ development cost, research
  and development cost
intangible fixed asset   무형고정자산
  ▶ amortization, tangible fixed
  asset
intangible personal property   무형동
  산
intangible property   무형재산, 무형
  동산
integer   정수(整數) = integer number
integer constant   정수계획법
integer number   정수 = integer
integer programming   정수계획법
integral boundary   정수경계, 규정경계
integral part   보험회사

integral view 1) 분기를 연차보고의 구성요소로 보는 관점 2) 총체적 관점

integrated account 통합계정

integrated circuit(IC) 집적회로

integrated communication adapter 통신통합어댑터

integrated data processing(IDP) 집중자료처리, 통합데이터처리

integrated disclosure system 통합공시제도 ▶ securities and exchange commission

integrated emulator 통합모방기

integrated processing 집중처리 ▶ distributed processing

integrated test facility(ITF) 종합자료검증법

integrating motor 적분 모터

integration 통합

integration clause 완결조항

integration of CCA and GPLA 현행원가회계와 일반물가변동회계의 결합 = blending of CCA and GPLA, current cost/ constant purchasing poweraccounting

integrator 적분기(積分器)

integrity 1) 완전성, 성실성, 정직성 2) 보전성 3) 보증

integrity of management 경영자의 성실성

intellectual property 지적(知的)재산권

intellectual property right 지적재산권

intelligence quotient 지능지수

INTELSAT(International Telecommunications Satellite Consortium) 국제 전기통신 위성기구

intended beneficiary contract 의도적인 수익자계약

intentional fraud 의도적 사기

intentional misstatement 의도적인 왜곡표시

intentional override 의도적 무효화

intentional tort 고의적 불법행위

interaction 1) 대화, 대화단위 2) 교호작용, 상호작용

interaction time 상호작용시간

interactive 상호작용식

interactive mode 회화형, 대화형, 상호작용모드

Inter-American Accounting Association(IAAA) 미국대륙회계연합 ▶ IFAC

interbank exchange rate 은행간 대체율

interbranch transaction 지점간 거래

interchangeable unit 호환가능한 단위, 대체가능단위 = fungible unit

interclass variance 계층간 분산(分算)

intercompany 기업간(間) ▶ intercompany elimination, intercompany investment, significant

intercompany bond transaction 모회사와 자회사간 회사채 거래

intercompany elimination 회사간 소거항목

intercompany fixed asset transaction 모회사와 자회사간 고정자산 거래

intercompany inventory transaction 모회사와 자회사간의 상품매매

intercompany investment　회사간투자

intercompany item in transit　회사간
미기입 사항

intercompany loan　기업집단 내의 회
사간 차입금 ▶ intercompany
receivable

intercompany profit　회사간 이익
▶ down stream, up stream

intercompany profit and loss　1) 연결
미실현손익 2) 내부손익
▶ consolidated financial
statements, consolidated income
statement

intercompany receivable　기업집단 내
회사에 대한 채권
▶ intercompany loan

intercompany receivable and payable
모회사와 자회사간의 채권 · 채
무

intercompany revenue and expense
내부이익 · 비용

intercompany transaction　기업집단
회사간 거래, 내부거래

intercorporate tax allocation　회사간
세(稅)배분

interdepartmental profit　부문간 대체
이익

interdisciplinary approach　둘 이상의
학문이 관여하는 연구, 학제적
(學際的) 연구

interdivisional transfer　부문간 대체,
사업부문간 대체

interest　1) 이자, 수취이자, 여분　2) 이자
율　3) 이해관계, 권익, 권리, 이
권, 지분　4) 관계자, 동업자　5)
청구권

interest allowed　규정이율

interest and discount　이자 · 할인료
▶ prepaid interest and discount

interest and dividend income　수취이
자와 배당

interest bearing　이자부(付)

interest bearing receivable　이자부 채
권

interest bearing security　이자부 증권
▶ coupon fund

interest bill　이자부 어음

interest cost　이자비용

interest coupon　이자지급표, 이찰(利札)
▶ coupon fund

interest cover　이자지급보상배율
= interest coverage ratio, times
interest covered, times interest
earned ratio

interest coverage ratio　이자보상배율,
이자보상비율 = interest cover

interest during construction　건설 기
간중의 이자 ▶ capitalization
of interest cost

interested director transaction　이해
관계를 가진 자와의 거래

interested party　이해관계자

interest expense　지급이자, 이자비용

interest group　이해관계자집단
▶ related party

interest in closely held company　비
공개회사에 대한 지분

interest income　수취이자, 이자수익
▶ interest revenue

interest in land　부동산상의 이익

interest in partnership　파트너십의 지
분권, 합자회사 지분

interest in real property　부동산권

interest method　이자법

interest note 이자계산서

interest on accumulated postretirement benefit obligation 누적 퇴직후 연금지급의무에 관한 이자

interest on bank deposit 은행예금 이자

interest on borrowing 차입금이자

interest on construction 건설중 지급이자 ▶ capitalization of interest cost

interest on funded debt 장기채권이자

interest on loan 대출금이자

interest only strip 월별 이자지급만 있는 증권

interest on projected benefit obligation (PBO) 추정연금지급의무에 관한 이자

interest on public bond 공채이자

interest on refund 환부금이자, 상환가산금

interest on security 유가증권이자

interest paid 이자비용

interest payable 미지급이자 ▶ dividend payable

interest rate 이자율

interest rate cap and floor written 상한 · 하한 특약부 금리(대여자 측의)

interest rate implicit in the lease 리스료 산정에 포함한 이자율, 리스에서의 내재이자율

interest rate swap 금리스왑

interest receivable 미수이자

interest revenue 수취이자, 이자수익 ▶ interest income

interest slip 이자계산표

interest table 금리계산표

interface 1) 경계 2) (데이터전송의) 인터페이스

interference 방해요인

inter-firm comparison 기업간 비교

interfund borrowing 기금 상호간의 차입

interfund service provided and used 기금간 서비스의 제공과 사용

interfund transfer and other interfund transaction 기금간 대체 및 기타 기금간 거래

interim 기중(期中), 중간, 가협정(假協定)

interim account (영)중간재무제표

interim audit 기중감사

interim balance sheet 중간대차대조표

interim control 기중통제

interim date 기중(期中)의 일(日)

interim dividend 중간배당

interim earning report 중간이익보고서

interim examination date 중간감사일

interim financial information 중간재무정보 = interim report ▶ quarterly report

interim financial report 중간재무보고서 = interim report, interim financial information,interim financial reprot

interim financial reporting 중간재무보고

interim financial statement 중간재무제표 = interim report ▶ quarterly report

interim injunction 중간 중지명령 = interlocutory injunction

interim period 기중

interim report 반기보고서, 중간보고서 = interim financial statements

▶ quarterly report

interim reporting   분기보고서, 중간보고

interim review report   중간검토 보고서 ▶ review report

interim statement   중간재무제표
= interim financial report, interim report, interim financial information ▶ quarterly report

interim trustee   임시 관재인

interleave   상호배치

interlock   연결, 결합하다

interlocutory injunction   중간 중지명령
= interfim injunction, preliminary injunction, provisional injunction, temporary injunction
▶ finalinjunction, permanent injunction, perpetual injunction

intermediary   투자대행기관

intermediary bank   중간 은행

intermediate area (IA)   (영)중규모개발지역 ▶ assisted area, develoment area, special development area

intermediate distributing frame(IDF)
중간단자반, 중간배선반

intermediate holding company   (영)
중간지주회사

intermediate stock   중간재고품

internal accounting   내부회계
= internal report accounting, management accounting, managerial accounting
▶ external accounting, external report accounting

internal accounting control   내부회계

통제

internal analysis   내부분석 ▶ external analysis

internal aspect   내부적 측면

internal audit   내부감사 ▶ external audit

internal audit activity   내부감사 활동

internal audit committee   내부감사 위원회

internal audit function   내부감사기능

internal auditing   내부감사

internal auditing department   내부감사부(部)

internal auditing division   내부감사과
= internal auditing section

internal auditing manual   내부감사 실시기준서

internal auditing responsibility   내부감사책임

internal auditing section   내부감사과
= internal auditing division

internal auditing standard   내부감사기준

internal auditing system   내부감사 제도

internal auditor   내부감사인

Internal Auditor   내부감사인협회
(Institute of Internal Auditor)의 기관지. 1944년 창간, 격월발행

internal audit order   내부감사명령서

internal audit report   내부감사보고서

internal audit system   내부감사제도
▶ internal control system

internal check   내부견제

internal check system   내부견제제도
= internal control system

internal control   내부통제 = internal

control structure ▶ audit
testing, detailed audit
internal control questionnaire(ICQ)
내부통제질문서
internal control structure 내부통제
기구
**internal control structure policy and
procedure relevant to an
audit** 감사에 적합한 내부
통제제도의 방침과 절차
▶ assertion, internal control
structure
internal control system 내부통제제도
= internal check system, internal
audit system
internal control weakness 내부통제
의 약점
internal event 내부사건
internal evidence 내부증거 ▶ external
evidence, extrinsic evidence
internal financing 내부자금조달
internal fund 내부자금 ▶ external
fund
internal node 중간접점
internal pricing 내부대체가격의 결정
= intra-company transfer
pricing ▶ transfer pricing
internal procedure 내부절차
internal profit 내부이익
internal rate of return(IRR) 내부이
익률, 내부수익률 = time-
adjusted rate of return ▶ net
present value
internal rate of return method 내부
이익률법, 내부수익률법
▶ dicounted cash flow method,
financial statenents method,

internal rate of return
internal reconstruction 내부감자(減
資)에 의한 회사구조조정
internal report 내부보고서 ▶ external
report
internal report accounting 내부보고
회계 = internal accounting,
management accounting,
managerial accounting
▶ external accounting, external
report accounting
internal reporting 내부보고
▶ external reporting
internal reporting system 내부보고
제도 ▶ external reporting
system
Internal Revenue Code(IRC) 내국세
입법(內國稅立法), 내국세입법전
Internal Revenue Code method 내국
세입청 규칙과 연결회사간의 세
(稅)배분법
Internal Revenue Service(IRS) 내국
세입청
internal sort 내부분류
internal storage 내부기억장치
= internal store
internal store (영)내부기억장치
= internal storage
internal tranfer price 내부대체가격
= intra-company transfer price
internal transaction 내부거래
▶ external transaction
internal transfer 내부대체
= intra-company transfer
internal user 내부정보이용자
international accountant 국제회계사
International Accountant 국제회계사

협회(Association of International
Accountants) 발행의 계간 회계
연구지

international accounting   국제회계

International Accounting Guideline
    (IAG)   감사의 국제적 지침

international accounting section   국
제회계부문

International Accounting standards
    (IAS)   국제회계기준
    ▶ International Organization
    of Securitie Commission and
    Similar Agencies

International Accounting Standards
    Committee(IASC)   국제회
계기준심의회 ▶ International
    Organization of Securities
    Commissions and Similar
    Agencies

International Auditing Practices
    Committee(IAPC)   국제감
사실무위원회 ▶ International
    Federation of Accountants

International Bank for Reconstruction
    and Development(IBRD)
    국제부흥개발은행

international business finance   국제
적 기업재무(財務)

International Commerce Commission
    (ICC)   국제상업위원회

International Commercial Terms
    (Incoterms)   국제상업용어

International Committee for the
    Coordinations of the
    Accountancy Profession
    (ICCAP)   회계업무국제협조
위원회 ▶ International

Federation of Accountants

International Communication
    Association(ICA)   국제통
신협회

International Computer Center(ICC)
    국제계산센터

International Conference on
    Accounting Education   국
제회계교육회의

International Congress of Accounting
    (ICA)   국제회계사협회

international diversification   국제 분
산투자 ▶ diversification

international double tax   국제 이중과
세

International Electrotechnical
    Commission(IEC)   국제전
기표준회의

International Federation for
    Information Processing
    (IFIP)   정보처리학회 국제연
합

International Federation of
    Accuntants(IFAC)   국제
회계사연맹

international financial reporting   국
제재무보고

international financial statement   국
제재무제표

International Fiscal Association(IFA)
    국제재정(財政)협회

International Frequency Registration
    Board (IFRB)   국제주파수
등록회의

International Guidelines on Auditing
    and Related Services
    (IAG/RSs)   감사와 감사관련

업무에 관한 국제적지침

international intercompany transfer price 국제대체가격

International Journal of Accounting, Education and Research 일리노이 대학의 국제회계연구센터(University of Illinois Center for International Education and Research in Accounting)의 기관지, 1966년 창간, 연2회 발행

International Monetary Fund(IMF) 국제통화기금
▶ International Bank for Reconstruction and Development

international operation 해외사업활동, 국제거래

International Organization of Securities Commission and Similar Agencies(IOSCO) 증권감독자 국제기구
▶ International Accounting Standards Committee

International Standards Organization (ISO) 국제표준화기구

International Statement on Auditing 감사의 국제적 성명서

International Telecommunications Satellite Consortium (Intelsat) 국제전기통신 위성기구

International Telecommunication Union(ITU) 국제전기통신 연합

international trade 국제무역

International Trade Commission(ITC) 국제무역위원회

internet 인터넷

interperiod relationship 기간(期間) 상호관계

interperiod tax allocation 법인세의 기간배분, (법인)세 등의 기간배분, 기업간 세금배분

interpret 해석하다, 통역하다, 번역하다
▶ interpreter

interpretation 해석, 해석지침

interpretation of the FASB FASB의 해석지침

interpretive routine 해석 루틴(일련의 절차)

interrelationship 상호관계

interrogation 질문, 의문

interrupt 1) 방해하다, 방해하는 기구 = interruption 2) 중단시키다

interruption 방해, 중단 = interrupt

intersection 교차점, 교집합

interstate commerce 주간통상(州間通商), 주제(州際) 통상(通商)

Interstate Commerce Commission (ICC) 주제(州際)상업위원회

interstate succession 상속

interval estimate 구간추정치

interval estimation 구간추정

intervening period test 중간기간검사

interview 면접조사

inter vivos gift 생전(生前)증여

inter vivos trust 생전(生前)신탁

intestacy 무(無)유언사망, 무유언사망인의 유산(遺産) ▶ testment, will

intestate 무유언사망자

intestate offering 주내(州內) 모집(募集)

intestate succession 무유언 상속, 법정상속

intestate succession statute 주(州)의

상속법

intor vivos trust 생존 중 신탁

intoxicated person 몹시 술에 취한 사람

intoxication 술에 취함

intra-company transfer 내부대체 = internal transfer

intra-company transfer price 내부 대체가격 = internal transfer price

intra-company transfer pricing 내부 대체가격의 결정 = internal pricing

intraday high and low 당일의 고값, 저값

intranet 인트라넷

intraperiod tax allocation 세금의 기간내 배분

intrastate commerce 주내(州內) 통상 (通商)

intrastate exemption 주내(州內) 면책

intrastatement tax allocotion 항목별 법인세 효과 분석

intrinsic motivation 내적 동기 부여 ▶ extrinsic motivation

intrinsic value 내재가치, 본래가치, 본원적 가치, 본질적 가치, 진정 (眞正)가치

introduction (영)도입, 소개, 채용 ▶ offer for sale, placing

introductory paragraph 도입단락

invasion of privacy 사생활 침해

inventoriable cost 재고가능원가 = inventory costinventory

inventory 1) 재고자산, 재고품 = stock 2) 상품목록, 재고표 3) 재고조사, 재고파악

inventory accounting 재고자산회계

inventory allowance to report 재고 허용수준 보고

inventory and production cycle 재고 및 생산순환과정

inventory at lower of cost or market 저가법으로 평가된 재고자산

inventory audit 재고자산감사

inventory budget 재고예산

inventory carrying cost 재고자산유지 비용 = holding cost, storage cost ▶ inventory cost, ordering cost

inventory control 재고관리 = inventory management

inventory cost 1) 재고자산원가 2) 재고 비용 ▶ inventory carrying cost, ordering cost

inventory depreciation 재고법

inventory equation 재고자산 등식

inventory error 재고자산의 오류

inventory gain or loss 재고자산의 이득 또는 손실

inventory holding gain 재고자산 보유 이익

inventory level 재고수준

inventory management 재고관리 = inventory control ▶ carrying cost, economic orderquantity, safety stock, stockout cost, two-bin system

inventory management program and control technique(IMPACT) 재고관리 프로그램과 통제기법

inventory method 1) 실지재고조사법, 재고자산 평가방법 ▶ derivative method 2) 재고

계산법 = periodic inventory
method, periodic stockthking
▶ perpetual inventory method,
physical inventory
inventory model (경제적 발주량)재고
모델, 재고관리 모형
inventory of asset and liability 자산
과 부채의 실지재고조사표
inventory pricing 재고자산평가
inventory profit 재고이익
inventory profit or loss 재고자산손익
inventory purchased 재고자산 매입
inventory requisition 재고상품 발주서
inventory reserve 재고자산준비금
inventory sheet 재고조사표
▶ inventory ticket
inventory shortage 재고자산감모손,
재고차손
inventory shrinkage 재고자산감모
▶ abnormal shrinkage,
shrinkage, spoilage, waste
inventory subsidiary ledger 재고자
산보조원장
inventory tag 재고조사표 = inventory
ticket
inventory ticket 재고조사표
= inventory tag ▶ inventory
sheet
inventory turnover 재고자산회전율,
재고자산회전수 = stock
turnover
inventory turnover period 재고자산
회전기간, 재고회전기간
inventory turnover rate 재고자산회
전율, 재고회전율
inventory turnover ratio 재고자산회
전율 ▶ turnover ratio, account

receivable turnover ratio
inventory unit 재고단위
inventory valuation 재고자산평가, 재
고평가 ▶ inventory written
down, lower of cost or market
basis
inventory value 재고자산평가액
inventory written down 재고평가손
▶ inventory waluation, lower
of cost or market
inverse matrix 역행렬(逆行列)
inverse relationship 반비례 ▶ 정비례
(direct relationship)
invert 반전되다, 역전하다
invested capital 투하자본
= contributed capital ▶ issued
capital, paid-in capital
invested capital of division 사업부문
의 투하자본
investee 피투자회사
investee company 피투자회사
investigation 조사(調査)
investigation department 조사부
investigative report (특수목적의) 조사
보고서
investing activity 투자활동
investing company (영)(관련회사에서의)
투자회사 ▶ investing group
investing cycle 투자순환과정
investing group (영)(관련회사에서의) 투
자그룹, 투자기업집단
▶ investing company
investment 투자, 투자자산, 투자유가
증권
investment advisor 투자자문
▶ Investment Advisors Act of
1940

Investment Advisors Act of 1940
1940년 투자자문법

investment analysis 투자분석

investment bank 투자은행
= investment banker
▶ merchant bank, issuing
house

investment banker 투자은행
= investment bank ▶ merchant
bank

investment banking 투자은행업무
▶ investment bank, investment
banker

investment budget 투자예산 = capital
budget, capital expenditure
budget, construction budget,
plant and equipment budget

investment by owner 소유주에 의한
투자

investment center 투자중심점
▶ cost center, profit center,
responsibility center

Investment Companies Act of 1940
1940년 투자회사법

investment company 투자회사, 투자
신탁회사

investment contract 투자계약

investment credit 투자세액공제
= investment tax credit

investment decision 투자의사결정
▶ capital budgering, cashflow,
net present value

investment fund 투자기금

investment horizon 투자 기간
▶ economic life of investment

investment in affiliated company 관
계회사투자 ▶ affiliated

company, related company

investment in bond 사채 투자

investment in closely held company
비공개회사 투자

investment income (영)투자에 따른
소득, 불로소득 = unearned
income

**investment in marketable equity
securities** 시장성이 있는
지분증권

investment in real estate 부동산 투자

investment in S 투자계정

investment in stock 주식투자자산

investment in stock right 주식인수권
투자

investment interest 투자에 따른 이자

investment letter 투자확인서
▶ private placement

investment manager 투자경영자

investment multiplier 투자승수

investment opportunity 투자기회

investment pool 투자목적 합동운영자산

investment potential (영)투자수익력

investment program 투자계획

investment property (영)투자부동산
▶ investment revaluation,
reserve, property

investment revaluation reserve 투자
(부동산)의 재평가적립금

investment securities 투자증권

investment tax credit(ITC) 투자세액
공제 = investment credit

investment trust 투자신탁(회사)
▶ investment company, mutual
fund

investment trust fund 투자신탁기금

investment turnover 투자자산회전율

= asset turnover, capital turnover

investment value (of a convertible security) (전환증권의) 투자가치

investment with significant influence 타사에 중대한 영향력을 갖는 투자자산

investment without significant influence 중대한 영향력을 갖고 있지 않은 투자자산

investor 1) 투자자, 출자자 2) 서임자(敍任者)

investor-owned enterprise 투자자가 소유하는 기업

invitation to offer 신청의 유인(誘引)

invitation to subscribe 청약모집

invitation to treat (상)상회의의 초대

invocation 호출하다

invoice 송장(送狀)

invoice amount 송장(결산장부)가액
= invoice value

invoice discounting 채권의 매각
▶ debt factoring

invoice register 송장기입장

invoice value 송장가액
= invoice amount

involuntary bankruptcy 비자발적 파산, 강제파산

involuntary bankruptcy petition 비자발적 파산 신청

involuntary conversion 비자발적전환

involuntary conversion of asset 자산의 비자발적 전환

involuntary dissolution 비자발적 해산, 강제해산, 강제파산

involuntary liquidation of LIFO inventory 비자발적 Lifo 재고의 청산

involuntary petition 강제신청

inward remittance 미지불 외국환어음

I/O(input/output) 입출력

IOSCO(International Organization of Securities Commission and Similar Agencies) 증권감독기관 국제기구

IOU(I owe you) 약식 차용증서

IPA(Insolvency Practitioners Association) 파산관재인협회

IPO(initial public offering) 신규상장, 최초의 공모

IR(Inland Revenue) (영) 내국세입청(內國歲入廳)

IRA(individual retirement account) 개인퇴직금구좌제도

IRC(Inland Revenue Commissioners) 내국세입(歲入)위원회

IRC(Internal Revenue Code) 내국세입법

IRR(internal rate of return) 내부이익률, 내부수익률

irrational number 무리수(無理數)

irrecoverable ACT (영)회수불능 예납법인세 ▶ Recoverable ACT

irredeemable debenture 무(無)상환사채

irregular fluctuation 불규칙변동

irregular gain and loss 비경상적 이득과 손실 ▶ extraordinary gain and loss

irregularity 부정(不正)

irrelevant cost 비관련원가, 무관련원가, 매몰원가 ▶ relevant cost, sunk cost

irrevocable agencies 철회불능 대리

irrevocable (letter of) credit   철회불능
   신용장, 취소불능신용장
   ▶ confirmed credit
irrevocable offer   철회불능 신탁
irrevocable trust   철회불능 신탁
IRS(Internal Revenue Service)   내국세
   입청(內國歲入廳)
IRS Proceeding   IRS 소송절차
IRS Revenue Procedure   내국세입청
   절차, 내국국절차
IRS Ruvenue Ruling   내국세입청 재정
   (裁定)
IS(information separator)   정보분리 문
   자
ISO(incentive stock option plan)   주식매
   수선택권 인센티브제도
**ISO(International Standards
   Organization)**   국제표준화
   기구
issuance   공표(公表)
issuance of general longterm debt   일
   반고정부채의 발행
issue   1) 자녀, 자손 2) 제(諸)문제
issue cost   발행비용
issued capital   (영)발행된 자본
   = allotted capital, issued share
   capital ▶ authorised capital,
   nominal share capital
issued share   발행주식 = issued stock
   ▶ unissued share, unissued
   stock

issued share capital   (영)발행주식자본
   = issued capital
issued stock   기발행주식
issue equity theory   발행지분설
   ▶ entity equity theory, equity
   theory
issue price   발행가격 ▶ carrying
   amount, face value, maturity
   value, reacquisition price
issuer   발행자
issues paper   문제집자료
issuing   발행
issuing enterprise   발행회사
issuing house   (영)(증권)발행상사, 발행
   수탁회사 = investment bank
Italian system of bookkeeping   이탈
   리아식 부기법
ITC(International Trade Commission)
   국제무역위원회
ITC(investment tax credit)   투자세액
   공제
item   항목 = field
item depreciation   개별상각 = single-
   unit depreciation ▶ composite
   depreciation
itemized deduction   항목별 공제
iteration factor   반복요소
ITF(integrated test facility)   종합자료
   검증법, 통합테스트법
**ITU(International Telecommunication
   Union)**   국제전기통신연합

J

JCL(job control language) 작업관리 언어

JDS(Joint Disciplinary Scheme) (영)(칙허회계사협회의) 합동징벌제도

JES(job entry subsystem) 작업기입 하위조직

JIT(just in time) 무재고시스템

job 1) 일, 작업 2) 직업, 직장 3) 직무, 역할, 기능

job accounting facility 작업회계기능

job accounting interface 작업회계 영역

job accounting routine 작업회계루틴

job accounting table 작업회계일람표

job backup file 작업파일백업 = job recovery control file

jobber 1) 중매업자 2) (싼물품을 대량으로 매입하여 소매상에 파는) 중계업자 3) 공적 지위를 이용하여 사리를 도모하는 사람

job card 작업시간표, 작업시간보고서

job control 작업관리

job control language(JCL) 작업관리 언어

job control statement 작업관리문장

job cost 개별원가 = job order cost
▶ job order costing

job cost card 개별원가계산표, 제조지시서별 원가계산표 = job order cost sheet

job costing 개별원가계산, 제조지시서별 원가계산 = job order costing

job costing accounting 개별원가계산, 제조지시서별 원가계산 = job order costing

job cost record 개별원가기록, 제조지시서별 원가계산

job cost sheet 제조지시서별 원가계산표 = job cost card, job order cost sheet

job cost system 개별원가계산, 제조지시서별 원가계산 = job order costing

job definition 작업(직무) 정의

job description 직무기술서

job development credit 직업개발세액공제, 고용촉진세액공제 = targeted jobs tax credit

job documentation 직무문서

job enlargement 직무확대

job enrichment 직무충실화

job entry central service 작업입력 중앙서비스

job entry peripheral service 작업입력 주변업무

job entry subsystem(JES) 작업입력 하위조직

job finished report 작업완료보고서

job input device 작업입력장치

job input file 작업입력파일

job input stream 작업입력흐름

job lot costing 작업로트별 개별원가계산 = lot costing

job management   직무(작업)관리

job name   직무(작업)명

job order   제조지시서 = production order

job order accounting   개별원가계산, 제조지시서별 원가계산 = job order costing

job order cost   개별원가, 제조지시서별 원가 = job cost
▶ job order costing

job order cost accounting   개별원가계산, 제조지시서별 원가계산 = job order costing

job order costing   개별원가 = job costing, job costing accounting, job cost system, job order accounting, job order cost accounting, job order cost system, job order system, production order costing, specific order cost system, specific order costing ▶ continuous operation costing, job order cost sheet, process costing

job order costing system   개별원가 계산제도

job order cost sheet   개별원가계산표, 제조지시서별 원가계산표 = job cost card, job cost sheet ▶ cost ledger, job order costing, production order

job order cost system   개별원가계산제도, 제조지시서별 원가계산제도 = job order costing

job order system   개별원가계산, 제조지시서별 원가계산 = job order costing

job-oriented terminal   특정업무용 단말장치

job output device   작업출력장치

job output file   작업출력파일

job pack area   작업 팩 구역

job priority   직무(작업) 우선순위

job processing   작업처리

job queue   작업에 대한 대기행렬

job recovery control file   작업회복제어 파일 = job backup file

job-related accommodation   (영)사택(社宅), 관사(官舍), 공택(公宅)

job satisfaction   직무만족

job security   직업안정

job sheet   작업시간표, 작업시간보고서 = time ticket

job shop scheduling   특정의 기능별 공정계획

job specification   작업지시명세서

job standard   작업표준, 과업

job step   작업단계

job step initiation   작업단계 개시

job step restart   작업단계 재시동

job stream   작업흐름 = input stream, run stream

job study   작업연구, 직무연구 = job analysis

job tax credit   고용촉진세액공제 = job development credit

job ticket   작업시간표, 작업시간보고서 = time ticket

job time card   작업시간표, 작업시간보고서 = time ticket

job time ticket   작업시간표, 작업시간보고서, 작업기록 = time ticket

Johnson's sequencing problem   존슨의 순서문제

J

Joint 결합, 연대

joint adventure 공동출자사업
= joint venture

joint and several liability 연대보증인
이 보증한도에서 채권자에게 이
행할 책임, 기업측 연대책임, 공
동 및 단독책임

joint consignment 조합(組合)매매

joint control 공동 지배권

joint cost 결합원가, 연결원가

joint cost allocation 결합원가의 배분
▶ joint cost

joint disciplinary scheme(JDS) (영)합
동징벌제도

joint fixed cost 공통고정비

joint investment 합병, 공동투자

joint liability 공동채무, 연대책임
▶ several liability

**Joint Panel to Review Non-Compliance
with Accounting Standard**
(영)회계기준위반 합동심사위
원회

joint product 연산품 = co-product
▶ by-product, joint cost, joint
product cost system

joint product cost 연산품 원가, 결합
원가

joint product cost accounting 연산품
원가계산 = joint product
casting, joint product system

joint product cost allocation 연산품
원가의 배부

joint product costing 연산품 원가계산
= joint product cost accounting,
joint product cost system

joint product cost system 연산품 원가
계산 = joint product costing,

joint product cost accounting

joint report 공동감사보고서

joint stock association 공동주식연합,
공동주식조합

joint stock bank (영)공동주식은행

joint stock company 공동주식회사

joint stock trust (시장 독점을 위해 결성
된) 공동주식회사

joint tenancy 1) 공동소유권 2) 공동
부동산권 3) 합유(合有)소유권

joint tenant 공동소유자

joint test 결합 테스트

joint variance 혼합차이, 결합차이
▶ cost variance

joint venture 공동출자사업, 합작투자,
합작회사, 합병사업 = joint
adventure

joint will 공동유언(서)

journal 1) 분개장 2) 거래기록 3) 항해
= log

journal book 분개장

journal entry 분개장 입력
= journalizing

journalizing 분개, 분개기장 = journal
entry

Journal of Accountancy 미국공인회
계사협회(American Institute of
Certified Public Accountants)의 기
관지, 1950년에 창간된 월간지

Journal of Accounting and Economics
로체스터대학 대학원 경영연구
과 (Graduate School of Business
Administration, University of
Rochester) 편집의 연구지, 연3회
발행

*Journal of Accounting, Auditing &
Finance* 예일대학의 로스

회계연구협회 (Ross Institute of Accounting Research)에서 편집한 계간 연구지

Journal of Accounting Research 시카고대학 대학원의 경영연구과 (University of Chicago, Graduate School of Business, Institute of Professional Accounting) 발행 회계연구지, 1936년 창간해서 연 3회 발행, 현재 연2회 발행

Journal of Business 시카고대학 대학원 경영연구과 (Graduate School of Business, University of Chicago) 발행 경영학 연구지. 1928년 창간 계간지

Journal of Taxation 미국 조세전문가의 월간지

journal proper 일반분개장

journal slip 분개전표

Journal UEC : European Journal of Accountancy 유럽회계사연합 (L'union Europeenne des Experts Comptables Economiques et Financiers, UEC)의 기관지. 1967년 창간 계간지

journal voucher 분개증빙, 분개전표

joy stick 수동식 조작장치

judge 재판관

judgement 판단, 판결

judgement lien 판결 담보권, 판결 유치권

judgment creditor 판결 채권자
▶ judgment debtor

judgment debt 판결 채무

judgment debtor 판결 채무자
▶ judgment creditor

judicial definition 판례

jump instruction 비월명령

junior accountant 하급회계사, 견습 회계사 ▶ senior accountant

junior lien bond 후순위 선취특권부 사채 ▶ lien bond

junior lien mortgage 후순위 선취특권 담보

junior mortgage bond 후순위 물적담보부 사채

junior security (청구권에서의) 하위증권
▶ senior security, subordinated security

junk bond (미)위험도 높은 값싼 증권

jury duty pay remitted to employer 고용주에게 되갚은 배심원으로서의 수입

justice 공평성 ▶ fairness

justification 1) 정당화, 변호 2) 위치 조정 ▶ left-justify

just in time(JIT) 무재고시스템

just in time(JIT) costing 무재고시스템하의 원가계산

just price 공정가격

J

K

Kaizan budgeting　카이잔 예산
Kardex System　카덱스식 장부
Karnaugh map　카노프 지도
KC(King's Counsel)　칙선변호사
　　　= Queen's Counsel(Q.C)
Keogh plan　키오 계획 = individual
　　　retirement account
key　열쇠, 색인 = label, tag
keyboard　키보드, 건반
keyboard send/receive(KSR)　건반
　　　송수신
key factor　주요요인, 제한요소
　　　= limiting factor
keying　건반을 치다
key verification　키 입력검증
keyword　키워드, 색인어, 주요단어
keyword in context(KWIC)　키워드 검
　　　색
keyword in context index(KWIC index)
　　　키워드 검색, 키워드 색인
King's Counsel(KC)　칙선변호사

　　　= Queen's counsel
kinship　혈족관계
kite bill　금융어음, 융통어음
　　　▶ accommodation bill
kiting　1) (수표의) 초과발행　2) 공수표
kiting check　융통수표, 융통어음을 발
　　　행하다
knockdown system　낙찰방식
know-how　노하우, 기술지식, 기술정보,
　　　실제적 지식
knowledge of error　오류의 인식
known misstatement　이미 알려진 왜
　　　곡표시금액
known party　인식하고 있는 당사자
Kreuger & Toll Co. Case　클루거 앤
　　　톨 회사사건
KSR(keyboard send/receive)　건반 송수
　　　신
Kuhn-Tucker theorem　쿤 · 터커 정리
KWIC(keyword in context)　키워드 검
　　　색

L

LAAI(Licentiate of the Institute of
　　Administrative Accountant)
　　관리회계사협회회원

label　1) 표(標), 명찰 = key, tag 2) 표 (프
　　로그램에서의)
labeling method　라벨링법

labor   1) 노동, 노동력 = labour 2) 노동
          자 3) 노동비 = labor cost
laboratory experiment   연구실 실험
          ▶ laboratory test
laboratory test   (상품에 대한) 과학적 테
          스트, 연구실 테스트
          ▶ laboratory experiment
labor budget   노무비예산 = labor cost
          budget
labor cost   노무비 ▶ classification of
          cost by nature, wage
labor cost analysis   노무비분석
labor cost budget   노무비예산
labor cost percentage method   노무비
          백분율법
labor cost summary   노무비집계표
labor cost variance   직접노무비차이
labor distribution report   작업내용 보
          고서
labor efficiency   작업효율
labor efficiency variance   (표준원가계
          산) 작업시간차이, 작업능률차
          이 = labor hour variance
labor hour method   작업시간법
labor hour variance   작업시간차이, 노
          동시간차이 = labor
          efficiency variance, labor time
          variance ▶ labor rate variance
labor laws   노동관계법
labor mix variance   노무비혼합차이
          ▶ labor hour variance, labor
          yield variance
labor productivity   노동생산성
labor rate   임률 = wage rate
labor rate standard   임률표준
          ▶ labor time standard, direct
          labor standard

labor rate variance   임률차이 = wage
          rate variance ▶ labor hour
          variance
labor related cost   노무관련원가
labor time   작업시간
labor time standard   표준작업시간
          ▶ direct labor standard, labor
          rate standard
labor time ticket   작업시간표, 작업시
          간보고서 = time ticket
labor time variance   작업시간차이, 노
          동시간차이 = labor hour
          variance
labor turnover   노동이직률
labor union   노동조합 = trade union
labor variance   노무비차이, 직접노무
          비의 원가차이 ▶ labor hour
          variance, labor rate variance,
labor yield variance   노무비능률차이
          ▶ labor hour variance, labor
          mix variance
laches   권리를 행사하는 청구가 늦음
lack of consistency   (회계원칙 적용방법
          상의) 중요한 변경에 따른 계속
          성 결여
lag   뒤떨어지다
LAN(local area network)   구내정보통신
          망, 기업내 정보통신망
land   토지
land and building   토지와 건물 ▶ plant
          and equipment, property
land appreciation   토지평가이익
          ▶ accretion, appreciation
landing charge   하역료
landlord   임대인
land mortgage   토지의 저당증권
land residual technique   토지잔여법

K

L

▶ building residual technique, income approach

Landrum-Griffin Act 랜드럼 그리핀법

language 언어

lapping 외상매출금 회수 시간차이를 이용한 부정행위

lapse 유증의 실효, 경과

lapse of time 시간의 경과

large business GAAP 대기업에 대한 일반적으로 인정된 회계원칙 ▶ big GAAP, little GAAP, small business GAAP

large company 대회사, 대기업 ▶ small company

large sample 대규모 표본

large scale integrated circuit(LSI) 대규모집적회로 ▶ integrated circuit

large stock dividend (20%~25% 초과) 주식배당

Laspeyres formula 라스파레스 산식 ▶ Laspeyres index, Paasche formula

Laspeyres index 라스파레스 지수 ▶ Laspeyres formula, Paasche index

last-bag system 라스트 백 시스템 = two-bin system

last cost method 최종매입원가법

last-in first-out(LIFO) 후입선출법

last-in first-out basis 후입선출기준 ▶ last-in first-out method

last-in first-out dollar value method 화폐가치후입선출법 = dollar-value, last-in first-out method ▶ dollar value LIFO inventory

last-in first-out inventory layers 후입선출법에 의한 기말 재고자산의 계층

last-in first-out method(LIFO) 후입선출법 ▶ first-in, first-out method; first-in on hand, average method, periodic average method

last-in first-out reserve 후입선출법 충당금 = 선입선출법 준비금 = allowance to reduce inventory to LIFO

last-in on hand 후입재고법 = 선입선출법 = first-in first-out

last-in still-here(LISH) 후입재고법 ▶ first-in, first-out

latency 대기시간

latent 은밀한, 숨긴

latest event time 최지연 결합점시각

latest finishing time 최지연 종료시각

latest purchase price 최종취득원가

laundering 사용용도가 불분명한 소액 지출

law and regulation 법령

lawful money 법정통화 = legal tender

law of contract 계약법

law of corporation 회사법 = company law

law of exception 예외원리

law of large number 대수(大數)의 법칙

law of succession 상속법

lawyer inquiry 변호사 질문

layoff 일시해고

lay off pay 일시해고중의 급여

layout 설계, 배치

layout character (영)서식제어문자

= format effector

LBO(leveraged buyout)   기업담보 차입 매수

L/C(letter of credit)   신용장

LCM(lower of cost or market)   저가기준, 저가법

lead schedule   합계명세서

lead time   (경제적 발주량) 리드 타임, 준비시간

learning curve   학습곡선

learning machine   학습기계

learning rate   학습율 = learning curve

lease   1) 리스계약, 유체재(有體財) 임대차계약 ▶ charter, rental, trust 2) 차지(借地) 3) 광물자원의 개발 계약

lease accounting   리스회계

lease back   리스백, 판매 후 리스 = sale-leaseback ▶ lease

lease bonus   리스 보너스

lease capitalization   리스의 자산화

lease contract   리스계약

leased asset   리스자산

leased circuit   전용회선 = leased line

leased facility   전용설비

leased fee   리스기본료 ▶ fee simple

leased line   전용회선 = leased circuit

leased property   리스자산 = leased asset

leased property-estimated economic life of   리스자산-추정경제적 내용연수

leased property-estimated residual value of   리스자산-추정 잔존가액

leased property-fair value of   리스자산-공정가액

lease financing   리스자금조달

leasehold   정기임대차권리 = term of years absolute

leaseholder   정기임대차권자

leasehold estate   부동산이용권 ▶ lease interest

leasehold improvement   리스물건 개량비, 리스개량자산

leasehold interest   이용권 ▶ leasehold estate

leasehold land   (영)(토지의) 정기임차권, 토지임차권, 차지권, 임차지(賃借地) ▶ freehold land, freehold property

leasehold property   정기임대차의 대상이 되는 리스자산

leasehold right   정기임대차의 대상이 되는 리스자산권리

lease improvement   리스 개량비

lease interest   부동산임차권

lease obligation   리스채무

lease-or-borrowing decision   리스 또는 차입에 대한 결정 ▶ lease-or-buy decision

lease-or-buy decision   임차 또는 구입에 대한 의사결정

lease payment   지급리스료

lease purchase   리스구입

lease receivable   미수리스료

lease revenue   수취리스료

lease term   리스기간

leasing commitment   리스계약약정

leasing industry   리스업계

least significant   최하위

least square method   최소자승법 = method of least squares ▶ scatter diagram method

L

least square regression line 최소자승
회귀선 = method of least squares

ledger 원장(元帳) ▶ general ledger,
subsidiary ledger

ledger account 원장계정

ledger folio(LF) 원장쪽수

ledgerless bookkeeping 무(無)원장 장
부조직

ledger transfer method 원장대체법

left-justify 좌측으로 가지런히하다
▶ justify

legacy 동산(動産)의 유증(遺贈), 유증, 유
산 = bequest

legal capacity 법적 능력

legal capacity to contract 법적 계약능
력

legal capital 법정자본, 법정자본금
▶ authorised capital

legal corporation 법적인 회사

legal definition 법률상의 정의

legal detriment 법적 불이익

legal difficulty 법적 곤란성

legal entity 법적 실체 ▶ accounting
entity

legal estate 재산권, 부동산권 = estate

legal holiday 공휴일, 법정휴일
▶ bank holiday

legal interest 법정이자

legality 합법성, 적법성

legality of contract 계약의 적법성

legal liability of accountant 회계사의
법적 책임

legal list rule 법정 품목

legally sufficient 법적으로 충분한

legal mortgage (영)법률상의 양도담보
▶ equitable mortgage

legal opinion 법률전문가의 의견

legal proceeding 법적 절차

legal remedies 법적 구제수단

legal responsibility 법적 책임

legal sanction 법률적 인가

legal tender 법정통화 = lawful money

legal title (부동산의) 법적 소유권, 법적
권원

legal value 법정가격

legal welfare expense 법정복리비

legislation 법률제정

legislator 입법기관 = legislature

legislature 1) 입법기관 = legislator
2) 주(州)의회

lender 빌려주는 사람, 대주(貸主) , 여신
자(與信者)

lending 대출, 여신

lending activity 대출활동

lending institution 금융기관

length of operating cycle 정상영업 순
환기간 또는 일수

lessee 임차인, 리스임차인 ▶ lessor

lessee's incremental borrowing rate
리스의 추가차입이자율, 임차인
의 한계차입이자율
= incremental borrowing rate
▶ implicit rate computed by
lessor

lessee's interest 임차인의 권리
▶ lessor's interest

lesser quorum 정족수 (투표권이 있는 주
식의 과반수 출석 이하)

lessor 임대인, 리스임대인

lessor's implicit rate 리스회사의 내재
적 이율

lessor's interest 임대인의 권리
▶ lessee's interest

letter　활자, 문자, 영자

letter for auditor　감사의뢰장

letter for underwriter　증권인수권자
　를 위한 회계사 서한
　= comfort letter for underwriter
　▶ comfort letter

letter of administration　(영)재산관리
　증서

letter of advice　어음발행통지서

letter of allotment　배당증서
　= allotment letter, allotment
　certificate

letter of application　신청서

letter of audit engagement　감사계약
　서 = letter of engagement,
　engagement letter

letter of comfort　(영)증권인수권자를
　위한 회계사 서한
　= comfort letter

letter of comment　질문서, 논평의 문서
　▶ deficiency letter

letter of credit(L/C)　신용장
　= documentary credit

letter of engagement　계약서 = letter of
　audit engagement, engagement
　letter

letter of inquiry　조회문서

letter of insurance　보험결정통지서

letter of regret　증권신청 거절통지서

letter of representation　진술서, 확인
　서 = representation,
　representation letter

letter patent　개봉칙허장, 정부발행의
　허가증, 전매(專賣)특허증

letter security　비등록주식에 대한 채권,
　비등록증권 ▶ private
　placement, private placing

letter stock　비등록주(株) = unregistered
　stock

level　수준, 레벨

level annuity　정액연금(계산)
　▶ variable annuity

level indicator　레벨지시어, 레벨표식,
　레벨지시자

level number　레벨번호

level of assurance　확신정도

level of significance　유의(有意)수준, 중
　요성 수준

level of statistical significance　통계적
　유의수준 ▶ error of the first
　kind

leverage　지레원리, 지레작용, 레버리지,
　차입효과 = gearing
　▶ operating leverage,
　financial leverage

leveraged buyout(LBO)　기업담보 차
　입매수 ▶ merger and
　acquisition

leveraged lease　리스의 레버리지
　▶ direct financing lease

leverage ratio　레버리지 비율

levy　압류하다

LF(ledger folio)　원장쪽수

LF(line feed character)　개행(改行)

liability　1) 부채 ▶ debt, obligation
　2) 채무

liability allowance　부채성충당금
　▶ allowance, reserve,
　valuation allowance, valuation
　reserve

liability for endorsement　어음배서 의
　무

liability for guarantee　보증채무
　= liability on guaranty

L

liability for warranty   보증책임

liability insurance   책임보험

liability method   부채(負債)법

     ▶ income tax allocation (자산부채법)

liability of agent   대리인의 책임

liability of corporation   법인의 책임

liability off the book   부외(簿外)부채

liability of party of negotiable instrument   교부성 증권 당사자의 책임

liability of principal   본인의 책임

liability on guaranty   보증채무

     = liability for guarantee

liability represented by outstanding coupon   경품비 담보금

liability to FC dealer   외화표시 채권 · 채무 판매회사에 대한 지급채무

liberty of contract   계약의 자유

LIBOR(London inter-bank offered rate)   런던 은행간 이율

library control   보관통제 ▶ library

library management software   보관관리기능

library name   등록명(名)

license   면허, (특허권의) 사용권

license agreement   라이센스계약

licensed deposit-taker   (영) 공인예금업자 = licensed institution

licensee   허락받은 자

license fee   특허권사용료 = patent fee

licensing   (공인회계사에 대한) 자격인가 (資格認可)

Licentiate of the Institute of Administrative Accountant (LAAI)   (영) 관리회계사협회 회원

lien   리엔, 담보권, 선취특권, 유치권

lien creditor   담보 채권자, 법정담보 채권자

life   존속기간

life annuity   종신연금, 평생연금

     ▶ limited annuity

life cycle   생활주기, 생애주기

     ▶ system life cycle, system design

life estate   종신부동산권, 종신물권 (부동산)

life estate pur autre   종신 부동산을 만드는 경우에 기준이 다른 사람의 삶인 경우

life insurance   생명보험

life insurance dividend   생명보험 배당금

life insurance premium   생명보험료

life insurance proceed   생명보험금

life interest   1) 평생부동산이용권 2) 생애권

liferent   (영) 평생배당수령권

life tenant   종신부동산권자

lifetime gift   생전(生前)증여

lifetime learning credit   평생학문 세액공제

LIFO(last in, first-out method)   후입선출법

LIFO layer liquidation   후입선출법에 의한 기초재고량의 청산 혹은 결손 ▶ LIFO inventory layer

LIFO liquidation   후입선출법에 의한 청산

LIFO reserve   LIFO에 의한 자본잠식에 대한 보충준비금, 결손보충준비금

LIFO retail method   후입선출소매재고

법 ▶ retail inventory method

light industry 경공업 ▶ heavy industry

light pen (전산) 라이트펜

light pen tracking 라이트펜 추적

light stability 빛의 안정도, 광안정성

likely misstatement 발생가능왜곡표시

limitation of action 소송제출기한
= limitation period

limitation of audit 재무제표감사의 고유한계

limitation of internal control 내부통제의 고유한계

limitation of statute 소멸시효

limitation of warranty 담보책임의 제한

limitation period 소송제출기한
= limitation of action

limit check 한도검사

limited(Ltd.) 유한책임의 회사

limited annuity 유기한연금 = terminable annuity ▶ life annuity

limited assurance 제한된 확신, 한정보증 = negative assurance

limited business activity 제한된 기업활동

limited company 유한책임회사
= limited liability company

limited duration 유한의 지속기간

limited exceptions 약간의 예외

limited liability 한정책임, 유한책임
▶ unlimited liability, limited company

limited liability company(LLC) 유한책임회사 ▶ limited liability, unlimited liability

limited liability of stockholder 주주유한책임

limited liability partnership 유한책임파트너십

limited liability partnership(LLP) 유한책임파트너십

limited opinion 부분의견, 단편적의견
= piecemeal opinion

limited partner 유한책임사원, 유한책임조합원 = special partner
▶ general partnership

limited partnership 유한파트너십, 유한책임조합

limited review 제한적 검토 = review

limited scope examination 범위한정감사

limiting factor 제한요소 = key factor

limit order 가격지정주문 ▶ market order

limit(reasonableness) test 한계(합리성)검증

line 1) 명령계통 2) 복사품의 묘사 3) 운행노선 4) 조립공정 5) 선, 회선, 행

linear combination 선형결합, 1차결합

linear function 1차함수

linearity 선형성(線型性) ▶ non-linearity

linearly dependent 일차종속

linearly independent 일차독립

linear programming(LP) 선형계획법
▶ mathematical programming

line department 라인부문, 집행부문, 실시부문 = operating department

line feed character(LF) 개행문자

line graph 선 그래프

line number 1) 행번호 2) 회선번호

line number editing 행번호 편집

line of business 사업의 종류 ▶ line

of business reporting, segment
reporting

line of business information　사업의
종류별 정보 ▶ segment
information

line of business program　사업의 종류
별 보고프로그램

line of business reporting　사업의 종
류별 보고 ▶ segmental
reporting, line of business

line of credit　신용한도

line of discount　할인한도

line organization　라인조직

line printer　행 인쇄장치 = printer

line printing　행 인쇄

line relay　선로단전기

line switching　회선교환

link　1) 연계, 연결 = linkage 2) 연계하다

linkage　연계, 연결 = link

linkage editing　연계편집

linkage editor　연계편집자, 연계편집
프로그램

link-chain index　연환(쇠사슬)지수
= link index

link-chain method　연쇄법

liquid asset　당좌자산 ▶ current asset,
fixed asset, long-lived asset

liquidate damage　확정손해배상액

liquidated damage　불합리한 거액의
약정 손해배상

liquidated damage clause　미리 정해
진 손해배상 조항

liquidated debt　확정채무

liquidating corporation　청산법인

liquidating distribution　청산배분

liquidating dividend　청산배당

liquidation　1) 청산 = winding up 2) 결

제

liquidation balance sheet　청산대차대
조표

liquidation dividend　청산배당

liquidation of subsidiary　자회사의 청
산

liquidation of the investment　투자의
처분

liquidation value　청산가치

liquidator　청산인

liquid fund　유동자금

liquidity　유동성 ▶ current ratio

liquidity preference　유동성선호

liquidity ratio　유동성비율 ▶ acid test
ratio, current ratio, quick ratio

liquidity risk　유동성위험

liquid resource　유동자원

liquor tax　주세(酒稅)

LISH(last-in, still-here)　후입재고법
▶ first-in, first-out

LISP(list processing)　목록처리과정

lis pendens　소송진행 사실을 등기하여
부동산을 취득하려는 자가 선량
구매자가 되는 것을 방지

list　계열, 목록, 명부, 명세서

listed company　상장회사 = listed
corporation, public company,
quoted company ▶ listed share,
listed stock, unlisted company,
unquoted company

listed investment　상장증권에 대한 투
자

listed security　상장유가증권

listed share　상장주식 = listed stock

listing　상장 ▶ listing agreement

listing agreement　1) 유가증권상장 규
정 ▶ listing 2) (영)상장 규정

listing application　상장신청, 상장신청서

listing particular　(영)상장명세서

listing requirement　상장요건

list of equipment　비품목록, 비품대장
　　　▶ list of fixed asset

list of fixed asset　고정자산대장, 고정
　　　자산목록 ▶ list of equipment

list of weight and measurement　중량
　　　용적증명서

list organization　리스트편성

list price　정가

list processing　목록처리

list structure　목록구조 ▶ tree
　　　structure

lite pendente　소송중인, 자문중인
　　　= pendente lite

literal constant　불변정수

literal performance　완전한 이행

literature search　문헌탐색

litigation　소송

litigation, claim and assessment　소
　　　송, 배상청구 및 부과

litigation liability　소송부채

litigation officer　소송담당관

little GAAP　폐쇄회사와 소규모회사에
　　　적용하는 GAAP = small
　　　business GAAP ▶ big GAAP,
　　　large business GAAP

lives　내용연수

lives in being　생물

livestock　가축(家畜) ▶ dead stock

living trust　생전(生前)신탁

LLC(limited liability company)　유한
　　　책임회사 ▶ limited liability,
　　　unlimited liability

LLP(limited liability partnership)　유한
　　　책임파트너쉽

load　1) 짐, 적재량 2) 짐을 싣다, 적재하
　　　다

load charge　판매수수료 ▶ investment
　　　fund, mutual fund

loading　1) 선적(船積) 2) 부가(할증)보험
　　　료 3) 로딩

load module　로드 모듈

load point　선적지점

loan　1) 대출금 2) 대출 3) 차입금, 여신,
　　　채권

loan account　대출금계정

loan agreement　대출계약서

loan capital　부채, 차입자본, 타인자본,
　　　차입금 = borrowed capital,
　　　debt capital

loan crowd　증권대차당사자

loaned stock　신용거래의 차입주식

loan fee charged to the borrower　채
　　　무자가 부담하는 대출관련 수
　　　수료

loan from officer　임원차입금

loan fund　차입금 펀드

loan guarantee scheme　(영)융자보증
　　　제도

loan loss coverage ratio　대손율

loan obligation　차입금 지급의무

loan on bill　어음대여금, 어음대여
　　　= loan on note

loan on deed　대출금 증서 ▶ loan on
　　　bill

loan on note　어음대출금, 어음대출
　　　= loan on bill

**loan origination cost incurred by
　　　lender**　채권자 쪽에 발생한
　　　대여에 따른 비용

loan origination fees　대출수수료

loan payable　차입금 ▶ loan

L

receivable

loan payable from officer 임원차입금
= loan from officer

loan position 대출 상태 ▶ money
position

loan price 대부금 대가

loan receivable 대여금, 대출금 ▶ loan
payable

loan redemption 차입금상환

loan stock (양도가능)채권 = unsecured
stock ▶ debenture stock

loan to affiliated company 관계회사
대출금

loan to director 임원대출금 ▶ loan to
officer

loan to officer 임원대출금 ▶ loan to
director

loan trust 대출신탁

local area network (LAN) 구내정보
통신망, 기업내 정보통신망

local authority 지방자치단체

Local Authority Association (영)지방
자치단체연합

local bond 지방채(地方債)
▶ municipal bond interest

local channel 시내회선

local chapter 지방지부(支部)

local currency 현지통화 = functional
currency ▶ home currency

local filing 지역 등록

local government 지방정부

local governmental unit 지방자치단체

local tax 지방세

locate mode 위치지정모드

location (기억)장소 = storage

location counter 기억위치카운터

lockbox 사서함

lockbox plan 사서함방식

locking 로킹

lock out 1) 공장폐쇄, 로크아웃 2) 축출
= protection

locus sigilli (LS) 날인장소

lodgement 1) 공탁, 예입 (영) 2) 제기하
다, 제의하다

log 1) 로그 2) 운전기록, 경과기록
= journal

logger 자동기록기

logging facility 로깅기능

logging technique 로깅수법

logic 논리

logical batch 이론 배치

logical comparison 논리비교

logical expression 논리식

logical multiply 논리적(論理積)

logic check 논리검증

logic design 논리설계

logic element 논리요소

logic symbol 논리기호

logic test 논리테스트

logistic 물적유통, 물류

logistic cost 물류비 = physical
distribution cost ▶ sales
promotion cost

London acceptance credit 런던은행
수용신용도

London and General Bank Case 런
던과 제너럴 은행사건

London Gazette (영)런던가제트, 관보
▶ Companies Registration
Office, Gazette registered
company

London inter-bank offered rate(LIBOR)
런던 은행간 이율

London shipper (영)런던의 수입대행

업자 = confirming house

long-dated bill　　장기어음 = long-dated
　　paper

longevity　　수명

long-form audit report　　장문식 감사보
　　고서 = long-form report
　　▶ short-form audit report,
　　short-form report

long hedging　　매입헤징 ▶ short hedging

long lease　　장기 리스

long-lived asset　　고정자산, 장기성자산
　　= capital asset, fixed asset,
　　long-term asset ▶ current
　　asset, liquid assetlong run

long-range budget　　장기예산
　　= long-term budget
　　▶ short-range budget

long-range cash forecast　　장기자금
　　예측

long-range cash planning　　장기자금
　　계획 = long-range fund
　　planning

long-range cost　　장기적 비용= long-run
　　cost ▶ short-range cost

long-range fund planning　　장기자금조
　　달 계획 = long-range
　　cashplanning ▶ short-range
　　fund planning

long-range management planning　　장
　　기경영계획 ▶ short-range
　　management planning

long-range profit planning　　장기이익
　　계획 ▶ short-range profit
　　planning, profit planning

long-run capacity cost　　장기생산설비
　　원가, 장기고정원가
　　▶ capacity cost

long-run cost　　장기비용 = long-range
　　cost ▶ short-run cost

long-run cost curve　　장기원가곡선
　　▶ short-run cost curve

long-term asset　　고정자산, 장기성자산
　　= fixed asset, long lived asset
　　▶ current asset, liquid asset

long-term bill　　장기어음

long-term budget　　장기예산 = long-
　　range budget ▶ short-range
　　budget

long-term capital　　장기자본 ▶ short-
　　term capital

long-term construction contract　　장기
　　건설공사

long-term construction work contract
　　장기건설공사계약
　　▶ completed job method,
　　percentage of completion
　　method

long-term contract　　장기계약
　　= long-term contract work in
　　progress

long-term contract profit　　장기계약에
　　귀속하는 이익 = attributable
　　profit

long-term contract work in progress
　　건설중인 장기공사계약
　　= long-term contract

long-term debt　　고정부채, 장기채무
　　= long-term liability, long-term
　　obligation ▶ current liability,
　　short-term debt

long-term debt from affiliated
　　company　　관계회사간 장기
　　차입금

long-term debt-paying ability　　장기

L

채무변제능력

long-term earning ability　장기적 수
익력

long-term investment　투자유가증권,
장기투자

**long-term investment in marketable
security**　시장성이 있는 유가
증권에 대한 장기투자

long-term liability　장기부채, 고정부채
= long-term debt, long-term
obligation ▶ current liability,
short-term debt

long-term loan　장기대출금, 장기융자
▶ short-term loan

long-term note payable　장기지급어음
▶ short-term note payable

long-term obligation　고정부채 장기채
무 = long-term debt

long-term payable　장기지급채무

long-term performance　장기적 업적

long-term receivable　장기수취채권

look-up　색인, 탐색

loop　루프

loopback test　국내(局內) 반복실험

loop checking system　반송(返送)조합
방식 = echo checking system

loophole　법을 빠져나갈 수단

loose leaf book　루즈리프식 장부

loose leaf system　루즈리프식

Lorenz curve　로렌츠곡선 ▶ degree of
inequality

loss　손실, 차손(次損), 손해

loss adjustment expense　손해조정비
(보험회계)

loss carryback　결손금의 소급, 차손금
의 소급 ▶ loss carry forward

loss carryforward　결손금의 이월, 결손

금의 이월공제 ▶ loss carry
back

loss contingency　우발적 손실
▶ contingency, contingency
liability, gain contingency

loss due to defective work　공손손실
= defective work cost
▶ spoilage cost

loss due to spoiled work　공손손실

**losses on deposit in insolvent financial
institution**　파산금융기관의
예치금 손실

loss from amalgamation　합병차손

loss from decline in the value of money
화폐가치하락에 따른 손실
= purchasing power losses on
monetary items ▶ gain from
decline in the value of money,
purchasing power gains or
losses on net monetary items

loss from lapsed discount　현금할인 미
이용 손실, 매입할인 미이용 손
실 = purchase discounts loss

loss from spoilage　공손손실 = spoilage
cost

loss leader　저가상품, 특저가품

loss on bad debt　대손손실

loss on cost and market　저가법에 대
한 손실

loss on discontinued operation　중단
된 영업활동에 따른 손실

loss on impairment　진부화에 따른 손
실

loss on purchase commitment　매입
계약상 손실

**loss on reduction of inventory to
market**　재고자산평가손실

loss on sale of building   건물처분손실

loss on sale of equity securities   지분
증권 처분손실

loss on spoilage   공손손실 = spoilage
cost

loss per share   1주당 손실
▶ earnings per share(EPS)

loss provision   손실준비금 = lossre serve

loss recognition   손실인식 ▶ accrual
basis

loss reserve   손실준비금 = loss provision

lost profit   상실된 이익

lost property   분실물, 유실물(遺失物)

lot   로트, 한벌 ▶ batch

lot cost   (영)로트원가, 조별원가 = batch
cost

lot costing   로트원가계산, 조별원가계산
= job lot costing, lot cost
system, batch costing ▶ lot

lot cost system   조별원가계산 = lot
costing

lot production   조별생산 = batch
production

lot size   공업제품의 생산단위 ▶ lot

lower bound   하한(下限)

lower of cost or market(LCM)   저가
기준, 저가법 ▶ net realizable
value, replacement cost

lower of cost or market basis   저가주
의, 원가 · 시가비교 저가법
▶ current replacement cost,

net realizable value, net
realizable value less overall
profit margin, replacement cost

lower of cost or market value   저가법
▶ aggregate basis, individual
item basis, inventory written
down

**lower realizable value or replacement
price rule**   실현가능가액 대
체원가비교 저가법 ▶ value to
the business

lowincome housing credit   저소득가구
세액공제

LP(linear programming)   선형계획법

LS(locus sigilli)   날인개소 (군데)

LSI(large scale integrated circuit)   대규
모집적회로

Ltd.(limited)   유한책임회사

lucky buy   행운매수, 저렴취득

Lukasiewicz notation   루카시비츠 표
기법 = Polish notation, prefix
notation

lump-sum contract   일괄계약

lump-sum payment   일괄지불, 일시지
불 ▶ lump-sum purchase

lump-sum purchase   일괄구입 = basket
purchase ▶ lump-sum payment

lump-sum repayment   일괄변제

lump-sum sale of stock   주식의 일괄
매각

L

_M_

m.(million)   백만

M&A(merger and acquisition)   기업합
　　병·매수

**MAAT(Member of the Association of
　　Accounting Technicians)**   (영)
　　회계기능자협회 회원의 칭호

Macfadden Act   1927년 은행법

machine control   기계관리

machine cost   기계비

machine hour   (표준원가계산에서) 기계시
　　간

machine hour basis   기계시간법
　　= machine hour method

machine hour method   기계시간법
　　= machine hour basis, machine
　　hour rate method, machine rate
　　method

machine hour rate   기계시간율
　　= machine rate ▶ machine
　　hour method

machine hour rate method   기계시간
　　율법 = machine hour method

machine independent   기계독립성

machine instruction   기계명령
　　= computer instruction

machine rate   기계시간율 = machine
　　hour rate

machine rate method   기계시간율법
　　= machine hour method

machine readable medium   기계판독
　　가능매체

**Machinery and Allied Products
　　Institute (MAPI)**   미국기계
　　공업협회

machinery & equipment   기계와 장비

macro accounting   매크로 회계, 거시
　　회계 ▶ social accounting

macro call   매크로 호출

macro definition   거시적 정의

macro expansion   대규모 확장

macro generating program   대규모 생
　　성프로그램 = macro generator

macro generation   대규모 생성, 매크
　　로 생성기 = macro generating
　　program

macro instruction   매크로 명령

macro language   매크로 언어

macro prototype   매크로 원형

**MACRS(modified accelearated cost
　　recovery system)**   수정가속
　　원가회수법

magazine subscription   잡지의 예약
　　판매

magnitude   1) 절대치, 중요도 2) 큰, 크
　　기, 거대함, 중대, 중요함

Magnuson-Moss Warranty Act   맥너
　　슨·모스 보증조항법

mail   우편

mail box rule   우편함 규정

mail transfer   우편대체송금

main account   주(主)계정

main book   주요 장부 ▶ subsidiary book

main control unit   주제어장치, 주제어
기구

main distributing frame(MDF)   주배
선반, 주단자반

main frame   주계산장치

main product   주산물(主産物)
▶ by-product

main production order   주(主)제품제
조지시서

main storage   주기억장치, 주기억, 주기
억기구 = main store

main store   (영)주기억장치 = main
storage

mainstream corporation tax(MCT)
(영)본(本)납부 법인세
▶ imputation system

maintainability   보수유지가능성

maintained markup   이익가산율유지
액 ▶ initial markup

maintenance   보수, 보전, 유지
▶ maintenance control

maintenance and repair allowance
수선유지충당금

maintenance and repair expense   수
선유지비

maintenance charge   유지비

maintenance control   유지관리

maintenance cost   유지비 = maintenance
charge, maintenance expense
▶ capital improvement

maintenance equalization provision
수선충당금 = allowance for
repair, reserve for repair

maintenance expense   유지비
= maintenance charge,
maintenance cost ▶ capital
improvement

maintenance of book and record   장부
서류의 정리보존

maintenance of capital   자본유지

maintenance of operating capability
조업능력의 유지 ▶ concept of
maintenance of operating
capability, financial capital
maintenance

maintenance of real capital   실질자본
유지 ▶ concept of
maintenance of operating
capability, constant purchasing
power accounting

maintenance time   보수시간

major component of internal control
내부통제를 구성하는 주요 요소

major costumor   주요 매출처, 주요 고
객

majority   다수결(연산자), 과반수

majority decision   다수결

majority interest   다수주주지분
= consolidated equity

majority owned company   다수지분에
의한 소유회사 = majority
owned subsidiary ▶ totally
hold subsidiary, wholly owned
subsidiary

majority owned subsidiary   다수지분
에 의한 종속회사 = majority
owned company ▶ totally hold
subsidiary, wholly owned
subsidiary

majority rule   다수결 = majority voting

majority stockholder   지배주주

majority vote   과반수 투표

major management change   주요 경
영진의 변동

M

major repair　대수선(大修繕)
　　　= extraordinary repair
　　　▶ ordinary repair
major structure　주요구조, 주(主)구조
　　　체
make or buy　자가제조 또는 외부구입
make or buy decision　자가제조 또는
　　　구입 의사결정 ▶ differential
　　　cost
maker　발행인, (어음의) 작성자
makeup time　조립시간
malfunction　오작동, 고장
malpractice　직무상 과실
malpractice insurance　직무상 과실 보
　　　험
managed capacity cost　관리가능생산
　　　시설원가 = managed cost
managed control　관리 통제
managed cost　관리가능비, 자유재량 고
　　　정비 = discretionary cost,
　　　managed capacity cost, policy
　　　cost, programmed cost
　　　▶ committed cost
managed currency　관리통화
management　1) 경영자, 경영관리자
　　　= manager　2) 경영관리
management accountant　관리회계 담
　　　당자
management accounting　관리회계
　　　= internal accounting, internal
　　　report accounting, managerial
　　　accounting ▶ financial
　　　accounting
Management Accounting　(영)영국 관
　　　리회계사칙허협회 (Charterd
　　　Institute of Management
　　　Accountants)의 기관지, 1965년

창간의 월간지
Management Accounting　미국전국
　　　회계사협회 (National Association
　　　of Accountants)의 기관지. 1916년
　　　에 NACA(NAA의 전신)의
　　　Official Publication 창간, 1925
　　　년에 NACA Bulletin으로 개칭.
　　　1965년부터 Management
　　　Accounting이란 이름으로 발간
　　　하는 월간지
management accounting guideline
　　　관리회계지침서
management accounting practice　관
　　　리회계실무
Management Accounting Practice
　　　Committee　관리회계실무
　　　위원회
management accounting system
　　　1) 관리회계의 체계　2) 관리회
　　　계제도
management advisory service(MAS)
　　　경영자문서비스
management approach　사업부문의
　　　결정방법
management audit　경영업무감사, 경영
　　　감사
management buyout(MBO)　기업매수
management by exception　예외에 의
　　　한 관리
management by objective(MBO)　목
　　　표에 의한 관리 = managing by
　　　objective
management charge　관리비
management consulting　경영자문
management control　경영 통제
　　　▶ operational control, strategic
　　　planning

management discretion　　경영자의 재량(裁量)

management expense　　경영비용

management fraud　　경영자의 부정행위

management game　　경영게임
　　= business game

management information　　경영정보

management information system(MIS)
　　경영정보시스템
　　▶ accounting information
　　system

management letter　　건의서, 경영층에 대한 회계사의 서한

management of research and development expense　　연구개발비 관리

management override　　경영자 우회

management planning　　경영계획

management policy　　경영방침

management procedure　　관리과정, 관리절차

management ratio　　경영비율
　　▶ financial statements analysis

management remuneration　　경영자의 보수

management reponsibilities　　경영책임

management report　　경영자의 보고서

management representation　　경영자의 진술서

management representation letter　　경영자 진술서

management's assertion　　경영자 주장

management science　　경영과학, 관리과학

management's discussion and analysis (MD&A)　　사업보고서에 포

함되는 경영자 토의 및 분석

management service　　경영자문, 경영자에 대한 제안업무

management's responsibility　　경영자의 책임

management's responsibility for financial statement　　재무제표에 대한 경영자의 책임
　　▶ auditing

management stewardship　　경영자의 수탁책임 ▶ accountability, agency theory, stewardship accounting

management through figure　　계수관리

management trail　　경영증적(證跡)
　　▶ audit trail

management type report　　관리용 보고서

manager　　1) 경영자, 관리자　2) (증권인수의) 간사

managerial accounting　　관리회계
　　= internal accounting, internal report accounting, management accounting ▶ financial accounting

managerial audit　　경영감사

managerial control　　경영통제
　　▶ managerial planning

managerial economics　　관리경제학

managerial effort　　경영자의 목표달성 노력

managerial planning　　경영계획
　　▶ managerial control

managerial style　　(경영자의) 일상적인 업무관리양식

managerial subentity　　경영관리상의 부

M

수적 본질, 실재

manager'sexplanation   관리자의 설명

managing by objective   목표관리
= management by objective

managing director   상무이사, 전무이사

managing executive   경영업무 집행임
원

managing expense   경영비, 관리비용

managing trustee   지배수탁자
▶ custodian trustee

mandate   1) (직권)명령 2) 무상계약

mandatory provision   강제규정

mandatory redemption   강제상환

man day   1인 1일 노동량

man hour   1인당 노동시간

man hour rate   작업공의 시간율

manipulation   서류조작, 이익조작

manipulation of account   분식회계
= equation manipulation

man power planning   인적자원회계

mantissa (of a logarithm)   (대수對數의)
가수(假數), 소수부(小數部)

manual   1) 취급설명서 2) 수동조작의,
수동의

manual input   수조작 입력

manual of budgetary control   예산 통
제규정

manual operation   수조작, 수동조작

manual system   수동시스템

manufactory expense   제조간접비
= burden

manufactured goods   제품, 생산품

manufactured material   자가제조 원
재료

manufactured parts   자가제조부품
= finished parts ▶ purchased
parts

manufactured parts cost   자가제조 부
품비 ▶ purchased parts cost

manufacture order   제조지시서, 제조
지도서 = production order

manufacturer   제조회사

manufacturer or dealer lessor   제조
업자 또는 판매업자의 임대인

manufacturing account   제조계정
▶ manufacturing statement

manufacturing accounting   공업회계,
제조원가계산
▶ manufacturing costing

manufacturing bookkeeping   공업부
기 ▶ factory book keeping

manufacturing budget   제조예산
= production budget
▶ cost of production budget,
production volume budget

manufacturing burden   제조간접비
= factory overhead

manufacturing capacity   제조능력

manufacturing contribution margin
제조공헌이익 ▶ contribution
margin, gross sales (CVP분석)
제조 공헌이익, 매출액-변동
매출원가

manufacturing cost   제조원가
= factory cost ▶ manufacturing
cost accounting, manufacturing
expense, manufacturing
overhead

manufacturing cost accounting   제조
원가회계

manufacturing costing   제조원가계산
▶ manufacturing accounting

manufacturing cost of goods produced
제품제조원가

manufacturing defect 제조상의 결함

manufacturing department 제조부문
= producing department,
production department
▶ auxiliary department

manufacturing direct cost 직접제조원
가

manufacturing enterprise 제조기업,
제조업 = manufacturing firm

manufacturing expense 1) 제조간접비
= factory overhead 2) 제조경비
▶ manufacturing cost

manufacturing expense budget 제조
간접비 예산 = factory overhead
budget

manufacturing expense budget report
제조간접비 예산표
= manufacturing overhead
budget report

manufacturing expense ledger 제조
간접비 원장 = manufacturing
overhead ledger

manufacturing expense standard 제
조간접비 표준 = manufacturing
overhead standard

manufacturing expense variance 제
조간접비 차이 = overhead
variance

manufacturing firm 제조기업
= manufacturing enterprise

manufacturing indirect cost 제조간
접비 = factory overhead

manufacturing lead time 제조기간

manufacturing overhead 제조간접비
= factory overhead

manufacturing overhead budget 제
조간접비 예산 = factory

overhead budget

**manufacturing overhead budget
report** 제조간접비 예산표
= manufacturing expense
budget report

**manufacturing overhead collecting
sheet** 제조간접비 집계표

manufacturing overhead cost 제조간
접비 = factory overhead

manufacturing overhead cost variance
제조간접비 차이 ▶ overhead
variance

**manufacturing overhead distribution
sheet** 제조간접비 배분표
= factory overhead expense
distribution sheet

manufacturing overhead ledger 제조
간접비 원장 = manufacturing
expense ledger

manufacturing overhead rate 제조간
접비 배부율 = burden rate,
overhead rate

manufacturing overhead standard 제
조간접비 표준 ▶ manufacturing
expense budget

manufacturing overhead variance 제
조간접비 차이 = overhead
variance

manufacturing planning 제조계획

manufacturing process 제조공정

manufacturing profit 제조활동으로
부터 발생하는 이익 = profit on
manufacture

manufacturing specification 제조 시
방서(명세서)

manufacturing statement 제조원가
명세표

M

manufacturing supply　제조용 소모품
manufacturing time　제조시간
MAPI(Machinery and Allied Product Institute)　미국기계공업협회
marchandise　상품
marchandising　상업
margin　1) 차익, 이익 2) 위탁증거금
marginal analysis　한계분석
marginal check　한계검사 = marginal test
marginal cost　한계원가, 직접원가, 변동원가 = direct cost, variable cost ▶ differential cost, incremental cost
marginal cost curve　한계비용곡선
marginal costing　한계원가계산, 직접원가계산, 변동원가계산 = direct costing, variable costing, variable cost system
marginal cost of capital　한계자본비용 ▶ cost of capital, weighted average cost of capital
marginal demand　한계수요
marginal efficiency　한계효율
marginal income　한계이익 = marginal profit
marginal income approach　한계이익법 ▶ contribution approach
marginal income chart　한계이익도표 = marginal profit graph
marginal income graph　한계이익도표 = marginal profit graph
marginal income path　한계이익선 = marginal profit path ▶ marginal profit graph, marginal profit rate
marginal income ratio　한계이익률

= marginal profit ratio
marginal principle　한계원리
marginal private net product　사적 한계 순생산물
marginal productivity　한계생산력
marginal productivity of capital　자본의 한계생산력
marginal profit　한계이익 = contribution margin, marginal income
marginal profit chart　한계이익도표 = marginal profit graph
marginal profit graph　한계이익도표 = marginal income chart, marginal income graph, marginal profit chart ▶ profit chart, profit graph
marginal profit path　한계이익선 = marginal income path ▶ marginal profit graph, marginal profit ratio
marginal profit ratio　한계이익률 = contribution margin ratio, marginal income ratio, profit volume ratio
marginal social net product　사회적 한계 순생산물
marginal tax rate　한계세율
marginal test　한계검사 = marginal check
marginal utility　한계효용
margin call　보증금 추가청구
margin of safety　안전한계
margin of safety ratio(M/S ratio)　안전한계율 ▶ break-even point
margin requirement　증거금율
Marine Protection, Research, and

Sanctuaries Act   해양보
호, 연구 및 보호구역법
marital deduction   부부공제
mark   표기, 표시
markdown   가격인하 ▶ markup
markdown cancellation   가격인하 취
소 ▶ markup cancellation,
retail inventory method
mark down sale   가격인하판매
market   시장
marketability   시장성
marketable commodity   시장성이 있
는 상품
marketable debt security   시장성 있는
채권, 시장성 있는 채무증권
= marketable nonequity
security ▶ marketable equity
security
marketable equity security   시장성 있
는 지분증권 ▶ marketable debt
security, marketable nonequity
security
marketable investment security   투자
유가증권
marketable nonequity security   시장
성 있는 채권 = marketable debt
security ▶ marketable equity
security
marketable security   단기투자목적의
시장성 있는 유가증권, 시장성
지분증권
marketable title   시장성이 있는 소유
권, 매매 가능한 소유권
market analysis   시장분석 ▶ market
research
market average   평균주가 = stock
price average

market basket index   마켓 바스켓 지수
market beta   시장 베타값
▶ beta coefficient
market control   시장통제
market data approach   시장자료비교
법 = sales comparison approach
▶ cost approach, income
approach
market discount bond   시장할인채권
market efficiency   시장효율성
▶ efficient market hypothesis
market equilibrium   시장균형
market force   시장의 지배력
market index   시장지수
marketing   마케팅, 판매
marketing activity   판매활동
marketing channel   판매경로, 유통경로
marketing cost   판매비
marketing cost accounting   판매비 회
계 ▶ cost accounting
marketing cost analysis   판매비 분석
▶ contribution profit approach,
net profit approach
marketing cost budget   판매비 예산
= marketing expense budget
marketing cost control   판매비 관리
= marketing cost management
marketing cost management   판매비
관리 = marketing cost control
marketing cost variance   판매비 차이
marketing expense budget   판매비 예
산 = marketing cost budget
marketing information system   마케
팅 정보시스템
marketing objective   마케팅 목표
marketing of stock   주식의 매매
marketing process   유통과정

M

marketing rate 시장이자율

marketing research 시장조사 = market research

marketing strategy 마케팅 전략

marketing variance 마케팅 차이
▶ production variance, volume variance

market mix 시장조합, 마케팅믹스

market model 시장모델

market order 시장시세주문 = order without limit ▶ limit order

market penetration rate 시장침투도, 시장점유율

market portfolio 시장 포트폴리오

market price 시장가격, 판매가격, 시세 = current price, quotation
▶ speculation

market price basis 시가주의, 시가기준 = market value basis ▶ cost basis

market price method 시가법 = market value method

market price of stock 주식시세 = stock quotation

market psychology 시장심리

market quotation 시장시세

market related asset value 시장연동 자산가치

market related risk 시장관련위험
▶ systematic risk, undiversifiable risk

market research 시장조사

market research cost 시장조사비
▶ market research

market risk 시장위험 = systematic risk, undiversifiable risk
▶ diversifiable risk, unsystematic risk

market risk premium 시장위험 할증금 ▶ risk premium

market share variance 시장점유율 차이 ▶ market size variance, sales quantity variance

market size variance 시장규모 차이
▶ market share variance, sales quantity variance

market strategy 시장전략, 제품전략을 가리키는 경우

market test 시장 점검

market value 시가(時價), 시장가치, 시가(市價) = current value
▶ current cost, face value, market price, selling price

market value approach 시장가격법

market value basis 시가기준, 시가주의 = market price basis ▶ cost basis

market value method 시가법, 시장가액법 = market price method
▶ book value method

markon 가격인상

Markov chain 마아코프 연쇄

mark reader 마크 판독장치

mark scanning 마크 판독 = optical mark reading

mark sensing 마크 센싱

mark-to-market basis 시가기준

mark to the market 시가평가

markup 가격인상률, 가격인상
▶ mark down, retail inventory method

markup cancellation 가격인상 취소
▶ retail inventory method

markup percentage 가격인상률

= percentage mark up on cost

married filing jointly　부부가 공동으로 소득세신고

married filing separately　부부가 별도로 소득세신고

martingale process　기간적으로 상호 독립한 확률변수의 시계열을 발생시키는 과정

MAS(management advisory service)　경영자문서비스

mask　1) 마스크, 가면 2) 마스크하다

Maslow's hierarchy　매슬로우 욕구단계 ▶ needs hierarchy theory

mass production　대량생산

mass storage　대량기억장치

master budget　종합예산, 기본예산 = comprehensive budget, summary budget ▶ departmental budget

master budget activity　종합예산조업도 = master budget volume

master budget volume　종합예산조업도 = budgeted activity, budgeted capacity, budgeted volume, expected annual activity, expected annual capacity, expected annual volume, master budget activity

master clock　주(主) 시계

master file　마스터 파일 ▶ transaction file

master index　기본색인, 주(主)색인

master operation list　총괄작업 과정표

master plan　총괄계획

master's account　주인계정, 점주계정

master-servant relationship　고용인 · 피고용인의 관계

master station　발신국, 발신단말

master valuation approach　포괄평가법 ▶ discounted free cash flow method, excess earning power approach, number of years method

matching　대응(對應), 어울리는, 조화된

matching concept　대응개념 ▶ accrual accounting, matching principle

matching cost with revenue　비용 · 수익대응 ▶ matching revenue and related expense

matching of cost and revenue　비용과 수익의 대응

matching principle　비용 · 수익의 대응원칙 = concept of matching cost with revenue ▶ effort and accomplishment, expense and revenue matching

matching revenue and related expense　수익 · 비용대응 ▶ matching cost with revenue

material　1) 재료, 원재료 2) 재료비 = material cost 3) 현저(뚜렷이 나타남) 4) 금액상 중요성

material alteration　중대한 변조(變造)

material audit　물품감사, 자재감사

material blend variance　재료혼합차이, 재료배합차이 = material mix variance ▶ yield variance

material breach　중대한 계약위반

material budget　재료예산 ▶ material cost budget, material inventory budget, material purchase budget

material cost　재료비

material cost analysis　재료비 분석

material cost budget　재료비 예산

M

material costing　재료비 원가계산

material exemption　배우자 사이의 소송 면제

material explosion　부품전개

material fact　중요한 사실

material for repair　보수재료

material inconsistency　중요한 일관성의 결여

material indirect financial interest　중요한 간접적인 경제적 이해

material inventory budget　재료재고예산

materiality　중요성

materiality threshold　중요성의 기준금액

material ledger　재료원장

material misstatement　중요한 왜곡표시, 중요한 허위기재

material mix variance　재료혼합차이, 재료배합차이 = material blend variance

material noncompliance　중요한 위반

material price standard　재료가격 표준 ▶ direct material standard, material quantity standard

material price variance　재료가격차이 ▶ material quantity variance, material usage variance

material purchase book　재료매입장

material purchase budget　재료구매예산

material purchase order　재료주문서

material purchase price variance　재료구입가격차이 = material received price variance

material purchase requisition　재료구입청구서

material quantity standard　재료소비수량표준 ▶ direct material standard, material price standard

material quantity variance　재료소비수량차이 = material usage variance ▶ material blend variance, material price variance, material yield variance

material received price variance　재료구입가격차이 = material purchase price variance

material received report　재료입고 전표, 재료수입보고서

material requisition　재료출고청구서, 재료출고전표 = material transfer sheet

material returned to stockroom　환입재료

material returned to vendor　환출재료

material specification　재료시방서(명세서) = bill of materials

material store card　재료출납 카드

material summary　재료사용집계표 = summary of materials used

material transfer sheet　재료출고청구서, 재료출고전표 = material requisition

material usage price variance　재료사용가격차이

material usage variance　재료수량차이 = material quantity variance

material variance　재료비차이 ▶ material price variance, material quantity variance, material usage variance

material weakness　(내부통제 상의) 중대

한 약점

material weakness in internal control 내부통제의 중요한 취약점

material yield 재료수율 차이

material yield variance 재료수율 ▶ material blend variance, material quantity variance

maternity pay 출산수당

Maternity Pay Fund 출산수당기금

mathematical check 수학적 검사

mathematical discount 복리할인 = compound discount

mathematical model 수학적 모형

mathematical programming 수리계 획법

matrix 행렬

matrix bookkeeping 행렬 부기

matrix method 매트릭스법 = cross allocation method, double-distribution method, reciprocal allocation method, reciprocal distribution method

matrix model of cost allocation 원가 배분의 행렬모형

matrix organization 매트릭스 조직

matrix storage 매트릭스 기억장치

matured bond 만기 후 사채

maturity 만기

maturity book 만기일장부

maturity date 만기일, 지불기일, 상환 일

maturity value 만기상환가액, 만기가 치(MV), 만기일에 있어서의 가치

maturity yield 최종이자율, 상환이자 율 = yield-to-maturity

maximal collateral 근저당(根抵當)

maximax criterion 최대값중 최대 판 정기준 ▶ maxmin criterion

maximum 최대, 최대치, 극대 ▶ minimum

maximum capacity 최대조업도, 최대 생산능력 = full capacity, ideal capacity, theoretical capacity ▶ expected actual capacity, normal capacity, practical capacity

maximum level of control risk 통제 위험최대수준 ▶ assertion, internal control structure

maximum likelihood estimator 최우 추정량

maximum price 최고가격 ▶ fixed price

maximum principle 최대원리

maximum rate of deviations 최대이 탈율

maximum stock 최고재고량 ▶ economic order quantity, minimum stock

maximum stock level 최고재고수준

maxmin criterion 최소값중 최대 판정 기준 ▶ maximax criterion

May Day 메이데이, 노동절

MBCA(Model Business Corporation Act) 모범사업회사법

MBO(management by objective) 목표 관리

Mckesson & Robbins Inc. Case 맥케 슨 · 로빈스 회사사건

MCT(mainstream corporation tax) 본 (本)납부 법인세

MD(measurement date) 1) 사업부문 을 폐기하기로 의사결정을 한

M

날 2) 구입 가능한 주식수와 구
입가격을 결정한 날 3)측정일
**MD&A(management's discussion and
analysis)** 사업보고서에 포함
된 경영자 토의 및 분석
MDF(main distributing frame) 주배 선
반, 주단자반
mean 평균
mean absolute deviation 평균절대 편
차
**meaningful value on the investment
account** 투자유가증권 계
정에 실질가치 반영
mean-per-unit difference method
차액추정법 ▶ difference
estimation method, mean-per-
unit method, ratio estimation
method
mean-per-unit estimation 차액추정
평가, 단위당 평균추정법
mean-per-unit method 차액추정법
= difference estimation method,
mean-per-unit difference
method, ratio estimation method
mean time between failures(MTBF)
평균고장간격 ▶ mean time to
repair
mean time to repair(MTTR) 평균수
리시간, 평균회복시간 ▶ mean
time between failure
mean value 평균치
measurability 측정가능성
measure 1) 측정치 2) 예측치 3) 척도
measured consideration 측정대가, 지
불대가
measurement 측정, 계량
▶ fundamental measurement,

revaluation
measurement attribute 측정속성
= attribute measured
measurement by fiat 규약적 측정
▶ derived measurement,
fundamental measurement,
measurement
measurement concept 측정개념
measurement date(MD) 1) 사업부문
을 폐기하기로 의사결정을 한
날 2) 구입 가능한 주식수와 구
입가격을 결정한 날 3) 측정일
measurement deviation 측정오차
**measurement focus and basis of
accounting(MFBA)** 회계측
정의 관점과 측정기준
measurement issue 측정문제
measurement method 측정방법
measurement procedure 측정과정
▶ measurement process
measurement scale 측정척도
measurement system 측정시스템
measurement unit 측정단위
= monetary unit
measuring tool 측정수단
measure of performance 성과의 측정
치
mechanical check system 기계적 점
검제도
mechanic's lien 건설업자의 담보권,
메카닉 선취특권
median 중앙치
Medicaid 저소득자 의료보조
medical and dental expenses 의료비
와 치과비용
medical corporation 의료법인
Medicare 국민의료보장

Medicare Hospital Insurance 노령자, 장애자 의료보험

Medicare Tax 메디케어 세(稅)

medium sized company (영)중규모 회사 ▶ large company

meeting of stockholder 주주총회 = general meeting

melon 잉여이익 ▶ melon-cutting

melon cutting 특별배당 = cutting a melon

member 1) 구성원, 회원, 부원, 단원, 사원 2) (국회 등의) 의원 3) 조직의 일부분 4) (정당 등의)지부 5) 요소

membership due 회원부담금, 수취회원부담금

membership organization 회원제 조직

members' voluntary liquidation (영)주주의 임의해산 = members' voluntary winding up

members' voluntary winding up (영) 주주의 임의해산 = members' voluntary liquidation ▶ compulsory winding up, voluntary winding up

memo entry 부외 비망기록

memo entry only 부외 비망기록

memorandum 1) 비망록, 각서 2) 기본정관, 정관

memorandum book 비망장부

memorandum entry 비망기록

memorandum of association (영)기본정관, 정관 = articles of incorporation ▶ certificate of incorporation

memorandum value 비망가액

menu driven input 메뉴에 따른 입력

mercantile agency 흥신소, 신용조사기관 = credit agency

mercantile agent 상사대리인

merchandise 상품

merchandise available for sale 판매가능상품

merchandise inventory 재고상품, 이월상품

merchandise ledger 상품원장

merchandise receivable ratio 상품외상매출금 비율, 상품수취계정 비율

merchandise to arrive 미착품 = goods in transit

merchandise turnover 상품회전율

merchandising company 상업을 영위하는 회사, 상품매매업회사

merchandising enterprise 상품매매업회사, 상사(商社) = merchandising company, merchandising firm

merchandising firm 상품매매업회사, 상사, 상기업 = merchandising enterprise

merchant 상인(商人)

merchantability 상품성

merchantable quality 상품성, 상품의 질

merchant bank (영)상인은행 ▶ investment bank

merchant memo rule 상인의 메모 룰

merchant seller (상인 중에)판매자

merchant's firm offer 상인의 확정청약

merge pass 조합(組合) 패스

M

merger 합병, 기업결합, 흡수합병, 진정 합병 ▶ acquisition, business combination, pooling of interests, purchase, statutory consolidation, statutory merger

merger accounting (영)흡수합병회계 ▶ acquisition accounting, purchase

merger and acquisition(M&A) 기업 의 합병과 매수 ▶ leveraged buyout

merger clause 모든 사전 합의를 기(旣) 계약서에 통합한다는 조항

merger plan 합병계획

merger-purchase 흡수합병 · 매입

merit regulation 규제주의 = disclosure philosophy, disclosure requirement, regulatory philosophy

meteorologist 기상예보관

method based on the use of indexes 지수(指數) 이용방식 ▶ indexation

method of allocation 배분방법

method of average price at the close of the preceding month 이 월평균단가 = month-end average cost method

method of comparative analysis 비 교분석법

method of compound interest 복리 계산법 ▶ method of simple interest

method of current account 유동계정 법

method of least square 최소자승법 = least square method

method of link relation 연쇄비율법

method of moving average 이동평균 법

method of neglect [실제원가계산] 도 외시법, 정상공손품의 처리법

method of negotiation 유통 방법

method of nonneglect [실제원가계 산] 비도외시법, 정상공손품의 처리법

method of selected point 선점법(選点 法) ▶ freehand method

method of simple interest 단리계산법 ▶ method of compound interest

MFBA(measurement focus and basis of accounting) 회계측정의 관 점과 측정기준

MI(minority income) 소액주주 귀속이 익

micro accounting 미시회계

microsecond 100만분의 1초

middle management 중간관리자, 중 간관리층 ▶ top management

middle management level 중간관리 층

middle section 중간부분 = middle paragraph

MI in NI(minority income, minority interest in net income) 소액주주 귀 속손익

million(m.) 백만

minimum 최소, 극소 ▶ maximum

minimum desired rate 최소요구이익 률

minimum desired rate of return 최 저요구이익률, 최저기대수익률 ▶ cost of capital

minimum distance code 최소거리 코

드

minimum guarantee   최저보증금

minimum lease payments(MLPs)   최저지불리스료, 최저리스지불액의 계산

minimum lending rate(MLR)   (영)최저대출이율

minimum liability   최소채무

minimum liability requirement   최소부채계상요건

minimum pension liability adjustment   연금의 추가 최소부채계상액의 조정

minimum price   최저가격 ▶ fixed price

minimum stock   최저재고량 ▶ maximum stock

minimum stock level   최저재고수준

minimum stock quantity   최저재고 보유량

minimum subscription   최소주식인수 한도

minimum tax   최저세

mining right   광업권 ▶ mineral right

minor   1) 미성년(未成年) 2) 소행렬식

minority   미성년

minority income(MI)   소액주주 귀속이익

minority income, minority interest in net income(MI in NI)   소액주주 귀속손익

minority interest   소액주주지분 = minority shareholders' equity

minority shareholders   소수주주, 소액주주

minority shareholders' equity   소수주주지분 ▶ minority interest

minor portion   최소 부분

minuend   피감수(被減數) ▶ subtrahend

minus from joint cost   [실제원가계산] 결합원가로부터의 차감, 부산물의 코스트를 공제

minute   의사록 = minute book

minute book   의사록(철) = minute

minute of board of director   이사회의사록

MIRAS(mortgage interest relief at source)   (영)택지취득공제

mirror image rule   경상(鏡像)주의, 경상(鏡像)원칙, 거울영상규칙

MIS(management information system)   경영정보시스템

misapplication   오용(誤用)

misappropriation   착복, 횡령, 악용(惡用)

misappropriation of asset   자산 횡령

miscellaneous deduction   기타 공제

miscellaneous expenditure   잡지출, 잡비 = miscellaneous expense ▶ miscellaneous revenue

miscellaneous expense   잡비 ▶ miscellaneous expenditure, miscellaneous revenue

miscellaneous revenue   잡수입 ▶ miscellaneous expenditure, miscellaneous expense

miscellaneous time   잡시간

misfeasance   직무남용, 실당(失當)행위, 과실

mislaid property   분실물(紛失物), 놓아둔 곳을 잊어버린 물품

misrepresentation   부실표현, 부실표시 ▶ representational faithfulness

missing data check   자료누락검증

M

missing data test   자료누락테스트

misstatement   왜곡표시, 허위기재

mistake   오류, 착오 ▶ error

misunderstanding   오해

misuse   오용(誤用)

mitigation of damage   손해배상의 완화

mixed account   혼합계정

mixed collateral   혼합저당

mixed cost   혼합비, 준변동비 = semi-variable cost ▶ fixed cost, semi-fixed cost, variable cost

mixed radix notation   혼합기수(基數)표기법 = mixed radix numeration system

mixed radix numeration system   혼합기수표기법 = mixed radix notation

mixed transaction   혼합거래

mix variance   (재료)혼합차이, (제품) 구성차이 = blend variance ▶ sales-volume variance, yield variance

MLPs(minimum lease payments)   최저지불리스료, 최저리스지불액의 계산

MLPs + URV   최소지불리스료+무보증잔존가액

MLR(minimum lending rate)   최저대출이율, 최저대출금리

MMC(money market certificate)   시장금리연동형 단기금융상품

MMF(money market fund)   단기금융상품투자신탁

MM hypothesis   MM가설

MM(Modigliani-Miller) theory   모딜리아니 · 밀러 이론

mnemonic symbol   간략(기억)기호

mode   방식, 방법, 양식, 형태

model   모형

Model Act   모범법

model building   모델설정

Model Business Corporation Act (MBCA)   모범사업 회사법

model code (on directors' dealings)   (영) 이사와의 거래에 관한 모델코드

model deviation   모형오차

modem(modulator and demodulator)   변조장치

modi(modified distribution method)   수정배분법

modifiability   갱신성(更新性) ▶ maintainability

modification   변경, 수정

modification of an existing contract   기존의 계약 변경

modification of contract   계약의 변경

modification of terms   조건변경처리

modified accelerated cost recovery system   수정가속도상각제도, 수정가속도원가회수제도 ▶ accelerated cost recovery system

modified accelerated cost recovery system(MACRS)   수정가속원가회수법

modified accounts   수정재무제표 ▶ small company

modified accrual basis   수정발생주의

modified accrual basis of accounting   수정발생주의회계

modified all-inclusive concept   수정포괄주의

modified all-inclusive form   수정포괄
　주의양식
modified disclaimer   수정된 의견 거절
modified distribution method(modi)
　modi법, 수정배분법
modified flexible budget   수정변동예
　산
modified partial plan   수정부분계획
　▶ partial plan, single plan
modified perpetual inventory system
　수정계속기록법
modified sales price   수정판매가
modified units of production method
　수정생산량비교법
　▶ combination of the production
　and the straight-line method
modified U.S. report   수정을 더한 미
　국 형식의 보고서
modifier   (명령)수식자, 변경자
modulation   변조(變調)
modulation rate   변조속도
modulator and demodulator(modem)
　변조장치 ▶ acoustic coupler
module   모듈, 기본단위
modulo N check   모듈러N검사
modulus   1) 절대치 2) 모듈러스법, 계
　수법 ▶ check digit
moment   적률(積率)
moment generating function   적률 창
　출함수
monadic operation   단항연산
　= unary operation ▶ operand
monadic operator   단항연산자
　= unary operator
monetary   화폐
monetary asset   화폐성 자산
　▶ monetary liability, non-

monetary asset, quick asset
monetary asset and liability   화폐
　성 자산 · 부채
monetary asset · liab   화폐성 자산 ·
　부채
monetary capital   화폐자본 = financial
　capital ▶ capital maintenance,
　physical capital
monetary current liability   화폐성
　유동부채
monetary gain or loss   화폐성이득 또
　는 손실 = purchasing power
　gain or loss
monetary item   화폐성항목
　▶ monetary asset, monetary
　liability, non-monetary item
monetary liability   화폐성부채
　▶ monetary asset, non-
　monetary liability
monetary measurement convention
　화폐적 측정의 공준
monetary measurement principle
　화폐적 측정의 원칙
monetary measuring unit   화폐적 측
　정단위
monetary-nonmonetary method   화
　폐성 · 비화폐성법 ▶ closing
　rate method, current-non-
　current method, temporal
　method
monetary return   화폐적인 이익
monetary sampling   화폐단위표본조
　사
monetary unit   화폐단위, 명목화폐단
　위 = measurement unit, unit
　of account
monetary unit assumption   화폐단위

M

측정의 가정

monetary working capital(MWC)
화폐성운전자본 ▶ gearing
adjustment, monetary working
capital adjustment

**monetary working capital adjustment
(MWCA)** (영)화폐성운전자
본수정

money 1) 화폐, 금전, 통화 2) 재산, 부
(富) 3) 임금, 급료 4) 금액

money market 금융시장 ▶ capital
market

money market certificate(MMC) 시
장금리연동형 단기금융상품

money market fund (MMF) 단기금
융상품투자신탁

money measurement 화폐적 측정

money order 우편환, 송금환

money order paid in part (주문계약금
의) 일부선불

money position 머니 포지션 ▶ loan
position

money price 화폐가격

money purchase plan 정액납부연금
▶ deferred profit-sharing plan

money rate 금리, 이자율

money shipment 화폐수송

money supply 화폐공급량

monitoring 감시

monitoring cost 감시원가 = agency
cost

monitor printer 감시용 인쇄장치

monitor program 감시(감독)프로그램

monolithic integrated circuit 당일 결
정(結晶)집적회로

Monopolies and Mergers Commission
(영)독점 · 합병위원회

monopoly 독점기업

monopoly price 독점가격

monopoly profit 독점이윤

Monte Carlo method 몬테카를로법

Monte Carlo simulation 몬테카를로
시뮬레이션

month-end average cost method 월
말평균원가법, 이월평균단가지
불법 ▶ method of average
price at the close of the
preceding month

monthly cash report 월별현금보고서

monthly income statement 월차손익
계산서

monthly payment 매월지불, 월불(月拂)

monthly profit and loss 월차손익

monthly statement 월차보고서, 월차
계산서

Moody's Investors Service, Inc. 무디
스사

moral hazard 도덕적 위험, 도덕적 해
이

moratorium 1) 지불유예, 지불정지, 지
불연기 2) (활동 또는 사용의) 일
시정지, 일시연기

**more than minor portion but less than
substantially all** 최소부분
보다 많고 실질가치보다 적은

Morpeth Committee (영)모페드 위원
회

mortality 사망자수, 사망률 ▶ mortality
table

mortgage 양도, 저당, 저당권, 저당 증서,
질권(質權), 담보차입, 부동산 담
보물권

mortgage backed security 담보부 유
가증권

mortgage bond   담보부 사채, 담보부 채권

mortgage credit   담보대부

mortgaged debt   저당채무, 담보채무

mortgage debenture   담보부 사채

mortgage debt service   차입금의 상환액

mortgage deed   담보증권

mortgaged property   저당재산, 담보재산

mortgaged property subject to mortgage   저당증권부 저당재산

mortgagee   저당권자, 저당채권자

mortgage-equity capitalization   저당-자기자본 자본화방식 ▶ down payment, income approach

mortgage holding   담보부 장기대부금 ▶ mortgage loan

mortgage interest deduction   주택(담보)금리공제

mortgage interest relief at source (MIRAS)   (영)주택취득공제

mortgage loan   담보부 대부금 = mortgage loan receivable, secured loan

mortgage loan receivable   담보부 대부금 = mortgage loan, secured loan

mortgage note   담보부 장기어음 = secured note

mortgage note payable   담보부 지급어음 ▶ collateral note

mortgage payable   담보부 차입금 ▶ secured liability

mortgage trust   저당권신탁 ▶ equity trust

mortgagor   양도저당권 설정자, 저당권 설정자, 저당채무자

most significant   최상위

motion study   동작연구 ▶ time study

motivation   동기부여

motivation control   동기에 대한 관리 ▶ motivation theory

motivation cost control   사전원가관리 ▶ post cost control

motivation-hygiene theory   동기 · 위생관리이론

motivation theory   동기부여이론

motive   동기

move mode   이동모드

moving average   이동평균 ▶ moving average cost method

moving average cost method   이동평균법 = moving average method ▶ periodic average method

moving average method   이동평균법 = moving average cost method

moving expenses   이사비용

M/S ratio(margin of safety ratio)   안전한계율, M/S율

MTBF(mean time between failure)   평균고장간격

MTTR(mean time to repair)   평균수리시간

multidimensional bookkeeping   다차원부기(簿記)

multidrop line   분기회선

multiemployer plan   둘 이상의 고용자 제도

multi-journal system   복합분개장제

multilevel address   다중어드레스 = indirect address

multinational enterprise   다국적 기업

M

= multinational firm

multinational firm 다국적 기업
= multinational enterprise

multinational operation 다국적 경영
활동

multiple break-even point 복수 손익
분기점

multiple budget 복수예산, 변동예산
= variable budget

multiple correlation 다중상관(相關)

multiple declaration 다중선언

multiple goal 다원적 목표, 다중목표
▶ aspiration level

multiple product 결합생산물, 연결생
산물 = joint product

multiple punching 다중천공(穿孔)

multiple regression analysis 다중회
귀분석

multiple step form 다단계양식

multiple step income statement 다단
계식 손익계산서

multiple valuation 다원평가

multiplex mode 다중방식

multiplexer channe 다중채널
▶ channel, selector channel

multiplexing 다중화

multiplicand 피승수(被乘數)
▶ multiplier

multiplication theorem 승법(乘法)정
리

multiplicative congruential method
승산(乘算)합동법

multiplier 승수(乘數) = multiplier factor
▶ multiplicand

multiplier factor 승수 = multiplier
▶ multiplicand

multipoint connection 다중접속

multiprocessing 다중처리
▶ multiprogramming

multiprocessor 다중처리장치

multi-process type of production 다
각적 공정형생산

multiproduct firm 복수제품

multiprogramming 다중프로그래밍
▶ multiprocessing

multi-regression analysis 다중회귀분
석

multi-stage consolidation 다단계연결

multi-stage sampling 다단계 추출법

multitasking 병행성(두 가지 이상의 동작
이 동일시간 대에 발생)
▶ multiprogramming, task

multitask operation 다중태스크 조작

multivariate analysis 다변량(多變量)
분석

municipal bond 지방채 = tax-exempt
bond

municipal bond interest 지방채이자
▶ local bond

municipal security 지방채

mutual consent 상호합의

mutual cooperative entity 상호협동기
업

mutual fund 투자신탁 = closed-end
fund, investment trust, open-
end fund ▶ investment fund,
load charge

mutual insurance company 상호보험
회사

mutuality of remedy 구제수단의 상호
성

mutually exclusive project 상호배타
적 프로젝트 ▶ contingent
projectmutual mistake 상호착

오, 쌍방착오
mutual rescission　　합의 해제
MWC(monetary working capital)　　화폐
　　성운전자본

MWCA(monetary working capital adjustment)　　화폐성운전자
　　본수정

N

NAA(National Association of Accountants)
　　미국회계담당자협회, 미국전국
　　회계사협회
NACA Bulletin(National Association of Cost Accountants Bulletin)
　　NACA월보, 미국원가회계사
　　협회의 월보
narration　　(분개장의) 주기
narrative　　서술식 = report form,
　　statement form
narrative form　　서술적 형식, 보고식,
　　보고형식 = report form
narrow market　　한산한 시장, 활발하지
　　못한 시장 = thin market
NASD(National Association of Securities Dealers)　　전미증권업협회
NASDAQ(National Association of Securities Dealers Automated Quotations)　　나스닥(미국 증
　　권업계 상장정보시스템), 전국점
　　두품목상장가 자동통보방식
national account　　국민계정, 국민소득
　　계정
National Association of Accountants (NAA)　　미국회계담당자협회,
　　미국전국회계사협회
National Association of Cost

Accountants Bulletin(NACA Bulletin)　　NACA월보, 미국원
　　가회계사협회의 월보
National Association of Securities Dealers(NASD)　　전미 증권업
　　협회
National Association of Securities Dealers Automated Quotations(NASDAQ)　　나
　　스닥 (미국증권업계 상장정보시스
　　템), 전국점두품목상장가 자동
　　통보방식
National Audit Office　　(영)회계검사원
national balance sheet　　국민대차대조표
National Board for Prices and Incomes (NBPI)　　(영)물가 · 소득 심의
　　회
national bond　　국채(國債) = national
　　debt
National Bureau of Standard(NBS)
　　미국 표준국
National Conference of Commissioners on Uniform State Laws　　통
　　일주법위원 전국회의
National Council on Governmental Accounting(NCGA)　　전미
　　정부회계평의회, 정부회계 전국

심의회

national debt   정부채, 국채

**national disposable income and its
appropriation account**   국
민가처분소득과 처분계정
▶ system of national accounts

national economic accounting   국민
경제회계 ▶ social accounting,
system of national accounts

national economic budget   국민경제
예산

**National Economic Development
Council(NEDC)**   (영)국가
경제개발심의회

national economy   국민경제

National Enterprise Board(NEB)   (영)
국유기업청(國有企業廳)

**National Environmental Policy Act
(NEPA)**   국가환경정책국

national goal   국가목적

National Health Service(NHS)
(영)국민의료제도 ▶ National
Insurance

national income(NI)   국민소득

national income accounting   국민소
득회계 ▶ national economic
accounting, social accounting

National Insurance   (영)국민보험제도
▶ National Health Service

national insurance number   (영)국민
연금보험의 개인번호

**National Labor Relations Act (Wagner
Act)**   전국노동관계법, 연방
노사관계법

National Labor Relations Boards
전국노동관계국(局)

National Securities Exchange   증권

거래소

national security reason   국가보안상
의 이유

national tax   국세(國稅)

National Tax Journal   미국 조세협회
(National Tax Association Tax
Institute of America)가 발행하는
조세전문지, 1948년 창간한 계
간지

national wealth   국부(國富)
▶ national balance sheet

natural business year   자연 회계년도
▶ fiscal year

natural classification of cost   성격별
원가분류

natural language   자연언어

natural resource   천연자원

natural resource deposit   천연자원
매장물

nature, timing, extent   성질, 실시 시
기, 범위

**NBPI (National Board for Prices and
Incomes)**   (영)물가 · 소득
심의회

NBS(National Bureau of Standard)   미
국 표준국

NBV(net book value)   순장부가액

NC(numerical control)   수치제어

**NCGA(National Council on Governmental
Accounting)**   전미 정부회계
평의회

near maturity   근일 만기

nearness to cash   유동성(流動性)
= liquidity ▶ financial
flexibility

NEB(National Enterprise Board)   (영)국
유기업청

N

necessary   생활필수품

NEDC(National Economic Development Council)   (영)국가경제개발심의회

needs hierarchy theory   욕구단계설
= hierarchy of needs theory

negation   부정(否定) = NOT operation

negative account   평가(차감)계정
= contra account

negative asset account   자산차감계정
▶ contra account

negative assurance   소극적 확신, 부정적 확신, 소극적 보증
= limited assurance

negative confirmation   소극적 확인
▶ affirmative confirmation,
inquiry, positive confirmation

negative correlation   부(負)의 상관(相關), 역상관(逆相關)
▶ correlation, correlation
coefficient, positive correlation

negative covenant   소극적 계약

negative easement   소극적 지역권

negative form   소극적 확인양식

negative goodwill   부(負)의 영업권
▶ positive goodwill

negative income tax   부(負)의 소득세

negative interest   역금리

negative pledge   담보제한

negative property   소극재산
▶ positive property

negative valuation account   차감적 평가계정

negligence   과실(過失), 부주의, 태만, 과실책임

negligence rule   과실규칙

negligent fraud   태만한 행위의 기망

negligent tort   과실에 의한 불법행위

negotiability   유통(流通)

negotiable bill   유통어음

negotiable bill of lading   교부성 선하증권

negotiable document   교부성 증서

negotiable instrument   유통성이 있는 유가증권, 유통증권, 교부성 증서

negotiable order of withdrawal(NOW)   양도가능 인출증서

negotiable paper   교부성 증서

negotiable security   유통유가증권

negotiable voucher   외부거래증빙(證憑)

negotiated price   협의가격

negotiated static budget   합의된 고정예산

negotiated transaction   상대매매, 상대거래

negotiated transfer price   협상이전가격

negotiated underwriting   협정인수

negotiating bank   어음매입은행

negotiation   교부, 유통(流通)

negotiation by draft   역환(逆換), 징수환(換)

negotiation credit   어음매수취급은행 무지정신용장 = general credit, open credit

NEPA(National Environmental Policy Act)   국가환경정책국

nest   포개넣다

net amount   순액(純額)

net asset(equity)   순자산, 순재산, 주주지분

net asset available for benefit   급부가능한 순자산 ▶ net asset information

net asset information 순자산정보
    ▶ net asset available for benefit

net asset statement 순자산계산서

net asset value 순자산, 순재산
    = net worth ▶ net asset worth

net asset worth 순자산액 ▶ net asset value

net asset worth per share 1주당 순자산

net basis of calculating EPS (영)배당 과세후 이익에 대한 1주당 이익 계산서 ▶ earnings per share, nil distribution basis of calculating EPS

net book value(NBV) 순장부가액
    ▶ book value, depreciated value, net carrying amount, written down value

net borrowing 순차입금 ▶ gearing adjustment, gearing proportion, monetary working capital, net operating asset

net capital employed 사용순자본
    ▶ capital employed

net carrying amount 순장부가액, 감가상각비 공제후 장부가액
    ▶ book value, carrying amount, gross book value, gross carrying amount, net book value

net carrying amount of debt 부채의 순장부가액

net cash flow 순현금흐름 ▶ cash flow, gross cash flow

net cash flow from operating activity 영업활동으로부터 순현금흐름

net cash investment in a lease 리스 관련 순현금투자액 ▶ lease

net cash provided by financing activity 재무활동에 의한 순현금

net cash provided by operating activity 영업활동에 의한 순현금

net cash used in investing activity 투자활동에 사용한 순현금

net current asset 순유동자산, 운전자본 ▶ net working capital, working capital ▶ current asset, gross working capital, net current liability

net current cost 순현행원가
    ▶ current cost

net current liability 순유동부채

net current replacement cost 현행원가에서 감가상각누계액 공제 후의 현행대체원가

net dividend 순배당금

net dividend per share 1주당 순배당금 = dividend per share

net income 순이익, 당기순이익
    = net profit

net income after income tax 법인소득세 공제후 순이익

net income and extraordinary item 순이익 · 특별항목
    ▶ all-inclusive basis

net income available to common stockholder 보통주주에 대한 분배가능이익

net income before depreciation(NIBD) 상각전 순이익 ▶ net income before recapture (NIBR)

net income before income tax 세전순이익, 법인소득세 공제전순

이익

net income before recapture(NIBR)
상각전 순수익 = net income
before depreciation ▶ income
approach, over-all rate

net income of division 부문순이익

net income per share 1주당 순이익
▶ earnings per share

**net increase in cash and cash
equivalent** 현금 및 현금
등가물의 순증가액

net investment 순투자, 순투자액
▶ gross investment

net investment concept 순투자개념
= cover concept

net investment in a foreign entity
해외사업체에 대한 순투자액
▶ parent's equity share

net investment in a lease 리스 순투자
액

net investment in foreign operation
해외사업체에 대한 순투자액

net invoice price 순송장가액
▶ gross invoice price

net liability 순부채, 채무초과액

net liquid fund (영)순당좌자산

net loss 세차감후 손실, 순손실, 당기 순
손실 ▶ loss, net income, net
profit

**net loss not recognized as pension
expense** 연금비용으로 인식
되지 않은 순손실

net method 순액법

net monetary item 순화폐성항목

net national income 국민순소득
▶ national income, social
accounting

net national product(NNP) 국민순
생산 ▶ gross national products

net national welfare(NNW) 순국민
복지, 국민복지지표

net of tax 세차감후

net of tax method 세후방식, 세납부후
방법 ▶ deferred method,
interperiod tax allocation,
liability method, net of tax
reporting, tax effect accounting

net of tax reporting 세후보고, 세납부
후 순액보고, 세효과 고려후 보
고 ▶ discontinue operation,
extraordinary item, interperiod
tax allocation, prior-period
adjustment, tax allocation
within period, tax effect
accounting, tax effect, timing
difference

net operating asset (영)순영업자산
▶ concept of maintenance of
operating capability, monetary
working capital

net operating loss(NOL) 영업순손실

**net operating loss carryback and
carryover** 영업순손실의
소급과 이월

net periodic pension cost 당기순연금
비용, (당기연금비용)의 계산, 기
간연금순비용

**net periodic postretirement benefit
cost** 당기퇴직후 연금지급
채무비용

net periodic postretirement cost 기간
퇴직후 급부비용

net present value(NPV) 순현재가치,
순현가 ▶ excess present value,

value in use

net present value method　순현재가치
법 ▶ financial statement
method, internal statement
method, internal rate of return
method, payback period

net profit　순이익, 당기순이익

net profit approach　순이익법
▶ contribution profit approach

net profit before tax　법인세공제전 순
이익, 세납부전 순이익 = net
income before income tax

net profit from operation　영업순이
익 = income from operation

net purchases　당기순매입액

net quick asset　순당좌자산

net realizable value(NRV)　순실현가
능가액　= estimated exit value,
expected exit value ▶ current
market value, net settlement
value, output price, realization,
replacement cost

**net realizable value less overall profit
margin**　순실현가능가액 공
제 정상이익액 ▶ current
replacement cost, lower of cost
or market basis, net realizable
value, replacement cost

net realizable value method　순실현
가치방법

net receivable　순채권

net recognized built-in gain　순액으로
인식된 내재이득

net resource　순(純)자원

net sales　순매출액 ▶ gross sales

net settlement　결제순액

net settlement value　순결제가액

▶ net realizable value

net short hedging　단기순헷징

net spoilage cost　순공손비

net turnover　순매출액 = net sales

net value　순가치(純價値)

network　네트워크, 회로망 ▶ computer
network

net working capital　순운전자본 = net
current asset ▶ current asset,
current liability, gross working
capital, working capital

net worth　순가치, 순재산 = net asset

net worth shareholder's equity　소유
자지분, 주주지분, 출자자지분
= net asset, owner's equity,
stockholder's equity

neutrality　중립성 ▶ freedom from
bias

Neville Report　(영)네빌 보고서

new business　새로운 사업

new client　새로운 의뢰인

new partner's contribution　새 파트
너의 출자액

news release　기사 공개, 발표기사

new stock　신주(新株) ▶ old stock

**New York State Society of Certified
Public Accountants**　뉴욕
주 공인회계사회

New York Stock Exchange(NYSE)　뉴
욕 증권거래소 = Big Board

next-in, first-out(NIFO)　차입(次入) 선
출(先出)법 ▶ first-in, first-out,
last-in, first-out

Neyman-Pearson lemma　노이만 · 퍼
슨 정리

NH(normal labor hour)　정상작업시간

NHS(National Health Service)　(영)국민

의료제도 ▶ National Insurance

NI(national income)　국민소득 ▶ net national income, nominal national income, real national income

NIBD(net income before depreciation)　상각전 순이익

NIBR(net income before recapture)　상각전 순수익

NIFO(next-in, first-out)　차입선출법

night duty allowance　야근수당

nil distribution basis of calculating EPS　(영)배당과세전 이익에 대한 1주당 이익의 계산법, 배당금과세후 이익법 ▶ earnings per share, net basis of calculating EPS

ninety percent subsidiary　90%소유종속회사 ▶ claimant company, group relief, surrendering company

NLRA(National Labor Relations Act)　전국노동관계법

NLRB(National Labor Relations Boards)　전국노동관계국(局)

NNP(net national product)　국민순생산

NNW(net national welfare)　순국민복지, 국민복지지표

no arrival, no sale　미도착 불판매

no boot involved　교환차금의 수수가 없는 경우

node　절점(節点), 마디

no goodwill recorded　영업권을 계상하지 않는 방법

Noise Control Act　소음관리법

noise killer　소음방지기

NOL(net operation loss)　영업순손실

nominal account　명목계정 = income account ▶ impersonal account, real account

nominal amount　총명목가액

nominal capital　명목자본 = authorized capital, nominal share capital

nominal damage　명목적 손해배상

nominal dollar　명목 화폐가치

nominal dollar accounting　명목화폐가치회계 ▶ historical cost accounting

nominal dollar amount　명목화폐가치

nominal functional currency　명목기능통화 ▶ constant functional currency, functional currency

nominal income　명목이익, 명목소득 ▶ real income

nominal interest rate　명목이자율 ▶ effective interest rate

nominal ledger　(영)총계정원장 = general ledger ▶ impersonal ledger, private ledger

nominal national income　명목국민소득 ▶ real national income

nominal price　명목가격

nominal profit　명목이득, 명목이윤 ▶ real profit

nominal rate　명목이자율

nominal share capital　(영)명목주식자본 = authorised share capital

nominal unit of money　명목화폐 단위

nominal value　명목가치, 액면금액 = face value ▶ real value

nominal wage　명목임금 ▶ real wage

nominee　명의인, 지명인, 임명인

nomogram　계산도표 = nomograph

non-accredited investor　비유산(非有

產)투자가

non-adjusting event 수정불필요사건
▶ adjusting event, post
balance sheet event, subsequent
event

non-assessable capital stock 추가 납
입의무가 없는 주식

non-audit fee 감사 이외의 업무에 대한
보수

non-audit service 감사 이외의 서비스,
비감사서비스

non-business day (영)휴업일 = dies
non ▶ business day

non-business environment 비영리조
직체에 대한 환경

non-business organization 비영리사
업체, 비영리조직체 = non-profit
business ▶ non-profit
accounting

non-business reporting entity 비영리
보고실체

non-callable bond 만기상환사채
▶ callable bond

non-cancelable lease 해약불능리스

non-carrier cases 운송인에 의해 운송
될 것을 예정하지 않은 계약

non-cash asset 현금 이외의 자산, 비현
금자산, 비화폐성 자산

non-cash charge 비현금비용, 현금지
출이 없는 비용 = non-cash
expense

non-cash expense 비현금비용, 현금지
출이 없는 비용 = non-cash
expense

**non-cash investing and financing
activity** 현금을 수반하지 않
는 투자 및 재무활동

non-cash monetary asset 비현금화폐
성자산

non-cash transaction 비현금거래
▶ cash transaction

non-compensated surety 무상(無償)
보증인

non-conforming goods 부적합 물품,
불일치 상품

non-conjunction 부정이론적(否定理論
積)

non-contributory plan 비납입연금제도

non-controllable cost 관리불능비, 관
리불능원가 = uncontrollable
cost controllable cost

non-corporate entity 회사형태가 아닌
사업체

non-cost item 비원가항목

non-coterminous year end 연결회사
간의 결산일 불일치

non-court trust 비(非)법정신탁

non-cumulative 비누적식

non-cumulative dividend 비누적적 배
당 ▶ cumulative dividend,
preferred stock, preference
share

non-cumulative method 비누적법
▶ cumulative method

non-cumulative preference stock 비
누적적 우선주 ▶ non-
cumulative dividend

non-cumulative preferred stock 비누
적적 우선주

non-cumulative stock 비누적주 = non-
cumulative preference stock

non-current 장기

non-current asset 비유동자산, 고정자
산 = fixed asset

non-current asset acquired 장기자산

non-current deferred tax asset 장기의 이연법인세자산

non-current liability 비유동부채, 고정부채 = fixed liability

non-current receivable 장기수취계정 ▶ account receivable

non-deductible expense 비공제비용

non-delivery 불착, 미도착, 미인도(未引度)

non-derivative instrument 비(非) 파생금융상품

non-destructive read 비파괴 판독

non-detachable 분리할 수 없는

non-detachable stock purchase warrant 비분리형 신주인수권

non-detachable stock warrant 비분리형 신주인수권 증서 ▶ detachable stock warrant

non-dischargeable debt 비면책 채무, 비면제대상 부채

non-disjunction 부정이론화(否定理論和)

non-diversifiable risk 분산불가능 위험 = systematic risk ▶ diversifiable risk, unsystematic risk

non-equivalence element 부등가요소

non-exhaustive property 비감가성 자산

non-expenditure item 비현금지출항목, 비지출항목

non-expired cost 미소멸원가 ▶ unexpired cost

non-financial data 비재무적 자료

non-financial information 비재무정보

non-forfeiture benefit 불몰수특권

non-functional requirement 비기능적 요구 ▶ functional requirements, requirements

Non-identification theory 피고 부지정의 법리

non-industrial building (영)생산에 사용되지 않는 건물, 비생산용 건물

non-interest-bearing note 무이자부어음, 무이자어음채권

non-linearity 비선형성(非線形性) ▶ linearity

non-linear optimization 비선형계획법, 비선형최적화

non-linear programming 비선형계획법

non-liquid asset 고정자산 ▶ fixed asset

non-liquidating distribution 비청산배당

non-manufacturing cost 비제조원가 = commercial expense ▶ manufacturing cost

non-marketable security 시장성이 없는 유가증권 ▶ marketable security

non-market related risk 시장무관련위험 ▶ non-market risk

non-market risk 비시장성위험 = diversifiable risk, unsystematic risk ▶ systematic risk, undiversifiable risk

non-merchant 비(非)상인

non-merchant seller 비상인의 판매자

non-monetary A/L(asst/liability) 비화폐성 자산·부채

non-monetary asset   비화폐성 자산
    ▶ monetary asset, non-
    monetary liability
non-monetary exchange   비화폐성
    자산의 교환
non-monetary item   비화폐성 항목
    ▶ monetary item, non-
    monetary asset, non-monetary
    liability
non-monetary liability   비화폐성 부채
    ▶ monetary liability,
    monetary-nonmonetary
    method, non-monetary asset
non-monetary transaction   비화폐적
    거래, 비금전거래
    ▶ donation
non-negotiable   비교부성
non-negotiable document   비교부성
    증서
non-operating asset   영업외자산
non-operating book   영업외장부
non-operating expense   영업외비용
    ▶ non-periodical profit
non-operating income budget   영업외
    손익예산
non-operating profit   영업외수익
non-operating revenue   영업외수익
    ▶ other revenue and gain,
    non-operating profit
non-opinion engagement   무의견계약
non-opinion report   무의견감사보고서
non-owner change in equity   출자자
    이외의 사람과의 거래에서 발
    생하는 지분의 변동
non-parametric method   비모수법
non-par stock   무액면주식 ▶ par value
    stock

non-participating preferred stock   비
    참가적우선주 ▶ participating
    preferred stock
non-periodical profit and loss   비반복
    적 손익 = extraordinary profit
    and loss, non-recurring profit
    and loss
non-possessery use interest   비점유적
    사용권
non-pre-notice audit   불시감사, 무예
    고 감사 = surprised audit
non-production overhead cost   비제
    조간접비
non-productive labor   간접노무비, 비
    생산적 노무비 = indirect labor
non-productive stock   간접재료(재고)
    = indirect material, indirect
    stock
non-professional auditor   비전문적 감
    사인
non-profit accounting   비영리회계
    = not-for-profit accounting
non-profit business   비영리사업
    ▶ non-business organization,
    non-profit accounting
non-profit corporation   비영리법인
    ▶ non-profit organization,
    profit-corporation, profit
    organization
non-profit enterprise   비영리기업
non-profit hospital   비영리병원
non-profit making   비영리 = not-for-
    profit
non-profit organization   비영리단체
    = not-for-profit organization
non-profit sector   비영리부문 = not-
    for-profit sector

non pro rata distributions from partnership   파트너십으로부터 불균등 배분

non-public company   비공개회사

non-public enterprise   비공개기업

non-purchased goodwill   비매입영업권 ▶ purchased goodwill

non-qualifying distribution   부적격배분 ▶ imputation system, qualifying distribution

non-reciprocal interfund activity   비상호기금간 거래

non-reciprocal transaction   일방적 거래 ▶ donation

non-reciprocal transfer   일방적 양도

non-recuring item   비경상손익항목

non-recurrent   비경상적

non-recurrent expense   비경상비용 ▶ extraordinary loss

non-recurring charge   비경상적 비용, 임시손실 = extraordinary charge ▶ extraordinary loss

non-recurring gain   비경상상이득 ▶ extraordinary gain

non-recurring item   경상외항목, 비경상항목 ▶ extraordinary item, recurring profit

non-recurring loss   비경상손실 = extraordinary loss ▶ extraordinary gain or loss, extraordinary item, non-recurring gain

non-recurring profit and loss   비경상손익 = non-recurring gain and loss, extraordinary gain and loss ▶ non-periodical profit and loss

non refundable deposit   보증금이 리스기간 종료시에 최종 리스료와 상계

non-registered bond   무기명사채

non-reusable   재사용불가, 재사용불능

non-routine decision   비일상적인 의사결정, 의사결정회계

non-sampling risk   비표본위험

non-savable cost   절약불능원가 ▶ avoidable cost

non-standard label   표준 이외의 레벨

non-statistical sampling   비통계적 표본조사, 판단적 표본조사

non-sufficient fund check   부도수표

non-taxable exchange   비과세 대상 교환

non-taxable income   비과세소득

non-trade note   비영업어음

non-trade receivable   비영업 수취 채권 ▶ trade receivable

non-union worker   비조합원, 미조직 노동자 ▶ union worker

non-value-added activity   [JIT]부가가치가 아닌 활동, 비(非)부가가치 활동

non-value-added cost   [JIT] 부가가치가 아닌 원가

non-value bill   융통어음 = accommodation bill

non-vested benefit information   수급권 미귀속의 정보,

non-vested stock   권리미확정 주식

non-voting share   무의결권주 = non-voting stock ▶ voting share, voting stock

non-voting stock   무의결권주 = non-voting share

▶ preferred stock, voting
stock, voting share
no-par 무액면(無額面) ▶ par value,
share with par value
no-par stock 무액면주식
no-par value stock 무액면주식 ▶ par
value stock, par value capital
stock
normal activity 정상조업도, 정상생산
능력 = normal capacity, normal
production, normal volume
normal auditing procedure 통상의
감사과정 = normally accepted
auditing procedure
normal burden rate 제조간접비 정상
배부율 = normal overhead rate
normal capacity 정상조업도, 정상생산
능력 = normal activity
normal cost 정상원가 = normal
standard cost ▶ abnormal cost
normal costing 정상원가계산 = normal
cost system ▶ normal cost
normal cost system 정상원가계산
= normal costing
normal curve 정규곡선 = bell-shaped
curve
normal depreciation 통상의 감가상각
▶ extraordinary depreciation
normal distribution 정규분포
▶ Gaussian distribution
normal dividend 통상적인 배당
normal equation 정규방정식
normal inventory 정상재고량, 항상
재고량 = base stock, normal
stock ▶ normal stock method
normalize 정규화(正規化)
normalized form 정규형(正規形)(부동소

수점표시의) = standard form
normalizing 표준화
normal labor hour(NH) 정상작업 시
간
normal lead time [경제적 발주량] 정
상 리드 타임
normal loss 정상감손
normally accepted auditing procedure
일반적으로 인정된 감사절차
= normal auditing
normal operating cycle 정상적인 거
래순환주기, 정상영업순환
▶ normal operating cycle basis
normal operating cycle basis 정상영
업순환 기준 ▶ one year rule
normal overhead rate 제조간접비 정
상배부율 = normal burden rate
normal pension cost 정상연금비용
= current service cost
normal price 정상가격
normal probability paper 정규확률표
normal production 정상조업도, 정상
생산능력 = normal activity
normal profit margin 정상이익, 정상
이윤 ▶ excess profit
normal profit rate 정상이익률, 정상
이윤률
normal quorum 정족수(투표권 있는 주
식의 과반수 출석)
normal return 정상이익
normal shrinkage 정상감모손
▶ abnormal shrinkage
normal spoilage 정상공손
▶ abnormal spoilage, spoilage
normal spoilage cost 정상적인 공손비
normal standard cost 정상표준원가
= normal cost

normal stock   정상재고량, 항상보유고
= base stock, normal inventory,
normal stock method

normal stock method   정상재고법, 기
준재고법, 항상재고법 ▶ base
stock method, normal stock

normal variate   정규변량(變量)

normal volume   정상조업도, 정상생산
능력 = normal activity

normal waste   정상감손, 정상작업감손
▶ abnormal waste, waste
procedure

notary public   공증인

notation   표기법, 표시법

not between merchant   상인간의 거래
가 아닌 거래

not collected by bank   은행에 의해 회
수 되지 않은

note   1) 주석 2) 주기(註記) ▶ footnote
3) 어음, 지폐 4) 중기채권

note discounted   할인어음 = note
receivable discounted

note dishonoured   부도어음

**note exchanged for cash and unstated
right and privilege**   현금
및 현금 이외의 어떤 권리와 교
환한 어음

note exchanged for cash only   현금결
제용 어음

**note exchanged in a noncash
transaction**   현금 이외의
자산 또는 서비스 제공의 대가
로 받은 어음

note issurance facility   채권발행 보증
조건

note payable   지급어음, 어음채무
▶ note receivable

note payable book   지급어음 기입장
= note payable register

note payable register   지급어음 기입
장 = note payable book
▶ note payable

note payable to subsidiary   자회사 지
급어음

note receivable   받을어음 ▶ note
payable

note receivable book   받을어음 기입
장 = note receivable register
▶ note payable book

note receivable discounted   할인어음

note receivable due from employee
종업원 어음대출금

note receivable endorsed   배서어음

note receivable register   받을어음 기
입장 = note receivable book
▶ note receivable

note to financial statement   재무제표
의 주석사항 ▶ accounting
policy, supplementary
information

note trader debtor   수취어음 = note
receivable

note with no interest   무이자부 어음

note with reasonable interest rate   통
상의 이율을 붙인 어음

note with unreasonable interest   비
정상 이자부어음

not-for-profit   비영리 = non-profit-
making

not-for-profit accounting   비영리회계
= non-profit accounting

not-for-profit organization   비영리단
체 = not-profit organization,
non-profit-making organization

not-for-profit sector　비영리부문
　　= non-profit sector, not-for-
　　profit accounting(비영리회계)
notice　공고, 공시, 통지(通知), 신고
notice of acceptance　인수통지
notice of dishonor　거절통지, 부도통지
notice of dissolution　해산통지
notice of principal　대리 소멸의 통지
notice of protest　지불거절통지
notice recording statute　선의자 보호
　　형 등기
notice statute　통지법규
notice-type statute　통지형 입법
notification　1) 최고(催告) 2) 독촉 3) 공
　　고, 통지, 신고서
notify　통지
not-in-then operation　배타(排他)연산
　　= exclusion
notional amount　추상적인 양, 비현실
　　적인 양, 명목상의 금액
NOT operation　부정(否定) = negation
NOT-OR　부정논리화(否定論理和)
not taxable　익금불산입
novation　개정, 계약의 경정(更正), (채무,
　　계약 등의) 갱신, 경개
NOW(negotiable order of withdrawal)
　　양도가능 인출증서
NPV(net present value)　순현재가치, 할
　　인현재가치
NPV method　순현재가치법
NRV(net realizable value)　순실현가능
　　가액 = estimated exit value,
　　expected exit value
Nuclear Waste Policy Act　핵폐기물
　　정책법
nucleus　핵심, 토대
null event　무효사건

null hypothesis　귀무가설
number　수(數), 번호
numbered account　번호가 부여된 계
　　정
numbering machine　자동번호기
number of authorized share　수권 주
　　식수
number of days' sales in average
　　receivable　외상매출금 회
　　수 일수
number of days' stock held　(영)평균
　　재고일수 = days' sales in
　　inventory, days to sell inventory
number of days' supply in average
　　inventory　재고자산 회전
　　일수
number of days to turnover　재고자
　　산 회전일수 ▶ inventory
　　turnover
number of invoice　송장번호
number of order　주문번호
number of periods　회수되는 기간
number of shares of stock outstanding
　　사외유통주식수
number of unit produced　(종합원가
　　계산) 생산수량, 제조수량
number of years method　연수법(年數
　　法), 연매법(年買法)
　　▶ discounted free cash flow
　　method, excess earnings power
　　approach, master valuation
　　approach
number representation system　기수
　　법(記數法) = numeral system,
　　numeration system
number shares of stock outstanding
　　사외유통주식수

numeral　수표시(數表示), 數

numeral system　기수법(記數法)
　　= numeration system ▶ binary
　　numeral, decimal numeral

numeration system　기수법 = number
　　representation system, numeral
　　system

numeric　수치, 수치적 = numerical
　　▶ alphabetic character set,

alphanumeric character set

numerical　수치적, 수의, 숫자의
　　= numeric

numerical analysis　수치분석

numerical control (NC)　수치제어

NYSE(New York Stock Exchange)　뉴욕
　　증권거래소 = Big Board

NYSE common stock index　뉴욕증권
　　거래소의 주가지수

O

O

OASDI(Old Age, Survivor and Disability
　　　　Insurance)　노령자 · 유족 ·
　　장애자 보험

object clause　목적조항

objection　이의(異議)

objective　목적, 기본목적

objective function　목적함수 ▶ linear
　　programming, non-linear
　　programming

objective of financial reporting　재무
　　보고의 목적

objective of firm　기업목표

objective probability　객관적 확률

objective test　객관성 검증

objective value　객관적 가치
　　▶ subjective value

objective, verifiable evidence　객관적
　　인, 검증 가능한 증거

objectivity　객관성 ▶ verifiability

obligation　의무, 부채, 채무(債務)

obligation of agent　대리인의 의무

obligation of confidentiality　비밀보

호의무

obligation of principal　본인의 의무

obligation to repurchase security sold
　　매각증권의 환매수의무

obligation under capital lease　리스
　　부채

obligor　채무자

observation　관찰, 입회(立會)

observation of physical inventory　실
　　지재고조사의 입회

OBSF(off balance sheet financing)　부
　　외자금조달

obsolescence　진부화, 부패화, 노후화
　　▶ functional depreciation,
　　inadequacy, physical
　　depreciation

obsolete asset　진부화 자산

obsolete inventory　진부화 재고자산,
　　진부화 재고 = obsolete stock
　　▶ net realizable value

obsolete stock　(영)진부화 재고자산, 진
　　부화 재고 = obsolete inventory

occupational pension scheme 종업원
    연금계획

Occupational Safety and Health Act
    (OSHA) 직업안정위생법

OCR (optical character reader) 광학식
    문자판독장치

octal 1) 8 2) 8진 3) 8진법 ▶ binary,
    decimal, ternary

octal digit 8진 숫자

octet 8중주, 8개(1조)

odd-even check 기우(奇偶)검사 = parity
    check

odd-lot 단주(端株), 단수

OECD(Organization for Economic
    Cooperation and Development)
    경제협력개발기구

off balance 부외, 장부 외

off balance sheet asset 부외자산(簿外
    資産)

off balance sheet financing(OBSF) 부
    외자금조달

off balance sheet liability 부외부채

off balance sheet risk 부외 위험, 부외
    항목관련 위험

offer 신청, 신청가격, 청약

offered price 매도호가, (판매의) 신청가
    격 = ask price, asked price,
    asking price ▶ bid price

offeree 판매신청접수자 ▶ offeror

offeree company 매입대상회사

offer for sale 판매의 신청(주문)
    ▶ introduction

offer for sale by tender (영)주식의 경
    쟁입찰

offering 1) 신청하다 2) 공모(公募)
    = public offering

offering circular 1) 간이계획서 2)구
    분판매안내서

offering market 발행시장, 모집시장

offering statement 간이신고서

offeror 판매신청자, 신청인,청약자
    ▶ offeree

offer price 매출가격

office 1) 사무소, 영업소 2) 성(省), 국(局)

office hour 영업시간

Office of Production Management
    (OPM) 미국생산관리국

office of the chief accountant 주임회
    계심사관실

officer 회사임원, 임원, 집행임원
    ▶ director

officer's bonus 임원상여금

office supply 사무용 소모품

official assessment 공식적인 부과과세
    제도 ▶ self assessment

official discount rate 공식적인 할인율
    ▶ central bank rate

official listing 공정시세표 ▶ listing,
    quotation

official receipt 공급영수증

official receiver (영)정부임명 관재인,
    관재관(管財官)

official receiver in bankruptcy 관선
    파산관재인

off limit 한도초과

off-line 오프라인, 연결이 끊긴 ▶ on-
    line

off-market purchase of share 주식
    의 시장외 매입

offset account 상쇄계정, 공제계정, 평
    가계정 ▶ valuation account

offset right 상쇄권

offsetting asset and liability 자산과
    부채의 상쇄

offsetting error　상쇄 오류
▶ clerical error, error of mistake in writing, error of omission

offshoot　자회사(子會社)

offshore fund　구역외 기금 ▶ tax haven

offshore loan agreement　역외 대부계약

offshore market　역외시장

oil and gas accounting　석유와 가스 회계

Oil Pollution Act　원유오염법

Old age, Survivor and Disability Insurance　노령자 · 유족 · 장애자 보험

old business　기존 사업

old share　구주(舊株) = old stock ▶ new stock

old style auditing　구식(舊式)감사

oligopoly　과점(寡占) ▶ monopoly

omitted procedure　감사절차의 누락

omitted procedure discovered after report date　보고서일자 이후에 발견된 생략된 감사절차

OMR(optical mark reading)　광학식 마크판독기

oncost　(영)제조간접비 = factory overhead

on credit　외상판매, 외상매입, 신용거래

on demand guarantee　요구불보증계약

on demand system　즉시회답시스템

one economic entity　하나의 경제적 실체

one hundred percent balance sheet　백분율 대차대조표 ▶ one hundred percent income statement

one hundred percent income statement　백분율 손익계산서 ▶ one hundred percent balance sheet

one-sided confidence interval　단측신뢰구간

one-sided test　단측 검정(檢定) ▶ two-sided test

one transaction perspective　단일 거래기준 ▶ two transaction perspective

one-way communication　일방적 통신

one year concept　1년 기준 = one year rule ▶ current-noncurrent method, normal operating cycle basis

one year rule　1년 기준 = one year concept ▶ current-noncurrent method, normal operating cycle

on-line　온라인, 연결된 = online ▶ off-line

open account　정산계정, 실잔고계정

open and current account　교차계정계정

open and notorious　공개적이고 잘 알려진

open check　보통수표 = open cheque

open cheque　보통수표 = open check ▶ crossed cheque

open corporation　공개회사, 주식공개회사 ▶ close corporation closed corporation

open credit　매수은행부지정 신용장, 무조건 신용장 = general credit, negotiation credit

open delivery place　인도장소의 미정(未定)

open-ended　확장가능, 개방식, 개방형

open-end fund　개방형 투자회사, 계약형 투자신탁 ▶ closed-end fund, investment trust, mutual fund

open-end investment trust　개방형 투자신탁 ▶ closed-end investment company

open-end mortgage　개방식 담보부 사채, 추가차입채 담보 ▶ closed-end mortgage

opening balance　기초잔고 ▶ closing balance

opening bank　신용장개설은행

opening entry　개시기입

opening inventory　기초재고액

opening price　시초가 ▶ closing price

opening stock　(영)기초잔고, 기초재고액 ▶ closing stock

opening trial balance　기초산표 ▶ opening balance

open market operation　공개시장조작

open market value　공개시장가치 ▶ market value

open mines doctrine　개발된 광구에 대한 계속 채취는 인정, 새로운 광구를 만들 수 없다는 것

open mortgage　개방담보 ▶ closed mortgage

open order　무조건 주문(품종, 가격만 표시하고 기타사항은 공급자에게 일임) ▶ good till cancelled

open policy　보험계약 체결시 일정한도만을 정하고 구체적 가치는 손해발생시 시장가격으로 정하는 보험

open price　가격의 미정

open quantity　수량의 미정

open shop　[노동조합]오픈 샵 ▶ closed shop, union shop

open term　미정의 조건

open time for payment　지불시기의 미정

open time for shipment or delivery　인도시점과 장소의 미정

operable time　정상가동시간 ▶ uptime

operand　연산수, 작용대상 ▶ operation

operating account　영업활동관련계정, 영업계정 ▶ balance sheet account

operating activity　영업활동

operating asset　영업용 자산

operating asset turnover　영업자산 회전율

operating audit　업무감사 = operational auditing, operation audit

operating book　영업장부

operating budget　업무예산, 영업예산 = income budget, profit and loss budget

operating capability　조업능력, 영업능력 ▶ concept of maintenance of operating capability, net operating asset

operating capacity maintenance　영업능력 유지 ▶ concept of maintenance of operating capability

operating capital　영업자본

operating cost　영업비 = operating expense ▶ marketing cost

operating cycle　영업순환기간, 거래 주기

operating decision　업무집행 의사결정 ▶ management control,

programmed decision, strategic
decision, strategic planning

operating department　집행부문, 실시
부문 = line department

operating earning rate　영업자본이익
율, 영업이익율

operating effectiveness　운용상의 유효
성 ▶ internal control structure

operating expense　1) 영업비 2) 운용
비용

operating expense budget　영업비예산

operating expense ratio　영업비율
= ratio of selling and
administrative expenses to sales
▶ operating ratio, ratio of cost
of sales

operating fund　영업자금

operating goal　영업목표

operating income　영업이익

operating income margin　영업손익,
영업이익

operating inferiority　조업부진, 가동
부진

operating lease　운용리스, 영업리스 계
약 ▶ finance lease

operating leverage　영업레버리지
▶ financial leverage, leverage

operating loss　영업손실

operating performance　영업성과, 업
적

operating plan　업무계획

operating policy　영업정책

operating profit　1) 조업이익 2) 영업
이익 = income from operations,
operating income

operating profit or loss　영업손실

operating purpose　영업목적

operating ratio　영업비율 ▶ operating
expense ratio, ratio of cost of
sales

operating result　영업실적, 경영성적

operating revenue　영업수익, 영업수입
▶ operating income, operating
profit

operating segment　사업부문

operating statement　1) 손익계산서
= income statement 2) 영업손
익요약표

operating system(OS)　운영체제

operating time　동작시간, 가동시간

operating transfer　운영이전

operation　1) 연산 = operand 2) 조작, 동
작 3) 운용, 업무

operational audit　업무감사, 운영감사
= management audit, operating
audit, operation audit,
performance audit

operational control　현장통제
= management control, strategic
planning

operational efficiency ratio　영업효율
성비율

operation analysis　작업분석
= operations research

operation audit　업무감사 = operational
audit, management audit,
operating audit, performance
audit

operation capacity　조업도 = activity
level, volume level

operation card　작업시간표, 작업시간
보고서 = time ticket

operation code　연산코드, 명령코드

operation cost system　작업별 원가계

O

산, 작업단위별 원가계산
= operation costing
operation decoder 명령해독기
operation list 작업수순표 = operation
routing
operation part 연산부(部), 명령부(部)
= function part, operator part
operation research (OR) 사업분석
= operations analysis
operation sheet 작업표
operation standard 작업표준 = work
standard
operation time 1) 작업시간, 가공시간,
가동시간 2) 연산시간
operation time card 작업시간표, 작업
시간보고서 = time ticket
operator 1) 연산자(기호처리에 대한)
2) 조작원
operator command 조작원의 지령
opinion 의견, 감사의견
opinion date 감사보고서의 날짜
opinion of independent accountant
독립회계사의 감사의견
**opinion of the Accounting Principles
Board** APB의 견해
opinion paragraph 의견문단
opinion section 의견구분 ▶ scope of
examination, scope of opinion,
scope section
opinion type 의견의 유형
OPM(Office of Production Management)
미국생산관리국
opportunity cost 기회원가 = imputed
cost ▶ outlay cost, special cost
studies
opportunity cost variance 기회원가
차이 ▶ ex post optimum

analysis, ex post variance,
forecasting variance
opportunity loss 기회손실
= conditional loss, cost of
prediction error
optical character reader(OCR) 광학
식 문자판독장치
optical character recognition(OCR)
광학식 문자인식
optical mark reading 광학식 판독기
= mark scanning
optimal control problem 최적제어 문
제
optimality principle 최적성 원리
optimal purchasing lot size 최적구입
규모 = economic order quantity
optimum capacity 최적조업도
= optimum output
optimum production lot size 최적생
산규모
option 옵션, 선택권, 주식구입선택권
**Optional Adjustment to Basis of
Partnership Property** 파
트너십 재산의 기초가격에 대
한 선택적 조정
optional redemption 수시상환
▶ mandatory redemption
option contract 옵션계약
option pricing model 옵션가격모델
▶ contingent claim security,
option
option written (판매자측의) 옵션 리튼
OR(operation research) 사업분석
= operation analysis
oral 구두(口頭)
oral evidence 구두증거(口頭證據)
oral stop order 구두(口頭) 지급정지명

령

order 1) 주문, 주문서 2) 순서 3) 명령, 지령 4) 배열하다

order backlog 수주(受注)잔고

order check 지시인 지불수표, 지시식 수표, 기명식수표 = order cheque ▶ open check

order cover 순잔고 = free balance

ordered pair 순서쌍

order filling cost 주문수행비, 주문처리비 ▶ order getting cost

order form 주문서, 주문서식

order for relief 구제명령

order getting cost 주문획득비 ▶ order filling cost

ordering bias 순서편견, 순서편차

ordering cost 발주비 ▶ inventory carrying cost, inventory cost

ordering cycle 주문간격 = ordering interval

ordering point 주문점(재고를 보충하는 시점) = order point, reorder point, reordering point

ordering point method 주문점 방식

order number (개별원가계산에서) 작업지시서 번호

order of liquidity 유동성 배열법

order of relief 구제명령, 절차개시명령

order paper 기명식 증서, 기명배서식 증서, 지불지시증권

order point 주문점 = ordering point, reordering point, reorder point

order quantity 발주(주문)량

order to paper 지시식 증권

order to pay 지불 지시

order without limit 시세주문 = market order ▶ limit order

ordinal number 순서수(數) = ordinal

ordinance 법령, 포고, 조례, 정부명령, 규제, 규정

ordinary annuity 정상연금, (연금의 미래가치 계산상) 후불연금

ordinary audit risk 통상적인 감사위험 ▶ audit risk

ordinary budget 일상적인 예산, 경상예산 ▶ capital budget, cash budget, income budget, master budget

ordinary dividend 보통배당

ordinary duress 통지의 강요, 통상의 강박(强迫)

ordinary income 통상의 소득, 사업소득

ordinary incremental budget 통상의 증분예산 = incremental budget ▶ priority incremental budget, zero-base budgeting

ordinary journal 보통분개장 = proper journal ▶ special journal

ordinary least square 최소자승법 = least square method

ordinary negligence 일반 과실

ordinary repair 통상의 수선 ▶ extraordinary repair, major repair

ordinary resolution (영)보통결의 ▶ extraordinary resolution, special resolution

ordinary share (영)보통주 = common share, equity share

ordinary share capital (영)보통주 자본

ordinary shareholder   보통주주

ordinary shareholders' equity   보통
주주지분 = ordinary
shareholders' fund

ordinary stock dividend   보통주 주식
배당

organizational environment   조직환경

organizational expenditure   창업비

organizational expense   창업비용

organizational structure   조직구조

organization and system audit   조직
감사(내부감사) = organization
audit

organization chart   조직도

organization cost   창업비
= formation expense,
preliminary expense

organization for budgetary control
예산통제조직

Organization for Economic
Cooperation and
Development(OECD)   경
제협력개발기구

organization form   조직형태, 기업형태

organization goal   조직목표, 기업목표
= organization objective

organization meeting   창립총회, 설립
총회

organization objective   조직목표, 기업
목표 = organization goal

organization of business firm   기업
조직

organization planning   조직계획

oriented graph   방향이 정해진 그래프

origin   1) 기점(起點) 2) 원점(原點) 3) 발
신지

original cost   원시원가, 취득원가, 역사

적 원가 ▶ historical cost

original entry   원시기입, 원초기입

original sales price   원시매가(賣價), 원
시매가가액

original voucher   원시증빙(原始證憑)

orthogonal array   직각배치

orthogonal matrix   직각행열

orthogonal system   직각계

OS(operating system)   운영체제

OSHA(Occupational Safety and Health
Act)   직업안전위생법

ostensible authority   표현상의 권한

OTC(over-the-counter)   점두매매(店頭
賣買)

OTC stock(over-the-counter stock)   점
두주식 = counter stock

other accumulated comprehensive
income   기타 누적포괄이익

other asset   기타자산 ▶ sundry asset

other auditors' report   다른 감사인
의 감사보고서

other comprehension income   기타
포괄이익

other comprehensive bases of
accounting   기타 포괄적 회
계기준

other dependent auditor   다른 비독립
적인 감사인

other expense   영업외비용

other income   영업외수익

other income and expense budget   영
업외손익 예산

other information   다른 정보

other revenue and gain   영업외수익
▶ nonoperating revenue

other tax   그 밖의 세금

other than temporary   일시적이 아닌

ouster   일부 공동 소유자가 다른 공동
소유자의 이용을 배제하면서
재산을 독점적 사용하는 것

outcome   결말

outflow   유출(流出)

outgo   지출 = outlay

outgoing dividend   현금배당, 금전배당
▶ non-qualifying distribution

outlay   지출, 경비 = outgo

outlay cost   지출원가 ▶ imputed cost,
opportunity cost

out of date check   기한경과수표
= stale check

out-of-pocket cost   현금지출원가
▶ relevant cost

out-of-pocket expense   현금지출비용

output   1) 생산량 2) 출력(data) 3) 출력
(처리 process)

output contract   생산계약, 특정물품
판매계약

output level   산출(량)수준, 생산량수준,
조업(도)수준 = capacity, level
of activity, volume

output method   산출법 ▶ input method,
standard cost

output price   유출가격 = exit price
▶ input price, net realization
value

output tax   매출에 대한 부가가치세
▶ input tax

outside of audited financial statement
감사완료재무제표 외

outsider   기업외부의 정보이용자
▶ insider

outstanding bond   사외유통사채

outstanding check   미결제수표

outstanding claim   미결의 클레임

outstanding commitment written   대
부계약 미이행 잔액(대부자측)

outstanding contract   미이행 계약

outstanding share   사외유통주식

outstanding stock   사외유통주식

out-the-window   판매해지증권

outward remittance   외국환 매도

**overabsorbed and underabsorbed
overhead**   제조간접비 배부
과부족액

overabsorbed burden   제조간접비 배
부초과액 = overabsorbed
overhead

overabsorbed labor cost   노무비 배부
초과액

overabsorbed material cost   재료비 배
부초과액

overabsorbed overhead   제조간접비
배부초과액 = overabsorbed
burden, overapplied burden,
overapplied overhead
▶ underabsorbed overhead,
underapplied overhead

overabsorption   배부초과

**overall opinion on the financial
statements as a whole**   재
무제표에 대한 종합의견

overall past performance   과거의 전반
적 업적

overall rate   종합이율 ▶ direct
capitalization, gross rent (or
income) multiplier

overall review   종합 검토

overapplied burden   제조간접비 배부
초과액 = overabsorbed
overhead

overbid   비싼 값 ▶ reverse bid

O

overbought (투자의 채산성을 초과하는)
주식매입, 고가매입

overcapitalization 과대자본화

over depreciation 과대상각
▶ depreciation, under-
depreciation

overdraft 당좌차월 = bank over-draft,
overdrawing

overdue 지급 기일의 경과

overdue account 만기경과 계정
= delinquent account receivable

overdue bill 만기경과 어음

overdue check 만기경과 수표

overdue interest 연체이자

overdue loan 변제기한경과 대부금

overdue note 만기경과 어음

overestimation 과대추정, 과대견적
▶ underestimation

overflow 1) 넘치다, 범람하다 2) (상품,
자금 등이) 충만하다, 넘치다
3) 과다, 과잉

overflow check 과다 검사

overhead 1) 간접비 = indirect cost 2) 제
조간접비 = factory overhead

overhead absorption 제조간접비의 배
부

overhead allocation 제조간접비의 배
부 ▶ burden rate, factory
overhead

overhead cost 제조간접비 = factory
overhead

overhead cost standard 제조간접비
표준 = manufacturing overhead
standard

overhead distribution sheet 제조간접
비 배부표

overhead efficiency variance 제조간
접비 능률차이 = efficiiency
variance

overhead expenditure variance 제조
간접비 차이
= overhead variance
▶ overhead efficiency
variance, overhead spending
variance, overhead volume
variance

overhead expense 제조간접비
= factory overhead

overhead operation 부수연산, 관리
조직 = housekeeping operation

overhead rate 제조간접비 배부율
= burden rate

overhead spending variance 제조간
접비 소비차이 = budget
variance, spending variance
▶ overhead variance

overhead total variance 제조간접비
총차이

overhead variance 제조간접비 차이

overhead volume variance 제조간접
비 조업도차이

overlap 병행, 중복

overloan 대출초과

overriding criterion 최우선 규준(規準)

overseas branch 재외지점

overseas company 재외회사

overseas money order 외국송금환
= foreign money order

overseas sterling area 해외 파운드(영
국의 화폐단위)지역 = overseas
sterling bloc ▶ scheduled
terriories

overseas sterling bloc 해외 파운드 지
역 = overseas sterling area

▶ scheduled territiries

overseas subsidiary   해외 자회사
▶ overseas company

overseers   감독자

oversight body   감독기관

overstatement   과대표시 ▶ creative
accounting, understatement,
window dressing

oversubscription   응모초과

over-the-counter(OTC)   증권회사의 점
두(店頭), 점두매매

over-the-counter market   점두시장
▶ over-the-counter stock

over-the-counter stock   점두주(株), 점
두품목 ▶ over-the-counter
markets

overtime premium   초과노무수당, 시
간외수당, 잔업수당

overtrading   자금초과거래, 과대거래

owners   소유권

owners as owners   소유주로서 출자자

owners' equity   소유자 지분, 주주지분,
출자자 지분, 자본 = net assets,
net worth, shareholders'
equiity, stockholders' equity

ownership   소유권

ownership equity   소유주 지분

ownership interest   지분권, 소유주 지
분 = owners'equity, owners'
interest

ownership interests   소유주 청구권,
출자자 청구권

ownership rights   소유권

ownership theory   소유주 이론

owners' interest   소유자 지분
= owners' equity, ownership
interest

P

p.a.(per annum)   1년 단위, 1년마다, 매년

PA(public accountant)   공공 회계사

Paasche formula   파셰식, 파셰산식
▶ Laspeyres formula, Paaasche
index

Paasche index   파셰지수 ▶ Laspeyres
index, Paasche formula

pack   팩, 꾸러미, 대량

packet   한 묶음, 한 다발 ▶ packet
switching

packing and wrapping expense   포장
비 ▶ packing cost

packing cost   포장비 ▶ packing and
wrapping expense

packing density   포장밀도

padding   채워넣기

page   페이지

paging   페이징

paid check   지불결제수표

paid education leave   유급학습휴가
▶ compensated absence

paid-in capital   납입자본
▶ paid-in surplus

paid-in capital from reduction in par

of outstanding share 감자
차익 = surplus from capital
reduction ▶ capital surplus

paid-in surplus 납입잉여금
= contributed surplus, share
premium account ▶ capital
surplus, donated surplus

paid-up capital (영)납입완료주식자본
= paid-up share capital
▶ called-up(share) capital

paid-up share capital 납입완료주식
자본 ▶ called-up(share)
capital, fully paid share, partly
paid share

paid vacation 유급휴가
▶ compensated absence, paid
education leave

**P and L(Parliamentary and Law Steering
Group)** (영)의회법률대책
위원회

P and L account (profit and loss account)
1) 손익계산서 2) 손익계정
3) 유보이익계정 = retained
earnings, retained income

paper 1) 문서, 기록, 신분증명서 2) 어
음, 환어음 3) 상장증권, 유가
증권

paper audit 서면감사

paper profit 장부상이익, 가공이익
▶ fictitious profit, unrealized
income

paperwork commission 사무처리 위
원회

par 액면

paragraph 단락

paragraph header 단락의 표제

paragraph name 단락명

parallel 병행, 병렬

parallel loan 평행차입

parallel loan arrangement 평행차입
계약

parallel operation 병렬연산, 병렬조직

parallel simulation 병행처리법

parallel storage 병렬기억상치

parallel transmission 병렬전송

parameter 매개변수, 모수

parent company 친회사, 모회사
▶ affiliated company,
dependent company, subsidiary
company

parent company concept 모회사이론
▶ entity concept

parent company statement 모회사
재무제표

parentheses-free notation 이전가격표
기법

parenthetical disclosures 주기, 재무
제표에 삽입하는 방법에 대한
공시

parenthetical reference 괄호내 참조
사항 = parenthetical remark

parent's equity share 모회사지분
▶ net investment in a foreign
entity

pari passu 동일한 보조, 공정한, 동등한

par issue 평가발행, 액면발행

parity 균형성, 기우(奇偶)성

parity adjustment 평가수정액, 평가
조달

**parliamentary and Law Steering
Group (P and L)** (영)의회
법률대책위원회

parol evidence rule 패럴 에비던스 룰,
구두증거의 원칙, 구두증거 규

정, 구술(口述)증거 규칙

par stock 액면주식

part cost 부품비

part finished product ledger 반(半)제품원장 = partially finished goods ledger

partial audit 일부감사

partial carry 부분실행

partial consolidation 부분연결 ▶ full consolidation

partial cost 부분원가 ▶ full cost

partial derivative 편도(偏導)함수

partial differentiation 편미분

partial equity method 부분적 지분법

partial integration 부분적 통합

partial loss 부분적 손실

partially disclosed principal 부분적으로 공개된(드러난) 본인

partially finished goods ledger 반제품원장 = part finished product ledger

partially-participating preferred stock 부분참가적 우선주

partially processed product 반제품 = semi finished goods

partial performance rule 부분 이행 규칙

partial plan 부분법, 분기법 ▶ output method, single planparticipant 가입자

participating contract 가입계약 ▶ participation right

participating interest 참가지분

participating preference share (영)참가적 우선주 = participating preferred stock

participating preferred stock 참가적

우선주 = participating preference share

participating unit plan (임원상여의) 업적단위방식

participation 참가

participation in profit sharing 이익분배의 참가

participation right 가입권, 참가권

participative budgeting 참여예산 ▶ imposed budget

participator 참가자, 관계자 ▶ participant

particular card (영)회사정보카드 ▶ white card, yellow card

partition 구획, 구분

part ledger 부품원장

partly finished work 반성(半成)공사

partly paid share (영)일부 불입된 주식 ▶ called-up share capital, fully paid share, paid- up share capital

partner 파트너, 조합원, 공동경영자, 사원

partner's basis in partnership 파트너십에서 파트너의 지분 기초 가격

partnership 공동협력, 조합영업

partnership agreement 조합계약(서), 합명회사의 정관 = articles of partnership, partnership articles

partnership article 조합계약서, 합명회사의 정관= partnership agreement

partnership at will 무기한부 파트너십 계약

partnership basis 파트너십 기초

partnership by estoppe 금반언에 의

한 파트너십

partnership deed　조합계약증서 = deed of partnership

partnership formation　파트너십의 형성

partnership income and loss　파트너십 소득과 손실

partnership interest　파트너십 지분

partnership liquidation　파트너십의 해산

partnership property　조합재산, 합명회사의 재산

partnership's use of cash method　파트너십의 현금주의 회계방법의 사용

partner withdrawal or death　파트너의 탈퇴 혹은 사망

part performance　일부 이행, 부분 이행

part-purchase, part-pooling　부분 매입, 지분풀링 절충법 ▶ pooling of interests concept, purchase concept

par value　액면금액, 환평가

par value capital　액면주식

par value method　액면가액법

par value stock　액면주식 ▶ no-par stock, no-par-value, shares of no par value

passage of title　소유권 이전

passive activity　소극적 행위

passive activity loss　소극적 손실

passive income　소극적 소득

passive station　수동단말, 수동국(局)

password　패스워드, 암호말 ▶ access control

past consideration　과거의 대가

past cost　과거원가 ▶ future cost, present cost

past exchange price　과거의 교환가격

past or moral consideration　과거 혹은 도덕적 대가

past service cost　과거용역비용 = prior service cost ▶ current service cost, retirement benefit plan

pat　구성부분

patch　1) 패치, 조각 2) 배선

patent　특허권

patent amortization　특허권 상각

patent fee　특허권사용료 = license fee

patent law　특허법

path　경로, 통로

pattern recognition　패턴 인식 ▶ artificial intelligence

pause instruction　휴지(休止)명령 = halt instruction

pawn　저당물, 질물(質物) = pledge

payable　지급채무

payable at a definite time　확정기일 지불, 확정일 지급

payable at sight　일람(一覽)지급

payable on demand　요구(要求) 불(拂)

payable on presentment　정시(呈示) 지급

payable period　회수기간 = payback period

payable to bearer　지참인 지급, 무기명 배서식

payable to order　지시인 지급, 기명 배서식

pay-as-you-earn(PAYE)　(영)원천과세 = pay-as-you-go

pay-as-you-go　1) 현금지급방식, 현금지급주의 ▶ retirement benefit

plan 2) 원천과세 = pay-as-
you-earn

payback 회수기간법 = payback period

payback method 회수기간 = payback
period method ▶ payback
period

payback period 회수기간 = payable
period, payback, payoff period,
payout period, payouttime
▶ cash-flow, payback method,
financial statement method

payback period method 회수기간법
= payback method ▶ financial
statements method

paycheck 급여 수표

PAYE(pay-as-you-earn) (영)원천과세

payee 수취인, 지불처

payer 지급인

paying bank 지급은행

paying-in slip 입금전표 = credit slip
▶ payment slip

paying subsidiary 보조금의 교부

payment 변제(辨濟)

payment against document 변제대항
서류

payment credit 지불신용장

payment guarantor 지급보증인

payment in advance 선급금
= prepayment

payment of debt 채무변제

payment of dividend 지급배당금

payment of penalty 벌금지급

payment of penalty or fine 벌과금지급

payment on account 외상지급

payment provision 지급조항

payment slip 출금전표 ▶ paying-in slip

payment system 임률인정시스템

= pay plan

payoff 1) 이득, 이익 2) 청산, 보복 3)
뇌물 4) 페이 오프 5) 이익의
배분 6) 해고 7) (확률) 결말, 결
과, 기대치

payoff matrix 이익도표 = decision
table, payoff table

payoff period 회수기간 = payback
period

payoff table 이익도표 = decision table,
payoff matrix

payor 지급인(인수인)

payor bank 지급은행

payout percentage 배당성향, 배당 지
급율 = dividend payout, payout
rate, payout ratio

payout period 회수기간 = payback
period

payout rate 배당성향 = dividend
payout, payout percentage,
payout ratio

payout ratio 배당성향, 배당비율
= dividend payout percentage,
payout rate

payout time 회수기간 = payback period

pay plan 임률결정제도 = payment
system

payroll 1) 임금 = wage 2) 임금대장
= payroll book 3) 급료

payroll book 임금대장

payroll check 급료 수표

payroll department 급여 부문

payroll distribution journal 임금지
급분개장

payroll fringe benefit 급여부수비

payroll journal 급여대장

payroll record 임금지급장 = payroll

register

payroll register 임금지급장 = payroll record

payroll tax 급여관련세금

PBGC(pension benefit guaranty corporation) 연금급부 보증 회사

PCB(petty cash book) 소액현금출납장

PDB(purchases day book) 매입일기장, 일별매입장

pecuniary benefit 금전적 이익

peer 동업자

peer review 회계법인간의 상호검토, 동료심사, 동업자 리뷰, 동료검토

penalty 형벌, 벌금, 위약금

penalty for premature withdrawal from time deposit 정기 예금의 중도해지에 따른 위약금

pendente lite 소송중인, 심문중인 = lite pendente

pending lawsuit 미해결의 소송사건

pending legal matter (소송) 미결사건

pending litigation 계류중인 사안

pension 연금회계, 연금

pension benefit guaranty corporation (PBGC) 연금급부 보증회사

pension benefit plan 연금제도

pension expense 연금비용

pension fund 연금기금

pension plan 연금제도

pension scheme 연금지급협정

Peppercorn Theory 후추열매 이론

PER (price earning ratio) 주가수익률

per annum(p.a.) 1년 단위, 1년마다, 매년

P/E ratio(price earning ratio) 주가수익률

per capita 일인당, 인원수에 따른 분할, (유산을균등하게 분할하는 경우) 두할(頭割)

percentage 1) 백분율 2) 수수료, 구전 (口錢)

percentage depletion 일정률 감모상 각 = statutory depletion ▶ cost depletion

percentage error (백분율 표시상의) 견적 오차

percentage markup [가격결정] 원가 가산이익율법

percentage markup on cost 원가가산 이익률, 이익률

percentage of capital structure 자본 구성비율 ▶ debt ratio

percentage of completion method 공 사진행기준, 진행기준 ▶ accrual basis, completed contract method

percentage of completion method for long-term contract 장기 공사계약에 의한 공사진행기준 = percentage of completion method ▶ accrual basis, complete contract method

percentage of process yield 공정수율

percentage of sales method 매출비례 법

percentage on wage method 임금율 법

percentage point 1) 1퍼센트 기준 2) 백분위수, 백분순위(百分順位) = percentile

percentage profit on turnover 매출액 이익률 = profit to turnover ratio

percentage rental 임차료 비율

= contingent rental

percentage rule   백분율기준

= fixed percentage rule

percentile   백분위수, 백분순위

= percentage point

perception   지각(知覺)

per contra acceptance and guarantee
지불승낙서면(은행부기)

per contra account   대조계정

per diem   1) 1일 단위   2) 일당, 일급, 하
루당 사용료

perfected security interest   완성된 담
보권

perfect information game   완전정보
게임

perfecting a security interest   담보권
의 완성

perfecting by attachment   설정에 의한
완성

**perfecting by filing a financing
statement**   융자보고서 발송
에 의한 완성

perfecting by possession of collateral
담보물 점유에 의한 완성

perfection   완성, 완전화(제3자 대항요건
의 확립)

perfection by attachment   담보권 설
정상의 자동적 완전화, 설정에
의한 완성

perfection by filing   등록에 의한 완성

**perfection by filing a financing
statement**   융자보고서의 등
록상의 완전화

**perfection by possession of the
collateral**   담보권자 점유상
의 완전화

perfection by taking possession   담보

물을 점유함으로써 완성하는
것

perfection of security interest   담보
권의 완전화

perfection standard   이상적 기준
▶ currently attainable standard
cost

perfect tender rule   완전이행의 원칙
(대금지불조건), 완벽한 제공규칙

performance   이행, 업적, 성능, 효율
▶ cost/performance

performance accounting   업적평가회
계, 업적관리회계 ▶ budgeting,
decision accounting

performance analysis   업적평가, 성과
평가

performance appraisal   업적평가
= performance evaluation

performance audit   성과감사, 이행감사

performance based stock option   업
적에 기초한 스톡옵션

performance bond   이행보증서

performance budget   업적예산

performance condition   업적조건

performance evaluation   업적평가
= performance appraisal

performance guarantee   계약 미이행
의 경우에 보상계약

performance level   업적수준
= efficiency level ▶ capacity
level

performance measurement   성과측정

performance of audit work   감사작업
의 수행

performance of contract   계약의 이행

performance of sales contract   매매
계약의 이행

performance report　성과보고서
　　= budget report
performance review　성과검토
performance standard　업적표준, 업
　　적기준
perfunctory activity　형식적인 활동
peril　손해발생 원인
period　기간, 사업연도, 회계기간
period budget　기간예산 = fixed budget
period cost　기간비용, 기간원가 ▶ 제
　　품원가(product cost)
periodic allocation of cost　원가의 기
　　간배분, 원가배분
periodic average method　총평균법
　　▶ first-in, first-out method, last-
　　in, first-out method, moving
　　average method
periodic earning　기간이익
periodic esate　기한부 재산권
periodic income　기간이익 ▶ periodic
　　loss
periodic inventory　실지재고, 정기재
　　고 = (영)periodic stock check,
　　(영)periodic stock taking,
　　perpetual inventory
periodic inventory method　실지재고
　　조사법 = inventory method,
　　periodic stock taking
　　▶ perpetual inventory method,
　　physical inventory
periodic inventory record　실지재고
　　조사법
periodic inventory system　실지재고
　　조사법, 정기재고자산 계산법
　　▶ 계속기록법(perpetual
　　inventory system)
periodicity　회계기간

periodicity assumption　회계기간의 가
　　정
periodicity concept　회계기간의 개념,
　　회계기간의 공준 = convention
　　of periodicity,time period
　　concept, time-period principle
　　▶ accounting convention,
　　accounting period, accounting
　　postulate
periodic loss　기간손실 ▶ periodic
　　income
periodic measurement　기간적 측정
periodic physical inventory　실지재고
　　조사 ▶ continuous physical
　　inventory
periodic review system　주기적검토제
　　도
periodic stock check　(영)정기재고조사
　　= periodic inventory, periodic
　　stock taking
periodic stock dividend　정기적 주식
　　배당
periodic stock taking　(영)정기재고조
　　사 = periodic inventory, periodic
　　stock check
periodic system　실지재고조사법
periodic tenancy　자동갱신 정기 부동
　　산권, 정기임대
period of account　회계기간
period of conversion　전환기간
period of irrevocability　철회불능기간
period planning　기간계획 ▶ project
　　planning
peripheral transaction　부수적 거래,
　　말초적 거래 = incidental
　　transaction
permanent asset　1) 영구자산 = capital

asset ▶ fixed asset 2) 자본적
자산
permanent decline in value　영구적
가치의 하락
permanent difference　영구적 차익
▶ timing difference
permanent file　1) 영구조서(調書)
2) 계속파일 = permanent file
paper, permanent working
paper
permanent file paper　영구조서
= permanent file, permanent
working paper
permanent fund　영구기금
permanent injunction　종국적 중지명
령 = perpetual injunction
▶ interlocutory injunction,
preliminary injunction,
provisional injunction,
temporary injunction
permanently restricted　영구적 구속
permanently restricted net asset　영
구구속순자산 ▶ temporarily
restricted net asset
permanently restricted resource　영
구적 제한자원
permanent publication　확실한 공식
의 간행물
permanent storage　영구기억장치
= permanent store
permanent working paper　영구조서
= permanent file, permanent
file paper
permissible capital payment　자기 주
식의 취득에 대한 상환의 허용
한도액
permissive waste　소극적 훼손

permutation　1) 순열(順列) 2) 치환(置換)
perpetual bond　영구채권 = annuity
bond
perpetual existence　계속주체
perpetual injunction　종국적 중지명령
= final injunction, permanent
injunction ▶ interlocutory
injunction
perpetual inventory method　계속기
록법, 계속재고조사법
= continuous inventory
▶ periodic inventory method,
physical inventory
perpetual inventory record　계속재
고조사기록, 계속기록장부
perpetual inventory system　계속기록
법 ▶ periodic inventory system
(재고계산법)
perpetual life　영속성(永續性)
perpetual system　계속기록법
perpetuity　영구연금, 종신연금
person　사람, 당사자, 거래관계자
personal account　인명계정
personal audit　인사감사
**personal casualty and theft gain and
loss**　인적 재난과 도난으로
부터 발생하는 이익과 손실
personal chattel　인적 동산 = chattel
personal
personal defence　개인적인 항변사유,
인적 항변
personal entity　인적 실체
personal estoppel　개인적인 금반언
personal financial planning(PFP)　개
인 재무계획
personal F/S(financial statement)　개
인적 재무제표

personal holding company(PHC) 동족회사, 동족지주법인

personal holding company and accumulated earnings tax 인적 지배회사와 누적소득과세

personal injury 인적 손해

personal interest 개인적인 이자

personal liability 개인 책임

personal notice 개별적 통지

personal property 동산(動産), 인적 재산 = personalty

personal property tax 개인재산세, 동산세

personal relief (소득세의) 인적 공제

personal representative 인적 대표자

personal representative(PR) 유언 관리인

personal service 인적 용역

personal service contract 인적 용역계약

personalty 동산, 인적 재산 = personal property

personnel and payroll cycle 인사 및 급여 순환과정

personnel department 인사부문

per stripes 가계상속, 퍼 스트립스(주식 수에 따른 분할)

PERT(program evaluation and review technique) 프로그램평가 및 검토기법

pertinent information 관련정보

pervasive constraint 일반적 제약조건

pervasive cost-benefit constraint 비용 · 효익에 관한 일반적 제약조건

petition 청원, 탄원, 신청

petition in bankruptcy 파산신청

petroleum revenue tax(PRT) 석유이윤세, 석유수입세

petty cash 소액현금, 소액지불자금 = petty fund ▶ imprest fund, imprest system

petty cash analysis envelope 소액지불비용 일람표 ▶ petty cash book, petty cash fund, petty cash voucher

petty cash book(PCB) 소액현금출납장

petty cash fund 소액현금, 정액전도 소액현금

petty cash voucher 소액현금전표

petty fund 소액지불자금 = petty cash

PFP(personal financial planning) 개인 재무계획

phantom stock plan (임원상여의) 주식 시가지급방식

phase modulation 위상변조 (位相變調)

phase modulation recording 위상변조기록

phaseout period 조업정지기간

phasing 예산기간의 관리가능기간 분할

PHC(personal holding company) 등록회사, 동족지주법인

philanthropic organization 자선단체

physical access control 물리적 접근통제

physical age 물리적 내용연수 ▶ economic life, effective age, depreciation

physical capital 물적자본, 실물자본, 실체자본 ▶ financial capital, monetary capital

physical capital concept 물적자본 개념

physical capital maintenance 실물 자본유지, 물적 자본유지, 실체 자

본유지 ▶ financial capital maintenance, maintenance of operating capability

physical capital maintenance concept 물적자본유지개념, 실물자본 유지개념

physical check system 물리적 견제조직

physical control 물량관리 ▶ cost control

physical count 실지재고

physical depreciation 물리적 감가 ▶ functional depreciation, physical factor

physical deterioration 물리적 노후화, 물리적 감가 ▶ cost approach, functional obsolescence, external obsolescence, reproduction cost

physical distribution 물적유통, 물류 = logistics

physical distribution cost 물류비 = logistics cost

physical distribution cost budget 물 류비 예산 ▶ physical distribution cost

physical evidence 물리적 증거

physical examination 물리적인 실사 (實查)

physical facility 실물자산

physical factor 물리적 (감가) 원인 ▶ physical depreciation

physical fixed asset 유형고정자산 = tangible fixed asset

physical inspection 실사(實查)

physical inventory 실지재고 = physical taking ▶ book inventory, perpetual inventory

physical inventory count 실지재고

physical inventory taking 실지재고, 실지재고조사 ▶ book inventory

physical life 물질적 내용연수, 물리적 내용연수 ▶ economic life

physical measure 물량적 측정치

physical observation 물리적 관찰

physical productive capacity 물적 생 산능력

physical standard 물량표준 ▶ cost standard, material quantity standard, operation standard, price standard, quantitative standard, wage standard

physical stock check 실지재고점검 ▶ physical inventory

physical supporting evidence 물적 증 거 ▶ physical evidence

physical taking 실지재고조사 = physical inventory ▶ book inventory, perpetual inventory

physical usage depreciation 물리적 사용에 따른 감가상각

pictogram 그림도표

picture 픽쳐

piece 작업량, 생산량, 수확량

piecemeal opinion 단편적 의견, 부분 의견 = limited opinion

piece rate 성과급 임률

piece rate plan 성과급제도 = piece rate system

piece rate system 성과급제도 = piece rate plan

piecework 청부업무, 성과급 지불업무

pie chart 파이 챠트 = circular chart

piercing the corporate veil 법인격의 부인(否認)

pilot plant 실험공장

pilot test　감사계약 체결전의 사전조사

PINCCA(price index numbers for current cost accounting)　현행원가회계용 물가지수

pink sheet　상장주 주가표

pixel　그림도 구성요소

PL(private ledger)　비밀원장 ▶ general ledger, impersonal ledger, nominal ledger

PL(product liability)　제조물책임

placed in operation　실시중인 ▶ internal control structure

placement　1) 배치 2) 직업소개 = placing

placing　(영)배치 = placement ▶ introduction, offer for sale

placing of share　주식의 모집(판매) = public offering

plan　계획 ▶ budget

plan administrator　연금제도 관리자

plan asset　연금제도자산, 사용제한자산, 구속자산

plan asset-actual return　제도자산-실제수익률

plan asset at fair value　연금제도자산의 공정가액

plan asset-expected long-term rate of return　연금제도자산-장기기대수익률

plan asset-expected return　연금제도자산-기대수익률

plan asset gain or loss　연금제도자산의 손익

plan asset-market-related value　연금제도자산-시가관련가액

plane graph　평면 그래프

planned assessed level of control risk　계획된 통제위험 평가치

planned economy　계획경제 ▶ free economy

planned variance　예정조업도차이, 계획차이 ▶ unplanned variance

planning　계획화, 계획설정 ▶ control

planning budget　계획예산

planning for capital investment　설비투자계획

planning of programmed activity　정형적 활동계획

planning procedure　계획절차

planning, programing and budgeting system(PPBS)　계획·프로그래밍·예산편성 시스템 ▶ zero-base budgeting

plant　공장

plant and equipment　공장설비, 유형고정자산 = fixed asset

plant and equipment budget　설비예산 ▶ capital budget, capital expenditure budget, construction budget, investment budget

plant asset　유형고정자산

plant budget　설비예산 ▶ plant and equipment budget

plant capacity　설비능력

plant fund　공장설비기금

plant idleness　공장설비의 유휴상태

plant investment　설비투자

plant ledger　고정자산대장 = fixed asset ledger

plant order　설비지시서 ▶ production order

plantwide overhead rate　공장전체 제조간접비배부율 ▶ department

overhead rate, department rate

PLC(public limited company. plc) (영)공모 주식회사

pleading 플리딩(변론, 항변), 소송절차

pledge 입질(질권 설정), 질권(質權), 저당권 = pawn

pledged asset 담보자산 = hypothecated asset

pledgee (동산)질권자

pledging 담보

pledging · assigning · selling(factoring) AR. 외상매출금의 담보제공, 양도담보, 매각

pledging of receivable 수취채권 담보

pledgor 질권설정자

plotter 작업도장치

P/L ratio 손익률

plugboard 배선반

plug-in unit 플러그 접속식의 부품

PM(preventive maintenance) 예방보수, 예방보전

PMM(purchse money mortgage) 매입대금 저당권

PMSI(purchase money security interest) 물품의 구입자금을 제공한 자가 가지는 담보권

PMSI in consumer goods 소비자 물품에서 물품의 구입자금을 제공한 자가 갖는 담보권

PMSI in inventory 재고에 대해 물품의 구입자금을 제공한 자가 갖는 담보권

PMSI in noninventory good 비재고 물품에서 물품의 구입자금을 제공한 자가 갖는 담보권

P/N(promissory note) 약속어음

PNA(project network analysis) 프로젝트 네트워크 분석

PNT(project network technique) 프로젝트 네트워크 기법

point estimation 점추정

point of sale recorder 판매시점 기록기

point of sales (POS) 판매시점

point of sales (POS) system 판매시점 관리 시스템

point-to-point connection 두 지점간 접속

poison pill 독약의 해독약

poisson distribution 포아송분포

police audit 검사적 감사

policy 보험증권, 경영방침

policy cost 정책적 원가 ▶ discretionary cost, managed cost

policy holder 보험계약자

policy holder dividend 보험계약자 배당금

policy holder's surplus 보험계약자 잉여금

polish notation 폴란드식 표기법 = Lukasiewicz notation, prefix notation

political climate 정치적 정세

political contribution 정치 기부금

political gift 정치적 증여

Pollution Prevention Act 오염방지법

pooling method 지분풀링법 = pooling of interest method

pooling of interest 지분풀링

pooling of interest concept 지분풀링법 ▶ business combination, purchase concept

pooling of interest method 지분풀링법

pool of resource provider   자원 제공
  자 집단

population   모(母)집단

population correlation coefficient   모
  집단상관계수

population parameter   모수(母數)

population size   모집단의 크기

population variance   모집단분산
  = variance

porducer   생산자

porducing   생산

portability   휴대가능성

portfolio   포트폴리오 ▶ diversifiable
  risk, efficient portfolio,
  systematic risk, unsystematic
  risk

portfolio analysis   포트폴리오 분석

portfolio income   포트폴리오 소득

portfolio management - 포트폴리오 관
  리 ▶ portfolio analysis,
  portfolio theory

portfolio theory   포트폴리오 이론

position   1) 위치 2) 행

positional notation   위치지정표기법,
  위치지정기수법 = positional
  representation system

positional parameter   정위치 파라미터

positional representation   위치지정표
  현법 = positional notation,
  positional representation system

positional representation system   위
  치지정표현법 = positional
  notation

positioning time   위치결정시간

position statement   재무상태보고서, 재
  정상태계산서 = statement of
  financial position

positive confirmation   적극적인 조회
  확인, 적극적 확인
  = affirmative confirmation

positive correlation   정(正)의 상관관계
  ▶ negative correlation

positive definite matrix   정치(正値), 정
  부호 행렬

positive form   적극적 조회양식

positive goodwill   영업권
  ▶ negative goodwill

positive law   실정법(實定法)

positive property   적극재산 ▶ negative
  property

possession   점유, 소유

possessory lien   점유 담보권

possibility of reverter   미래에 점유권
  을 취득하게 될 재산권

possible manipulation   이익조작 가능
  성

POS(point of sales) system   판매시점
  관리 시스템

post   1) 전기(轉記) 2) 지위, 격

postal check   송금수표

postal note   송금소액환

postal order   송금환

postal transfer deposit   대체저금

post audit   사후감사

post balance sheet date   대차대조표일
  후(後), 결산일후

post balance sheet disclosure   대차대
  조표일후공시

post balance sheet event   후속사건
  = event occurring after the
  balance sheetdate, subsequent
  event

post cessation receipt   휴업후 수취액
  = receipt after discontinuance

post closing trial balance   마감후 시산
　　표 = after-closing trial balance
post cost control   사후원가관리
　　▶ motivation cost control
post date   선일자(先日字), 사후일자
　　▶ antedate, backdate
post dated   선일부, 앞선 날짜
post dated bill   선일자 어음
post dated check   선일자 수표
post employment benefit   고용후 급부
postfix notation   접미표기법 = reverse
　　Polish notation, suffix notation
post implementation review   도입후
　　의 검토
posting   전기(轉記)
posting book   전기부(轉記簿)
postmortem dump   사후분석 덤프
postponable cost   연기가능원가
　　▶ escapable cost,
　　unpostponable cost, urgent cost
post retirement award   퇴직연금 증가
　　액
post retirement benefit   퇴직후 급부
post retirement benefit cost   퇴직후
　　급부비용
**post retirement benefit other than
　　pension**   연금 이외의 퇴직
　　후 급부제도
post retirement benefit plan   퇴직후
　　급부제도
post retirement health care   퇴직후
　　의료보장제도
post retirement health care benefit
　　퇴직후 의료보장제도
postulate   공준(公準) ▶ accounting
　　postulate, axiom, basic concept
postulate of accounting   회계공준

　　= accounting postulate
　　▶ assumption of accounting,
　　convention of accounting
postulate of auditing   감사공준
potential common stock   잠재적 보통
　　주식
potential investor   잠재적 투자자
potentially dilutive security   보통주식
　　이 될 가능성이 있는 증권
**potentially dilutive security
　　outstanding**   희석화할 가능
　　성이 있는 증권 등
potential productive capacity   잠재적
　　생산능력
potential user   잠재적인 정보이용자
power   권한
power expense   동력비
power level   전력수준
power of attorney   대리권을 서면으로
　　부여하는 경우의 그 서면, 위임
　　장
power of corporation   법인의 권한
**PPBS(planning, programming and
　　budgeting system)**   PPBS 계
　　획, 계획 · 프로그래밍 · 예산편
　　성 시스템
PPM(product portfolio management)
　　제품 포트폴리오 관리
PPS sampling   PPS 샘플링, 금액비례확
　　률표본조사
PPS sampling table   금액비례확률표본
　　조사 테이블
PR(personal representative)   유산관리인,
　　유언관리인
pracitical consequence   실무적 결과
practical attainable capacity   현실적
　　으로 달성가능한 조업도

P

▶ normal capacity

practical capacity   실제생산능력, 실현
가능조업도 ▶ average
capacity, theoretical capacity

practical insolvency   실질적 파산(상태)

practice   (영)(회계사의) 공공실무
= private practice, public
practice

practice bulletin   업무공보(公報)

practitioner   실무자

PRB(purchases return book)   환출품
명세표

pre acquisition contingency   취득전
우발사건

pre acquisition profit   취득일전 이익
▶ consolidated financial
statements

pre acquisition reserve   취득일전 유보
이익 ▶ consolidated financial
statements

pre audit   사전감사 = pre auditing

pre auditing   사전감사 = pre audit

precedence   우선권

preceding-year basis   (영)전년도소득
과세주의 ▶ basis period

precious metal   귀금속

precision   정도, 정확성

pre closing trial balance   마감전시산
표

pre consolidation adjustment   연결전
수정 ▶ consolidated financial
statements, consolidation
policy

pre date   전 날짜 = antedate, backdate
▶ postdate

predecessor auditor   전임감사인
▶ change of auditor

pre defined process   정의된 처리

predetermined burden rate   제조간
접비 예정배부율 ▶ burden rate

predetermined cost   예정원가
▶ estimate cost, standard cost

predetermined cost accounting   예정
원가계산

predetermined cost system   예정원가
계산제도

predetermined overhead rate   제조
간접비의 예정배부율

predetermined price   예정가격

predetermined rate   예정률

predetermined time standard system
예정작업시간의 표준화 시스템

predetermined wage rate   예정임률

predictable relationship   예측가능한
관계

predicted operating profit   예상영업
이익, 목표이익

prediction   예측

prediction deviation   예측편차
▶ implementation deviation,
measurement deviation, model
deviation, random deviation

prediction error   예측오차 ▶ cost of
prediction error

predictive model   예측 모델

predictive value   예측가치 ▶ feedback
value

predictor   예측지표

predominance   우월

preemption   신주인수 우선매입권, 신
주우선인수

preemptive right   신주인수권 = share
right, stock right ▶ pre-
emption

preexisting duty   기존의 의무

preexisting duty rule   기존의무규정,
이전에 존재한 법적 의무

preexisting legal duty (as consideration)
선재 법적 의무

preferability   선호성

preferability choices   선호성 선택

preference   1) 선호, 우선 2) 우선적 양도

preference dividend   우선주 배당
▶ preferred stock, preferred
stock capital

preference item   선호항목, 우선항목

preference share   (영)우선주 = preferred
stock

preference share capital   (영)우선주
주식자본 = preferred stock
capital ▶ preference dividend

preference shareholder   (영)우선주주
▶ preferred stock

preferential creditor   우선채권자

preferential debt   우선금전채무, 우선
채무

preferential transfer   특혜적 양도, 우
선적 양도, 편파양도

preferred   우선적

preferred dividend   우선주배당

preferred ordinary share   우선적인
보통주 ▶ deferred share

preferred stock   우선주 = preference
share ▶ preference
shareholder

preferred stock capital   우선주 자본
= preferred share capital
▶ preference dividend

**preferred stock with detachable
common stock warrant**
보통주 신주인수권부 분리형
우선주

prefessional association   직업단체

pre fix notation   접두표기법
= Lukasiewicz notation, Polish
notation

pre fix operator   접두연산자, 단항연산
자

Pregnancy Discrimination Act   임신
차별법

pre incorporation contract   발기인이
회사설립전에 행한 계약담보

pre incorporation transaction   회사
설립전의 거래

prejudgment remedy   판결전의 구제

preliminary audit   예비감사, 준비감사

preliminary expense   창업비
= (영)formation expense,
organization cost

preliminary injunction   예비적인 금지,
예비적 중지명령
▶ interlocutory injunction

preliminary investigation   예비조사
▶ preliminary review

**preliminary judgment about
materiality**   중요성에 대한
예비적 판단

preliminary negotiation   예비교섭

preliminary prospectus   예비계획서,
임시계획서

preliminary review   예비조사

preliminary sample   예비적 샘플

preliminary statement   예비보고서

premises and real estate   동산과 부동
산

premium   1) 액면초과액 2) 보험료
3) 할증금 4)경품

premium amortization   할증액 상각

premium expense　경품비　▶ estimate premium claims out standings

premium issue　할증발행

premium on acquisition　(기업매수시 발생하는) 매입할증 = purchased goodwill(영)　▶ discount on bonds payable

premium on bonds payable　사채할증발행차금

premium on capital stock　주식발행초과금

premium on debt　채무증권의 할증발행차금

premium on forward contract　선물계약 할증액

premium on forwarding contract　선물계약 할증액

premium on redemption　사채상환손실 = redemption premium

premium on sale of stock　주식발행초과금, 주식할증발행차금 = premium on capital stock

premium rate　보험료율

premium reserve　보험료적립금

pre notice audit　예고감사

pre numbering　일련번호

prepaid asset　선급항목

prepaid commission　선급수수료

prepaid expense　선급비용　▶ accrued expense

prepaid insurance　선급보험료

prepaid insurance premium　선급보험료　▶ insurance expense, insurance premium, insurance prepaid

prepaid interest and discount　선급이자와 할인료　▶ interest and discount

prepaid interest expense　선급이자비용

prepaid pension cost　선급연금비용

prepaid rent　선급임차료　▶ prepayment

prepaid rental expense　선급임차료　▶ deferred rental revenue

prepaid royalty　선급특허권사용료 = royalty advance

preparation　작성

preparation time　제조준비시간

preparer　작성자

preparer penalty　작성자의 벌금

prepayment　1) 선급금, 전도금, 선불(先拂)금 = advance, prepaid expense　▶ prepayment paid, prepayment received　2) 선급비용　3) 만기전 지불(기한전 변제)　4) 선불계정

prepayment paid　선급비용　▶ prepayment received

prepayment received　선수수익　▶ prepayment paid

pre preferential debt　파산자가 최우선으로 지불해야 할 채무　▶ preferential debt

pre production cost　생산 개시전 원가

prerequisite　필요조건

prescribed form　규정형식, 통일양식

prescribed format　규정형식, 통일양식

prescription　취득시효

present accounting model　현행의 회계모델

present and potential resource provider　현재와 장래의 자원 제공자

presentation and disclosure　표시와 공시

presentation bill　일람지불어음

presentation for acceptance　인수요구 제시

presentation for payment　지급요구 제시

present cost　현재원가 ▶ future cost, past cost

present discount value　현재할인가치

present financial statement　현행의 재무제표

presenting bank　지급제시은행 ▶ drawee

present intent　현재의 의도

present interest　현재(現在)권(權)

present measurement practice　현행의 측정실무

presentment　1) 지급제시 2) 표현

presentment warranty　지급담보 책임

present net income　현행의 순이익

present operative effect　현재영업효과

present or discounted value　현재 또는 할인 가치

present or discounted value of future cash flow　미래현금흐름의 현재가치

present practice　현행의 회계실무

present status　현재상황

present value(PV)　현재가치 = economic value, present worth

present value accounting　현재가치회계 ▶ continuously contemporary accounting, current cost accounting, current value accounting, replacement cost accounting, value accounting

present value method　현가법 ▶ discounted cash flow technique

present value of an ordinary annuity　통상의 연금현가

present value of future cash flows　미래 현금흐름의 현재가치

present value(PV) of minimum lease payments is 90% or more　최소리스료의 현재가치가 자산 공정가액의 90% 이상

present value(PV) of minimum lease payments(MLPs)　최소리스료의 현재가치

present value of money time value of money　화폐의 시간가치

present value rate　현재가치율

present worth　현재가치 = present value

president　대통령, 사장

presumptive trust　묵시(默示)신탁 = implied trust ▶ express trust

pretax accounting income　세금공제전 회계이익 ▶ income before taxes

pretax accounting income　기업회계상의 세차감전 순이익

pretax financial accounting income　기업회계상의 세차감전 순이익

pretax financial income　세차감전 순이익

pre trading expenditure　개업전 지출, 개업준비비

preventive control　예방통제

preventive maintenance(PM)　예방보수, 예방보전

price 가격, 물가

price adjustment clause 물가 수정조항 ▶ escalator clause

price aggregate 가격총계 ▶ historical cost

price appreciation 가격상승

price change 가격변동

price discrimination policy 차별가격 정책

price dividend ratio 주가배당률

price earning ratio(PER) 주가수익률

price increase 가격상승

price index 가격지수 ▶ price level

price index numbers for current cost accounting(PINCCA) 현행 원가회계용 물가지수

price level 가격수준, 물가수준 = general purchasing power, retail price index ▶ price index

price level adjusted data 물가수준 수정후 데이터

price level change 물가수준변동 ▶ changing prices

price level decline 물가수준의 하락

price list 가격목록

price policy 가격정책

Prices and Incomes Board (영)물가 와 소득 심의회

price-sensitivity hedge ratio 가격 · 민감도 헷지비율

price standard 가격표준 ▶ cost standard, direct labor standard, direct material standard, labor time standard, labor rate standard, material price standard, material quantity standard, operation standard, physical standard, wage standard

price tag 가격표 = tag ▶ key, label

price variance 가격차이, 재료의 가격 차이, 재료 구입가격과 소비가 격의 차이

pricing 가격계산, 가격설정

pricing decision 판매가격 결정문제

pricing materials issued 재료 출고가 격의 설정

prima facie 언뜻 보기에

primarily liable 1차적 책임부담

primary auditor 주요 감사인

primary capital market 제1차 자본 시장 ▶ secondary capital market

primary dealer 미국정부공인 증권 딜 러

primary distribution 제1차 매출

primary earnings per share 기본적 1 주당 이익 = basic earnings per share ▶ fully diluted earnings per share

primary financial statement 기본 재 무제표 ▶ secondary financial statements,supplementary information

primary function 1차 기능

primary government 기본 정부

primary liability 1차적 책임

primary liable 제1차 채무

primary market 1) (증권의) 발행시장 2) 일차시장, 주요시장 ▶ after market, secondary market

primary quality 기본적 특성

primary station 일차국(局)

prime cost 기본원가, 기초원가, 직접재

료비와 직접노무비 ▶ prime cost basis

prime rate   기본비율

principal   1) 원본, 원금 2) (주식의) 액면금액 3) (대리인 관계에서의) 본인 4) 주요 조건 5) 회장, 사장, 학장

principal-agent relationship   본인과 대리인 관계 = agency problem

principal and third party   본인과 제3자

principal auditor   주(主)감사인

principal book   주요 장부 = main book ▶ subsidiary book

principal budget factor   예산편성의 전제가 되는 제약요인

principal component analysis   주요성분 분석

principal debt   주된 채무

principal debtor   주된 채무자

principal-other auditor relationship   주요 감사인과 다른 감사인의 관계

principal owner   주요 주주

principal product   주(主)제품

principal production order   주(主)제조지시서 ▶ production order

principle   원리, 원칙, 주의 ▶ accounting principle

prior bond   우선 사채

prior charge capital   우선증권자본 ▶ gearing ratio

priority   우선순위, 우선권 ▶ multi-programming

priority incremental budget   우선순위에 따른 증분주의 예산

▶ incremental budget, ordinary incremental budget, zero-base budget

priority of claim   채권의 배당순서, 우선순위, 우선권

priority of claim of security interest   담보물권의 우선순위

priority percentage   우선지불율

prior knowledge   예비적 지식

prior payment   과거의 지불

prior period adjustment   전기 손익수정 = prior year adjustment

prior period item   전기수정사항 ▶ prior year adjustment

prior service cost(PSC)   과거용역원가 = prior service pension cost unrecognized

prior service pension cost   과거용역 연금비용

private accounting   사적(私的) 회계

private brand   상업자 상표

private company   1) 개인적 회사(영) ▶ corporation 2) 폐쇄회사

private cost   개인적 원가 ▶ social cost

private disposition   개인적 매각

private drawing   (현금 또는 재고자산의) 개인적 인출 = drawing

private enterprise   개인기업, 민간기업

private foundation   사적 재단

private ledger(PL)   비밀원장 ▶ general ledger, impersonal ledger, nominal ledger

private line   전용회선, 사설(私設)회선

private offering   (주식청약 등의) 개별모집, 사모(私募)

private placement   (주식청약 등의) 개별모집, 사모(私募) = direct

placement, private placing
private placement of security   유가
증권의 사모(私募), 개별모집
= direct placement
private placing   (영)사모(私募)발행
= private placement
private practice   (영)(회계사의) 공공실
무 = public accounting
private purpose trust fund   개인목적
의 신탁기금
private sale   공모(公募)
private statute of fraud   매매계약 체결
시 장래의 변경은 서면으로만
할 수 있다고 하는 경우
private treaty   입찰방식에 의하지 않는
재산의 판매 ▶ auction
private trust   사익(私益)신탁
private volume   개인용 용량, 전용 용량
privileged communication   면책적 의
사전달
privileged instruction   특권명령
privily   법률 당사자간의 상호관계
privily in contract   계약상의 상호관계
privily in estate   재산상의 상호관계
privily of contract   직접적인 계약의
상호관계
privy of contract   계약관계
prize and award   상품과 상금
probabilistic forecasting   확률적 예측
probability   개연성(蓋然性), 확률
probability analysis   확률분석
probability density function   확률 밀
도함수
probability distribution   확률분포
probability event   확률사건
probability-proportional-to-size
sampling (PPS 샘플링)   화폐

금액비례 확률표본조사
probable   가능성, 발생가능성이 거의
확실한
probable life   예상내용연수
probable mineral reserve   예상매장량
probate   1) 유언검인증 2) 유언검인(檢認)
probate court   검인(檢認)재판소
problem description   문제기술
procedural aspect of preparing return
소득신고서 작성의 절차
procedural audit   절차감사
procedural law   절차법
procedure   1) 수순, 절차 2) 처리과정
3) 발생의 가능성 빈도
proceed   1)수취액, 수입 2)회계절차, 대
가 3) 보험금
proceed from issuing stock   주식발행
에 의한 실수금
proceed from sale of equipment   비
품 매각에 따른 실수금
proceeding   파산절차
process   1) 처리 2) (데이터를)처리하다
process cost accounting   종합원가계산
= process costing
process costing   종합원가계산, 공정별
원가계산 = process cost
accounting, process cost system
▶ job-order costing
process costing system   공정별 원가
계산제도
process cost system   종합원가계산
= process costing
processing control   처리통제
processing method   처리방법
processing program   처리프로그램
processor   1) 처리장치 = data processor,

language processor 2) (언어) 처
리프로그램 3) 자료처리장치

process sheet 공정표

producer price index 생산자물가지수
▶ consumer price index

producers' goods 생산재 = production
goods ▶ capital goods,
consumers'goods, consumption
goods

producers' risk 생산자위험
▶ consumers' risk

producing department 제조부문, 생산
부문 = manufacturing
department, production
department ▶ auxiliary
department, service department,
subsidiary department

producing department cost 제조부문
비

product 1) 급부(給付) 2) 제품 3) 계산결
과

product and service pricing 제품 및
용역의 가격결정

product cost 제품원가 ▶ expired cost,
period cost(기간원가)

product cost accounting 제품원가계
산 = product costing

product costing 제품원가계산
= aggregative costing, product
cost accounting

product financing arrangement 제품
차입약정

production 생산, 제조

production batch 묶음생산량

production budget 제조예산
= manufacturing budget

production center 생산중심점

production control 생산관리

production cost 제조원가
= production overhead

production cost of sales 매출원가
= cost of goods sold, cost of
sales

production department 제조부문, 생
산부문 = manufacturing
department, producing
department

production expense 제조경비, 제조간
접비

production function 1) 생산기능 2) 생
산함수

production goods 생산물, 제품
▶ capital goods, consumption
goods, producer's goods

production level 생산수준, 제조수준

production management accounting
생산관리회계

production method 1) 생산방법, 제조
방법 2) 생산량비례법
= activity method, service yield
basis, unit of production method

production mix variance 생산요소 배
합차이 ▶ direct labor mix
variance, material mix variance

production order 제조지시서 = job
order, manufacturing order,
work order ▶ job-order
costing, process costing

production order costing 개별원가
계산, 제조지시서별 원가계산
= job-order costing

production output method 생산량 비
례법 = service hours method,
unit of service method

production overhead cost　제조간접비
　= factory overhead

production planning　생산계획, 제조
　계획

production report　제조보고서

production scheduling　생산일정계획

production specification　제조사양서
　▶ bill of materials

production variance　제조차이
　▶ marketing variance, volume
　variance

production volume budget　제조량 예
　산, 예산조업도 ▶ cost of
　production budget,
　manufacturing budget

production volume variance　조업도
　차이 = denominator variance

productive activity　생산활동

productive asset　감가상각자산, 생산용
　자산

productive asset(similar)　(유사한) 생산
　용자산

productive capacity　생산능력

productive output method　생산량 비
　례법 = service hours method,
　unit of service method

productive resource　생산자원

productive stock　생산용 재고자산
　= direct stock

productive time　작업시간, 제조시간

productivity　1) 생산성, 생산력 2) 다산
　성(多産性)

productivity accounting　생산성회계

productivity analysis　생산성분석

productivity of labor　노동생산성
　= labor productivity

product liability　제조물책임, 제품책임

product life cycle　제품생애주기

product line　제품계열 ▶ line of
　business, segmentation

product line investment　신제품 또는
　제품개량투자

product line reporting　제품계열별 보
　고서

product master　제품 마스터

product mix　제품배합 = sales mix

product portfolio management(PPM)
　제품 포트폴리오 관리

product pricing　가격결정

product service　제품업무, 제품 서비스

product warranty　제품보증

profession　직업, 전문직

professional　전문가

professional accreditation fee　전문적
　인가(승인)비용

professional association　직업단체

professional auditor　직업적 감사인

professional corporation　전문가 회사,
　직능(職能)법인, 전문가 법인

professional developed ability test　직
　무능력 테스트

professional due care　직업전문가의
　정당한 주의 = due professional
　care

professional ethics　직업윤리

professional ethics division　직업윤리
　위원회

professional judgment　직업적 전문가
　의 판단

professional qualification　전문직에
　대한 자질, 자격

professional responsibility　전문가로
　서의 책임

professional skepticism　직업적 전문

가의 회의적 태도

profile 프로필

profit 1) 이익(이익권) 2) 이윤

profitability 수익성, 이익률, 이윤률

profitability analysis 수익성분석

profitability index 수익성지수
= excess present value index, benefit-cost ratio

profitability ratio 수익성비율 ▶ profit margin on sales, return on investment

profit and loss 이익과 손실

profit and loss account (P and L accounting) 1) (영)손익계산서 = income statement, trading and profit and loss account 2) 손익계정

profit and loss budget 손익예산 = income budget

profit and loss from liquidation 청산손익

profit and loss statement 손익계산서 = income statement, statement of earnings

profit and loss summary account 집합손익계정

profit appropriation 이익처분

profit appurtenant 부속적 이익권

profit available for distribution 배당(분배)가능이익

profit available for dividend 배당가능이익 ▶ earnings available for dividend

profit center (책임회계) 이익중심점 ▶ cost center, investment center, responsibility center

profit chart 이익도표 = profit graph

profit contribution 이익공헌도

profit control 이익통제 ▶ profit planning, profit planning and control

profit corporation 영리법인, 영리기업, 회사 = profit organization ▶ non-profit enterprise, non-profit organization

profit directed activity 영리활동

profit equivalent 이익등가물

profit forecasting 이익예측

profit from consolidation 합병차익

profit goal 이익목표

profit graph 이익도표 = profit chart ▶ marginal income, marginal income graph, marginal profit chart, marginal profit graph

profit in gross 독립적 이익권

profit making potential 잠재적 이익창출능력

profit management 이익관리 = profit planning and control ▶ profit control, profit planning

profit margin 매출액이익률

profit margin on sales 매출액총이익률

profit maximization hypothesis 이윤극대화가설

profit maximizing volume 이익극대화 조업도 profit maximization 이익최대화, 이익극대화

profit on manufacture 제조활동으로부터 발생한 이익 = manufacturing profit

profit on paper 장부상이익, 가공이익 = paper profit

profit on treasury stock 자기주식처

분익 ▶ gain on sale of treasury stock

profit organization   영리사업체, 영리기업 = profit corporation ▶ non-profit enterprise, non-profit organization

profit or loss sharing   손익공유제도

profit planning   이익계획 ▶ period planning, profit control, project planning

profit planning and control   이익관리 = profit management

profit planning chart   이익계획도표

profit planning on a short-run basis   단기 이익계획

profit ratio of capital   자본이익률 ▶ profit ratio of gross capital, profit ratio of net worth

profit ratio of gross capital   총자본이익률 ▶ profit ratio of capital, profit ratio of net worth

profit ratio of net worth   자기자본이익률 ▶ profit ratio of capital

profit recognition   이익인식 ▶ revenue recognition

profit related pay(PRP)   (영)이익연동형 급여

profit sharing bond   이익분배사채

profit sharing plan   이익배분제도

profit sharing ratio   (조합, 합명회사의) 이익배당률

profit sharing trust   이익분배신탁

profit to turnover ratio   매출액이익률 = percentage profit on turnover

profit volume chart   PV차트, 공헌이익도표, 손익분기점도표, 이익도표 = break even chart

profit volume graph   손익분기점도표, 이익도표

profit volume ratio(PV ratio)   한계이익률, PV비율 = marginal profit ratio

pro forma balance sheet   예산대차대조표

pro forma effect of retroactive application   새로운 회계원칙을 소급 적용하는 경우의 예측효과

pro forma financial information   예측재무정보, 가상적 재무정보

pro forma financial statement   예산재무제표

pro forma income statement   예산손익계산서

pro forma invoice   견적송장

pro forma retroactive disclosure   특정가정의 소급적용에 대한 공시

program   프로그램, 계획 = programme ▶ programming

program analysis   프로그램 분석

program audit   프로그램 감사

program budget   프로그램 예산 ▶ zero-base budgeting

program design   프로그램 설계 ▶ detail design

program evaluation and review technique(PERT)   프로그램평가 및 검토기법 ▶ critical path method

programmed capacity cost   프로그램 설비원가 ▶ discretionary cost, managed cost, policy cost

programmed control activity   프로그

램 통제활동

programmed cost　프로그램 원가
= managed cost, policy cost
▶ committed cost

programmed decision　정형적 의사결
정 ▶ programmed planning

programmed decision making　정형
적 의사결정 ▶ unprogrammed
decision making

programmed planning　정형적 계획
▶ programmed decision

programming　프로그램 작성

programming flowchart　프로그램 흐
름도 = programming flow
diagram

programming flow diagram　프로그
램 흐름도 = programming
flowchart

programming language　프로그램 언
어 ▶ program, software

programming module　프로그램 모듈

programming system　프로그래밍 시
스템

**program, planning and budgeting
system(PPBS)**　프로그램
계획, 편성, 예산편성 시스템

progress　기업성장, 진척도

progressive audit　진행감사

progressive budget　누진형 예산
= continuous budget, evolving
budget, rolling budget

progressive cost　체증비(遞增費)

progressive method　누진법

progressive tax　누진과세 ▶ regressive
tax

progress payment　분할지급, 분납(分納)

prohibition against retaliatory eviction

임차인의 정당한 권리행사를 이
유로 임대차의 연장을 거절하는
등의 보복적인 조치 금지

project　투자안, 기획안 ▶ period
planning

project cost　투자안 원가, 프로젝트 원
가

projected benefit cost method　미래
효익원가방식 = accrued
benefit cost method, unit credit
method

projected benefit obligation(PBO)　예
측연금채무, 추정급부채무

projected benefit valuation method
미래효익평가방식
= retirement benefit plan

projected financial statement　추정
재무제표

projected misstatement　추정왜곡표
시, 추정허위기재, 계획된 허위
기재

project finance　프로젝트 자금조달

project financing arrangement　프로
젝트 금융의 체결

projection　1) 계획 ▶ estimate, forecast
2) 견적, 예상, 예측

project network analysis(PNA)　프로
젝트 네트워크 분석

project network technique(PNT)　프
로젝트 네트워크 기법

project on measurement　측정프로젝
트

project on recognition　인식프로젝트

project planning　개별계획

prologue　서언, 서막, 전조, 발단

promise　약속

promise to cure　구제약속

promise to pay 지불약속

promissory estoppel 약속적인 금반언
의 법리

promissory note (P/N) 약속어음 = note

promoter 발기인(發起人)

promotion 판매촉진

promotion expense 1) 창업비 2) 판매
촉진비

prompt promise 즉각적 약속

prompt promise to ship 즉시 출하의
약속

prompt shipment 즉시 발송

pronouncement 공식견해

proof of cash 현금검증

**proof of cash format bank
reconciliation** 현금 증명
형식의 은행조정표

proof of claim 청구권의 증명서

proof of loss 손해의 입증

proof (control) total 검증통제 합계

propagation delay 전파지연

proper accounting record (영)적정
한 회계기록

proper journal 보통분개장 = ordinary
journal ▶ special journal

proper transaction 고유거래

property 1) 재산, 부동산 ▶ estate,
freehold property, investment
property 2) 소유권, 저작권
3) 특성, 속성, 자질

property arrangement 재산의 정리

property dividend 현물배당, 재산배당
= dividend in kind ▶ cash
dividend

property interest 재산권

property law 재산법

property, plant and equipment 유형

고정자산 = tangible fixed asset
▶ intangible fixed asset

**property, plant, and equipment fixed
asset** 유형고정자산

property right 재산권

property settlement 재산의 정산금액

property tax 재산세

property unit trust 재산단위형 투자
신탁

proportional consolidation 비례연결
= proportionate consolidation
▶ consolidated financial
statement, full consolidation,
minority interest

proportional cost 비례원가

proportion of work carried out 공사
진행도, 공사진척률

proposal of departmental budget 부
문예산안

proposed amendment 잠정적 수정안

proposed dividend 예정배당

proposed statement 공개초안

proprietary fund 사업형 기금
▶ internal service fund,
enterprise fund

proprietary networks 사적 네트워크

proprietary theory 자본주이론
▶ enterprise theory, entity
theory, fund theory

proprietor 1) 재산의 소유자 2) 기업의
소유자 3) 개인사업주 = sole
trader

proprietorship 개인기업 ▶ partnership

proprietorship bookkeeping 개인기
업 부기

Pro rata clause 비례배분 조항

pro rata distribution 비례배분

pro rata distribution from partnership
파트너십으로부터의 비례배분

pro rata insurance   비례 보험

prospect   견적액, 장래성, 예측, 예견

prospective financial information   예
측 재무정보

prospective financial statement   예
측 재무제표

prospective investor   장래의 투자자

prospectively   미래에 관한

prospectus   1) (설립)취지서, 발기서 2)
(신간서적)내용견본, 목록색인
3) 계획서, 사업설명서, 강령

protected location   보호기억장소, 보호
기억구역

protection   보호

protection key   기억보호 키

protective trust   보호신탁, 낭비자신탁
= spendthrift trust

protocol   원안, 조약안, 의정서, 규약

prototype   원형, 기본형, 시작품(試作品)
▶ prototyping

prototyping   원형설계 ▶ prototype

proved developed reserve   기개발확인
매장량 ▶ proved reserve

proved reserve   확인매장량 ▶ proved
developed reserve, proved
undeveloped reserve

proved undeveloped reserve   미개발
확인매장량 ▶ proved
developed reserve, proved
reserve

provision   1) 규정 2) 담보금, 준비금

provisional injunction   잠정적 금지명
령 ▶ interlocutory injunction

provisional liquidator   잠정청산인

provisional remedy   잠정 조치

provision for bad debt   (영)대손준비
금, 대손충당금 = allowance for
bad debt

provision for discount allowable   (영)
현금할인충당금, 매출할인충당
금 = allowance for sales discount

provision for doubtful debt   대손충당
금 = allowance for doubtful
accounts, allowance for
uncollectable accounts

provision for income tax   법인세 납세
충당금

provision for tax payable   법인세 납
세충당금

proxy   1) 대리인, 대리인 위임장 2) 투
표권의 위임 ▶ power of
attorney, proxy solicitation

proxy contest   위임장의 쟁탈전
▶ proxy solicitation

proxy fight   위임장의 쟁탈전

proxy solicitation   위임장의 권유, 투표
권의 위임 요청, 대리투표권 권
유

proxy statement   주주에게 보내지는
연차보고서

PRP(profit related pay)   (영)이익연동형
급여

PRT(petroleum revenue tax)   (영)석유
이윤세, 석유수입세

prudence   신중, 조심, 검약

prudence in accounting   회계실행의
신중성 ▶ fundamental
accounting concept

prudent investor rule   신중한 투자가
법칙

PSC(prior service cost)   과거용역비용

public   1) 일반대중 2) 공개, 공표

public accountant(CPA) 회계사, 공공
회계사 ▶ industrial member
public accounting 공공회계(실무)
= private practice
Public Accounts Commission (영)공
공회계위원회
Public Accounts Committee 회계검
사위원회
publication 간행물
public company 공개회사, 상장기업,
공모회사 = listed company
▶ private company
public corporation 공개회사 ▶ closed
corporation
public database 공공 데이터베이스
public disposition 공매(公賣)
public enemy 공적(公敵)
public enterprise 공영기업, 공기업
public hearing 공청회
public interest 일반대중의 이익
public investment 공공투자 ▶ private
investment
publicity cost (영)선전비, 판매촉진비
▶ promotion expense
publicity held company 공개회사, (영)
공모유한책임회사, 주식공개유
한책임회사 ▶ publicly owned
corporationpublic limited
company(PLC)
publicity held enterprise 공개회사
▶ public owned corporation
publicity owned corporation 공개회
사 ▶ publicity held enterprise,
publicity traded company
publicly held corporation 공개회사
publicly held enterprise 공개회사
public network 공공 네트워크

public notice 일반 대중 통지
public offering 공모(公募) = placing of
shares ▶ private offering
public offering bond 공모채(公募債)
public officials 관리, 공무원
public policy 공공정책, 공공질서의 건
전한 풍속
public practice 감사업무, 공공회계 실
무 = private practice, public
accounting
public sale 공개 매각
public sector accounting 공공부문
회계 ▶ non profit accounting
Public Sector Liaison Group
(영)공공부문연결위원회
public transportation system 공공 운
송시스템
public trust 공익신탁
public trustee (영)공공수탁자
public utility 공익사업, 공공시설, 공공
사업
public utility accounting 공익사업 회
계
public warehouse 창고대여업자의 창
고, 영업창고
Public Works Loan Board (PWLB)
(영)공공사업자금대부위원회
public works loan commissioner
(영)공공사업자금대부위원
pulse 충격 = impulse
punitive damage 징벌적 손해배상
purchase 1) 매입, 구입, 구매 2) 매수
3) 유상취득
purchase allowance 매입할인
purchase analysis 구매분석
purchase audit 구매감사
purchase budget 구매예산

=purchasing budget ▶ purchase control

purchase commitments 확정구입계약, 매매계약상의 채무, 구매약정

purchase concept 매수설, 현물출자설 ▶ business combination, pooling of interests concept

purchase control 구매관리 ▶ purchase budget

purchase cost 구입원가, 매입원가 = acquisition cost, purchase price ▶ historical cost, original cost

purchase day book(PDB) 매입일기장, 일별매입장

purchased goodwill 매입영업권 = premium or discount on acquisition ▶ non-purchased goodwill

purchase discount 매입할인 ▶ cash discount, trade discount

purchase discount loss 매입할인 불행 사손실, 매입할인 미이용손실 = loss from lapsed discount

purchased life annuity 매입종신연금

purchased part 매입부품 ▶ manufactured parts

purchased part cost 매입부품비 ▶ manufactured parts cost

purchased part stock 매입부품재고

purchase invoice 매입송장 ▶ sales invoice

purchase journal 매입분개장

purchase ledger 매입처원장 = bought ledger, creditor's ledger

purchase method 매수법, 매매법, 매

수방식, 매입법 ▶ pooling of interest concept

purchase money mortgage(PMM) 부동산의 매도인에게 그 대금의 일부를 대신하여 설정해 주는 저당권, 구매대금 부동산 담보물권

purchase money security interest(PMSI) 물품의 구입자금을 제공한 자가 갖는 담보권, 매매대금 담보권, 구매대금 담보물권

purchase money security interest in consumer good 소비자 물품 구입자금 담보권, 소비재에 대한 구입대금 담보권

purchase of business 기업매수 ▶ amalgamation, business combination, merger

purchase of groups of fixed asset 고정자산의 일괄구입

purchase of security 유가증권의 구입

purchase order 매입주문서, 구입지도서, 구입주문서

purchase or sales commitment 가격이 고정된 구입 혹은 판매계약

purchase, payable, and cash disbursement cycle 매입 · 매입채무 · 현금지급 순환과정

purchase price 구입가격, 매입가격 = acquisition cost, purchased cost ▶ historical cost, original cost

purchase price of the goods 물품의 매입가격

purchaser 구입자

purchase rebate 매입할인

purchase record 매입기록

P

purchase requisition 매입청구서

purchase return 매입환출 = return
outward ▶ return inward, sales
return

purchase return book(PRB) 환출품
명세표 = purchases outward
book, returned outward book

purchasing 매입

purchasing auditing 구매감사

purchasing budget 구매예산
= purchase budget

purchasing department 자재 구입 부
문

purchasing management 구매관리
= purchasing control

purchasing power 구매력

**purchasing power gain on monetary
item** 화폐성 항목에 관련
되는 구매력 손익 ▶ loss from
decline in the value of money,
purchasing power loss monetary
item

purchasing power gain or loss 구매
력 손익, 화폐구매력 손익, 화폐
가치 손익 = monetary gain or
loss ▶ gain from decline in
purchasing power of net
amount owed

**purchasing power gain or loss on net
monetary item** 순화폐성
항목에 관련되는 구매력 손익
▶ constant dollar accounting,
constant purchasing power
accounting, gain from decline
in the value of money, loss
from decline in the value of
money

purchasing power loss 구매력 손실

**purchasing power loss on monetary
item** 화폐성 항목에 관련
되는 구매력 손실 ▶ gain from
decline in the value of money,
purchasing power gain on
monetary items

purchasing power of money 화폐구
매력

purchasing power unit 구매력 단위
▶ current purchasing power
unit

pure holding company 순수 지주회사
▶ holding company

pure rate of interest 순이자율

pure research 기초연구, 순수연구

purpose 목적, 의도

purpose restriction 목적제한

pushdown accounting 푸시다운회계

pushdown list 후입선출 리스트

pushdown storage 후입선출 기억장치
= pushdown store

pushup list 선입선출 리스트

pushup storage 선입선출 기억장치
= pushup store

put option (증권 등의) 매각선택권
▶ call option, option

puts and calls 선택권 = option

PV(present value) 현재가치, 할인현가

PV chart(profit volume chart) 손익분
기점도표, 이익도표

PV of MLPs 최소리스료의 현재가치

PV of MLPs + URV MLPs와 비보증
잔존가액의 현재가치 합

PV ratio(profit volume ratio) 이익과 조
업도 비율 = marginal profit
ratio

PWLB(Public Works Loan Board)   공공 사업자금대출위원회

Q

QC(quality control)   품질관리

QC(Queen's Counsel)   (영)칙선변호사

QC circle (quality control circle)   품질
관리모임

quadratic form   2차 함수형식

quadratic function   2차 함수

quadratic programming   2차 함수계
획 ▶ mathematical
programming

qualification   한정, 한정사항

qualified acceptance   (어음의) 조건부
인수

qualified auditor's report   한정의견
감사보고서 = qualified audit
report

qualified audit report   한정의견 감사
보고서 = qualified auditor's
report

qualified certificate   한정증명서

qualified endorsement   무담보배서,
제한배서, 한정배서

qualified name   수식명(修飾名)

qualified opinion   한정의견 ▶ except
opinion, qualified auditor's
report, qualified opinion report

qualified opinion report   한정의견 감
사보고서 ▶ unqualified
opinion report

qualified organization   인증된 기관

qualified pension plan   적법연금계획,
적격연금제도, 적절한 퇴직 연
금 = individual retirement
account, Keogh plan

qualified property   제한적 재산권

qualified report   한정의견 보고서, 한정
보고서 ▶ qualified opinion
report

qualified residence interest   적격한 주
택자금 이자

qualifier   수식명(修飾名), 수식어

qualifying capital interest   법정자본
지분 ▶ related company

qualifying distribution   1) 예납법인세
(advance corporation tax) 2) 납부
의무를 진 이익배분
▶ imputation system, non
qualifying distribution

qualifying language   한정된 표현

qualitative characteristic   질적 특성

qualitative information   질적 정보
▶ quantitative information

quality   특성, 품질

quality control(QC)   품질관리

quality control chart method   품질 관
리도법

quality control circle(QC circle)   품질
관리모임

quality control element   품질통제 구성
요소

quality control standard   품질통제 표준

quantifiability 계량가능성

quantification 계량화 ▶ freedom
from bias

quantified nonfinancial information
정량적 비재무정보

quantile 분위(分位)

quantitative control 계량적 관리

quantitative guideline 양적(量的) 지침
(指針)

quantitative information 정량정보, 양
적인 정보 ▶ qualitative
information

quantitative materiality 양적 중요성

quantitative standard 물량표준
= physical standard ▶ price
standard

quantity 1) 수량 2) 자산 ▶ quality

quantity discount 수량할인 = volume
discount

quantity survey method 공사수량 조
사법 ▶ comparative unit
method, cost approach,
reproduction cost, unit-in-place
method

quantity system 정량발주시스템
= constant order quantity
system, constant order, two bin
system ▶ recorder point

quantity variance 수량차이 ▶ aterial
quantity variance, material
usage variance, sales quantity
variance

quantum 양자(量子)

quarterly budget 4분기 예산

quarterly financial data 분기 재무데
이터

quarterly financial information 분기

재무정보 ▶ interim financial
information

quarterly financial statement 분기
재무제표

quarterly report 분기보고서, 분기별
(期別) 보고서 ▶ interim
financial information

quartile 4분위 수

quartile deviation 4분위 편차

quasi contract 준(準)계약

quasi external transaction 준(準)외부
거래

quasi judicial activity 준(準)사법활동

quasi legislative activity 준(準)입법활동

quasi loan 준(準)차입

quasi reorganization 의사개생, 법률절
차에 기초하지 않는 회사재건,
(회사의) 준개생(準更生)

quasi reorganization approach 준(準)
개생 절차 ▶ fresh start method

quasi tangible personal property 준
(準)유형 동산

Queen's Counsel(QC) (영)칙선변호사
= King's Counsel

questionnaire 질문서

questionnaires, internal control 내부
통제질문서

queue 대기행렬

quick asset 당좌자산

quick deposit 당좌예금

quick fund 당좌자금

quick ratio 당좌비율 ▶ cash ratio,
current ratio, liquid ratio,
solvency

quid pro quo 1) 대상물(代償物), 보수품
(報酬品) 2) 대용물

quinary 5진법

quitclaim deed   권리 포기형 양도증서, 소유권의 하자에 매도인이 책임을 부담하지 않는다는 증서

quitting concern   종료기업 ▶ going concern

quorum   1) (의결, 의사진행에 필요한) 정족수(定足數) 2) 치안판사 3) 선발자 집단

quota   할당, 분담, 할당수량

quotation   1) 시가, 시세, 시세표 = current price, market price, stock quotation ▶ speculation 2) 시장경기, 시장동향

quoted company   (영)상장회사 ▶ listed investment, quoted investment, unlisted company, unquoted company

quoted investment   상장유가증권, 거래소 상장증권에의 투자 = listed investment

quoted market price   시장가격, 시가

quoted price   시장시세가격

quotient   (숫자의) 상, 몫, 지수, 비율

quo warrant proceeding   공권력이 부여하는 특권을 행사하는 자의 정당한 자격 여부를 심사하는 절차

R

R

RA(repurchase agreement)   환매조건부 채권 매매계약

race notice recording statute   선의(善意) 등기자 보호형 등기

race notice statute   먼저 등록한 자가 우선적 권리를 취득한다는 규칙

race notice type statute   경쟁통지형 입법

race recording statute   선순위자 보호형 등기

race statute   먼저 등록한 자가 우선적 권리를 취득한다는 규칙

race type statute   경쟁형 입법

radix   기수(基數)

radix complement   기수의 보수(補數)

radix-minus-one complement   기수-1의 보수 = diminished radix complement

radix notation   기수표기법 = radix numeration system

radix point   소수점, 기점(基點)(소수부)

raid   (침략적) 점량, 탈취

railway accounting   철도회계

raising of fund   자금조달

RAMS (resource allocation and multi-project scheduling)   램스, 자원배분 및 다중프로젝트 일정관리

random based selection   무작위 추출법

random deviation   확률차이

randomizing   무작위화

random number   난수(亂數), 무작위수

random number sampling   난수표 표

본추출

random number sequence 난수열, 난수배열

random number table 난수(亂數)표

random sampling 무작위 추출법

random variable 확률변수

random walk 랜덤웍

random walk method 랜덤웍법

range 범위

range check 범위검사

range of assignment 감사인의 업무범위, 할당범위

rank 계급, 등급

ratable charge method 시간비례 상각법

ratable value 과세평가액, 과세평가 가격

rate 1) (영)부동산세 2) 수수료, 비율 3) 속도 4) 시세, 요금 5) 등급

rated speed 정격속도

rate making body 공공요금 결정기관

rate of call 콜 비율 = call rate

rate of change 변동률

rate of dividend 배당률

rate of exchange 외환시세

rate of income to sales 매출액이익률

rate of interest 이자율, 이율

rate of occurrence 모(母)집단의 오류율

rate of operation 조업율

rate of profit 이익률

rate of return 이익률

rate of return on asset 자산이익률

rate of return on equity 자기자본이익률

rate of return on investment (투자)자본이익률, 투자이익률 ▶ return on investment method

rate of return on total asset 총자산이익률

rate of stock turn 상품회전률 = stock turnover

rate of stock turnover 재고자산회전률 = inventory turnover, stock turnover, turnover of inventory

rate of turnover 회전률

rate of yield 이자율

rate variance 임률차이 = labor rate variance

ratification 추인(追認), 비준, 승인

ratification of agency relationship 대리인 관계의 비준

ratification of contract by minor 미성년자 계약 승인

rating 1) 등급 2) 보험요율의 산정 3) 신용도평가 4) 레이팅

rating agency 신용도 평가기관

ratio 비율

ratio analysis 경영분석 · 비율분석 ▶ financial statements analysis, ratio method

ratio estimation 비율추정법

ratio estimation method 비율추정법 = difference estimation method, mean-per-unit difference method, mean-per-unit method

ratio method 비율법 ▶ financial statement analysis, ratio analysis

rational decision 합리적인 의사결정

rational expectation 합리적인 예측

rational number 유리수(有理數)

rationing of capital 자본배분

ratio of bond issue to total expenditure 공채의존도

ratio of cost of sales   매출원가율
   ▶ operating expense ratio,
   operating ratio

ratio of fixed asset to long-term capital
   고정장기적합률, 고정자산대 장
   기자본비율

ratio of gross profit to net sales   매출
   총이익률

ratio of interest burden   이자부담율

ratio of liability to net worth   부채비율,
   부채 · 자본비율

ratio of net worth to fixed asset   고정
   비율 = fixed asset ratio, fixed
   asset to net worth ratio

ratio of operating profit to net sales
   매출액 영업이익률

ratio of ordinary profit to net sales
   매출액 경상이익률 ▶ ratio of
   interest burden

ratio of profit to net sales   매출이익률

ratio of retained income to net profit
   이익유보율 ▶ payout ratio

ratio of retained income to net worth
   유보이익자본비율

ratio of selling and administrative
   expense to sales   영업비 비
   율 = operating expense ratio
   ▶ operating ratio, ratio of cost
   of sales

ratio of shareholders' equity   주주 지
   분율

ratio of total liability to net worth
   부채비율 ▶ ratio of interest
   burden

raw data   원시 데이터

raw material   원료, 재료, 원재료, 소재

raw material cost   원재료비 = direct

material cost, direct materials

raw material inventory budget   원재
   료재고예산

raw material stock   원재료재고

RCRA(Resource Consarsation and
   Recovery act)   자원보호법

R/D(refer to drawer)   발행인 회수

R&D(research and development)   연구
   개발비

R&D expenditure   연구개발지출

RDG(regional development grant)   (영)
   지역개발조성금 ▶ assisted
   area, special assisted area

reacquired bond   재취득사채, 자기사채

reacquired long-term debt   재취득 장
   기차입금

reacquired share   자기주식, 재취득 주
   식, 금고주 = reacquired stock,
   treasury stock

reacquired stock   자기주식, 재취득 주
   식, 금고주 = reacquired share,
   treasury stock

reacquisition   재취득

reacquisition price   재취득가격, 재구입
   가격 ▶ current cost,
   replacement cost

reacquisition price of debt   부채의 재
   취득가격

readjustment   1) 자주정리, 회사재건
   2) 재정리기입 = readjustment
   entry

readjustment entry   재정리분개, 재대
   체분개 = retransfer entry
   ▶ reverse entry

ready money   즉시 사용할 수 있는 현 ·
   예금

reaffirmation   채무의 재확인

R

reaffirmation agreement 재승인 합의

reaffirmation of discharged debt 면제된 채무의 재승인

real account 실질계정 ▶ impersonal account, nominal account

real audit evidence 물적 증거, 물리적 증거 ▶ documentary evidence

real capital 실질자본 ▶ financial capital

real defense 실질적 항변 사유, 물적 항변

real estate 부동산, 물적 부동산권 ▶ real property

real estate appraiser 부동산 감정사

real estate investment trust 부동산 투자신탁

real estate sales 부동산 판매

Real Estate Settlement Procedures Act (RESPA) 부동산 청산절차법

real growth rate 실질성장률

real income 1) 실질이익 2) 실질소득

realistic possibility standard 현실적인 가능성에 대한 표준

reality of consent 합의의 진실성, 동의의 실재

realizability 실현가능성

realizable asset 실현가능한 자산

realizable cost saving 실현가능원가절약 = realizable holding gain ▶ current cost accounting, realized cost saving

realizable value 실현가능가액 ▶ current value

realization 실현 ▶ realization basis, realization concept, revenue recognition

realization basis 실현주의 ▶ accrual basis, conservatism, prudence in accounting

realization concept 실현개념 ▶ realization principle

realization of revenue 수익의 실현 ▶ realization principle

realization principle 실현주의

realize 실현

realized and earned 실현 및 이득

realized capital gain 실현자본이득 ▶ capital gain, realization basis

realized cost saving 실현원가절약 ▶ unrealized cost saving

realized gain 실현이익

realized gain and loss 실현손익 ▶ realization principle

realized gain or loss 매각에 의한 손익

realized gross profit 실현총이익

realized gross profit on installment sales 할부판매 실현총이익

realized holding gain 실현보유이득 ▶ unrealized holding gain

realized holding gain or loss 실현보유손익 ▶ realization basis

realized income 실현이익 ▶ realization, realization principle

realized profit 실현이익 = realized income

realized value 실현가치

reallocation 재분배

real national income 실질국민소득 ▶ nominal national income

real number 실수(實數)

real price 실질가격, 진정가격

real profit 실질이익 ▶ nominal profit

real property 부동산, 물적 재산

= realty ▶ immovable
personal property

real property tax   고정자산세(固定資産
稅)

real thing and event   실제사항과 사건

real time   실시간

real transaction   실물거래

realty   물적 재산, 부동산 = real property
▶ personal property

real value   실질가치, 실질가액
▶ face value, nominal value

real wage   실질임금 ▶ nominal
wage

reappraisal   재평가

reaquisition   재취득

reasonable assurance   합리적 확신, 합
리적 확증

reasonable basis   합리적 기준

reasonable care and skill   합리적인
주의와 숙련

reasonable evidence   합리적 증거

reasonableness   타당성, 합리성

reasonableness check   합리성 검사

reasonableness (limit) test   합리성 (한
계)검증

reasonable period of time   합리적인
기간

reasonable person   합리적인 사람

reasonable price   적정가격

reasonable test   합리성 점검

reasonably informed user   합리적으
로 일반적인 지식을 소유한 정
보이용자

reasonably possible   합리적인 가능성

reassessment   평가 또는 결정, 경정 결
정

rebate   환불, 리베이트

recalculation   계산대조

recall   (결함제품에 대한) 회수

recapitalization   1) 자본구성의 변경, 자
본변경 ▶ leveraged buyout
2) 자본수정 ▶ reorganization

recapture   회수

recapture rate   회수율 ▶ depreciation
rate, economic age, income
approach

receipt   1) 수령 2) 영수증 3) 수령액, 수
입액

receipt after discontinuance   폐업후
수입 = post cessation receipt

receipt and payment account   현금 수
지보고서 ▶ cash basis, income
and expenditure account

receipt and payment basis   수지(收支)
기준 = cash basis ▶ accrual
basis

receipt and payment bookkeeping
수지(收支)부기 ▶ double entry
bookkeeping, single entry
bookkeeping

receipt slip   입금전표, 수납전표

receipt stamp   수취(受取)인(印)

receivable   채권, 수취채권, 매출채권 계
정, 외상매출금 ▶ accounts
receivable, votes

receivable turnover   매출채권회전율,
수취계정회전율, 외상매출금 회
전율 = receivable turnover
ratio, turnover of receivable

receivable turnover ratio   매출채권회
전율, 수취계정회전율
= receivable turnover, turnover
of receivable

receiver   재산 관리인

R

receivership 관재인(管財人)의 직무, 재산관리 상태

receiving clerk 수입계

receiving department 물품수령 부문

receiving division 수령부문

receiving order 재산관리명령

receiving report 물품수령서

reception stamp 수령인(受領印)

recession 중도해약, 계약해제, 취소

recipient 수취인, 수령서

reciprocal 역수(逆數)

reciprocal account 대조계정, 평가계정

reciprocal allocation 상호배부
▶ cross allocation, direct allocation, sequential allocation, step-down allocation

reciprocal allocation method 상호배부법 = double distribution method, reciprocal distribution method

reciprocal distribution method 상호배부법 = cross allocation method, double distribution method, matrix method, reciprocal allocation method

reciprocal interfund activity 상호 기금간 거래

reciprocal share holding 주식의 상호보유

reciprocal transfer 상호이전

reciprocity trade agreement 호혜통상협정

reckless disregard 무모한 무시

reclaimed material 재생재료, 회수재료

reclassification 재분류

reclassification adjustment 재분류 수정

reclassification entry 재분류 분개

recognised bank (영)인가은행

recognised item 인식되는 항목

recognised stock exchange (영)인가 증권거래소

recognition 인식

recognition and measurement concept 인식과 측정

recognition consideration 인식문제

recognition criteria 인식기준

recognition criteria and guidance 인식기준과 지침

recognition decision 인식결정

recognition implication 인식함축, 인식포함

recognition issue 인식문제

recognition of gain and loss 손익의 인식

recognition of revenue 수익의 인식
▶ sales basis

recognition policy 인식방침

recognized profit on long-term construction 장기공사계약에 대한 이익 ▶ percentage of completion method for long-term contracts

recommendation 조언, 권고

recommendation letter 개선권고서

Recommendation on Accounting Principles 회계원칙에 관한 권고서 ▶ Statements of Standard Accounting Practice

recomputation 계산대조, 재계산

reconciliation 잔액조정표

reconciliation of account balance 계정잔액의 조정

reconciliation of book income to
    taxable income   장부상 이
    익의 과세소득에의 조정
reconciliation of net income to net cash
    flow operating activity
    순이익을 영업활동에 의한 현금
    흐름으로의 조정
reconciliation of segment information
    to consolidated amount
    사업부문정보의 연결총액에 조
    정
reconciliation sheet   잔액조정표
reconstruction   회사재건
record   1) 레코드, 기록 2) 장부
record count   기록 개수
record date   기준일, 명의개서 정지일
    = date of record ▶ date of
    declaration
recorded accountability   기록된 회계
    책임
recorded investment in the receivable
    채권의 장부가액
record holder   등록(登錄) 주주(株主)
recording   리코딩, 등기(登記)
recording density   기록밀도, 기억장치
record retention policy   사업체의 데이
    터 보존방침
record shareholder   등록된 주주
recourse   상환청구, 소구(遡求), 추심(推
    尋)
recourse obligation on receivable sold
    매각채권에 대한 상환 의무
recover   회수하다
recoverable ACT   (영)환급가능 예납
    법인세 ▶ Irrecoverable ACT,
    outgoing dividend
recoverable amount   회수가능가액

▶ current market value, net
    realizable value, value in use
recoverable value   회수가능가액
    ▶ estimated realizable value
recovery   회복
recovery in market value   시장가액의
    회복
recovery of bad debt   상각채권의 추심
recovery procedure   회복절차
recrecurrence   반복(反復)성
rectangular distribution   직각형 분포
rectification note   (영)보수지도서
    = rework note
recurring audit   연속감사 = return
    audit ▶ initial audit
recurring profit   경상이익
    ▶ extraordinary item, non-
    recurring item
recursion   귀납, 반복, 재귀
red clause credit   적색기입조항부 신용
    장, 수출대금업무전 대부조항
redeemable preference share   상환우
    선주 = redeemable preferred
    stock
redeemable security   상환가능증권, 매
    입출환가능증권
redeemable share   상환가능주식, 환매
    (還賣) 주(株)
redeemable stock   상환가능주식, 환매주
redemption   담보물의 반환, 중도상환,
    매입환출
redemption before maturity   만기전
    상환
redemption by drawing   추첨상환
redemption fund   상환기금 = sinking
    fund
redemption of stock   주식의 상환

redemption premium　상환시 할증금
　　= premium on redemption
redemption price　상환가격
red herring　예비목록색인
red herring prospectus　적색 헤링 계
　　획서
red lining　적색선
reduced profit method　이익감액기준,
　　이익체감법
reducing balance method　체감잔액법
　　= declining balance method,
　　fixed percentage method,
　　reducing installment method
　　▶ depreciation, production
　　method, straight-line method
reducing charge method　체감상각법
reducing installment method　체감
　　할부방식 = declining balance
　　method, fixed percentage
　　method, reducing balance
　　method ▶ depreciation,
　　production method, straight
　　line method
reduction of capital　자본감소, 감자
redundancy　1) 중복 2) 과잉
redundancy check　중복검사 ▶ parity
　　bit, parity check
Redundancy Fund　(영)잉여노동자 퇴
　　직수당환급기금
redundancy payment　(영)잉여노동자
　　퇴직수당
　　▶ Redundancy Fund,
　　redundancy rebate
redundancy rebate　(영)잉여노동자 퇴
　　직수당환급금
redundant data check　불필요한 자료
　　검증

reenterable program　재입력가능프로
　　그램 = reentrant program
　　▶ reenterable routine,
　　reeterable subroutine
reference　1) 참조, 참고 2) 기준 3) 조
　　회, 신용조회장, 조회처　4)
　　[FORTRAN]인용 5) 기술(記述)
reference level　기준 레벨
referral fee　위탁보수
refer to drawer(R/D)　발행인 회수
refinancing debt　차환부채
　　= debt restructuring
　　▶ continuation of debt,
　　extinguishment of debt,
　　retirement of debt
refinancing fee　차환 수수료
reformation　교정
refund　차환, 반환, 상환
refundable deposit　리스기간 종료시에
　　보증금 반환 유형, 반환가능보
　　증금
refund claim　반환청구권
regeneration　기억재생
regent　1) 평의회 2) 참고문헌
region　영역, 구역
regional development grant(RDG)
　　(영)지역개발조성금
　　▶ assisted area, special
　　development area
region of significance　유의영역
register　레지스터, 금전등록기
registered accountant　(영)등록회계사
registered bond　기명식 채권 ▶ bearer
　　bond, coupon bond
registered company　1) 등록회사
　　▶ company registration office
　　2) (영)등기회사 ▶ company

limited by guarantee

registered office   등록사무소

registered security   기명증권

registered statement   등록신고서

register of interest in share   (영)대주
주명부

register of member   주주명부

registrant financial statement   등록
자의 재무제표

registrar   1) 등기계, 등록계 2) 주주명부
계 3) 주주명부등록기관 4) 교
무계(학교)

registrar of company   (영)회사등기관
▶ Gazette, registered company

registrating and issuing cost   SEC등
록비용, 변호사 및 회계사비용,
인수수수료, 인쇄비 등

registration   1) 등록, 등기 2) 위치

registration cost   등록비용

registration provision   등록조항

registration statement   증권등록 실명
서, 등록서, 등록신고서
▶ prospectus, Securities Act
of 1933

regression   회귀(回歸)

regression analysis   (원가예측) 회귀분
석법, 회귀분석 ▶ least squares
method

regression coefficient   회귀계수

regression estimation   회귀분석추정법

regression line   회귀선

regressive audit   역행감사, 후진감사

regressive tax   역진과세 ▶ progressive
tax

regret criterion   후회기준

regret matrix   리그레트 매트릭스

regular audit   정규감사

regular cost accounting system   원가
계산제도 = cost accounting
system

regular dividend   보통배당

regular matrix   정칙행렬

regular tax credit   일반세액공제

regular tax rate   정기 세율

regular wage   정규임금

regulated enterprise   법적규제 대상 기
업

regulation   정리, 규칙, 규제
▶ deregulation

regulation of employment   고용 규정

Regulation S-K   미국 증권거래위원회
의 재무제표준칙 ▶ Regulation
S-X

regulation statement   등기부

regulatory agency   통제기관, 규제기
관, 규제당국 = regulatory
authority

regulatory authority   감독관청, 규제
기관

regulatory body   감독기관, 규제기관

regulatory philosophy   규제주의
= merit regulation
▶ disclosure philosophy,
disclosure requirement

regulatory rule   규제기관의 규칙

**reimbursed employee business
expenses**   변제받은 피고용
자 영업비

reimbursement   변상, 보상

reinsurance   재보험

reinvestment rate   재투자수익률
▶ rate of return on investment

reissued report   재발행된 보고서

rejected items report   거절된 항목보

고서

rejection 거절, 기각(棄却)

rejection of offer 청약의 거절

rejection rate 기각률

reject the whole 전부 거절

related company (영)계열회사

related enterprise 관련기업

related matter 관련사항

related party 특수관계자, 관련당사자, 특수관계자집단 ▶ financial accounting, interest group, related company, related party transaction

related party disclosure 특수관계자공시—SFAS 57

related party in leasing transaction 리스거래에 대한 특수 이해관계자

related party transaction 1) 특수관계자간 거래 2) 특별 이해관계자간 거래 3) 관련당사자간의 거래

related taxpayer 관련 납세자, 과세 대상자

relation 1) 관계 2) 비교식[ALGOL] 3) 친족

relational database 관계적 데이터베이스

relationship to third party 제3자와의 관계

relative fair market value method 상대적 공정시장가액법

relative frequency 상대빈도수

relative sales value 상대적 판매가치법

relative sales value method (연산품에서) 상대적 매출가액법

release 면제, 권리포기, 채무의 면제

relevance 목적적합성 ▶ feedback value, freedom from bias, predictive value, reliability, timeliness level

relevance and reliability 목적적합성과 신뢰성

relevance of evidence 증거의 목적적합성

relevant accounting 목적적합성 회계

relevant benefit 관련효익 ▶ retirement benefit scheme

relevant cost 관련원가, 관련범위 ▶ differential cost, incremental cost

relevant costing 관련원가계산 ▶ absorption costing, direct costing

relevant information 목적에 적합한 정보

relevant range 관련 범위

reliability 1) 신뢰성 2) 신뢰도 ▶ usability

reliability factor 신뢰성계수

reliability level 신뢰성수준

reliability of financial reporting 재무보고의 신뢰성

reliance interest 신뢰이익

reliance on other accountant 다른 회계사에 대한 의존

relief (세금의) 면제, 면세 = tax relief

religion discrimination 종교차별

relocate 재배치하다

remainder 잉여(剩餘), 잔여권

remainder man 잔여권자

remaining discount 잔존할인액

remaining economic age 경제적 잔존내용연수 ▶ depreciation,

effective age, effective life,
physical age, physical life, total
economic life

remaining economic life 경제적 잔존
내용연수 = remaining
economic age

remaining lease term 잔존리스기간

remaining period 재무제표일까지의
남은 기간

remark 적요(摘要)

remeasurement 재측정

remeasurement gain or loss 재측정에
의한 손익

remedy 구제

remedy for breach of contract 계약
위반의 구제

remittance 송금, 송금액, 송금수단

remittance advice 송금전표
= remittance slip

remittance basis (영)송금주의

remittance bill 송금어음 = bank
remittance

remittance check 송금수표

remittance slip 송금전표, 송금통지
= remittance advice

remote 거리가 먼, 발생가능성이 낮은

remote job entry (RJE) 원격작업입력

remote station 원격단말, 원격(遠隔) 국
(局)

removal 해임

removal with cause 이유있는 해임

removal without cause 이유없는 해임

remuneration cost 지급보수, 보상(報償)

renewal fund 갱신자금

renewal option 갱신선택권 ▶ lease

rent 1) 임대(차)료, 지대 2) 임대차

rental expense 임차료 = rent expense

rental income 임대료 = rental revenue

rental method 렌탈법

rental of vacation home 휴양 주거지
의 임대

rental revenue 임대료 = rental income

rental value of parsonage 목사관의
임차료

rent expense 임차료 = rental expense
▶ accrued expense, prepaid
expense

rent payable 미지급임차료

rent payment 임차료 지급

rent receivable 미수임대료
▶ accrued income, accrued
revenue

rent received in advance 선수임대료
= deferred rental revenue
▶ prepaid rental expense

rent revenue 임대료 수익

reordering point 재주문점 = ordering
point, order point, reorder point

reorder interval system 정시발주 시
스템 ▶ reorder level system

reorder level system 정량발주 시스템
▶ reorder interval system

reorder point (경제적 발주량에서) 재주
문점, 발주점(發注点)
= reordering point

reorganization 1) 회사갱생 2) (흡수합
병, 신설합병, 영업양도, 자본증가에
의한)구조조정, 재조정, 재편성

reorganization plan 구조조정 계획, 재
건계획, 갱생계획

reorganization type 재건(再建)형

REPA(repurchase agreement) 환매조
건부 채권 매매계약

repair 수선, 수리 ▶ betterment, capital

expenditure, maintenance

repair and maintenance expense 수선과 유지비용

repair charge 수선비 = repair expense

repair expense 수선비 = repair charge

repairing budget 수선비 예산

repair production order 수선지시서 = rework note ▶ production order

repayment 변제, 상환

repayment guarantee 계약금반환약정 ▶ stage payment

repeat audit 연속감사 ▶ first audit

repeater 중계기, 재생기

reperformance 재수행

repetition factor 반복요소

repetition instruction 반복명령

repetitive addressing 반복어드레스 지정

replacement 대체(代替)

replacement cost 1) 대체원가, 재조달 원가 ▶ current cost, current cost accounting 2) 치환원가 ▶ comparative unit method, reproduction cost

replacement cost accounting 대체원 가회계 ▶ continuously contemporary accounting, current cost accounting, current replacement cost accounting, current value accounting

replacement cost method 대체원가법

replacement investment 대체투자, 갱 신투자

replacement method 대체법 = replacement system ▶ depreciation

replacement price 대체가격 ▶ current cost, replacement cost

replacement system 대체법 = replacement method ▶ depreciation, retirement method

repledging 재입질

replevin 동산점유권 회복, 압류동산 회 복 소송

replevy action 정당한 권리자에게 물건 을 넘겨 달라는 소송

reply doctrine 답변의 원칙

reportable condition 보고 가능조건

reportable industry segment 보고가 능 산업부문

reportable segment 보고가능 산업부 문

report date 보고일, 결산일, 보고서 작 성일

reported earning 보고이익

report form 보고식 ▶ account form

reporting 보고

reporting accountant (영)보고회계사 ▶ auditor, prospectus

reporting agency 보도기관

reporting currency 재무보고통화, 보 고통화 ▶ foreign currency, functional currency

reporting cycle 보고순환과정

reporting entity 보고주체, 보고실체

reporting function 보고기능

reporting interfund activity 기금간 활동에 대한 보고

reporting on an entity's internal control over financial reporting 재무보고에 대한 내부통제에 관한 보고

reporting provision 보고조항

reporting standard 보고기준

report of independent accountant 독립회계감사인의 감사보고서

report on internal control 내부통제에 대한 보고서

report on responsibility performance 책임수행보고서 ▶ responsibility center

report on the processing of transaction by service organization 용역대행업체에 의한 거래 처리에 관한 보고서

report review procedure 보고서 검토 절차

repossession 환입품, 재소유

repossession by judicial action 재판 절차에 의한 재소유

representation 표현, 표시, 진술 = letter of representation, representation letter

representational faithfulness 표현의 충실성 = correspondence, representative faithfulness, validity ▶ neutrality, verifiability, completeness

representation letter 진술서, 확인서 = letter of representation, representation letter

representative action 대표 소송

reproduction cost 재조달원가, 재생산 원가 ▶ comparative unit method, depreciation, quantity survey method, replacement cost, unit-in-place method

repudiation 거절, 부인

repurchase agreement(REPA;RA) 환매조건부 채권 매매계약

repurchase cost 재구입가격

repurchased stock 재취득주식, 자기주식 = reacquired stock, treasury stock

reputed ownership 표현적 소유권

request for proposal(RFP) 제안요구서

required rate of return 요구이익률 ▶ cost of capital

requirement 요구 ▶ functional requirements, non functional requirements

requirement contract 독점공급계약, 필요량 계약

requirements of negotiability 유통성의 요건

res 신탁 재산

resale 전매(轉賣), 재판매

rescheduling 채권변제기일 연기 조치

rescission 계약 해제

rescission of contract 계약의 철회

research 연구

research and development(R&D) arrangement 연구개발의 체결

research and development cost 연구개발비 = research and development expense, research and development expenditure

research and development expenditure 연구 개발비 지출 = research and development cost

research and development expense 연구개발비 = research and development cost

researcher 조사기관

research study   조사연구
reseller   전매인(轉賣人), 재판매인
reservation   유보사항
reservation of title   소유권 유보
reserve   적립금, 충당금, 준비금
= allowance, provision
reserve accounting   (영)적립금회계
▶ all inclusive, extraordinary
items, prior year adjustments
reserved profit   유보이익, 미처분이익
= retained earnings, retained
surplus, undistributed profit
reserved stock   예비재고 = allocated
stock, appropriated stock,
assigned stock, earmarked
stock
reserve for bad debt   대손충당금
= allowance for bad debt,
allowance for doubtful
accounts, bad-debt provision,
allowance for uncollectibles
reserve for contingency   우발손실준비
금, 재해전보(災害塡補)적립금
= reserve for possible future
loss, retained earnings
appropriated for contingency
reserve for decline in asset value   자
산가치하락 손실준비금
reserve for depreciation   감가상각충
당금, 감가상각누계액
= allowance for depreciation
reserve for encumbrance   저당권에 대
한 충당금
reserve for income tax   법인세등 충
당금
reserve for interim dividend   중간배
당적립금

reserve for possible future loss   우발
손실준비금 = reserve for
contingency, retained earnings
appropriated for contingency
reserve for repair   수선충당금
reserve for retirement allowance   퇴
직급여충당금 = allowance
for retirement and severance,
retirement allowance ▶ reserve
for retirement fund, retirement
plan
reserve for retirement fund   퇴직급
여적립금 = retirement and
severance appropriated
▶ reserve for retirement
allowance, retirement plan
reserve for self-insurance   자가보험
적립금 = retained earnings
appropriated for self-insurance
reserve for sinking fund   감채기금 적
립금
reserve for tax   납세충당금 = reserve
for tax payment
reserve for tax payment   납세준비금
= reserve for taxes
reserve fund   준비자금 ▶ retained
earnings appropriated for bond,
sinking fund
reserve price   최저경매가격
reserve recognition accounting(RRA)
매장량계상회계 ▶ full costing
method, successful effort
method
reservoir   1) 저수지, 저장소 2) (지식, 부)
저장, 축적
resident   상주, 거주
resident agent   송달 대리인

resident control program   상주제어
　　프로그램 = nucleus
residual   잔여(殘餘), 잉여의
residual cost   잔여원가
residual distribution   잔여배분
residual equity   잔여지분 ▶ residual
　　equity theory
residual equity theory   잔여지분설
　　▶ entity theory, proprietorship
　　theory, residual equity
residual error ratio   진차비율
residual income   [업적평가] 잔여이익
　　▶ contribution margin
　　이익—투하자본(average invested
　　capital) × 잠재적이익률(imputed
　　interest rate)
residual income approach   잔여이익
　　법 ▶ contribution approach
residual income method   잔여이익법
residual interest   잔여지분, 소유주의
　　지분
residual property   잔여재산
residual term   잔여항목 = disturbance
　　term, error term
residual value   1) 추정잔존가액, 잔존
　　가액 = scrap value 2) (리스에서)
　　잔존가치
residue check   잉여검사
res ipsa loquitur   사실 자체 이야기
resolution   결의(決議)
resource   자원
resource allocation   자원할당, 자원배분
resource allocation and multi-project
　　scheduling(RAMS)   자원배
　　분 및 다중프로젝트 일정관리
resource available   이용가능한 자원
Resource Conservation and Recovery
　　Act(RCRA)   자원보호법
resource flows   자원흐름
resource inflow   자원의 유입
resource in process   공정중에 있는 자원
resource outflow   자원의 유출
resource provider   자원제공자
resource structure   자원구조
RESPA   부동산 청산절차법
respondent superior   대리인의 불법행
　　위를 고용인이 책임을 짐
response   응답
response time   응답시간
responsibilitiy   1) 책임, 의무 2) 신뢰성
　　3) 지불능력
responsibility accounting   책임회계
　　▶ responsibility center
responsibility audit   책임감사
　　= function audit
responsibility budget   책임예산
responsibility center   책임중심점
　　▶ report on responsibility
　　performance
responsibility entity   책임단위
　　▶ report on responsibility
　　performance, responsibility
　　center
restatement   1) 재표시 2) 갱신
restate/translate method   선수정후환
　　산 방식, 수정후 환산방식
　　▶ translate/restate method
restitution   반환, 원상회복
restitution interest   원상회복이익
restoration cost   회복원가
restricted asset   구속자산
restricted cash   사용제한예금, 지급 등
　　이 제한된 예금
restricted retained earnings   사용이

제한된 이익잉여금 = restricted
surplus

restricted security   양도제한 유가증권

restricted stock   제한주식

restricted use   배부처의 한정

restricted use of audit report   감사보
고서의 제한적 사용

restriction on audit scope   감사범위의
제한 = scope limitation

restrictive endorsement   배서금지배
서, 양도금지배서, 제한적배서
= restrictive indorsement

restrictive indorsement   제한적 배서
= restrictive endorsement

restrictive injunction   제한적(금지적 또
는 예방적) 금지명령

restructuring charges   구조조정비용

restructuring fee   구조조정 수수료

restructuring of debt   채무의 재조정

result at completion   완성시의 성과

result for the year   당기의 성과

resulting trust   복귀신탁, 추정신탁
    ▶ trust

result of operation   경영성적

retail inventory method   소매재고법
= retail method

retail lifo method   매가환원 후입선출
법, 소매재고 후입선출법
    ▶ last-in, first-out method;
    retail inventory method

retail method   매가환원법, 소매재고법
= retail inventory method

retail price index(RPI)   소매물가지수
    ▶ general purchasing power,
    price level

retail store accounting   소매점 회계

retain   유보

retainage   유보금

retained earnings   이익잉여금, 유보이
익 ▶ retained earnings
statement, retained income

**retained earnings appropriated for
bond**   감채적립금
    ▶ sinking fund
    ▶ retained income, revenue
reserve

**retained earnings appropriated for
contingency**   우발손실준비
금 = reserve for contingency,
reserve for possible future losses

**retained earnings appropriated for
purchase of treasury stock**
자기주식 매수적립금 ▶ treasury
stock

retained earnings statement   유보이
익계산서, 이익잉여금계산서
    ▶ retained earnings

retained income   유보이익
= reserve, revenue reserve
    ▶ retained earnings

retained interest   유보이익

retained life fund   퇴직종신연금

retained profit   유보이익, 이월이익

retained surplus   유보이익, 유보이익
잉여금

retention   보유

retention of title   소유권 유보
= reservation of title, title
retention

retirement   1) 제각(除却) 2) 퇴직 3) 상
환(償還) 4) 정년퇴직수당

retirement allowance   퇴직급여충당금
= allowance for retirement and
severance, reserve for retirement

allowance ▶ reserve for
retirement fund, retirement plan

retirement annuity　퇴직연금
▶ funded debt, unfunded debt

retirement benefit　퇴직급여

retirement benefit plan　퇴직급여제도
= retirement plan ▶ accrued
benefit valuation method,
actuarial valuation, current
service cost, final pay plan, past
service cost

retirement benefit scheme　퇴직급여
제도 ▶ relevant benefit,
retirement benefit plan

retirement cost　제각(除却)비

retirement date　퇴직 연월일

retirement method　제각법
▶ appraisal system

retirement of debt　부채의 변제, 부채
의 상환 ▶ debt restructuring,
refinancing debt

retirement of share　주식의 소각
= retirement of stock

retirement of share of profit　주식의
이익소각 = retirement of shares
out of profit ▶ retirement of
stock

retirement of share out of profit
주식의 이익소각 = retirement
of stock out of profit
▶ retirement profit

retirement of stock　주식의 소각

retirement of stock out of profit　주식
의 이익소각 = retirement of
shares out of profit
▶ retirement of stock

retirement pension　퇴직연금

retirement plan　퇴직급여제도
= retirement benefit plan
▶ reserve for retirement
allowance, reserve for
retirement fund

retirement system　제각법
= abandonment method,
retirement method ▶ appraisal
system

retracing of book　장부대조 = checking
posting

retransfer entry　재대체분개, 재수정
분개 = readjustment entry
▶ reversing entry

retrieval　검색

retroactive restatement　소급적 재수
정, 공표가 완료된 지난 연도의
재무제표를 재작성하여 재표시
하는 방법

retroactive restatement type　소급수
정을 행하는 타입

retroactivity　소구(遡求) = recourse

retrospective search　소급검색
▶ selective search

retry　재시행

return　1) 신고서 ▶ tax return 2) 보수,
이익 ▶ return on capital
employed 3) 환입량 4) 리턴

returnable deposit　미상환예금, 보증
금 = deposit, deposit received

return adjustment　회수가능액 조정

return audit　연속감사 = running audit

return book　반품기입장

returned material ticket　재료반환표

returned purchase　매입환출품
▶ returned sales

returned sales　매출환입, 매출환입품

= sales return ▶ returned
purchase

return inward 매출환입, 매출환입품
= sales return ▶ return outward

return inward book 매출환입기입장
= sales return book

return of capital 투자의 회수, 자본의
회수

return of investment 투자의 회수

return on asset 자산이익률 = return
on capital employed

return on asset employed 투하자산이
익률 ▶ return on capital
employed

return on asset pricing 자산이익률을
이용한 가격설정

return on capital 자본이익률

return on capital employed(ROCE)
투하자본이익률 = return on
assets, return on assets
employed, return on investment

return on common stockholders'
equity 보통주주 자기자본
이익률

return on equity 자기자본이익률

return on financial capital 화폐자본
이익, 재무적 자본이익
▶ return on physical capital

return on investment(ROI) 투자이익
률, 투자수익률, 매출액이익률
(profit margin) × 총자본회전율
(capital turnover)

return on investment method 투자
이익률법

return on net worth 순자산이익률

return on physical capital 실물자본
이익률 ▶ return on financial

capital

return on resource 자원에 대한 이익

return on sales 1) 매출액이익률 2)매
출환입 , 매출환입품 = sales
return

return on total asset 총자산이익률
▶ return on investment

return outward 매입환출 = purchases
return ▶ return inward

return outward book 매입환출기록장
= purchases return book

return preparation 납세신고서 작성

revaluation 재평가 ▶ appraisal surplus,
revaluation reserve

revaluation of asset 자산의 재평가
▶ revaluation reserve,
revaluation surplus

revaluation reserve 재평가적립금
▶ revaluation of asset,
revaluation surplus

revaluation surplus 재평가잉여금
▶ revaluation of asset,
revaluation reserve

revenue 1)수익, 매상 2) 세입(歲入)

revenue account (영) 수입지출계산서
= income and expenditure
account

revenue agency 세입(歲入)대리점

revenue and expenditure budget 세
입세출(歲入歲出)예산

revenue and expense summary account
집합손익계정

revenue bond 면세지방채권

revenue center 수익중심점
▶ responsibility accounting

revenue-cost graph 손익분기점도표
= break-even chart, profit chart,

profit graph ▶ break-even
point

revenue-cost matching   수익비용의 대
응 ▶ principle of matching
costs with revenues

revenue deficit   세입(歲入)결함(缺陷)
▶ revenue

revenue-earning activity   수익창출활동

revenue expenditure   수익적 지출
▶ capital expenditure

revenue expense   수익비용의 환산

revenue from consignment sales   위
탁판매손익

revenue from franchise fee   프랜차이
즈료 수익

revenue measurement   수익의 측정

revenue over life of project   프로젝트
전기간에 걸친 수익(수입)

revenue realization   수익의 실현
▶ realization, sales basis

revenue realization principle   수익실
현의 원칙

revenue received in advance   선수수익

revenue recognition   수익의 인식
▶ earnings recognition

revenue recognition principle   수익
인식의 원칙

revenue reserve   유보이익 = retained
income

revenue stamp   수입인지

reversal entry   역분개

reverse   차기 첫날 역분개

reverse bid   역경매 ▶ take-over bid

reverse discrimination   역(逆)차별

reverse entry   역분개

reverse Polish notation   역 폴란드식
표기법 = postfix notation,

suffix notation

reverse split   주식병합 = reverse stock
split ▶ split

reverse stock split   주식병합 = reverse
split

reversing entry   역분개, 재정리분개,
재대체분개, 재수정분개
= retransfer entry

reversion   복귀가치, 회복권

review   검토, 재조사 = review service
▶ compilation review of
interim financial information,
review report

review engagement   검토업무, 상장회
사의 중간 재무정보를 알려주
는 계약서 ▶ review

review of financial statements   재무
제표의 검토 ▶ audit of
financial statements

review of interim financial information
중간재무정보의 검토
▶ review engagement, review
report

review of interim financial statements
중간재무제표에 대한 검토 업무

review period   신규상장주의 관찰기간

review procedure   검토 절차

review report   검토 보고서, 리뷰 보고
서 ▶ review

review service   검토업무 = review

revised budget   수정예산 = amended
budget

revised return   수정신고 = amended
tax return

revised simplex method   수정 심플렉
스방법 ▶ simplex method

Revised Uniform Limited Liability Act

R

(RULLA) 개정 통일유한책임법

Revised Uniform Limited Partnership Act(RULPA) 개정 통일유한파트너십법

Revised Uniform Partnership Act (RUPA) 개정 통일파트너십법

revised version of UCC 통일상사법 개정판

revision 개정(改訂)

revision variance 개정표준원가와 원시표준원가와의 차이

revocable trust 철회가능한 신탁

revocation 철회, 폐지, 취소

revocation of discharge 채무면제의 철회

revocation of offer 청약의 철회

revolving bond 보상채권

revolving credit 회전신용

revolving credit agreement 회전신용 계약

revolving fund 회전자금

rework (JIT에서) 재작업, 보수

rework cost 1) 재작업비 ▶ spoilage 2) 보수지도서 = rectification note, repair production order, rework order

Rex v. Kylsant and Morland case (영)Rex v. Kylsant and Morland사건 = Royal Mail Steam Packet Co. Ltd. case

RFP(request for proposal) 제안요구서

RI(residual income) 잔여이익

right 1) 권리, 권익, 이권 ▶ preemptive right, rights offering 2) 신주인수권 = stock right

right and duty 권리와 의무

right and obligation 권리와 채무

rightful transfer 정당한 이전

right of action 일정 기간 소송권

right of a holder in due course 정당 소지인의 권리

right of contribution 분담금 청구권

right of entry (원수여자의) 점유권

right of exoneration 의무해제권리

right offering 주주할당발행 = rights issue ▶ pre-emptive right, subscription right

right of first refusal 첫 번째 거부권

right of holder in due course 정당 소지인의 권리

right of inspection 물품검사권

right of party upon default 채무불이행[부도]시의 당사자의 권리

right of recovery 상환권

right of reentry 재점유권

right of rely 신뢰권

right of self-help 자조(自助)권(權)

right of subscription 인수신청권

right of survivorship 생존자 재산권, 생존 소유자에의 권리의 귀속

right of withdrawal 철회권

rights issue 주주할당발행, 인수권발행 = right offering

rights-off 권리락(權利落) = ex-rights ▶ rights-on, cum-rights

rights-on 권리부(權利附) = cum-rights

right to an account 회계보고청구권

right to cure 하자 치유권

right to inspect book 장부열람권

right to inspect book and record 장부열람권

right to leased property 임차자산 사

용권 ▶ royalty

right to participate in the management
경영참가권

right to return of capital contribution
출자금 반환 청구권

right to share in dividend　배당 청구권

right to share in profits　이익 분배 청
구권

right to share of profit　이익지분권

right to share of surplus　잔여재산 지
분권

right to use　이용권

rigid budget　고정예산 = fixed budget
▶ fiexible budget, variable
budget

risk　위험 ▶ coefficient of variation,
standard deviation variance

risk and benefit of ownership　자산 소
유의 위험 · 효익

**risk and benefit of ownership transfer
to lessee**　자산 소유에 따른
위험과 효익이 임차인에게 이
전

risk and return　(리스)위험과 보수

risk and return of security　유가증권
의 위험과 보수

risk assessment　위험평가, 위험사정

risk averse attitude　위험회피적 태도
▶ risk neutral attitude, risk
seeking attitude

risk aversion　위험회피

risk bearer　위험부담자

risk capital　위험부담자본

risk class　위험유형

risk congruence　위험에 대한 태도의
일치

risk evaluation of project　프로젝트의

위험평가

risk free asset　무위험자산 ▶ riskless
interest rate

risk free rate of interest　무위험이자율

riskless interest rate　무위험이자율
= risk free rate of interest
▶ risk free asset

riskless security　무위험증권 ▶ risk
security

risk neutral attitude　위험중립적 태도
▶ risk averse attitude, risk
seeking attitude

risk of incorrect acceptance　부당수
용위험

risk of incorrect rejection　부당거절
위험

risk of loss　손실위험

risk of loss and title　손실위험부담과
소유권

risk of overreliance　과대신뢰의 위험

risk of underreliance　과소신뢰의 위험

risk premium　리스크 프리미엄

risk rate　위험률 ▶ capitalization rate,
safe rate

risk security　위험증권 ▶ riskless
security

risk seeking attitude　위험선호 태도
▶ risk averse attitude, risk
neutral attitude

risk sharing　위험분담

risk taker　위험선호자

RJE(remote job entry)　원격작업입력

RMBCA　1997년 개정 모범사업회사법

Robert Morris Associates　Robert
Morris협회

Robinson-Patman Act　Robinson-
Patman법(法)

ROCE(return on capital employed) 투
하자본이익률

Rodenticide Acts   Rodenticide법

ROI(return on investment)   투자이익률

roll back   소급

roll backward adjustment   소급(遡及)
법 ▶ roll forward adjustment

roll forward adjustment   전진법
▶ roll backward adjustment

rolling budget   연속갱신예산
= continuous budget, evolving
budget, progressive budget

rotational test   윤번(輪番)감사
▶ rotation of audit firm,
rotation of audit personal

rotation of audit firm   감사인의 교대
(순환) ▶ rotational test

rotation of audit personal   감사인의
교대(순환) ▶ rotational test

round down   절사하다

rounding error   오차

round number   단수의 오차

round off   사사오입하다

round up   절상하다

routine   일상의 과정, 일과, 관례, 기계
적 절차

routine reporting   정기적 보고

routine transaction   경상적 거래

row   열, 줄, 좌석 = frame

royal assent   (영)국왕(여왕)의 재가(裁
可)

Royal Mail Steam Packet Co.Ltd. case
Royal Mail Steam Packet 회사
사건 = Rex v. Kylsant and
Morland case

royalty   1) 특허권사용료 2) 광산, 광구
사용권 3) 상연료 4) 저작권사

용료 5) 채굴권

royalty advance   선급특허권사용료
= prepaid royalty

royalty audit   특허권사용료에 대한 감
사 ▶ general audit

RP(repurchase agreement)   환매조건부
채권 매매계약

RPI(retail price index)   소매물가지수

RRA(reserve recognition accounting)   매
장량계상회계

Rucker plan   Rucker계획 ▶ Scanlon
plan

rule   통칙(通則), 규칙 ▶ postulate

Rule 10 b-5   사기 금지 규정

**Rule 203 of (the Rules of Conduct of) the
code of professional
ethics (of the AICPA)**
(AICPA의) 직업윤리규정 (행위
규칙) 제203조

Rule 504 of Regulation D   1년에 100만
달러 이하 증권발행 및 자금 조
달에 적용되는 SEC의 규정

Rule against perpetuity   영구적 구속
금지원칙 , 장기미확정금지규칙

Rule against restraint on alienation
양도제한 금지규칙

rule of conduct   행위규칙

**Rule of Conduct of the Code of
Professional Ethics**   직업
윤리규정 · 행위규칙

rule of fair practice   공정관습 준수 원
칙 ▶ National Association of
Securities Dealers

rule of law   법의 지배

rule of thumb   경험에 기초한 지침

rules of procedure (of FASB)   (FASB의)
절차원칙

RULLA(Revised Uniform Limited Liability Act) 개정 통일유한책임법

RULPA(Revised Uniform Limited Partnership Act) 개정 통일유한 파트너십법

run 1) 주행, 실행 2) (프로그램의)실행

running audit 연속감사 = initial audit, return audit

running form (재무제표의) 보고식 = report form, vertical form

running inventory method 계속기록법 = perpetual inventory method ▶ inventory method

running stock 운전재고, 적정재고

run stream 질서에 따른 연속작업지시 = input stream, job stream

run with the land 토지 이전과 함께 이전

RUPA(Revised Uniform Partnership Act) 개정 통일 파트너십법

S

S. (section) (법률에서의) 안(案)

SAA (Single Audit Act) 단일감사법

SAB (SEC Staff Accounting Bulletins) SEC Staff의 적용지침

SAB (Staff Accounting Bulletin) 직원회계공보

safe custody 안전관리

Safe Drinking Water Act 안전음료수법

safeguard 보호 수단

safeguarding of asset 자산 보호

safe harbor rule 안전항 조약(피난조항)

safe installment 안전분배법

safekeeping 보전, 보관, 보호

safe rate 안전율 ▶ capitalization rate, risk rate

safety deposit box 대여금고

safety stock 안전재고, 적정재고 = safety stock of inventory

safety stock of inventory 안전재고

= safety stock

salaried partner 정액급 파트너

salaries book 급여(給與)대장(臺帳) = salary roll

salary 급료, 봉급

salary day 급여일, 봉급지급일 = pay day

salary roll 급여(給與)대장(臺帳) = salaries book

sale 1) 판매, 매각 2) 경매 3) 특매 4) (pl.) 매출, 매출액 5) 양도

sale and leaseback (리스거래의)매각후 리스 ▶ finance lease

sale and return 잔여품 환입조건의 매매계약 = sale or return

sale leaseback 매각후 임차, 판매후 리스

sale leaseback transaction 판매후 리스거래

sale of a partnership interest 파트너

십 지분의 매각

sale of obsolete inventory (의사결정)
진부화된 제품의 매각

sale of office 직위의 부당거래

sale of property, plant and equipment
고정자산의 매각

sale on approval 승낙에 의한 판매

sale or exchange of principal residence
주요 주택의 매출 또는 교환

sale or return(SOR, S/R) 반환조건부
판매, 불필요부분 반환권부 매
매, 잔여품 환입조건의 매매계
약 = sale and return

sales activity variance 판매량차이
▶ sales mix variance

sales agent 판매대리점

sales allowance 매출할인 ▶ sales
rebate

sales analysis 매출액분석, 판매분석

sales and administrative expense 판
매비와 일반관리비

sales and exchange of security 유가
증권의 매각 및 교환

sales and other disposition 매출과
기타 처분

sales audit 1) 판매감사 ▶ sales cutoff
2) 판매(販賣)부(部) 감사

sales base of revenue recognition 판
매기준 = sales basis

sales basis 판매기준

sales basis of revenue recognition 판
매시점 수익인식

sales book 매출장 ▶ sectional journal,
subsidiary register

sales budget 판매예산, 매출예산

sales cash discount 매출할인
= sales discount

sales commitment 판매계약

sales comparison approach 거래사례
비교법 ▶ market data
approach

sales contract receivable 판매계약 미
수금 ▶ sales of future goods

sales credit note 송장가액의 변경통지서

sales cutoff 매출액의 기간귀속 ▶ sales
audit

sales day book(SDB) 외상매출대장,
매출처원장 = customer's
ledger

sales discount 매출할인 = sales cash
discount

sales estimate 판매예측 = sales
forecasting

sales invoice 매출송장

sales journal 매출분개장

sales ledger 매출처원장 = debtors
ledger, sold ledger

sales management 판매관리

sales management accounting 판매
관리회계

sales maximization hypothesis 매출
액최대화가설

sales mix [의사결정] 매출배합, 많은 종
류의 제품을 판매할 경우 제품
비율 ▶ product mix

sales mix profit variance 매출품구성
이익차이, 매출배합이익차이
▶ sales mix variance, sales
price variance, sales volume
variance

sales mix variance 매출배합차이
▶ sales activity variance

sales of future goods (or delivery) 선
물(先物)매매(賣買) ▶ sales

contract receivable

sales of goods   상품의 판매

sales of goods to arrive   미착품 판매

sales on approval   자가사용, 시용(試用)
판매, 시송품 ▶ conditional
sales

sales on consignment   위탁판매
▶ conditional sales

sales on credit   외상판매 ▶ cash sales

sales order   판매주문, 발주전표

sales or return   반환조건부판매

sales price analysis   판매가격분석
▶ sales analysis, sales quantity
analyses, sales volume profit
variance

sales price variance   판매가격차이
▶ sales quantity variance,
sales volume variance

sales profit budget   매출이익예산

sales promotion   판매촉진

sales promotion cost   판매촉진비

sales proportion   매출관계비율
= salient ratio

sales quantity analysis   판매수량분석
▶ sales analysis, sales price
analysis, sales volume profit
variance

sales quantity variance   판매량차이
▶ sales price variance, sales
volume variance

sales quota   판매할당 ▶ sales budget

sales ratio   매출관계비율 = salient
proportion ▶ trend ratio

sales rebate   매출에누리 ▶ sales
allowance

sales, receivable, and cash receipt cycle
매출, 매출채권, 현금회수 순환

과정

sales receivable turnover   수취계정 회
전율 = receivable turnover ratio

sales region contribution report   판매
지역별 공헌액보고서

sales report   매출보고서

sales return   매출환입, 매출환입품
= return on sales

sales return book (SRB)   매출환입 기
입장

sales revenue   매출액

sales tax   매출세(稅), 물품세

sales ticket   매출전표

sales to net worth   순자본회전률
= equity turnover

sales type lease   판매형 리스 ▶ capital
lease, direct financing lease

sales value   매각가치, 매각가액

sales value at split off method   분리점
에서의 판매가치법

sales volume   매출액, 매출수량, 판매량

sales volume budget   판매량예산
▶ sales budget, sales quota

sales volume profit variance   판매수
량이익차이 ▶ sales analysis,
sales price analysis, sales
quantity analysis

sales volume variance   매출조업도차
이 = sales price variance, sales
quantity variance

salvage   1) 잔여재산 2) 폐물이용 3) 해
난구조, 인명구조

salvage note   용도변경허가서

salvage value   상각자산의 잔존가액, 잔
존가액 = scrap value
▶ depreciation

SAM(social accounting matrix)   사회 회

계 매트릭스

sample 1) 표본, 견본 2) 시공품, 시료 (試料)

sample deviation rate 표본이탈률, 표본오류율

sample expense 견본비

sample mean 표본평균

sample selection test 표본추출법
▶ test

sample size 표본 크기, 샘플 수

sample size equation 표본 크기 등식

sample space 표본공간

sampling 표본추출법
▶ audit sampling

sampling distribution 표본분포

sampling interval 표본추출 간격

sampling method 표본조사법

sampling risk 표본위험, 샘플링 위험
▶ test

sampling technique 표본추출기법

sampling testing 시사(試査)
= sampling ▶ statistical
sampling

sampling unit 표본단위

sampling without replacement 중복없는 표본추출

sampling with replacement 중복추출

Samurai bond 사무라이 본드
▶ Bulldog bond, Yankee bond

sanction 인가, 허가, 승인

Sandilands Report (영)샌디랜즈 리포트

SAP(statement on auditing procedure) 감사절차서

SAR(stock appreciation right) 주식평가차익보상제도, 주가연동보수

SAS(Statement on Auditing Standard)

감사기준서, 감사절차서

SAT(senior accounting technician) 상급회계기능자

satisfaction 만족

satisfactory performance 만족할 만한 이행

satisfying 만족수준의 달성

satisfying level 만족수준

satisfying principle 만족기준

savable cost 절약가능원가 ▶ avoidable cost

saving 1) 절약 2) (pl.) 저축액 3) 구제 4) (법) 보류, 제외

saving account 저축성예금
▶ checking account

saving bond 저축성채권

saving bond for higher education 고등교육을 위한 저축채권

saving clause 유보조항

saving deposit 저축성예금 ▶ saving account saving incentive match plan for employee

savings and loan association(S&L) 저축 · 대부조합

savings bank 저축은행, 저축조합

savings note 저축채권

savings related share option scheme 저축연동형 주식옵션제도

SBC(small business corporation) 소(小) 기업

scaffolding 발판

scale 1) 기준화 2) 크기, 규모

scale effect 규모효과

scale factor 1) 배율(倍率) 2)기준화 인수 (因數) = scaling factor

scaling 기준화, 규모화

scaling factor 1) 배율 2) 기준화 인수

= scale factor

Scanlon plan　　Scanlon계획 ▶ Rucker plan

scanner　　스캐너

scanning　　정밀조사, 통사(通査) ▶ audit technique

scanning the chart of accounts method　　계정조직 통사법, 계정조직 정사법(精査法)

scarce resource　　회소자원

SCARF(system control audit review file)　　시스템 통제감사 검토파일

scatter chart　　산포도표 = scatter diagram

scatter chart method　　산포도법 = scatter diagram method ▶ least squares method, regression analysis

scatter diagram　　산포도표 = scatter chart

scatter diagram method　　산포도법 = scatter chart method

scatter graph method　　(원가예측) 산포도법, 산포도표법

schedule　　1) 부속명세서 ▶ schedules of financial statement 2) 계획하다

scheduled maintenance　　정기보수, 정기보전, 계획보전

scheduled start date　　(원가계산) 제조개시 예정일, 제조착수 예정일

scheduled territory　　(영)외환관리법상의 지역

schedule of bonds payable　　사채명세서 ▶ bonds payable

schedule of capital　　자본금명세서

schedule of changes in working capital　　운전자본변동명세서

schedule of cost of goods manufactured　　제조원가명세서 = schedule of manufacturing cost

schedule of manufacturing cost　　제조원가명세서 = schedule of cost of goods manufactured

schedule of unpaid voucher　　미지급증빙일람표 ▶ voucher system

scheduler　　스케줄러 ▶ job management

schedules of financial statement　　재무제표 부속명세서 ▶ SEC schedules, supplementary schedule

scheduling problem　　스케줄링 문제

scholarships and fellowships　　장학금과 연구보조금

scienter　　1) 심리적인 요소, 기망의 의도, 사기 의도 2) 고의로, 일부로

scientific management　　과학적 관리법

scope　　유효범위

scope and nature of service　　서비스의 범위와 성격

scope limitation　　감사범위의 제한 = audit scope limitation

scope of audit　　감사범위

scope of consolidation　　연결범위 = consolidation criteria

scope of examination　　감사범위 ▶ scope section, opinion section, scope of opinion

scope of opinion　　의견문단 = opinion section ▶ scope opinion

scope paragraph　　범위문단 ▶ auditor's report

scope section　　범위문단 = scope

paragraph ▶ opinion
paragraph, opinion section
scorched earth   초토화전술, 초토화
s-corporation   특별소규모회사법
scrap   작업폐물 ▶ spoilage, waste
scrap note   폐기허가서
scrap report   작업폐기물보고서
scrap value   1) 잔존가액 = disposal
        value, residual value, salvage
        value ▶ depreciation 2) 작업
        폐물평가
scrip   단수주권, 증서, 권면(券面) = scrip
        certificate
scrip certificate   단수주권, 증서, 권면
        = scrip
scrip dividend   증서배당 ▶ cash
        dividend, property dividend,
        stock dividend
scrip issue   (영)무상신주발행
        ▶ capitalization issue
script   정본, 스크립트
SDA(special development area)   (영)
        (1982년 산업개발법에 의한) 특별
        개발지역
SDB(sales day book)   외상매출대장
SDR(Special Drawing Right)   IMF의 특
        별인출권
SE(Stock Exchange)   (영)런던의 증권
        거래소
SE(system engineer)   시스템 엔지니어
seal   1) 인장(印章), 증인(證印) 2) 실인(實
        印)
sealed contract   seal을 부착한 계약서
search   탐색
search cycle   탐색주기
search for unrecorded liability   부외
        부채에 대한 탐색

search key   탐색 키
search theory   탐색이론
SEC(Securities and Exchange Commission)
        증권거래위원회
SEC Accouting Series Release   SEC
        회계연속통첩
SEC Engagement   SEC에 의해 감독되
        는 기업에 대한 감사업무
secondarily liable   2차적 책임부담
secondary capital market   제2차 자본
        시장 ▶ primary capital market
secondary contributor   (영)사회보장
        제도에 의한 납입금 부담 고용자
secondary control   2차 관리
secondary distribution   1) 2차 배부, 2
        차 거래 2) 2차 매출, 2차 할부
        매출 ▶ primary distribution
secondary financial statement   제2차
        재무제표
secondary function   2차 기능
secondary liability   2차적 책임
secondary liable   제2차 채무
secondary market   유통시장
        ▶ primary market, secondary
        securities market
secondary quality   2차적 특성
secondary security market   유통시장
        = secondary market ▶ primary
        market
secondary station   2차 국(局)
second half year   하반기 ▶ first half
        year
second mortgage   두번째 저당
second mortgage bond   두번째 저당
        부사채
second quarter   제2사분기 ▶ first
        quarter

second standard of field work 두번째 실시기준

SEC Regulation S-X 미국증권거래위원회의 재무제표준칙 S-X ▶ Regulation S-K

secret account 비밀계정

secretariat 1) 사무국, 밀서과(密書課), 문서과 2) 사무국원 3) 비서직

secretary 이사회 총무부장

secretary of state 주무장관

secret asset 비밀재산 ▶ secret bookkeeping

secret bookkeeping 비밀장부 = secret ledger

secret ledger 비밀원장 ▶ secret bookkeeping

secret or hidden reserve 비밀적립금

secret partner 익명조합원 ▶ dormant partner, silent partner, sleeping partner

secret reserve 비밀적립금 = hidden reserve

secret service expense 기밀비

secret trust (영)비밀신탁

SEC Schedules SEC가 요구하는 부속명세표 ▶ schedules of financial statements

SEC Staff Accounting Bulletin(SAB) SEC 스태프 적용지침

section (법률, 문장, 서류의) 안(案)

sectional calculation 구분계산, 부문계산

sectional form 구분식 = multiple-steps form ▶ single-step form

sectional journal 분할분개장, 특수분개장 ▶ sales book

section system 분과(分課)제도

sector 부문, 분야, 영역

secular trend 장기추세

secured bond 담보부사채 ▶ secured liability

secured borrowing 담보부차입

secured claim 담보채권

secured creditor 담보권자

secured debt 담보채무

secured liability 담보부 부채 ▶ secured bond

secured loan 담보부 차입금(대부금)

secured note 담보부 약속어음

secured property 담보재산

secured transaction 담보부 거래

Securities Act of 1933 1933년 증권법 ▶ Securities Exchange Act of 1934

Securities and Exchange Commission (SEC) 미국 증권거래위원회

securities borrowed 차입유가증권

securities broker 주식중개인 = stock broker

securities broker and dealer 증권회사

Securities Exchange Act of 1934 1934년 연방증권거래법

securities law 증권법

securities lending transaction 증권대부거래

securitization 증권화

security 1) (pl.) 유가증권 2) 안전, 무사 3) 방어, 방위 4) 담보, 저당 5) 보증인, 보증 6) 기밀보호, 안전보호

security advisor 증권고문업자

security agreement 담보합의, 담보계약합의

security analysis　증권분석

security analyst　증권분석가

security control　기밀관리, 안전관리

security credit　증권금융

security deposit　보증금

security interest　약정담보권, 유가증권이자

security interest in after-acquired property　사후취득재산의 담보권

security market　증권시장

security market line　증권시장선
　　▶ capital asset pricing model, market portfolio

security offering　유가증권의 모집

security price　주가(株價)

security specific risk　증권 고유의 위험 = diversifiable risk, unsystematic risk

security trading　유가증권거래

security underwriter　유가증권인수업자 ▶ underwriter

seek time　조사시간

segment　1) 구분단위, 구분, 부문 2) 세그먼트

segmental information　부문별 정보
　　= segment information

segmental report　부문별 보고서

segmental reporting　부문별 보고
　　▶ segment reporting ▶ line-of-business, products line, segmentation, segment information

segment asset　부문 자산
　　▶ identifiable asset segment

segmentation　부문화 ▶ segment reporting, segmental reporting

segmented reporting and controllability　부문별 보고 및 통제가능성

segmented source and application of fund statement　부문별 자금운용표

segment expense　부문 비용
　　▶ segment information

segment information　부문정보
　　= segmental information
　　▶ geographical segment information, industry segment information, line-of-business information

segment manager　부문관리자

segment margin　부문이익

segment of a business　사업부문

segment of an enterprise　기업의 부문정보

segment profit or loss and asset　부문 손익과 자산

segment result　부문성과 ▶ segment reporting

segment revenue　부문수익
　　▶ segment reporting

segregated goods　분리된 상품

segregation　분장

segregation control　업무분장통제

segregation of duty　업무분장

selected financial data　주요 재무자료, 선택된 재무자료 ▶ annual report, financial highlight, high light

selected quarterly financial data　선택된 분기 재무자료

selection　선택, (통신)셀렉션

selection check　선택검사

selective dissemination of information

정보의 선택적 제공
▶ retrospective search

selective dump   지정구역 덤프

selective theory   당기업적주의
▶ all inclusive theory

selector   선택자

selector channel   선택채널 ▶ input-
output channel

self accounting system of factory   공
장독립회계

self adapting   자기적응, 자기조정

self adapting computer   자기적응 컴
퓨터

self assessment   신고납세

self balancing ledger   독자(獨自)평균
원장

self constructed asset   자가건설자산

self construction   자가건설

self-dealing   자기 거래

self employed individual   개인 자영
업자

Self Employment Contributions Act
자가고용납입금법

self employment tax   자영업세 ▶ self-
employment tax simple trust

self financing   자기금융 ▶ debt
financing

self insurance   자가보험, 자기보험

self insured   자가담보

seller   판매자

seller's remedy for breach of contract
계약위반에 대한 판매인의 구제

selling   매각, 판매, 판매업무

selling and general administrative cost
판매비와 일반관리비

**selling and general administrative
expense**   판매비와 일반관

리비

selling charge   판매비, 판매제비용

selling commission   판매수수료

selling cost   판매비 = selling expense

selling exchange   매출환어음 ▶ bills
bought

selling expense   판매비 = selling cost
▶ general and administrative
expense

selling expense budget   판매비예산
▶ sales budget

selling overhead   판매간접비

selling price   매가, 판매가, 매각가치
▶ market value

selling price variance   판매가격차이

sell or process further decision   매각
또는 추가가공에 대한 의사결정
▶ make or buy decision,
special cost, special cost study

**sell or process further sensitivity
analysis**   매각 또는 추가 가
공에 대한 민감도 분석

semantics   의미론, 의미

semiannual compound   반 년 마다의
복리계산

semidirect cost   준직접비
▶ classification of cost by
product

semi-finished goods   반제품 = semi-
manufactured goods ▶ finished
goods, manufactured goods

semi-finished parts   반성부품
▶ finished parts, purchased
parts

semi-fixed cost   준고정비 = step cost
▶ fixed cost, semi-variable
cost

S

semi-manufactured goods　반제품
　　= semi-finished goods
　　▶ finished goods, manufactured
　　goods
semi-strong efficient market　준강형
　　의 효율적 시장 ▶ strong
　　efficient market
semi-strong form efficient market　준
　　강형의 효율적 시장 ▶ efficient
　　market
semi-variable cost　준변동비 = mixed
　　cost ▶ semi-fixed cost, variable
　　cost
senior accountant　상급회계사
senior accounting technician(SAT)
　　상급회계기능자 ▶ association
　　of accounting technician (AAT)
senior security　상위증권 ▶ junior
　　security, subordinated security
sense switch　센스 스위치
sensor　검출기, 센서
SEP(simplified employee pension)　단순
　　종업원연금
separable account　독립계정, 분리 계
　　정, 특별계정
separable cost　분리가능비
separable fixed cost　부문별 분리가능
　　고정비
separable net asset　분리가능순자산
separable processing cost　개별원가
**separate cost of each process in a
　　manufacture**　공장내 공정
　　별 분리원가
separate disclosure　구분공시
separate entity　독립된 실체
separate financial statement　개별재
　　무제표

separate legal entity　독립된 법적 주체
separation　임의퇴직수당, 별거수당
separator　분리부호, 분리기호
sequential control　순차(順次)통제
sequential (stop-or-go) sampling　순차
　　적 표본조사, 단속적 표본조사
sequential sampling inspection　연속
　　표본추출검사법
sequential scheduling system　순차식
　　(順次式) 일정관리 시스템
sequestration　특별강제관리, 가차압(假
　　差押)
sequestrator　특별관재인
serial　직렬(直列), 순차, 연속
serial bond　연속상환사채
serial issue　연속발행
serial number　일련번호
series EE bond　현금화되거나 만기일
　　이 도래할 때까지 이자가 부가
　　되는 채권
service　1) 용역, 역무, 업무 2) (연금계산
　　상의) 근속(勤續)
service beneficiary　용역수익자
service benefit　용역 효익, 용역의 편익
service capacity　용역제공능력
　　▶ operating capacity
service center　보조부문, 용역제공부문
service contract　고용계약 = contract
　　of service
service contribution　노무(勞務)출자(出
　　資)
service cost　용역원가
service cost allocation　보조부문비 배
　　부 ▶ overhead allocation
service cost center　보조부문 원가중심
　　점
service costing　서비스의 원가계산

service department　보조부문
= auxiliary department,
subsidiary department
▶ manufacturing department,
production department,
producing department

service department allocation cost
variance　보조부문비 배부
차이

service department charge　보조부문
비 = service department cost,
service department expense

service department cost　보조부문비
= service department charge

service department cost allocation
보조부문의 원가배부

service department expense　보조부
문비 = service department
charge

service effort　용역제공노력

service enterprise　서비스업

service hours method　이용시간비례법
= production output method,
unit of service method

service inventory　용역성 재고자산

service lease　서비스 리스 ▶ operating
lease

service life　내용연수 = depreciable life,
durable years, useful life

service objective　용역제공의 기본 목적

service of subsidiary department　보
조부문의 용역제공 ▶ auxiliary
department

service organization　용역조직, 용역제
공업체

service period　근무기간

service potential　용역잠재능력

service program　보조 프로그램
= utility program

service value　용역가치 = service
potential

service well　용역의 원천

service year　근속년수

service yield basis　생산량비례법
= production method, service
basis

servient tenement　다른 사람의 토지

servitude　용역권

set　1) 집합 2) 세트 3) 설정

set off　상쇄

setting out　무시

settled account　청산계정, 당사자의 쌍
방승인의 거래계산서

settled property　신탁부동산

settlement　결제, 변제, 청산

settlement date　결제일

settlement day　결제일

settlement discount　현금할인 = cash
discount

settlement of debt　채권채무관계의 청
산

settlement of liability　부채의 변제

settlement price　결산일 종가
▶ closing price, opening price

settlement rate　상환률, 결제율

settlement value　매각시가, 처분가액

settlor　신탁재산의 제공자, 설정자, 신
탁인

set-up　1) 셋업 2) 준비

set-up cost　1) 작업준비원가 2) [ABC]
셋업에 필요한 비용

set-up diagram　준비도(準備圖)

set-up time　준비시간

several　개별적

several liability   개별책임 ▶ joint
     liability

severance benefit   이직수당, 퇴직수당,
     퇴직금

severance indemnity   퇴직급여

severance pay   퇴직금

SFAC(statement of financial accounting
     concept)   재무회계 제개념
     보고서

SFAS(statement of financial accounting
     standard)   재무회계기준서

shadow director   (영)음(陰)의 임직원

shadow price   잠재가격 ▶ linear
     programming, simplex method

shaken faith doctrine   동요하는 서약
     의 법리

sham consideration   허위의 대가

Shannon's theorem   샤논의 정리

share   주식 = stock

share and debenture issue expense   주
     식과 사채발행비

share capital   주식자본금 = capital
     stock

share certificate   주권(株券) = stock
     certificate

share consolidation   주식병합

shared file   공용(共用)파일

shareholder   주주(株主) = stockholder

shareholder of record   주주, 등록주주
     = stockholder of record

shareholder resolution   주주결의
     = stockholder resolution

shareholders' account   자본계정
     = stockholders' account

shareholders' equity   주주지분, 자본
     = stockholder's equity

shareholders' meeting   주주총회

     = stockholders' meeting

shareholders' right   주주권(株主權)
     = stockholders' right

share issue expense   신주발행비
     ▶ stock issue cost

share ledger   주식대장, 주권대장
     = stock ledger

share of no par value   무액면주식
     = no-par stock, no-par-value
     stock ▶ par value stock

share option   (영)주식구입선택권
     = stock option

share premium   주식발행초과금
     = capital paid in excess of par
     value ▶ paid-in surplus

share right   신주인수권, 주식매수권
     = pre-emptive right, stock right
     ▶ pre-emption

share split-down   주식병합
     = stock splitdown
     ▶ share split-up

share split-up   주식분할 = stock split-
     up ▶ share split-down

share warrant   무기명주식 ▶ bearer
     stock

share with par value   액면주식
     = par value stock ▶ non-par
     stock

sharing of risk   위험분담, 위험분산

sheet   1) 표, 도면 2) (종이의) 장, 일면

sheffer stroke   부정(否定)논리적

shelf registration   자가등록, 일괄등기
     제도 ▶ Samurai bond

shell company   (영)쉘 컴퍼니 = skeleton
     company

shelter provision   보호조항

shelter rule   차단규칙, 셸터룰

sheriff 집달관

shift 옮기다, 이동시키다

ship and vessel 선박(船舶)

shipment 발송, 적송품, 출하(出荷)

shipment carrier case 선적지 운송의 경우

shipment case 선적지의 경우

shipment contract 선적지 계약, 출하지 계약

shipment term 선적조건

shipment under reservation 제한된 선적

shipping 출하

shipping advice 송장안내, 선적통지서

shipping cost 발송비

shipping department 출하 부문

shipping document 출하서류

shipping industry 해운업

shipping through 선량한 구매자가 아닌 자가 선량한 구매자에게 양도하였다가 다시 취득

shipping transportation cost 발송운임

shop 1) 상점, 소매점 2) 공장, 작업장 3) 근무처, 직장 4) 런던 증권거래소 = the Stock Exchange

shopworn 상품이 팔리지 않고 오래된, 진부화

short 1) 부족 2) 현품없이 파는, 공매(空賣)의

shortage and shrinkage 재고감모

short block 단기블럭

short covering 신용거래의 환매

short form audit report 단문식 감사보고서, 약식 감사보고서 ▶ long form audit report

short form report 단문식 (감사)보고서

        ▶ long form report

short hedging 판매 단기헤징

short lease 단기 리스

short notice 기한경과통지, 사전통고

short range budger 단기예산 ▶ long range budget

short range fund planning 단기자금계획 ▶ long range fund planning

short range management planning 단기경영계획 ▶ long range management planning

short range planning 단기경영계획 ▶ long range planning

short range profit planning 단기이익계획 ▶ long range profit planning, profit planning

short run cash planning 단기자금계획

short run cost 단기적 비용 ▶ long run cost, long range cost

short run cost curve 단기원가분석 ▶ long run cost curve

short run decision making 단기의사결정 ▶ long range planning

short sale 공매, 단기예측판매 = short selling

short selling 공매(空賣) = short sale

short swing profit 단기차익

short term capital 단기자본 ▶ long term capital

short term contract 단기계약

short term credit 단기신용

short term debt 1) 유동부채, 단기채무 ▶ long term debt 2) 단기차입금

short term differential cost analysis 단기차액원가분석

short term financing 단기자금조달, 단기금융

short term investment 단기투자
= current asset investment
▶ fixed asset investment, long term investment

short term investment security 단기투자유가증권 ▶ current asset investment

short term liability 단기부채 = current liability

short term loan 단기대출금 ▶ long term loan

short term loan payable to officers 임원에 대한 단기차입금

short term monetary asset 단기화폐성 자산

short term notes payable 단기지급어음 ▶ long-term notes payable

short term obligation 유동부채
= current liability

short-term obligation expected to be refinanced 차환예상의 유동부채, 차환권 단기채무

short time bill 단기어음

short time credit 단기신용

should cost 발생한도원가, 허용원가

"should-cost" review 허용원가의 검증

shrinkage 가치하락, 감모, 감모손, 감모비 ▶ abnormal shrinkage, inventory shrinkage, spoilage, waste

shrinkage loss 재고자산감모비, 재고자산감모손 = inventory shortage

shrinkage variance 감모차이

shutdown cost 1) 근본원가 2) 조업중

지비용

SI(Statutory Instrument) (영)위탁입법집, 정부명령

SIAS(Statement of International Accounting Standards) 국제회계기준서

SIC(Standard Industrial Classification) 표준산업분류

sick leave 질병 휴가

sick pay 질병 보상

sideband (통신의) 측파대

sight (어음의) 일람(一覽) ▶ sight bill, sight draft, sight note

sight bill 일람지불(환)어음 = demand bill, sight draft

sight draft 일람지불(환)어음 = demand bill, sight bill

sight note 일람지불(약속)어음 = demand note

signal 신호

signal distance 신호거리

signatory 서명자, 조약(條約) 국(國)

signature 서명(署名)

signed field 부호 란(欄)

significance 중요, 중요성 = weight

significance level 유의(有意)수준

significant 중요한

significant accounting policy 중요한 회계방침

significant audit adjustment 중요한 감사의 수정사항

significant condition 유의(有意)상태

significant digit 유효숫자, 유효행

significant influence 중요한 영향

significant intercompany transaction 기업집단내 회사간의 중요한 거래

significant subsidiary   중요 자회사

silence   침묵

silent partner   익명조합원 ▶ dormant
      partner, secret partner, sleeping
      partner

similar asset   유사자산

simple accumulation   단리(單利)정기
      적금

simple average   단순평균법

simple average method   단순평균법

simple buffering   단순완충법

simple capital structure   단순한 자본
      구조

simple correlation coefficient   단순상
      관계수

simple discount   단순할인

simple hypothesis   단순가설

simple interest   단리(單利) ▶ compound
      interest

simple linear regression   단순선형회귀

simple liquidation   일괄분배방식

simple process costing   단순 공정별
      원가계산

simple random sample   단순무작위 표
      본

simple regression   단순회귀 ▶ multiple
      regression, regression analysis

simple regression analysis   단순회귀
      분석 ▶ multiple regression
      analysis

simplex method   심플렉스방법
      ▶ linear programming

simplex table   심플렉스표

simplex transmission   일방향전송, 단
      일신호전송

simplified employee pension(SEP)   단
      순종업원연금

simplified employee pension plan   단
      순종업원연금계획

simplified income statement   간이 손
      익계산서

simplified report   간이보고서

simultaneous operation   동시연산, 동
      시조작

simultaneous processing   동시처리

simultaneous verification   동시검증

single account system   단일회계제도
      ▶ double account system

Single Audit Act(SAA)   단일감사법

single audit approach   1인 감사인방법

single delivery   단일 인도

single entry   단식기입 ▶ single entry
      bookkeeping

single entry bookkeeping   단식부기
      ▶ double entry bookkeeping

single index model   단일지표모델
      ▶ diagonal model

single plan   단기법(單記法) ▶ partial
      plan

single precision   단일 정밀도
      ▶ double-precision, triple-
      precision

single process cost accounting   단순
      종합원가계산 = single process
      costing

single process costing   단순종합원가
      계산 = single process cost
      accounting, single process cost
      system, single product costing
      ▶ job order costing, process
      costing, special order cost
      system

single process cost system   단순종합
      원가계산 = single process

S

costing

single process lot cost system   단순조
별원가계산

single proprietorship   개인사업주

single step form   일단계식, 총괄식
▶ multiple step form

single-step income statement   일단계
식 손익계산서, 단일구분식 손
익계산서 ▶ multiple step
income statement

single step operation   일단계조작, 단일
스텝조작 = step-by-step
operation

single time rate plan   단일시간급제

single unit depreciation   개별상각
= item depreciation
▶ composite depreciation,
group depreciation

singular matrix   특이행렬

sinkage   가치하락

sinking fund   감채기금 ▶ fund for
retirement of bond, reserve
fund, sinking fund bond,
sinking fund reserve

sinking fund accrual   철거예정 감채기
금

sinking fund bond   감채기금부 사채
▶ sinking fund, reserve fund,
sinking fund reserve

sinking fund method   상각기금법
▶ annuity method, compound
interest method

sinking fund reserve   감채적립금
▶ sinking fund bond, reserve
fund

site audit   현장감사

sixes   1) 6개월 지불어음 2) 6% 이자부

어음

sixties   60일 지불어음

size   크기, 규모

size of capacity   생산능력의 규모
▶ capacity, capacity resources

skeleton bill   백지어음

skeleton form   T자형 계정양식 = T-
account

skepticism   회의주의

skew   1) 오용, 왜곡 2) 비스듬한

S&L(saving and loan association)   저축·
대출조합

slave station   착신단말

sleeping account   휴면계정, 정지(靜止)
계정 ▶ active account

sleeping partner   익명조합원
▶ dormant partner, secret
partner, silent partner

SLH(standard labor hour)   표준노동시간

slight negligence   경과실

slip accounting system   전표회계제도

slow-moving   1) 느리게 움직이는 2) 상
품이 잘 팔리지 않는, 매출이 뜻
대로 되지 않는 = slowmoving

slow moving inventory   회전이 느린
재고자산

**SMA(statement on management
accounting)**   관리회계보고서

small business   소(小)기업

small business computer   소형사무처
리 컴퓨터 ▶ general purpose
computer, minicomputer

small business corporation(SBC)   소
(小)기업

small business GAAP   폐쇄회사와 소
규모회사에 대한 GAAP
= little GAAP

small business stock   소(小)기업 주식

small company   소규모회사 ▶ large
company, private company,
medium sized company

small company rate   소규모 기업에 적
용하는 낮은 세율

small enterprise   소규모기업

small sample   소규모 표본

small sampling theory   소규모 표본이
론

small (or ordinary) stock dividend
소규모(통상적인) 주식배당

small workshop   소규모공장 ▶ very
small workshop

Smithonian Agreement   스미소니언 협
정

smoothing   유연화

smoothing of income   이익의 유연화

SNA(system of national account)   국민
계정체계, 국민경제계산체계

snapshot dump   속사(速寫) 덤프

social accounting   사회회계 ▶ private
accounting

social accounting matrix(SAM)   사회
회계 매트릭스

social audit   사회감사 ▶ social
responsibility accounting

social benefit   사회적 편익

social cost   사회적 비용

social responsibility   사회적 책임

social responsibility accounting   사회
적 책임회계 ▶ social audit

social security   사회보장

social security contribution   사회보장
부담금

social security tax   사회보장세

Society of Company and Commercial
Accountants   (영)회사 · 상
업회계사협회

Society of Investment Analysts   (영)
투자분석가 협회

soft information   소프트한 정보
▶ hard information

SOI(statement of intent)   (영)취지서

sold day book   매출장 = sales day book

sold ledger   매출처 원장 = debtors
ledger, sales ledger

sole practitioner   개인 개업자, 개업의
원, 개인개업 회계사 또는 변호
사

sole proprietor   개인 상인, 개인기업주
= ole trader

sole proprietorship   개인기업
= proprietorship

sole trader   개인상인 = sole proprietor

solicitation   권유(勸誘)

solicitation of client   고객의 권유

solicitor   (영)사무변호사 ▶ Queen's
Counsel

solvency   지불능력 ▶ cash ratio,
current ratio, quick ratio

SOP(statement of position)   1) AICPA
의 의견표명서 = SOPs 2) 상황
보고

sophisticated investor   정보에 정통한
투자자 ▶ unsophisticated
investor

SOPs(Statement of Positions)   AICPA
의 의견표명서 = SOP

SOR(sale or return)   반환조건부 판매

SORP(statement of recommended practice)
(영)회계실무권고서

sort   분류하다

sorter   분류기

S

sound accounting practice　건전한 회
계실행

sound bill　건전어음, 확실한 어음

sound value　건전가액, 건전가치
　　　▶ replacement cost,
　　　reproduction cost

source and application of fund
　　　statement　자금의 원천과
　　　용도에 관한 계산서, 자금계산
　　　서, 자금운용표 = statement of
　　　source and application of funds

source and application of working
　　　capital　운전자본의 원천과
　　　용도

source and disposition statement　자
　　　금의 원천과 용도에 관한 계산
　　　서, 자금계산서, 자금운용표
　　　= statement of source and
　　　application of funds

source document　원시(原始)서류, 원시
　　　전표, 원시자료 ▶ audit trail

source language　원시언어

source module　원시 모듈

source of financial information　재무
　　　정보원천

source of financing　자금조달의 원천

source of fund　자금의 원천
　　　▶ statement of source and
　　　application of fund

source of tax　세원(稅源)

source program　원시(原始) 프로그램

sources of information　정보원천

SP(standard price)　표준가격, 표준단가

SP(standard price per unit of input)　투
　　　입단위당 표준가격

span of control　관리한계, 통제한계

spare part inventory　예비부품의 재고

　　　= spare stock

spare stock　예비부품의 재고 = spare
　　　parts inventory

special agent　특정대리인

special assessment　특별사정

special bailment　특별기탁

special bid　특별입찰, 특별매수가격

special category account　(영)(회사법
　　　상의) 특별구분회사의 재무제표
　　　▶ special category company

special category company　(영)(회사법
　　　상의) 특별구분회사

special character　특수문자

special collection　특별징수

special commissioner　(영)특별국세불
　　　복심판관 = commissioner for
　　　the special purposes of the
　　　Income Tax Acts

Special Committee on Cooperation
　　　with Stock Exchanges　주
　　　식거래소 특별위원회

special cost　특수원가
　　　▶ special cost study,
　　　differential cost, incremental
　　　cost

special cost concept　특수원가개념
　　　▶ special cost

special cost study　특수원가연구, 특수
　　　원가계산 ▶ cost accounting
　　　system, differential cost
　　　analysis, opportunity cost

special crossing　특별횡선수표
　　　▶ general crossing

special day-book　보충일기장

special deposit　별도예금, 별단예금
　　　= specified deposit

special development area(SDA)　(영)

특별개발지역

special drawing right(SDR)　　(IMF의) 특별인출권

special endorsement　기명식배서, 지명 식배서, 특별이서 = full endorsement ▶ blank endorsement, endorsement in blank

special examination　특별감사

special indorsement　기명식배서, 지명 식배서 = special endorsement

specialist　전문가

specialized accounting and reporting　특수회계와 보고

specialized accounting practice　특수 한 회계실무

specialized institution　전문기관

special job order　특정제조지시서 = special production order

special journal　특수분개장, 분할분개 장 ▶ general journal

special journal system　특수분개장 제 도

special ledger　특수원장 = subsidiary ledger ▶ special journal

specially manufactured goods　특별 주문품

special manager　(영)(파산회사의) 특별 매니저

special meeting　특별총회

special notice (of resolution)　(영)의제에 관련한 특별통지

special order　특정제조지시서 = special production order

special order cost system　개별원가계 산, 제조지시서별 원가계산 = job order costing ▶ processcosting,

single process costing

special partner　유한책임조합원 = limited partner ▶ general partner

special price　특가(特價)

special production order　특정제조지 시서 = special order, special job order, specific job order, specific production order ▶ standing production order

special property　제한부 재산권

special purpose computer　특정목적 컴퓨터

special purpose entity　특별목적기업

special purpose financial presentation　특수목적의 재무제표정보

special purpose financial statement　특수목적의 재무제표 ▶ general purpose financial statement, specific purpose statement

special purpose government　특수목 적 정부

special report　특수 보고서

special resolution　(영)특별의결 ▶ extraordinary resolution, ordinary resolution

special revenue fund　특별수익기금

specialty contract　날인(捺印)계약, 날 인증서에 의한 계약

specie　정화(正貨)

specification　1) 사양서　2) 건물설계명 세서

specific capacity cost　구체적 생산설 비원가 ▶ common capacity cost

specific cost　개별원가

specific cost method　개별법
　　　= identified cost method, specific
　　　identification
　　　▶ average-cost method, first-in
　　　first-out method, last-in first-out
　　　method

specific deposit　별도예금, 별단예금
　　　= special deposit

specific disclaimer　구체적 의견거절

specific duty　종량세 ▶ ad valorem
　　　duty

specific gift　(유언상의) 특정증여
　　　▶ general gift

specific identification　(재고자산평가상
　　　의) 개별원가법, 개별법

specific job order　특정제조지시서
　　　= special production order
　　　▶ standing production order

specific level of activity　[ABC]특정의
　　　조업도 수준

specific order costing　개별원가계산
　　　= job order costing ▶ process
　　　costing

specific order cost system　개별원가
　　　계산 = job order costing
　　　▶ process costing

specific performance　특별이행, 구체
　　　적 이행

specific policy　특정재산대상 가입보험

specific price change　개별가격변동
　　　▶ current cost accounting

specific price index　개별가격지수
　　　▶ current cost accounting

specific production order　특정제조지
　　　시서 = special production order

specific purpose statement　특정목적
　　　새무제표 ▶ general purpose
　　　statements

specific tax　종량세 = specific duty
　　　▶ ad valorem duty

specified element, account, or item of a
　　　financial statement　재무제
　　　표의 특정요소, 계정 혹은 사항

specified requirement　명시된 요구사항

specified users　특정사용자

spectral response　스펙트럴 반응

speculation　투기목적으로 선물환계약
　　　을 체결할 경우, 투기(投機)
　　　= gambling ▶ hedge

speculative holding　투기적 보유
　　　▶ hedge holding

speed limit　속도제한

speedy clearance　즉시매각

speedy disposal　즉시처분

spending　지출, 소비

spending mandate　용도지정, 용도를
　　　지정하는 명령

spending unit　지출단위, 소비단위

spending variance　(표준원가계산) 예산
　　　차이, 제조간접비 소비차이
　　　= budget variance, overhead
　　　spending variance ▶ overhead
　　　variance

spendthrift clause　낭비방지조항

spendthrift trust　낭비방지신탁
　　　= protective trust

spilt-off point　(연산품의) 분리점

spin-off　주식소각에 의한 회사분할
　　　▶ divestiture, split-down,
　　　split-off, split-up

spin-out　스핀아웃, 회사분할

split　주식분할 = stock split

split-down　주식병합 ▶ spin-off, split-
　　　off, split-up

split-off 주식소각에 의한 회사분할
  ▶ spin-off, split-down, split-up

split-up 회사 해산을 위한 회사분할
  ▶ spin-off, split-down, split-off

spoilage 공손, 정상공손과 비정상공손
  ▶ abnormal spoilage, shrinkage, waste

spoilage cost 공손비 = defective work cost, loss due to defective work, loss due to spoiled work, loss from spoilage, loss on spoilage

spoilage in job costing 개별원가계산에서의 공손

spoilage in process costing 공정별원가계산의 공손

spoilage report 공손품보고서

spoilage variance 공손차이

spoilage work 공손품 = spoiled work

spoiled goods 공손품

spoiled unit 공손품 = spoiled work

spoiled work 공손품 = spoilage work, spoiled goods, spoiled unit
  ▶ unit

sponsor (연금제도의) 스폰서

sponsorship 지원(支援)

spooling 스풀링

spot dealing 현장거래 = spot exchange dealing

spot exchange 현장교환 ▶ forward exchange

spot exchange dealing 현장교환거래
  ▶ forward exchange, forward rate, spot dealing, spot exchange, spot exchange rate, spot rate

spot exchange rate 현장교환시세
  ▶ forward exchange rate, spot rate

spot goods 현물(現物)

spot market 현물시장

spot price 처분가격, 현지가격

spot quotation 현물시세

spot rate 현물시세, 현재 통용되는 통화교환비율 ▶ forward rate

spot reproduction cost 재생산원가

spouse 배우자

spread 가격 폭

spreadsheet 전개표, 운용표, 표 계산

SQ(standard quantity of input) 표준투입량

SQ(standard quantity used) 표준투입량

SQC(statistical quality control) 통계적 품질관리

square root formula (경제적발주량의) 제곱근공식 ▶ economic order quantity

S/R(sale or return) 반환조건부 판매

SR(standard labor rate) 표준임률

SRB(sales return book) 매출환입품 기입장

SSAE(statement on standard for attestation engagement) 입증업무에 관한 기준서

SSAP(statements of standard accounting practice) (영)회계실무기준서, 회계기준서

SSARS(statement on standard for accounting and review service) 회계와 검토업무에 관한 기준서

SSCC(standard on standard consulting or consulting service) 자문 및 자문서비스에 관한 기준서

S

SSDS(statement of social and demographic statistics) 사회 · 인구통계 보고서

SSP(statutory sick pay) (영)법정질병 휴가수당

S-s policy S-s정책

stability 안정도

stabilized accounting 화폐가치 안정의 회계 ▶ constant dollar accounting, general price level accounting

stable monetary unit 안정된 화폐단위 = constant purchasing power unit

Staff Accounting Bulletin(SAB) 증권거래위원회의 적용지침 ▶ Regulation S-X, Financial Reporting Release

staff and other support service 인력파견 및 지원업무

staff and support service 지원 서비스

staff department 스태프 부문

stag 권리주 매매상, (거래소의) 증권업자가 거래소를 통하지 않고 주식을 매매하는 행위

stage of completion 완성도, 가공진척도, 가공도 ▶ work in process

stage payment 단계적 지불 ▶ repayment guarantee

stagnation 불황(不況)

stale check 장기경과수표, 지연수표 = out-of-date check

stamp duty 인지세(印紙稅) = stamp tax

stamp tax (영)인지세(印紙稅) = stamp duty

standard 1) 표준, 기준, 규격 2) (통화의) 본위(本位)

standard activity 표준조업도 = standard volume, standard capacity

Standard and Poor's 500 스탠다드 앤 푸어스(사)의 지수

standard audit report 표준감사보고서

standard bank confirmation 표준은행조회확인서

standard burden rate 제조간접비 표준배부율 = standard overhead rate ▶ overhead rate

standard capacity 표준조업도 = standard activity, standard volume

standard confirmation form 표준조회서양식

standard conversion cost 표준가공비

standard cost 표준원가, 표준원가법 ▶ standard costing

standard cost accounting 표준원가계산 = standard costing, standard cost system ▶ actual cost accounting, standard cost

standard cost card 표준원가표 = standard cost sheet

standard costing 표준원가계산 = standard cost accounting ▶ actual cost accounting

standard cost per unit 단위당 표준원가

standard cost sheet 표준원가표 = standard cost card

standard cost system 표준원가계산 ▶ standard cost accounting

standard cost variance 표준원가차이 ▶ cost variance

standard deviation 표준편차

▷ coefficient of variation,
risk, variance

standard direct costing 표준직접원가
계산 = standard marginal costing
▷ actual absorption costing

standard direct labor cost 표준직접
노무비 ▷ direct labor cost

standard direct labor hour 표준직접
노동시간 ▷ direct labor hour

standard direct labor rate 표준직접
임률

standard direct material cost 표준직
접재료비 ▷ direct material cost

standard error 표준오차

standard error of beta 베타의 표준
오차 ▷ beta

standard factory overhead 표준제조
간접비, 제조간접비 표준

standard fixed cost 표준고정비, 고정
비 표준

standard fixed overhead cost 표준
고정제조간접비

standard form 1) 표준양식 2) 정규화,
표준형 = normalized form in a
floating-point representation

standard hour allowed 허용표준시간

standard industrial classification(SIC)
표준산업분류

standardized audit program 표준화
된 감사계획

standardized distribution 표준화된
분포

standardized normal distribution 표
준정규분포

standardized normal variate 표준화
된 정규변량(變量)

standardized variate 표준화된 변량

standard labor cost 표준노무비
▷ labor cost

standard labor hour(SLH) 표준노동
시간

standard labor rate(SR) 표준임률
▷ labor rate

standard labor time 표준노동시간
▷ labor time

standard machine time 표준기계시간

standard manufacturing overhead
표준제조간접비
▷ manufacturing overhead

standard marginal costing 표준한계
원가계산, 표준직접원가계산,
표준변동원가계산 = standard
direct costing, standard variable
costing ▷ actual absorption
costing

standard material cost 표준재료비
▷ material cost

standard material usage 표준재료 소
비량

standard minute (작업연구의) 1인당 표
준작업량

standard normal distribution 표준
정규분포 = standardized normal
distribution

standard operating performance 표
준영업성과 = standard
performance

standard operation 표준작업

standard operation list 표준작업목록
표 = standard operation sheet

standard operation sheet 표준작업목
록표 = standard operation list

standard opinion 표준의견 ▷ clean
opinion

S

standard overhead cost　　표준제조간
접비 ▶ overhead cost

standard overhead rate　　제조간접비
표준배부율 = standard burden
rate ▶ overhead rate

standard percentage analysis　　표준
비율분석

standard performance　　표준성과
= standard operating
performance

standard price(SP)　　표준가격, 표준
단가

standard price per unit of input(SP)
투입단위당 표준가격

standard production cost　　표준제조
원가

standard purchase price　　표준매입가격

standard quantity of input(SQ)　　표준
투입량

standard quantity used(SQ)　　표준소
비수량

standard ratio　　표준비율

standard report　　표준보고서

standard report departure　　표준보고
서로부터 이탈

standards　　회계기준

standards and variances　　표준과 차이

standard selling price　　표준판매가

standard setter　　설정주체, 회계기준 설
정주체 = standards-setting
authority, standards-setting
body

standard setting　　회계기준설정

standard setting body　　회계기준설정
기관, 회계기준설정주체
= standard setter, standard
setting authority

standards for accounting information
회계정보기준

**standards for the professional practice
of internal auditing**　　내부
감사의 직업적 실무기준

standards level　　회계기준 레벨

standards of field work　　실시기준

standards of field work in auditing
감사실시기준
▶ standards of reporting in
auditing

standards of reporting　　보고 기준

standards of reporting in auditing
감사보고기준 ▶ standards of
field work in auditing

standards setting authority　　기준(基
準)설정기관 = standard setter,
standard setting body

standard stock level　　표준재고수준

standard total rate(STR)　　표준배부율

standard variable cost　　표준변동비,
변동비 표준발생액

standard variable costing　　표준변동
원가계산, 표준직접원가계산
= standard direct costing,
standard marginal costing

standard variable overhead cost　　표
준변동제조간접비 ▶ standard
fixed overhead cost

standard variable rate　　표준변동비율

standard volume　　표준조업도
= standard activity, standard
capacity

standby　　대기(待機)

standby agreement　　잔액인수계약
▶ underwriting agreement

standby credit　　스탠바이 크래디트

standby letter of credit written (발행
자측의) 스탠바이 신용장

standing cost 고정비 = fixed cost

standing expense 경상비(經常費)

standing job order 계속제조지시서
= standing production order

standing-on-nines carry (정보통신용
어) 9건너뛰기 자리올림

standing order 계속제조지시서
= standing production order

standing production order 계속제조
지시서 = standing job order,
standing order ▶ special
production order

state and local government 주(州)와
지방정부

state and local government accounting
주(州)와 지방정부회계
▶ statutory accounting
principle, uniform accounting
system

**state and municipal bond interest
income** 지방채의 수취이자
수입

state CPA society 주(州)회계사회

stated capital 1) 표시자본금 2) 법정자
본 ▶ legal capital

stated value 표기가격, 표기금액, (주식
의) 액면가액, 표시가격, 기재가
치 = face value

stated value of no-par stock 무액면
주식의 기재가액 ▶ par value

state governmental unit 주(州)정부

statement 1) 명세서, 조서(調書), 회계
보고서, 계산서, 일람표, 진술서,
재무표 2) 명령문

statement form 보고서 형식 = report

form, narrative form

statement of account 외상매출금 계산
서 ▶ invoice, sales invoice

statement of activity 활동보고서, 영업
보고서, 상황보고서

statement of affair 재산상태보고서,
상황보고서

statement of auditing procedure (SAP)
감사절차서
= codification of statement on
auditing procedure

statement of cash flow 현금흐름계산
서(보고서)

statement of change in capital 자본
증감보고서 ▶ statement of
changes in shareholder's equity

statement of change in equity 지분
변동보고서

**statement of change in fiduciary net
asset** 수탁순자산 변동보
고서

**statement of change in financial
position** 재무상태변동표
= financial position statement,
fund statement

statement of change in net asset 순
자산변동표, 자본변동 보고서

statement of change in net worth 순
자산변동 보고서, 자본변동 보
고서

**statement of change in shareholders'
equity** 주주지분변동보고서
= shareholder's equity,
statement of change in capital,
statement of stockholders'
equity, statement of
stockholders' investment,

statement of surplus

**statement of change in working
    capital**   운전자본변동표

statement of comprehensive income
    포괄이익계산서

statement of earnings   당기이익계산
    서, 이익계산서 ▶ income or
    earnings statement

**statement of earnings and
    comprehensive income**   이
    익 및 포괄적 이익 결합계산서

**statement of estimated application of
    fund**   추정자금운용표

statement of fiduciary net asset   수
    탁순자산보고서

**statement of financial accounting
    concept**   재무회계개념에
    관한 보고서

**statement of financial accounting
    concept(SFAC)**   재무회계
    제개념보고서 ▶ conceptual
    framework, financial
    accounting standards board,
    statement of financial
    accounting standards

**statement of financial accounting
    standard(SFAS)**   재무회
    계기준서

statement of financial activity   재무
    활동보고서

statement of financial condition   재무
    상태표, 대차대조표 = balance
    sheet, statement of financial
    position

statement of financial position   재무
    상태표, 대차대조표 = balance
    sheet, statement of financial

condition

statement of fund   자금계산서

statement of income   손익계산서
    = income statement, profit and
    loss account, profit and loss
    statement, statement of earnings

statement of intent(SOI)   (영)취지서

**Statement of International Accounting
    Standards(SIAS)**   국제회
    계기준서

**statement of investment by and
    distributions to owner**   주
    주지분 증감계산서

statement of loss   손익계산서

statement of net asset   순자산보고서

statement of operations   경영성과 계
    산서, 사업보고서 = income and
    expenditure account, statement
    of transaction

statement of partnership liquidation
    파트너십 청산 보고서

statement of position(SOP)   의견보고
    서, 상황보고

**statement of recommended practice
    (SORP)**   (영)회계실무권고
    서 ▶ explanatory foreword,
    statement of standard
    accounting practice

statement of resource and liability
    대차대조표 = balance sheet
    ▶ income statement

**statement of responsibility of the
    internal auditing**   내부 감
    사책임에 관한 보고서

statement of retained earnings   이익
    잉여금처분계산서

statement of social demographic

statistics(SSDS)   사회, 인구 통계보고서

statement of source and application of fund   자금운용표 = source and application of fund statement, source and disposition statement

statement of standard accounting Practice(SSAP)   (영)회계 실무기준, 회계기준
  ▶ explanatory foreword, statement of intent, statement of recommended practice

statement of stockholder's equity   주 주지분계산서

statement of surplus   잉여금계산서

statement of the responsibility of the internal auditor   내부감사 인 책임에 대한 보고서

statement of transactions   거래보고서 = income and expenditure account, statement of operation

statement of transaction with owner   주주(株主)지분 증감계산서

statement of variation in profit   이익 증감분석표

statement on auditing procedure(SAP)   감사절차서 ▶ statement of auditing standards

statement on auditing standard(SAS)   감사기준서

statement on management accounting (SMA)   관리회계기준서

statement on quality control standard   품질관리기준서 ▶ peer review

statement on responsibility in tax practice   조세업무책임에 관한 기준서

statement on standard for accounting and review service (SSARS)   회계 및 검토업무에 대한 기준 서

statement on standard for accounting practice(SSAP)   회계실무 기준서, 회계기준서

statement on standard for attestation engagement(SSAE)   입증 업무에 관한 기준서

statement on standard for consulting or consulting service(SSCC)   자문 및 자문서비스에 관한 기 준서

state probability   상태확률 = absolute probability

state statute   주법(州法)

static budget   고정예산 = fixed budget, period budget

static dump   정적(靜的) 덤프

static ratio   정태비율

static standard cost   정태적 표준원가 = basic standard cost

statistical analysis   통계적 분석

statistical decision theory   통계적 의 사결정이론 ▶ decision theory

statistical estimation   통계적 추정

statistical quality control(SQC)   통계 적 품질관리

statistical sampling   통계적 표본조사
  ▶ sampling, sampling testing

statistical sampling method   통계적 표본조사 방법

statistical table   통계표

statistical test   통계적 검정(檢定)

statistical test of random number   난

S

수의 통계적 검정

statistics   통계자료

status inquiry   거래은행에의 질문
▶ audit technique

statute   제정(制定)법

statute of fraud   사기방지법, 서면계약
성

**statute of fraud, applicability of
insurance**   사기방지법의
적용

statute of limitation   소멸시효, 소송
제기 기한법

**statute of limitation for breach of
contract**   계약위반에 대한
소멸시효

statutory accountant   (영)법정회계사
= authorised auditor
▶ chartered accountant

statutory accounting principle   법정
회계원칙 ▶ state and local
governmental accounting

statutory audit   법정감사 ▶ audit of
financial statement

statutory auditor   법정감사인

statutory authority   법적 권한

statutory books   법적 장부

statutory consolidation   법적 합병
= statutory merger
▶ acquisition, business

statutory depletion   법정감모상각
= percentage depletion ▶ cost
depletion

statutory instrument(SI)   (영)위탁입
법집, 정부명령

statutory lien   제정법상의 선취특권,
성문법상의 담보권

statutory limitation   법적 제한

statutory merger   법적 합병 = statutory
consolidation ▶ acquisition,
business combination, merger,
pooling of interest, purchase

statutory reporting requirement   강
제적 보고요구사항
▶ Regulation S-X, security
and exchange commission

statutory sick pay(SSP)   (영)법정질병
휴가수당

statutory spendthrift   성문법상의 낭
비방지

step budget   변동예산 탄력성예산
= flexible budget, variable
budget ▶ fixed budget, static
budget

step-by-step operation   단계별명령조
작 = single step operation

step cost   단계원가, 단계비 = step
function cost, stepped cost
▶ semi-fixed cost

step-down allocation method   단계식
배부법 = sequential allocation
method, step ladder distribution
method, step ladder method
▶ direct allocation, reciprocal
allocationstep ladder
distribution method

step function cost   단계비, 단계원가
= step cost, stepped cost

step ladder sheet   단계식 배부법

step method   단계배분법

stepped cost   단계비, 단계원가 = semi-
fixed cost, step cost, step
function cost, stepped fixed cost

stepped fixed cost   준고정비 = semi-
fixed cost, step cost, stepped

cost

stepping stone method   운송모형의 최적화해법을 발견하는 기법

stepwise refinement   단계적 상세서
▶ structured design

sterling   1) 영국통화 2) 순은(純銀)제품

sterling area   (영)스털링 지역
= scheduled territory

sterling bloc   (영)스털링 지역
= scheduled territory

steward   수탁자

stewardship   1) 수탁책임 2) (재산)관리

stewardship accountability   수탁회계 책임

stochastic inventory model   통계적 재고모델

stochastic simulation   통계적 모의실험

stock   1) 주식, 지분 = share 2) 주권(株券) 3) 저량 ▶ flow 4) 재고자산 (영) = inventory

stock acquisition   주식의 취득

stock appreciation right (SAR)   주식 평가차익에 따른 보상, 주가연동보수

stock at par   액면주 = par value stock, stock with par value ▶ non par stock

stock award plan   주식보상제도

stock based compensation   주식에 근거한 보수

stock broker   (영)주식중매인
= security broker ▶ Big Bang, jobber

stock card   상품재고표

stock certificate   주권(株券)

stock certificate book   주권대장

stock compensation   주식 등을 사용한 보상제도

stock compensation under fair value approach SFAS 123   공정 가치접근법에 의한 주식 등을 사용한 보상

stock control   재고관리

stock conversion   주식의 전환

stock cover   (영)스톡 커버

stock dividend of appraisal increment   평가익의 주식배당

stock dividend yield   주식의 배당율

stock dividend   주식배당

stock exchange   1) 증권거래소 2) 영국의 증권거래소(SE)
▶ admission of security to listing, unlisted security market, yellow book 3) 주식 교환

stock exchange listing   증권거래소의 상장

stock exchange unlisted security market   (영)증권거래소내 비상장증권시장 ▶ admission of securities to listing, yellow book

stock exhaust   품절 = stock-out

stock fund   주식투자신탁 ▶ bond fund

stockholder   주주(株主) = shareholder

stockholder list   주주명부

stockholder listing   주주명부

stockholder of record   등록주주, 주주 명부에 기재된 주주
= shareholder of record

stockholder's equity   주주지분
= shareholder's equity

stockholder's interest   주주지분
= capital, capital stock, shareholder's equity,

stockholder's equity
stockholder's meeting　주주총회
　　= shareholder's meeting
stockholders' equity　주주지분
stockholders' liability　주주의 책임
stockholders' right　주주의 권리
stockholder's voting right　주주의결권
stockholding cost　(영)보관비
　　= inventory carrying cost
stock in hand　재고품 ▶ stock, stock
　　in trade
stock in trade　재고품, 재고상품, 재고
　　제품 ▶ stock, stock in hand
stock in transit　미착상품, 미착품, 미달
　　상품, 미달품
stock issuance cost　신주발행비 = share
　　issue expense, stock issue
　　expense
stock issue cost　주식발행비
stock issue expense　신주발행비
stock jobber　주식중매인 = brokerage
　　firm, jobber, stock broker
stock ledger　1) 상품원장 2) 주식대장,
　　주식원장 = stock record
stock manipulation　주식조작, 주가조작
stock market　주식시장
stock option　스톡옵션, 주식 매입 선택
　　권 = share option, stock
　　purchase plan
stock option right　주식매입선택권
stock order　(영)재고보충을 위한 제조
　　지시서 ▶ production order,
　　stores order
stock-out　품절 = stock exhaust
stock-out cost　재고품절원가
stock ownership plans for employees
　　종업원을 위한 주식소유제도

stock premium　주식발행초과금, 액면
　　초과액 ▶ stock discount
stock price　주가(株價) = stock
　　quotation
stock price index　주가지수
stock purchase plan　주식구입(선택)권
　　제도 = stock option plan
stock purchase treated as asset
　　acquisition　자산취득으로
　　간주된 주식매입
stock purchase warrant　주식매입권
　　= warrant
stock quotation　주가(株價) = stock
　　price
stock recapitalization　주식재(再)자본
　　화
stock record　주식대장, 주식원장
　　= stock ledger
stock redemption　주식상환
stock register　주주명부
stock repurchase　주식재매입
　　▶ treasury stock
stock right　신주인수권, 주식매수권
　　= preemptive right, share right
stocks and work in progress　(영)재
　　고자산, 재고품과 재공품
　　▶ inventory
stock split　주식분할 = stock split-up
stock split-down　주식병합 = share
　　split-down ▶ stock split, stock
　　split-up
stock split-up　주식분할 = stock split
stock subscription　주식청약, 주식의
　　인수
stock taking　(영)재고자산 = inventory
stock transfer　주식명의개서
stock transfer agent　주식명의개서 대

리인

stock transfer book　주주명부

stock turnover　(영)재고자산회전율,
　　상품회전율 = inventory
　　turnover, rate of stock turn

stock valuation　주식의 평가

stock warrant　신주인수권

stock with par value　액면주 = par
　　value stock

stock yield　주식배당율

stolen bill　도난 어음

stolen check　도난 수표

stolen note　도난 어음

stop element　중지요소

stop instruction　정지명령

stop-or-go sampling　단속적 표본조사

stop payment order　지불정지명령

stopping delivery　인도 종료

storage cost　보관비 = inventory
　　carrying cost

store-and-forward mode　축적교환 형
　　태

stores　원재료

stores-in-out-book　재료 수불장

stores ledger　재료원장 = material
　　ledger

stores order　재고 보충을 위한 제조지
　　시서 = stock order

STR(standard total rate)　표준배부율

straddle　스트라들, 양건(兩建)

straight bankruptcy　협의의 파산 절
　　차

straight line(SL) amortization method
　　정액상각법

straight line capitalization　직선식 수
　　익환원법 ▶ capitalization rate,
　　direct capitalization

straight line depreciation　정액법, 직
　　선법 = equal-installment
　　depreciation, straight-line
　　method

straight line method　정액법 = straight
　　line depreciation ▶ declining
　　balance method, fixed
　　installment method, sum-of-
　　the-years-digits method

straight piece rate plan　단순생산량급
　　제 = straight piece work plan

straight piece work plan　단순생산량
　　급제 = straight piece rate plan

straight piece work system　단순생산
　　량급제 = straight piece rate
　　plan

straight salary system　고정급(固定給)
　　제

strategic investment　전략적 투자

strategic planning　전략계획
　　　　▶ management control,
　　operational control

strategy of market segmentation　시
　　장세분화전략

stratified　층화된

stratified random sampling　층화무작
　　위표본조사

stratified sampling　층화표본조사

stratigraphic test　층위 시추
　　　　▶ development type
　　stratigraphic test well,
　　exploratory type stratigraphic
　　test well

street paper　길거리 어음, 거리 어음

strict liability　엄격한 책임, 절대책임

strike price　행사가격 = striking price

striking out　삭제

S

striking price 행사가격 = strike price
▶ option

string 열(列), 연계, 기호열

striping 횡선

stroke 스트로크, 건반을 치다

stroke centerline 스트로크 중심선

stroke edge 스트로크의 가장자리

stroke width 스트로크 폭

strong box 보호예수금고

strong efficient market 강형 효율적
시장 ▶ efficient market

strong room 금고실

structure expression 구조식

structure member 구조체의 구성요소

stub (수표책의) 떼어 주고 남은 쪽

stub period 잔존기간

Student distribution 스튜던트의 T-분
포 = T-distribution

Student test T-분포검증 = T-test

**study and evaluation of internal
control system** 내부통제
조직의 조사와 평가
▶ compliance test, test of
control, test of compliance

sub agent 부 대리인

sub assembly production order 부수
제조지시서 = sub production
order ▶ production order

subassignment 재양도

sub branch 출장소, 지점

Subchapter S corporation 세입법 제
1장 S호 규정 적용회사
▶ small business corporation

subclassification 세분류(細分類)

subconsolidation (영)하위기업집단간
의 연결

subcontractor 하청업자, 하청계약자

sub group (영)하위기업집단, 하위그룹
▶ ultimate holding company,
ultimate parent company

subjective acceleration clause 주관적
가속조항

subjective income 주관적 이익
= economic income

subjective probability 주관적 확률

subjective value 주관적 가치
▶ objective value

subjectivity (in accounting) (회계에서)
주관성 ▶ audit function

subject matter 주제

subject to 한정된

subject to opinion 조건부 한정의견,
유보사항부 한정의견
▶ except opinion, uncertainty

sublease 전대(轉貸)

submartingale process 서브마팅글 과
정 ▶ martingale process

subordinated debenture 노후채권

subordinated loan 노후대출금 ▶ loan

subordinate ledger 보조원장
= subsidiary ledger
▶ subsidiary register

subpopulation (통계의) 부분모집단

sub production order 부수 제조지시서
= sub assembly production order

subrogation 대위변제(代位辨濟)

subscript 첨자(添字)

subscription (주식의) 신청, 주식의 청약

subscription basis 청약기준

subscription income 예약판매수익

subscription revenue 선수구매료 수익

subscription right 신주인수권

subscription warrant 신주인수권증서

subsequent bona fide purchaser 이

후의 선의의 구매자

subsequent cash receipt　기말 이후의
현금수취

**subsequent discovery of fact existing
at report date**　보고서일에
존재하는 사실을 그 이후에 발
견

subsequent event　후속사건, 후발사건,
대차대조표일 이후의 사건
= non-adjusting event,
post balance sheet event

sub servant　피고용인에 의해 고용된 자

subset　부분집합

subsidiary　자회사, 종속회사
= subsidiary company

subsidiary book　보조장부 ▶ main
book, subsidiary book of entry,
subsidiary ledger

subsidiary book of entry　보조기입장
▶ main book, subsidiary book,
subsidiary ledger

subsidiary company　자(子)회사, 종속
회사 = subsidiary ▶ dependent
company, parent company

subsidiary department　보조부문
= auxiliary department, service
department

subsidiary ledger　보조원장 ▶ main
book, subsidiary book,
subsidiary book of entry

subsidiary material　보조재료

subsidiary material cost　보조재료비
▶ subsidiary material

subsidiary register　보조기입장
▶ subordinate ledger

subsidy　보조금, 조성금, 교부금
▶ grant, subvention

substance over form　실질우선주의,
형식보다 실질, 실질우선성

substantial authoritative support　실
질적인 권위에 의한 지지
▶ generally accepted
accounting principle

substantial disposition of asset　실질
적인 자산처분

substantial doubt　중대한 의심

substantially all　실질적으로 모든

substantial performance　실질적 이행

substantial performance rule　실질적
이행규칙

substantial tender　실질적 제공

substantive law　실체법

substantive plan　실질적 급부제도

substantive test　입증시사
▶ compliance test

substitute contract　대용계약

substitute for consideration　대가의
대체물

substitute of money　금전의 대체물

sub-subsidiary　손(孫)회사

subtask　서브태스크

subtracter　감산(減算)기

subtraction method　공제법, 차감법

subtrahend　감수(減數) = minuend

subvention　보조금, 조성금, 기부금
▶ grant, subsidy

successful effort approach　성공 노력법

successful effort method　성공노력방
법 ▶ full costing method,
reserve recognition accounting

successive assignment　이중양도

successor　상속인, 후임, 후계자

successor auditor　후임감사인

sufficient relevant data　충분한 관련

정보

suffix notation　접미표시법 = postfix
　　　notation, reverse Polish notation

suit　소(訴), 소송, 청원(請願)

sum　합계, 총계

summarized financial information
　　　요약재무정보

summarizing account　집합계정
　　　= summary account

summary account　집합계정
　　　= summarizing account

summary budget　총괄예산 = master
　　　budget

summary controlling account　총괄
　　　통제계정

summary control report　총괄통제보
　　　고서

summary judgment　약식판결

summary of daily cash balances　일별
　　　현금잔액요약표

summary of earnings　소액총괄표

summary of material used　재료비 집
　　　계표 = material summary

summary posting　합계전기 ▶ unit
　　　posting

summary statement of business　사업
　　　설명서 ▶ annual report to
　　　stockholders

summation check　합계검사

sum-of-the-years-digit method　연수
　　　합계법, 급수법, 등차급수법
　　　▶ declining balance method,
　　　straightline method

sum-of-the-years' digit(SYD) method
　　　연수합계법

sum total　1) 총계, 총액 2) 전 체 3) 요
　　　지(要旨)

sundry　1) 제구좌 2) 잡비, 잡품

sundry asset　잡자산 ▶ other assets

sundry income　잡수입

sundry loss　잡손실

sunk cost　매몰원가, 무관련원가
　　　▶ irrelevant cost, special cost
　　　study

superficy　지상(地上)권 ▶ surface right

Superfund Act　환경보호 기금법

supermajority　재적주식의 2/3 이상

**super negotiable order of withdrawal
　　　(super NOW)**　수퍼 양도가능
　　　인출증서

super profit　초과이윤

supervening illegality　부차적 위법성

supervision　지도감독

supervision requirement　감독요구
　　　사항

supervisor　1) 감시프로그램
　　　= executive program,
　　　supervisory program 2) 감독자,
　　　관리자

supervisor state　감시프로그램 상태

supervisory program　감시프로그램
　　　= supervisor, executive program

supervisory routine　감시 루틴

supplemental actuarial value　보조적
　　　인 보험계산가치

supplementary budget　추가예산, 보
　　　충예산

supplementary disclosure　보충적 공
　　　시

supplementary evidence　보충증거

supplementary explanation　보충적
　　　설명사항 ▶ subsequent event

supplementary financial information
　　　보충적 재무정보

supplementary information   보충적
정보 ▶ unaudited financial
information

**supplementary information required
by FASB or GASB**
FASB 혹은 GASB가 요구하는
보충정보

supplementary rate   보충률

supplementary schedule   보충적 명세
서, 부속명세서 ▶ primary
financial statement, schedule

supplementary statement   보충명세서

supplier   매입처

supplier's credit   공급자의 신용
▶ buyer's credit

supply   1) 공급, 공급품, 보급품, 소모품,
저장품 2) (pl.) (정부의) 세입(歲
入), 세출(歲出) 3) 개인의 지출
4) 대리

supply and demand   수요와 공급

supply curve   공급곡선

supply price   공급가액

supply service   (영)당년도 세출(歲出)

supply used   저장품 소비액

support   부양

support cost center   보조원가중심점

supporting document   부속서류

supporting schedule   부속명세서

supreme court   최고재판소

surcharge   지역권을 벗어난 이용

surety   보증(인), 저당, 인수인

surety bond   보증서

surety promise   보증계약

suretyship   보증, 보증관계

suretyship contract   보증계약

surface right   지상(地上)권 ▶ superficy

surplus   잉여금

surplus analysis   잉여금분석
= analysis of surplus

surplus at beginning of the period
기초잉여금

surplus from capital reduction   감자
차익 = paid-in capital from
reduction in par of outstanding
shares

surplus from consolidation   연결잉여금

surplus from reduction of capital stock
감자차익

surprised audit   불시(不時)감사 = non-
pre-notice audit

surprise rejection rule   사전통지 없이
물품수령을 거절할 수 있는 규
정

surrender   1) 권리의 포기, 권리의 인도
2) 항복 3) (보험의) 해약

surrender charge   해약료, 해약공제금

surrendering company   (영)그룹세액
공제 대체회사 ▶ group relief

surrender of bill   어음의 인도

surrender value   (영)해약환급금, 해약
반환금 ▶ cash surrender value

surrogate   대리, 대리인 ▶ principal

surrogate court   유언법정

surrogate measure   대체적 측정치

surtax   부가세, 소득세 특별부가세, 누
진부가세

surveyor   1) 감정인, 평가인 = appraiser,
valuer 2) 검사관

surveyor of customs   세관(稅關)검사관

survival condition   생존조건

surviving spouse   생존해 있는 배우자

suspended trading   미결제거래

suspense account   가계정, 미결산계정
▶ suspense payment, suspense

receipt
suspense payment 가지급금, 가인도금
▶ suspense receipt
suspense receipt 가수금(假受金)
▶ suspense account
suspension of payment 지불정지
swap 스왑, 바꾸다, 교환하다
▶ currency swap, interest rate swap
swapping 스와핑, 교환
sweeping out method 일소법
sweetner 전환촉진비
switching 1) 교환, 교환접속 2) 바뀌침
SYD(sum-of-the-years-digit) method
연수합계법
symbol 기호(記號)
symmetric matrix 대칭행렬
syndicate 1) (채권, 주식의) 인수조합, 인수은행단 2) 신문사, 통신사의 신디케이트 3) 조직폭력단 연합 4) (대학의) 평의원회
syndication fees 협조융자수수료
synergism 합동효과 = synergy
synergy 시너지, 상승
syntax 통어론, 구문법

synthetic instrument 복합(금융)상품
system analysis 시스템분석
systematic and rational allocation 체계적이며 합리적인 배분
systematic risk 체계적 위험
▶ diversifiable risk, unsystematic risk
systematic sampling 체계적 표본조사
system audit 시스템감사
system control audit review file
(SCARF) 시스템 통제감사 검토파일
system design 시스템설계 ▶ system life cycle
system development life cycle 시스템 개발주기 ▶ life cycle
system flowchart 시스템 흐름도표
system of account 계정조직
system of accounting book 장부조직
system of national sccount(SNA)
국민계정체계, 국민경제계산체계
system of social and demographic statistics(SSDS) 사회, 인구통계체계

T

table 시산표, 표 ▶ subscript
Table A (영)A표
table element 1) 표의 요소 2) 테이블 요소
table method 실사법
tablet 평판, 명판, 표식

table type of variable budget 다행식 변동예산, 실사법 변동예산 = columnar type of variable budget ▶ formula type of variable budget
tabular ledger 표식예산 ▶ Boston

ledger

tabular type of variable budget 다행식 변동예산 = columnar type of variable budget ▶ fixed budget, flexible budget, variable budget

tabulator 도표작성장치

TAC(total actual material cost) [표준원가계산] 실제 재료비 총액

T-account T자형 계정 = skeleton form, T-form

Taft-Hartley Act 태프트·하틀리 법

tag 1) 가격표 = price tag 2) 키 = key, label 3) 화물 명찰형식의 표

tainting 오류율, 오염율

take or pay contract 인취보증계약

take-over 매수, 기업취득, 지배(소유)권의 취득 = acquisition

take-over bid(TOB) 주식공개매입 = tender offer

taking 결합, 부가

taking of physical possession 물리적인 점유의 취득

tandem award 직렬식 제도

tangible and movable property 유형동산

tangible asset 유형(고정)자산

tangible collateral 유형담보물

tangible fixed asset 유형고정자산

tangible net worth 유형자기자본, 유형순자산 ▶ net worth

tangible personal property 유형동산

target income 목표이익

target net income 목표순이익 ▶ target profit

target net income percentage of sales 매출에 대한 비율로 표시된 목표이익

target payout ratio 목표배당성향

target price 목표가격

target pricing 목표가격결정

target profit 목표이익 ▶ target net income

target ratio of profit to capital 목표자본이익률

tariff 1) 관세(표), 세율(표) 2) 요금(표), 운임표, 요율

TARR(time adjusted rate of return) 시간조정이익률

task 태스크, 과업

task force 전문위원회

task queue 업무대기

taxable entity 과세주체

taxable exchange 과세대상 교환

taxable goods 과세물품, 과세대상

taxable income 과세소득

taxable person (영)부가가치세 대상 (물품)의 공급자 ▶ taxable supply

taxable supply (영)부가가치세 대상 물품 ▶ taxable person

taxable temporary differences 과세대상 일시적 차이

taxable year of partnership 파트너십의 과세대상기간

tax accountant (영)세무회계사, 세리사 (稅理士)

tax accounting method 세무회계 방법 ▶ cash basis, accrual basis, installment method, percentage of completion method

Tax Adviser 미국 공인회계사협회 (AICPA)발행 조세전문 월간지

tax allocation 세금의 기간배분(처리) ▶ allocation of tax expense, inter period tax allocation

tax assessment　조세의 사정(査定)

taxation　1) 과세(課稅), 징세(徵稅), 세제
(稅制) ▶ ability theory of
taxation 2) 세수(稅收)

taxation of source　원천과세

taxation on capital gain　자본이득 과
세

tax avoidance　(합법적 수단의) 조세회피,
절세 ▶ tax planning

tax bearer　조세부담자, 납세자 = tax
payer

tax benefit　세의 경감액

tax benefit rule　세금이익규정

tax carryback and carryforward　결
손금의 소급과 이월, 세금의 환
급과 이월

tax computation　세금 계산

tax consequence　세(稅)효과

tax convention　조세 조약, 국제조세 조
약 = tax treaty

tax credit　세액공제, 세금공제

tax deductible　손금산입항목

tax deferred tax　조세유예세

tax effect　세효과(稅效果) ▶ inter period
tax allocation, tax allocation,
tax effect accounting, timing
difference

tax effect accounting　세효과 회계
▶ accounting for income tax

Taxes Management Act 1970(TMA 1970)
(영)1970년 조세관리법

taxes paid　세금지급

TAXES-The Tax Magazine
Commerce Clearing House, Inc.
(CCH)에서 발행한 조세 전문지,
1923년 창간의 월간지

tax evasion　탈세(脫稅) ▶ tax avoidance,
tax saving

tax exempt　면세, 무세 = tax free

tax exempt bond　면세채권
▶ industrial revenue bond,
revenue bond, tax exempt
security

tax exempt borrowing　비과세 차입금

tax exempt organization　세금면제
조직

tax exempt security　면세증권, 면세
채권 ▶ tax exempt bond

tax expense　법인세비용 ▶ tax
saving

tax free　면세 = tax exempt

tax haven　조세회피국, 조세피난처
▶ offshore fund

tax holiday　면세기간

tax individual　개인소득세

taxing authority　세무당국

tax law　세법(稅法)

tax lien　세금 담보권

tax loss　세무상의 차손금

tax loss benefit　세공제 효익

tax on business　기업과세

tax paradise　조세천국 = tax haven,
tax shelter

tax payable　미지급법인세

tax payer　납세자 ▶ taxpayer

taxpayer　납세자(納稅者) ▶ tax payer

taxpayer penalty　납세자 벌금

tax planning　조세계획, 절세계획, 조세
회피

tax planning strategy　세(稅)계획전략

tax point　(영)(부가가치세의) 과세시기

tax practitioner　세무대행 등을 행하는
회계사, 세무사

▶ tax accountant

tax preparation fee   세무신고 수수료
tax procedure   세무절차
tax rate   세율(稅率)
tax rate schedule   과세율표
tax recoverable   미수환급세액
tax refund   세금차환
tax refund receivable   세금차환 수취
계정
tax relief   면세, 세액공제
tax return   세무신고서, 납세신고서
tax return position   세무 신고시의 상
태
tax saving   1)절세(節稅) ▶ tax avoidance,
tax evasion 2) 법인세 등의 경
감액 ▶ tax expense
tax selling   과세회피 목적의 채권매각
= wash sale
tax service   세무 업무
tax shelter   세금피난수단 ▶ tax haven,
tax paradise
tax sparing credit   면세외국세액공제,
외국세액공제
tax table   과세표
tax treaty   조세조약 = tax convention
tax year   (영)세무연도, 회계연도
= fiscal year, year of assessment
▶ income tax
Taylor's expansion   테일러의 전개
TB(Technical Bulletins)   적용지침
TB(treasury bill)   미국재무성의 단기
증권, (영)대장성 증권
T/B(trial balance)   시산표(試算表)
**TBAC(Test of Basic Accounting
Competence)**   (영)기초적 회
계능력시험
T-bond   T-본드 = treasury bond

▶ treasury bill, treasury note
T.C. (traveler's check)   여행자 수표
t-distribution   t-분포 = student
distribution
teacher   연구자
technical analysis   기술적 분석
▶ fundamental analysis
technical bulletin   기술공보
Technical Bulletins(TB)   (FASB의) 적
용지침, 전문적 공보
technical coefficient   기술계수
Technical Release(TR)   (영)지침서, 안
내서 ▶ Guidance Note
technical standard   기술수준
technological feasibility   기술상의 실
행가능성
telecommunication   원격통신, 전기통
신
teletypewriter exchange service(TWX)
텔레타이프 교환서비스
teller   현금출납계, 은행의 현금출납창구
▶ ATM
teller's check   한 은행이 다른 은행을
지급인으로 한 수표
temporal method   (외화환산법의) 잠정
계산법 ▶ closing rate method,
current-non-current method,
foreign currency financial
statements, monetary-non-
monetary method
temporarily restricted   일시적 사용제
한
temporarily restricted net asset   일시
사용제한 순자산
▶ permanently restricted net
asset
temporary accommodation   가설 건축

물

temporary difference 일시적 차이

temporary injunction 일시적 중지명
령 ▶ interlocutory injunction

temporary investment 단기투자
▶ long-term investment,
marketable security

temporary lay-off 일시해고, 일시귀휴
= lay-off

temporary payment 가지급금, 가인도
금 = suspense payment
▶ suspense account

temporary perfection 일시적 완성

temporary storage 일시기억구역

tenancy 부동산권

tenancy at sufferance 묵시적 허용 하
에서의 임차, 인정한 부동산 임
차권, 용인한 부동산권

tenancy at will 임의 부동산 임차권, 임
의종료 부동산권

tenancy by the entirety 부부(夫婦) 전
부보유 부동산권

tenancy for a term 정기 부동산 임차
권

tenancy for years 정기 부동산권, 기한
부 임차권, 정기 부동산 임차권

tenancy from month to mouth 월간
부동산 임차권

tenancy from period to period 자동
갱신 부동산 임차권

tenancy from year to year 연간 부동
산 임차권

tenancy in common 협의(協議)의 공유,
공유 부동산권

tenancy in partnership 파트너십 재산
권

tenant 임차인

tenant right 소작권, 차지권, 차용권

tendency 경향, 동향, 성향

tender 1) 입찰, 제출, 제공 2) (회사지배
목적의) 주식매입, 공개매입
3) (화해의) 신청 4) (채무의) 변제

tender bond 입찰보증금, 입찰보증서
= bid bond

tenderer 입찰자, 신청인

tender guarantee 입찰보증금, 입찰보
증서 = bid bond

tender of delivery 인도(引度)의 제공

tender offer 1) 주식의 공개매입
= take-over bid 2) 주식 공개매
입 제의

tender offeror 공개매수신청서

tender offer statement 공개매수보고서

tender of payment 대금지불의 제공

tender of performance 이행의 제공

Tenth Circuit Court of Appeals
제10회 연방항소재판소

ten year summary 10년간의 업적요약

term 1) 기한, 기간, 임기, 학기 2) 용어
3) (pl.)조건, 요금, 약정, 관계
4) 항(項)

term bond 일괄상환채권 ▶ callable
bond, noncallable bond

terminable annuity 1) 기한부 연금공채
▶ consols, funded debt,
unfunded debt, treasury bill
2) 기한부 연금

terminal 이용자 단말기, 단말기 = user
terminal

terminal date 결산일, 기말일 = closing
date

terminal funding 퇴직시 일괄적립방
식 ▶ retirement benefit plan

terminal value 종가(終價)

termination 1) 종료, 만료 2) 한계, 말단 3) 결과

termination benefit 퇴직급부

termination of estate or trust 유산 또는 신탁의 종료

termination of leases 임대의 종결

termination of offer 신청의 종료, 청약의 소멸

termination of principal 대리의 소멸

termination of trust 신탁의 소멸

termination rate 한계율

termination statement 종료보고서

terminology 전문용어

term life insurance 정기생명보험, 정기사망보험

term loan 기한부 대출

term of payment 지급기한, 지불기간

term of years absolute (영)절대 정기 부동산권 = leasehold

term structure of interest rates 이자율의 기간구조, 금리의 기간구조 ▶ yield curve

terra 흙, 토지

territory 1) 지역 2) 영토, 영지 3) 수비구역, 분야

test 검사, 시험 = test check, test checking, testing ▶ study and evaluation of internal control system

testability 검증가능성 ▶ maintainability

testament 1) 유언, 유서 2) (유형의) 증거, (신념 또는 신조의) 표명

testamentary capacity 유언능력

testamentary gift 유증(遺贈)

testamentary trust 유언(遺言) 신탁

testate 유언, 유언된 유산

testator 남성 유언자

testatrix 여성 유언자

test board 시험반(盤)

test check 조사, 검토 = test

test checking 시험검사 = test

test count 시험적 계산

test data 시험자료, 모의자료

test data method 시험자료법

test for goodness of fit 적합도 검정(檢定) = goodness-of-fit test

testing 시험검사 = test

test marketing testability 시장(市場) 실험 ▶ desk research

Test of Basic Accounting Competence (TBAC) (영)기초적 회계능력시험

test of compliance 준거시사 = compliance test, test of control ▶ study and evaluation of internal control system, substantive test

test of control 통제시사, 내부통제의 시사 ▶ assertion, internal control structure

test of detail 상세시사

test of detail of transaction 거래에 관한 상세한 시사

test of detail of transaction and balance 거래 및 잔액에 관한 상세한 시사, 거래 및 재고의 세부적 테스트

test statistic 검증통계량

text 텍스트, 본문

text retrieval software 텍스트 검색 소프트웨어

T Form T형 양식 = skeleton form, T-account

The Auditing Standards Executive Committee(ASEC) 감사기준 집행위원회

The Committee on Auditing Procedure (CAP) 감사절차위원회

The Emergency Planning and Community Right to Know Act 위험물질과 독극물을 소유하는 사람과 기업은 주정부에 사실을 통지해야 한다는법

The Financial Reporting Model Prior to The Adoption of GASB 34 GASB 34조 채택 이전의 재무보고 모델

theft 절도

the hierarchy of accounting quality 회계정보를 유용하게 하는 특성의 계층구조

The New Government Reporting Model 새로운 정부보고기준

theorem of total probability 총체 확률의 정리

theoretical capacity 이론적 조업도, 이론적 생산능력 ▶ maximum capacity

theoretical ex-rights price 이론상의 권리락된 주가(株價)

theoretical standard cost 이론적 표준원가 ▶ standard cost

theory of congestion 폭주(輻輳)의 이론

theory of game 게임이론 ▶ decision theory

theory of normal burden 제조간접비 정상배부 이론 ▶ normal burden rate

the pooling of interest criteria 지분 풀링법으로 처리하기 위한 요건

The Pregnancy Discrimination Act 임신부(姙娠婦)고용차별금지법

therblig 동작연구에서 과업을 수행하는 동작의 유형을 기술하는 용어

The Securities and Exchange Commission 증권거래위원회

The Supreme Court 연방 대법원

thin film 박막, 얇은 필름

thing in action 무체동산, 채권 = chose in action

thing in possession 유체재산 = chose in possession ▶ thing in action

thin market 한산한 시장, 불활발한 시장 = narrow market

third party beneficiary 제3수익자

third party beneficiary contract 제3자를 위한 수익자 계약, 제3자 수혜인 계약

third party claimant 제3자 담보권

third party PMM 제3자 저당권

third party security 담보부증권

third quarter 3사분기

third standard of field work 세 번째 실시기준

three column cash book 3행식 현금출납장

three party instrument 제3자 교부증서

three point estimation 3점 측정법

three way analysis (표준원가계산) 3분법

three way overhead analysis 3분법에 의한 제조간접비 차이분석 ▶ overhead variance, two way overhead analysis

threshold 1) 논리한계 (연산자) 2) 경계점

threshold element 논리한계연산소자

threshold for recognition 인식의 경계수준 ▶ materiality

through-put 처리시간, 처리량

through-put agreement 생산량보증계약

throughput contract 생산량보증계약

ticker 1) (주식의) 시세표시기 2) 시계 3) 심장

ticket 전표

tick mark 꺾자(∨) 표시

tick mark legend 꺾자표시의 설명

tied loan 타이드 론 ▶ debtor-creditor agreement, debtor-creditor-supplier agreement

till float 통화유통량 = cash float

timber financing 입목(立木)자원금융

time adjusted rate of return(TARR) 시간조정이익률 = internal rate of return (IRR)

time adjusted return method 시간조정이익률법

time bill 정기지불환(약속)어음 = draft at a tenor

time card 작업시간표, 작업시간보고서 = time ticket

time clerk 시간기록계

time clock card 출근표

time control method 시간제어방식

time deposit 저축성예금, 정기예금

time difference 일시적 차이

time discounting (어음의) 기간할인

time draft 일람 후 정기지불환어음, 정기지급어음, 날짜 후 정기지불어음

time factor 시간적 요소, 시간적 제약

time for performance 이행기일

time instrument 확정기일 지불증권

timekeeper 시간기록계, 작업시간계 ▶ time record

time keeping machine 계시기(計時機)

timeliness 적시(適時)성

timeliness of evidential matter 증거의 적시성

time loan 정기대출금

time of sale 판매시점

time period concept 회계기간의 개념 = convention of periodicity, periodical concept, time period principle ▶ accounting convention, accounting period, accounting postulate

timer 계시기구 = clock register, time register

time rate 시간급, 시간임률 = timework rate

time rate system 시간급제, 시간지불임금제도

time record 시간기록 ▶ timekeeper

time recorder 시간기록기

time restriction 시기제한

time series data 시계열자료

times fixed charge 이자보상비율, 이자보전배율 ▶ fixed charge coverage

time sharing 1) 시간공용방식 2) 시간분할

time sharing interest 일정기간 거주권

time sheet (영)작업시간표, 작업시간보고서 = time ticket

times interest covered (영)지불이자부담능력배율, 이자보상율

= interest cover, interest coverage ratio, times interest earned ratio

times interest earned ratio　지불이자 부담능력배율, 이자보상율
= times interest covered

time slicing　시간분할

time span　시간대, 기간

time study　시간연구 ▶ motion study

time summary　시간요약

time ticket　작업시간표, 작업시간 보고서 = daily time ticket, job card, job sheet, job ticket, job time card, job time ticket, labor time ticket, operation card, operation time card, time card, time sheet, work ticket

time value　시간적 가치

time value of money　화폐의 시간가치

time value of money factor(TVMF)　시간을 고려한 화폐가치

timework　시간급노동 = daywork

time worked　작업시간

time worker　시간급노동자

timework rate　시간급(時間給), 시간임율 = time rate

timing difference　일시적 차이
▶ permanent difference, tax effect accounting, interperiod tax allocation

timing of audit procedure　감사절차의 실시시기

tips　1) 예상, 조언, 암시　2) 비결

title　소유권, 권리의 원인, 권원(權原)

Title 7 of the Civil Right Act of 1964
1964년 공민권법 제7장

title covenant　소유권 보증조항

title insurance　소유권 보험, 보험의 권원, 부동산의 소유권에 하자가 있는 경우 손해를 보전하는 보험

title insurance enterprise　소유권 보험업자

title of account　계정과목명

title of goods　상품의 권원

title plant　소유권 플랜트

title retention　소유권 유보

title search　소유권 조사

title transfer　소유권의 이전

title transfer to lessee by end of term
리스기간 종료시 소유권의 이전

TMA 1970(Taxes Management Act 1970)
(영) 1970년 조세관리법

T-note　재무성 발행증권 = treasury note
▶ treasury bill, treasury bond

TOB(take-over bid)　주식공개매입
= tender offer

to hold indefinitely　영구보유

token chose　(예금 증서, 통장, 증권 증서) 권리를 구체화한 증서

token consideration　완전한 가치가 없는 것

tolerable deviation rate　허용이탈율, 허용오류율 = tolerable rate of deviation

tolerable error　허용오류율

tolerable misstatement　허용가능한 왜곡표시, 허용왜곡표시

tolerable rate　허용비율

tolerable rate of deviation　허용이탈율 = tolerable deviation rate

tombstone advertisement　묘비 광고
= tombstone ad.

tool order　공구지시서

top-down   상의하달방식

top-down design   탑다운 설계

top-down type budget   상의하달방식 예산 ▶ bottom-up type budget

top line   경상이익 ▶ above the line, below the line, bottom line

top management   최고경영자

tort   불법행위, 개인범죄

tort liability   불법행위 책임

tort of employee   피고용자의 불법행위

total   합계, 총액, 합계수치, 합계액

total account   통제계정 = control account

total actual material cost(TAC)   (표준원가계산) 실제 재료비 총액

total amount   총액

total approach   (표준원가계산) 총액법

total asset   총자산

total asset employed   사용총자산

total asset turnover   총자산회전율, 총자본회전율

total budgeted factory overhead   제조간접비 총액예산

total cost   총원가, 총코스트

total costing   전부원가계산 = absorption costing, full costing

total economic life   총 경제적 내용 연수 ▶ effective age, depreciation, physical age

total estimated cost   추정총원가

total float   전체 여유

total income   1) 총소득, 총수입 2) (소득세법상의) 개인의 총소득

total liability   부채합계

total loss   총손실

totally hold subsidiary   완전소유 자회사 = wholly owned subsidiary

    ▶ majority owned company, majority owned subsidiary

total manufacturing cost   총제조원가

total mix   전체의 조합

total present value   총현재가치, 현재가치총계

total quality management(TQM)   전사적 품질관리

total sales   총매출액

total standard material cost(TSC)   표준재료비총액

total standard production cost   표준제조원가총액

total standard profit   표준이익총액

totten trust   토튼 신탁

touch and concern the land   토지 자체와 관련된

Toxic Substance Control Act(TSCA)   유독물관리법

TQM(total quality managrment)   전사적 품질관리

T/R(technical release)   (영)지침서, 안내서 ▶ guidance note

traceability   연락(連絡)성 ▶ software requirement specification

traceable cost   추적가능원가, 추적가능비, 개별비용 ▶ controllable cost

traceable fixed cost   추적가능고정비 ▶ direct fixed cost

trace program   추적 프로그램

trade   1) 거래, 매매, 교역, 상업 2) 교환 3) 부정거래 4) 직업 5) 동업자 6) 고객, 매출처

trade acceptance   (판매자 발행의) 자기앞 환어음, 수출어음인수

trade account payable   매입채무

T

trade association   상공(商工)단체

trade channel   무역경로 = distribution channel

trade credit   기업간 신용

trade creditor   (영)1) 외상매입금 = trade payable 2) 매입처

trade debt   매입채무

trade debtor   (영)1) 외상매출금 = trade receivable 2) 매출처

trade discount   업자(業者)할인(割引), 중간할인

trade fixture   업무용 정착물, 상업 정착물

trade fixture exception   업무용 정착물 예외

trade in   1) 보상판매 교환품, 교환의 2) 교환 평가액

trade in allowance   교환품 가액

trade investment   관련회사에의 투자

trademark   상표(商標)

trade name   1) 상호 2) 상품명

trade note payable   영업상의 지급어음

trade-off   1) 상충관계 이율배반(二律背反)성 2) 거래, 교환, 협정, 흥정, 트레이드 오프
   ▶ trading-off

trade paper   업계(業界)신문, 업계 소식지

trade payable   매입채무, 외상매입금 = trade creditor

trade price   업자간 가격, 도매가격

trade receivable   매출채권, 외상매출금 = trade debtor

trade reference   신용조회처

trade secret   영업비밀, 기업비밀

trade secret law   거래기밀법

trade term   무역조건, 매매계약조건

trade union   (영)노동조합 = labor union

trading   단기매매목적

trading account   (영)1) 매출총이익 계산구분 2) 매출총손익계정, 상품매매손익계정 3) 매매계정, 영업계정

trading and profit and loss account
   1) 손익계산서 = income statement 2) (원장의) 손익계정 = profit and loss account

trading corporation   상사회사(商事會社), 무역회사, 상사(商社)

trading method   상품매매 손익계정 마감법

trading-off   상충관계 교환, 흥정
   ▶ trade-off

trading on the equity   [자금조달 방법] 보통주의 거래 ▶ financial leverage, gearing, leverage

trading profit   영업이익

trading security   단기매매목적 유가증권

trading stamp   상품인환증지

traditional costing system   [ABC]전통적 원가계산

traffic   통신량

traffic law   교통법규

training and proficiency   훈련 및 숙련

training expense   훈련비

transaction   거래

transaction-based system   거래기초 시스템

transaction cost   거래비용

transaction cycle   거래 사이클

transaction date   거래일, 거래의 발생 시점

transaction file   거래파일

▷ master file

transaction gain or loss   거래이득 또는 손실, 환차손익 ▷ exchange gain or loss,translation gain or loss

transaction in property   재산의 거래

transaction matrix   거래 행렬

transaction related cost driver   [ABC] 거래와 관련된 원가동인 (예 :구입관련 비용을 발생시키는 구입거래 건수) ▷ 조업도와 관련된 원가동인 (volume related cost driver, 예 :수선비를 발생시키는 기계운전시간)

transaction service   거래 서비스

transaction tagging   거래부표

transaction with controlled partnership   지배 파트너십과의 거래

transcription   전기(轉記)

transfer   1) 이전(移轉), 배치전환 2) (재산상의 권리) 양도, (명의의) 개서 3) 양도증서 4) 전송 = move

transferability   양도가능성

transferability of interest   지분의 양도 가능성

transfer between category   투자분류의 변경, 보유목적을 변경한 경우의 처리

transfer between partners   파트너 간의 거래

transfer between spouses   배우자 사이의 양도

transfer check   전송체크, 전송검사

transfer day   명의개서일

transferee   어음양수인, 피개서인

transfer fee   대체요금, (프로야구 선수에

대한) 이적료

transfer in process costing   공정 완료품의 이전

transfer of financial asset   재무자산의 이전

transfer of receivable   수취채권 이전

transfer of title   소유권의 이전

transfer of warranty   양도담보책임

transferor   양도인, 명의개서인

transfer payment   이전지출, (정부의) 사회보장부담금

transfer price   (내부)대체가격 ▷ decentralization

transfer pricing   (내부)대체가격의 결정, 이전가격 결정 ▷ internal pricing, intra-company transfer pricing

transfer risk   외화거래에 따른 결제위험

transfer time   전송시간

transfer to a controlled corporation (Sec 351)   지배법인으로의 양도

transfer transaction   대체거래

transfer variance   대체차이

transfer warranty   이전보증

transform   변형(變形)

transient area   일시적 구역, 비상주 구역

transient routine   일시적 루틴, 비상주 루틴

transit   1) 통과, 진행, 추이(推移) 2) 전송, 통로

transition   변환, 추이, 변위(變位)

transition probability   추이확률

translate   번역하다

translater   번역 프로그램 = translator, translating program

▶ assembler, compiler

translate/restate method 선환산 후수
정방식, 환산후 수정방식
▶ current cost/constant
purchasing power accounting,
restate/translate method

translating program 번역 프로그램
= translater, translator
▶ assembler, compiler

translation 환산(換算) ▶ functional
currency

translation adjustment 환산조정액,
환산조정 계정

translation gain or loss 환산차손익
▶ exchange gain or loss,
transaction gain or loss

translation obligation(asset) 경과채
무(자산)

translation of foreign currency 외화
환산

**translation of foreign currency
financial statement** 외화
표시 재무제표의 환산

**translation of foreign currency
statement** US$이외로 쓰
여진 재무제표를 US$로 환산
하기

**translation of foreign currency
transaction** 외화표시 채권
채무를 US$로 환산하기

translation table 변환 테이블

translator 1) 번역 프로그램 = translater,
translating program
▶ assembler, compiler 2) 번역
기구

transmission 1) 전송, 송신 2) 트랜스
미션 3) 송금

transmittal letter 송장

transport 운송

transportation in 운임, 운임도착지급
= carriage in, carriage inward,
freight in ▶ carriage out,
carriage outward, distribution
cost, freight out

transportation out 발송운임, 발송비
= carriage outward, freight out
▶ transportation in, freight in

transportation problem 운송형 문제

transposed matrix 전치행렬

transposition 바꾸어놓음, 전위, 전환법

transshipment problem 옮겨 쌓는 문제

trap 트랩, 함정

traveler's check(T.C.) 여행자수표

Treadway Commission 트레드웨이
위원회

treasurer 1) 재무부장, 경리부장 2) 주
(州) 또는 시(市)의 수입(收入)직
원

treasury 1) 출납(出納)소(所), 회계국 2)
금고 3) 금고 안에 있는 자금

treasury bill(TB) 1) 재무성 단기증권
▶ treasury bond, treasury note
2) (영)대장성 증권

Treasury Board (영) 대장성위원회

treasury bond 1) 대장성 장기증권
▶ treasury bill, treasury note
2) 자기사채

Treasury Department 재무성

treasury lord (영)대장성위원회 위원

treasury note 1) 재무성 중기증권
▶ treasury bill, treasury bond
2) 법정 지폐

treasury stock 자기주식, 금고(金庫) 주
(株), 자사주

treasury stock method (to test dilutiveness)　자기주식법

treasury stock subterfuge　자기주식에 준하는 방법 ▶ watered stock

treasury stock transaction　자기주식 거래

Treasury tax-anticipation bill　재무성 납세준비금 증서

treatment of complex trust and beneficiary　복합신탁과 수익자의 처리

treatment of simple trust and beneficiary　단순신탁과 수익자의 처리

treaty　조약, 조약문, 취결

tree structure　목조구조, 수목구조 ▶ list structure

trend　동향, 경향, 경향선, 유행

trend analysis　추세분석 ▶ trend method, trend ratio, trend report

trend method　추세법 ▶ trend analysis, trend ratio, trend report

trend ratio　추세비율 ▶ trend analysis, trend method, trend report

trend report　추세보고서 ▶ trend analysis, trend method, trend ratio

trespass　불법침해

trespasser　불법침해자

trial　배심(陪審)

trial balance(T/B)　시산표 ▶ trial balance of balances, trial balance of totals, trial balance of totals and balances

trial balance equation　시산표등식

trial balance of balances　잔액시산표 ▶ trial balance, trial balance of totals, trial balance of totals and balances

trial balance of totals　합계시산표 ▶ trial balance, trial balance of balances, trial balance of totals and balances

trial balance of totals and balances　합계잔액시산표 ▶ trial balance, trial balance of balances, trial balance of totals

trial piece　시매품(試賣品)

trial process　배심과정

trigger　1) 방아쇠 2) (분쟁 등의) 계기, 유인, 자극

triple precision　3배 정도 ▶ double precision, single precision

troubled debt　불량채무

troubled debt restructuring　불량채무의 재조정

trouble debt　불량채권 = bad debt

troubleshoot　1) 조정자의 역할을 하다, 2) 장애제거

trover　불법행위자에 대한 손해배상 청구권

true and correct view　(영)진실하고 정확한 개관(槪觀)

true and fair view　(영)진실하고 공정한 개관

Trueblood Committee　트루블러드 위원회 ▶ conceptual framework project, Wheat Committee

Trueblood Report　트루블러드 보고서

true complement　실제 보수(補數)

true reserve　실제준비금(적립금)

truncation (of a computation process)　(계산처리의) 절삭, 중단

truncation error　절삭오류

trunk 중계경로, 트렁크, 간선(幹線)

trust 신탁

trust account 신탁재산, 신탁계정

trust accounting 신탁업회계

trust cash fund account 금전신탁계정

trust certificate 신탁수익증권

trust corpus 신탁재산

trust deed 신탁증서 = deed of trust

trustee 1) 신탁의 수탁자, 피신탁자, 위탁자 2) 관재인(管財人), 이사(理事)
▶ trustee in bankruptcy

trustee accounting 재산관리인의 회계기록

trustee as a lien creditor 유치권자로서의 파산신탁인

trustee in bankruptcy 파산관재인 = trustee

trustee of trust 신탁의 수탁인

trustee savings bank (영)신탁저축은행

trust estate 신탁재산

trust indenture 신탁증서

trust property 신탁재산

trust purpose 신탁목적

truth 1) (회계사의) 진실, 진실성 2) 사실, 진상, 현실

Truth in Lending Act(TLA) 대부신탁법

TSCA(Toxic Substance Control Act) 유독물질관리법

t-test t-검정, t-분포검증

turnaround document 턴어라운드 서류, (방침, 태도의) 전환문서

turning point 분기점, 전환점

turnout 1) 생산량, 생산액 2) 집합, 출석자(수) 3) 분기점

turnover 1) (영) 매출액 = sales 2) 회전율 3) 생산고, 수확량 = volume

turnover of asset 자산회전율

= asset turnover ratio

turnover of capital 자본회전율
= capital turnover, turnover rate of capital

turnover of current asset 유동자산회전율 = current asset turnover

turnover of gross and net working capital 총운전자본과 순운전자본회전율

turnover of inventory 재고자산회전율
= inventory turnover, rate of stock turnover, stock turnover

turnover of net working capital 순운전자본회전율

turnover of net worth 자기자본회전율

turnover of payables 미지급계정회전율, 매입채무회전율

turnover of receivables 매출채권회전율, 수취계정회전율
= receivables turnover ratio

turnover of total capital 총자본회전율

turnover of total capital employed 사용총자본회전율

turnover of total liability and net worth 총자본회전율 = turnover of total capital

turnover of total operating asset 영업자본회전율

turnover period 회전(回轉)기간

turnover rate 회전율

turnover rate of capital 자본회전율
= capital turnover, turnover of capital

turnover ratio 회전비율 ▶ account receivable turnover ratio, inventory turnover ratio

t-value t-값

TVMF(time value of money factor)　시간을 고려한 화폐가치

two-bin system　이중창고 시스템, 정량발주제도 = constant order, constant order quantity system, last-bag system, quantity system ▶ reorder point

two-input adder　반(半)가산기, 2입력가산기 = half-adder

two sided test　양측검정 ▶ one sided test

two stage sampling　2단계 표본추출법

two to one principle　2대 1의 원칙 = two to one rule ▶ current ratio

two to one rule　2대 1의 원칙 = two to one principle

two transaction perspective　두 개 거래관점 ▶ one transaction perspective

two way account　상호계정

two way alternate communication　양방향 교차통신 = either way communication ▶ both way communication

two way analysis　(표준원가계산) 2분법

two way layout　이원배치(법)

two way overhead analysis　이분법에 의한 제조간접비 차이분석 ▶ overhead variance, three way overhead analysis

two-way simultaneous communication　양방향 동시통신 = both way communication

TWX(teletypewriter exchange service)　텔레타이프 교환서비스

TX　조세부담책임에 관한 기준서

type　종(種)

type I error　제1종 오류

type II error　제2종 오류, 베타위험

type I risk　제1종 위험, 알파위험, 제1종의 오류를 범할 확률 ▶ beta risk

type II risk　제2종 위험, 제2종의 오류를 범할 확률 = beta risk

type of agent　대리인의 종류

type of contract　계약의 종류

type of corporation　법인의 종류

type of leasehold　임차권의 종류

type of organization　조직 유형

type of principal　본인의 종류

type of trust　신탁의 종류

U

UBI(unrelated business income)　비관련 사업소득

UCC(Uniform Commercial Code)　통일상사법전

UCC Act.　통일상사법

UCC Article　통일상사법 규정, 조항

UCCC(Uniform Consumer Credit Code)　통일소비자신용법

UCCR(Uniform Commercial code Rules)　통일상사법전

UDC(Universal Decimal Classification)
(도서의) 국제십진분류법

UDUPA(Uniform Disposition off Unclimed Property Act) 권리주장자 재산의 처분에 관한 통일법

UEC(Union Europeenne des Experts Comptables Economiques et Financiers) 유럽회계사연합

UFCA(Uniform Fraudulent Conveyance Act) 통일 사해적 양도법

ULPA(Uniform Limited Partnership Act) 통일 유한책임 파트너십법

ULS(unsecured loan stock) 무담보사채, 원리보증이 필요없는 사채

ultimate holding company 궁극적인 지주회사, 최종적 지주회사 = ultimate parent company
▶ subgroup

ultimate parent company (영)궁극적인 지주회사, 최종적 지주회사 = ultimate holding company

ultra vires 권한 외(外), 권능 외 ▶ intra vires

ultra vires act 권한 외 행위

unabsorbed burden 제조간접비 배부부족액 = unabsorbed overhead

unabsorbed overhead 제조간접비 배부부족액 = unabsorbed burden, unapplied burden, unapplied overhead, under absorbed burden, under absorbed overhead, under applied burden, under applied overhead
▶ over absorbed overhead, over applied overhead

unadjusted audit difference 미수정된 감사상의 차이

unadjusted trial balance 수정전 잔액 시산표

unaffiliated revenue 외부수익, 즉 부문간의 거래를 포함하지 않는 금액

unallocated contract 불(不)분할계약

unallotted share (영)미할당주식
▶ allotted share, uncalled share capital

unallowable cost 허용불능원가
▶ allowable cost

unamortized cost 미상각원가

unanimous consent 전원일치, 만장일치

unapplied burden 제조간접비 배부부족액 = unabsorbed overhead

unapplied overhead 제조간접비 배부부족액 = unabsorbed overhead

unappropriated earned surplus 미처분이익잉여금 ▶ appropriated earned surplus

unappropriated RE (retained earings) 미처분이익잉여금

unary operation 단항연산 = monadic operation

unary operator 단항연산자 = monadic operator

unasserted claim 미청구 클레임

unasserted claim and assessment 주장하지 않는 청구금 및 부과금

unattended operation 부재(不在)시 조작, 조작원 부재의 통신처리

unaudited 감사받지 않은

unaudited financial information 감사받지 않은 재무정보
▶ supplementary information

unaudited statement 감사받지 않은

재무제표

unauthorized completion   무권한의
백지보증

unauthorized mean   미승인 매체

unauthorized signature   승인되지 않
은 서명

unauthorized sub-agent   미승인 부대
리인

unavailable time   사용불능시간

unavoidable cost   회피불능원가
= inescapable cost ▶ avoidable
cost, escapable cost

unavoidable fixed cost   회피불능고정
비 = inescapable fixed cost

unbalanced budget   불균형예산

unbiased estimator   불편추정량

unbiasedness   불편성(不偏性)

unbilled receivable   미청구채권

unbound book   비장정장부 ▶ bound
book

uncalled share capital   (영)불입 미청
구 주식자본 ▶ paid-up share
capital

uncertainty   1) 미확정사항 2) 불확실성

uncertificated stock   주식증서를 발행
하지 않는 주식

unclaimed paycheck   수취인 부재의
급료지급수표

unclaimed stock   실권주

unclassified balance sheet   무구분식
대차대조표 ▶ classified
balance sheet

unclean hand   부정한 반칙

uncollectible accounts   불량채권
= doubtful debt, doubtful
receivable

uncollectible receivable   회수불능 채

권, 불량채권 ▶ distressed loan

uncompensated   배상하지 않는

unconditional   무조건

unconditional order to pay   무조건
지불지시

unconditional promise   무조건 약속

unconditional promise to pay   무조건
지불약속

unconditional purchase obligation   무
조건의 구입계약

unconscionability   비(非)양심성

unconscionable contract   부당한 계
약, 비양심적 계약

unconsciousness   부당계약

unconsolidated subsidiary   비연결자
회사

uncontrollable capacity cost   통제불
능생산설비원가 ▶ capacity
cost, controllable capacity cost

uncontrollable cost   통제불능비, 통제
불능원가 = non-controllable
cost ▶ controllable cost

uncontrollable profit   통제불능이익

uncontrollable variance   통제불능차이

undefeasibly vested remainder   잔여
권 취득이 확실하고 그 지분에
있어서도 확정된 것

undefined record   명확한 양식이 없는
기록

undepreciated cost   미상각원가

under absorbed burden   제조간접비
배부부족액 = unabsorbed
overhead

under absorbed overhead   제조간접
비 배부부족액 = unabsorbed
overhead

under applied burden   제조간접비 배

부부족액 = unabsorbed
overhead

under applied overhead   제조간접비
배부부족액 = unabsorbed
overhead

under depreciation   과소(過小)상각
▶ depreciation, over
depreciation

under estimation   과소평가 ▶ over
estimation

underflow   (산술) 언더플로

underlying   기초가 되는 자산

underlying accounting data   기초 회
계자료 ▶ corroborating
evidence

underlying concept   기초적 개념

underlying evidence   기초적 증거
▶ corroborating evidence

understandability   1) 이해가능성
▶ user specific quality 2) 이해
성 ▶ maintainability

understanding   이해력

**understanding of the internal control
structure**   내부통제제도의
이해 ▶ accounting system,
control environment, control
procedure

understatement   1) 과소표시, 과소평가
▶ overstatement 2) 삼가서 말
함

undertaking   1) 청부(請負), 인수 2) 기
업, 사업, 업무, 직업 3)약속, 보
증

undervaluation   과소평가, (부당한) 싼
값

underwriter   증권인수회사, 증권회사,
인수업자 ▶ security

underwriter

underwriting   증권인수

underwriting agreement   증권인수 계
약 ▶ firm commitment, stand-
by agreement

underwriting syndicate   인수(引受)단
▶ underwriting

undisclosed principal   대리인이 서명
을 하면서 자기의 이름만 서명
하고 본인 이름을 감춘 경우

**undiscounted expected future cash
flow**   미할인 추정미래현금
흐름

undistributable reserve   배당불가능
적립금

undistributed income   미분배이익

undistributed profit   유보이익, 미처분
이익 = reserved profit, retained
earnings, retained surplus

undiversifiable risk   분산불가능위험
= market risk, systematic risk
▶ diversifiable risk, market
related risk, unsystematic risk

undivided interest   비분할 지분

undue influence   부당한 위압, 부당한
영향력

unearned finance income   선수 금융
소득 ▶ gross investment in the
lease, lease

unearned franchise fee   미경과 프랜
차이즈료, 선수 프랜차이즈료

unearned income   1) (영)불로소득, 투
자에 대한 소득 = investment
income 2) 선수수익

unearned interest   선수이자

unearned interest revenue   선수이자
수익

unearned premium   선수 보험료
unearned rent   선수임대료
unearned rent revenue   선수임대료
또는 선수로열티 수입
= deferred rental revenue
unearned service fee   선수서비스료
unemployment benefit   실업수당, 실업
연금, 실업혜택
▶ unemployment compensation
unemployment compensation   실업
보상, 실업수당, 실업보험금
▶ unemployment benefit
unemployment insurance   실업보험
unequivocal   명확하지 않은
unescapable cost   회피불능원가
= inescapable cost, unavoidable
cost ▶ avoidable cost, escapable
cost
uneven payment   (리스 초기단계에서) 금
액이 일정하지 않은 리스료
unexpected gain and loss   우발적 이
득과 손실 = contingent gain,
contingent loss ▶ contingency
unfavorable to surety   보증인에 불리
unfavorable variance   불리한 차이
unfunded accrued pension cost   기금
이 없는 미지급 연금비용
**unfunded accumulated benefit
obligation**   금액 미납입 누
적급부채무
unfunded debt   1) (영) 무기한부 국채
▶ funded debt, terminable
annuities   2) 단기차입금
unguaranteed residual value   무보증
잔존가액 ▶ leased asset
unified transfer tax   통합양도세
uniform accounting   통일회계

▶ approved methods for the
preparation of balance sheet
statement, verification of
financial statement
uniform accounting system   통일회계
제도 ▶ State and Local
Governmental Accounting
Uniform Capitalization Rules   통일
자본화 규정
uniform chart of accounts   통일계정
도표
Uniform Commercial Code(UCC)   통
일상사법전
Uniform Commecial Code Act.(UCCA)
통일상사법
**Uniform Commecial Code Article
(UCCA)**   통일상사법 규정,
조항
**Uniform Commercial Code Rules
(UCCR)**   통일상사법전
**Uniform Consumer Credit Code
(UCCC)**   통일소비자신용법
uniform cost accounting   통일원가계
산제도 = uniform cost
accounting system
uniform cost accounting system   통일
원가계산제도
= uniform cost accounting,
uniform cost plan, uniform cost
system
uniform cost plan   통일원가계산제도
= uniform cost accounting
system
uniform cost system   통일원가계산제
도 = uniform cost accounting
system
Uniform Disposition of Unclaimed

Property Act(UDUPA) 권리 주장자 재산의 처분에 관한 통일법

uniform distribution 균등분포

Uniform Fraudulent Conveyance Act (UFCA) 통일 사해적 양도법

uniformity 통일성 ▶ conformity

Uniform Limited Partnership Act (ULPA) 통일 유한책임 파트너십법

Uniform Partnership Act(UPA) 통일 파트너십법

Uniform Principal and Income Act (UPIA) 통일 본인과 수익법

uniform product 단일제품

uniform random number 단일 난수(亂數)

unilateral contract 일방 계약

unilateral mistake 일방적 실수

unilateral offer contract 일방청약·계약

unilateral or illusory promise 일방적 또는 가공의 약속

unilateral relief 국외 납부에 관한 이중과세구제책, 상호주의에 대한 면세

unilateral transaction 일방적 거래 ▶ bilateral transaction

unimodal 단일모델상태

unincorporated association 비(非)법인단체

union 1) 노동조합, 노동자가 조직하는 단체 2) 결합, 합동, 합병

Union Europeenne des Experts Comptables Economiques et Financiers(UEC) 유럽회계사연합

union shop 유니언 샵 ▶ closed shop, open shop

unique cost 단일의 원가

unissued capital stock 미발행주식, 미발행자본

unissued share 미발행주식

unissued share capital (영)미발행 주식자본 ▶ allotted share, issued capital

unissued stock 미발행주식 ▶ issued stock

unitary taxation 합산과세

unit contribution margin [CVP분석] unit CM, 단위당 공헌이익 ▶ segment margin

unit cost 단위당 원가, 단위원가

unit costing 단위당 원가계산

unit credit method 단위기금방식 ▶ projected benefit cost method, accrued benefit cost method

unit depletion charge 단위당 감모상각비

unit depreciation 개별상각 = individual depreciation ▶ composite depreciation, group depreciation

unit distribution 단위(單位)분포

United States of America Standards Institute(USASI) 미국 규격협회

United States trustee 연방관재인

unitholder 단위형 신탁의 수익자

uniting of interest (영)흡수합병 = merger ▶ acquisition

unit-in-place method 부분별 단가적 용법 ▶ comparative unit

method, cost approach, quantity survey method, reproduction cost

unit investment trust　단위형 투자신탁

unit matrix　단위행렬

unit of account　회계상의 측정단위
　　　▶ constant purchasing power unit, monetary unit

unit of constant purchasing power　항상 구매력단위

unit of measure　측정단위 = unit of measurement

unit of measurement　측정단위 = unit of measure

unit of money　화폐단위

unit of output method　[표준원가계산] 생산수량법

unit of production　생산량비례법

unit of production method　생산량비례법 = actively method, production method

unit of service method　생산량비례법 = productive output method, service hours method

unit posting　개별전기 ▶ summary posting

unit price　매매원가, 단가, 요금

unit pricing　1) 단위가격표시, 단위표시 2) 단위가격측정법 = functional pricing

unit standard operating profit　단위당 표준영업이익

unit standard production cost　단위당 표준제조원가

unit standard selling price　단위당 표준판매가

unit string　단위열, 단위연계, 단위스트

링

unit to break-even　[CVP분석] 손익분기점에서의 매출수량

unit trust　단위형 신탁, 단위형 투자신탁회사

unity of interest　동일권리

unity of ownership　소유권의 통일

unity of personality　부부(夫婦)일체의 원칙

unity of possession　공동소유

unity of time　동일시기

unity of title　동일한 권원

universal agent　총대리점(人), 전권 대리인

universal character set　범용(汎用) 문자코드

Universal Decimal Classification(UDC)　(도서 의) 국제십진분류법

universal defense　물적 항변

universe　모(母)집단

unjust enrichment　부당이득

unlawful act　불법적 행위

unlimited company　(영)무한책임회사

unlimited liability　무한책임

unlimited personal liability　무한정의 개인책임

unliquidated damage　불확정손해배상금 ▶ liquidated damage

unlisted company　비상장회사
　　　= unquoted company ▶ listed company, listed investment, quoted company, quoted investment

unlisted securities market(USM)　(영) 증권거래소내 비상장 증권시장

unlisted security　비상장유가증권
　　　= unquoted security ▶ listed

U

company, listing

unlisted stock   비상장주, 장외주식

unpaid balance for non-par stock   무
액면주식의 미지급잔고

unpaid voucher file   미지급전표철

unplanned or unanticipated variance
예상 외의 원가차이

unplanned variance   예상하지 않은 조
업도차이 ▶ planned variance

unpostponable cost   연기불능원가
▶ postponable cost

unprogrammed decision   비정형적 의
사결정 ▶ programmed decision

unprogrammed planning   비정형적
계획 ▶ programmed planning

unproved property   미확인 이권 광구
(鑛口)

unqualified certificate   적정의견 보고
서

unqualified opinion   적정의견

unqualified opinion report   적정의견
보고서 ▶ qualified opinion,
subject to opinion

**unqualified opinion with explanatory
language added to the
standard audit report**   표
준감사보고에 설명문이 추가된
무한정 의견

unqualified report   적정의견
▶ adverse opinion report

unquoted company   비상장회사
= unlisted company ▶ listing

unquoted investment   비상장유가증권

unquoted security   비상장증권
= unlisted security ▶ listed
company, listing

unrealized appreciation   미실현평가

익, 미실현증가액

unrealized cost saving   미실현원가 절
약 ▶ realized cost saving,
realized holding gain or loss

unrealized gain   미실현이득

**unrealized gain on holding debt
security**   채무증권 미실현 보
유이익

unrealized gain or loss   미실현손익

unrealized holding gain   미실현보유
이익 ▶ realized holding gain

**unrealized holding gain and loss on
available-for-sale securities**
판매가능 유가증권의 미실현보
유손익

unrealized holding gain or loss   미실
현보유손익

unrealized income   미실현이익

unrealized loss   미실현손실

**unrealized loss on holding debt
security**   채무증권의 미실현
보유손실

**unrealized loss on holding equity
security**   지분증권의 미실현
보유손실

unrealized profit   미실현이익
▶ realized profit

unrecognized firm commitment
인식되지 않은 확정계약

unrecognized net gain or loss   미인식
순손익

**unrecognized net obligation · asset at
date of initial application**
처음 적용시 인식되지 않은 순
채무(자산)

unrecognized prior service cost   미인
식 과거근무원가

unrecognized transition obligation
(**asset**) 미인식 경과채무(자산)

unrecognized transition obligation
(**average remaining service**
period) 미인식 경과채무
(평균잔여 근무기간)

unrecorded liability 부외 부채

unrecorded retirement 기록되지 않
은 유형자산제각

unrecoverable error 회복불능인 실수

unrecovered cost 회수불능원가

unregistered company 비등기회사

unregistered debenture 비등록사채

unregistered stock 비등록주(株)
= letter stock

unrelated business income(UBI) 비관
련사업소득

unrestricted 제약이 없는

unrestricted net asset 제약이 없는 순
자산

unrestricted net nonrecurring gain
and loss 제약이 없는 비반
복적 순이득과 손실

unrestricted revenues and expense
제약 없는 수익과 비용

unrestricted security 양도자유 유가
증권

unsecured bond 무담보채권
= unsecured cliam

unsecured claim 무담보채권
= unsecured bond

unsecured creditor 무담보채권자

unsecured debt 무담보채무

unsecured loan stock(ULS) 무담보
사채, 원리보증사채

unsecured nonpriority claim 무담보
비(非)우선채권

unsecured priority claim 무담보 우
선채권

unsophisticated investor 정보에 정통
하지 않은 투자자
▶ sophisticated investor

unsystematic risk 비체계적 위험
▶ diversifiable risk, portfolio,
systematic risk

unusual circumstance requiring a
departure from
promulgated accounting
principle GAAP로부터의
이탈이 정당화되는 상황

unusual gain and loss 비경상적 손익

unusual item 비경상적 항목

unusual nature 비경상적 성격

unusual profit or loss item 비경상적
손익항목

unwarranted innovation 정당하다고
인정할 수 없는 혁신

UPA(Uniform Partnership ACT) 통일
파트너십법

updated report 최신 보고서

UPIA(Uniform Principal and Income Act)
통일 본인과 수익법

upper deviation limit 이탈율의 상한
= upper occurrence limit,
achieved upper precision limit

upper limit on misstatement 왜곡표
시의 상한(上限)

upper occurence limit 상한(上限) 이탈
율

upstream 자회사가 모회사에 판매하는
경우 ▶ intercompany profit

up-stream 자회사가 모회사에의 판매
= upstream ▶ intercompany
profit

U

uptime　작동가능시간, 사용가능시간
　　= operable time ▶ down time
usability　사용(使用)성
usage rate　재고품출고율
usage variance　[표준원가계산] 소비량
　　차이
usance　실습기간, 지불기간, (수출입환의)
　　기한
usance L/C　인수조건부 신용장
　　= acceptance credit
**USASI(United States of America
　　Standards Institute)**　미국 규
　　격협회
useful economic life　경제적 내용연수
　　= economic service life
　　▶ physical life
useful life　내용연수 = depreciable life,
　　durable years, service life
　　▶ useful economic life
usefulness　유용성 ▶ relevance
use of estimate　추정의 사용
use of fund　자금의 용도 = application
　　of fund
user　사용자, 정보이용자
user cost　사용자비용

user oriented accounting　이용자중심
　　회계
user specific quality　정보이용자의 고
　　유 특성 ▶ understand ability
user terminal　이용자단말기 = terminal
U.S. general accounting office　미국
　　회계검사원
U.S. government security　미국국채
using up　소비(消費)
USM(unlisted securities markets)　(영)증권
　　거래소내 비상장증권시장
U.S. obligation　미국인의 의무
usury　1) 고리(高利), 폭리(暴利) 2) 고리
　　(高利)대(貸)
utility　1) 유익, 유용, 효용 ▶ marginal
　　utility 2) 공익사업, 공공시설
　　= public utility
utility control　동력비통제
utility cost center　동력원가중심점
utility function　효용함수
utility rate　공공요금
utility theory　효용이론
utilization cost　활동원가
utilization variance　조업도차이
　　= capacity variance

V

VA(valuation allowance)　평가성 충당금
VA(value analysis)　가치분석
vacation and holiday pay　휴가수당
vacation pay　유급휴가수당, 휴가비
valid　유효, 유효한
valid consideration　유효한 대가

validity　1) 타당성 2) 휴가수당
　　▶ correspondence,
　　representational faithfulness
validity check　타당성 검증
validity of contract　계약상의 유효
valid will　유효한 유언

valuation   1) 감정평가, 견적, 사정(査定)
　　　 2) 평가액, 사정액
valuation account   평가계정
　　　= absorption account, contra
　　　account, offset account
valuation allowance(VA)   평가성 충당
valuation at net realizable value (or
　　　valuation at market)   순실
　　　현가액법
valuation at relative sales value   상대
　　　적 판매가액에 의한 평가
valuation basis   평가기준
valuation convention   평가관습
valuation of security   유가증권의 평가
valuation or allocation   평가 또는 분배
valuation principle   평가의 원칙
valuation reserve   평가성 충당금
　　　= valuation allowance
value   1) 평가액, 가액, 금액 2) 가치, 중
　　　요성 3) (어음상의) 액면, 수치,
　　　등급 4) 값
value accounting   가치(價値)회계
　　　▶ current value accounting
value added   부가가치 = added value
value added activity   부가가치활동
value added analysis   부가가치분석
　　　▶ value added
value added cost   부가가치원가
value added network(VAN)   부가가치
　　　통신, 부가가치 네트워크
value added statement   부가가치계산
　　　서 = added value statement
value added tax(VAT)   부가가치세
　　　▶ value added
value analysis(VA)   가치분석
value approach   가치접근법 = value
　　　theory ▶ event approach,

　　　event   theory**value**
engineering   가치 엔지니어링
value in use   사용가치 ▶ economic
　　　value, net present value, present
　　　value, recoverable amount
value of information   정보가치
value of money   화폐가치 = purchasing
　　　power of money ▶ constant
　　　dollar accounting, constant
　　　purchasing power accounting
valuer   감정인, 평가인, 검사관
　　　= appraiser, surveyor
value received   대가수령
value theory   가치이론 = value approach
　　　▶ event theory
value to the business   기업에 대한 가
　　　치 ▶ current value accounting,
　　　deprival value
VAN(value added network)   부가가치
　　　통신, 부가가치 네트워크
variable   1) 변수 2) (프로그램의) 변수
variable and absorption costing   변동
　　　원가계산과 전부원가계산
variable annuity   변동연금 ▶ level
　　　annuity
variable budget   변동예산, 탄력성예산
　　　▶ fixed budget
variable budget with columnar form
　　　다행식 변동예산 = variable
　　　budget with tabular form
variable budget with tabular form   다
　　　행식 변동예산 = variable budget
　　　with columnar form
variable capital   변동자본 ▶ fixed
　　　capital
variable cost   변동비, 변동원가, 가변적
　　　비용 = activity cost,

V

proportional cost ▶ direct costing, fixed cost

variable costing　변동원가계산 = direct costing, marginal costing, variable cost system

variable cost of goods sold　변동매출원가

variable cost ratio　변동비율

variable cost system　변동원가계산 = direct costing, marginal costing, variable costing

variable factory overhead　변동제조간접비 = variable overhead cost, variable production overhead, variable production overhead cost ▶ fixed factory overhead

variable overhead cost　변동제조간접비 = variable factory overhead

variable point representation system　가변소수점표시법

variable production overhead　변동제조간접비 = variable factory overhead

variable production overhead cost　변동제조간접비 = variable factory overhead

variable sampling　변량표본조사, 변수표본조사

variable selling expense　변동판매비

variable stock option plan　유동적 주식구입선택권 제도, 유동적 스톡옵션 제도

variable symbol　가변기호

variance　1) 차이 2) 분산 ▶ standard deviation

variance accounting　차이분석회계

variance analysis　차이분석 금 = valuation reserve ▶ allowance, liability allowance, liability reserve, reserve

variate　확률변수 = random variable

variation from individual taxation　개인 과세와의 차이

variation margin　변동증거금

variation within population　모집단내의 분산

VAT(value added tax)　부가가치세 ▶ value added

vector generator　벡터발생기

vendee　매수주체, 매수인, 인수인

vender　팔 사람

vendor　판매주체, 판매인, 양도인

vendor invoice　판매업자 대금청구서

Venetian system of bookkeeping　베네치안식 부기

Venn diagram　벤 다이어그램

venture　1) 모험, 투기, 투기대상 2) 모험적 사업, 투기적 사업

venture business　벤처기업 ▶ venture capital

venture capital　벤처캐피탈, 모험자본 = risk capital ▶ spin-out, venture business

venture capital financing　벤처기업의 자금조달

verdict　평결(評訣)

verifiability　검증가능성 ▶ reliability, representational faithfulness

verifiable, objective evidence　검증가능한 객관적 증거

verification　검증

verification of balance　잔액 검증

verification of financial statement
재무제표의 검증 ▶ uniform accounting

verification of footing and posting
계산검증 ▶ audit technique

verification procedure 검증절차

verifier 1) 검사기구 2) 검공기(檢孔機), 천공검사기

vertical check 수직검사

vertical common size analysis 구성비율분석

vertical form 보고식 = report form, running form

vertical merger 수직적 합병 ▶ conglomerate merger, horizontal merger

vertical privity (법률) 당사자간의 수직적 상호관계

vertical testing 관련있는 자료를 대조하는 감사절차

very small workshop 영세공장 ▶ small workshop

vested 확정, 권리가 확정된

vested benefit 수급권 귀속이 확정된 급부 (수급권부 급부)

vested benefit information 수급권 귀속이 확정된 급부 정보

vested benefit obligation 확정급부형 채무

vested interest 확정적 권리, 기득(旣得)권익 ▶ contingent interest

vested remainder subject to open 부동산에 대한 장래의 이익을 취득하는 것은 확정되었지만 규모는 변동할 수 있는 것

vested remainder subject to total divestment 잔여권을 취득

하는 것이 확정되었지만, 이것이 어떠한 사유의 발생에 의하여 전면적으로 박탈될 수 있는 것

viability 실행가능성

Vietnam Era Veterans Readjustment Assistance Act 베트남전쟁 퇴역군인 재적음보조법

virtual address 가상(假想)주소

virtual machine 가상계산기

virtual storage 가상기억장치

visual fit 눈에 보이는 적합성

vocation 1) 직업, 상매매, 사명 2) 재능, 적성

Vocational Rehabilitation Act 직업적 갱생법

void 1) 쓸모 없는, (법) 무효, 무효의 2) 방출하다

voidability of insurance 보험의 무효성

voidable 취소가능한

voidable contract (영)취소가능한 계약

voidable title 취소가능한 소유권, 취소가능한 권원(權原)

void contract 취소계약

void title 무효인 권원(權原)

void voidable contract 무효취소 가능계약

volenti non fit injuria 동의하는 사람에게 해를 끼치지 않는다는 라틴어

volume 1) (직접원가계산) 생산량, 제조량, 조업도 2) 용량, 용적, 볼륨

volume discount 수량할인, 거액할인 = quantity discount

volume level 조업도(操業度) = activity level, operation level

volume of trading 매매량, 생산량, 수
확량

volume-related cost driver 조업도에
관련된 원가동인 (예 : 수선비를
발생시키는 기계운전시간) ▶ 거래
와 관련된 원가동인 (transaction
related cost driver, 예 : 구입 관련 비
용을 발생시키는 구입거래 건수)

volume table of contents(VTOC) 컨
텐츠의 목록

volume variance 조업도차이
= overhead volume variance
▶ marketing variance,
production variance, capacity
variance

voluntary audit 임의(任意)감사
▶ authorized audit

voluntary bankruptcy 자발적 파산,
자발적 해산

**voluntary health and welfare
organization** 자발적 보건
과 복지단체

voluntary liquidation 임의청산
= voluntary winding up

voluntary winding up (영)임의해산

= voluntary liquidation
▶ compulsory winding up

vote 1) 투표, 표결 2) 투표용지 3) 투표
권, 의결권 4) 득표, 투표수
5) 의결사항

voting agreement 투표계약

voting for 찬성투표

voting right 의결권, 의결권주(議決權株)

voting share 의결권부 주식, 의결권 비
율 = voting stock ▶ nonvoting
stock

voting stock 의결권부 주식 = voting
share ▶ nonvoting stock

voting trust 의결권신탁, 투표신탁, 의
결권 트러스트

voucher 거래증빙

voucher check register 증빙식 당좌
예금 지불장

voucher system 증빙식 제도

voucher trading 지급보증서를 이용
하는 소비자금융

vouching 증빙 대조

VTOC(volume table of contents) 컨텐
츠의 목록

W

WA(weightd average) 가중평균법, 총
평균법

wage 임금

wage and salary 임금과 급료

wage for idle time 유휴노동시간 임금
= wage for waiting time, wage

for waste time

wage for waiting time 유휴노동시간
임금 = wage for idle time

wage for waste time 유휴노동시간 임
금 = wage for idle time

wage index 임금지수 = index of wages

wage in kind 현물급여

wage rate 임률 = labor rate

wage rate variance 임률차이 = labor rate variance

wagering contract 도박계약

Wagner Act 와그너법

waiting period 대기(待期) 기간

waiting time 대기시간

waiting time pay 대기시간 급여

wait state 대기상태

waiver 포기

walk through 재추적법

WAR(weighted average rate) 가중평균환율

warehouse 창고, 도매점, 대형상점

warehouse certificate 창고증권

warehouse financing 창고수입

warehouseman 창고업자, 창고관리인

warehouse receipt 창고증권, 창고화물증권

warehouses, goods held in public 공공창고업자에 보관된 재고

warehouse stock 제품재고

warehousing 창고업

warehousing department 창고부문

war game 전쟁 게임, 탁상연습

warrant 워런트, 주식매수권, 신주인수권, 신주인수권(부) 증서 = stock warrant

warranty 1) 담보책임, 제품보증, 서약 2) 보증서, 담보 3) 영장(令狀), 명령서

warranty against infringement 권리 (상표권, 저작권 등) 침해에 대한 보증, 담보책임

warranty deed 1) 증서상의 담보책임 2) 권원(權原) 담보양도증서, 소유권 담보양도증서, 보증증서

warranty expense 제품보증비용

warranty liability 1) 담보책임, 보증책임 2) 제품보증충당금

warranty obligation 보증채무

warranty of fitness for a particular purpose 특별한 목적에 적합하다는 보증

warranty of marketable title 소유권 매매의 담보책임

warranty of merchantability 상품성의 보증

warranty of title 권원(權原)보증, 소유권의 보증, 소유권 담보책임

wash sale 1) 절세거래 = tax selling 2) 위시 세일, (미) 증권의 가장(假裝)매매, 경기를 돋우기 위한 자본손실을 일으키는 매매

waste 작업폐물 = scrap ▶ shrinkage

wasting asset 감모자산

watered stock 혼수(混水)주식, 액면가 이하로 발행된 주식 ▶ treasury stock subterfuge

water right 수리권(水利權), 용수권

WATS(Wide Area Telephone Service) 광역전화서비스

Watts Report (영)와트 리포트

waybill 화물인환증

WDA(writing down allowance) (영)연차상각 ▶ capital allowance, first-year allowance, initial allowance

weak efficient market 약형의 효율적 시장 ▶ strong efficient market

weakness test 내부통제의 결함점검

wealth maximization 부(富)의 극대화

web browser 웹 브라우저

web server　웹 서버

web trust　전자인증제도

weight　1) 가중, (통계)가중치, 비중　2) 중
요 = significance

weighted arithmetic mean　가중산술
평균

weighted average　가중평균 ▶ fungible
asset, weighted average price

weighted average(WA)　가중평균법,
총평균법

weighted average cost of capital,　가
중평균자본비용 ▶ cost of
capital

weighted average inventory method
평균법, 가중평균원가법

weighted average method　평균법, 가
중평균원가법 ▶ moving
average method

**weighted average number of common
shares outstanding**　가중
평균 사외유통주식수

weighted average price　가중평균가격
▶ fungible asset, weighted
average

weighted average rate(WAR)　가중
평균환율

weighted average share　가중평균주식
수

weighted geometric mean　가중기하
평균

welfare benefit plan　복지제도

welfare compensation　복리후생비

welfare compensation plan　복리후생
비제도

welfare expense　복리후생비

welfare to work credit　생활보호 세액
공제

Wheat Committee　Wheat위원회

Whistle blower Protection Act　내부
고발자보호법

white card　(영)화이트 카드 ▶ green
card

white knight　백마의 기사

White Paper　(영)정부(政府)백서(白書),
백서 ▶ Black Paper, Blue
Book, Green Paper

wholesale　도매(都賣)

wholesale price index(number)(WPI)
도매물가지수

wholesaler　도매업자, 대리점

whole statement　재무제표 전체

wholly owned subsidiary　완전소유자
회사 = totally hold subsidiary
▶ majority owned company,
majority owned subsidiary

wide area telephone service(WATS)
광역전화서비스

will　1) 유언, 유언서, 유언장 2)의사

willful wrongdoing　의도적인 부정

Williams Act　윌리엄스 법

Wilshire 5,000 equity index　Wilshire
5,000 주가지수

windfall profit　우발이익, 예상 외의 이
익

winding up　해산, 청산 = liquidation

winding up by the court　재판소에 의
한 청산, 법정청산
= compulsory winding up

winding up order　(영)(재판소의) 청산
명령

**winding up subject to the supervision
of the court**　(영)재판소 감
독 하에서 이루어지는 청산
▶ winding up by the court

winding up under supervision (영)재
판소 감독 하에서 이루어지는
청산 = winding up subject to
the supervision of the court

window dressing 분식결산(粉飾決算)
▶ creative accounting,
overstatement, understatement

WIP(work in process, work in progress)
재공품

with all fault 모든 과오가 있는

with cause 정당한 사유가 있는

with coupon price of bond 채권의 이
자를 포함한 시세

with dividend 배당부(付)

withdrawal (예탁물의) 인출

withdrawing partner 파트너의 탈퇴,
퇴직한 파트너

withholding delivery 인도(引度)) 보류

withholding tax 원천징수세(액), 원천
과세(액)

within course of employment 업무 집
행중

with interest (어음결제에서의) 이자부
(付)

within the scope of employment 고용
의 범위내

within class variance 계층내 분산

without cause 정당한 사유가 없는

without dividend 배당락(落) = ex
dividend

without par value stock 무액면주

without recourse 소구권이 없는

with the exception of opinion 제외사
항에 대한 감사의견 = except
of opinion

witness 증인

work center 작업중심점

worker' compensation 노동자 재해
보상, 산업재해 보상

workers' compensation 근로자 재해
보상

Workers' Compensation Act 산업
재해보상법, 근로자보상법, 노
동자 재해보상법

Workers' compensation insurance
노동자 재해보상보험

work factor method 웍 팩터 법

work file 작업용 파일

working 운동, 가동

working capital 운전자본 ▶ floating
capital

working capital ratio 운전자본회전율
= current ratio

working capital reserve 운전자본 준
비금

working capital turnover 운전자본회
전율

working expense 영업비 = operating
expense, overhead expense

working fund 운전자본

working hours method (감가상각의) 작
업시간비례법, 운전시간법

working paper 감사조서(調書)

**working rules of audit procedure in
reporting** 현행 감사보고
준칙

**working rules of audit procedure of
field work** 현행 감사실시
준칙

working sheet 정산표 = work sheet

working storage 작업용 기억구역

working trial balance 조서시산표

work in process(WIP) 재공품 = goods
in process, work on progress

▶ process costing, semifinished goods

work in process control account 재공품통제계정

work in process inventory 재공품
= work in process

work in process turnover 재공품회전율

work in progress(WIP) 재공품
= work in process

work measurement 작업측정

work opportunity credit 고용기회 세액공제

work order 제조지시서, 작업지시서
= production order

work paper file 감사조서 파일

work proceed 공사수익

work sampling 작업 샘플링

work sheet 정산(精算)표 = working sheet

work sheet elimination 정산표상 소거(消去) 분개 = cancellation table entry, elimination journal entry

work sheet for consolidation 연결정산표 ▶ consolidated balance sheet, consolidated financial statements, consolidated income statement

work sheet for statement of application of fund 자금운용표의 정산표

workshop 1) 공장, 작업장, 직장 2) 연구집회

work standard 작업표준 = operation standard

work ticket 작업시간표, 작업시간 보고서 = time ticket

world wide web(WWW) 월드와이드웹

worth 1) 재산, 자본 2) 가치(價値) 3) (일정금액에 상당하는) 분량

worthless stock and security 가치가 없는 주식과 증권

worth to debt ratio 자본부채비율

worth to fixed ratio 고정자본비율

WPI(wholesale price index) 도매물가지수

W/R 창고증권

write down 평가절하, 감액

write down or write off of asset 유형, 무형을 불문한 모든 자산의 상각손

write enable ring 기입허가 링, 기입가능 링 = file protection ring

write off 1) 소각(消却), 평가감, (채권의) 소각 2) 장부의 마감 3) (수리불능의) 장부상 제거

write off of account receivable 매출채권의 상각

writer of option 옵션의 판매자

write up 1) 평가증(增) 2) (상품을 소개하는) 호의적 기사

writing down allowance(WDA) (영)연차상각 ▶ capital allowance, first-year allowance, initial allowance

writing down inventory 재고자산의 감액

writ of attachment 압류영장

writ of execution 판결집행영장

writ of garnishment 채권압류

written assertion 문서화된 주장

written audit program 감사계획 = audit planning

written communication 문서

written confirmation between merchants   상인간의 계약에 적용되는 규칙

written down value   평가절하후의 가액 ▶ book value, depreciated value, net book value, net carrying amount

written law   성문법

written management representation   경영자 진술서, 경영자확인서

written plan   문서화된 제도

written stop order   서면 지급정지 명령

WRU(who-are-you?)   누구인가?

WWW(world wide web)   월드와이드웹

X

XC(ex coupon)   이자락

X chart   X관리도

XD(ex dividend)   배당락

XYZ analysis   (재고조사에서) XYZ분석 = ABC analysis

Y

Yankee bond   양키 본드

yard   1) 야드 2) 작업장, 직장 3) 지면

year-end   기말(期末)

year-end financial position   기말재무상태

year of assessment   (영)세액사정연도, 회계연도 = fiscal year, tax year ▶ income tax

Yellow Book   (영)옐로우 북, Goverment Auditing Standards의 별칭 ▶ Green Book

yellow card   (영)옐로우 카드

yen bond   엔화 채권

yield   1) 수율 (원료에 대한 제품 비율) 2) 이율 ▶ XC, XD, yield to maturity 3) 산출, 수확

yield adjustment   이자조정

yield curve   이율곡선 ▶ term structure of interest rates

yield percentage   수율 = yield ratio ▶ yield variance

yield rate   유효이율 ▶ capitalization rate, mortgage-equity capitalization

yield ratio   수율 = yield percentage ▶ yield variance

yield to maturity   만기이율 = maturity yield ▶ yield

yield variance   수율차이 = material yield variance ▶ yield

X

Y

Z

percentage

Z

ZBB(zero base budgeting)　영기준 예
　　산관리
zero base budgeting(ZBB)　영기준 예
　　산관리　▶ cost effectiveness
　　analysis, incremental budget,
　　ordinary incremental budget,
　　priority incremental budget
zero coupon bond　무이자채권
zero level address　제로 레벨 어드레스
　　= immediate address
zero rating　부가가치세의 비과세 판매,
영세율과세(부가가치세)
zero salvage value　제로 잔존가액
zero sum game　제로섬 게임
zero sum two persons game　제로섬
　　2인 게임
zero suppression　제로 억제, 제로 소거
　　(消去)
zoning　토지 용도지정
Z-transformation　(표준정규분포에서) Z
　　변수로 변환

한영편
Korean-English

ㄱ

가격　price
가격수준　price level
가격을 제시하다(사는 사람이)　bid
가격인상　markon, markup
가격인상률　markup percentage
가격인상 취소　markup cancellation
가격인하　markdown
가격인하 취소　markdown cancellation
가격지수　price index
가격지정주문　limit order
가격차이　price variance
가격 폭　spread
가계정　suspense account
가공비　conversion cost
가공이익　paper profit
가득(稼得)이익　earned income,
　　　earnings
가맹권(加盟權)　franchise
가변적 비용　variable cost
가속상각(법)　accelerated depreciation
가속상각제도　accelerated cost
　　　recovery system(ACRS)
가속원가회수제도　accelerated cost
　　　recovery system(ACRS)
가액　value
가중평균　weighted average
가중평균원가법　weighted average
　　　inventory method, weighted
　　　average method
가중평균자본비용　weighted average
　　　cost of capital

가차압(假差押)　sequestration
가처분소득　disposable income
가치　value, worth
가치(價値)회계　value accounting
가치하락　shrinkage
가협정(假協定)　interim
간사(증권인수의)　manager
간접노동　indirect labor
간접노무비　indirect labor, indirect
　　　labor cost
간접비　indirect cost, overhead
간접비용　indirect expense
간접비 중심점　indirect cost center
간접세　indirect tax
간접재료　indirect material
간접재료비　indirect material, indirect
　　　material cost
감가　depreciation, discount,
　　　impairment
감가상각　depreciation
감가상각가능가액　depreciable
　　　amount, depreciable cost,
　　　depreciation base
감가상각기금　depreciation fund
감가상각기초액　depreciation base
감가상각누계액　accrued depreciation,
　　　allowance for depreciation,
　　　reserve for depreciation
감가상각누계액 공제전 장부가액
　　　(영)gross book value
감가상각누계액 공제후 가액

depreciated value

감가상각단위   depreciation unit

감가상각방법   depreciation method

감가상각비   depreciation, depreciation charge, depreciation expense

감가상각비 수정   (영)depreciation adjustment(DA)

감가상각율   depreciation rate

감가상각의 간접법   appraisal method of depreciation

감가상각의 평가법   appraisal method of depreciation

감가상각자산   depreciable asset

감가상각충당금   allowance for depreciation, reserve for depreciation

감가수정   depreciation

감가율   depreciation rate

감모   shrinkage

감모비   shrinkage

감모상각   depletion

감모상각비   depletion

감모손   shrinkage

감모자산   wasting asset

감사   audit, auditing, controllership, examination

감사 가이드   audit guide

감사계약   audit engagement

감사계약서   engagement letter

감사계획   audit planning, audit program

감사계획의 입안   audit planning

감사관   comptroller

감사기술   auditing technique

감사기준   auditing standard

감사 노트   audit note, audit notebook

감사된 재무제표   certified financial statements

감사 매뉴얼   audit manual

감사받은 재무제표   audited financial statements

감사받지 않은 재무정보   unaudited financial information

감사범위   audit scope, scope of examination

감사범위의 제한   scope limitation

감사보고서   audit report, auditor's certificate, auditor's report

감사보수   audit fee

감사 소프트웨어   audit software

감사수속   audit procedure

감사 수첩   audit notebook

감사업무   examination

감사위원회   audit committee

감사위험   audit risk

감사의견   audit opinion, opinion

감사 이외의 업무에 대한 보수   non-audit fee

감사인   auditor

감사인의 책임   auditor's responsibility

감사절차   audit procedure, auditing procedure

감사절차서   audit program

감사조서   audit working paper

감사증거   audit evidence

감사증명서   auditor's certificate

감사증적   audit trail

감사 표본추출   audit sampling

감사 프로그램   audit program, audit software

감사하다   audit

감시원가   monitoring cost

감액   write down

감자　　reduction of capital
감정　　appraisal
감정가치　　appraisal value
감정서　　check
감정 자본　　appraisal capital
감정평가　　valuation
감채기금　　sinking fund
감채기금부 사채　　sinking fund bond
감채적립금　　debenture redemption
　　reserve, sinking fund reserve
값　　value
강령　　prospectus
강세쪽　　bull
강제매매　　forced sale
강제예산　　imposed budget
강제청산　　compulsory liquidation
개념구조　　conceptual framework
개념적 체계　　conceptual framework
개량　　improvement
개발단계기업　　development stage
　　enterprise
개발비　　development cost, intangible
　　development cost
개방담보　　open mortgage
개방형 투자회사　　open-end fund
개별가격변동　　specific price change
개별가격지수　　specific price index
개별계획　　project planning
개별모집(주식청약 등의)　　private
　　offering, private placement
개별법　　specific identification
개별비용　　traceable cost
개별상각　　item depreciation
개별원가　　job cost, job order cost, job
　　order costing, specific cost
개별원가계산　　job cost system, job
　　costing, job order cost

　　accounting, specific order
　　costing
개별원가법(재고자산평가상의)　　specific
　　identification
개산치(槪算値)　　estimate
개서(명의의)　　transfer
개선　　betterment
개시기입　　opening entry
개시잔액　　beginning balance
개연성(蓋然性)　　probability
개인기업　　private enterprise, sole
　　proprietorship
개인사업주　　proprietor sole proprietor
개인상인　　sole proprietor, sole trader
개인의 지출　　suppliy
개인재산세　　personal property tax
객관성　　objectivity
객관적 가치　　objective value
객관적 확률　　objective probability
갱신　　restatement
갱신자금　　renewal fund
거래　　transaction
거래계약　　commitment
거래기록　　journal
거래비용　　transaction cost
거래소　　exchange
거래소 상장증권에의 투자　　quoted
　　investment
거래의 이중가정　　dual transaction
　　assumption
거래주기　　operating cycle
거시회계　　macro accounting
거액할인　　volume discount
건설가계정　　construction in process
건설공사미수금　　construction account
　　receivable
건설중인 자산　　construction work in

progress

건설중 지급이자　interest on construction

건전가액　sound value

검사　check, examination, inspection, test

검수　inspection

검약　prudence

검증　verification

검증가능성　verifiability

검토　test check

격　post

견본　sample

견적　appraisal, balance, estimate, forecasting, projection, valuation

견적내용연수　expected life

견적서　estimate

견적송장　pro forma invoice

견적 재무제표　budgeted statement

견적(예산) 재무제표　budgeted financial statement

결산의 결과　balance

결산일　(영)accounting date, closing date, cutoff date

결산일 현행환율법　current rate method

결산일환율　closing rate(CR)

결산일환율/순투자법　closing rate/net investment method

결산일환율법　closing rate method

결산재무제표　(영)final accounts

결산절차　closing process

결산정리　adjustment

결손(자본금의)　impairment

결손금　deficit

결손금의 소급　carryback of operating

loss, loss carryback

결손금의 이월　loss carryforward

결손금의 이월공제　loss carryforward

결제　liquidation, settlement

결제일　settlement date

결합　combination

결합 손익 및 이월이익잉여금처분계산서　combined statement of income and retained earnings

결합원가　joint product cost, joint cost

결합재무제표　combined financial statement

결합차이　joint variance

경과이자　accrued interest

경기를 돋우기 위한 자본손실을 일으키는 매매　wash sale

경리·회계 담당자　accountant

경리부장　treasurer

경매　auction, sale

경매처분　forced sale

경비　administrative expense, burden, expenditure, expense, outlay

경상비(經常費)　standing expense

경상외손실　extraordinary loss

경영　administration, business

경영감사　management audit

경영게임　business game

경영과학　management science

경영관리　administration, management

경영관리자　management

경영다각화　diversification

경영분석　financial statement analysis

경영분석·비율분석　ratio analysis

경영비율　management ratio

경영성적　operating result, result of operation

경영업무감사　management audit

경영자　management, manager

경영자문　management service

경영자문서비스　management advisory service(MAS)

경영자에 대한 제안업무　management service

경영자의 진술서　management representation

경영정보시스템　management information system(MIS)

경영통제　management control

경제가치　economic value

경제사건　economic event

경제사상(事象)　economic event

경영실체　economic entity

경제적 내용연수　economic life

경제적 발주량　economic order quantity(EOQ)

경제적 생산 단위규모　economic lot size(ELS)

경제적 이익　economic income, economic interest, fringe benefit

경제적 이해관계　economic interest

경제적인　cost-effective

경제적 자원　economic resource

경제적 주문량　economic order quantity(EOQ)

경품　premium

계량　balance, measurement

계량화　quantification

계산결과　product

계산서　bill, estimate, statement

계산서류　accounts

계상의 상한액　intangible asset

계속기록법　book inventory, continuous inventory method, perpetual inventory method

계속기업　going concern

계속기업의 가정　going concern assumption

계속기업의 가치　going concern value

계속기업의 개념　going concern concept

계속기업의 공준　going concern assumption

계속성　consistency, continuity

계속 재고정리　continuous inventory

계속재고조사법　perpetual inventory method

계속적 감사　continuous audit

계속적 영업활동에 의한 이익　income from continuing operation

계속적 조업(영업, 사업)활동　continuing operation

계속적 현행회계　continuously contemporary accounting (CoCoA)

계속제조지시서　standing order

계속파일　permanent file

계속형 예산　continuous budget

계약　agreement, contract

계약가격　contract price

계약별 비용　contract cost

계약별 원가　contract cost

계약서　contract, letter of engagement

계약위반　breach of contract

계약의 불이행　breach of contract

계약조항　covenant

계약해제　recession

계약형 투자신탁　open-end fund

계열회사　(영)related company, affiliated company, associated

company
계정　　account(a/c)
계정과목 코드　　account code
계정분류　　classification of accounts
계정서　　bill
계정연관표　　articulation statement
계정잔액　　balance
계정조직　　chart of account, system of
　　account
계정체계　　accounting system
계정 형식　　account form
계좌 개설(은행의)　　direct debit
계층구조　　hierarchical structure
계획　　plan, projection
계획 · 프로그래밍 · 예산편성 시스템
　　planning, programing and
　　budgeting system(PPBS)
계획서　　prospectus
계획설정　　planning
계획하다　　schedule
계획화　　planning
고 · 저점법　　high-low point method
고객　　client
고용계약　　service contract
고용보고서　　(영)employment report
고유위험　　inherent risk
고유자산　　idle asset
고정가격　　firm price, fixed price
고정부채　　fixed liability, funded debt,
　　long-term debt, long-term
　　liability, non-current liability
고정비　　fixed charge, fixed cost, fixed
　　expense, standing cost
고정비배율　　fixed charge coverage
고정시세　　fixed exchange rate
고정예산　　fixed budget, static budget
고정자본　　fixed capital

고정자산　　capital asset, fixed asset,
　　long-lived asset, long-term
　　asset, non-current asset
고정자산대장　　fixed asset register,
　　plant ledger
고정자산 증감변동표　　fixed asset
　　statement
고정자산 처리단위　　fixed asset unit
고정자산처분손　　capital loss
고정자산회전　　fixed asset turnover
고정자산회전율　　fixed asset turnover
　　ratio
고정적 비용　　fixed cost
고정제조간접비　　fixed overhead
고정환율　　fixed exchange rate
공개매입　　tender
공개시장가치　　open market value
공개시장조작　　open market operation
공개초안　　exposure draft(ED)
공개회사　　public company, publicity
　　held company
공공부문회계　　public sector
　　accounting
공공사업　　public utility, utility
공공회계(실무)　　public accounting
공공회계사　　public accountant(CPA)
공급　　supply
공급가액　　supply price
공급품　　suppliy
공동 및 단독책임　　joint and several
　　liability
공동사업회사　　corporate joint venture
공동채무　　joint liability
공동출자사업　　joint adventure, joint
　　venture
공동협력　　partnership
공리(公理)　　axiom

공매   short sale
공매(空賣)의   short
공모(公募)   public offering
공모유한책임회사   (영)publicity held company
공모회사   public company
공사완성 기준   completed contract method
공사외상매출금   construction account receivable
공사진행기준   percentage of completion method
공사채   bond
공손   spoilage
공수표   kiting
공시   disclosure
공시된 배당   declared dividend
공시제도   disclosure
공식적인 할인율   official discount rate
공업제품의 생산단위   lot size
공익사업   public utility, utility
공인회계사   certified public accountant(CPA)
공장   plant
공장설비   plant and equipment
공장소모품   factory supply
공장소모품비   factory supply
공장원가   factory cost
공장원장   factory ledger
공장인도(가격)   ex works(EXW)
공장전체 제조간접비배부율   plantwide overhead rate
공정가격   fair value
공정가치   fair value
공정별원가계산   process costing
공정성   fairness

공정시세표   official listing
공정시장가격   fair market price
공정시장가치   fair market value (FMV)
공정한 거래   arm' length transaction
공제   deduction
공제계정   offset account
공제액   deduction
공준   assumption, postulate
공채 이자액   dividend
공탁금   deposit
공통비   common cost
공통형 대차대조표   common size balance sheet
공통형 손익계산서   common size income statement
공학적 원가   engineered cost
공헌이익   contribution margin
공헌이익도표   profit volume chart
공헌이익률   contribution margin ratio
공헌이익 손익계산서   contribution income statement
공헌이익 접근법   contribution approach
과거용역비용   past service cost
과대거래   overtrading
과대자본화   overcapitalization
과대표시   overstatement
과세시기(부가가치세의)   (영)tax point
과세유보기간   bailout period
과세회피적 배당정책   dividend stripping
과소평가   understatement
과실   error, negligence
과실책임   negligence
과잉재고   excess stock
과학적 관리법   scientific management

관계자	interest
관계회사	affiliate, affiliated company, associated company
관련당사자	related party
관련당사자간의 거래	related party transaction
관련범위	relevant cost
관련원가	relevant cost
관련회사	affiliated company, (영)associated company
관련효익	relevant benefit
관리	control
관리(재산)	stewardship
관리가격	administered price
관리가능비	managed cost, controllable cost
관리과학	management science
관리불능비	non-controllable cost
관리비	administrative expense
관리자	director, manager
관리자의 보고서	(영)directors' report
관리자의 보수	(영)directors' emoluments
관리통제	administrative control
관리한계	span of control
관리회계	management accounting, managerial accounting
관리회계 담당자	management accountant
관세	customs duty, duty of custom
관세(표)	tariff
관재인(管財人)	trustee
관찰	observation
관행	convention
광고	advertising
광구사용권	royalty
광물자원의 개발 계약	lease

광산	royalty
광업권	mining right
교무계(학교)	registrar
교부(交付)(상품, 제품의)	delivery
교부금	grant, subsidy
교차	crossing
교환	exchange
교환가치	exchange value
교환소	exchange
교환의	trade in
교환차액	boot
교환 평가액	trade in
구매	purchase
구매력	purchasing power
구매력 손익	purchasing power gain or loss
구분	class
구분식(보고식) 대차대조표	classified balance sheet
구분식(보고식) 손익계산서	classified statement of profit and loss
구속자산	restricted asset
구역외 기금	offshore fund
구입	purchase
구입가격	purchase price
구입원가	cost of goods purchased
구입주문서	purchase order
구입지도서	purchase order
구제	saving
구조조정	reorganization
국고보조금	government grant
국민대차대조표	national balance sheet
국민보험의 급부(금전, 현물, 서비스)	(영)benefit
국민소득	national income(NI)
국민소득회계	national income

accounting

국민순생산   net national product (NNP)

국민총생산   gross national product (GNP)

국장   director

국제회계   international accounting

국제회계기준   Intrenational Accounting Standards(IAS)

국채   national debt

권리   interest

권리락   ex right

권리부(신주인수권의)   cum-right

권리증서(일정금액에 대한)   instrument

권리행사가격   exercise price

권면   face value, scrip

권면가액   face value

권위   authority

권익   interest

권한   authority

귀속이자   imputed interest

귀환   feedback

규격   standard

규정   provision

규제   regulation

규칙   regulation, rule

그룹재무제표   (영)group account

근사치   approximation

근속(勤續)(연금계산상의)   service

금고(金庫)주(株)   treasury stock, reacquired stock

금리스왑   interest rate swap

금리의 기간구조   term structure of interest rates

금액   value

금액상 중요성   material

금융   finance

금융기관   financial institution

금융리스   financing lease

금융상품   financial instrument

금융선물거래   financial future

금융시장   financial market, money market

금융어음   accommodation bill

금융중개업   financial intermediary

금융회사   finance company

금전적 이익   pecuniary benefit

금전출납장   cash journal

급료   payroll, salary

급부(給付)   product

급수법   sum-of-the-years-digit method

급여(給與)대장(臺帳)   salary roll

급여액   allowance

기간   aging, period

기간보장연금   annuity certain

기간비용   period cost

기간원가   period cost

기간이익   periodic income

기계   instrument

기계시간율   machine hour rate

기관투자가   institutional investor

기구   instrument

기금   endowment fund, fund

기금순재산(회계단위에서의)   fund balance

기금잔고   fund balance

기금회계   fund accounting

기기   equipment

기능별 원가분류   functional cost

기능적 감가   functional depreciation

기능통화   functional currency

기대내용연수   expected life

기대매각가치   expected exit value

기대실제조업도   expected actual

activity

기대실제활동량 expected actual
activity

기대치 expected monetary
value(EMV), expected value

기대화폐치 expected monetary
value(EMV)

기록 record

기록계 book keeper

기말(期末) year-end

기말배당 final dividend

기말잔고 closing balance

기말재고 예산 ending inventory
budget

기말정리 adjustment

기명식수표 order check

기명식채권 registered bond

기명주권(記名株券) inscribed share,
inscribed stock

기명증권 registered security

기명 채무증서 debenture

기밀보호 security

기본 개념 fundamental concept

기본금 (영)capital fund, accumulated
fund, endowment fund

기본목적 objective

기본예산 master budget

기본원가 prime cost

기본 재무제표 primary financial
statement

기본적 제개념 basic concept

기본정관 (영)memorandum of
association

기부금 endowment fund, donation,
subvention

기수불 연금 annuity due

기술적 분석 technical analysis

기술정보 know-how

기어링 조정액 (영)gearing adjustment

기억용량 capacity

기업 business, business enterprise,
corporation, enterprise

기업가 entrepreneur

기업가치 enterprise value

기업간(間) intercompany

기업간 비교 inter-firm comparison

기업간 세금배분 interperiod tax
allocation

기업간 신용 trade credit

기업결합 business combination,
merger

기업내부자 insider

기업내용공시 disclosure

기업담보 차입매수 leveraged
buyout(LBO)

기업매수 management buyout(MBO)

기업명 business name

기업소득 business income

기업실체 business entity, economic
entity, entity

기업실체개념 entity concept

기업실체이론 entity theory

기업어음 commercial paper(CP)

기업에 대한 가치 value to the
business

기업외부의 정보이용자 outsider

기업의 사회적 보고 corporate social
reporting

기업의 소유자 proprietor

기업이익 business income

기업전략 corporate strategy

기업집단 (영)group

기업집단 내 회사에 대한 채권
intercompany receivable

기업집단재무제표　(영)group account, group financial statements
기업집단 회사간 거래　intercompany transaction
기업취득　take-over
기업측 연대책임　joint and several liability
기업합동　business combination, business trust
기입　entry
기장상 오류　clerical error
기재가치　stated value
기재된 장부의 끝　balance
기점 가격　basing point price
기준　standard
기준 기간　base period
기준연도　base year
기준일　record date
기준 재고　base stock
기준 재고법　base stock method, normal stock method
기준조업도　denominator level
기준 표준원가　basic standard cost

기중(期中)　interim
기중감사　interim audit
기초　beginning of year(BOY)
기초연구　pure research
기초원가　first cost, prime cost
기초잔고　(영)opening stock, opening balance, beginning balance
기초 잔액　base stock
기초재고　(영)opening stock, beginning inventory
기타자산　other asset
기타항목　extraordinary item
기탁　bailment
기한경과수표　out of date check
기한부 국채　(영)fund debt
기한부 대출　term loan
기한전 계약불이행　anticipatory breach
기회손실　opportunity loss
기회원가　opportunity cost
기획안　project
긴급회수기간　bailout period

ㄴ

낙인　brand
날인증서　covenant
납세신고서　tax return
납입완료주식자본　(영)paid-up capital
납입잉여금　contributed surplus, paid-in surplus
납입자본　contributed capital, paid-in capital

납품서　delivery note
내국법인　domestic corporation
내부감사　internal audit
내부감사보고서　internal audit report
내부감사인　internal auditor
내부거래　intercompany transaction, internal transaction
내부견제　internal check

내부보고	internal reporting
내부수익률	internal rate of return (IRR)
내부자거래	insider dealing, insider trading
내부자금조달	internal financing
내부통제	internal control
내부통제기구	internal control structure
내부통제절차	control procedure
내부통제질문서	internal control questionnaire(ICQ)
내부회계	internal accounting
내부회계통제	internal accounting control
내용견본(신간서적)	prospectus
내용연수	depreciable life, service life, useful life
내재원가	imputed cost
내재이자	imputed interest
노동	labor
노동소득	earned income
노동자	employee, labor
노무비	labor cost
노무비차이	labor variance
노하우	know-how
노후화	obsolescence
농장가격법	farm price method
누적 미지급 배당금(누적적 배당우선주의)	dividend in arrear
누적배당	cumulative dividend
누적이익 배당	accumulated dividend
누적적 우선주	cumulative preference share, cumulative preferred stock
누적투표	cumulative voting
누진과세	progressive tax
능력	efficiency
능률	efficiency
능률차이	efficiency variance

ㄷ

다각화기업	diversified company
다국적기업	multinational enterprise
다단계식 손익계산서	multiple step income statement
다단계양식	multiple step form
다단계연결	multi-stage consolidation
다른 통화끼리의 상호대부	back-to-back loan
다산성(多産性)	productivity
다수지분에 의한 종속회사	majority owned subsidiary
단계비	step cost, step function cost
단계원가	step cost, step function cost
단기대출금	short term loan
단기부채	short term liability
단기예측판매	short sale
단기융자	demand loan
단기차입금	short term debt
단기채무	short term debt
단기투자	current investment, short term investment, temporary investment

단기투자목적의 시장성 있는 유가증권
　　marketable security
단기투자자산　current asset investment
단리(單利)　simple interest
단문식 (감사)보고서　short form report
단수　odd-lot
단수결제금　boot
단수주권　scrip
단식부기　single entry bookkeeping
단위원가　unit cost
단위형 투자신탁회사　unit trust
단일구분식 손익계산서　single-step
　　income statement
단주(端株)　fractional share, odd-lot
단주인수권 증서　fractional share
　　warrant
단편적 의견　piecemeal opinion
달러의 일반구매력　general purchasing
　　power of the dollar
담보　charge, collateral, gage,
　　guarantee, guaranty, security,
　　warranty
담보계약　hypothecation
담보권　lien
담보금　provision
담보물건　collateral
담보물의 반환　redemption
담보부대여금　collateral loan
담보부 부채　secured liability
담보부 사채　(영)debenture stock,
　　mortgage bond
담보부 약속어음　secured note
담보부 장기어음　mortgage note
담보부 차입금(대부금)　secured loan
담보부채권　mortgage bond
담보자산　pledged asset
담보차입　mortgage

담보차입계약서　debenture
담보책임　warranty
당기 감사조서　current file
당기순매입액　net purchases
당기 순손실　net loss
당기순이익　net income, net profit
당기업적주의　current operating
　　performance concept
당기영업이익　current operating
　　income, current operating
　　profit
당기이익　current income
당기인식법　flow through method
당기표준원가　current standard cost
당좌계정철　current file
당좌대월(대부)　demand loan
당좌비율　acid test ratio, quick ratio
당좌예금구좌　current account,
　　checking account
당좌예산　current budget
당좌자금　current fund
당좌자산　liquid asset, quick asset
당좌지분계정　current account
당좌차월　bank overdraft, overdraft
대가　proceed
대금선불조건판매　cash before delivery
　　(CBD)
대금징수 어음　bill for collection(B/C)
대기시간　idle time
대리　agency, suppliy, surrogate
대리권　agency
대리권을 서면으로 부여하는 경우의 그
　　서면　power of attorney
대리기금　agency fund
대리인　agent, proxy, surrogate
대리인 위임장　proxy
대리작성 업무　compilation

대리점 agency, agent
대리행위 agency
대변 credit, creditor(cr.)
대변비망표 credit memorandum
대손 bad debt, doubtful debt
대손상각비 bad debt expense
대손준비금 (영)provision for bad debt
대손충당금 allowance for doubtful account, allowance for uncollectables, reserve for bad debt
대손평가액의 계상 impairment
대용통화 currency
대위변제(代位辨濟) subrogation
대응개념 matching concept
대장성 장기증권 treasury bond
대장성 증권 (영)treasury bill(TB)
대차계정 balance
대차대조표 balance sheet(B/S), statement of financial condition, statement of financial position
대차대조표 감사 balance sheet audit
대차대조표 계정 balance sheet account
대차대조표 등식 balance sheet equation
대차대조표 분석 balance sheet analysis
대차대조표일 balance sheet date
대차대조표일 이후의 사건 subsequent event
대체(代替) replacement
대체가격 replacement price
대체가격의 결정(내부) transfer pricing
대체가능자산 fungible asset
대체법 replacement method, replacement system

대체원가 current cost, replacement cost
대체원가법 replacement cost method
대체원가회계 replacement cost accounting
대체적 회계기준 alternative accounting rule
대출 loan
대출금 loan
대출한도액 credit line
대회 convention
데이터베이스 database
데이터베이스 관리 시스템 database management system(DBMS)
데이터베이스 관리자 database administrator(DBA)
도덕적 위험 moral hazard
도덕적 해이 moral hazard
도매가격 trade price
도매물가지수 wholesale price index(number)(WPI)
도매상 factor
도산 bankruptcy
도착 후 일람불어음 arrival draft
도착통지 arrival notice
독립 감사인 independent auditor
독립기업간의 거래 arm' length transaction
독립변수 independent variable
독립성(감사인의) independence
독립프로젝트 independent project
독자(獨自)평균원장 self balancing ledger
동계회사 affiliated company
동료 company
동료검토 peer review
동료심사 peer review

동산(動産)　personal property

동산세　personal property tax

동업자　interest

동업자 리뷰　peer review

동의　agreement

동의 서한　consent letter

동적 계획법　dynamic programming (DP)

동족지주법인　personal holding company(PHC)

동족회사　personal holding company (PHC)

두번째 저당　second mortgage

등급　rating, value

등기　registration

등기계　registrar

등기회사　(영)registered company

등록　registration

등록계　registrar

등록서　registration statement

등록신고서　registration statement

등록주주　stockholder of record

등록회사　registered company

등차급수법　sum-of-the-years-digit method

ㄹ

랜덤웍　random walk

레버리지　leverage

레버리지 비율　leverage ratio

레이팅　rating

로트　lot

로트원가　(영)lot cost

로트원가계산　lot costing

리드 타임(경제적 발주량)　lead time

리베이트　rebate

리스계약　lease

리스기간　lease term

리스백　lease back

리스의 레버리지　leveraged lease

리스임대인　lessor

리스임차인　lessee

리스크 프리미엄　risk premium

리스회계　accounting for lease, lease accounting

리엔　lien

리턴　return

□

마감	closing
마감분개	closing entry
마감일	cutoff date
마감전시산표	pre closing trial balance
마감후 시산표	post closing trial balance
만기	maturity
만기가치	maturity value(MV)
만기상환가액	maturity value
만기이율	yield to maturity
만기일에 있어서의 가치	maturity value
만기전 지불(기한전 변제)	prepayment
만족수준의 달성	satisfying
많은 종류의 제품을 판매할 경우 제품비율	sales mix
매가	selling price
매가환원법	retail method
매가환원 후입선출법	retail lifo method
매각	sale
매각가치	sales value, selling price
매각 또는 추가가공에 대한 의사결정	sell or process further decision
매각선택권(증권 등의)	put option
매각시가	current exit value
매각후리스(리스거래의)	sale and leaseback
매도증	bill of sale
매도호가	ask price, asked price, asking price
매매계약	buy-sell agreement
매매법	purchase method
매몰원가	irrelevant cost, sunk cost
매상	revenue
매수	acquisition, purchase, take-over
매수방식	purchase method
매수법	purchase method
매수선택권	call option
매수선택권부 임차	(영)hire-purchase
매수약정	call
매수에 의한 연결	consolidation by purchase
매수은행부 지정 신용장	open credit
매수일자	date of acquisition
매입	purchase
매입가격	purchase price
매입기록	purchase record
매입대상회사	offeree company
매입법	purchase method
매입송장	purchase invoice
매입영업권	purchased goodwill
매입운임	(영)carriage-inward, freight-in
매입일기장	purchase day book(PDB)
매입장	bought day book
매입주문서	purchase order
매입채무	account payable, trade payable
매입채무 만류(挽留)일수	creditors days ratio
매입처	trade creditor

매입처원장   bought ledger, purchase
    ledger

매입할인   discount received, purchase
    allowance, purchase discount

매입할인충당금   allowance for
    purchases discount

매입환출   purchase return, redemption,
    return outward

매입환출가능증권   redeemable
    security

매장량계상회계   reserve recognition
    accounting(RRA)

매장물   deposit

매출   sales

매출가격   offer price

매출배합   sales mix

매출배합이익차이   sales mix profit
    variance

매출배합차이   sales mix variance

매출세(稅)   sales tax

매출액   sales, sales revenue,
    (영)turnover

매출액이익률   profit to turnover ratio,
    return on sales

매출에 대한 부가가치세   output tax

매출예산   sales budget

매출원가   cost of goods sold, cost of
    sales, production cost of sales

매출원가예산분석   cost of goods sold
    budget

매출원가의 수정   (영)cost of sales
    adjustment(COSA)

매출조업도차이   sales volume
    variance

매출채권   accounts receivable, trade
    receivable

매출채권계정   receivable

매출채권원장   debtors ledger

매출채권의 매각   factoring

매출채권의 연령조사   aging of
    debtors

매출채권회전   receivables turnover
    ratio

매출처   trade debtor

매출처원장   customers' ledger, sales
    day book(SDB), sales ledger

매출총손실   gross loss

매출총이익   gross margin, gross
    profit, gross profit on sales

매출총이익 검사   gross profit test

매출총이익률   gross margin percentage,
    gross margin ratio, gross profit
    percentage, gross profit ratio

매출총이익률법   gross margin method

매출총이익법   gross profit method

매출품구성이익차이   sales mix profit
    variance

매출할인   cash discount(CD), sales
    allowance, sales discount

매출환입   return on sales, return
    inward, sales return

매출환입 기입장   sales return book
    (SRB)

매출환입품   return on sales, return
    inward, sales return

매크로 회계   macro accounting

매트릭스 조직   matrix organization

면세   relief, tax free, tax relief

면세기간   tax holiday

면세채권   tax exempt bond

면제(세금의)   benefit, relief

면책조항   escape clause, exclusion
    clause, exemption clause

면허   license

명령	commission
명령문	statement, warranty
명목가치	nominal value
명목계정	nominal account
명목임금	nominal wage
명목자본	nominal capital
명목화폐단위	monetary unit
명세서	bill, statement
명예	brand
명의개서 정지일	record date
명의서 교환 정지일	date of record
모험자본	venture capital
모회사	controlling company, parent company
모회사 재무제표	parent company statement
목록	bill
목록색인	prospectus
목적	objective
목적적합성	relevance
목적조항	object clause
목표가격	target price
목표순이익	target net income
목표에 의한 관리	management by objective(MBO)
무(無)상환 사채	irredeemable debenture
무(無)원장 장부조직	ledgerless bookkeeping
무관련원가	irrelevant cost, sunk cost
무기명 사채	bearer debenture
무기명식 배서	blank endorsement
무기명식 채권	bearer bond
무기명 주식	bearer share, bearer stock
무기명 증권	bearer security
무기한채권	annuity bond

무담보배서	qualified endorsement
무담보사채	debenture, debenture bond
무담보채권	unsecured bond
무사	security
무상배당주	bonus share
무상신주발행	bonus issue, (영)scrip issue
무상주식	bonus share
무액면주식	no-par value stock
무위험이자율	riskless interest rate
무의결권주	non-voting share, non-voting stock
무이자부 어음	non-interest-bearing note
무이자어음채권	non-interest-bearing note
무이자채권	zero coupon bond
무조건 신용장	open credit
무한책임	unlimited liability
무한책임사원	general partner
무한책임 파트너	general partner
무한책임회사	(영)unlimited company
무형고정자산	intangible asset, intangible fixed asset
무형자산	intangible, intangible asset
무효원가	idle cost
문서위조	falsification
물가	price
물가변동회계	inflation accounting
물가수준	price level
물류비	distribution cost
물리적 감가	physical deterioration
물리적 내용연수	physical life
물리적 노후화	physical deterioration
물적 계정	impersonal account
물적 부동산권	real estate

물적자본　physical capital
물적 자본유지　physical capital maintenance
물적재산　real property
물질적 내용연수　physical life
물품　goods
물품서　delivery note
물품세　sales tax
미결산계정　suspense account
미결제수표　outstanding check
미달(未達)수표　deposit in transit
미달상품　goods in transit, stock in transit
미달현금　deposit in transit
미래가치　future value(FV)
미래원가　future cost
미래재무제표　forward financial statement
미래효익원가방식　projected benefit cost method
미발행자본　unissued capital stock
미발행주식　unissued capital stock
미발행 주식자본　(영)unissued share capital
미상각잔액　depreciated value
미상환 사채　bond payable
미상환 사채 잔액비례법　bonds outstanding method
미수(未收)채권　claim
미수배당금　dividend receivable
미수수익　accrued income, accrued revenue
미수이자　accrued interest, interest receivable
미수채권　accrued receivable

미수행채무　commitment
미시회계　micro accounting
미실현보유이익　unrealized holding gain
미실현손실　unrealized loss
미실현이익　unrealized profit
미실현증가액　unrealized appreciation
미실현평가익　unrealized appreciation
미완성공사　construction in progress
미이행계약　executory contract
미지급배당　accrued dividend
미지급배당금　dividend payable
미지급법인세　accrued income tax, income tax payable
미지급부채　accrued liability
미지급비용　accrued expense, accrued liability
미지급소득세　accrued income tax, income tax payable
미지급이자　accrued interest, interest payable
미지급이자 할인율　accrued interest
미지급효익 · 비용방식　accrued benefit cost method
미착상품　goods in transit, stock in transit
미처리 주문　back order
미처분 이익　undistributed profit
미청구 클레임　unasserted claim
미할당주식　unallotted sharex
미확정 부채　indeterminate term liability
미확정사항　uncertainty
미확정 임대차료　contingent rental
민간기업　private enterprise

ㅂ

박탈가치	deprival value	발주점(發注点)	reorder point
반기보고서	interim report	발행가격	issue price
반수(半數)소유회사	associate company	발행된 자본	(영)issued capital
반증	falsification	발행비	flotation cost
반환	refund	발행시장(증권의)	primary market
받을어음	bill receivable(B/R, BR), note receivable	발행주식자본	(영)issued share capital
발견가치계정	discovery value accounting	발효일	effective date
발기서	prospectus	방어	security
발기인(發起人)	promoter	방지책(손실, 위험에 대한)	hedge, hedging
발생	accrual	배급비	distribution cost
발생급부 원가방식	accrued benefit cost method	배당	allocation, allotment, dividend
발생기준	accrual basis	배당(분배)가능이익	profit available for distribution
발생된(실현된) 채무	accrued liability	배당결의	declaration of dividend
발생배당	accrued dividend	배당과세 워싱	dividend washing
발생비용	accrued expense	배당금 수익	dividend income
발생원가	accrued depreciation	배당금 지급증서	dividend warrant
발생의 가능성 빈도	procedure	배당락(落)	dividend-off, ex-dividend (XD)
발생자산	accrued asset	배당배율	(영)dividend cover
발생주의	accrual basis, accrual concept	배당부	cum-dividend
발생주의 회계	accrual accounting, accrual basis accounting	배당비율	payout ratio
		배당선언	declaration of dividend
발생한도원가	should cost	배당선언일	declaration date
발생항목	accrual	배당성향	dividend payout, dividend payout ratio, payout ratio
발송(물품의)	delivery	배당소득	dividend income
발송비	shipping cost	배당이율	dividend yield
발송운임	freight-out	배당정책	dividend policy
발주비	ordering cost	배당증서	letter of allotment
		배당지급률	dividend payout, dividend

payout ratio

배당평균적립금   dividend equalization
reserve

배부   allocation, allotment, distribution

배부계정   absorption account

배부기준   allocation basis, distribution
basis

배부원가   absorbed cost

배부율   absorption rate

배부초과   overabsorption

배분   allocation, assignment, attribution

배서(背書)   endorsement, indorsement

배서인   endorser

배송(물품의)   delivery

배송비   distribution cost

배임   defalcation

배치전환   transfer

백분율 대차대조표   common size
balance sheet

백분율 손익계산서   common size
income statement

백지 배서   blank endorsement

범위문단   scope paragraph

법령 준거 테스트   compliance test

법률절차에 기초하지 않는 회사재건
quasi reorganization

법안   bill

법인   (영)body corporate, corporation

법인세   (영)corporation tax(CT), income
tax

법인세공제전 순이익   net profit before
tax

법인세 납세충당금   provision for
income tax, provision for tax
payable

법인세비용   income tax expense

법인세의 기간배분   interperiod tax

allocation

법인소득세   (영)corporation tax(CT),
income tax

법인소득세 공제전순이익   net income
before income tax

법적 실체   legal entity

법적 장부   statutory books

법적 주체   entity

법정가격   legal value

법정감사   statutory audit

법정이자   legal interest

법정자본   legal capital, stated capital

법정자본금   legal capital

법정 지폐   treasury note

법정통화   cash

법정허용 내용연한   asset depreciation
range system(ADRS)

벤처캐피탈   venture capital

변동계수   coefficient of variation

변동비   variable cost

변동비율   variable cost ratio

변동시세   flexible exchange rate

변동연금   variable annuity

변동예산   flexible budget, flexible
budgeting, variable budget

변동예산 차이   flexible budget variance

변동예산 허용액   flexible budget
allowance

변동원가   marginal cost, variable cost

변동원가계산   marginal costing,
variable costing

변동이자 부채권   floating rate note
(FRN)

변동제조간접비   variable factory
overhead, variable overhead
cost

변동환율   flexible exchange rate

변수	variable
변제	settlement, payment, tender
변제액	face value
변조	forgery
별도적립금	general reserve
보고기준	reporting standard
보고서 형식	statement form
보고식	narrative form, report form, vertical form, running form
보고주체	reporting entity
보고통화	reporting currency
보고형식	narrative form
보관비	carrying charge, carrying cost, holding cost
보관소	deposit
보급품	suppliy
보너스	bonus
보류(법)	saving
보상금	compensation
보상예금	compensating balance
보상판매 교환품	trade in
보수	allowance, compensation, emolument, fee, maintenance, return
보수주의	conservatism
보유손실	holding loss
보유이익	holding gain
보유현금	cash in hand, cash on hand
보장	compensation
보전	maintenance
보조금	grant, subsidy, subvention
보조부문	service center, service department
보조부문비	service department cost
보조부문 원가중심점	service cost center
보조원장	subsidiary ledger

보증	assurance, guaranty, security
보증계약	guaranty
보증금	deposit
보증금 추가청구	margin call
보증부 사채	guaranteed bond
보증서	warranty
보증인	guarantor, guaranty, security
보충명세서	supplementary statement
보충적정보	supplementary information
보통수표	open check
보통주	(영)ordinary share
보통주 1주당 장부가치	book value per share of common stock
보통주식	common stock
보통주식 등가물	common stock equivalent
보통주식 상당증권	common stock equivalent
보통지불환	bill payable(B/P, BP)
보통징수환	bill receivable(B/R, BR)
보험	assurance, insurance
보험계리인	actuary
보험금	proceed
보험금 수취인	beneficiary
보험료	insurance premium, premium
보험수리사	actuary
보험요율의 산정	rating
보험위탁	abandonment
보험인수증	insurance certificate
복리상각법	compound interest method, equal annual payment method
복리이자	compound interest
복수할인	compound discount
복식기입	double entry
복식부기	double entry bookkeeping
복식회계제도	double account system
복합기업	conglomerate, diversified

company
복합기업재무제표　conglomerate financial statement
복합내용연수　composite life
복합상각　composite depreciation
복합적 합병　conglomerate merger
본부비　central corporate expense
본사　head office
본선인도가격　free on board(FOB)
본위(本位)(통화의)　standard
본인(대리인 관계에서의)　principal
본점　head office, home office
본점계정　home office control
본지점의 결합(총합) 재무제표　combined financial statement
봉급　emolument, salary
봉토　fee
부(部)　department
부(富)의 극대화　wealth maximization
부(負)의 소득세　negative income tax
부(負)의 영업권　negative goodwill
부가가치　added value, value added
부가가치계산서　added value statement, value added statement
부가가치세　value added tax(VAT)
부가가치세의 비과세 판매　zero rating
부가계정　adjunct account
부가원가　imputed cost
부가적 불입자본　additional paid in capital
부기　bookkeeping
부기계　book keeper
부기의 일련의 순환과정　bookkeeping cycle
부담보(副擔保)　collateral
부담보대여금　collateral loan
부당유용액　defalcation

부대기구　fixture and fitting
부대물　fixture and fitting, fixtures
부도　bankruptcy
부도어음　dishonored note
부동산　property, real estate, real property
부동산 담보물권　mortgage
부동산에 첨부된 동산　fixtures
부동산회계　fiduciary accounting
부문(部門)　department
부문간 대체 이익　interdepartmental profit
부문간접비　departmental burden, departmental overhead
부문관리　divisional control
부문배부　departmentalization
부문별　departmentalization
부문별 배부율　departmental rate
부문별 보고　segmental reporting
부문별 제조간접비 배부율　departmental overhead rate
부문별 · 제품별 원가집계　cost finding
부문비　departmental charge
부문정보　segment information
부문제조 간접비배부율　departmental burden rate
부문화　departmentalization
부분의견　piecemeal opinion
부산물　by-product
부속명세서　schedule
부외부채　off balance sheet liability
부외자금조달　off balance sheet financing(OBSF)
부외자산(簿外資産)　off balance sheet asset
부적응화　inadequacy
부적정 의견　adverse opinion

부정   fraud, irregularity

부정경리   (영)false accounting

부정적 확신   negative assurance

부족   short

부족액   balance

부채   debt, liability, loan capital, obligation

부채비율   debt ratio

부채에 의한 자금조달   debt financing

부채의 변제(상환)   retirement of debt

부채조정액   (영)gearing adjustment

부패화   obsolescence

부표(付漂)   exhibit

분개   journalizing

분개기장   journalizing

분개장   journal

분개장 입력   journal entry

분개전표   journal voucher

분개증빙   journal voucher

분권화   decentralization

분기   branch

분기보고서   quarterly report

분기재무정보   quarterly financial information

분담   quota

분량(일정금액에 상당하는)   worth

분리가능비   separable cost

분리가능순자산   separable net asset

분리형 신주인수권 증서   detachable stock warrant

분배   distribution

분배가능이익   distributable income, distributable profit

분산   variance

분산가능한 위험   diversifiable risk

분산불가능 위험   non-diversifiable risk, undiversifiable risk

분산투자   diversification

분석적 검토   analytical review(AR)

분석적 검토 절차   analytical procedures

분식결산(粉飾決算)   window dressing

분포   distribution

분할분개장   special journal

불량채권   bad debt, doubtful account, doubtful debt, uncollectible accounts

불로소득   investment income, unearned income

불리한 차이   unfavorable variance

불법 회계조작   (영)false accounting

불변가격   constant dollar

불변가격회계   constant dollar accounting

불변구매력회계   constant purchasing power accounting(CPP accounting)

불변달러화 가격회계   constant dollar accounting

불변화폐회계   constant dollar accounting

불이행   default

불편성(不偏性)   freedom from bias

불합리한 거액의 약정 손해배상   liquidated damage

불확실성   uncertainty

불활발한 시장   thin market

브랜드   brand

브로커 중매인   broker

비(非) 법인단체   unincorporated association

비경상적 감가   extraordinary depreciation

비경상적 비용   non-recurring charge

비경상적 손익   extraordinary profit

and loss

비경상적 항목   extraordinary item

비공개기업(회사)   non-public enterprise, closely held company, non-public company

비관련원가   irrelevant cost

비교가능성   comparability

비교대차대조표   comparative balance sheet

비교분석   comparative analysis

비교성   comparability

비교손익계산서   comparative income statement

비교재무제표   comparative financial statement

비금전거래   non-monetary transaction

비납입연금제도   non-contributory plan

비누적적 우선주   non-cumulative preferred stock

비누적주   non-cumulative stock

비등기회사   unregistered company

비등록주(株)   letter stock

비례연결   proportional consolidation

비명시적(묵시적) 비용   implicit cost

비밀원장   private ledger(PL)

비밀적립금   hidden reserve, secret reserve

비상장유가증권   unlisted security, unquoted investment

비상장회사   unlisted company, unquoted company

비시장성위험   non-market risk

비연결자회사   unconsolidated subsidiary

비영리단체   non-profit organization,

not-for-profit organization

비영리법인   non-profit corporation

비영리회계   non-profit accounting

비용   charge, cost, expense

비용배부   expense distribution

비용센터   expense center

비용·수익대응   matching cost with revenue

비용예산   expense budget

비용유효도(효과)   cost-effectiveness

비용효용분석   cost utility analysis

비용·효익분석   cost-benefit analysis

비유동부채   non-current liability

비유동자산   non-current asset

비율   ratio

비율표시 대차대조표 common size balance sheet

비율표시 손익계산서   common size income statement

비인명계정원장   impersonal ledger

비정상 감모   abnormal shrinkage,

비정상 감손   abnormal shrinkage, abnormal waste

비정상 공손   abnormal spoilage

비정상작업 폐기물   abnormal waste

비즈니스게임   business game

비참가적우선주   non-participating preferred stock

비축물   backlog

비화폐성 부채   non-monetary liability

비화폐성 자산   non-monetary asset

비화폐성 항목   non-monetary item

비화폐적거래   non-monetary transaction

빅 백스 접근   big-bath approach

ㅂ

人

사건	event
사기(詐欺)	fraud
사례(謝禮)	fee
사모(私募)	private offering, private placement
사모(私募)발행	(영)private placing
사무용 소모품	office supply
사사오입하다	round off
사상(事象)	event
사업	enterprise
사업단위	entity
사업별 부문	industry segment
사업부관리	divisional control
사업부문별 보고	divisional reporting
사업부 업적평가	divisional performance evaluation
사업부의 폐지	discontinued operation
사업부이익	divisional profit
사업부통제	divisional control
사업설명서	prospectus
사업소득	ordinary income
사업신탁	business trust
사업연도	business year, financial year, period
사업 영역 구분	business segment
사업의 종류별 보고	line of business reporting
사열	inspection
사외유통주식	outstanding share
사용가치	value in use
사용권(특허권의)	license
사용기한	expiry date
사용이 제한된 이익잉여금	restricted retained earnings
사용자본	capital employed
사용제한예금 잔고	compensating balance
사장	principal
사전감사	pre audit
사정	appraisal, valuation
사정(액)	assessment
사정가액	appraisal
사정가치	appraisal value
사정액	appraisal, valuation
사채	bond, corporate bond
사채계약	bond indenture
사채권	bond certificate
사채권자	bond holder, debenture holder
사채등급	bond rating
사채발행비	bond issue cost, bond issue expense
사채발행차금	discount on bond payable
사채발행차입금	funded debt
사채발행할인료	discount on bond payable
사채배당	bond dividend
사채상환	bond redemption
사채상환손실	premium on redemption
사채상환적립금	debenture redemption reserve

사채신탁계약	bond indenture
사채의 전환	conversion of debt
사채의 차환	bond refunding
사채평가	bond valuation
사채할인료	bond discount
사채할인발행차금	bond discount
사채할증금	bond premium
사채할증발행차금	bond premium, premium on bonds payable
사회감사	social audit
사회보장부담금	social security contribution
사회적 비용	social cost
사회적 책임회계	social responsibility accounting
사회회계	social accounting
사후감사	post audit
사후비용	after cost
사후일자	post date
산성시험비율	acid test ratio
산술평균	arithmetic mean
산업별 분문 보고서	industry segment
산업 분류표	industry segment
산업화	capitalization
산포도법	scatter chart method, scatter diagram method
산포도표	scatter chart, scatter diagram
상각	amortization
상각기금법	sinking fund method
상각대상가액	depreciable amount
상각비	amortization
상각원가	depreciable cost
상각자산의 잔존가액	salvage value
상각채권 추심액(이익)	bad debt recovery
상관계수	correlation coefficient
상관관계	correlation
상급회계사	senior accountant

상대적 매출가액법 (연산품에서)	relative sales value method
상법	commercial law
상사	firm
상사조합	firm
상속세	estate tax, inheritance tax
상쇄	set off
상쇄계정	offset account
상쇄 오류	offsetting error
상승가액	carrying charge
상업 신용장	documentary credit
상업증권	commercial paper(CP)
상여금	bonus
상연료	royalty
상위증권	senior security
상장	listing
상장기업	public company
상장요건	listing requirement
상장유가증권	listed security, quoted investment
상장회사	listed company, (영)quoted company
상제품	goods
상표	trademark
상품	commodity, goods, merchandise
상품(금융)	instrument
상품명	trade name
상품목록	inventory
상품 선물거래	commodity futures
상품수령증	goods received note(GRN)
상품원장	stock ledger
상품회전율	merchandise turnover, (영)stock turnover
상한금리	cap
상호	trade name

상호관련   articulation

상호배부법   reciprocal allocation method, reciprocal distribution method

상호배타적 프로젝트   mutually exclusive project

상호협조   cross-holding

상환   refund, retirement

상환가격   call price, redemption price

상환가능주식   callable stock, redeemable share

상환가능증권   redeemable security

상환기금   redemption fund

상환사채   callable bond

상환시 할증금   redemption premium

상환우선주   callable preferred stock

상환조건부 유가증권   callable security

상환주   callable stock

상환청구   recourse

상환프리미엄   call premium

상황보고서   statement of affair

색인   index

색인첨부   indexing

색출표본조사   discovery sampling

샘플링 위험   sampling risk

생략   default

생명보험료   life insurance premium

생산   production

생산 개시전 원가   pre production cost

생산계획   production planning

생산고   turnover

생산관리   production control

생산기능   production function

생산능력   capacity, productive capacity

생산량비례법   production method, service yield basis, unit of production method

생산력   productivity

생산방법   production method

생산부문   production department

생산설비 기초원가   committed cost

생산설비원가   capacity cost

생산성   productivity

생산요소   factor of production

생산요소 배합차이   production mix variance

생산자물가지수   producer price index

생산자위험   producers' risk

생산함수   production function

서면에 청구되지 않은 지급을 청구할 수 있는 권리   accounts

서술적 형식   narrative form

서약   warranty

서임자(敍任者)   investor

선급금   advance, payment in advance, prepayment

선급보험료   prepaid insurance premium

선급비용   prepaid expense, prepayment, prepayment paid

선급이자(차입금의)   discount

선급이자비용   prepaid interest expense

선급임차료   prepaid rent

선물(先物)계약   futures contract

선물가격   future price

선물계약 레이트   forward rate

선물상품   commodity futures

선물환 계약   forward exchange contract

선물환계약에 수반한 손익   forward exchange contract

선물환시세   forward exchange rate, forward rate

선불(先拂)금   prepayment

선불계정   prepayment

선불법인세　　advance corporation tax(ACT)

선불연금　　annuity due

선수금　　advance, advance from customer

선수수익　　unearned income

선일자　　post date

선일자 수표　　post dated check

선입선출법　　first-in, first-out method(FIFO)

선전비　　(영)publicity cost

선취특권　　lien

선택권　　option, puts and calls

선하증권　　bill of lading(B/L)

설비　　equipment

설비능력　　plant capacity

설비투자　　capital investment

성격별 원가분류　　natural classification of cost

성공노력방법　　successful effort method

성과보고서　　performance report

성과측정　　performance measurement

성장주(株)　　growth stock

세금공제　　tax credit

세금의 기간배분(처리)　　tax allocation

세금피난수단　　tax shelter

세납부전 순이익　　net profit before tax

세납부후 방법　　net of tax method

세 등의 기간배분(법인)　　interperiod tax allocation

세무감가상각　　capital allowance

세무상의 차손금　　tax loss

세무신고서　　tax return

세무 업무　　tax service

세무연도　　(영)tax year

세부감사　　detail audit

세 액　　assessment

세액공제　　tax credit, tax relief

세율(稅率)　　tax rate

세율(표)　　tariff

세입(歲入)　　revenue, supplies

세전 순이익　　net income before income tax

세차감후 손실　　net loss

세출(歲出)　　supplies

세효과(稅效果)　　tax effect

세후방식　　net of tax method

소각(채권의)　　write off

소구(遡求)　　recourse

소극적 보증　　negative assurance

소극적 확신　　negative assurance

소극적 확인　　negative confirmation

소급 상각액　　backlog depreciation

소득　　income

소득공제　　allowance

소득세　　income tax

소득세 기간배부　　allocation of income tax

소득세의 완전기간배분　　comprehensive income tax allocation, comprehensive tax allocation

소매물가지수　　retail price index(RPI)

소매재고법　　retail inventory method, retail method

소매재고 후입선출법　　retail lifo method

소멸원가　　expired cost

소모품　　suppliy

소비량　　expenditure

소비자 물가지수　　consumer price index(CPI)

소비재　　consumers' goods

소비함수　　consumption function

소액주주지분　　minority interest

소액지불자금　　petty cash

人

소액현금   petty cash, petty cash fund

소액현금전표   petty cash voucher

소액현금출납장   petty cash book(PCB)

소유권   owners, property

소유권 유보   reservation of title

소유자 지분   owners' equity

소유주에 대한 배부   distribution to owner

소유한 자산의 시장가격 상승   appreciation

소장(訴狀)   bill

소재   raw material

속성   attribute, attribution, property

손(孫)회사   sub-subsidiary

손금산입항목   tax deductible

손상   impairment

손실   loss

손실금   deductions, deficit

손익계산서   earnings statement, income account, income statement, operating statement, (영)profit and loss account(P and L accounting), profit and loss statement

손익계산서분석   income statement analysis

손익계산서비율   income statement ratio

손익계정   profit and loss account (P and L accounting)

손익분기도표   break-even chart

손익분기 매출액   break-even sales

손익분기점   break-even point

손익분기점도표   profit volume chart, profit volume graph

손익분기점분석   break-even analysis

손해   loss

송금   remittance

송금수단   remittance

송금액   remittance

송금전표   remittance advice, remittance slip

송금주의   (영)remittance basis

송금통지   remittance slip

송장(送狀)   invoice

송장가액   invoice value

송장기입장   invoice register

송하인   consignor

수권   authorization

수권자본   authorized capital

수권주식자본   (영)authorised share capital

수당   allowance, compensation

수량차이   quantity variance

수량할인   quantity discount, volume discount

수령   acceptance, receipt

수령액   receipt

수리   repair

수리계획법   mathematical programming

수선   repair

수선충당금   allowance for repair, reserve for repair

수수료   commission, fee

수순   procedure

수시상환가능사채   callable bond

수율(원료에 대한 제품 비율)   yield

수율차이   yield variance

수익   revenue

수익권자   beneficiary

수익력   earning power

수익부과분   charge

수익사채   income bond

수익성   profitability

수익성지수   profitability index

수익의 실현   revenue realization

수익의 인식   revenue recognition

수익의 자본화   capitalization of earnings

수익의 자본환원   capitalization

수익자   beneficiary

수익적 지출   revenue expenditure

수익중심점   revenue center

수입   proceed

수입액   receipt

수정   adjustment

수정기입   adjusting entry

수정분개   adjusting entry, adjusting journal entry(AJE)

수정전 잔액시산표   unadjusted trial balance

수정후 시산표   adjusted trial balance

수증   donation

수증자본   donated capital

수지(收支)계산서   income and expenditure account

수지(收支)기준   receipt and payment basis

수지(收支)회계   fund accounting

수직적 합병   vertical merger

수취리스료   lease revenue

수취액   proceed

수취이자   interest, interest income

수취인   payee

수취채권   receivable

수치   value

수탁자   fiduciary

수탁책임   stewardship

수탁판매   consignment

수탁품   consignment inward

수탁회사책임   fiduciary accounting

수표   check

수표교환소   clearing house

수표기입장   check register

수혜자   beneficiary

수확량   turnover

순가치   net worth

순당좌자산   (영)net liquid fund, net quick asset

순매출액   net sales, net turnover

순배당금   net dividend

순손실   net loss

순수연구   pure research

순실현가능가액   net realizable value(NRV)

순운전자본   net working capital

순위상관계수   coefficient of rank correlation

순유동자산   net current asset

순이익   net income, net profit

순자산   net asset(equity)

순장부가액   net book value(NBV)

순재산   net asset(equity), net worth

순현재가치(순현가)   net present value(NPV)

순환자산   circulating asset

스톡옵션   stock option

스트라들   straddle

승낙(승인)   acceptance, authorization

시가   cash value, current cost, current price, current value, quotation, quoted market price, market value

시가법   market value method

시가주의 회계   current cost accounting(CCA), current value accounting(CVA)

시가평가	mark to the market
시간급	time rate
시간외수당	overtime premium
시간임률	time rate
시간조정이익률	time adjusted rate of return(TARR)
시공품	sample
시굴비	exploration cost
시기	aging
시료(試料)	sample
시사(試査)	audit testing
시사범위	extent of test
시산표	trial balance(T/B)
시설	equipment
시세	market price, quotation
시세표	quotation
시송품	sales on approval
시스템설계	system design
시용(試用)판매	sales on approval
시장	market
시장가격	market price, quoted market price
시장가액법	market value method
시장가치	market value
시장경기	quotation
시장동향	quotation
시장 베타값	market beta
시장분석	market analysis
시장성이 없는 유가증권	non-marketable security
시장성지분증권	marketable security
시장시세가격	quoted price
시장시세주문	market order
시장용 작물	cash crop
시장위험	market risk
시장위험 할증금	market risk premium
시장조사	marketing research

시장 포트폴리오	market portfolio
시험	test
식별가능자산	identifiable asset
신고납세	self assessment
신고서	return
신뢰도	reliability
신설합병	consolidation
신용	credit
신용(책임)보험	fidelity bond
신용거래비망표	credit memorandum, credit note(C/N)
신용거래표	credit note(C/N)
신용관리	credit management
신용도평가	rating
신용등급책정	credit rating
신용분석	credit analysis
신용위험	credit risk
신용장	documentary credit, letter of credit(L/C)
신용조사기관	credit agency, credit reporting agency
신용판매	credit sale
신용한도	credit limit, line of credit
신원보증	fidelity bond
신주발행비	share issue expense
신주우선인수	preemption
신주인수권	preemptive right, stock right, subscription right, warrant
신주인수권(부) 증서	warrant
신주인수 우선매입권	preemption
신중	prudence
신청	offer
신청(화해의)	tender
신청가격	offer
신축조항	escalator clause
신탁	trust

신탁계약서	indenture	실질금리	effective interest
신탁계정	trust account	실질소득	real income
신탁부동산	settled property	실질우선주의	substance over form
신탁양도	deed of trust	실질이익	real income
신탁의 수탁자	trustee	실질임금	real wage
신탁재산	trust account	실질적인 권위에 의한 지지	substantial
신탁증서	deed of trust, trust deed,		authoritative support
	trust indenture	실체자본	physical capital
신탁회계	fiduciary accounting	실체 자본유지	physical capital
실물자본	physical capital		maintenance
실물 자본유지	physical capital	실행가능성 연구(조사)	feasibility study
	maintenance	실현	realization
실사(實査)	inspection	실현가능가액	realizable value
실수	error	실현가능조업도	practical capacity
실잔고계정	open account	실현개념	realization concept
실제생산능력	practical capacity	실현보유이득	realized holding gain
실제원가	actual cost	실현이익	realized income, realized
실제적 지식	know-how		profit
실지재고	periodic inventory,	실현주의	accrual basis, realization
	physical inventory		principle
실지재고조사법	periodic inventory	실효기일	expiry date
	method, periodic inventory	심플렉스방법	simplex method
	system	CVP도표	cost-volume-profit graph
실질가격	real price	CVP분석	cost-volume-profit analysis
실질가치	real value	CVP의 관계	cost-volume-profit
실질계정	real account		relationship

ㅇ

악용(惡用)	misappropriation	안전보호	security
안전	security	안전재고	safety stock
안전가치회계	constant dollar	안전한계	margin of safety
	accounting	안전한계율	margin of safety

ratio(M/S ratio)

안전항 조약(피난조항)   safe harbor rule

안정도   stability

안정된 화폐단위   stable monetary unit

액면   face value

액면(어음상의)   value

액면가액   face amount, face value

액면가액(주식의)   stated value

액면가 이하로 발행된 주식   watered stock

액면금액   nominal value, par value

액면금액(주식의)   principal

액면액   face amount

액면 이하   below par

액면주식   par value stock

액면초과금   capital paid-in excess of per value

액면초과액   premium

약세   bear

약세 시장   bear market

약속(증서에 규정된)   covenant

약속어음   promissory note(P/N)

약식재무제표   (영)abridged accounts

양건(兩建)   straddle

양건예금   compensating balance

양도   assignment, mortgage, sale

양도(재산상의 권리)   transfer

양도담보   assignment

양도성예금증서   certificate of deposit (CD)

양도증서   assignment, transfer

양체자금   change fund

어음   bill, note

어음관리   exchange control

어음발행인   drawer

어음인수   acceptance, acceptance of

bill of exchange

어음할인   discount

업계평균비율   industry ratio

업무   service

업무감사   operational audit

업무예산   operating budget

업무집행 의사결정   operating decision

업자간 가격   trade price

업적   (operating) performance

업적예산   performance budget

업적평가   performance evaluation

업종별 감사안내서   industry audit guide

에누리   allowance

여분   interest

여신   loan

여신잔고   credit balance

여신한도   credit limit

역경매   reverse bid

역금리   negative interest

역무   service

역분개   reversal entry

역사적 원가   historical cost, original cost

역사적 원가관행   historical cost convention

역사적 원가주의   historical cost convention

역사적 원가회계   historical cost accounting(HCA)

역원   director

역진과세   regressive tax

연간이익   annual earnings

연결(재무제표작성)   consolidation

연결납세 신고서   consolidated tax return

연결대차대조표   consolidated balance

sheet

연결방침　　consolidation policy

연결소거란　　eliminating entry

연결손익계산서　　consolidated income statement

연결영업권　　goodwill on consolidation

연결원가　　joint cost

연결이익　　consolidated profit

연결잉여금　　surplus from consolidation

연결재무상태변동표　　consolidated statement of changes in financial position

연결재무제표　　(영)consolidated accounts, consolidated financial statements

연결전 수정　　pre consolidation adjustment

연계매매(商)　　hedging

연구개발비　　research and development cost

연구개발비 지출　　research and development expenditure

연금　　annuity, pension

연금기금　　pension fund

연금법　　annuity method of depreciation

연금법 감가상각　　annuity depreciation

연금수령자　　annuitant

연금식 감가상각법　　annuity method of depreciation

연금액보증제도　　defined benefit pension plan, defined benefit plan

연금의 미래가치　　future value of annuity

연금제도　　pension plan

연금지급협정　　pension scheme

연금채권　　annuity bond

연금회계　　pension

연기가능원가　　postponable cost

연대보증인이 보증한도에서 채권자에게 이행할 책임　　joint and several liability

연대책임　　joint liability

연도감사　　annual audit

연도이익　　annual earnings

연령　　aging

연령조사표　　aging schedule

연불　　deferred payment

연불판매　　deferred payment sale

연산품　　joint product

연산품 원가계산　　joint product cost system, joint product costing

연속갱신예산　　rolling budget

연속변수　　continuous variable

연속복리 계산　　continuous compounding

연속상환사채　　serial bond

연속생산방식　　continuing operation

연속재고수량조사　　cycle count

연속 재고조사　　continuous inventory

연수　　asset depreciation range system(ADRS)

연수조사　　aging

연수합계법　　sum-of-the-years-digit method

연역(법)　　deduction

연차감사　　annual audit

연차계산서류　　annual accounts

연차보고서　　annual report, annual report and accounts

연차사원총회　　annual general meeting(AGM)

연차신고서　　　annual return
연차재무제표　　　annual accounts,
　　　(영)final accounts
연체료　　　arrears
염가갱신선택권　　　bargain renewal
　　　option
염가구입선택권　　　bargain purchase
　　　option(BPO)
영구구속순자산　　　permanently
　　　restricted net asset
영구연금　　　perpetuity
영구자산　　　permanent asset
영구적 차익　　　permanent difference
영구조서(調書)　　　permanent file
영구채권　　　perpetual bond
영국의 증권거래소　　　stock exchange
　　　(SE)
영기준 예산관리　　　zero base budgeting
　　　(ZBB)
영리　　　business enterprise
영세율과세(부가가치세)　　　zero rating
영속기업　　　going concern
영수증　　　receipt
영업계정　　　operating account
영업권　　　goodwill, positive goodwill
영업능력　　　operating capability
영업능력 유지　　　operating capability
　　　maintenance
영업레버리지　　　operating leverage
영업리스 계약　　　operating lease
영업비　　　commercial expense,
　　　distribution cost, operating
　　　cost, operating expense
영업비율　　　operating ratio
영업성과　　　operating performance
영업손익 요약표　　　operating statement
영업수익(수입)　　　operating revenue

영업순환　　　cash cycle
영업순환기간　　　operating cycle
영업실적　　　operating result
영업예산　　　operating budget
영업외비용　　　non-operating expense
영업외수익　　　non-operating revenue
영업용 자산　　　operating asset
영업위험　　　business risk
영업이익　　　operating income, operating
　　　profit
영업자금　　　operating fund
영업활동관련계정　　　operating account
영업활동에 의한 자금　　　fund from
　　　operation
영업활동에 의해 공급된 자금　　　fund
　　　provided by operation
영장　　　warranty
영지　　　fee
예금　　　cash, deposit
예납금　　　deposit
예납법인세　　　advance corporation
　　　tax(ACT)
예방보수(보전)　　　preventive
　　　maintenance (PM)
예보　　　forecasting
예비감사　　　preliminary audit
예비목록색인　　　red herring
예비조사　　　preliminary review
예산　　　budget, budgeting
예산관리　　　budgeting
예산관리규정　　　budgeting manual
예산기간　　　budget period
예산대차대조표　　　pro forma balance
　　　sheet
예산배부　　　allotment
예산사무담당자　　　budget director
예산손익계산서　　　pro forma income

statement

예산(추정) 손익계산서   budgeted income statement

예산 원가   budgeted cost

예산위원회   budget committee

예산작성   budgeting

예산재무제표   pro forma financial statement

예산(추정) 재무제표   budgeted statement

예산 조업도   budgeted capacity, budgeted volume

예산차이   budget variance

예산차이(표준원가계산)   spending variance

예산통제   budgetary control

예산편람   budgeting manual

예산편성   budget preparation, budgeting

예상   projection

예상내용연수   probable life

예상외의 이익   windfall profit

예약시세   forward rate

예외사항에 의한 한정의견   except for opinion

예외에 의한 관리   management by exception

예정   accrual

예정가격   predetermined price

예정납세액   estimated tax

예정배당   proposed dividend

예정원가   predetermined cost

예정임률   predetermined wage rate

예측   forecast, forecasting, projection

예측오차   prediction error

예측오차의 원가   cost of prediction error

오류(오차)   error

완료기준   completed contract method

완성품   finished goods, finished stock

완성품환산량   equivalent unit, equivalent unit of work

완전정보의 기대치   expected value of perfect information

완전희석화 1주당이익   fully diluted earnings per share

외국기업   foreign corporation

외국세   foreign tax

외국세액공제   foreign tax credit

외국적 법인(회사)   alien corporation

외국지점   foreign branch

외국환관리   exchange control

외국환시세   foreign exchange rate

외국환어음   foreign bill of exchange

외국환율   foreign exchange rate

외국환표기 단기어음   foreign exchange

외국회사   alien corporation

외부감사   external audit

외부감사인   external auditor

외부거래   external transaction

외부보고   external reporting

외부자금   external fund

외상   charge

외상거래계정   charge account

외상매입금   account payable, trade creditor, trade payable

외상매입채무 보유일수   days purchases in accounts payable ratio

외상매입처 원장   creditor ledger

외상매출   credit sale

외상매출금   accounts, accounts receivable, receivable, trade debtor, trade receivable

외상매출금의 연령조사   aging of

accounts receivable

외상매출금 회수 시간차이를 이용한 부정
행위　　lapping

외상매출금 회전율　　accounts
receivable turnover(ratio)

외상매출대장　　sales day book(SDB)

외상매출채권　　account(a/c)

외상매출채권의 매수　　factoring

외상지급　　payment on account

외상판매　　credit sale

외채　　external bond, foreign bond

외화거래에 따른 결제위험　　transfer
risk

외화표시 재무제표　　foreign currency
financial statement

외화표시 채권 · 채무　　foreign
currency receivables and
payables

외화표시 확인(행위)계약　　firm
commitment

외화 환산　　foreign currency translation

외화환산차익　　foreign exchange gain

외화환산회계　　foreign currency
translation

외환거래　　foreign currency
transaction

외환시세　　rate of exchange

요구불예금　　cash at bank, demand
deposit

요구이익률　　required rate of return

요금　　charge, fee

요금표　　tariff

요소　　factor

요소별 원가　　first cost

요소비용　　factor cost

요약재무정보　　condensed financial
information

요율　　tariff

요인　　factor

용역　　service

용역잠재능력　　service potential

용역제공능력　　service capacity

용역제공부문　　service center

우량주　　blue chip

우리사주제도　　employee stock
ownership plan(ESOP)

우발사건　　contingency

우발사항　　contingency

우발손실준비금　　contingency reserve,
reserve for contingency

우발이득　　gain contingency, windfall
profit

우발자산　　contingent asset

우발적 손실　　loss contingency

우발적 임차료　　contingent rental

우발채무　　contingency, contingent
liability

우발현상　　contingency

우선급전채무　　preferential debt

우선자본비율　　gearing ratio

우선주　　(영)preference share, preferred
stock

우선주의 자본비용　　cost of preferred
stock

우선지불율　　priority percentage

우선채권자　　preferential creditor

우선채무　　preferential debt

우연성이론　　contingency theory

운송보험료　　insurance

운송중인 물품　　goods in transit

운영감사　　operational audit

운영관리 통제　　administrative control

운용리스　　operating lease

운용비용　　operating expense

운임　freight, transportation in
운임도착지급　transportation in
운임 발송지 지불　carriage outward
운임표　tariff
운전자본　net current asset, working capital, working fund
운전자본변동표　statement of change in working capital
운전자본회전율　working capital ratio, working capital turnover
운전자산　circulating asset
워런트　warrant
워시 세일　wash sale
원(原)단위　costing unit
원가　cost, expense
원가(비용) 배분　cost allocation
원가 · 조업도 · 이익분석　cost-volume-profit analysis
원가 · 조업도 · 이익의 관계　cost-volume-profit relationship
원가가산 가격결정방법　cost-plus pricing
원가가산계약　cost-plus contract
원가가산방식　cost-plus contract
원가계산　cost accounting, costing
원가계산기준　cost accounting standard
원가계산단위　costing unit
원가계산제도　cost accounting
원가계산표　cost card, cost sheet
원가관리　cost control
원가기준　cost basis
원가단위　cost unit, costing unit
원가배부액　applied cost
원가배분　cost assignment, cost attribution, cost distribution
원가법　cost convention, cost method

원가보상계약　cost-plus contract
원가보상법　cost recovery method
원가분류　cost classification
원가산정　cost ascertainment, cost finding
원가에 기초한 대체가격　cost base transfer price
원가예측　cost estimation, cost prediction
원가원장　cost ledger
원가재배분　cost reapportionment
원가절감(절약)　cost saving
원가주의　cost basis, cost convention, cost method, cost principle
원가중심점　cost center
원가집계　cost accumulation
원가집계액　cost pool
원가추정　cost estimation
원가측정　costing
원가카드　cost card
원가통제　cost control
원가표준　cost standard
원가행태　cost behavior
원가회계　cost accounting
원가회수　cost recovery
원가회수법　cost recovery method
원가효율　cost-effectiveness
원가흐름의 가정　cost flow assumption
원금　principal
원료　raw material
원리　principle
원산국증명서　certificate of origin
원산지증명서　certificate of origin
원시(原始)서류　source document
원시기입　original entry
원시기입 장부　book of original entry, book of prime entry

원시원가	original cost
원시자료	source document
원시전표	source document
원장	book of final entry, general ledger, ledger
원장계정	ledger account
원재료	material, raw material, stores
원천과세	pay-as-you-go
원천징수	(영)deduction at source
원천징수 과세	(영)deduction at source
원초기입	original entry
원칙	principle
위약	default
위원회	commission
위임	commission, commitment
위임장	power of attorney
위임장의 쟁탈전	proxy contest, proxy fight
위조	falsification, forgery
위치	registration
위탁	bailment, commitment, consignment
위탁금 유용	defalcation
위탁자	consignor, trustee
위탁증거금	margin
위탁판매	consignment, consignment sale
위험	risk
위험도 높은 값싼 증권	(미)junk bond
위험부담자본	risk capital
위험회피	risk aversion
유가증권	commercial paper(CP), securitys
유급휴가	compensated absence
유기(遺棄)	abandonment
유기(有機)성	articulation
유동·비유동법	current-noncurrent method
유동기금	current fund
유동담보	floating charge
유동부채	current liability, floating debt, short term debt
유동비율	current ratio
유동성	liquidity
유동성비율	liquidity ratio
유동성선호	liquidity preference
유동자산	circulating asset, circulating capital, current asset
유리한 차이	favorable variance
유보사항	reservation
유보사항부 한정의견	subject to opinion
유보이익	accumulated earnings, retained earnings, retained income, revenue reserve, undistributed profit
유보이익계산서	retained earnings statement
유상취득	purchase
유연화	smoothing
유용(유익)	utility
유지	maintenance
유지비	carrying charge, maintenance expense
유체재(有體財)	lease
유치권	lien
유통비	distribution cost
유통시장	currency, secondary market
유한책임	limited liability
유한책임사원	limited partner
유한책임조합	limited partnership
유한책임조합원	limited partner
유한책임회사	limited company, limited liability company

(LLC)

유한파트너십	limited partnership,
유형(고정)자산	tangible asset
유형고정자산	plant and equipment
유효(실효)세율	effective tax rate
유효금리	effective interest
유효성	effectiveness
유효이율	effective rate of interest
유효이자	effective interest
유효 이자율	effective interest rate
유휴비	idle cost
유휴생산능력비용	idle capacity cost
유휴설비	idle equipment
유휴설비비용	idle capacity cost
유휴시간	idle time
6대 회계사무소	Big Six
융자자본	borrowed capital
융통어음	accommodation bill
은행가 비율	banker's ratio
은행계정	bank account
은행계정조정표	bank agreement
은행계좌	bank account
은행권	bank note(BN)
은행 당좌대	bank credit
은행미기입예금	cash in transit,
	deposit in transit
은행수수료	bank charge
은행신용	bank credit
은행(발행) 어음	banker's draft
은행예금	bank deposit
은행예금잔고	bank balance
은행의 자기앞 수표	cashier' check
은행 인수	banker's acceptance
은행 인수어음	bank acceptance,
	banker's acceptance
은행잔고명세서	bank statement
은행잔고조정표	bank reconciliation

	schedule, bank reconciliation
	statement
은행잔고증명서	bank statement
은행조회서	bank confirmation
은행할인료	bank discount
은행확인장	bank confirmation
은행환	banker' order
은행 환어음	banker's draft
은행(발행) 환어음	bank draft(B/D)
응모초과	oversubscription
응용연구	applied research
의견거절	disclaimer of opinion
의결권 트러스트	voting trust
의결권신탁	voting trust
의뢰	commission
의뢰인	client
의무	commitment, obligation
의사갱생	quasi reorganization
의사결정	decision making
의사결정 지원시스템	decision support system(DSS)
의사결정이론	decision theory
의사록(철)	minute book
의안	bill
의제자산	fictitious asset
이권	interest
이동평균	moving average
이동평균법	moving average method, moving weighted average method
이득	gain
이론적 생산능력	theoretical capacity
이론적 조업도	theoretical capacity
2배 정률법	double declining balance method(DDB method)
이사	director, trustee
이사회	board of directors

ㅇ

이상(理想) 표준 원가　ideal standard cost

이상(異常)항목　extraordinary item

이상감가　extraordinary depreciation

이상손실　extraordinary loss

이상적 조업도　ideal capacity

이서　endorsement, indorsement

이연 대변항목　deferred credit

이연법(세무조정상의)　deferral method

이연부채　deferred liability

이연비용　deferred charge

이연수익　deferred credit, deferred revenue

이연원가　deferred cost

이연자산　deferred asset, deferred charge

이용가능자산　available asset

이월　carryover

이월금　balance

이월상품　merchandise inventory

이월시산표　closing trial balance

이월액　carried forward(c/f)

이월품　carryover

이윤　profit

이윤률　profitability

이율　rate of interest, yield

이율곡선　yield curve

이익　benefit, earnings, gain, income, margin, return

이익(이익권)　profit

이익 계산서　earnings statement

이익계획　profit planning

이익도표　break-even chart, profit graph, profit volume chart, profit volume graph

이익률　profitability, rate of return

이익배당금　dividend

이익배당률(조합, 합명회사의)　profit sharing ratio

이익배분제도　profit sharing plan

이익예측　profit forecasting

이익유보　appropriation

이익의 실현　income realization

이익의 유연화　smoothing of income

이익잉여금　accumulated earnings, earned surplus, retained earnings

이익잉여금계산서　retained earnings statement

이익잉여금처분계산서　statement of retained earnings

이익중심점(책임회계)　profit center

이익창출과정　earnings cycle

이익측정　income measurement

이자　interest

이자(차입금의)　discount

이자보상배율　interest coverage ratio

이자보상율　times interest earned ratio

이자부 사채　coupon bond

이자비용　interest expense

이자비용의 자본화　capitalization of interest

이자비용의 자산계상액　capitalization of interest

이자수익　interest income

이자율　interest rate, rate of interest

이자율의 기간구조　term structure of interest rates

이전(移轉)　transfer

이전가격 결정　transfer pricing

이중과세　double taxation

이중과세회피　double taxation relief

이중목적시사　dual purpose test

이중체감잔액법   double declining balance method(DDB method)

2차 거래   secondary distribution

2차 매출   secondary distribution

2차 배부   secondary distribution

2차 할부매출   secondary distribution

이해가능성   understandability

이해관계   interest

이해성   understandability

익명조합원   sleeping partner

인가증서   authorization

인간자산회계   human asset accounting

인계   assumption

인도   abandonment

인도(상품, 제품의)   delivery

인도기준   delivery basis

인도유예금   backwardation

인명계정   personal account

인수(引受)   acceptance, assumption

인수(因數)   factor

인수(引受)단   underwriting syndicate

인수업자   underwriter

인수운임   freight-in

인수인   drawee

인수인도조건   document against acceptance(D/A)

인식   recognition

인자   factor

인적자산회계   human asset accounting

인적자원   human resource

인적자원회계   human resource accounting(HRA)

인적 재산   personal property

인적정보처리   human information processing

인증   authorization

인지세(印紙稅)   stamp duty

인출   drawing

인출금   drawing

인취운임   (영)carriage-inward

일   assignment

일관성   consistency

일괄공제법   flow through method

일괄구입   basket purchase, lump-sum purchase

일괄등기제도   shelf registration

일괄원가계산   batch costing

일괄제조지시서   blanket order

일괄주문   blanket order

일기장   daybook

일단계식   single step form

일단계식 손익계산서   single-step income statement

일람지불(약속)어음   sight note

일람지불(환)어음   sight bill, sight draft

일람표   statement

일반공채   general obligation fund

일반관리비   administrative expense, general administrative expense, general and administrative expense

일반관리비 예산   administrative expense budget

일반구매력회계   constant dollar accounting, constant purchasing power accounting (CPP accounting), general purchasing power accounting (GPPA)

일반기금   general fund

일반목적보고서   general purpose financial statement

일반목적 재무제표　　general purpose financial statement
일반물가(수준)변동회계　　general price level accounting(GPLA)
일반물가변동지수　　general price index, general price level index
일반물가수준 수정재무제표　　general price level adjusted statements
일반본사관리비　　central corporate expense
일반분개장　　general journal
일반비　　general expense
일반영업활동비　　general operating expense
일반우발손실준비금　　general contingency reserve
일반적으로 인정된 감사기준　　generally accepted auditing standard(GAAS)
일반적으로 인정된 회계기준　　generally accepted accounting principle(GAAP)
일반적 제약　　constraint
일반파트너　　general partner
일반 파트너십　　general partnership
일별매입장　　purchase day book(PDB)
일시연기　　moratorium
일시적 차이　　timing difference
일시정지(활동 또는 사용의)　　moratorium
일정가격　　constant dollar
일정률 감모상각　　percentage depletion
1주당 배당금　　dividend per share(DPS)
1주당 손실　　loss per share
1주당 순배당금　　net dividend per share
1주당 순이익　　earnings per share(EPS)
1주당 이익의 이중 표시　　dual presentation of earnings per share
일차시장　　primary market
일치　　agreement, harmonization
임금　　emolument, payroll, wage
임금대장　　payroll
임금지급장　　payroll register
임대(차)료　　rent
임대료　　rental income
임대인　　lessor
임대차　　rent
임대차계약　　lease
임률　　wage rate
임률차이　　labor rate variance, rate variance
임무　　assignment
임시사원총회　　(영)extraordinary general meeting(EGM)
임시상각　　extraordinary depreciation
임시손실　　non-recurring charge
임시손익　　extraordinary profit and loss
임시수선　　extraordinary repair
임시주주총회　　(영)extraordinary general meeting(EGM)
임시항목　　extraordinary item
임원(任員)회(會)　　board of directors
임원상여금　　officer's bonus
임원에 대한 단기차입금　　short term loan payable to officers
임의상환조건　　call provision
임의상환주식　　callable stock
임의청산　　voluntary liquidation
임차(賃借)　　borrowing

임차료	rent expense	입증적 증거	corroborating evidence
임차인	lessee	입질(질권 설정)	pledge
입금대장	cash receipt journal	입찰	bid, tender
입금전표	paying-in slip	입찰 가격	bid price
입증 기능	attest function	입회(立會)	observation
입증시사	substantive test	잉여금	surplus
입증 업무	attestation	잉여의	residual

ㅈ

자(子)회사	subsidiary company	자기자본비용	cost of equity, equity ratio
자가건설자산	self constructed asset	자기자본이익률	return on equity
자가등록	shelf registration	자기자본조달	equity financing
자가보험	self-insurance	자기주식	reacquired stock, repurchased stock, treasury stock
자가사용	sales on approval		
자가제조 또는 구입 의사결정	make or buy decision	자기지분	equity
자금	fund	자기투자자본	down payment
자금계산서	fund statement	자동 대체계좌	banker' order
자금운용표	statement of source and application of fund	자본	capital, owner' equity, shareholder's equity, worth
자금의 용도	use of fund	자본가치	capital value
자금의 운영	application of fund	자본감소	reduction of capital
자금의 원천	source of fund	자본구성	capital structure, financial structure
자금조달	financing, fund raising		
자금조달구조	financial structure	자본구성의 변경	recapitalization
자금조달법	financing method	자본구조	capital structure
자금초과거래	overtrading	자본금	capital, capital stock, common stock
자금흐름	fund flow		
자금흐름계산서	fund flow statement	자본기금	accumulated fund, (영)capital fund
자기금융	self financing		
자기보험	self-insurance	자본레버리지	capital leverage
자기사채	treasury bond	자본리스	capital lease
자기자본	equity		

자본배분	capital rationing
자본변경	recapitalization
자본비용	cost of capital
자본손실	capital loss
자본수정	recapitalization
자본시장	capital market
자본시장선	capital market line(CML)
자본예산	capital budget, capital budgeting
자본유지	capital maintenance, maintenance of capital
자본이득	capital gain
자본이득세	capital gain tax(CGT)
자본이익률(투자)	rate of return on investment
자본잉여금	additional paid in capital, capital reserve, capital surplus, contributed surplus
자본자산가격결정모델	capital asset pricing model(CAPM)
자본자산평가모델	capital asset pricing model(CAPM)
자본재	capital goods
자본적 자산	capital asset, permanent asset
자본적 지출	capital expenditure, capital improvement
자본적 지출공제	capital allowance
자본주이론	proprietary theory
자본준비금	capital reserve
자본지출예산	capital expenditure budget
자본투하	capital investment
자본화	capitalization
자본화가치	capitalized value
자본화리스	capital lease
자본화율	capitalization rate

자본회전율	capital turnover, equity turnover
자사주	treasury stock
자사주식	capital stock
자산	asset
자산배율	asset cover
자산의 감가상각 탄력제도	asset depreciation range system (ADRS)
자산이익률	return on asset
자산재평가	asset revaluation, revaluation of asset
자산평가	asset valuation
자산회전율	asset turnover
자연적 증가	accretion
자연 회계연도	natural business year
자유재량 고정비	managed cost
자유재량원가	discretionary cost
자주정리	readjustment
자질	property
자회사	affiliated company, controlled company, subsidiary
자회사 합병	down stream merger
작성	compilation
작업능률차이	labor efficiency variance
작업시간보고서	job card, time card, work ticket
작업시간차이(표준원가계산)	labor efficiency variance
작업시간표	job card, time card, work ticket
작업중심점	work center
작업지시서	work order
작업측정	work measurement
작업폐물	waste
작업폐물평가	scrap value

잔고	balancing figure
잔돈	change fund
잔무	backlog
잔액	balance
잔업수당	overtime premium
잔여(殘餘)	residual
잔여원가	residual cost
잔여이익	residual income
잔여이익법	residual income approach
잔여지분	residual equity
잔여지분설	residual equity theory
잔존가액	balance, residual value, salvage value, scrap value
잔존가치(리스에서)	residual value
잠재가격	shadow price
잠정계산법(외화환산법의)	temporal method
잡비	miscellaneous expense, sundry
잡수입	miscellaneous revenue
잡품	sundry
장관	director
장기경과수표	stale check
장기계약	long-term contract
장기부채	funded debt, long-term liability
장기성자산	long-lived asset, long-term asset
장기어음	long-dated bill
장기지불능력비율	coverage ratio
장기채무	long-term debt
장기추세	secular trend
장기투자	fixed asset investment, long-term investment
장부	record
장부가액	book value(BV), carrying amount, carrying value
장부상이익	paper profit

장부상 이익의 과세소득에의 조정	taxable income
장부상 제거(수리불능의)	write off
장부의 끝을 맞추기 위한 수치	balancing figure
장부의 마감	write off
장부재고법	book inventory
장부재고조사법	continuous inventory method
장치	equipment
재고관리	inventory control, inventory management, stock control
재고비용	holding cost
재고상품	merchandise inventory, stock in trade
재고자산	inventory, stock, stock taking
재고자산감모	inventory shrinkage
재고자산감모손	inventory shortage
재고자산 기말잔고	closing stock
재고자산 기말잔액	ending inventory
재고자산 등식	inventory equation
재고자산 보유이익	inventory holding gain
재고자산손익	inventory profit or loss
재고자산준비금	inventory reserve
재고자산평가	inventory pricing, inventory valuation
재고자산회계	inventory accounting
재고자산회전수	inventory turnover
재고자산회전율	inventory turnover, inventory turnover ratio, (영)stock turnover
재고제품	stock in trade
재고조사	inventory
재고차손	inventory shortage
재고파악	inventory

ㅈ

재고평가	inventory valuation
재고표	inventory
재고품	stock in trade
재공품	goods in process, work in progress(WIP), work in process inventory
재공품통제계정	work in process control account
재공품회전율	work in process turnover
재대체분개	reversing entry
재료	material, raw material
재료가격차이	material price variance
재료 구입가격과 소비가격의 차이	price variance
재료명세서	bill of materials(B/M)
재료배합차이	material mix variance
재료비	material cost
재료소비수량차이	material quantity variance
재료수량차이	material usage variance
재료시방서	bill of materials(B/M)
재료원장	material ledger, stores ledger
재료의 가격차이	price variance
재료출고전표	material requisition
재료출고청구서	material requisition
재료혼합차이	material mix variance
재무	finance
재무계획	financial planning
재무관리	financial management
재무구성	financial structure
재무담당자	chief financial officer (CFO)
재무레버리지	capital leverage, financial leverage
재무보고서	(영)financial accounts
재무보고통화	reporting currency
재무부장	treasurer
재무분석	financial analysis, financial statement analysis
재무분석가	financial analyst
재무비용	finance charge, financial expense
재무비율	financial ratio
재무상의 중심 부분	financial highlight
재무상태	financial condition, financial position
재무상태 변동	change in financial position
재무상태변동표	statement of change in financial position
재무상태표	statement of financial condition, statement of financial position
재무성 단기증권	treasury bill(TB)
재무성 중기증권	treasury note
재무예산(예측)	financial budget, financial forecast
재무위험	financial risk
재무자본	financial capital
재무자본유지	financial capital maintenance
재무정보요약	highlights
재무정책	fiscal policy
재무제표	accounts, (영)financial accounts, financial statements
재무제표감사	financial statement audit
재무제표 대리작성	compilation of financial statement
재무제표 대리작성계약	compilation engagement

재무제표분석 financial statement analysis

재무제표의 검토 review of financial statements

재무제표의 주석사항 note to financial statement

재무총괄경영자 chief financial officer(CFO)

재무표 statement

재무회계 financial accounting

재무회계보고서 financial reporting

재보험 reinsurance

재산 property, worth

재산배당 property dividend

재산상태보고서 statement of affair

재산의 소유자 proprietor

재생산원가 cost of reproduction, reproduction cost

재수정분개 reversing entry

재외 자회사 controlled foreign company

재외 종속회사 controlled foreign company

재외지점 overseas branch

재외회사 overseas company

재정 finance

재정리기입 readjustment

재정리분개 reversing entry

재정상태 financial position

재정정책 fiscal policy

재조달원가 current cost, replacement cost, reproduction cost

재조정 reorganization

재주문점(경제적 발주량에서) reorder point

재취득주식 repurchased stock

재투자수익률 reinvestment rate

재편성 reorganization

재평가 revaluation

재평가잉여금 revaluation surplus

재평가적립금 appraisal surplus, appreciation surplus, revaluation reserve

재표시 restatement

재해손실 casualty loss

재해전보(災害塡補)적립금 reserve for contingency

재화 goods

재화 1회분 batch

재화의 한 묶음 batch

저가기준 lower of cost or market (LCM)

저가법 lower of cost or market(LCM), lower of cost or market value

저가상품 loss leader

저당 mortgage, security

저당권 mortgage, pledge

저당권자 mortgagee

저당물 gage

저당 증서 mortgage

저당채권자 mortgagee

저량 stock

저작권 copyright, property

저작권사용료 royalty

저장품 suppliy

저장품 카드 bin card

저축성예금 time deposit

저축액 savings

적격연금제도 qualified pension plan

적극적인 조회확인 positive confirmation

적극적 확인 positive confirmation

적립금 reserve

적립금회계 (영)reserve accounting

적발위험   detection risk
적법연금계획   qualified pension plan
적송품   consignment, consignment outward
적절한 퇴직 연금   qualified pension plan
적정의견   clean opinion, unqualified opinion
적정의견 보고서   unqualified opinion report
적정재고   safety stock
적정표시   fair presentation
적정한 공시   adequate disclosure
전기(轉記)   post, posting
전기 손익수정   prior period adjustment
전기수정사항   prior period item
전기(前期)의 비교대응수치   comparative figure
전기의 비교액   comparative figure
전기이월   brought down(b/d), carried down(c/d)
전 날짜   pre date
전도금   advance, prepayment
전략계획   strategic planning
전무(상무)회   board of directors
전문직   profession
전부감사   complete audit
전부연결   full consolidation
전부원가   absorbed cost, absorption cost
전부원가계산   absorption costing, full absorption costing, full costing
전송   transfer
전액인수   firm commitment
전일부   antedate
전임감사인   predecessor auditor

전자 데이터 처리   electronic data processing(EDP)
전제   assumption
전통적 전부원가계산   conventional costing
전환가격   conversion price
전환가능우선주   convertible preferred stock
전환가정법   if converted method
전환기간   conversion period
전환비율   conversion ratio
전환사채   convertible bond(CB), convertible debenture, convertible debt, convertible preferred stock
전환우선주   convertible preferred stock
전환주식   convertible stock
전환증권   convertible security
절대치   absolute value
절사하다   round down
절세   tax avoidance
절세거래   wash sale
절세계획   tax planning
절약   saving
절차   procedure
절차감사   procedural audit
점두매매   over-the-counter(OTC)
점두시장   over-the-counter market
점두주(株)   over-the-counter stock
점두품목   over-the-counter stock
정가   fixed price, list price
정관   articles of incorporation, certificate of incorporation, (영)memorandum of association
정관(미국 회사의)   articles of association
정규곡선   normal curve

정규분포	normal distribution
정기예금	time deposit
정기재고	periodic inventory
정기재고자산 계산법	periodic inventory system
정기재고조사	(영)periodic stock check
정기주주총회	annual shareholders' meeting
정년퇴직수당	retirement
정당한 절차	due process
정량발주 시스템	reorder level system
정례주주총회	annual general meeting (AGM)
정률법	fixed percentage of book value method
정리	adjustment, regulation
정밀감사	complete audit, detailed audit
정보검색	information retrieval (IR)
정보경제학	information economics
정보시스템	information system
정보이론	information theory
정보조직	information system
정보처리	information processing
정부기관	agency
정부기금(청, 국 등 미국 정부기관의 기금)	agency fund
정부 조성금	government grant
정부채	national debt
정부회계	governmental accounting
정산(精算)표	work sheet
정산계정	open account
정상가격	normal price
정상감모손	normal shrinkage
정상감손	normal waste
정상공손	normal spoilage
정상공손과 비정상공손	spoilage

정상법	farm price method
정상생산능력	normal activity, normal capacity, normal volume
정상연금비용	normal pension cost
정상영업순환	normal operating cycle
정상영업순환 기준	normal operating cycle basis
정상원가	normal cost
정상이익	normal return
정상작업감손	normal waste
정상 재고	base stock
정상재고법	base stock method, normal stock method
정상적인 거래순환주기	normal operating cycle
정상조업도	normal activity, normal capacity, normal volume
정상표준원가	normal standard cost
정수계획법	integer programming
정시발주 시스템	reorder interval system
정액급부제도	fixed benefit plan
정액납부연금	money purchase plan
정액납입제도	defined contribution plan
정액법	straight line depreciation, straight line method
정액연금제도	defined benefit plan
정액전도 소액현금	imprest cash, petty cash fund
정액전도자금	imprest fund
정정지시서	deficiency letter
정지된 사업부문의 이익	discontinued operation
정착물	fixtures
정찰가격	fixed price
제1차 기입 장부	book of original

ㅈ

entry, book of prime entry

제2차 기입 장부　　book of secondary
　　　　entry

제각(除却)　　retirement

제각법　　retirement method

제거　　abandonment

제거분개　　eliminating entry, elimination

제공　　tender

제구좌　　sundry

제로섬 게임　　zero sum game

제로 잔존가액　　zero salvage value

제안요구서　　request for proposal(RFP)

제약조건　　constraint

제어　　control

제어환경　　control environment

제외　　saving

제외사항　　exclusion clause, exemption
　　　　clause

제조　　production

제조간접비　　burden, factory burden,
　　　　factory expense, factory
　　　　overhead, indirect
　　　　manufacturing cost,
　　　　manufacturing expense,
　　　　manufacturing overhead,
　　　　overhead, overhead cost,
　　　　production overhead cost

제조간접비 능률차이　　overhead
　　　　efficiency variance

제조간접비 배부부족액　　under
　　　　absorbed burden, under
　　　　absorbed overhead, under
　　　　applied burden, under applied
　　　　overhead

제조간접비 배부액　　applied overhead,
　　　　absorbed overhead

제조간접비 배부율　　burden rate,

overhead rate

제조간접비 배부초과액　　overabsorbed
　　　　burden, overabsorbed
　　　　overhead, overapplied burden

제조간접비 소비차이　　overhead
　　　　spending variance, spending
　　　　variance

제조간접비예산　　factory overhead
　　　　budget

제조간접비 예정배부율　　predetermined
　　　　burden rate, predetermined
　　　　overhead rate

제조간접비의 배부　　overhead
　　　　allocation

제조간접비 조업도차이　　overhead
　　　　volume variance

제조간접비 차이　　overhead variance

제조간접비 총차이　　overhead total
　　　　variance

제조간접비 표준배부율　　standard
　　　　burden rate

제조경비　　manufacturing expense

제조계획　　production planning

제조기업　　manufacturing firm

제조명령　　factory order

제조방법　　production method

제조부문　　production department

제조시간　　manufacturing time

제조예산　　manufacturing budget,
　　　　manufacturing cost,
　　　　production budget

제조원가　　cost of goods manufactured,
　　　　factory cost, production cost

제조원가 명세표　　manufacturing
　　　　statement

제조원가 보고서　　cost of production
　　　　report

제조지시서	job order, production order, work order
제조지시서별원가	job order cost
제조지시서별 원가계산	job cost system, job costing, job order cost accounting
제조지시서별 원가계산표	job cost sheet
제조직접비	first cost
제출	tender
제품	finished goods, product
제품계열별 보고서	product line reporting
제품배합	product mix
제품보증	warranty
제품생애주기	product life cycle
제품원가	product cost
제품원가계산	product costing
제품재고(량)	finished goods inventory
제품제조원가	cost of goods manufactured
제품제조원가명세서	cost of goods manufactured statement
제한배서	qualified endorsement
제한적 검토	limited review
조건부 매매	conditional sale
조건부 이서(裏書)	conditional endorsement
조건부 임차료	contingent rental
조건부 판매계약	conditional sale agreement
조건부 한정의견	subject to opinion
조건부 확률	conditional probability
조별상각	group depreciation
조별원가	(영)lot cost
조별원가계산	lot costing, lot cost system,

조사	examination, inquiry, test check, investigation
조사보고서	comfort letter
조사비	exploration cost
조서	bill, statement
조성금	subsidy, subvention, grant in aid
조세계획	tax planning
조세의 사정(査定)	tax assessment
조세조약	tax treaty
조세피난처	tax haven
조세회피	tax planning
조세회피(합법적 수단의)	tax avoidance
조세회피국	tax haven
조심	prudence
조업능력	operating capability
조업도	capacity
조업도비율	capacity ratio
조업도차이	capacity variance, denominator variance, volume variance
조업이익	operating profit
조작(造作)	fixtures
조직구조	organizational structure
조직도	organization chart
조직체	enterprise
조합	combination
조합영업	partnership
조합원(partner)의 총칭	firm
조화	balance
조화화	harmonization
조회	inquiry
종가	future value(FV)
종가(終價)	terminal value
종량세	specific duty
종류	brand
종속회사	controlled company,

subsidiary, subsidiary company

종신연금   life annuity, perpetuity

종업원   employee

종업원연금계획   occupational pension scheme

종업원 지주제도   employee stock ownership plan(ESOP)

종합상각법   group and composite method of depreciation

종합예산   comprehensive budget, master budget

종합원가계산   process costing

주(州)내 법인   domestic corporation

주(州) 또는 시(市)의 수입(收入)직원   treasurer

주(州)외 법인   foreign corporation

주가상승 기업   gain

주가수익률   price earnings ratio(PER)

주가시세의 상승   gain

주관적 가치   subjective value

주권(株券)   share certificate, stock, stock certificate

주권대장   share ledger

주기(분개장의)   narration

주기(注記)   note

주기적 청구서작성   cycle billing

주문   commission

주문 잔고   backlog, back order

주문점(재고를 보충하는 시점)   ordering point, order point

주석   footnote, note

주식   share, stock

주식공개매입   (영)take-over bid(TOB), tender offer

주식공개매입 제의   tender offer

주식공개유한책임회사   publicity held

company

주식 교환   stock exchange

주식구입선택권   option, (영)share option

주식대장   share ledger, stock ledger

주식매매 중개인   broker

주식매수권   share right, stock right, warrant

주식매입(회사지배목적의)   tender

주식매입권   stock purchase warrant

주식 매입 선택권   stock option

주식발행에 의한 자본조달   equity financing

주식 발행으로 인하여 회사가 받는 대가의 합계액   contributed capital

주식발행초과금   capital paid-in excess of per value, share premium, premium on capital stock

주식배당   stock dividend

주식병합   reverse split

주식분할   split, stock split

주식불입잉여금   additional paid in capital

주식비공개회사   close corporation

주식원장   stock ledger

주식의 공개   going public

주식의 상장   going public

주식의 소각   retirement of stock

주식의 할당   allotment of share

주식자본금   share capital

주식중개인   securities broker

주식중매인   (영)stock broker

주식회사   corporation

주요 감사인   primary auditor

주요시장   primary market

주요 조건　principal
주의　principle
주주(株主)　shareholder, stockholder
주주명부　register of member, stock transfer book
주주명부계　registrar
주주명부등록기관　registrar
주주명부에 기재된 주주　stockholder of record
주주에게 보내지는 연차보고서　proxy statement
주주지분　equity, net asset, owner' equity, owners' equity, shareholder's equity, stockholder's equity
주주지분계산서　statement of stockholder's equity
주주총회　general meeting of stockholders
주주할당발행　right offering
주택(담보)금리공제　mortgage interest deduction
준갱생(準更生)(회사의)　quasi reorganization
준거감사　compliance audit
준거성 테스트　compliance test
준거시사　test of compliance
준고정비　semi-fixed cost
준변동비　mixed cost, semi-variable cost
준비감사　preliminary audit
준비금　accumulated earnings, provision, reserve
준비시간　lead time, set-up time
준수감사　compliance audit
줄여서 해석　default
중간　interim

중간검토 보고서　interim review report
중간배당　interim dividend
중간보고서　interim report
중간재무정보　interim financial information
중간재무정보의 검토　review of interim financial information
중간재무제표　interim financial statement, interim statement
중개　brokerage
중개수수료　brokerage
중기채권　note
중단된 영업활동　discontinued operation
중도상환　redemption
중도해약　recession
중립성　neutrality
중매　brokerage
중매업　brokerage
중매인　factor
중역　director
중요성　materiality, value
증가(增價)　accretion, appreciation
증감연관　articulation
증거　evidence
증거(물건)　evidential matter
증거금　deposit
증거금율　margin requirement
증거문　instrument
증거자료　evidential matter
증권　bill, instrument
증권거래소　stock exchange
증권담보사채　collateral trust bond
증권등록 실명서　registration statement
증권분석가　financial analyst

증권 소지인

증권 소지인   debenture holder
증권시장선   security market line
증권의 가장(假裝)매매   (미)wash sale
증권의 발행인   drawer
증권인수   underwriting
증권인수회사   underwriter
증권화한 채무   debenture
증권회사   broker, underwriter
증권회사의 점두(店頭)   over-the-counter(OTC)
증명서   certificate
증분분석   incremental analysis
증분수익   incremental revenue
증분예산   incremental budget
증분원가   incremental cost
증분이익   incremental profit
증분주의 예산   incremental budget
증빙 대조   vouching
증빙식 제도   voucher system
증서   bill, instrument, scrip
증여   donation, gift
증여세   gift tax
증여잉여금   donated surplus
증여자본   donated capital
증축   improvement
지급보증서   bond
지급어음, 어음채무   note payable
지급이자   interest expense
지급인   drawee
지대   rent
지방채   municipal bond
지배   control
지배(소유)권의 취득   take-over
지배ㆍ종속관계의 회사   affiliated company
지배회사   controlling company
지분   entity, interest, stock

지분법   equity method
지분유가증권   equity security
지분자본   (영)equity capital
지분증권   equity security
지분풀링법   pooling of interest method
지불(현금, 수표 등의)   disbursement
지불(지급)어음 기입장   bill payable book
지불능력   solvency
지불불능   insolvency
지불어음   bill payable(B/P, BP)
지불연기   moratorium
지불운임   carriage outward
지불유예   moratorium
지불의 연기   deferred payment
지불이자부담능력배율   times interest earned ratio
지불인도조건   document against payment(D/P)
지불전송료   freight-out
지불정지   moratorium
지불채무   accounts payable
지불처   payee
지사   branch
지수   index, index number
지수법   indexation, indexing
지수화   indexing
지시   commission
지시식수표   order check
지시인 지불수표   order check
지역권   easement
지역별 구획   geographical segment
지역별 부문   geographical segment
지연수표   stale check
지위   post
지점   branch
지점 계정   branch current account

지점 예산　　branch control

지점 통제　　branch control

지점회계　　branch accounting

지정양도　　assignment

지주(持株)회사　　holding company

지참인 지급 사채　　bearer bond

지참인 지급 어음(수표)　　bearer check

지참인 지급 증권　　bearer security

지출　　expenditure, outgo, outlay

지출권한　　appropriation

지출액　　expenditure

지출예산　　allowance

지폐　　bill, note

지표　　index

지표첨부　　indexing

지휘자　　director

직권　　authority

직능별 분류 functional classification

직능별 회계　　functional accounting

직선법　　straight line depreciation

직업　　profession

직업윤리　　professional ethics

직업윤리규정　　code of professional ethics

직업회계사(공인회계사)　　accounting profession

직전의 계약 불이행　　anticipatory breach

직접감액법(대손처리상의)　　direct write-off method

직접공　　direct labor

직접금융리스　　direct financing lease

직접노동시간　　direct labor hour

직접노무비　　direct labor, direct labor cost

직접노무비 능률차이　　direct labor efficiency variance

직접노무비예산　　direct labor budget

직접노무비의 원가차이　　labor variance

직접노무비 임률차이　　direct labor rate variance

직접노무비 작업시간차이　　direct labor efficiency variance

직접노무비차이　　direct labor total variance

직접배분법　　direct allocation method

직접비　　direct cost

직접비용　　direct expense

직접상각법(대손처리상의)　　direct write-off method

직접원가　　direct cost, marginal cost

직접원가계산　　direct costing, marginal costing

직접작업　　direct labor

직접작업시간　　direct labor hour

직접재료　　direct material

직접재료비　　direct material, direct material cost

직접재료비 가격차이　　direct material price variance

직접재료비 소비량차이　　direct material usage variance

직접재료비예산　　direct material cost budget

직접재료비와 직접노무비　　prime cost

직접재료비차이 총계　　direct material total variance

직접 전기(轉記)　　direct posting

진부화　　obsolescence

진술서　　letter of representation, representation letter, statement

진실하고 공정한 개관　　(영)true and fair view

진정가격	real price	집중투표	cumulative voting
진정합병	merger	집중화	centralization
진행기준	percentage of completion method	집합손익계정	income summary account, profit and loss summary account
질권(質權)	mortgage, pledge	집행	administration
질문	inquiry	집행임원	officer
짐작	discount	징수 어음	bill for collection(B/C)
집단	company		

ㅊ

차감계정	contra account	차환	refund
차기이월	carried forward(c/f)	착복	embezzlement, misappropriation
차변	debit, debtor(Dr.)	착선통지	arrival notice
차변기입(차기)	charge	착수금	deposit
차변잔액	debit balance, credit balance	착오	error
차손(次損)	loss	참가적우선주	participating preferred stock
차손금의 소급	loss carryback	참가지분	participating interest
차액	balance, balancing figure	참여예산	participative budgeting
차액분석	differential analysis	창고	deposit
차액원가	differential cost	창고증권	warehouse receipt
차액취득매매	arbitrage	창고화물증권	warehouse receipt
차이	variance	창업비	organization cost, preliminary expense, promotion expense
차이분석	analysis of variance	창조적 회계	creative accounting
차이분석금	variance analysis	채광비	exploration cost
차익	margin	채굴권	royalty
차입	debt, borrowing	채권	certificate, loan, receivable
차입금	borrowing, loan, loan capital	채권금융회사	factor
차입금리	borrowing rate	채권매수업자	factor
차입비용	borrowing cost	채권변제기일 연기 조치	rescheduling
차입자본	borrowed capital, loan capital	채권액	creditors
차입효과	leverage	채권자	creditor(cr.)
차지(借地)	lease		

채권자 분배금　　dividend
채권투자신탁　　bond fund
채무　　debt, liability, obligation
채무거래장부　debit note
채무액　　debtors
채무초과액　　impairment
채취산업　　extractive industry
책임중심점　　responsibility center
책임회계　　responsibility accounting
처리과정　　procedure
처분　　appropriation
처분가능이익　　distributable income, (영)distributable profit
처분된 이익잉여금　　appropriated retained earnings
천연자원　　natural resource
첨부서류　　exhibit
청구　claim
청구권　　claim, interest
청구금액　　charge
청구서　　bill
청산　　liquidation, settlement, winding up
청산가치　　liquidation value
청산소(무역수지결산에 대한)　　clearing house
청산인　　liquidator
청약　　offer
청약된 자본금　　capital stock subscribed
체감잔액법　　declining balance method, reducing balance method
체계적 위험　　systematic risk
체납금　　arrears
체납세액　　delinquent tax
체화(滯貨)　　backlog
초(超)인플레이션　　hypothecated asset
초(超)할인사채　　deep discount bond

초과노무수당　　overtime premium
초과발행(수표의)　　kiting
초과이윤　　super-profit
초과현재가치　　excess present value
초과현재 가치지수　　excess present value index
총계　　sum
총계정원장　　general ledger
총괄계정　　controlling account
총괄식　　single step form
총괄예산　　comprehensive budget
총매출액　　gross sales, (영)gross turnover
총발생원가 자산계상방식　　full costing method
총소득　　gross income
총수입　　gross income
총원가　　total cost
총익금　　gross income
총자본이익　　all-capital earnings rate
총자본회전율　　capital turnover, total asset turnover
총자산이익률　　return on total asset
총자산회전율　　total asset turnover
총재무자원　　all financial resource
총코스트　　total cost
최고경영책임자　　chief executive officer(CEO)
최고재무관리자　　chief financial officer(CFO)
최대생산능력　　maximum capacity
최대조업도　　maximum capacity
최소주식인수한도　　minimum subscription
최저리스지불액의 계산　　minimum lease payment(MLPs)
최저재고수준　　minimum stock level

최저지불리스료　minimum lease payment(MLPs)

최적 발주량　economic order quantity (EOQ)

최적생산규모　optimum production lot size

최종기한(식품의)　expiry date

추가가격인상　additional mark-up

추가설비투자　capital addition

추세분석　trend analysis

추심(推尋)　recourse

추적가능비　traceable cost

추정　estimate, forecast, forecasting

추정부채　estimated liability

추정비용　estimated expense

추정원가　estimated cost

추정잔존가액　estimated salvage value, residual value

추정재무제표　projected financial statement

추징금　assessment

추출산업　extractive industry

출입장　daybook

출자자　investor

출자자에 대한 분배　distribution to owner

출자자 지분　owners' equity

충당금　allowance, appropriation, reserve

충당금 방식　allowance method

충실증서　fidelity bond

취득(타회사의)　acquisition

취득원가　acquisition cost, cost of goods purchased, historical cost, original cost

취득원가기준　historical cost basis

취득원가산입　capitalization

취득원가주의　historical cost basis

취득원가주의회계　historical cost accounting(HCA)

취득일　date of acquisition

취득일전 이익　pre acquisition profit

취소　recession

취임　assumption

취지서(설립)　prospectus

측정　estimate, measurement

측정개념　measurement concept

치환원가　replacement cost

칙허(공인)회계사　(영)chartered accountant(CA)

친교　company

친회사　holding company, parent company

ㅋ

컴퓨터 주변 감사　auditing around the computer

콜 대부금　call loan

콜 옵션　call option

클레임　claim

E

타당성　validity
타인자본　borrowed capital, loan capital
타인자본비용　cost of debt
탄력성예산　flexible budget, variable budget
탈세(脫稅)　tax evasion
탐사비　exploration cost
탐색이론　search theory
토지　land
통계적 표본조사　statistical sampling
통계적 품질관리　statistical quality control(SQC)
통상의 소득　ordinary income
통상정관　articles of association
통상조합　general partnership
통일성　uniformity
통일회계제도　uniform accounting system
통제　control
통제가능변수　controllable variable
통제가능원가　controllable cost
통제계정　control account, controlling account, total account
통제불능비　uncontrollable cost
통제불능원가　uncontrollable cost
통제위험　control risk
통제절차　control procedure
통제한계　span of control
통제환경　control environment
통칙(通則)　rule

통화　currency
통화교환　currency swap
통화 유통액　currency
통화의 가치상승　appreciation
통화의 가치하락　depreciation
퇴직　retirement
퇴직급여제도　retirement benefit scheme, retirement plan
퇴직급여충당금　retirement allowance
투기(投機)　speculation
투기목적으로 선물환계약을 체결할 경우　speculation
투입산출분석　input-output analysis
투자　investment
투자대상 설비의 판매가치를 가미한 회수기간　bailout period
투자부동산　(영)investment property
투자분석　investment analysis
투자세액공제　investment credit, investment tax credit(ITC)
투자수익률　return on investment(ROI)
투자신탁　mutual fund, investment trust
투자신탁회사　investment company
투자안　project
투자에 대한 소득　(영)unearned income
투자에 따른 소득　(영)investment income
투자유가증권　investment, long-term investment
투자은행　investment bank,

ㅋ

ㅌ

investment banker

투자은행업무　investment banking

투자의 기본 분석　fundamental
analysis

투자이익률　rate of return on
investment, return on
investment(ROI)

투자자　investor

투자자문　investment advisor

투자자산　investment

투자자산회전율　investment turnover

투자중심점　investment center

투자회사　investment company

투표권의 위임　proxy

투표신탁　voting trust

투하자본　invested capital

투하자본이익률　return on capital
employed(ROCE)

특권영업면허　franchise

특매　sale

특별감가　extraordinary depreciation

특별강제관리　sequestration

특별발행　bonus issue

특별상각　extraordinary depreciation

특별손실　extraordinary loss

특별손익　extraordinary gain or loss,
extraordinary profit and loss

특별손익항목　extraordinary item

특별수당　bonus

특별수선　extraordinary repair

특별의결　(영)special resolution

특별이익　extraordinary gain

특별 이해관계자간 거래　related party
transaction

특별횡선수표　special crossing

특성　property

특성선　characteristic line

특수관계자　related party

특수관계자간 거래　related party
transaction

특수관계자집단　related party

특수목적의 재무제표　special purpose
financial statement

특수분개장　special journal

특약점　agency, agent

특저가품　loss leader

특정제조지시서　special job order,
special order, special
production order, specific job
order, specific production
order

특허권　patent

특허권사용료　license fee, royalty

ㅍ

파는 쪽　bear

파산　bankruptcy

파산감사관　comptroller

파산관리인　(영)insolvency

practitioner

파산관재인　trustee in bankruptcy

파산 예측　bankruptcy prediction

판매　sale

판매가격   market price, selling price
판매가격차이   sales price variance, selling price variance
판매가능상품   goods available for sale
판매 가능상(제)품의 원가   cost of goods available for sale
판매간접비   selling overhead
판매계약   commitment
판매기준   completed sales basis, sales basis
판매량차이   sales quantity variance
판매비   distribution cost, distribution expense, marketing cost, selling cost, selling expense
판매비예산   selling expense budget
판매비와 일반관리비   selling and general administrative expense
판매시점   point of sales(POS)
판매시점 수익인식   sales basis of revenue recognition
판매예산   sales budget
판매의 신청(주문)   offer for sale
판매촉진비   promotion expense, (영)publicity cost
판매품의 제조원가   factory cost
판매형 리스   sales type lease
판매 후 리스   lease back
8대 회계사무소   Big Eight
팩토링   factoring
편집   compilation
평가   appraisal, balance, estimate
평가(액)   assessment
평가감   write off
평가계정   absorption account, contra account, offset account, valuation account
평가성 충당   valuation allowance(VA)

평가성 충당금   valuation reserve
평가액   appraisal, valuation, value
평가익   appreciation
평가절하   write down
평가증(增)   appreciation, write up
평균   average
평균법   average, average method, weighted average inventory method, weighted average method
평균원가   average cost(AVCO)
평균원가법   average cost(AVCO), average cost method
평균원가흐름의 가정   average cost flow assumption
평균자본이익율   average rate of return
평균재고   average inventory
평균재고일수   days sales in inventory, day to sell inventory, (영)number of days' stock held
평균재고자산   average inventory
평균치   average
평균투자수익(률)   average return on investment
평생연금   life annuity
평행차입   parallel loan
평형   balance
폐기   abandonment
폐기가치   abandonment value
폐쇄회사   closed corporation
포괄계정   control account
포괄담보   floating charge
포괄예산   comprehensive budget
포괄이익   comprehensive income
포괄주의   all inclusive concept, clean surplus approach
포괄주의 손익계산서   all inclusive

income statement
포트폴리오　　portfolio
포트폴리오 분석　　portfolio analysis
포트폴리오 이론　　portfolio theory
표　　bill
표기가격　　stated value
표기금액　　stated value
표본　　sample
표본감사　　audit sampling
표본분포　　sampling distribution
표본위험　　sampling risk
표본추출법　　sampling
표시가격　　stated value
표시가액　　face value
표시 이율　　coupon rate
표시자본금　　stated capital
표준　　standard
표준가격　　standard price(SP)
표준고정제조간접비　　standard fixed
　　overhead cost
표준기계시간　　standard machine time
표준노동시간　　standard labor time
표준매입가격　　standard purchase price
표준변동원가계산　　standard marginal
　　costing, standard variable
　　costing
표준변동제조간접비　　standard variable
　　overhead cost
표준비율　　standard ratio
표준산업분류　　standard industrial
　　classification(SIC)
표준오차　　standard error
표준원가　　standard cost
표준원가계산　　standard cost system,
　　standard costing
표준원가법　　standard cost
표준원가차이　　standard cost variance

표준의견　　standard opinion
표준임률　　standard labor rate(SR)
표준재고수준　　standard stock level
표준재료비　　standard material cost
표준재료 소비량　　standard material
　　usage
표준제조간접비　　standard overhead
　　cost
표준제조원가　　standard production
　　cost
표준직접 노무비　　standard direct labor
　　cost
표준직접원가계산　　standard direct
　　costing, standard marginal
　　costing, standard variable
　　costing
표준직접임률　　standard direct labor
　　rate
표준직접재료비　　standard direct
　　material cost
표준치　　average
표준판매가　　standard selling price
표준편차　　standard deviation
표준한계원가계산　　standard marginal
　　costing
푸시다운회계　　pushdown accounting
품목수령증　　goods received note(GRN)
품절　　stock-out
품질　　brand
품질관리　　quality control(QC)
프랜차이즈　　franchise
프랜차이즈료 수익　　franchise fee
　　revenue
프로그램 예산　　program budget
프로그램 원가　　programmed cost
프로젝트 자금조달　　project finance
피감사회사　　client

피드백	feedback
피배서인	endorsee
피신탁자	trustee

피지배회사	controlled company
피투자회사	investee, investee company

ㅎ

하역료	landing charge
하위증권(청구권에서의)	junior security
하한금리	floor
하향 시세의 시장	bear market
학습곡선	learning curve
한계분석	marginal analysis
한계생산력	marginal productivity
한계세율	marginal tax rate
한계원가	marginal cost
한계원가계산	marginal costing
한계이익	contribution margin, marginal income
한계이익률	contribution margin ratio, marginal income ratio, profit volume ratio(PV ratio)
한 벌	lot
한산한 시장	thin market
한정	qualification
한정배서	qualified endorsement
한정보고서	qualified report
한정사항	qualification
한정의견	qualified opinion
한정의견 감사보고서	qualified auditor's report, qualified audit report, qualified opinion report
한정의견 보고서	qualified report
한정증명서	qualified certificate

한정책임	limited liability
할당	allocation, allotment, assignment, quota
할당금	assessment
할당수량	quota
할당예산액	appropriation
할부금융회사	finance company
할부기준	installment method
할부기준법	installment method
할부상각	amortization
할부상환	amortization
할부의 첫 지불금	down payment
할부판매	deferred payment sale
할인	allowance, discount
할인가치	discounted value
할인계수	discount factor
할인 구입	bargain purchase
할인구입권리	bargain purchase option(BPO)
할인된 현금흐름	discounted cash flow
할인액	discount
할인어음	note receivable discounted
할인율	discount, discount rate
할인현재가치	discounted present value
할인회수기간법	discounted payback method, discounted payback period method

ㅎ

할증금	premium
합계	footing, sum
합동	amalgamation, combination
합동효과	synergism
합명회사	general partnership
합병	amalgamation, combination, merger
합병(주식)회사	corporate joint venture
합병사업	joint venture
합병시 영업권	consolidated goodwill
합병영업권	goodwill on consolidation
합산	footing
합의된 고정 예산	negotiated static budget
합의에 의한 주식 공개매입	agreed bid
합작투자	joint venture
합작회사	joint venture
항상가격	constant dollar
항상재고법	normal stock method
항해	journal
해산	winding up
해약가능 리스	cancellable lease
해약반려금	cash surrender value
해약반려금(생명보험 관련)	cash value
해약반환금	(영)surrender value
해약현금가치	cash surrender value
해약환급금	(영)surrender value
해외지점	foreign branch
행동회계	behavioral accounting
행렬 부기	matrix bookkeeping
행사가격	strike price, striking price
행정	administration
허가	authorization
허용된 할인액	discount allowed
허용량	allowance
허용원가	should cost
허위	fraud

허위표시	fraud
현근무비	current service cost
현금	cash
현금가치	cash value
현금거래	cash transaction
현금과부족계정	cash over and short a/c
현금구입	cash purchase
현금기준	cash basis
현금등가물	cash equivalent
현금등가액	cash equivalent value
현금매입	cash purchase
현금배당	cash dividend
현금보고서	cash statement
현금비율	cash ratio
현금수입장	cash receipt journal
현금 수지보고서	receipt and payment account
현금순환	cash cycle
현금예금관리	cash management
현금예금자금	cash fund
현금예산	cash budget
현금인도판매	cash on delivery sale(COD sale)
현금주문	cash with order(CWO)
현금주의	cash basis
현금주의회계	cash basis accounting
현금지급방식	pay-as-you-go
현금지급장	cash payment journal
현금지급주의	pay-as-you-go
현금지출	cash disbursement
현금지출비용	out-of-pocket expense
현금지출원가	out-of-pocket cost
현금출납장	cash book(CB), cash journal
현금판매	cash sale
현금할인	cash discount(CD)

현금회수기준   cash collection basis

현금흐름   cash flow, cash flow statement

현금흐름 계산서   cash flow statement

현금흐름계산서(보고서)   statement of cash flow

현금흐름의 할인율법   discounted cash flow method

현금흐름회계   cash flow accounting

현물고   backwardation

현물배당   dividend in kind, property dividend

현물시세   spot rate

현장감사   site audit

현장교환시세   spot exchange rate

현장통제   operational control

현재가치   current value, present value(PV), present worth

현재가치 수익성지수   excess present value index

현재구매력회계   constant purchasing power accounting(CPP accounting)

현재원가   current cost

현재의 상태로 매각   as is sale

현재 통용되는 통화교환비율   spot rate

현재현금수령액   current proceed

현저(뚜렷이 나타남)   material

현지통화   local currency

현품없이 파는   short

현행가격   current price

현행가치회계   current value accounting(CVA)

현행구매력변동회계   current purchasing power accounting(CPP accounting)(영)

현행달성가능표준원가   currently attainable standard

현행대체원가   current replacement cost

현행대체원가회계   current replacement cost accounting

현행시장가격   current market value

현행원가   current cost, current value

현행원가 감가상각   current cost depreciation

현행원가영업이익   current cost operating profit

현행원가 재무제표   (영)current cost account

현행원가 준비금   (영)current cost reserve

현행원가회계   current cost accounting (CCA)

현행판매가치   current exit value

협의가격   negotiated price

협정   agreement, convention

형식보다 실질   substance over form

형제회사   fellow subsidiary

형평법   equity

호가(呼價)   bid and asked price

호의적 기사 (상품을 소개하는)   write up

호출(프로그래밍에서)   call

혼수(混水)주식   watered stock

혼합계정   mixed account

혼합비   mixed cost

혼합차이   joint variance

화물인수   acceptance

화물 적하증   bill of lading(B/L)

화폐(현금)자본   financial capital

화폐가치 손익   purchasing power gain or loss

화폐가치 안정의 회계   stabilized accounting

화폐가치입선출법	dollar value LIFO
화폐가치후입선출법	last-in first-out dollar value method
화폐구매력	general purchasing power of the dollar
화폐구매력 손익	purchasing power gain or loss
화폐단위	monetary unit
화폐성·비화폐성법	monetary-nonmonetary method
화폐성부채	monetary liability
화폐성운전자본	monetary working capital(MWC)
화폐성운전자본수정	monetary working capital adjustment (MWCA)(영)
화폐성이득 또는 손실	monetary gain or loss
화폐성 자산	monetary asset
화폐성항목	monetary item
화폐의 시간가치	time value of money
화폐자본유지	financial capital maintenance
화폐적 측정	money measurement
확률	probability
확률변수	random variable, variate
확률분포	probability distribution
확신	assurance
확실성	certainty
확실성등가(액)	certainty equivalent
확인	confirmation
확인서	letter of representation, representation letter
확인적 증거	corroborating evidence
확정가격	firm price
확정가격계약	fixed price contract
확정고정비	committed cost

확정급부형 연금제도	defined benefit pension plan
확정 부채, 고정담보	fixed charge
확정연금	annuity certain
환경회계	environmental accounting
환금작물	cash crop
환매(還賣) 주(株)	redeemable share
환불	rebate
환산(換算)	translation
환산율	exchange rate
환산차손익	translation gain or loss
환어음	bill of exchange(B/E), draft, exchange
환위험	exchange risk
환율	exchange rate
환입량	return
환출품명세표	purchase return book (PRB)
환평가	par value
활동분석	activity analysis
활동비	activity cost
회계	accountancy
회계감사관	comptrollership
회계검사관	comptroller
회계공준	accounting convention, accounting postulate, fundamental accounting assumption
회계관리	accounting control
회계관행	accounting convention
회계규준	accounting criteria
회계기간	accounting period, business year, fiscal period, fiscal year, period
회계기간의 개념	periodicity concept
회계기간의 공준	periodicity concept
회계기록	accounting record

회계기준	accounting standards
회계등식	accounting equation
회계방침	accounting policy
회계법인	accounting firm
회계법인간의 상호검토	peer review
회계보고서	statement
회계사	accountant, public accountant (CPA)
회계사무소	firm
회계사의 보고서	accountant's report
회계사의 의견	accountant's opinion
회계사의 책임	accountant's responsibility
회계상의 견적	accounting estimate
회계상의 변경	accounting change
회계상의 오류	accounting error
회계상의 이익	accounting profit
회계상의 추정	accounting estimate
회계순환과정	accounting cycle
회계시스템	accounting system
회계실무	accounting practice
회계실체	accounting entity, accounting unit
회계업	accountancy
회계연도	accounting period, business year, financial year, fiscal period, fiscal year, (영)tax year
회계원리	accounting principle
회계의 기초개념	fundamental accounting concept
회계이론	accounting theory
회계이익률법	accounting rate of return(ARR)
회계인	accounting profession
회계장부	book of account
회계적 이익률	accounting rate of return(ARR)

회계 전문가	accountant, accounting profession
회계절차	accounting procedure, proceed
회계정보	accounting information
회계정보 시스템	accounting information system(AIS)
회계정책	accounting policy
회계제도	accounting system
회계조직	accounting system
회계증거	accounting evidence
회계직	accountancy
회계책임	accountability
회계처리방법	accounting method
회계처리 수속의 과정	accounting cycle
회계추정치	accounting estimate
회계통제	accounting control
회계학	accounting
회계 항등식	accounting identity
회귀분석	regression analysis
회귀분석법(원가예측)	regression analysis
회사	company, firm, incorporation
회사간 소거항목	intercompany elimination
회사간 이익	intercompany profit
회사갱생	reorganization
회사법	(영)company law, corporation law
회사 설립	incorporation
회사설립증명서	certificate of incorporation
회사임원	officer
회사재건	readjustment, reconstruction
회사책임	accountability
회사합병	amalgamation
회수가능가액	recoverable amount

ㅎ

회수기간　　payback method, payback period
회수불능원가　　unrecovered cost
회수 상각액　　backlog depreciation
회장　　principal
회전비율　　rate of turnover, turnover ratio
회전신용　　revolving credit
회전신용계약　　revolving credit agreement
회전율　　turnover
회전자금　　revolving fund
회피가능고정비　　avoidable fixed cost, escapable fixed cost
회피가능원가　　avoidable cost, escapable cost
회피불능원가　　inescapable cost, unavoidable cost
횡단　　crossing
횡단면 분석　　cross section analysis
횡령　　defalcation, embezzlement, misappropriation
횡선수표　　crossing
효과성　　effectiveness
효력발생일　　effective date
효용　　utility

효율　　efficiency
효율감사　　efficiency audit
효율성　　efficiency
효율적 시장가설　　efficient market hypothesis
효율적 자본 시장　　efficient capital market
효율적 포트폴리오　　efficient portfolio
후발사건　　subsequent event
후배주(後配株)　　deferred share, deferred stock
후불　　deferred payment
후생급부　　fringe benefit
후속사건　　post balance sheet event, subsequent event
후일부　　antedate
후임감사인　　successor auditor
후입선출법　　last-in, first-out method(LIFO)
후입재고법　　last-in, still-here method (LISH)
휴가수당　　validity
휴면(休眠)회사　　(영)dormant company
흡수합병　　merger
희석화　　dilution